DSL

Simulation Techniques and Standards Development for Digital Subscriber Line Systems

Dr. Walter Y. Chen

MACMILLAN
TECHNICAL
PUBLISHING
U·S·A

Macmillan Technical Publishing, Indianapolis, Indiana

DSL: Simulation Techniques and Standards Development for Digital Subscriber Line Systems

By Dr. Walter Y. Chen

Published by:
Macmillan Technical Publishing
201 West 103rd Street
Indianapolis, IN 46290 USA

Printed in the United States of America   3 4 5 6 7 8 9 0

Library of Congress Cataloging-in-Publication Data

Library of Congress Catalog No.: 96-80469

ISBN: 1-57870-017-5

Warning and Disclaimer

This book is designed to provide information about **Digital Subscriber Line technology**. Every effort has been made to make this book as complete and as accurate as possible, but no warranty or fitness is implied.

The information is provided on an "as is" basis. The author and Macmillan Technical Publishing shall have neither liability nor responsibility to any person or entity with respect to any loss or damages arising from the information contained in this book or from the use of the disks or programs that may accompany it.

Publisher   *Jim LeValley*
Executive Editor   *David Gibson*
Managing Editor   *Caroline Roop*

Acquisitions Editor
Tracy Hughes

Development Editor
Christopher Cleveland

Project Editor
Brian Sweany

Copyeditor
Thomas Cirtin

Technical Editor
Jacky Chow

Market Reviewers
Brian Armstrong
Dr. J.J. Werner

Team Coordinator
Amy Lewis

Manufacturing Coordinator
Brook Farling

Book Designer
Ann Jones

Cover Designer
Sandra Schroeder

Cover Production
Aren Howell

Director of Production
Larry Klein

Production Team Supervisor
Andrew Stone

Graphics Image Specialists
Steve Adams
Debi Bolhuis
Kevin Cliburn
Sadie Crawford
Wil Cruz
Tammy Graham
Oliver Jackson

Production Analysts
Dan Harris
Erich J. Richter

Production Team
Chris Barrick
Jeanne Clark
Christy M. Lemasters
Julie Searls
Sossity Smith
Heather Stephenson

Indexer
Kevin Fulcher

Trademark Acknowledgments

All terms mentioned in this book that are known to be trademarks or service marks have been appropriately capitalized. Macmillan Technical Publishing cannot attest to the accuracy of this information. The use of a term in this book should not be regarded as affecting the validity of any trademark or service mark.

About the Author

Dr. Walter Y. Chen was born in Shanghai, China, on September 8, 1956. He received a B.S. (summa cum laude) degree in electrical engineering from the Polytechnic Institute of New York, Brooklyn, in 1982, an M.S. degree in electrical engineering from California Institute of Technology, Pasadena, in 1983, and a Ph.D. in electrical engineering from Polytechnic University of New York in 1989.

From 1982 to 1987, he was a Member of Technical Staff at AT&T Bell Laboratories, where he worked on PBX systems engineering and voice band modem VLSI ship design. From 1987 to 1989, he was a Member of Technical Staff at NYNEX Science and Technology, where he conducted computer network traffic and adaptive signal processing simulation studies. From 1989 to 1995, he was a research scientist at Bellcore, where he was involved with HDSL, ADSL, and HFC modem simulation studies and standards development. From 1995 to 1997, he was a research branch manager at the DSPS R&D Center of Texas Instruments, Inc., for the development of DSL technologies and High-throughput Digital Home Networks.

Dr. Chen is currently with the Information Systems Group of Motorola working on next-generation DSL and Digital Home Network technologies. Since 1989, he has made more than 40 technical contributions at T1E1.4, ADSL Forum, and IEEE 802.14 standards committees. His main research interest is the application of circuit and system theories to the area of advanced digital communication. He holds four U.S. patents and has several others pending.

Dedication

To Aaron and Brian, and to Nancy and our parents.

Acknowledgments

First, I would like to thank all the folks at Macmillan Technical Publishing for making this book a reality. Especially, I would like to thank Jim LeValley for getting me started with his inquiring email message. I also would like to thank Amy Lewis and Tracy Hughes for their assistance, guidance, and patience during the course of this project.

I would like to express my deep gratitude to my development editor, Chris Cleveland, for his tireless efforts at improving my writing and coordinating other related issues. I also would like to express my appreciation to my review editors, Brian Armstrong, Jacky Chow, and J. J. Werner, for their valuable comments, suggestions, and corrections in a very timely fashion.

I would like to thank my project editor, Brian Sweany, and all those who sent me a Christmas card. It was nice to receive that card when I was working like crazy and cutting off from TI.

I am so happy to see my idol Joe Lechleider willing to take time off from his busy schedule to read this manuscript and to come up with an insightful foreword for this book. Without Uncle Joe's early speculation on ADSL, we would probably be working on some other projects right now.

I would like to acknowledge that my work experience at Bellcore had inspired and prepared me for this book. I have enjoyed and benefited very much from working with my Bellcore colleagues. Especially, I would like to mention Barry Blake, Ken Kerpez, Ron McConell, Rich McDonald, Kamran Sistanizadeh, and Craig Valenti. Their contributions have provided key input to the formation of many DSL systems.

I feel very privileged to have had the opportunity to work with many research pioneers and industry leaders on DSL system issues at T1E1.4 working group meetings and other related standards activities. Their contributions have been reflected by many references addressed throughout this book. I would like to thank Richard Goodson, Mike Rude, and Hiroshi Takatori for keeping me informed on the most recent developments of HDSL2.

I would like to thank Don Shaver and Bob Hewes of Texas Instruments, Inc., for allowing me to prepare this manuscript on company computers during my spare time. I really appreciate Vedat Eyuboglu and Mike Taylor of Motorola for giving me support during the final editing period of this book.

I probably never would have been able to make any contributions to the data communications industry without many supportive managers during the last 17 years of my career at many research organizations. I would like to thank Don Stewart for his encouragement and patience during my early career at Bell Labs preparing memos for PBX system engineering. I would like to express my gratitude to J.J. Werner for helping my selection of a Ph.D. thesis topic. I would also like to express my appreciation to Jeff Waldhuter for supporting my part-time Ph.D. study during the period of completing my thesis. I would like to thank Dave

Waring for bringing me to the Bellcore DSL group and for his leadership on HDSL and ADSL projects. I would like to express my gratitude to Russell Hsing for encouraging me to go forward with technical publication. I would like to express my appreciation to Don Shaver for giving me a second chance to work on ADSL and the opportunity of trying out the role of a research manager.

I have very much enjoyed working with my colleagues at Texas Instruments, Inc., DSPS R&D Center. I have also enjoyed working with Peng Zhang and Alan Wetzel for the advancement of a high-speed digital home network especially for the idea of a long distance 1394.

I would like to express my deep gratitude to my wife for her support, especially for her giving up a high-paying consulting job to accept more responsibilities at home. This allowed me to spend most of my time during the last 60 weekends concentrating on this book. I also appreciate my son's early offer to help me proofread and create technical drawings. My wife and son have provided me with a lot of enlightenment during many of those long working days.

I would like to take another opportunity to thank my uncle and his family for bringing our family to this promised land. I would like to express my appreciation to my parents and my sister for their beliefs in my talent and ability. Finally, I hope this book makes my late grandmother in heaven really proud.

Contents at a Glance

Part I: Fundamentals: Transmission Environment and Signal Processing

Part II: DSL Systems: System and Transceiver Architectures

Table of Contents

Part I: Fundamentals: Transmission Environment and Signal Processing

Part II: DSL Systems: System and Transceiver Architectures

11   DSL (DIGITAL SUBSCRIBER LINES)   293

Foreword

The second half of the twentieth century has been a remarkable period for technological innovation, and particularly so for telecommunications. In 1950, telecommunications was almost entirely in the analog mode. Digital transmission of pulse code modulated voice in the telephone exchange carrier plant, and low-speed data communications were the first ventures into digital transmission in the wire-pair telephone loop plant. Both of these radical departures required engineering design of transmission circuits. The invention of the transistor and the subsequent explosion of integrated circuit technology quickly led to a revolution in consumer electronics and in communications in general. It was not until the eighties, however, that the idea of an adaptive digital subscriber line that permitted turnkey installation without prescription engineering or plant conditioning began to emerge.

There were several key innovations that made this possibility into a reality. Certainly, decision-directed echo cancellation made feasible the use of the switched telephone network for the conveyance of data between modems. Decision feedback equalization reduced the problem of transmission distortion to an economic one in contrast to a technical unfeasibility. These new technologies coupled with the invention and progress in forward error correcting codes made the future look promising for telephone transmission over plant that was designed for analog voice frequency signals. Indeed, it was possible to transmit at speeds as high as 1200 bps over telephone loop plant without conditioning. Also, conditioned loops could be used as a medium for 56 Kbps data at a limited range.

Notwithstanding this great advance, the possibility of inline signal processing at high speeds seemed remote. But integrated circuit technology continued its inexorable march. ISDN transmission at 80 Kbps second over unconditioned and unselected loops seemed like a brash idea at first, but 160 Kbps duplex transmission proved feasible before ISDN standards for basic access were set. Key to this advance was the emergence of compression techniques with far greater dynamic range than was earlier thought feasible.

The new technologies led to reconsideration of the way that ISDN Primary access—access to the switched network at low megabit speeds was provided. Before the emergence of the technology used for Basic Access, Primary Access was provided by using two simplex loops operating at the DS-1 (E-1 in Europe) rate; near-end crosstalk was suppressed by shortening regenerator spacing in the plant or by separating the two directions of transmission into separate cable binder groups. The new Basic Access technology suggested that most of the loops in the telephone plant could be used to provide Primary access by using two duplex loops operating at half the bit rate. Furthermore, no plant conditioning or special engineering was required. Thus, the High-rate Digital Subscriber Line (HDSL) was born. The magic of the HDSL compared to the simplex version of Primary access is that the HDSL uses the full transmission capacity of each cable pair in *both* directions and not only in one direction.

More magic was to follow. The success of the HDSL idea and the apparent emergence of video compression techniques that would allow entertainment video coding at DS-1 rates (MPEG-1) suggested that there might be an application for a system that transmitted to the customer at a higher rate than in the upstream direction. The idea of a network of backend computers serving individual customers also suggested a need for such an asymmetric service. This apparently emerging market, coupled with the fact that the most significant impairment to loop transmission—near-end crosstalk—would be considerably suppressed with an asymmetric channel, ultimately led to the conception of the Asymmetrical Digital Subscriber Line (ADSL).

At about this time, Trellis coding and Viterbi receivers emerged as economically feasible approaches to reliable transmission on copper pairs. Fortunately, signal processing speeds and the complexity of processor chips develops at a pace concomitant with the needs of the emerging processing and transmission technologies. The impact of this advance on modem technology is now well appreciated. Its impact on Digital Subscriber Line technology is still evolving. There are, at present, several laboratories that are researching new DSLs employing the new coding techniques with capabilities unimagined just a short time ago.

This rapid evolution of technology required conviction, on the part of equipment vendors, that the proposed new technologies would performance satisfactorily in the extant telephone loop plant before any serious commitment to development could be made. This required knowledge of the transmission and noise characteristics of telephone loop plant. Loop survey information was used to help predict performance through simulation of the proposed new systems. These simulation activities are continuing today, as the technology of DSLs continues to evolve. The requisite simulations are needed to assure that proposed technology is adequate to satisfactory performance on the overwhelming majority of loops selected at random from a large population. Thus, numerous simulations are necessary at each step in the evolution of a new technology. The simulations are also necessary for parameter setting in new technologies. For example, simulations determined the sensitivity required of analog to digital converters (ADCs) used prior to processing received signals in DSL transceivers. To attempt to conduct the studies that are the modern province of simulation would be prohibitively expense in a physical laboratory.

The remarkable pace of innovation in DSL technology did not take place in a vacuum. Standards bodies the world over considered, in considerable detail, the suitability of numerous proposals for the embodiment of DSLs. The deliberations of these groups were not merely the coming together of different vendors to guarantee the compatibility of different equipment and the feasibility of compliance to an agreed upon specification. The efforts of these bodies were, and continue to be, a collaborative effort in creating a new technology. The best engineers from some of the greatest communications laboratories in the world shared and modified ideas and data in order to produce a good, and workable product. The meetings of these bodies rank with the most sophisticated engineering and scientific symposia in their contribution to the fund of the world's technical knowledge and wisdom. They continue to guide the evolution of an extremely dynamic technology.

The book by Dr. Walter Chen thus arrives at a most opportune time. The amount of capital and human resources that are involved in DSL technology and its evolution is large, indeed. Dr. Chen's book is, I believe, the only book of its kind that is available to those that need to understand and predict the performance of DSLs. It is a welcome and sorely needed addition to the libraries of communications engineers.

Dr. Joseph W. Lechleider

February 13, 1998

PART

I

Fundamentals: Transmission Environment and Signal Processing

Introduction

When telecommunication was first invented as a telegraph, letters were coded in binary form: a combination of dots and dashes, as specified by the Morse code. In some sense, early telegraph was a digital system. The later invention of the telephone made the most popular telecommunication means into the analog format. Today, most telephone subscriber loops are still in analog format for the sole purpose of carrying analog telephone services.

Nonetheless, the *Public Switched Telephone Network* (PSTN) is dominated by digital technologies. High speed digital transmission links between different telephone Central Offices (COs) are capable of multiplexing and concentrating local traffic according to the digital hierarchy with a minimum number of physical cable connections. A flexible digital network also is efficient at carrying new feature services, delivering information other than voice signals.

With the advanced development of computer and consumer electronics, traditional telephone subscribers are ready for new services based on digital technologies. There is a lot of useful information, such as news, weather, and stock prices, on the Internet. As a result of this new information channel, there will be a stronger need by consumers to access the Internet for telecommunication, shopping, and "infotainment." There are some digital information appliances, such as PCs, satellite receivers, and digital audio/video recorders, in the home already. When the digital television technology becomes a reality, the average household will be more digitally oriented.

Along with the digitization of public and private information and of consumer electronics, the amount of information associated with their applications has been drastically increased. First-generation PCs had a RAM size of 256KB and a hard disk drive of 20MB. Now, a consumer-grade PC has 16MB of RAM and a hard disk drive of 1GB. During the last 15 years, the PC memory and storage size increase factors have been about 62.5 and 50, respectively; however, the increase of transmission throughput for a voice band modem, which has become a popular PC communication device, is only about a factor of 14–33.4 kbps vs. 2.4 kbps.

With a much more powerful PC processing lots of information, the capability of a voice band modem, which is limited by the 3.3 kHz voice channel, becomes a limiting factor in integrating consumers to the evolving high-speed digital communication network. The drawback of a voice band modem can be overcome with the *Digital Subscriber Line* (DSL) technology. By bypassing the *Plain Old Telephone Set* (POTS) interface at a local CO, a DSL system can utilize the full potential of a copper telephone subscriber loop to deliver a transmission throughput of up to a few hundred times that of a voice band modem.

1.1 Digital Access Methods Through POTS Loops

Currently, there are three ways to provide digital access through a telephone subscriber loop:

- Analog voice channel
- Digital switches
- POTS splitters

1.1.1 Digital Access Through Analog Voice Channels

Figure 1.1 shows the first approach of providing digital transmission through the existing POTS switch and PSTN network.

Figure 1.1 Digital Access Through an Analog Voice Channel

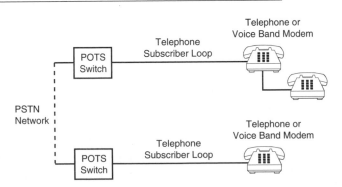

Figure 1.1 shows the configuration for today's voice band modem. There is no switch and network infrastructure change involved for this approach. A subscriber can connect to another subscriber or to an *Information service provider* (ISP) with compatible voice band modems via an existing voice band telephone protocol. The transmission throughput is limited, however, by the bandwidth of the analog voice channel.

At the subscriber end, multiple telephone sets and voice band modems can be connected to the same subscriber loop through in-house telephone wiring, although only one voice band modem can be active at a given time.

1.1.2 Digital Access Through Digital Switches

Figure 1.2 shows the second approach of digital access through special digital switch line cards.

Figure 1.2 Digital Access Through a Special Digital Switch

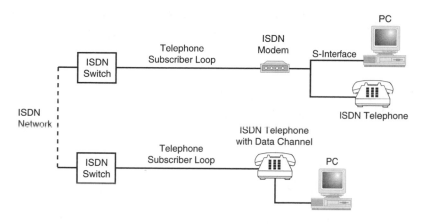

Figure 1.2 shows the configuration for the *Basic Rate Access Integrated Services Digital Network* (ISDN) service. An ISDN-capable digital switch is required for this second approach. A subscriber can connect to another subscriber or to an ISP equipped with an ISDN modem or telephone set via a digital switching protocol. A fixed transmission throughput can be defined for the worst-case condition telephone subscriber loop if the digital access service is to be available for all telephone subscribers.

At the subscriber end, only one ISDN modem or one ISDN telephone set with a U-interface is connected to the telephone subscriber loop. Multiple telephone sets and PCs can share the same digital access service through the S-interface, which can be implemented with the installation of a new in-house twisted-pair wiring. Basic Rate Access ISDN is the first DSL system.

1.1.3 Digital Access Through POTS Splitters

Figure 1.3 shows the third approach of digital access through the addition of POTS splitters.

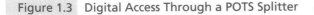

Figure 1.3   Digital Access Through a POTS Splitter

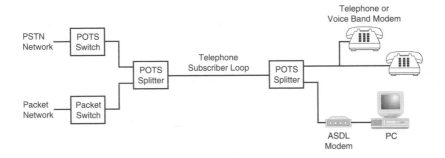

Figure 1.3 shows the configuration for *Asymmetrical Digital Subscriber Lines* (ADSL). A POTS splitter separates the voice channel from that of DSL through highpass and lowpass filters to provide co-existing services. At a CO, POTS splitters are used to merge a POTS switch and a packet switch.

At the subscriber end, a POTS splitter can be installed between the telephone subscriber loop and the existing in-house telephone wiring to avoid extensive reflection. New in-house wiring is required to connect a DSL modem to the POTS splitter. Through proper design, the interference between voice and DSL services can be kept at a minimum level.

1.1.4 Next-Generation Digital Switches

Figure 1.4 shows the possibility of providing digital transmission through a next-generation digital switch.

Figure 1.4   Digital Access Through a Digital Switch

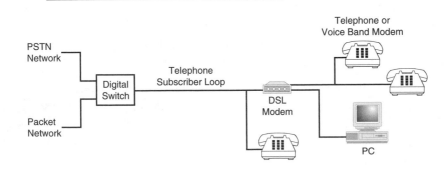

The digital switch can recognize a particular subscriber device—a POTS telephone set, a voice band modem, or a DSL modem—and will adjust its hardware parameters and software "modem" accordingly to establish an analog or digital connection. Proper network connection also will be selected. POTS service can be provided directly through the digital switch or indirectly through the subscriber-end DSL modem. With careful design and engineering, the simultaneous operation of multiple analog and digital devices also is feasible.

1.2   DSL System Engineering

The twisted-pair telephone loop between a CO and a subscriber premises can have a length of from a few kilofeet (kft) to a few tens of kilofeet. A twisted-pair telephone loop usually consists of many cable sections of sizes from 19 gauge to 26 gauge. Due to the installation practice, there are bridged taps associated with telephone subscriber loops. To compensate for the effect of magnitude and phase distortion for the broad DSL signaling band and reflections caused by bridged taps and terminal impedance mismatch, some inter-symbol interference counter measures, such as adaptive channel equalization and multi-carrier modulation, become necessary.

For every section, there are many twisted pairs sharing the same electrical sheath and plastic covering within a single twisted-pair cable. Crosstalks exist between adjacent twisted pairs. Because twisted-pair telephone cables are originally engineered for the voice band, the crosstalk noise level could become quite severe for DSL applications. Besides the telephone loop plant background noise, the crosstalk noise is a limiting factor for the performance of a DSL system. There are Near End Crosstalk (NEXT) noise and Far End Crosstalk (FEXT) noise. The effect of NEXT is usually worse than that of FEXT.

Extensive digital signal processing techniques, such as adaptive channel equalizers and adaptive echo cancellers, have been adapted for DSL transceivers. The implementation of these signal processing techniques is made possible by the advancement of *Very-Large-Scale Integrated Circuit* (VLSI). VLSI can be a combination of *Application Specific Integrated Circuit* (ASIC) and a general-purpose *Digital Signal Processor* (DSP). The advancement of VLSI also made the application of extensive *Trellis Coded Modulation* (TCM) and forward error correction coding, such as *Reed-Solomon coding,* possible for low-cost DSL transceivers.

It has been a common practice, to combine the current and upcoming expected capabilities of VLSI with the desired performance of a DSL system under development. This combination has resulted in both a challenge and a rewarding experience for participating DSL system developers. For example, high-resolution, low sampling rate and low-resolution, high sampling rate Analog to Digital Converters (ADCs) have been developed for voice and video applications, respectively. The development of *High-Bit-Rate Digital Subscriber Line*

(HDSL) technology resulted in a market need of a high-resolution high sampling rate, 12 bits and 800 kHz, ADC. Furthermore, there are many other unique requirements within a DSL transceiver.

1.3   *The General DSL Transceiver Architecture*

Figure 1.5 shows the general structure of a DSL transceiver. As far as the semiconductor is concerned, there is an analog part and a digital part of a DSL transceiver chip set. The analog part covers analog transmit and receiver filters, the Digital to Analog Converter (DAC), the automatic gain device, and the ADC. The digital part of a DSL chip set has three major functions: modulation/demodulation, coding/decoding, and bit packing/unpacking.

Figure 1.5   A Typical DSL Transceiver Block Diagram

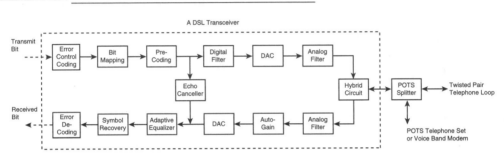

Specifically, the modulation/demodulation function, which involves lots of digital signal processing, includes the following:

- *Fast Fourier Transform* (FFT) and *Inverse Fast Fourier Transform* (IFFT) for the case of *Discrete MultiTone* (DMT) line code

- Constellation mapping

- Precoding for the case of using Tomlison precoding

- Digital shaping filter for the cases of *Carrierless AM/PM* (CAP) or *Quadrature Amplitude Modulation* (QAM) line codes

- Adaptive echo canceller

- Adaptive channel equalizer

- Symbol/bit conversion

- Timing recovery

A DSL can have either or both Trellis code and Reed-Solomon code, such as ADSL. Earlier DSL systems—such as the Digital Subscriber Lines (DSL), which have been adapted as the physical layer of the Basic Rate Access ISDN channel—and HDSL have no coding required. New DSL systems—such as HDSL2, which is intended to deliver twice the transmission throughput of HDSL under the similar loop condition—have considered coding as a critical part of a DSL transceiver. A coding gain of 5 to 6 dB can bring the performance of a DSL system very close to the theoretical channel capacity.

The *Transmission Convergence* (TC) layer, which belongs to the general bit-packing/ unpacking function, has received a lot of attention in recent development of DSL systems. A DSL system with a properly designed TC layer will not only make a simplified network interface, but also reduce the complexity of a DSL chip set. The proper design of a bit-packing/unpacking function also is a requirement for integrated DSL systems, such as a DSL PC plug-in card or a DSL CO switch line card for which specific frame rates and frame sizes are necessary to be compatible with their host systems.

Besides the DSL chip set covering analog and digital function, some discrete components— such as the hybrid circuit, which converts a four-wire, dual half-duplex interface to a two-wire, full-duplex one, and the POTS splitter, which separates voice channel from the DSL spectrum—also are important parts of a DSL system. The improved performance of these discrete components can sometimes ease up the demand for a DSL chip set. For example, a better hybrid circuit can reduce the requirement for an echo canceller. Special techniques implemented with discrete components can be tailored for different DSL systems.

1.4   DSL Systems and Standards

There are many different signal-processing algorithms capable of achieving a particular transmission performance objective. For a particular algorithm, system and hardware parameters can vary depending on preferences. For network and service providers, an interchangeable DSL transceiver from different vendors is a key to drive hardware cost down. A common agreement is necessary to insure DSL transceivers from different developers can interoperate with each other.

A process for establishing standards is necessary—not only to define transceiver line and network interfaces, but also to identify the proper combination of signal processing algorithms and VLSI semiconductor technologies. DSL standards have been defined earlier by ANSI T1D1.3 and recently by ANSI T1E1.4 working groups.

1.4.1 Early DSL System Standards

The first DSL system is the DSL developed for the Basic Rate Access ISDN application during 1982 and 1988. DSL is designed to operate on all non-load telephone subscriber loops confirming the resistance design rule. ANSI documents "Integrated Service Digital Network (ISDN): Basic Access Interface for Use on Metallic Loops for Application on the Network Side of the NT-Layer 1 Specification"[1] and "Integrated Services Digital Network (ISDN): Basic Access Interface for S and T Reference Points (Layer 1 Specification)"[2] describe the *U-interface* of the DSL and the *S-interface* of the DSL, respectively.

The U-interface defines transmission specifications over the telephone subscriber loop, while the S-interface defines transmission specifications over a local distribution medium, such as a residential wiring or a PBX extension wiring. The DSL, as defined by the ANSI standard, uses a baseband four-level line code, also called 2B1Q for *2 Bits per Quaternary* symbol, over the telephone subscriber loop. The transmission throughput of the DSL is 160 kbps with a baud rate of 80 kHz.

The DSL is capable of supplying two B channels of 64 kbps and one D channel of 16 kbps. The remaining transmission throughput is consumed by *Operational, Administrative, Maintenance, and Provisioning* (OAM) channels. A DSL transceiver relies on a baud rate adaptive channel equalizer to achieve full-duplex transmission, and on a baud rate adaptive channel equalizer to overcome the effect of channel inter-symbol interference.

1.4.2 HDSL System Standards

The HDSL system can be considered as a technology extension of the DSL. HDSL was mainly developed as a dual-duplex repeaterless T1 technology from 1988 to 1991. HDSL is designed to serve non-load telephone subscriber loops confirming the *Carrier Serving Area* (CSA) guideline. ANSI Technical report, "A Technical Report on High-Bit-Rate Digital Subscriber Lines (HDSL),"[3] defines transmission specifications over the telephone subscriber loop, as well as associate T1 network interface.

The HDSL also uses the 2B1Q baseband four-level line code. However, both the transmission throughput of 900 kbps and the baud rate of 400 kHz are five times those of the DSL. A pair of HDSL transceivers can be used as a T1 carrier to carry 24 B channels plus associated OAM channels. Higher operation rate adaptive echo canceller and adaptive channel equalizer of an HDSL transceiver demand more digital signal processing power compared with those of a DSL transceiver.

1.4.3 ADSL System Standards

The ADSL system was developed for video-on-demand services from 1991 to 1995 with a high transmission throughput from a CO to telephone subscribers downstream, and lower transmission throughput in the reverse direction upstream. Over CSA range distance, the ADSL is capable of a downstream transmission throughput of 6.433 Mbps. For longer telephone subscriber loops confirming the resistance design rule, the downstream transmission throughput is reduced to 1.544 Mbps.

ANSI document "Network and Customer Installation Interfaces: Asymmetrical Digital Subscriber Line (ADSL) Metallic Interface"[4] defines the DMT transmission specifications over the telephone subscriber loop as well as up to seven downstream channel and four upstream channel network interfaces. The DMT line code has a baud rate of 4 kHz and up to 256 subcarriers for downstream, and up to 64 subcarriers for the upstream. Depending on the channel signal-to-noise ratio, up to 11 bits can be allocated for each subcarrier. Both Trellis code and Reed-Solomon code have been introduced for ADSL to improve the transmission performance under white Gaussian and impulse noises.

CAP/QAM line codes also have been discussed in the early ADSL standardization process. Non-standard CAP/QAM line code–based ADSL systems have been used in trials and some special-purpose applications. With properly positioned passband downstream and upstream spectra and associated constellation sizes, transmission throughputs similar to that defined by the standard ADSL also can be achieved with CAP/QAM line codes. The use of Trellis code and Reed-Solomon code also is considered in conjunction with CAP/QAM line codes. An ANSI ad hoc group has been working on producing a document to define a standard for the CAP/QAM–based ADSL.

1.4.4 HDSL2 System Standards

It is expected that with some improvement on the modulation method and the addition of coding gain, the transmission throughput of HDSL can be doubled. The development of a single-pair HDSL, also called HDSL2, has been in steady progress since late 1995. Baseband multi-level line codes were the focus of the standard development; however, transmit signal spectrum shaping, with some experience gained from the development of ADSL, is considered to minimize the effect of NEXT.

A 512-state Trellis code also has been considered to bring about a coding gain of more than 5 dB. With the advancement of VLSI, the extra signal processing and coding complexity of HDSL2 is expected to be absorbed by higher-density semiconductor chips.

1.4.5   VDSL System Standards

To meet the demand of future all-purpose multimedia applications, Very-high-bit-rate Digital Subscriber Line (VDSL) has been under study since late 1995 for transmission throughputs of 13, 26, and 52 Mbps. The VDSL service range is expected to be between 1.5 to 4.5 kft. VDSL customers will be connected by short-distance copper twisted-pair loops to nearby *Optical Network Units* (ONUs) that are linked to a CO with fiber optical cables.

The VDSL transmit spectrum can occupy a bandwidth of up to 15 MHz where the Radio Frequency Interference (RFI), both ingress and egress, has become a chief concern. Under such a high transmission throughput, the requirement of delivering desired analog and digital semiconductor capabilities under a consumer product cost constraint becomes an incentive for VDSL system developers.

1.5   Chapter-by-Chapter Overview

This book is a collection of simulation/implementation techniques and reference materials for the design and development of DSL systems. It is intended for practicing engineers working in DSL and related fields. Many techniques developed for DSLs can be very useful also for next-generation communication systems, such as a high-throughput home digital network. This book also can be used as a reference for graduate students to aid in their research studies in digital communication systems.

Note
Past technical contributions of the T1E1.4 working group can be obtained from Creative Communications Consulting, P.O. Box 15189, Durham, NC 27704; telephone: 732-842-6250.

This book is divided into two parts: Part I, "Fundamentals: Transmission Environment and Signal Processing," and Part II, "DSL Systems: System and Transceiver Architectures." Part I deals with twisted-pair telephone loop channel modeling, DSL system performance simulation, and the general implementation of digital signal processing techniques. The transmission performance potential of telephone subscriber loops are examined through the calculation of channel capacity. Adaptive channel equalization, adaptive echo cancellation, and coding techniques are addressed with an emphasis on DSL-specific implementation details.

Part II deals with the specifics of developed and developing DSL systems. For each developed DSL system, initial and major standard development activities, general system performance characteristics, and key features of standard documents are discussed. The general features and related issues for developing DSL systems also are discussed. ANSI T1D1.3 and T1E1.4 working group contributions are extensively referenced.

Specifically, each chapter covers the following topics in depth:

- Chapter 2, "Telephone Subscriber Loop Environment," describes the twisted-pair telephone loop plant. Issues involved are telephone network architecture, the structure of the telephone loop plant, the loop plant design rules, the composition of twisted-pair cables, and basic voice channel transmission requirements.

- Chapter 3, "Twisted-Pair Channel Modeling," describes the channel model of the twisted-pair telephone loop. Twisted-pair cable primary parameters are examined. A two-port network and its matrix representation are used to construct a channel model based on sections of cables and other electrical components.

- Chapter 4, "Transceiver Front-End Noise Models," describes noise models for the twisted-pair telephone loop plant: crosstalk, background, and impulse noises.

- Chapter 5, "Channel Capacity," calculates channel capacities of the twisted-pair telephone loop based on channel and noise models.

- Chapter 6, "Hybrid Circuits," describes two forms of hybrid circuit that are used to connect transmitting and receiving circuits to a two-wire telephone subscriber loop. The construction of an echo path model based on the hybrid circuit and the line coupling transformer equivalent circuit also is presented.

- Chapter 7, "Analog Front-End Precision," discusses resolution requirements for ADC and DAC devices with respect to transmitting signal peak-to-average ratio and associated channel and echo path transmission characteristics.

- Chapter 8, "Channel Equalization," presents calculation techniques for the adaptive channel equalizer. Filter coefficients as well as the output signal-to-noise ratio are calculated for baud rate and fractional spaced linear and decision feedback channel equalizers. Results are given for both baseband and passband systems as well as for the DMT time domain equalizer.

- Chapter 9, "Echo Cancellation," discusses challenges of the implementation of an adaptive echo canceller for a DSL transceiver. Issues of asymmetrical echo cancellation and crosstalk cancellation also are addressed.

- Chapter 10, "Error Correction and Trellis Coding," introduces the Reed-Solomon code as a forward error correction code with background information of parity check codes and block codes. The Trellis code modulation is discussed with background information of convolution codes and Viterbi detection algorithm. Related basic implementation techniques are discussed as well.

- Chapter 11, "DSL (Digital Subscriber Lines)," discusses standard development activities, the 2B1Q line code, the expected transmission performance, and semiconductor implementation issues related to DSL.

- Chapter 12, "HDSL (High-Bit-Rate Digital Subscriber Lines)," addresses standard development activities, the 2B1Q line code, the expected transmission performance, and semiconductor implementation issues related to HDSL.

- Chapter 13, "ADSL (Asymmetrical Digital Subscriber Lines)," discusses issues related to the standard DMT line code ADSL as well as some efforts at developing a CAP/QAM line code ADSL standard.

- Chapter 14, "SHDSL (Single-Pair High-Bit-Rate Digital Subscriber Lines)," summarizes activities for the development of HDSL2.

- Chapter 15, "VDSL (Very-High-Bit-Rate Digital Subscriber Lines)," explores new issues associated with the development of VDSL, and addresses the effect of Radio Frequency Interference (RFI).

End Notes

1. ANSI T1.601-1992, "Integrated Services Digital Network (ISDN): Basic Access Interface for Use on Metallic Loops for Application on the Network Side of the NT (Layer 1 Specification)," American National Standards Institute, Inc.

2. ANSI T1.605-1991, "Integrated Services Digital Network (ISDN): Basic Access Interface for S and T Reference Points (Layer 1 Specification)," American National Standards Institute, Inc.

3. ANSI T1E1.4, "Working Group on Digital Subscriber Lines: A Technical Report on High-Bit-Rate Digital Subscriber Lines (HDSL)," T1E1.4/96-006 (April 22, 1996).

4. ANSI T1.413-1995, "Network and Customer Installation Interfaces: Asymmetrical Digital Subscriber Line (ADSL) Metallic Interface," American National Standards Institute, Inc.

Telephone Subscriber Loop Environment

Digital Subscriber Lines (DSL) are developed based on existing telephone subscriber loops. The telephone subscriber loop environment was developed originally for the practice of carrying analog voice services and lately with the consideration of carrying digital extensions, such as *Digital Loop Carrier* (DLC), of analog voice services. The transmission characteristics of the telephone subscriber loop environment[1,2] and the proper utilization of these transmission characteristics determine the performance potential of a DSL system.

A basic knowledge of the telephone subscriber loop environment is necessary for the understanding of many technical choices for the engineering of a particular DSL system. This chapter explains the basic components and concepts of a telephone subscriber loop environment, as follows:

- *Central Offices and customer premises.* The loop plant consists of twisted-pair cables connecting a local Central Office (CO) to customer (telephone subscriber) premises (residential or small business units). The termination conditions of a subscriber loop at a CO and a premises could also affect the engineering and performance of a DSL system.

- *Subscriber loop structure and twisted-pair cables.* An individual subscriber loop consists of many different cable sections. Twisted-pair cable size, installation methodology, and grouping of subscriber loop sections could result in different degrees of exposure to *crosstalk noise* and to *radio frequency interference* (RFI).

- *Subscriber loop design rules.* A telephone subscriber loop plant followed some general design rules during its evolution. Those rules also can be used in certain degrees as guidelines for the development and deployment of DSL systems.

- *Voice channel characteristics.* A DSL system is based on the same telephone subscriber loop as a *Plain Old Telephone System* (POTS). A DSL system is sometimes designed to coexist with a POTS service on the same twisted-pair cable, offering simultaneous analog/digital services. The understanding of the POTS signaling mechanism is necessary for the design of a DSL system that coexists with a POTS.

2.1   Central Offices and Customer Premises

Today a telephone subscriber, anywhere in the world, with a telephone set connected by a twisted-pair telephone cable to a Central Office (CO) can reach another telephone subscriber whose telephone set is also connected by a twisted-pair telephone cable to another CO. Connections between each pair of telephone sets among different telephone subscribers at different locations are made indirectly through COs. COs that connect telephone subscribers are called *end COs* (Class 5).

A telephone company building is called a *wire center* and can contain several CO switching machines. The number of subscriber connections to each CO switching machine is usually limited to fewer than 10,000, constrained by the four-digit-number assignment plan for each CO. The twisted pair telephone loop connecting a subscriber to an end CO is called a *subscriber loop*. The house hosting the subscriber telephone set is called *customer premises*. Large business customers are served through *Private Branch Exchanges* (PBX).

COs at a local region are connected through *interoffice trunks* or *tandem trunks* and *tandem COs* by the means of the existing and still-evolving digital hierarchy. Telephone connections beyond a local region are made possible through *toll centers* (Class 4). Above the toll center hierarchy are the *primary center* (Class 3), the *sectional center* (Class 2), and the *regional center* (Class 1). Centers are all connected through *intertoll trunks*. Figure 2.1 depicts a model telephone network.

Analog voice channels are digitized once they are terminated at an end CO. *Digital channel banks,* which consist of subscriber loop line cards and a high-speed *Time Division Multiplexing* (TDM) bus, convert analog voice signals as well as signaling information, such as originating and destination addresses, into digital format and combine the resulting digital signal into a single-digital bit stream to be integrated into the digital hierarchy.

The current digital hierarchy has transmission rates of 64 Kbps (DS0), 1.544 Mbps (DS1), 6.312 Mbps (DS2), 44.736 Mbps (DS3), and 274.176 Mbps (DS4) in North America. These transmission throughputs are typically implemented by T1, T2, T3, and T4 carrier systems based on a variety of transmission media, such as digital radio, coaxial cable, twisted-pair cable, and fiber-optic cable. Since the early 1980s, connections between major COs have been dominated by fiber-optic cables (nearly 95 percent).[3] The evolving higher speed digital hierarchy—*Synchronous Transport Signal* (STS)—can provide transmission throughputs of 51.84 Mbps (OC-1), 155.51 Mbps (OC-3), 466.56 Mbps (OC-9), 622.08 Mbps (OC-12), and so on.

Figure 2.1   A Model Telephone Network

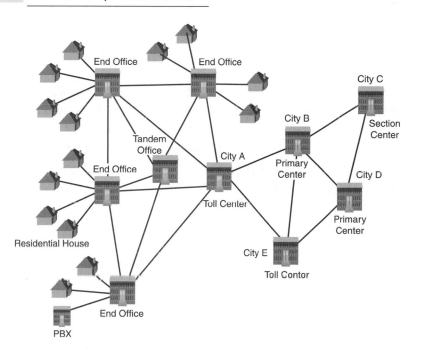

The major subscriber loop, or local loop, equipment in a CO consists of *main distribution frames* and a *switch machine*. *Multiplexers* are also used for the interconnection of equipment with different transmission rates conforming to a particular digital hierarchy. Subscriber loops are first terminated on distribution frames and then connected to line cards of a switch.

There are also cross-connector frames for the interconnection of switch, multiplex, and monitor equipment. *Monitor equipment* keeps electronic hardware as well as associated functions in good running condition. Most of the equipment operates directly from the battery supplies that are AC charged. Further, a lot of backup batteries are used in case of a power failure (see Figure 2.2).

Figure 2.2 Major Equipment at a CO

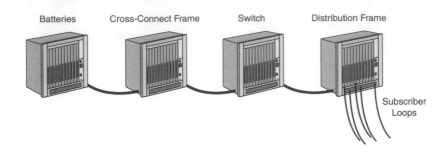

A switch line card supplies a DC voltage through the telephone loop to a subscriber premises to detect the on-hook and off-hook of the telephone set. Once off-hook is detected, the line card converts the dialing signal into a digital bit stream and sends it to switch equipment for further processing. For the dialed subscriber, the switch line card generates a periodic ringing signal in addition to the constant DC bias voltage for the dialed subscriber loop until the telephone is picked up and becomes off-hook. Switch line cards at both ends of an active telephone connection increase the performance of *Analog to Digital Conversion* (ADC) and *Digital to Analog Conversion* (DAC) for both subscriber loops during a telephone conversation.

The subscriber loop termination at a customer premises consists of a *Network Interface Device* (NID) from which multiple in-house wiring connections are made. An NID can be divided into two parts, as follows:

- A customer part that can be accessed by a customer to make in-house wiring connections.

- A telephone company part that is usually shielded from a customer. The telephone company part of an NID can also contain some special purpose electronics, such as a loop back circuit, for maintenance and testing.

Multiple telephone sets are connected to the telephone subscriber loop at different points in the in-house telephone wiring, which generally has a star/daisy-chain topology. Figure 2.3 shows a typical equipment and in-house wiring setup of a customer premises.

Because of the irregularity of the in-house wiring topology and sometimes poor quality of the wiring cables and their interconnections, the transmission characteristic of an in-house wiring can degrade the performance of a DSL system. Reflections could be very extensive throughout the in-house wiring. The energy loss caused by reflections can be as much as 30 dB at certain frequency regions. The inclusion of the in-house wiring has been ruled out from the telephone subscriber loop for most DSL systems. To optimize the transmission performance, a DSL transceiver at customer premises is usually connected to the NID directly with a short and high-quality twisted-pair cable.

Figure 2.3   Premises In-House Wiring

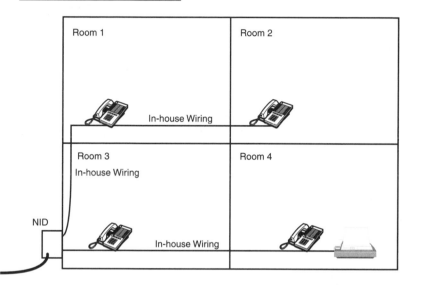

2.2   *Subscriber Loop Structure and Twisted-Pair Cables*

A subscriber loop consists of sections (typically 500 feet long) of copper twisted pairs of cables of different gauges. The physical location of a section of a subscriber loop could be

- Aerial (hung on poles)
- Buried (directly in the ground)
- Underground (protected within a dedicated conduit)

Earlier telephone loop installations were aerial for the most part, while most recent installations, especially for new housing developments, are underground. Buried cables are used for drop wires where the extra cost of conduit installation could not be justified for each individual connection. Aerial cables are more susceptible to Radio Frequency Interference (RFI) than buried or underground cables for their effective antenna heights.

Electrical joints, also called *splices*, are usually made with hand twists without soldering to connect sections of cables together. A protective housing, which can be sealed with wax, is used to cover cable splices, and it is usually located near a telephone pole for aerial cables or in a manhole for underground cables. A twisted-pair telephone cable with a plastic covering external to a metallic electrical sheathing can have thousands of twisted pairs organized into many binder groups.

To reduce the effect of crosstalk, binder groups within a cable have different twisting angles. Depending on the cable type, there could be 10, 25, or up to 50 twisted pairs in a binder group and up to 50 binder groups per cable. Because of the concentration, twisted-pair cables have larger *cross sections*—more twisted pairs—near the Central Office. Functionally, an individual subscriber loop can be divided into portions consisting of the following:

- *Feeder cables.* Provide links from a CO to a concentrated customer area

- *Distribution cables.* Provide links from feeder cables to potential customer sites

- *Drop wires.* Connect distribution cables to customer premises

> **Note**
> Wiring inside the customer premises that connects to the drop wire at the network customer interface does not count as part of the network loop.

Connection points between feeder cables and distribution cables are commonly located in cabinets, called the *Feeder Distribution Interface* (FDI). Connection points in distribution cables are commonly located in *pedestals* for underground cables or *terminals* for aerial cables. Single aerial drop wires often consist of parallel copper wires. Recent construction uses multiple twisted pairs (two, four, or six). The drop wire is usually short and has a proportionately small effect on the loop transmission characteristics, except for potential radiation effects. The loop and drop wire could potentially pick up other high-frequency radiation noises due to the longitudinal imbalance. It could also radiate signals to other high-frequency electronic devices. Figure 2.4 shows the physical layout of cabling from a CO to the customer premises.

2.2.1 Bridged Taps

Because loop plant construction usually occurs ahead of customer service requests, distribution cables are usually made available to all potential customer sites. Hence, it is a common practice to connect a twisted pair from a feeder cable with more than one distribution cable pair to maximize the probability of reaching a potential customer. The unused distribution cables result in bridged taps.

Figure 2.4   General Structure of a Telephone Loop Plant

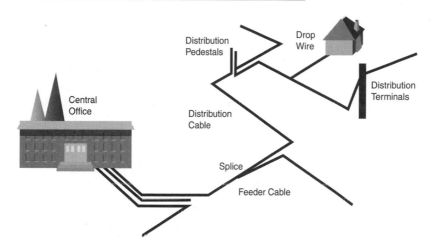

The loop plant design rules (discussed in section 2.3, "Loop Plant Design Rules"), such as *Resistance Design* and *Carrier Serving Area* (CSA), limit the total bridged tap length to minimize adverse effects, magnitude loss, and spectrum distortion on POTS (Plain Old Telephone System) transmissions.

2.2.2   *Loaded Loops*

Extending the central office serving distances for the voice channel is accomplished through a procedure of installing *load coils*. Load coils are typically installed for cables with a total length (including bridged taps) exceeding 15 kft (kilofeet).

Loading arrangements are designated by a code letter that specifies the distance between loading coils and by numbers that indicate the inductance value and wire gauge. The capital letters *H, D,* and *B* indicate spacing of 6, 4.5, and 3 kft between the coils, respectively. The number in front of the letter indicates the wire gauge, and the number after the letter indicates the inductance of the coil in millihenries (mH). Therefore, the loading arrangement 19H88, for example, indicates a 19-gauge wire with a spacing distance of 6 kft and the inductance of 88 mH.

Figure 2.5 shows typical transfer functions between a loaded and a non-loaded loop based on a 12 kft, 26-gauge twisted-pair loop, for which the insertion loss is the attenuation caused by the insertion of the twisted-pair cable between a signal source and a load resistance. The physical setup of loaded loops is discussed later in section 2.3.

Figure 2.5 Insertion Losses of Loaded and Non-Loaded Loops

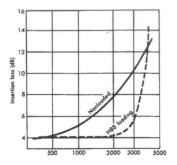

Note
Because its attenuation is much higher above the voice frequency, a loaded loop is not suitable for Digital Subscriber Line (DSL) systems.

2.2.3 *Twisted-Pair Loop Composition*

A telephone cable pair is made by twisting together two insulated conductors of high-purity copper. The insulation can be wood pulp formed on the conductors in a process similar to paper making (which is why sometimes it is referred to as pulp or paper cable), or it can be plastic formed by an extrusion process. *Polyolefin insulated cable* (PIC) is a general term used to describe all modern plastic insulated cables. Polyethylene is a widely used plastic insulation. Polypropylene is another commonly used plastic insulation material.

Neighboring pairs are twisted with different *pitch* (twist length) to limit electromagnetic interference (crosstalk) between them. The pairs are stranded into what are called *units,* and the units are then cabled into *cores.* The cores are covered with various types of sheaths depending on the intended use. Currently, the size of PIC cables ranges from 6 to 1,800 pairs, while the size of pulp cables ranges from 600 to 3,600 pairs. Unit sizes are 12, 13, and 25 pairs for PIC and 25, 50, and 100 pairs for pulp cables. Common wire sizes used are 19, 22, 24, and 26 gauge.

Feeder and distribution cables can contain as many as 4,200 pairs or as little as 6 pairs, all within a single sheath. In the smaller cable size, good design practice calls for using cables that are multiples of the 25-pair unit. There is very little difference between the installed cost of 6- or 12-pair cables and 25- or 50-pair cables in most applications. The extra pairs not only give the potential for growth, but also allow the allocation and use of pairs in the field to be more logical. This practice also leads to easier administration and maintenance. Feeder cables usually contain more pairs than distribution cables because of the concentration. Feeder and distribution cable sizes are usually determined based on the projected telephone subscriber population.

Drop wires can range from one pair to hundreds or thousands of pairs, depending on the establishment to be served. Drop wires in the smaller size are not always twisted because they are usually short and do not measurably degrade transmission quality. Aerial drop wires are usually 18 or 19 gauge, while buried drop wires are usually 19, 22, or 24 gauge. High-purity copper is the most widely used conductor material for underground drop wires, while copper with special alloying (or other means for strength) is used for aerial drop wires. Specifics vary, depending on cable type.

2.3   Loop Plant Design Rules

POTS loop plant design must accomplish three goals:

- Ensure that there is sufficient direct current flow to operate station sets

- Enable DC/low-frequency call process signaling (dialing and ringing)

- Limit transmission loss and frequency roll off to acceptable levels

2.3.1   Resistance Design Rule

As mentioned in section 2.2.2, "Loaded Loops," telephone cables are designed with different gauges of wire, from 26 gauge (thin, with higher DC resistance) to 19 gauge (thicker with lower DC resistance). These different gauges are designed to have close to the same *capacitance* per unit length. It so happens that the maximum DC resistance also controls the maximum voice frequency loss and roll-off frequency.

Note
The roll-off frequency is the corner frequency beyond which the attenuation increases rapidly.

For modern switching systems, a maximum loop resistance (DC resistance) of 1500 ohms meets powering, signaling, and transmission objectives. Corresponding maximum transmission loss at 1000 Hz is about 9 dB with a roll off of 6 dB at 2800 Hz. The average loop has a DC resistance of 600 ohms with 4 dB loss at 1 KHz.

Because distances from a CO to each customer are different, distribution cables of different gauges are utilized to keep the amount of copper (and dollars) used to a minimum while meeting design guidelines. To reduce overall loop resistance, the end sections of a long subscriber loop tend to have coarser twisted pairs, whereas finer gauge twisted pairs are used closer to the central office in order to reduce the diameter of the cable in crowded ducts.

Some customers are so far away from the Central Office, however, that a direct implementation of twisted-pair cables would result in a DC resistance much higher than the specified 1500 ohms and hence a poor voice channel service quality. A procedure of installing loading coils and coarser gauge cables has been used to extend the CO serving distance for the voice channel. Inductive loading results in a loop with reduced loss within the voice band for a given gauge of cable, and acts as a lowpass filter above 3000 Hz.

Loading coils are typically installed for cables with a total length, including bridged taps, exceeding 15 kft. The first loading coil is installed at 3 kft from the CO. Loading coils are installed every 6 kft thereafter. There can be no bridged taps between loading coils in order for the *bandpass* to be flat. Bridged taps on the end sections at the CO and customer ends can be left connected, up to a total tap length of 6 kft.

Figures 2.6 and 2.7 show length distributions of all loops and non-loaded loops, respectively, according to a 1983 loop survey conducted by AT&T Bell Labs.[4]

Figure 2.6 Loop Length Distribution

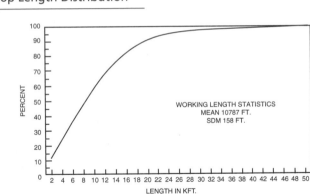

Figure 2.7 Non-Loaded Loop Length Distribution

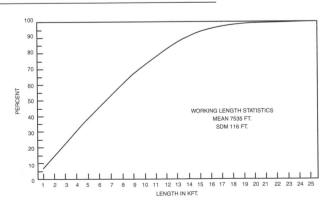

Those loops usually consist of cable sections of different gauges and bridged taps. The length of total bridged taps is also included for the overall length of each loop. Assuming all loaded loops are longer than 15 kft, the percentage of non-loaded loops among all loops can be estimated as follows:

- Let the number of non-loaded loops less or equal to 15 kft be x.

- Let the number of non-loaded loops more than 15 kft be y.

- Let the number of loaded loops be z.

Assuming those non-loaded and loaded loops, you have the following:

$$94\% = \frac{x}{x+y} \times 100\%$$

$$79\% = \frac{x}{x+y+z} \times 100\%$$

Therefore, you have

$$\frac{x+y}{x+y+z} \times 100\% = \frac{79\%}{94\%} \times 100\% - 84\%$$

It is expected that new loops are getting shorter and the use of loading coils becomes less frequent. Therefore, the percentage of non-loaded loops should have been increased since the 1983 loop survey; however, the amount of increase could be relatively small because of the large installed telephone subscriber loop bases.

2.3.2 *DLC Systems and CSA Guidelines*

Digital Loop Carrier (DLC) systems were developed to serve customers beyond the *Resistance Design* range. Early DLC systems were based on copper twisted pairs that used the 1.544 Mbps T-carrier technology with periodic repeaters to time division multiplex 24-voice channels. Fiber-based DLC systems are now more popular. For customers near a CO, it is cheaper to connect them directly with twisted-pair cables. Depending on the cost of DLC electronics, it becomes more economical to serve customers with DLC systems beyond a certain distance. This *prove-in distance* has been decreasing as DLC electronics costs have come down because of the advancement of semiconductor and optical-electronics technologies.

The concept of *Carrier Serving Area* (CSA) engineering guidelines was introduced in the early 1980s to shorten subscriber loop length, reducing loop deployment cost and supporting all future digital services. The CSA is roughly defined as a serving distance of 9 kft for 26-gauge loops and 12 kft for 24-gauge loops from a remote terminal. CSA design guidelines can be summarized as follows:

- All loops are non-loaded only.

- For loops with 26-gauge cable (used alone or in combination with other gauge cables), the maximum allowable loop length, including bridged taps, is 9 kft.

- If all cable is coarser than 26 gauge, the maximum allowable loop length, including bridged taps, is 12 kft.

- Any single bridged tap is limited to 2 kft maximum length, and the total length of all bridged taps is limited to 2.5 kft maximum length.

- The total length of multi-gauge cable containing 26-gauge cable must not exceed the following:

$$12 - \frac{(3 \times L_{26})}{9 - L_{BTAP}} \, kft$$

The value L_{26} is the total length of 26-gauge cable, excluding bridged tap, and L_{BTAP} is the total length of all bridged taps.

- Although not a transmission constraint, it is suggested for administrative purposes that no more than two gauges of cables be used.

A 1991 Bellcore loop survey shows that over 60 percent of DLC loops meet the CSA guidelines.[5] In the context of DSL systems, the term CSA is applied to loops that originate from a CO as well, if they meet CSA guidelines.

A CSA is further divided into one to six *Distribution Areas* (DA), as shown in Figure 2.8. A DA is characterized by a single FDI where crossconnectors are located. A DA typically serves about 500 customers. Distribution cables emanating from an FDI usually have 1.5 to 2 pairs for all potential customer living units. On the other hand, cable pairs from a Remote Terminal (RT) to FDI are installed based on the number of real customer lines with a smaller spare ratio. This strategy is aimed at an overall minimized installation cost. The average serving distance of each DA is usually significantly shorter than that of a CSA. The Bellcore 1991 loop survey shows that most DA distribution loops are less than 6 to 8 kft in length (26 and 24 gauge, respectively).

Figure 2.8   CSA and DA

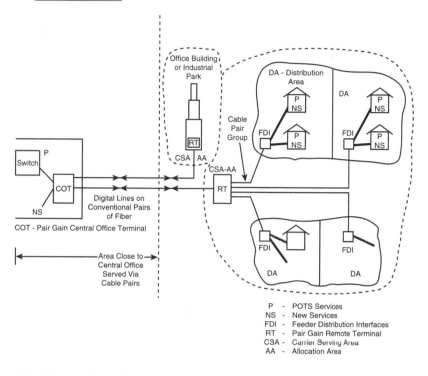

P   -   POTS Services
NS   -   New Services
FDI   -   Feeder Distribution Interfaces
RT   -   Pair Gain Remote Terminal
CSA   -   Carrier Serving Area
AA   -   Allocation Area

2.3.3   T1 Line Configurations

T1 lines,[6] carrying 24 DS0 channels with a transmission rate of 1.544 Mbps, are used for both DLC systems and customer private lines. The T1 technology was originally developed during the 1960s based on semiconductor transistors. A T1 line requires two twisted pairs, with each pair dedicated to one direction of transmission. T1 repeaters, where signals are received and regenerated, are placed along a T1 line at intervals of 6 kft. To minimize the effect of CO noise, the first T1 repeater is only 3 kft away from a CO. The transmission spectrum of T1 is centered around 750 KHz. The transmission power of T1 is relatively high, and a T1 transmitter could produce significant crosstalk noises to a DSL system sharing the same cable and the same frequency band.

T1 lines in the feeder cable are usually well engineered so that binder groups separate from those used for POTS are utilized. Statistically, the percentage of T1 lines in the loop plant is relatively small. Samples of customer T1 private lines are collected from two regional telephone companies.[7]

Figure 2.9 shows length distribution of these T1 lines. There are about 300 different T1 line configurations for each database. Those lines are located in different geographic areas.

Considering that only a limited number of T1 private lines have been installed (around 200,000 in the United States), this sample size is statistically significant. Some configurations have a number of T1 lines running parallel. Most T1 lines have more than one repeater.

Figure 2.9 Private T1 Line Length Distribution

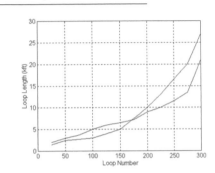

The average T1 line length is 8423 feet, and the median T1 line length is 5383 feet. The average distance between repeaters is 2491 feet, and the median distance is 2487 feet. The average T1 signal loss between repeaters is about 18 dB, which is much lower than the 32 dB design requirement. It is also important to note that, on average, the T1 line multiple number is small; therefore, the number of T1 disturbers will be relatively low.

2.4 Voice Channel Characteristics

A DSL system might need to be designed to coexist with a POTS service on the same twisted-pair cable, assuming there is only one twisted-pair loop available to some telephone subscribers. A *Frequency Division Multiplex* (FDM) scheme is necessary to separate the voice channel from the spectrum occupied by a DSL system. The understanding of POTS voice signal level as well as dialing/ring signaling levels is required for the design of a DSL system that coexists with a POTS. Furthermore, a certain signal-to-noise ratio is to be maintained for a voice band modem to operate under out-of-band leakage energy from a DSL system.

Voice signals are digitized by line cards of switches at the end COs. The quantization and aliasing noise generated from the digitization process could be a limiting factor for the optimal performance of a voice band modem. The DSL leakage energy level in the voice band should be kept below this quantization/aliasing noise floor to minimize DSL-to-voice-band interference. The digitization process consists of sampling lowpass filter, companding, Analog to Digital Conversion (ADC), and Pulse Code Modulation (PCM). The sampling filter affects the voice channel frequency response and the amount of aliasing noise. The ADC generates equalization noise. The companding process distorts the analog voice signal such that more digital bits are allocated to a lower magnitude signal. The companding process effectively enhances the effect of noise.

2.4.1 Companding Methods

The μ-law of companding is defined by the following expression:

$$F_\mu(x) = \text{sgn}(x)\frac{\ln(1+\mu x)}{\ln(1+\mu)}$$

Figure 2.10 shows how $F_\mu(x)$ changes as a function of μ. Note that for small x, $F_\mu(x)$ approaches a linear function, while for large x, $F_\mu(x)$ approaches a logarithmic function.

Figure 2.10 Logarithmic Companding Characteristics

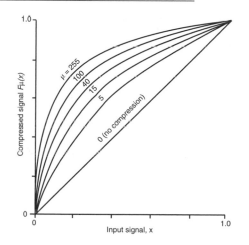

Although the μ-law of companding has found acceptance in the North American and Japanese digital networks, the standard companding law in Europe is the A-law, which is defined by the following expressions:

$$F_A(x) = \text{sgn}(x)\frac{1+\ln A|x|}{1+\ln A} \quad \frac{1}{A} \le |x| \le 1$$

$$F_A(x) = \text{sgn}(x)\frac{A|x|}{1+\ln A} \quad 0 \le |x| \le \frac{1}{A}$$

Note that for small x, $F_A(x)$ is truly logarithmic for $|x|>1/A$ and truly linear for $|x|<1/A$.

2.4.2 *Voice Channel Attenuation and Phase Delay*

The attenuation and phase delay of a typical voice channel, 3002 line as defined by the traditional Bell system telephony practice, are shown in Figures 2.11 and 2.12, respectively. In Figure 2.11, attenuation values between the two dashed lines are considered acceptable. In Figure 2.12, a phase delay value lower than the dashed line is also considered acceptable. These characteristics are mainly due to the effects of sampling lowpass filter, Digital to Analog Conversion (DAC) reconstruction lowpass filter, and line coupling transformers connection subscriber loops to switches. In addition, the voice signal can be attenuated by up to 22 dB due to subscriber loop (0–4 dB), interoffice trunk (6–12 dB), and CO (0–6 dB) losses.

Figure 2.11 Attenuation of a Voice Channel

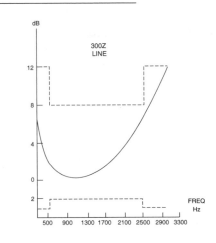

Figure 2.12 Phase Delay of a Voice Channel
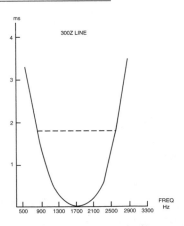

The signal power in a voice channel can be measured in dBrn, which is defined as the dB ratio to a reference noise power of 10^{-12} Watt. The voice band signal power is often measured in dBrnc, which is the same dB ratio as defined for dBrn, but with the inclusion of a message-waiting filter. A message-waiting filter has the frequency response similar to our hearing system to de-emphasize energy contribution from lower and higher frequency regions of a 3.3 KHz voice band. For a relatively flat signal, the inclusion of the message-waiting filter could reduce the power by about 2 dB.

For a good voice channel, the required noise level is about 23 dBrnc, which is about 25 dBrn, to achieve a good quality voice transmission for a voice channel loss of about 10 dB. Equivalently, the required voice channel noise level is about 25— –90=— –65 dBm, in which 0 dBrn is equivalent to –90 dBm, which is defined as the dB ratio to a reference noise power of 10^{-3} Watt. The noise power density level is then the following for a 3 KHz voice channel:

$$10\log_{10}\left(10^{\frac{-65}{10}}\,/3000\right) \approx -100 dBm\,/\,Hz$$

Regulations limit the total voice channel transmit signal power level to less than –9 dBm. On the other hand, a mean voltage of about 0.25 volts on a load impedance of 600 ohms generates a total power of –9.8 dBm. This is equivalent to a flat transmit power density level of –44.57 dBm/Hz for a bandwidth of 3 KHz.

2.4.3   Voice Channel Signaling Tones

The voice channel relies on signaling tones to establish a telephone connection. Tone dials provide address information during dialing; however, tone dial signals might be high in power. Without proper filtering, tone dial signals could saturate the ADC of a DSL system. Tone dials contain a dual tone multifrequency (DTMF) signal generator with a four-row by three-column push-button pad. Each push-button corresponds to two tones in a two-of-eight scheme.

Figure 2.13 shows the tone frequencies corresponding to each key. The tone frequencies are chosen in such a way that their harmonics and distortion products will not interfere with other DTMF, call progress, or signaling tones. The signal levels applied to the loop at the telephone instrument are 14 to 4 dBm per frequency with a maximum *twist* (level difference between the two tones) of 4 dB.

There are also dial, busy, ringback, and receiver off-hook tones. Parameters of the Precision Tone Plan tones are summarized in Table 2.1.

Figure 2.13 The Dual Tone MultiFrequency (DTMF) Scheme

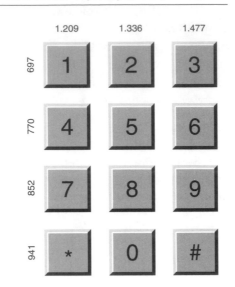

Table 2.1 Common Call Progress Tone Plans

Tone	Tone Frequency	Level per Frequency	Voltage per Frequency	Interruption Rate
Dial	350+440 Hz	−13 dBm	0.17 volts	Continuous
Busy tone	480+620 Hz	−24 dBm	0.049 volts	60 IPM
Ringback	440+480 Hz	−19 dBm	0.087 volts	2 s on and 4 off
Receiver off-hook tone	1400+2060+ 2450+2600 Hz	−6 to 3 dBm	0.39–1.09 volts	Continuous or interrupted

The called telephone is alarmed by a ringing signal. The frequencies normally used for ringing range from 16 Hz to 66 2/3 Hz. They are arranged in relationships and are given such names as *harmonic*, *decimonic*, *synchromonic*, and *single frequency*, as shown in Table 2.2.

Table 2.2 Common Ringing Schemes

Ringing Scheme	Frequencies (Hz)
Decimonic	20, 30, 40, 50, 60
Harmonic	16 2/3, 25, 33 1/3, 50, 66 2/3
Synchromonic	16, 30, 42, 54, 66
Single frequency	20 (or any above)

The ringing voltage applied to the loop by the CO line circuit varies from a nominal 105 volts at 16 Hz to 140 volts at 66 2/3 Hz. The AC ringing signal is also biased by a DC voltage, usually 48 volts, to enable the CO to detect called party answer by sensing a DC current. Each telephone ringer presents an AC coupled load of between 5000 and 10000 ohms to the loop. Ring voltage can drop to as low as 40 volts on a long loop with a large number of ringers attached.

When the call is answered and the telephone set is picked up off the hook, the ringing voltage can generate an impulse with an amplitude as high as the peak of the ringing signal. This impulse could have an amplitude as high as 150 volts. Impulses can also be generated by a telephone set with a mechanical rotary dialer. A rotary dialer can generate about 10 pulses per second with a peak-to-peak voltage variation of less than 48 volts.

With the general understanding of a telephone subscriber loop and its role in an end-to-end telephone connection, you are ready to explore in more detail the transmission characteristics of DSL systems. Characteristics of a DSL system transmission channel are related to loop distance, cable type, background noise, and noise to and from other coexisting systems. A DSL system is usually engineered with accurate channel and noise models in conjunction with extensive simulation studies.

End Notes

1. Members of the technical staff, Bell Telephone Laboratories, *Transmission Systems for Communications*, Fifth Edition (Bell Telephone Laboratories, Inc., 1982).

2. W. D. Reeve, *Subscriber Loop Signaling and Transmission Handbook, Analog* (IEEE Press, 1992).

3. T. H. Wu, *Fiber Network Service Survivability* (Artech House, 1992).

4. "ISDN Basic Access Digital Subscriber Lines," *Bellcore Technical Reference,* TR-TSY-000393, Issue 1 (May 1988).

5. "Generic Requirements for High-Bit-Rate Digital Subscriber Lines," *Bellcore Technical Advisory,* TA-NWT-001210, Issue 1 (October 1991).

6. H. Cravis and T. V. Crater, "Engineering of T1 Carrier Systems Repeated Lines," *Bell System Tech J.,* vol. 42 (March 1996): 431–486.

7. W. Y. Chen and D. L. Waring, "Applicability of ADSL to Support Video Dial Tone in the Copper Loop," *IEEE Communications Magazine,* vol. 32, no. 5 (May 1994): 102–109.

Twisted-Pair Channel Modeling

The twisted-pair telephone loop transmission channel modeling has played an important role in the engineering of DSL systems. Following a tradition of ensuring a better than 95 percent rate of success for first time installations, DSL systems have been designed for satisfactory operations in worst-case transmission conditions.

For channel modeling, worst-case telephone loop configurations are first obtained through extensive loop surveys. The transmission characteristics of these worst-case loops are then simulated with channel impulse responses derived from twisted-pair cable primary parameters available through accurate measurements. With accurate channel models, computer simulation studies can be carried out to understand the transmission performance potential of the telephone subscriber loop plant under different system assumptions.

With channel models in conjunction with noise models (presented in Chapter 4, "Transceiver Front-End Noise Models"), advanced transceiver architectures and signal processing algorithms can be tested for the telephone loop plant environment effectively and efficiently. This chapter explains the basic concepts and techniques of twisted-pair channel modeling, as follows:

- *Primary and secondary parameters of twisted-pair cables.* The transmission characteristics of a twisted-pair cable can be accurately specified by primary parameters as defined for a distributed equivalent circuit of a transmission line. The secondary parameters have often been used for performance analysis of ideal transmission lines; however, both primary and secondary parameters of twisted-pair cables are frequency dependent.

- *Two port network ABCD parameters.* ABCD parameters of a two-port network equivalent circuit can be obtained for a twisted-pair cable from its secondary parameters. To construct accurate channel models for twisted-pair telephone loops, each cable section is represented by its ABCD parameters. The ABCD parameters of the twisted-pair tele-phone loop are then obtained by cascading all cable sections in series. A general purpose electronic circuit can also be divided into a few two-port networks to simplify required transmission performance analysis.

- *Channel transfer function, insertion loss, and impulse response.* The transfer function of a twisted-pair telephone loop can be calculated from its ABCD parameters. The insertion loss, which is a slight variation of the transfer function, has been used as the channel model for DSL system performance simulation studies. The corresponding impulse response is used in simulation studies to generate a received signal at the input of a DSL transceiver.

- *Extended twisted-pair primary constants.* Some basic twisted-pair cable primary parame-ters are listed in Tables 3.2, 3.3, and 3.4 at the end of this chapter. The frequency range of these parameters has been extended from 5 MHz to 20 MHz based on the frequency relationships of these parameters discussed early in the initial sections of this chapter.

3.1 *Primary and Secondary Parameters of Twisted-Pair Cables*

A specific telephone subscriber loop model can be constructed according to twisted-pair cable primary constants.[1,2] In general, twisted cable primary constants R, L, and G are vari-ables of frequency, while shunt capacitance C can be considered as fixed without losing too much accuracy. Figures 3.1, 3.2, and 3.3 show frequency characteristics of the series resis-tance R, series inductance L, and shunt conductance G, respectively, for a 26-gauge PIC cable at the temperature of 70 degrees Fahrenheit.

Figure 3.1   The Series Resistance of the 26-Gauge PIC Cable

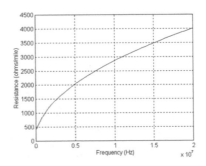

Figure 3.2   The Series Inductance of the 26-Gauge PIC Cable

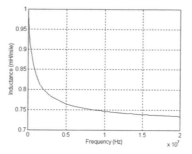

Figure 3.3   The Shunt Conductance of the 26-Gauge PIC Cable

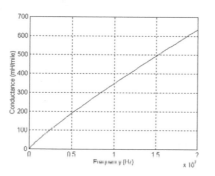

Values of these primary constants are expressed in terms of per unit distance. This kind of description is consistent with the distributed equivalent circuit of a transmission line. Figure 3.4 shows a unit component of such a distributed equivalent circuit. The equivalent circuit of an ideal transmission line consists of many of these units, with identical and frequency-independent primary constants, connected in a cascade. A twisted-pair cable can also be represented with this kind of distributed equivalent circuit, except these primary constants are frequency dependent.

These primary parameters can be measured directly or indirectly with wide bandwidth and high precision test equipment; however, some data fitting might be necessary due to the sensitivity of these measurements. Data fitting can be based on some general frequency relationships of these primary parameters. The series resistance as represented in Figure 3.1 is approximately proportional to the square root of frequency:

$$R(f) = a + b\sqrt{f}$$

Figure 3.4   The Transmission Line Equivalent Circuit

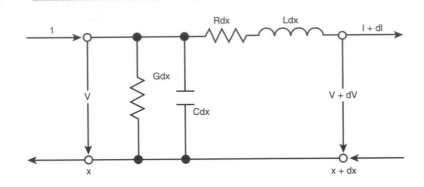

The values for *a* and *b* are empirically obtained by comparing them with measurements. The series inductance as represented in Figure 3.2 is approximately proportional to the inverse of the square root of frequency:

$$L(f) = c + \frac{d}{\sqrt{f}}$$

The values for *c* and *d* are also empirically obtained. The shunt conductance as represented in Figure 3.3 is approximately proportional to the frequency. In general, these series resistance, series inductance, and shunt conductance fittings are only valid for a limited frequency range.

These methods of primary parameter fitting can also be used to estimate twisted-pair cable parameters at frequencies that exceed existing measurements.[3] By fitting measurements from 1 MHz to 5 MHz, for example, you can obtain estimated series resistance and inductance for frequencies up to 20 MHz.

According to these primary constants, you can find twisted-pair cable secondary parameters, characteristic impedance:

$$Z_0(s) = \sqrt{\frac{R(f) + sL(f)}{G(f) + sC(f)}}$$

The complex frequency of $s=j2nf$ is introduced for the complex characteristics impedance and the propagation constant:

$$\gamma(s) = \sqrt{\left(G(f) + sC(f)\right)\left(R(f)\right) + sL(f)\right)}$$

As expected, both the characteristic impedance and propagation constant of a loop constructed with twisted-wire pairs are functions of frequency.

A loop is perfectly terminated if it is terminated with its characteristic impedance. For a perfectly terminated loop with length d, the transfer function is given by

$$H(d,s) = e^{-d\gamma(s)} = e^{-d\alpha(f)} e^{-jd\beta(f)}$$

The values are as follows:

$\gamma(s)$ is a complex function of frequency f.

$\alpha(f)$ and $\beta(f)$ are both real functions of frequency f.

Figures 3.5 and 3.6 show the real part and the imaginary part, respectively, of the propagation constant.

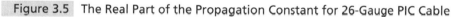

Figure 3.5   The Real Part of the Propagation Constant for 26-Gauge PIC Cable

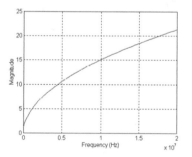

At high frequency, $f>250\ kHz$, the twisted-pair transfer function can be simplified as follows:

$$H(d,f) = e^{-d\left(k_1\sqrt{f} + k_2 f\right)} e^{-jdk_3 f}$$

The value for d is assumed to be in units of mile, and f is in units of Hertz.

Figure 3.6 The Imaginary Part of the Propagation Constant for 26-Gauge PIC Cable

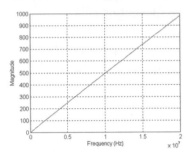

The proportional constants k_1 and k_2 can be estimated by minimizing the mean square fitting error between real parts of the simplified model and $\alpha(f)$, while k_3 can be easily identified by comparing it with the imaginary parts. For real parts, you have

$$\varepsilon_i^2 = \left(k_1\sqrt{f_i} + k_2 f_i - \alpha_i(f_i)\right)^2$$

for different frequency points. Taking partial derivatives of the error sum at different frequencies and making them equal to zeros results in the following:

$$k_1 \sum_{i=1}^{n} f_i + k_2 \sum_{i=1}^{n} f_i^{1.5} = \sum_{i=1}^{n} f_i^{0.5} \alpha_i(f_i)$$

$$k_1 \sum_{i=1}^{n} f_i^{1.5} + k_2 \sum_{i=1}^{n} f_i^2 = \sum_{i=1}^{n} f_i \alpha_i(f_i)$$

Values of k_is for different gauge of twisted pairs are summarized in Table 3.1.

Table 3.1 Parameters for a Simplified Cable Model

Gauge	$k_1 (\times 10^{-3})$	$k_2 (\times 10^{-8})$	$k_3 (\times 10^{-5})$
22	3.0	0.035	4.865
24	3.8	−0.541	4.883
26	4.8	−1.709	4.907

When the channel attenuation or loss is expressed in units of dB, you have[4]

$$L_{dB}(d,f) = -20\log_{10}|H(d,f)| = \frac{20}{\ln 10}d\alpha(f) \approx 8.686 d\alpha(f)$$

The loss value in dB units is proportional to the length of a cable. Supposing that the loss is 20 dB at a particular frequency for a 5 kft loop, the loss would be 30 dB for a 7.5 kft loop of the same gauge at the same frequency.

3.2   Two-Port Networks and ABCD Parameters

The simplified twisted-pair cable transfer function based on the propagation constant $H(d,f) = e^{-d\alpha(f)}e^{-jd\beta(f)}$ is only good for a single gauge twisted pair with perfect terminations at both ends. A subscriber loop, however, usually consists of many sections of different gauge, with bridged taps, and terminated with a resistive impedance. The transfer function of a telephone subscriber loop is not a simple product of transfer functions of these twisted-pair cable sections because of impedance mismatches. To accurately represent a subscriber loop channel, the concept of a two-port network and its ABCD parameter representation is normally used for the analysis of DSL systems.

An electronic circuit usually has an input port and an output port. The function of the electronic circuit is to produce a desired output signal based on a certain input signal. A twisted-pair cable section or a twisted pair telephone subscriber loop also has an input port and an output port. The function of an electronic circuit or the transfer function of a twisted-pair telephone loop can be determined according to its input/output current/voltage relationships. Figure 3.7 shows the model of a two-port network that can represent an electronic circuit or a twisted-pair telephone loop.

Figure 3.7   A Standalone Two-Port Network

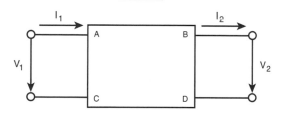

V_1 and I_1 are input port voltage and current, respectively. V_2 and I_2 are output port voltage and current, respectively. Input port voltage and current and output port voltage and current are related by ABCD parameters of the two-port network.

For a standalone two-port network, the input and output voltage and current relationship is represented as follows:

$$V_1 = AV_2 + BI_2$$

$$I_1 = CV_2 + DI_2$$

or in matrix format as

$$\begin{bmatrix} V_1 \\ I_1 \end{bmatrix} = \begin{bmatrix} A & B \\ C & D \end{bmatrix} \begin{bmatrix} V_2 \\ I_2 \end{bmatrix}$$

in which these ABCD parameters are defined as

$$A = \frac{V_1}{V_2}\bigg|_{I_2=0}$$

$$B = \frac{V_1}{I_2}\bigg|_{V_2=0}$$

$$C = \frac{I_1}{V_2}\bigg|_{I_2=0}$$

$$D = \frac{I_1}{I_2}\bigg|_{V_2=0}$$

ABCD parameters for a simple two-port network consisting of a series impedance, as shown in Figure 3.8, can be derived as follows:

$$A = \frac{V_1}{V_2}\bigg|_{I_2=0} = 1$$

$$B = \frac{V_1}{I_2}\bigg|_{V_2=0} = Z$$

$$C = \frac{I_1}{V_2}\bigg|_{I_2=0} = 0$$

$$D = \frac{I_1}{I_2}\bigg|_{V_2=0} = 1$$

Figure 3.8   A Series Impedance as a Two-Port Network

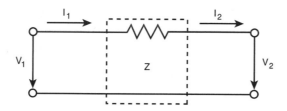

Therefore, the ABCD parameter matrix for a series impedance Z as a two-port network is as follows:

$$\begin{bmatrix} A & B \\ C & D \end{bmatrix} = \begin{bmatrix} 1 & Z \\ 0 & 1 \end{bmatrix}$$

ABCD parameters for another simple two-port network consisting of a shunt impedance, as shown in Figure 3.9, can be derived as follows:

$$A = \frac{V_1}{V_2}\bigg|_{I_2=0} = 1$$

$$B = \frac{V_1}{I_2}\bigg|_{V_2=0} = 0$$

$$C = \frac{I_1}{V_2}\bigg|_{I_2=0} = \frac{1}{Z}$$

$$D = \frac{I_1}{I_2}\Big|_{V_2=0} = 1$$

Figure 3.9 A Shunt Impedance as a Two-Port Network

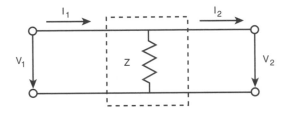

Therefore, the ABCD parameter matrix for a shunt impedance Z is

$$\begin{bmatrix} A & B \\ C & D \end{bmatrix} = \begin{bmatrix} 1 & 0 \\ Z^{-1} & 1 \end{bmatrix}$$

ABCD parameters of a twisted-pair cable are complex and frequency dependent, and they are related to characteristic impedance $Z_o(s)$ and propagation constant $\gamma(s)$, as follows:

$$A(s) = D(s) = \cosh \gamma(s)d$$

$$B(s) = Z_0(s) = \sinh \gamma(s)d$$

$$C(s) = \frac{1}{Z_0(s)} \sinh \gamma(s)d$$

The value for d is the length of the twisted-pair cable.

Many electronic circuits can be divided into a few simpler two-port networks. These simpler two-port networks are usually connected either in series or in parallel. A twisted-pair telephone loop consists of many twisted-pair cables in series. The use of twisted-pair ABCD parameters is convenient because each section of a twisted-pair subscriber loop can be described by its own ABCD parameters, and the ABCD parameters of the whole subscriber loop are the matrix product of individual ABCD matrices.

3.2.1 Two-Port Networks in Series

You can obtain the ABCD parameters of two two-port networks in series by equating the voltage and current of the first two-port network to that of the following network, as shown in Figure 3.10, and deriving the relationship between input voltage and current of the first two-port network to output voltage and current of the following network.

Figure 3.10 Two Two-Port Networks in Series

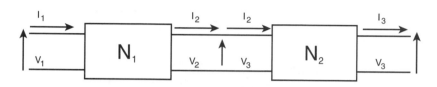

For two two-port networks in series, the input and output voltage and current relationship is represented as follows:

$$\begin{bmatrix} V_1 \\ I_1 \end{bmatrix} = \begin{bmatrix} A_1 & B_1 \\ C_1 & D_1 \end{bmatrix} \begin{bmatrix} V_2 \\ I_2 \end{bmatrix}$$

$$\begin{bmatrix} V_2 \\ I_2 \end{bmatrix} = \begin{bmatrix} A_2 & B_2 \\ C_2 & D_2 \end{bmatrix} \begin{bmatrix} V_3 \\ I_3 \end{bmatrix}$$

and

$$\begin{bmatrix} V_1 \\ I_1 \end{bmatrix} = \begin{bmatrix} A_1 & B_1 \\ C_1 & D_1 \end{bmatrix} \begin{bmatrix} A_2 & B_2 \\ C_2 & D_2 \end{bmatrix} \begin{bmatrix} V_3 \\ I_3 \end{bmatrix}$$

Therefore, the ABCD parameter matrix for two two-port networks in series is

$$\begin{bmatrix} A & B \\ C & D \end{bmatrix} = \begin{bmatrix} A_1 & B_1 \\ C_1 & D_1 \end{bmatrix} \begin{bmatrix} A_2 & B_2 \\ C_2 & D_2 \end{bmatrix} = \begin{bmatrix} A_1A_2 + B_1C_2 & A_1B_2 + B_1D_2 \\ C_1A_2 + D_1C_2 & C_1B_2 + D_1D_2 \end{bmatrix}$$

3.2.2 Two-Port Networks in Parallel

You can obtain the ABCD parameters of two two-port networks in parallel by equating the input and output voltages of the two-port networks, as shown in Figure 3.11, and deriving the relationship between the input voltage and combined input current, as well as between the output voltage and combined output current of these two two-port networks.

Figure 3.11 Two Two-Port Networks in Parallel

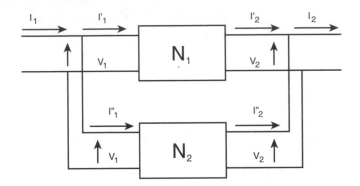

Voltage and current relationships of two two-port networks in parallel are represented as

$$\begin{bmatrix} V_1 \\ I'_1 \end{bmatrix} = \begin{bmatrix} A_1 & B_1 \\ C_1 & D_1 \end{bmatrix} \begin{bmatrix} V_2 \\ I'_2 \end{bmatrix}$$

$$\begin{bmatrix} V_1 \\ I''_1 \end{bmatrix} = \begin{bmatrix} A_2 & B_2 \\ C_2 & D_2 \end{bmatrix} \begin{bmatrix} V_2 \\ I''_2 \end{bmatrix}$$

$$I_1 = I'_1 + I''_1$$

$$I_2 = I'_2 + I''_2$$

Combining

$$V_1 = A_1 V_2 + B_1 I'_2$$

and

$$V_1 = A_2 V_2 + B_2 I''_2$$

results in the following:

$$V_1 = \frac{A_1 B_2 + A_2 B_1}{B_1 + B_2} V_2 + \frac{B_1 B_2}{B_1 + B_2} I_2$$

You also have

$$I_1 = (C_1 + C_2)V_2 + D_1 I''_2 + D_2 I''_2$$

which can be expressed as

$$B_2 I_1 = B_2(C_1 + C_2)V_2 + D_2(A_1 - A_2)V_2 + (B_1 D_2 + B_2 D_1)I'_2$$

or

$$B_1 I_1 = B_1(C_1 + C_2)V_2 + D_1(A_2 - A_1)V_2 + (B_1 D_2 + B_2 D_1)I''_2$$

by using

$$A_1 V_2 + B_1 I'_2 = A_2 V_2 + B_1 I''_2$$

Combining these two expressions together results in the following:

$$I_1 = \frac{(B_1 + B_2)(C_1 + C_2) + (D_1 - D_2)(A_2 - A_1)}{B_1 + B_2} V_2 + \frac{B_1 D_2 + B_2 D_1}{B_1 + B_2} I_2$$

Therefore, the ABCD parameter matrix for two two-port networks in parallel is

$$\begin{bmatrix} A & B \\ C & D \end{bmatrix} = \frac{1}{B_1 + B_2} \begin{bmatrix} A_1 B_2 + B_1 A_2 & B_1 B_2 \\ (B_1 + B_2)(C_1 + C_2) - (A_1 - A_2)(D_1 - D_2) & B_1 D_2 + D_1 B_2 \end{bmatrix}$$

The special case of two identical two-port networks in parallel is represented as

$$A_p = A$$

$$B_p = \frac{B}{2}$$

$$C_p = 2C$$

$$D_p = D$$

in which A, B, C, and D are the ABCD parameters of each individual two-port network, and A_p, B_p, C_p, and D_p are ABCD parameters of two two-port networks in parallel.

3.3 *Channel Transfer Function and Impulse Response*

The ABCD matrix information of a twisted-pair telephone loop can be easily converted into its input impedance or cable transfer function. Corresponding calculations can be put into a computer program[5] to generate channel models in conjunction with a few tables of twisted-pair cable primary parameters. The input impedance of a twisted-pair loop with a terminal impedance of $Z_t(s)$ is expressed as

$$Z_i(s) = \frac{A(s) + \dfrac{B(s)}{Z_t(s)}}{C(s) + \dfrac{D(s)}{Z_t(s)}}$$

in which $A(s)$, $B(s)$, $C(s)$, and $D(s)$ are complex frequency dependent ABCD parameters of a twisted-pair telephone loop. When the other end of the twisted-pair loop is left open, you have the following:

$$Z_{i,o}(s) = \frac{A(s)}{C(s)}$$

This is also the impedance of a bridged tap. A bridged tap can be considered as a two-port network with only a shunt impedance. Therefore, the ABCD parameters of a bridged tap are as follows:

$$\begin{bmatrix} 1 & 0 \\ \dfrac{C_{bridge}(s)}{A_{bridge}(s)} & 1 \end{bmatrix}$$

The values $A_{bridge}(s)$ and $D_{bridge}(s)$ are parts of frequency-dependent ABCD parameters of the section of twisted-pair cable connected as a bridged tap.

The transfer function of a twisted-pair loop with a source impedance of $Z_s(s)$ and a terminal impedance of $Z_t(s)$ is

$$H(s) = \frac{Z_t(s)}{Z_s(s)\big(C(s)Z_t(s) + D(s)\big) + A(s)Z_t(s) + B(s)}$$

When the effect of source impedance is excluded, that is $Z_s(s)=0$, you have the following:

$$H(s) = \frac{1}{A(s) + \dfrac{B(s)}{Z_t(s)}}$$

Following earlier practices of the Bell System[6], the insertion loss, which is defined as

$$H_{INS}(s) = \frac{Z_s(s) + Z_t(s)}{Z_s(s)\big(C(s)Z_t(s) + D(s)\big) + A(s)Z_t(s) + B(s)}$$

has been used as the channel model for DSL system performance simulation studies.[7] The use of insertion loss avoids the signal loss caused by the voltage division between source and loop input impedance while still including the effect of the source impedance or the voltage division between source and termination impedance when the loop is very short. For an example of a zero length or null loop, that is, for

$$\begin{bmatrix} A & B \\ C & D \end{bmatrix} = \begin{bmatrix} 1 & 0 \\ 0 & 1 \end{bmatrix}$$

the transfer function is

$$H(s) = \frac{Z_t(s)}{Z_s(s) + Z_t(s)}$$

while the insertion loss is

$$H_{INS}(s) = \frac{Z_s(s) + Z_t(s)}{Z_s(s) + Z_t(s)} = 1$$

Figures 3.12 and 3.13 show real and imaginary parts, respectively, of the input impedance for the 9 kft 26-gauge twisted-pair loop with a terminal resistance of 100 ohm.

Figure 3.12 The Real Part of the Input Impedance of the 9 kft 26-Gauge Twisted-Pair Loop

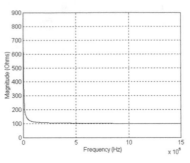

Figure 3.13 The Imaginary Part of the Input Impedance of the 9 kft 26-Gauge Twisted-Pair Loop

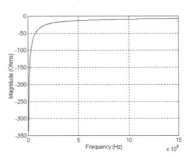

Figure 3.14 shows the magnitude of the input impedance for the 9kft 26-gauge twisted-pair loop with a terminal resistance of 100 ohms.

Figure 3.14 The Input Impedance of the 9 kft 26-Gauge Twisted-Pair Loop

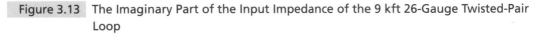

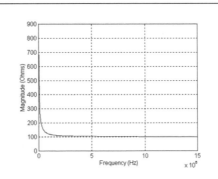

Figures 3.15 and 3.16 show the magnitude and phase, respectively, of the insertion loss for the 9 kft 26-gauge twisted-pair loop.

Figure 3.15 The Magnitude of the Insertion Loss for the 9 kft 26-Gauge Loop

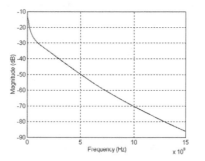

Figure 3.16 The Phase of the Insertion Loss for the 9 kft 26-Gauge Loop

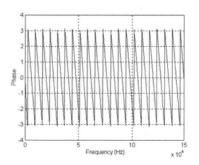

Figure 3.17 shows the corresponding impulse response of the 9kft 26-gauge twisted-pair loop.

Figure 3.17 The Impulse Response of the 9 kft 26-Gauge Loop

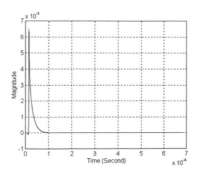

Figure 3.18 shows the configuration of a twisted-pair subscriber loop with bridged taps.

Figure 3.18 The Configuration of a Subscriber Loop with Bridged Taps

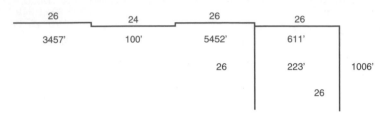

Figure 3.19 shows the magnitude of the input impedance at both ends of the loop.

Figure 3.19 The Input Impedance of a Twisted-Pair Loop with Bridged Taps

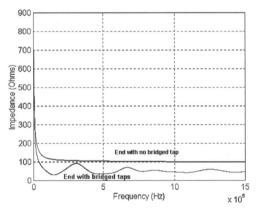

Figure 3.20 shows the magnitude of the transfer function for the loop in both directions.

Figure 3.20 The Transfer Function of a Twisted-Pair Loop with Bridged Taps

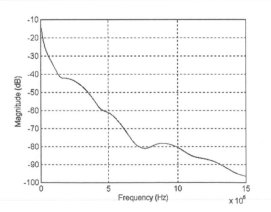

The input impedance is different at each end of a twisted-pair loop with bridged taps, while the insertion loss for the same twisted-pair loop with bridged taps and the same source and terminal impedance are the same in different directions. This can be explained as follows: The ABCD parameters of a two-port network at the reverse direction are related to those of the same two-port network at the forward direction as

$$
\begin{bmatrix} A_r & B_r \\ C_r & D_r \end{bmatrix} = \begin{bmatrix} D_f & B_f \\ C_f & S_f \end{bmatrix}
$$

Therefore the input impedance of a twisted-pair telephone loop at the reverse direction is

$$
Z_{rn}(s) = \frac{A_r(s) + \dfrac{B_r(s)}{Z_t(s)}}{C_r(s) + \dfrac{D_r(s)}{Z_t(s)}} = \frac{D_f(s) + \dfrac{B_f(s)}{Z_t(s)}}{C_f(s) + \dfrac{A_f(s)}{Z_t(s)}} \neq Z_{fi}(s) = \frac{A_f(s) + \dfrac{B_f(s)}{Z_t(s)}}{C_f(s) + \dfrac{D_f(s)}{Z_t(s)}}
$$

The input impedance at different ends are different because $A_f(s)$ $D_f(s)$ for twisted-pair telephone loops with random bridged taps. On the other hand, the insertion loss at the reverse direction of a twisted pair telephone loop with bridged taps and the same source and terminal impedance, $Z(s)$, is:

$$
H_{INS_r}(s) = \frac{2Z(s)}{C_r(s)Z^2(s) + (D_r(s) + A_r(s))Z(s) + B_r(s)} = \frac{2Z(s)}{C_f(s)Z^2(s) + (A_f(s) + D_f(s))Z(s) + B_f(s)} = H_{INS_f}(s)
$$

The insertion loss at different directions of a twisted-pair telephone loop with random bridged taps could be the same as long as source and terminal impedance are the same.

3.4   Extended Twisted-Pair Primary Constants

Tables 3.2, 3.3, and 3.4 list the frequency-dependent primary parameters for 22-gauge, 24-gauge, and 26-gauge PIC twisted-pair cables, respectively, at a temperature of 70° F. More detailed data can be found in DSL standard documents that are cited in Chapter 1, "Introduction," as well as the references at the end of this chapter.

Parameters are listed in the following tables with a log frequency scale. Some data fitting is necessary when using these tables to construct channel models. Primary parameters have been extended from 5 MHz to 20 MHz according to frequency relationships discussed in section 3.1, "Primary and Secondary Parameters of Twisted-Pair Cables," earlier in this chapter. The use of different fitting methods could cause some small discrepancies in the resulting channel models.

Table 3.2 22-Gauge PIC Cable at 70 Degrees F

Frequency (Hz)	R (ohm/Mile)	L (mH/Mile)	G (μ–Mho/ Mile)	C (μF/ Mile)
1	174.27	0.9861	0.000	0.083
5	174.27	0.9861	0.001	0.083
10	174.27	0.9861	0.001	0.083
15	174.27	0.9861	0.001	0.083
20	174.27	0.9861	0.002	0.083
30	174.27	0.9861	0.003	0.083
50	174.27	0.9861	0.005	0.083
70	174.27	0.9861	0.006	0.083
100	174.27	0.9861	0.009	0.083
150	174.27	0.9860	0.013	0.083
200	174.27	0.986	0.017	0.083
300	174.28	0.9860	0.024	0.083
500	174.29	0.9858	0.040	0.083
700	174.29	0.9857	0.054	0.083
1000	174.31	0.9856	0.076	0.083
1500	174.34	0.9853	0.110	0.083
2000	174.37	0.9850	0.145	0.083
3000	174.44	0.9844	0.211	0.083
5000	174.62	0.9833	0.341	0.083
7000	174.83	0.9821	0.467	0.083
10000	175.22	0.9804	0.652	0.083
15000	176.06	0.9778	0.954	0.083
20000	177.11	0.9744	1.248	0.083
30000	179.86	0.9672	1.824	0.083
50000	187.64	0.9491	2.943	0.083
70000	197.71	0.9372	4.032	0.083
100000	215.55	0.9237	5.630	0.083
150000	247.57	0.9055	8.229	0.083
200000	277.95	0.8898	10.772	0.083
300000	333.39	0.8642	15.744	0.083

Frequency (Hz)	R (ohm/Mile)	L (mH/Mile)	G (μ–Mho/ Mile)	C (μF/ Mile)
500000	421.57	0.8309	25.396	0.083
700000	493.24	0.8123	34.796	0.083
1000000	583.59	0.7950	48.587	0.083
1500000	707.91	0.7783	71.014	0.083
2000000	812.72	0.7681	92.958	0.083
3000000	988.53	0.7557	135.865	0.083
5000000	1267.31	0.7429	219.158	0.083
7000000	1493.93	0.7367	300.284	0.083
10000000	1779.64	0.7309	419.297	0.083
15000000	2172.76	0.7254	612.834	0.083
20000000	2504.18	0.7222	802.205	0.083

Table 3.3   24-Gauge PIC Cable at 70 Degrees F

Frequency (Hz)	R (ohm/Mile)	L (mH/Mile)	G (μ–Mho/ Mile)	C (μF/ Mile)
1	277.19	0.9861	0.000	0.083
5	277.19	0.9861	0.001	0.083
10	277.19	0.9861	0.002	0.083
15	277.19	0.9861	0.003	0.083
20	277.19	0.9861	0.004	0.083
30	277.19	0.9861	0.005	0.083
50	277.19	0.9861	0.008	0.083
70	277.19	0.9861	0.011	0.083
100	277.19	0.9861	0.016	0.083
150	277.20	0.9860	0.022	0.083
200	277.20	0.9860	0.028	0.083
300	277.20	0.9860	0.040	0.083
500	277.21	0.9859	0.063	0.083
700	277.22	0.9858	0.084	0.083
1000	277.23	0.9857	0.115	0.083
1500	277.25	0.9854	0.164	0.083

continues

Table 3.3 Continued

Frequency (Hz)	R (ohm/Mile)	L (mH/Mile)	G (μ–Mho/ Mile)	C (μF/ Mile)
2000	277.28	0.9852	0.210	0.083
3000	277.34	0.9848	0.299	0.083
5000	277.48	0.9839	0.466	0.083
7000	277.66	0.9829	0.625	0.083
10000	277.96	0.9816	0.853	0.083
15000	278.58	0.9793	1.213	0.083
20000	279.35	0.9770	1.558	0.083
30000	281.30	0.9723	2.217	0.083
50000	286.82	0.9577	3.458	0.083
70000	294.29	0.9464	4.634	0.083
100000	308.41	0.9347	6.320	0.083
150000	337.22	0.9204	8.993	0.083
200000	369.03	0.9087	11.550	0.083
300000	431.55	0.8885	16.436	0.083
500000	541.69	0.8570	25.633	0.083
700000	632.08	0.8350	34.351	0.083
1000000	746.04	0.8146	46.849	0.083
1500000	902.84	0.7947	66.665	0.083
2000000	1035.03	0.7825	85.624	0.083
3000000	1256.77	0.7676	121.841	0.083
5000000	1608.38	0.7523	190.021	0.083
7000000	1894.20	0. 7449	254.644	0.083
10000000	2254.56	0.7380	347.294	0.083
15000000	2750.38	0.7314	494.193	0.083
20000000	3168.38	0.7275	634.737	0.083

Table 3.4 26-Gauge PIC Cable at 70 Degrees F

Frequency (Hz)	R (ohm/Mile)	L (mH/Mile)	G (μ–Mho/ Mile)	C (μF/ Mile)
1	440.75	0.9861	0.000	0.083
5	440.75	0.9861	0.001	0.083

Frequency (Hz)	R (ohm/Mile)	L (mH/Mile)	G (μ–Mho/ Mile)	C (μF/ Mile)
10	440.75	0.9861	0.002	0.083
15	440.76	0.9861	0.003	0.083
20	440.76	0.9861	0.004	0.083
30	440.76	0.9861	0.005	0.083
50	440.76	0.9861	0.008	0.083
70	440.76	0.9861	0.011	0.083
100	440.76	0.9861	0.016	0.083
150	440.76	0.9861	0.022	0.083
200	440.76	0.9860	0.028	0.083
300	440.76	0.9860	0.040	0.083
500	440.77	0.9859	0.063	0.083
700	440.78	0.9859	0.084	0.083
1000	440.79	0.9858	0.115	0.083
1500	440.81	0.9856	0.164	0.083
2000	440.83	0.9854	0.210	0.083
3000	440.88	0.9850	0.299	0.083
5000	441.01	0.9843	0.466	0.083
7000	441.15	0.9836	0.625	0.083
10000	441.39	0.9825	0.853	0.083
15000	441.87	0.9907	1.213	0.083
20000	442.45	0.9789	1.558	0.083
30000	443.88	0.9753	2.217	0.083
50000	447.81	0.9660	3.458	0.083
70000	453.09	0.9546	4.634	0.083
100000	463.39	0.9432	6.320	0.083
150000	485.80	0.9306	8.993	0.083
200000	513.04	0.9212	11.550	0.083
300000	575.17	0.9062	16.436	0.083
500000	699.61	0.8816	25.633	0.083
700000	812.95	0.8614	34.351	0.083
1000000	956.65	0.8381	46.849	0.083
1500000	1154.38	0.8146	66.665	0.083
2000000	1321.07	0.8001	85.624	0.083

continues

Table 3.4 Continued

Frequency (Hz)	R (ohm/Mile)	L (mH/Mile)	G (μ–Mho/ Mile)	C (μF/ Mile)
3000000	1600.68	0.7823	121.841	0.083
5000000	1267.31	0.7638	190.021	0.083
7000000	2044.07	0.7552	254.643	0.083
10000000	2858.90	0.7469	347.294	0.083
15000000	3484.14	0.7391	494.193	0.083
20000000	4011.24	0.7344	634.737	0.083

End Notes

1. "Some Transmission Characteristics of Telephone Cables Used in the Loop Plant," *IBM T1D1 Contribution,* T1D1.3/86-003 (January 24, 1986).

2. "ISDN Basic Access Digital Subscriber Lines," *Bellcore Technical Reference,* TR-TSY-000393, Issue 1 (May 1988).

3. W. Y. Chen, "Twisted-Pair Channel Models for VDSL," *Texas Instruments T1E! Contribution,* T1E1.4/96-134 (April 9, 1996).

4. J. J. Werner, "The HDSL Environment," *IEEE JSAC,* vol. 9, no. 6 (August 1991): 785–800.

5. D.G. Messerschmitt, "A Transmission Line Simulator Written in C," *IEEE Transcript on Selected Areas in Communications* (January 1984).

6. *Transmission Systems for Communications,* Fifth Edition (Bell Telephone Laboratories, 1982): 267.

7. "A Technical Report on High-Bit-Rate Digital Subscriber Lines (HDS)," *Texas Instruments T1E1 Contribution,* T1E1.4/96-006, Working Draft (April 22, 1996).

Transceiver Front-End Noise Models

Noise is the combination of irrelevant signals coming from intelligent sources, such as other transmission systems, and non-intelligent sources, such as a microwave oven. When the noise occurs in the frequency band of communication interest, the strength of the noise could affect the quality of communication.

In a busy restaurant, for example, conversation is difficult without raising your voice because the noise floor has been raised significantly by other loud conversations. On the other hand, casual conversation is discouraged in a movie theater to keep the quality of the sound high. For telecommunication, the combination of a high signal level and a low noise level could result in an effective transmission system.

For a DSL system, the strength of a received signal is determined by the strength of the signal from the corresponding transmitter and the attenuation of the telephone subscriber loop. The effectiveness of the received signal, however, is judged relative to the noise level at the front end of a DSL transceiver. Besides the limitation of a transceiver hardware noise floor, there are three types of noise that affect the performance of a DSL system:

- *Crosstalk noise*. Crosstalk noise comes from adjacent telephone subscriber loops of the same or different types of transmission systems. This can also be divided as *Near End Crosstalk* (NEXT) and *Far End Crosstalk* (FEXT) noises. The effect of crosstalk noise is similar to conversation in a noisy restaurant in that raising your voice (transmit signal strength) alone sometimes cannot make the communication any better because others are doing the same.

- *Impulse noise*. Impulse noises are random impulses with magnitudes that are so high that their presence can be associated with receiver detection errors. The impulse noise can be from poor quality CO switching equipment or household electronics, such as a light dimmer.

- *Background noise.* Background noise exists in the telephone loop plant at a level that is a little stronger than the thermal or semiconductor noise level. This background noise can be caused by the combination of the background radio noise and noise generated by electrical and electronic devices and picked up by the telephone loop plant for its great exposure. Radio noises related to specific sources, such as AM medium and short wave radio stations, are discussed later in Chapter 15, "VDSL (Very-High-Bit-Rate Digital Subscriber Lines)."

The severity of a particular noise can be measured from its power level or its power density level. The magnitude of background noise can be in the range of 10 to 30 of micro-volts. The noise power is usually expressed in units of *dBm*, which is defined as follows:

$$P = 10 \times \log_{10} \frac{v^2}{R \times P_m} = 10 \times \log_{10} \frac{v^2}{100 \times 0.001}$$

The value for v is the average voltage of the noise, $R=100$ is the receiver input impedance, and $P_m=0.001$ is the reference of one milli-Watt.

The noise power density is usually expressed in units of *dBm/Hz*, which is defined as follows:

$$PSD = 10 \times \log_{10} \frac{v^2}{R \times P_m \times B} = 10 \times \log_{10} \frac{v^2}{0.1 \times B}$$

The value for B is the bandwidth of noise or of particular interest in unit of *Hertz*. For an example, the background noise power density is about *−140 dBm/Hz* while the receiver front-end electronics thermal noise power density could be lower than *−150 dBm/Hz*.

4.1 *Crosstalk Noise*

As discussed in Chapter 3, "Twisted-Pair Channel Modeling," telephone subscriber loops are organized in binder groups of 10, 25, or 50 pairs. Many binder groups share a common physical and electrical shield in a cable. Due to capacitive and inductive coupling, there is crosstalk between each twisted pair even though pairs are well insulated at DC. The effect of crosstalk is minimized by adapting different twist distances among different pairs in a binder group. Binder groups are also twisted such that no two groups are adjacent for long runs. For DSL systems, in which the signal bandwidth is well beyond the voice frequency, the crosstalk could become a limiting factor to the achievable transmission throughput.

In addition to Near End Crosstalk (NEXT) and Far End Crosstalk (FEXT) noises, described in the list at the beginning of this chapter, there is also *self crosstalk,* which is initiated from adjacent transmitters of the same type of DSL system. Further, there is *foreign crosstalk,* which is initiated from other DSL or twisted-pair systems.

The severity of crosstalk could be related to the system installation scale, that is, the total number of disturbers in the same twisted pair cable. Crosstalk coupling loss models have been developed for NEXT and FEXT with the consideration of different number of disturbers. These crosstalk coupling loss models are based on twisted pairs within the same cable of significant length, usually longer than 1 kilofeet. The effect of crosstalk could be different if only a portion of twisted pairs are within the same cable.

4.1.1 NEXT Coupling Configurations

NEXT is defined as the crosstalk effect between a receiving path and a transmitting path of DSL transceivers at the same end of two different subscriber loops within the same twisted-pair cable. The NEXT noise at the receiver front end of a particular DSL transceiver is caused by signals transmitted by other transceivers at the same end of the twisted cable. Specifically, a near-end transceiver i would experience NEXT noise from the near-end transceiver j if the two transceivers share the same frequency spectrum within the same twisted-pair cable, as indicated by Figure 4.1.

Figure 4.1 The Principles of NEXT

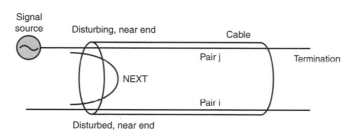

Self-NEXT is defined as NEXT caused by other transceivers of the same type. Self-NEXT has been considered a limiting factor for the transmission performance of DSL and HDSL systems when transmissions in opposite directions occupy the same spectrum, and the separation of transmitted and received signals is achieved through adaptive echo cancellation. *Foreign-NEXT* is defined as NEXT caused by other transceivers of different types. Transceivers of other types could have different transmission spectrums and different signal transmission levels. ADSL can experience foreign-NEXT from HDSL, and vice versa.

4.1.2 FEXT Coupling Configurations

FEXT is defined as the crosstalk effect between a receiving path and a transmitting path of DSL transceivers at opposite ends of two different subscriber loops within the same twisted-pair cable. The FEXT noise at the receiver front end of a particular DSL transceiver is caused by signals transmitted by other transceivers at the opposite end of the twisted cable. Specifically, a near-end transceiver i would experience FEXT noise from the far-end transceiver j if they share the same frequency spectrum within the same twisted-pair cable, as indicated by Figure 4.2.

Figure 4.2   The Principles of FEXT

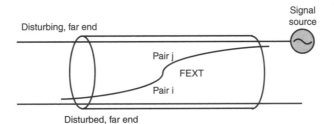

There is also *self-FEXT* from the same types of transceivers and *foreign-FEXT* from different types of transceivers. The effect of self-NEXT might dominate that of self-FEXT when both exist for such systems as DSL and HDSL. There is always self-FEXT unless all transceivers are synchronized and sending the same data sequence.

When self-NEXT is absent (through the arrangement of *Frequency Division Multiplex* (FDM) systems between transmissions in opposite directions, for example), the effect of self-FEXT could dominate that of background noise in certain frequency regions. For an FDM system, such as ADSL, the dominant noise component could be different at different frequency regions. It could be self-FEXT, foreign-NEXT, or background noises.

4.1.3 Distribution of Crosstalk Coupling Losses

The coupling mechanism of crosstalk has been studied since the early 1900s.[1] It was discovered that the crosstalk is mainly due to the unbalance of coupling capacitance of a twisted-pair cable. The effect of NEXT was seriously considered during the system engineering of the T1 system.[2] FEXT was also considered during T1 transmission engineering efforts but was classified as a minor factor compared with NEXT.

The study of transmission issues related to T1 systems established a first step in dealing with NEXT modeling for simulations. The study not only tried to model NEXT loss with mean and standard deviation, but also initiated the use of 1 percent worst-case NEXT value for overall system requirements. The reason is that people were expecting better than 95 percent satisfactory T1 service at an error ratio of less than 10^{-6}.

Note
The 95 percent satisfactory service rate for initial installation without the involvement of technicians for field visits has been a common industry practice to keep the cost of providing telecommunication service in control.

The use of the 1 percent worst case for transmission engineering would allow multiple spans of T1 systems in an end-to-end service connection and also provide room for some unforeseen impairments.

Crosstalk loss is defined as the attenuation for a disturbing signal to pass through the coupling mechanism arriving at a disturbed receiver. There are different crosstalk losses for NEXT and FEXT. Crosstalk losses from one pair to another pair are different for different pair-to-pair combinations. The crosstalk loss values can differ by up to 40 dB at a single frequency and have a nearly Gaussian distribution.[3,4] Figure 4.3 shows the distribution of NEXT loss at a frequency of 1 KHz.

Figure 4.3 The Distribution of NEXT and FEXT Losses

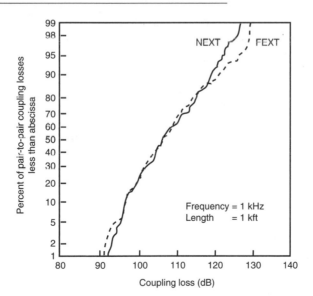

The 1 percent worst-case crosstalk loss shown at the bottom of the graph in Figure 4.3 is about 40 dB less than that of the 99 percent case. There are only 1 percent crosstalk losses with values that are lower than that of the 1 percent worst case.

There are lots of measurements and calculations involved in the statistical analysis of crosstalk losses, even for a single frequency. There could be 1,225 different NEXT values at a particular frequency for a 50-pair binder group, assuming the pair-to-pair NEXT is symmetrical. The measured NEXT losses can be approximated with a gamma or a truncated Normal distribution on log scale.

The truncated Normal distribution has a better physical meaning because the number of NEXT pairs is limited. In practice, you might be concerned about NEXT from more than one disturber, in which case you need to calculate a power sum for multiple disturbers. In a 50-pair group, you have 50, 3.16×10^{15}, and 4.1×10^{11} different power sum NEXT values for 49 disturbers, 24 disturbers, and 10 disturbers, respectively. The computation of power sums for 24 and 10 disturbers is usually carried out by a computer because of the large number of calculations required.

4.1.4 *The Unger NEXT and Simplified NEXT/FEXT Models*

Because of the work load, measurements of NEXT have only been made for a few particular frequencies. A NEXT model that covers a broad frequency range was necessary for the study of DSL transmission performance. J.H.W. Unger of Bellcore constructed a distributed, cross-coupling computer program with many simulated twisted pairs to model the crosstalk process based on the unbalanced-coupling capacitance principle. The coupling capacitance parameters were calibrated by comparing simulated results with real measurements at available frequencies. The NEXT effect was then simulated for the broad range of frequencies. These simulated results also represented the effect of a different number of disturbers.

Simulation results were summarized as the Unger 1985 model illustrated in Figure 4.4.[5] This Unger model was developed based on a 50-pair 18 kft. 22-Gauge PIC cable terminated with characteristic impedance at both ends for the 1 percent worst-case NEXT. The Unger model is very close to that used by an earlier study.[6]

The piece-wise linear (log-log scale) Unger NEXT model has loss values of 57 dB, 61 dB, and 67 dB for 49 disturbers, 10 disturbers, and 1 disturber, respectively, at a frequency of 80 KHz. A simplified 49 disturber NEXT model, which has 57 dB of loss at 80 KHz and a linear (log-log scale) slope of –15 dB/decade, has also been used and can be expressed as

$$NEXT_{49} = \frac{1}{1.134 \times 10^{13}} f^{\frac{3}{2}}$$

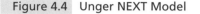

Figure 4.4 Unger NEXT Model

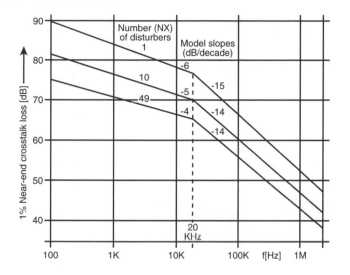

The value f is in units of *Hertz*, and the $NEXT_{49}$ value is a unit-less ratio, which can be expressed in dB by taking the base 10 Log of the $NEXT_{49}$ ratio and then multiplying it by 10.

This simplified NEXT model can also be generalized for N disturbers as

$$NEXT_N = \left(\frac{N}{49}\right)^{0.6} \frac{1}{1.134 \times 10^{13}} f^{\frac{3}{2}}$$

Notice that the loss difference between 1 disturber and 49 disturbers is about 10 dB. You can assume this general scaling factor is due to the physical arrangement of twisted pairs under the 1 percent worst-case condition. In other words, when you are dealing with 1 percent worst case, you are only interested in the disturbing pairs that are closest to the disturbed pair. Therefore, the additional group of disturbing pairs causes less disturbances because it is further away from the original group of disturbing pairs.

This leads to a generalized expression dealing with multiple disturber groups.[7] Assuming that N^1 is the number of disturbers for the first dominant disturbing pair group and N^2 is the number of disturbers for the second disturbing pair group, you have the following formulation:

$$NEXT_{N_1} = \left(\frac{N_1}{49}\right)^{0.6} \frac{1}{1.134 \times 10^{13}} f^{\frac{3}{2}}$$

$$NEXT_{N_2} = \left(\frac{N_1 + N_2}{49N_1}\right)^{0.6} \frac{1}{1.134 \times 10^{13}} f^{\frac{3}{2}}$$

In other words, two groups of disturbers that have different disturbing signal spectra should use two slightly different NEXT models to take into account the physical structure of the twisted-pair cable. This relationship between different types of disturber groups is consistent with the measurements.[8]

A simplified 49 disturber FEXT loss model can be expressed as

$$FEXT_{49} = kdf^2 |H(f)|^2$$

The values are as follows:

- $k=8 \times 10^{-20}$ is empirically derived from the FEXT measurements.
- d is the loop length in feet.
- f is the frequency in Hz.
- $H(f)$ is the transfer function of the loop.

Due to the similarity between NEXT and FEXT distribution, the same power sum scale for NEXT can also be applied to FEXT, in which case you have the following:

$$FEXT_N = \left(\frac{N}{49}\right)^{0.6} kdf^2 |H(f)|^2$$

These NEXT/FEXT models can be used in conjunction with the transmit signal power density to obtain crosstalk noise power density at the front end of a DSL receiver. For example, the NEXT power density at the front end of a DSL receiver can be expressed as

$$PSD_{NEXT}(f) = S(f)NEXT_N(f) = \left(\frac{N}{49}\right)^{0.6} \frac{S(f) \times f^{\frac{3}{2}}}{1.134 \times 10^{13}}$$

The value $S(f)$ is the power density of the transmit signal.

The FEXT power density at the front end of a DSL receiver can be expressed as

$$PSD_{FEXT}(f) = S(f)FEXT_N(f) = S(f) \times \left(\frac{N}{49}\right)^{0.6} kdf^2 |H(f)|^2$$

These 1 percent worst-case NEXT models have been based on the exact collocation of transmitters and receivers. This is generally true for transceivers located at a CO, but not for transceivers at customer premises. At the subscriber end, transceivers are very likely to be distributed at different customer premises apart from each other. In addition, the collocation assumption might not be true when considering NEXT or FEXT from other digital systems, such as T1 lines. Up to 5.5 dB of additional loss has been considered for the T1 NEXT by other studies.[9,10]

4.2 Impulse Noise

Unlike crosstalk noise—whose cause can be identified—the origin of impulse noise is more difficult to locate. Impulse noise could come directly through some connections to the telephone subscriber loop or come from the influence of an electromagnetic field.

Impulse noise is characterized as a random pulse waveform whose amplitude is much higher compared with the Gaussian-like background noise. According to some survey results, the amplitude of impulse noise is usually between 5 and 20 mV, and the frequency of impulses is between 1 and 5 per minute.[11] Also, the duration of the impulse waveform lasts from 30 to 150 microseconds. It was believed that impulse energy was concentrated at below 40 KHz; however, this might be caused by the bandwidth of impulse measuring equipment.

Characteristics of impulse noise could be quite different at other locations.[12,13] It has been a continuous effort to better understand the characteristics and effects of the impulse noise during the development of many DSL systems. Impulse noise is a major impairment for ADSL, especially due to the heavy ADSL subscriber loop loss. According to a Bellcore study, a majority of impulses would cause a receiver detection error, compared with the very weak received ADSL signal.

A NYNEX impulse noise study shows that impulse noises with amplitudes between 10 and 40 mV occur at about 10 times per minute on average.[14,15] A Deutsche Bundespost impulse noise study exposed that impulse noises were somehow related to daily activities (see Figure 4.5).[16]

Figure 4.5 Frequency of Impulses During a Day

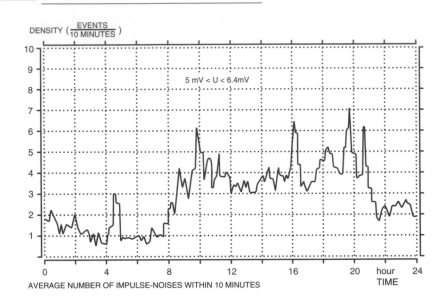

The Deutsche Bundespost impulse noise study also indicated that the probability density function of the amplitude u of impulse noise can be approximated by

$$p(u) = \frac{u_0^2}{u^3}$$

over an amplitude range of 5 to 40 mV, in which u_0=5 mV. Thus, the probability that the magnitude of the amplitude u exceeds some value u_t is described as follows:

$$P(|u| > u_t) = \left(\frac{u_0}{u_t}\right)^2$$

This hyperbolic distribution model is derived from impulse measurements, as expressed in Figure 4.6.

Figure 4.6 Impulse Noise Amplitude Distribution

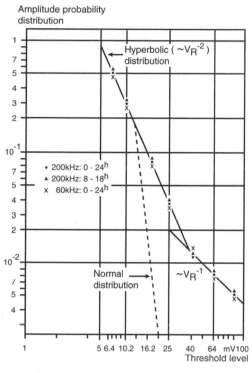

AMPLITUDE PROBABILITY DISTRIBUTION

It was also suggested by the Deutsche Bundespost impulse noise study that above 40 mV, the amplitude probability distribution is modeled by

$$P(|u| > u_t) = \frac{u_1}{u_t}$$

in which u_1=0.625 mV.

Two impulse noise wave forms have been suggested by Bellcore for an ADSL impulse noise performance test, as shown in Figures 4.7 and 4.8.[17] The impulse noise waveform #1 has more high frequency components compared with the impulse noise waveform #2. Both are real impulse waveforms collected from a field impulse noise survey.

Figure 4.7 Test Impulse Noise Waveform #1

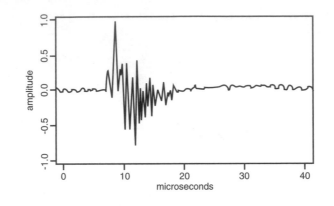

Figure 4.8 Test Impulse Noise Waveform #2

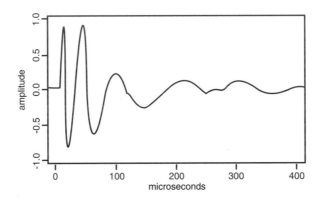

Amplitudes of the waveforms depicted in Figures 4.7 and 4.8 are normalized and adjusted during a test to see the threshold at which these waveforms can cause error. The threshold can then be converted to the estimated probability that a second will be erred, as follows:

$$E = 0.0037\,P(u > u_{e1}) + 0.0208\,P(u > u_{e2})$$

The value u_{e1} = 25 mV, and the value u_{e2} = 40 mV.[18]

While crosstalk and background noises impose a limit on transmission throughput over the twisted-pair telephone subscriber loop, the error caused by impulse noise can be corrected with forward error correction codes. The required error correction coding overhead could reduce the transmission throughput a little.

4.3   *Background and Receiver Front-End Thermal Noise*

By avoiding the effect of NEXT and FEXT, the loop plant noise level or the receiver front-end noise level becomes a limiting factor for the performance of a DSL system. During the standardization process of Asymmetrical Digital Subscriber Lines (ADSL), Bellcore conducted a background noise survey at two New Jersey locations. Table 4.1 summarizes the average background noise power density levels for three frequency bands.

Table 4.1   Residential Background Power Density Level (dBm/Hz)

Location	8–100 KHz	100–500 KHz	500 KHz–2MHz
1	−150	−148	−133
2	−136	−153	−146

The analysis of transmission performance over the twisted-pair telephone subscriber loop has been based on the assumption of a received signal over a Gaussian noise. The probability density of the background noise is very close, but not a Gaussian distribution. The histograms of the background noise are very similar to Gaussian density, except that they have short tails. Therefore, the Gaussian noise assumption is still valid.

Based on results from the Bellcore noise survey, the background noise level for the twisted-pair telephone loop plant has been assumed to be −140 dBm/Hz. This assumed that the loop plant background noise level is higher than the thermal noise of a receiver front-end electronic circuit. On the other hand, the circuit noise can easily exceed the −140 dBm/Hz background noise level if the proper design and implementation techniques have not been applied.

The receiver front-end noise level can be made close to that defined by the thermal noise and the noise figure of the first analog amplifier—assuming the interference from the transceiver electronic circuits can be avoided by a good hardware design. For the thermal noise, you have the following formulation:

$$v_{ns}^2 = kTR_s \Delta f$$

Assuming that input and output are both matched to source resistance R_s [19] for $k = 1.37 \times 10^{-23}$, $T = 290°\mathrm{K}$, and $\Delta f = 1 MHz$, you have the thermal noise power

$$\frac{v_{ns}^2}{R_s} = -65\,dBmV$$

as compared to the 0 dBmV defined by the power of 1 millivolts on a 75 ohms impedance. This is corresponding to a noise power density of −174 dBm/Hz. The received signal level becomes strong enough for analog-to-digital conversion at the output of the receiver amplifier. The noise power at the output of the receiver amplifier is the sum of the thermal noise, the amplifier gain, and the amplifier noise figure, ranging from 3 to 7 dB in dB units. In other words, the equivalent receiver front-end noise power density level can be made as low as about −160 dBm/Hz.

End Notes

1. S. H. Lin, "Statistical Behavior of Multipair Crosstalk," *Bell Systems Technical Journal,* vol. 59, no. 6 (July/August 1980): 955–974.

2. S. H. Lin, "Statistical Behavior of Crosstalk Power Sum with Dominant Components," *Bell Systems Technical Journal,* vol. 60, no. 7 (September 1981): 1363–1374.

3. J. H. W. Unger, "Near-End Crosstalk Model for Line Code Studies," *Bellcore T1D1 Contribution,* T1D1.3/85-244 (November 12, 1985).

4. S. V. Ahamed, P. P. Bohn, and N. L. Gottfried, "A Tutorial on Two-Wire Digital Transmission in the Loop Plant," *IEEE Trans. Commun.,* vol. COM-29, no. 11 (November 1981): 1554–1564.

5. This relationship was first suggested by a personal note from J. Bingham of Amati in the middle of 1993.

6. M. Elder and W. Y. Chen, "Effects of NEXT and FEXT in the Same Cable," *BNR and Bellcore Joint T1E1 Contribution,* T1E1.4/93-220 (August 1993).

7. J. Bingham and W. Y. Chen, "NEXT from T1 to ADSL and Vice Versa," *Amati and Bellcore Joint Contribution,* T1E1.4/93-178 (August 1993).

8. W. Y. Chen and D. L. Waring, "Applicability of ADSL to Support Video Dial Tone in the Copper Loop," *IEEE Communications Magazine,* vol. 32, no. 5 (May 1994): 102–109.

9. Bingham and Chen, "NEXT from T1 to ADSL and Vice Versa."

10. Chen and Waring, "Applicability of ADSL to Support Video Dial Tone in the Copper Loop": 102–109.

11. J. J. Werner, "Impulse Noise in the Loop Plant," *Proc. IEEE ICC '90,* Atlanta, Georgia (April 16–19, 1990): 1734–1737.

12. W. Henkel and T. Kessler, "Statistic Description and Modeling of Impulse Noise on the German Telephone Network," *Electron. Lett.,* vol. 30, no. 12 (June 9, 1994): 935–936.

13. J. W. Cook, "Wideband Impulse Noise Survey of the Access Network," *BT Tech. J.,* vol. 11 (1993): 155–162.

14. "NYNEX Loop Performance Survey Final Report," *Bellcore Special Report SR-TSY-0025* (October 1986).

15. R. A. McDonald, "Report on Bellcore Impulse Noise Study," *Bellcore T1D1 Contribution,* T1D1.3/87-256 (July 27, 1987).

16. K. Szechenyi, "On the NEXT and Impulse Noise Properties of Subscriber Loops," *Proc. GLOBECOM '89,* Dallas, Texas (November 27–30, 1989): 1569–1573.

17. K. Kerpez and C. Valenti, "Impulse Noise Testing for ADSL Transceiver," *Bellcore T1E1 Contribution,* T1E1.4/93-034 (March 10, 1993).

18. ANSI T1.413.

19. M. S. Ghausi, *Electronic Circuits* (Van Nostrand Reinhold Company, 1971).

5

Channel Capacity

Channel capacity is defined as the maximum throughput over a particular transmission channel. Specifically, if the throughput of a transmission system is less than the channel capacity, the transmission can be made error free in conjunction with some specific modulation and coding techniques. Channel capacity can be compared with the capacity of a solid container with a certain shape. The maximum capacity of a particular container can be reached if it is filled with liquid; however, to hold solid objects with specific shapes, the maximum capacity of the container can never be reached.

The data sequence sent through a transmission channel can be compared with solid objects with specific shapes. The task of telecommunication systems engineering is similar to finding the best way to pack solid objects such that the utilization of the container (channel) capacity is maximized.

Channel capacity is a good indication of the transmission potential for a particular channel. You can obtain a conservative estimate of the twisted-pair loop plant transmission potential by considering the worst-case channel capacity of the telephone subscriber loop plant. Channel capacity is also a good reference when judging the transmission efficiency of a particular transceiver architecture.

Although early transmission systems are not very efficient, performance of DSL systems can be engineered as close as only a few dBs away from the channel capacity. The channel capacity of a telephone subscriber loop is determined by the transmit signal level, the channel attenuation, and the receiver front-end noise level. For the self-NEXT dominated condition, channel capacity is only related to the channel attenuation. Specifically, channel capacity is based on the signal-to-noise ratio, which could be frequency dependent on a particular telephone subscriber loop.

This chapter presents the basic concepts and calculations of channel capacity for the twisted-pair telephone subscriber loop channel as follows:

- *Signal-to-noise ratio.* Because of the frequency dependence of the attenuation of a twisted-pair cable and the crosstalk coupling function, the SNR of a twisted-pair telephone subscriber loop is also frequency dependent. For a particular telephone subscriber loop, the SNR can be different, depending on the noise environment that can be arranged through system considerations.

- *Channel capacity calculations.* Specifically, the calculation of channel capacity can be further divided into topics, as follows:

  - *Basic channel capacity concept.* For a flat (frequency-independent) channel, the channel capacity is the product of the channel bandwidth and the base 2 log of 1 plus the SNR.

  - *Channel capacity for a twisted-pair telephone subscriber loop with frequency-dependent SNR.* The channel capacity of a twisted-pair telephone loop is the integration of the base 2 log of 1 plus the frequency-dependent SNR. If calculated over the frequency of interest, this channel capacity provides a good reference for the targeted transmission performance of a DSL system.

  - *Differential channel capacity.* By taking the derivative of the channel capacity at a certain frequency, the differential channel capacity gives a good indication of the transmission performance potential for each frequency region of a particular channel.

  - *Channel capacity with implementation constraints.* A 6 dB performance margin, which is achieved through raising the noise level by 6 dB, is usually required for the performance simulation study and confirmation test of DSL systems to compensate for some non-categorized channel impairments. The SNR is normally limited by the dynamic range of a particular hardware implementation. These practical engineering and implementation constraints can also be included in the channel capacity calculation to provide a more realistic reference.

Channel capacity calculations in this chapter are based on 26-gauge twisted-pair loops with lengths of 1 mile, 2 miles, and 3 miles. Corresponding self-NEXT and self-FEXT models are based on 49 disturbers.

5.1   *Signal-to-Noise Ratio*

The frequency-dependent SNR at a receiver front end is related to the received signal power spectrum density and the noise power spectrum density. The received signal power spectrum density, $S(f)$, is determined by the transmit power spectrum density, $Q(f)$, and the twisted-pair loop channel transfer function, $H(f)$, as shown in the following expression:

$$S(f) = Q(f)|H(f)|^2 = Q(f)e^{-2d(k_1\sqrt{f}+k_2 f)}$$

The simplified channel model derived in Chapter 3, "Twisted-Pair Channel Modeling," has been used for this expression:

$$|H(f)| = e^{-d(k_1\sqrt{f}+k_2 f)}$$

The higher the received signal power, the higher the transmission throughput; however, the effectiveness of the received signal power is relative to the noise power also present at the input of a receiver. There are NEXT, FEXT, loop plant background, analog-to-digital conversion quantization, and other electronic hardware noises, as discussed in Chapter 4, "Transceiver Front-End Noise Models."

The strength of a white noise of power density W can be described by its total power σ^2 within a particular bandwidth of B. For the simplified channel model, the received signal-to-white-noise ratio is expressed as

$$\frac{S(f)}{W} = \frac{Q(f)|H(f)|^2}{W} = \frac{P}{\sigma^2}e^{-2d(k_1\sqrt{f}+k_2 f)}$$

The transmit signal density is assumed to be white with a bandwidth of B and P and is the total power of the transmit signal. Figure 5.1 shows signal-to-noise ratios under the white noise condition for primary constant-based and simplified channel models assuming a transmit power density of -40 dBm/Hz and a white noise power density of -140 dBm/Hz.

In Figure 5.1, "5280 ft. S." stands for the 5280 ft., or 1 mile, simplified channel model, while "5280 ft." stands for the primary constants-based channel model. Similar notation applies to loops of other lengths in the same figure and subsequent figures. Simplified channel models produce fewer losses at a low frequency region, below about 300 KHz, and therefore result in higher signal-to-noise ratios. The 3 mile, 15840 ft., 26-gauge twisted-pair loops have 0 dB signal-to-noise ratio at the frequency of about 650 KHz. The shorter 1 mile and 2 mile loops have usable bandwidths up to 1 MHz and beyond.

Figure 5.1 Signal-to-White-Noise Ratio for Twisted-Pair Loops

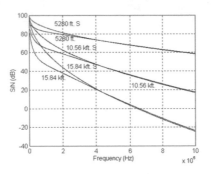

5.1.1 NEXT Signal-to-Noise Ratios

The NEXT noise power spectral density is determined by the transmit power spectral density and the NEXT coupling transfer function. The NEXT power spectral density is expressed as follows:

$$N_N(f) = Q(f)NEXT(f) = Q(f)\frac{1}{1.134 \times 10^{13}} f^{-\frac{3}{2}}$$

Under the self NEXT condition in which the same transmit power spectrum affects both received signal and noise power, the received signal-to-noise ratio is expressed as

$$\frac{S(f)}{N_N(f)} = \frac{Q(f)|H(f)|^2}{Q(f)NEXT(f)} = \frac{e^{-2d(k_1\sqrt{f}+k_2f)}f^{-\frac{3}{2}}}{1.134 \times 10^{-13}}$$

In practice, especially at a low frequency region where the NEXT noise power density is very small, you need to consider the effect of white background noise. By including the background noise power density, the received signal-to-noise ratio becomes

$$\frac{S(f)}{N_N(f)+W} = \frac{Q(f)|H(f)|^2}{Q(f)NEXT(f)+W} = \frac{e^{-2d(k_1\sqrt{f}+k_2f)}}{1.134 \times 10^{-13} f^{\frac{3}{2}} + \frac{\sigma^2}{P}}$$

Figure 5.2 shows signal-to-noise ratios under the self-NEXT-plus-white-noise condition for primary-constant-based and simplified channel models

Figure 5.2 Signal-to-Self-NEXT-Plus-White-Noise Ratio for 26-Gauge Twisted-Pair Loops

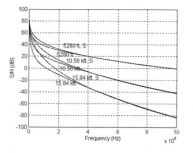

Under the self-NEXT condition, the 3 mile and 2 mile, 26-gauge twisted-pair loops have 0 dB signal-to-noise ratio at the frequency of about 110 KHz and 320 KHz, respectively, while the shortest 1 mile loop has usable bandwidth of about 970 KHz.

5.1.2 FEXT Signal-to-Noise Ratios

The FEXT noise power spectral density is determined by the transmit power spectral density and the FEXT coupling transfer function, as follows:

$$N_F(f) = Q(f)FEXT(f) = Q(f)|H(f)|^2 kdf^2$$

Under the self-FEXT condition where the same transmit power spectrum affects both received signal and noise power, the received signal-to-noise ratio is expressed as

$$\frac{S(f)}{N_F(f)} = \frac{Q(f)|H(f)|^2}{Q(f)FEXT(f)} = \frac{1}{kdf^2}$$

The values are as follows:

$k = 8 \times 10^{-20}$.

d is in unit of ft.

f is in unit of Hz.

The channel model becomes irrelevant when channel transfer functions are the same for the channel model and for the FEXT model.

In practice, especially at a low-frequency region and a high-frequency region where the FEXT noise power density is very small, you need to consider the effect of white background noise. By including the background noise power density, the received signal-to-noise ratio becomes

$$\frac{S(f)}{N_F(f)+W} = \frac{Q(f)|H(f)|^2}{Q(f)FEXT(f)+W} = \frac{1}{kdf^2 + \frac{\sigma^2}{P}e^{2d\left(k_1\sqrt{f}+k_2f\right)}}$$

Figure 5.3 shows signal-to-noise ratios under the self-FEXT-plus-white-noise condition for primary-constant-based and simplified channel models

Figure 5.3 Signal-to-Self-FEXT-Plus-White-Noise Ratio for 26-Gauge Twisted-Pair Loops

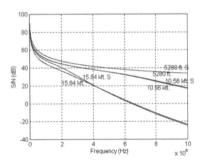

The usable bandwidth for the longest 3 mile, 26-gauge loop is around 650 KHz, which is the same as for the white noise only case. However, the signal-to-noise ratios have been reduced to below 50 dB at frequencies beyond 150 KHz also in comparison with the white noise only case. The usable bandwidths for shorter loops are beyond 1 MHz.

5.2 Channel Capacity Calculations

The transmission throughput of a DSL system is limited by the characteristics of the twisted-pair channel and the noise environment at the receiver front end, no matter what kind of transceiver structure is involved. Specifically, the transmission throughput of a DSL system is limited by the channel capacity for the particular loop and noise combination. Many studies have been carried out for the channel capacity of the twisted-pair telephone subscriber loop.[1]

5.2.1 *Basic Concepts of Channel Capacity*

The efficiency of a practical transmission system can be judged by how many bits per Hertz it can carry. For a simple *Quadrature Amplitude Modulation* (QAM) line code with a baud rate of 1 Hertz, the following expression describes this number of bits per Hertz efficiency:

$$C_{QAM} = \log_2 \left(1 + \frac{3}{\Delta^2} \frac{S}{N} \right)$$

The values are as follows:

S is the received signal power.

N is the receiver front-end noise power.

Δ^2 is related to the desired error rate.

C_{QAM} is in unit of number of bits per symbol or per Hertz for this special example.

In other words, the transmission efficiency of a QAM system is determined by the transmission channel signal-to-noise ratio and the desired error rate. For a desired error rate of 10^{-7}, you can find the value of Δ to be 5.333, according to the Gaussian distribution:

$$10^{-7} = \frac{2}{\sqrt{2\pi}} \int_{\Lambda}^{\infty} e^{\frac{x^2}{2}} \, dx$$

Table 5.1 summarizes Δ values for other error rates.

Table 5.1 Δ and Error Rates						
Error Rate	10^{-2}	10^{-3}	10^{-4}	10^{-5}	10^{-6}	10^{-7}
Δ	2.577	3.287	3.891	4.418	4.892	5.333

Figure 5.4 shows the relationship between the number of bits and the signal-to-noise ratio under different error rates for a QAM line code.

The top curve in Figure 5.4 is the channel capacity. The next lower curve represents the QAM transmission efficiency at an error rate of 10^{-2}. Lower curves are for error rates of 10^{-3}, 10^{-4}, 10^{-5}, 10^{-6}, respectively, and the bottom curve is for the error rate of 10^{-7}. A lower error rate requires a higher signal-to-noise ratio to achieve a certain number of bits per

Hertz; however, the maximum number of bits per Hertz is limited by the following expression, referred to as the channel capacity at a bandwidth of 1 Hertz when $\Delta = \sqrt{3}$:

$$C_e = \log_2\left(1 + \frac{S}{N}\right)$$

Figure 5.4 QAM Transmission Efficiency

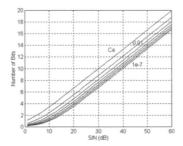

The corresponding error rate is 0.0833. There is an SNR difference of 9.77 dB between error rates of 0.0833 and 10^{-7}. The expression of C_e is the general form of calculation channel capacity. Figure 5.5 shows ratios of QAM transmission efficiency to the channel capacity for different error rates and different SNRs.

Figure 5.5 Efficiency Relative to Channel Capacity

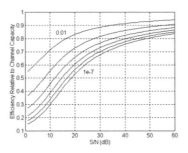

The top curve in Figure 5.5 represents the ratio of QAM transmission efficiency at an error rate of 10^{-2} to channel capacity. Lower curves are ratios for error rates of 10^{-3}, 10^{-4}, 10^{-5}, 10^{-6}, respectively, and the bottom curve is for the ratio of QAM transmission efficiency at an error rate of 10^{-7} to channel capacity. The transmission throughput is only half of the channel capacity at SNRs of 7.5 dB, 12 dB, 15 dB, 17 dB, and 18.5 dB and error rates of 10^{-3}, 10^{-4}, 10^{-5}, 10^{-6}, and 10^{-7}, respectively. The transmission efficiency is relatively high for a QAM line code at a high signal-to-noise ratio.

The channel capacity for a bandwidth of B with a flat signal and noise spectra is

$$C = B\log_2\left(1 + \frac{S}{N}\right)$$

Table 5.2 summarizes the channel capacities of the voice band for different SNRs assuming a bandwidth of 4 KHz with flat signal and noise spectra.

Table 5.2 Voice Band Channel Capacity

S/N (dB)	10	20	30	40	50	60
Channel Capacity (kbps)	13.84	26.63	39.87	53.15	66.44	79.73

5.2.2 Channel Capacity for Frequency-Dependent SNR

For frequency-dependent received signal and noise power spectra with a bandwidth of B, the integral channel capacity is expressed as

$$C = \int_0^B \log_2\left(1 + \frac{S(f)}{N(f)}\right)$$

For the receiver front-end white noise limited condition, the channel capacity is expressed as

$$C = \int_0^B \log_2\left(1 + \frac{S(f)}{N(f)}\right)df = \int_0^B \log_2\left(1 + \frac{P}{\sigma^2}e^{-2d\left(k_1\sqrt{f}+k_2 f\right)}\right)df$$

Figure 5.6 shows channel capacities under the white noise condition for primary-constant-based and simplified channel models assuming a transmit power density of -40 dBm/Hz and a white noise power density of -140 dBm/Hz.

Figure 5.6 White Noise Channel Capacity for 26-Gauge Twisted-Pair Loops

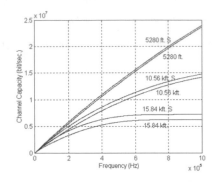

Channel capacities are all higher than 6 Mbps under the background white noise condition for 1 mile, 2 mile, and 3 mile 26-gauge loops.

For the self-NEXT limited condition, the channel capacity is expressed as

$$C = \int_0^B \log_2 \left(1 + \frac{S(f)}{N_N(f)}\right) df = \int_0^B \log_2 \left(1 + \frac{e^{-2d\left(k_1 \sqrt{f} + k_2 f\right)} f^{-\frac{3}{2}}}{1.134 \times 10^{-13}}\right) df$$

For the self-NEXT-plus-receiver-front-end-white-noise-limited condition, the channel capacity is expressed as follows:

$$C = \int_0^B \log_2 \left(1 + \frac{S(f)}{N_N(f) + W}\right) df = \int_0^B \log_2 \left(1 + \frac{e^{-2d\left(k_1 \sqrt{f} + k_2 f\right)}}{1.134 \times 10^{-13} f^{\frac{3}{2}} + \frac{\sigma^2}{P}}\right) df$$

Figure 5.7 shows channel capacities under the self-NEXT-plus-white-noise condition for primary constant based and simplified channel models also assuming a transmit power density of −40 dBm/Hz and a white noise power density of −140 dBm/Hz.

Under the self-NEXT-plus-white-noise condition, channel capacities are below 1 Mbps and 2 Mbps for 3 mile and 2 mile 26-gauge twisted-pair loops, while the 1 mile 26-gauge loop has a channel capacity of beyond 6 Mbps.

Figure 5.7 NEXT-Plus-White-Noise Channel Capacity for the 26-Gauge Twisted-Pair Loops

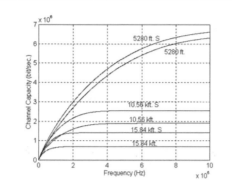

For the self-FEXT-limited condition, the channel capacity is expressed as

$$C = \int_0^B \log_2\left(1 + \frac{S(f)}{N_F(f)}\right) df = \int_0^B \log_2\left(1 + \frac{1}{klf^2}\right) df$$

For the self-FEXT-plus-receiver-front-end-white-noise-limited condition, the channel capacity is expressed as

$$C = \int_0^B \log_2\left(1 + \frac{S(f)}{N_F(f) + W}\right) df = \int_0^B \log_2\left(1 + \frac{1}{klf^2 + \frac{\sigma^2}{P}e^{2d\left(k_1\sqrt{f} + k_2 f\right)}}\right) df$$

Figure 5.8 shows channel capacities under the self-FEXT-plus-white-noise condition for primary-constant-based and simplified channel models, also assuming a transmit power density of −40 dBm/Hz and a white noise power density of −140 dBm/Hz.

Under the self-FEXT-plus-white-noise condition, the channel capacity of the 3 mile 26-gauge loop is about 6 Mbps, which is the same as the white noise only case, while the shorter 2 mile and 3 mile loops have channel capacities above 10 Mbps.

Figure 5.8 FEXT-Plus-White-Noise Channel Capacity for the 26-Gauge Twisted-Pair Loop

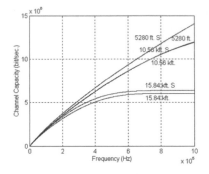

You can examine the contribution of an individual frequency region to the overall channel capacity by taking derivative of the channel capacity to obtain the differential channel capacity. The receiver-front-end-white-noise-limited condition is expressed as

$$\frac{dC}{dB} = \log_2\left(1 + \frac{S(f)}{W}\right) = \log_2\left(1 + \frac{P}{\sigma^2}e^{-2d\left(k_1\sqrt{f}+k_2f\right)}\right)$$

The differential channel capacity is just the base 2 logarithm of receiver front-end signal-to-noise ratio. Figure 5.9 shows differential channel capacities under the white noise condition for primary-constant-based and simplified channel models assuming a transmit power density of −40 dBm/Hz and a white noise power density of −140 dBm/Hz. The maximum differential channel capacity is $\log_2\left(1+1\times10^{10}\right) \approx 33.2$ bits. The differential channel capacity becomes 1 bit when the signal-to-noise ratio is 1.

Figure 5.9 White Noise Differential Channel Capacity

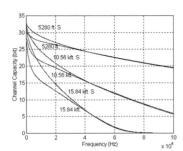

For the self-NEXT-limited condition, the differential channel capacity is expressed as

$$\frac{dC}{dW} = \log_2\left(1 + \frac{S(f)}{N_N(f)}\right) = \log_2\left(1 + \frac{e^{-2d\left(k_1\sqrt{f}+k_2 f\right)}f^{-\frac{3}{2}}}{1.134\times 10^{-13}}\right)$$

For the self-NEXT-plus-receiver-front-end-white-noise-limited condition, the differential channel capacity is expressed as

$$\frac{dC}{dW} = \log_2\left(1 + \frac{S(f)}{N_N(f)+W}\right) = \log_2\left(1 + \frac{e^{-2d\left(k_1\sqrt{f}+k_2 f\right)}}{1.134\times 10^{-13}f^{\frac{3}{2}} + \dfrac{\sigma^2}{P}}\right)$$

Figure 5.10 shows differential channel capacities under the self-NEXT-plus-white-noise condition for primary-constant-based and simplified channel models, also assuming a transmit power density of -40 dBm/Hz and a white noise power density of -140 dBm/Hz.

Figure 5.10   NEXT-Plus-White-Noise Differential Channel Capacity

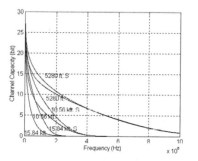

Under the self-NEXT-limited condition, the majority of the frequency region where the channel is usable has a differential channel capacity of fewer than 10 bits. The channel is almost closed at about 200 KHz and 400 KHz for 3 mile and 2 mile loops, respectively.

For the self-FEXT-limited condition, the differential channel capacity is expressed as

$$\frac{dC}{dB} = \log_2\left(1 + \frac{S(f)}{N_F(f)}\right) = \log_2\left(1 + \frac{1}{klf^2}\right)$$

For the self-FEXT-plus-receiver-front-end-white-noise-limited condition, the differential channel capacity is expressed as

$$\frac{dC}{dB} = \log_2\left(1+\frac{S(f)}{N_F(f)+W}\right) = \log_2\left(1+\frac{1}{klf^2+\dfrac{\sigma^2}{P}e^{2d\left(k_1\sqrt{f}+k_2 f\right)}}\right)$$

Figure 5.11 shows differential channel capacities under the self-FEXT-plus-white-noise condition for primary-constant-based and simplified channel models, also assuming a transmit power density of −40 dBm/Hz and a white noise power density of −140 dBm/Hz.

Figure 5.11   FEXT-and-White-Noise Differential Channel Capacity

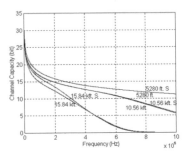

Under the self-FEXT-limited condition, there are big portions where the differential channel capacity is larger than 5 bits. These 1 mile and 2 mile loops have a usable bandwidth beyond 1 MHz, while the 3 mile loop has a usable bandwidth of about 650 KHz.

5.2.3   *Channel Capacity with Implementation Constraints*

The channel capacity can be used as a reference for a DSL system design. With advanced modulation and coding techniques, the transmission throughput of a DSL system can be brought to within 2 to 6 dB of the channel capacity. You can further take some practical and test-procedural constraint into account to obtain a conditional channel capacity as a more practical design reference.

You observed from the previous calculations, for example, the high channel capacity of the self-FEXT-plus-white-noise-limited conditional is partially a contribution of the high signal-to-noise ratio (larger than 60 dB) at the low-frequency region. In practice, these high signal-to-noise ratios might not be realized due to the receiver hardware dynamic range.

One of the practical limitations of the SNR at the very low-frequency region is the transformer, which blocks DC and creates a high-pass filter that greatly reduces the SNR at very low frequency.

Figure 5.12 shows channel capacities under the same self-FEXT-plus-white-noise condition for primary-constant-based and simplified channel models except with a constraint of a hardware dynamic range of less than, for example, 45.15 dB. This effect is emulated by limiting the differential channel capacity to less or equal to 15 bits for all frequencies. As the figure indicates, channel capacities can be reduced by 10–15 percent due to hardware dynamic range.

Figure 5.12 FEXT Channel Capacity with 45.15 dB Hardware Dynamic Range

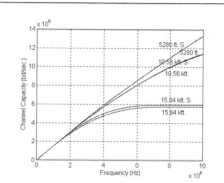

Many DSL systems were designed with a 6 dB performance margin reserved for non-characterized loop and system impairments. Figure 15.13 shows channel capacities under the same self-NEXT-plus-white-noise condition for primary-constant-based and simplified channel models with the addition of a 6 dB performance margin. The effect of the 6 dB performance margin is emulated by reducing the signal-to-noise ratio by a factor of 4 at all frequencies. The additional 6 dB performance margin can reduce the channel capacity by more than 20 percent.

Similar channel capacities can be calculated for 22-gauge and 24-gauge twisted-pair loops. You can find the distance scaling factor between different gauges of loops for the simplified channel model. Ignoring the effect of k_2s, you have the following:

$$d_{22} = d_{26} \frac{k_{1,26}}{k_{1,22}} = d_{26} \frac{4.8}{3.0} = 1.6 d_{26}$$

Figure 5.13 NEXT Channel Capacity with 6 dB Noise Margin

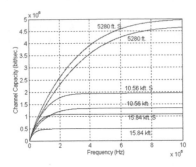

Therefore, the channel capacities of a 5280 ft. 26-gauge simplified channel model are equivalent to those of a 8448 ft. 22-gauge simplified channel model. Similarly, you have

$$d_{24} = d_{26} \frac{k_{1,26}}{k_{1,24}} = d_{26} \frac{4.8}{3.8} = 1.26 d_{26}$$

in which the simplified channel models are as follows for 26-gauge and 24-gauge twisted-pair cables, respectively:

$$H(d,f) = e^{-d\left(k_{1,26}\sqrt{f} + k_{2,26}f\right)}$$

$$H(d,f) = e^{-d\left(k_{1,24}\sqrt{f} + k_{2,24}f\right)}$$

This means that the channel capacities of a 5280 ft. 26-gauge simplified channel model is equivalent to those of a 6669 ft. 24-gauge simplified channel model.

End Notes

1. I. P. Auer, "Channel Capacity of Subscriber Loops Considering Near-End Crosstalk as the Dominant Source of Noise," Bellcore internal memorandum (June 1988). I. Kalet and S. Shamai-Shitz, "On the Capacity of a Twisted-Wire Pair: Gaussian Model," *IEEE Trans. Commun.*, vol. 38, no. 3 (March 1990): 379–383. J. T. Aslanis and J. M. Cioffi, "Achievable Information Rates on Digital Subscriber Loops: Limiting Information Rates with Crosstalk Noise," *IEEE Trans. Common.*, vol. 40, no. 2 (February 1992): 361–372. J. J. Werner, "The HDSL Environment," *IEEE JSAC*, vol. 9, no. 6 (August 1991): 785–800.

Hybrid Circuits

For half-duplex telegraphs of early days, transmission was carried out only in one direction over one pair of two-wire cables at a given time. The transmission direction can be regulated through some handshake protocol whenever a transceiver at one end has data to transmit. The transmission direction can also be time divided: transceivers at both ends are synchronized and take turns transmitting. This is sometimes called *Time Division Multiplex* (TDM) or *Time Division Duplex* (TDD), respectively. For a telephone conversation, a real-time, full-duplex system, in which telephone subscribers at both ends can talk and listen simultaneously, is preferred to emulate a more natural situation.

Real-time, full-duplex transmission of voice signals can be accomplished using a hybrid circuit, which connects a microphone and an earphone to a two-wire telephone subscriber loop. A hybrid circuit is basically an electrical bridge. There is little signal from the transmit path coming back to the receiving path when the electrical bridge is balanced. The balance condition, however, requires the impedance match to the telephone subscriber loop. This condition cannot really be satisfied because the input impedance of a telephone loop is not exactly fixed, due to bridged taps and temperature variation.

This small amount of impedance mismatch is tolerable for voice applications. In fact, the echo, which is caused by impedance mismatch of a hybrid circuit, of someone's own talk is usually perceived as an "alive" indication for a telephone connection.

For real-time, full-duplex data transmission applications, the amount of hybrid echo should be minimized; otherwise, the echo could interfere with the received signal. Although some telephone set hybrid circuits rely on voltage parities from different windings of one or two magnetic cores to cancel the transmit signal, hybrid circuits used for DSL systems are based on the balance of resistive networks to minimize the amount of echo.

DSL transceivers typically consist of both a single-ended and a differential hybrid circuit. Both circuits can be simplified to some resistive networks. DSL hybrid circuits also usually have a coupling transformer, which is mainly used for the purpose of longitudinal signal isolation and surge protection. Both wires of a telephone loop can pick up some substantial noises through the open electromagnetic field; however, the only difference between these two longitudinal signals appears after a transformer. A coupling transformer can also reduce the severity of some longitudinal surge voltage or current.

Because a hybrid is an analog circuit, it is connected to the rest of a DSL transceiver through a *Digital to Analog Converter* (DAC) in the transmitting path and an *Analog to Digital Converter* (ADC) in the receiving path. Figure 6.1 shows the typical structure of an *Analog Front End* (AFE) that connects the digital portion of a DSL transceiver to the telephone subscriber.

Figure 6.1 The General Structure of an Analog Front End

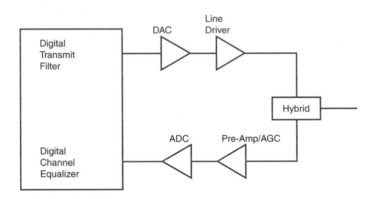

The transmit signal to a DAC is usually coming from digital transmit shaping filters, and the received signal from an ADC usually goes to channel equalizers. A hybrid circuit can provide some limited amount of transmission loss from the transmitting path to the receiving path, depending on the impedance balance condition. There is usually a line drive between the DAC and the hybrid circuit for supplying sufficient voltage and current onto the twisted-pair loop with certain line impedance.

There is usually also a pre-amplifier with automatic gain control between the hybrid circuit and the ADC to raise the received signal level to that suitable for the input dynamic range of the ADC. There are typically two types of hybrid circuits used for Digital Subscriber Line (DSL) transceivers: single-ended hybrid circuits and differential hybrid circuits. This chapter explains the structure, functionality, and components of these two types of hybrid circuits and related concepts, as follows:

- *Single-ended hybrid circuits.* Single-ended hybrid circuits can be simplified into a classical electrical bridge with four branches. The transmitting path and the receiving path are connected at two diagonal ports, while the twisted-pair telephone loop is used as one of these branches through the coupling transformer.

- *Differential hybrid circuits.* Differential hybrid circuits can be simplified into a balance circuit of six resistors with six joints. The transmitting path, the receiving path, and the twisted-pair telephone loop are cross-connected through a coupling transformer to six joints of this balance network. A differential hybrid circuit is suitable for using a differential line driver.

- *Transformer equivalent circuits.* A line coupling transformer can be represented with a T-equivalent circuit for transformer design and system performance analysis. The ABCD parameters of the transformer equivalent circuit are also derived to be used in conjunction with ABCD parameters of the twisted-pair telephone subscriber loop.

- *Echo path model.* A realistic echo path model can be obtained by combining the equivalent circuit of the line coupling transformer, the balance network, and the input impedance of the loop. The echo path model can be used to assess the echo level and as a reference for the design of an echo canceller.

6.1 Single-Ended Hybrid Circuits

Figure 6.2 shows a single-ended hybrid circuit.

Figure 6.2 Single-Ended Hybrid Circuit

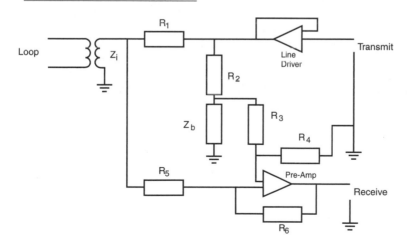

An electrical bridge connects the transmit line driver, the receive preamplifier, and the line transformer. The four branches of the electrical bridge are as follows:

- R_1

- R_2

- The equivalent twisted-pair loop impedance Z_i

- The balance impedance Z_b

The impedance seen by the twisted loop through the transformer is R_1 plus the line driver output impedance R_I. Because the output impedance of the line driver is usually negligible compared with R_1, the termination impedance for the twisted loop is approximately equal to R_1. The signal is received through R_3 and R_5 by the pre-amplifier, while R_4 and R_6 are resistors required as part of a differential feedback circuit.

The single-ended hybrid circuit can be simplified to an electrical bridge with the transformer and attached loop impedance as one of four branches, as shown in Figure 6.3.

Figure 6.3 Simplified Equivalent Circuit for Single-Ended Hybrid

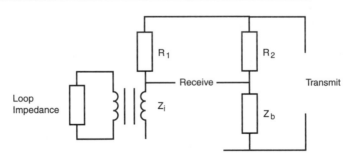

The balance condition occurs when the signal loss from the transmitting path to the receiving path (also called the *echo return loss*) becomes infinity. A balance condition for a single-ended hybrid circuit is reached when you have

$$\frac{Z_i}{R_1 + Z_i} = \frac{Z_b}{R_2 + Z_b}$$

If $R_1 = Z_i$, then $Z_b = R_2$.

The echo path is defined as from the transmit port to the receive port. The echo path transfer function for the single-ended hybrid is

$$H_{ec}(f) = \frac{Z_i(f)}{R_1 + Z_i(f)} - \frac{Z_b(f)}{R_2 + Z_b(f)}$$

Note
You should be aware that the perfect balance condition cannot be achieved if only fixed resistors are used for the bridge network.

Zero line driver impedance and infinite pre-amplifier input impedance have been assumed in the previous expression of the echo path transfer function. A more accurate echo path transfer function can be obtained through the use of two-port network equivalent circuits and associated ABCD parameters. The two-port network ABCD matrix for this single-ended hybrid echo path is as follows:

$$\begin{bmatrix} A & B \\ C & D \end{bmatrix} = \begin{bmatrix} \dfrac{(R_1 + Z_i(f))(R_2 + Z_b(f))}{Z_i(f)R_2 - Z_b(f)R_1} & \dfrac{R_1 R_2(Z_i(f) + Z_b(f)) + Z_i(f)Z_b(f)(R_1 + R_2)}{Z_i(f)R_2 - Z_b(f)R_1} \\ \dfrac{R_1 + R_2 + Z_i(f) + Z_b(f)}{Z_i(f)R_2 - Z_b(f)R_1} & \dfrac{(R_1 + R_2)(Z_i(f) + Z_b(f))}{Z_i(f)R_2 - Z_b(f)R_1} \end{bmatrix}$$

For $R_1 = R_2 = R$, we have

$$\begin{bmatrix} A & B \\ C & D \end{bmatrix} = \begin{bmatrix} \dfrac{R\left(1 + \dfrac{Z_i(f)}{R}\right)\left(1 + \dfrac{Z_b(f)}{R}\right)}{Z_i(f) - Z_b(f)} & \dfrac{R(Z_i(f) + Z_b(f)) + 2Z_i(f)Z_b(f)}{Z_i(f) - Z_b(f)} \\ \dfrac{2 + \dfrac{Z_i(f)}{R} + \dfrac{Z_b(f)}{R}}{Z_i(f) - Z_b(f)} & \dfrac{2(Z_i(f) + Z_b(f))}{Z_i(f) - Z_b(f)} \end{bmatrix}$$

You can also study the effect of line driver output and pre-amplifier input impedance using the ABCD matrix of the echo path. The single-ended hybrid circuit is suitable for a single output line driver. A differential output line driver requires a *differential hybrid circuit*.

6.2 *Differential Hybrid Circuits*

Figure 6.4 shows a differential hybrid circuit.

Figure 6.4 Differential Hybrid Circuit

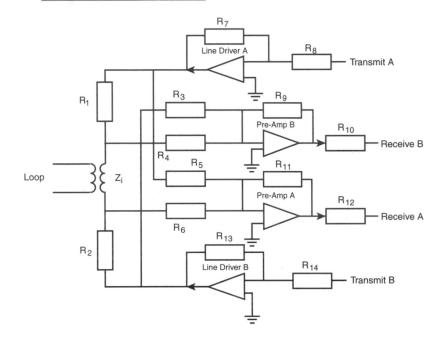

Outputs of a pair of differential line drivers are connected to joint points of $R_1 - R_4$ and $R_2 - R_3$. Inputs of a pair of differential pre-amplifiers are connected to joint points of $R_3 - R_4$ and $R_5 - R_6$. Notice that resistors R_3 and R_4 are effectively connected to the opposite phases of the line drivers, as are resistors R_5 and R_6.

The proper selection of resistor values can minimize the amount of transmitting signal coming back to the receiving path. The impedance seen by the twisted-pair loop through the transformer between one lead of the transformer and the ground is R_1 plus the line driver output impedance R_l. The impedance between the other lead of the transformer and the ground is R_2 plus the line driver output impedance R_l. Because the output impedance of the line driver is usually negligible, the termination impedance for the twisted loop is approximately equal to $R_1 + R_2$.

The balance resistive network of the differential hybrid can also be simplified to an electrical bridge with the transformer and its attached twisted-pair loop impedance connected in the middle of two branches, as shown in Figure 6.5.

Figure 6.5 Simplified Equivalent Circuit for Differential Hybrid

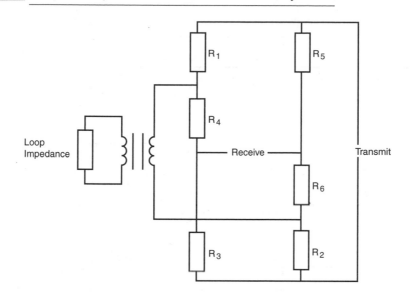

For the differential drive hybrid, we normally let $R_1 = R_2$, $R_3 = R_5$, and $R_4 = R_6$ through the choice of design. The balance condition for the differential drive hybrid is then reached when

$$\frac{R_1}{R_1 + Z_i(f)} = \frac{R_3 - R_4}{R_3 + R_4}$$

choosing $R_1 = \frac{1}{2}Z_i(f)$ for termination impedance matching results in $R_3 = 2R_4$. The general echo path transfer function for the differential hybrid is as follows:

$$H_{ec}(f) = \frac{1}{2R_1 + Z_i(f)}\left[R_1 + \left(Z_i(f) + R_1\right)\frac{R_4 - R_3}{R_4 + R_3}\right]$$

To consider the effect of line driver and preamplifier impedances, the use of two-port network equivalent circuits and associated ABCD parameters is required. To derive the ABCD matrix for the echo path of a differential hybrid circuit, we further arrange the simplified differential hybrid circuit into two two-port networks in parallel, as shown in Figure 6.6.

Figure 6.6 A Two-Port Network Parallel Representation of the Differential Hybrid Circuit

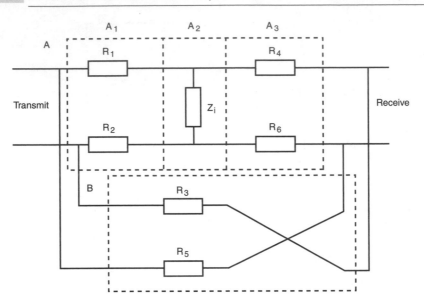

The two-port network A consists of three element two-port networks. The ABCD matrix for the two-port network A_1 is

$$\begin{bmatrix} A & B \\ C & D \end{bmatrix}_{A_1} = \begin{bmatrix} 1 & R_1 + R_2 \\ 0 & 1 \end{bmatrix}$$

The ABCD matrix for the two-port network A_2 is

$$\begin{bmatrix} A & B \\ C & D \end{bmatrix}_{A_2} = \begin{bmatrix} 1 & 0 \\ \dfrac{1}{Z_i} & 1 \end{bmatrix}$$

The ABCD matrix for the two-port network A_3 is

$$\begin{bmatrix} A & B \\ C & D \end{bmatrix}_{A_3} = \begin{bmatrix} 1 & R_4 + R_6 \\ 0 & 1 \end{bmatrix}$$

The ABCD matrix for the two-port network A is

$$\begin{bmatrix} A & B \\ C & D \end{bmatrix}_A = \begin{bmatrix} A & B \\ C & D \end{bmatrix}_{A_1} \begin{bmatrix} A & B \\ C & D \end{bmatrix}_{A_2} \begin{bmatrix} A & B \\ C & D \end{bmatrix}_{A_3}$$

$$= \begin{bmatrix} 1 + \dfrac{R_1 + R_2}{Z_i} & R_1 + R_2 + R_4 + R_6 + \dfrac{(R_1 + R_2)(R_4 + R_6)}{Z_i} \\ \dfrac{1}{Z_i} & 1 + \dfrac{R_4 + R_6}{Z_i} \end{bmatrix}$$

The ABCD matrix for the two-port network B is

$$\begin{bmatrix} A & B \\ C & D \end{bmatrix}_B = -\begin{bmatrix} 1 & R_3 + R_5 \\ 0 & 1 \end{bmatrix}$$

For $R_1 = R_2,\ R_3 = R_5$, and $R_4 = R_6$, we have

$$\begin{bmatrix} A & B \\ C & D \end{bmatrix}_A = \begin{bmatrix} 1 + \dfrac{2R_1}{Z_i} & 2R_1 + 2R_4 + \dfrac{4R_1R_4}{Z_i} \\ \dfrac{1}{Z_i} & 1 + \dfrac{2R_4}{Z_i} \end{bmatrix}$$

and

$$\begin{bmatrix} A & B \\ C & D \end{bmatrix}_B = \begin{bmatrix} 1 & 2R_3 \\ 0 & 1 \end{bmatrix}$$

The two-port network ABCD matrix for this differential hybrid echo path is

$$
\begin{bmatrix} A & B \\ C & D \end{bmatrix} = \begin{bmatrix} -\dfrac{R_3\left(1+\dfrac{2R_1}{Z_i}\right)+R_1+R_4+\dfrac{2R_1R_4}{Z_i}}{R_1-R_3+R_4+\dfrac{2R_1R_4}{Z_i}} & -\dfrac{2R_3\left(R_1+R_4+\dfrac{2R_1R_4}{Z_i}\right)}{R_1-R_3+R_4+\dfrac{2R_1R_4}{Z_i}} \\[3em] \dfrac{\dfrac{1}{Z_i}\left(R_1-R_3+R_4+\dfrac{2R_1R_4}{Z_i}\right)-2\left(1+\dfrac{R_1}{Z_i}\right)\left(1+\dfrac{1R_4}{Z_i}\right)}{R_1-R_3+R_4+\dfrac{2R_1R_4}{Z_i}} & \dfrac{R_3\left(1+\dfrac{2R_4}{Z_i}\right)+R_1+R_4+\dfrac{2R_1R_4}{Z_i}}{R_1-R_3+R_4+\dfrac{2R_1R_4}{Z_i}} \end{bmatrix}
$$

6.3 *Transformer Equivalent Circuits*

The transfer function of a transformer connecting the twisted-pair loop to the hybrid circuit can be determined according to its equivalent circuit. Figure 6.7 shows a typical transformer equivalent circuit.[1]

Figure 6.7 Simplified Hybrid or Transformer Equivalent Circuit

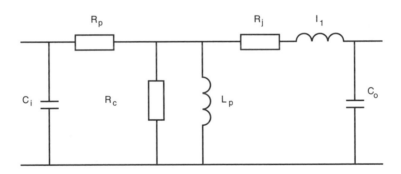

Key parameters for the transformer equivalent circuit include the following:

R_p—The resistance of the primary coil

R_s—The resistance of the secondary coil

R_c—The core resistance

L_p—The primary inductance

L_l—The leakage inductance

C_i—The input capacitance

C_o—The output capacitance

The ABCD matrix of the transformer equivalent circuit is

$$\begin{bmatrix} A & B \\ C & D \end{bmatrix} = \begin{bmatrix} 1 & 0 \\ sC_i & 1 \end{bmatrix}\begin{bmatrix} 1 & R_p \\ 0 & 1 \end{bmatrix}\begin{bmatrix} 1 & 0 \\ \dfrac{1}{R_c} + \dfrac{1}{sL_p} & 1 \end{bmatrix}\begin{bmatrix} 1 & R_s + sL_l \\ 0 & 1 \end{bmatrix}\begin{bmatrix} 1 & 0 \\ sC_o & 1 \end{bmatrix}$$

6.3.1 ISDN Transformer Equivalent Circuit Parameters

Transformer equivalent circuit parameters for a typical Basic Rate Access ISDN (Integrated Services Digital Network) channel, also called Digital Subscriber Line (DSL) transceiver, are as follows:

$R_p = 8\ \Omega$

$R_s = 12\ \Omega$

$R_c = 150\ k\Omega$

$L_p = 28.5\ mH$

$L_l = 28\ \mu H$

$C_i = 22\ pF$

$C_o = 22\ pF$

Figure 6.8 shows the frequency response of a transformer designed for an ISDN transceiver with source and termination impedances of 135 ohms.

Figure 6.8 Transfer Function of an ISDN Transformer

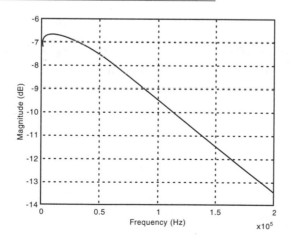

6.3.2 *HDSL Transformer Equivalent Circuit Parameters*

Transformer equivalent circuit parameters for a typical High-bit-rate Digital Subscriber Line (HDSL) transceiver are as follows:

$R_p = 1.8\ \Omega$

$R_s = 2.5\ \Omega$

$R_c = 50\ k\Omega$

$L_p = 3\ mH$

$L_1 = 29\ \mu H$

$C_i = 35\ pF$

$C_o = 35\ pF$

Figure 6.9 shows the frequency response of a transformer designed for an HDSL transceiver with source and termination impedances of 135 ohms.

Figure 6.9 Transfer Function of an HDSL Transformer

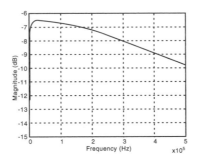

6.3.3 *ADSL Transformer Equivalent Circuit Parameters*

Transformer equivalent circuit parameters for a typical Asymmetrical Digital Subscriber Line (ADSL) transceiver are as follows:

$R_p = 1.32\ \Omega$

$R_s = 1.12\ \Omega$

$R_c = 50\ k\Omega$

$L_p = 407.5\ \mu H$

$L_1 = 5.4\ \mu H$

$C_i = 35\ pF$

$C_o = 35\ pF$

Figure 6.10 shows the frequency response of a transformer designed for an ADSL transceiver with source and termination impedances of 100 ohms.

Figure 6.10 Transfer Function of an ADSL Transformer

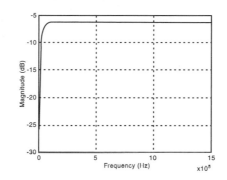

The low frequency portion of the transfer function is enlarged in Figure 6.11.

Figure 6.11 Transfer Function of an ADSL Transformer at Low Frequencies

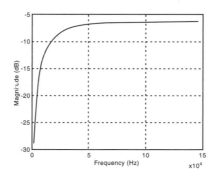

Among these DSL transformers, the one for ISDN has the narrowest bandwidth, and the one for ADSL has the widest bandwidth. The bandwidth of a DSL transformer depends on the primary inductance: The larger the primary inductance, the narrower the bandwidth. On the other hand, a smaller primary inductance leads to a higher low-corner frequency, as shown in Figure 6.11. The selection of low- and high-corner frequencies are interrelated with the current transformer technologies.

6.4 Echo Path Model

Because of the impedance mismatch, there is always echo of transmitted signal to a DSL receiver front end coming back from the hybrid circuit. The knowledge of the magnitude of the echo is necessary to determine the dynamic range of receiver front-end analog circuits.

A total characterization of the echo path transfer function is required for the design of an echo canceller.

Transmission at opposite directions of a DSL system can also be achieved through using different frequency bands. This is sometimes called *Frequency Division Multiplex* (FDM) or *Frequency Division Duplex* (FDD). A hybrid circuit with high echo return loss is also preferred for an FDM or FDD DSL system to relax the requirement of band separating filters.

A realistic echo path model can be constructed based on the hybrid circuit configuration, the transformer equivalent circuit, and the input impedance of the telephone subscriber loop. The effect of transmit and receiver filters or band separating filters can also be included depending on different design reference objectives. The calculation of the echo path transfer function can be carried out using two-port network equivalent circuits and associated ABCD parameters.

The input impedance of a twisted-pair loop can be expressed by its ABCD parameters as

$$Z_i = \frac{A + \dfrac{B}{Z_t}}{C + \dfrac{D}{Z_t}}$$

The value Z_t is the termination impedance at the other end of the twisted-pair loop. We can also express the twisted-pair loop impedance with the inclusion of the transformer by recognizing

$$\begin{bmatrix} A & B \\ C & D \end{bmatrix} = \begin{bmatrix} A_T & B_T \\ C_T & D_T \end{bmatrix}\begin{bmatrix} A_l & B_l \\ C_l & D_l \end{bmatrix} = \begin{bmatrix} A_T A_l + B_T C_l & A_T B_l + B_T D_l \\ C_T A_l + D_T C_l & C_T B_l + D_T D_l \end{bmatrix}$$

in which

   $_T$ denotes the transformer.

   $_l$ denotes the twisted-pair loop.

The input impedance of a twisted-pair loop connected through a transformer can be expressed by its ABCD parameters as

$$Z_i = \frac{A_T A_l + B_T C_l + \dfrac{A_T B_l + B_T D_l}{Z_t}}{C_T A_l + D_T C_l + \dfrac{C_T B_l + D_T D_l}{Z_t}}$$

Figure 6.12 shows the magnitude of the input impedance of a 1 mile, 26-gauge twisted-pair loop.

Figure 6.12 Magnitude of the Input Impedance of a 1 Mile, 26-Gauge Loop

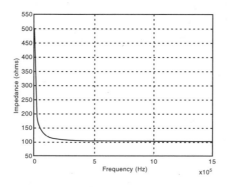

The magnitude of the input impedance converges to about 100 ohms at high frequency, while the magnitude can be at around 600 ohms or higher at voiceband.

Figure 6.13 shows the real and imaginary parts of the 1 mile, 26-gauge twisted-pair loop input impedance. The amplitude of the imaginary part is negligible at both low and high frequencies, while it can be as large as –200 ohms in between these extreme frequencies. In Figure 6.13, circles are marked at 15 kHz apart.

Figure 6.13 Real and Imaginary Parts of the Input Impedance of a 1 Mile, 26-Gauge Loop

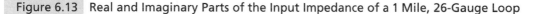

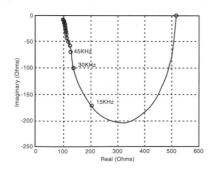

Figure 6.14 shows the magnitude of the input impedance of a twisted-pair loop with bridged taps. Originally detailed in Chapter 3, "Twisted-Pair Channel Modeling," the configuration of this loop is shown in Figure 6.15. The magnitude of the input impedance also converges to about 100 ohms at high frequency, but not always larger than 100 ohms.

Figure 6.14 Magnitude of the Input Impedance of a Loop with Bridged Taps

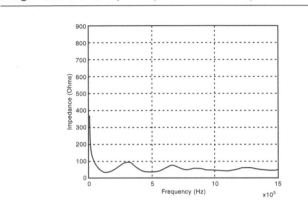

Figure 6.15 Configuration of a Subscriber Loop with Bridged Taps

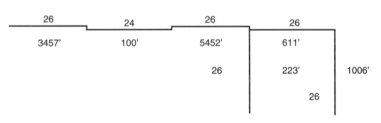

Figure 6.16 shows the real and imaginary parts of input impedance for the twisted-pair loop with bridged taps according to the configuration of Figure 6.15. The amplitude of the imaginary part is also negligible at both low and high frequencies. In Figure 6.16, circles are also marked at 15 kHz apart.

Figure 6.17 shows the magnitude of the input impedance of a 1 mile, 26-gauge twisted-pair loop with the inclusion of the transformer used for the Basic Rate Access ISDN channel, which is also called DSL. The DSL transmit signal energy is mostly concentrated at below 50 kHz.

Figure 6.16 Real and Imaginary Parts of the Input Impedance of a Loop with Bridged Taps

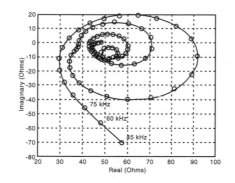

Figure 6.17 Magnitude of a 1 Mile, 26-Gauge Loop Including a DSL Transformer

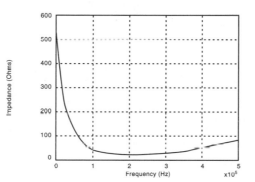

Figure 6.18 shows the real and imaginary parts of the input impedance for a 1 mile, 26-gauge twisted-pair loop with a DSL transformer. The upper portion of the curve corresponds to the low frequency part of the loop input impedance. In Figure 6.18, circles are marked at 5 kHz apart.

Figure 6.19 shows the magnitude of the input impedance of a 1 mile, 26-gauge twisted-pair loop with the inclusion of an HDSL transformer. The HDSL transmit signal energy is mostly concentrated at below 200 kHz.

Figure 6.20 shows the real and imaginary parts of the input impedance for a 1 mile, 26-gauge twisted-pair loop with an HDSL transformer. The upper portion of the curve also corresponds to the low frequency part of the loop input impedance. In Figure 6.20, circles are also marked at 5 kHz apart.

Figure 6.18 Real and Imaginary Parts of a 1 Mile, 26-Gauge Loop Including a DSL Transformer

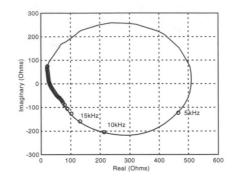

Figure 6.19 Magnitude of a 1 Mile, 26-Gauge Loop Including an HDSL Transformer

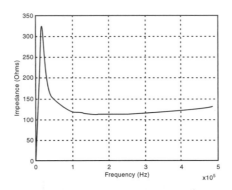

Figure 6.20 Real and Imaginary Parts of a 1 Mile, 26-Gauge Loop Including an HDSL Transformer

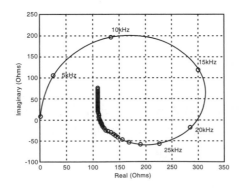

Figure 6.21 shows the magnitude of the input impedance of a twisted-pair loop with bridged taps and the inclusion of a DSL transformer. The configuration of this loop is also from Figure 6.15.

Figure 6.21 Magnitude of a Loop with Bridged Taps Including a DSL Transformer

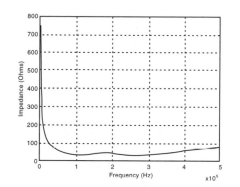

Figure 6.22 shows the real and imaginary parts of the input impedance for the twisted-pair loop with bridged taps according to the configuration of Figure 6.15 and with the inclusion of a DSL transformer. The upper portion of the curve corresponds to the low-frequency part of the loop input impedance.

Figure 6.22 Real and Imaginary Parts of a Loop with Bridged Taps Including a DSL Transformer

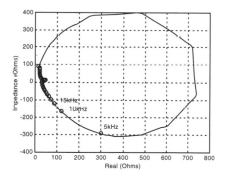

Figure 6.23 shows the magnitude of the input impedance of a twisted-pair loop with bridged taps for the configuration of Figure 6.15 and the inclusion of an HDSL transformer.

Figure 6.23 Magnitude of a Loop with Bridged Taps Including an HDSL Transformer

Figure 6.23 Magnitude of a Loop with Bridged Taps Including an HDSL Transformer

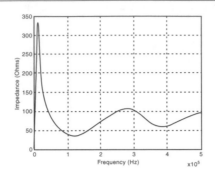

Figure 6.24 shows the real and imaginary parts of the input impedance for the twisted-pair loop with bridged taps for the configuration of Figure 6.25 and the inclusion of an HDSL transformer. The upper portion of the curve corresponds to the low frequency part of the loop input impedance.

Figure 6.24 Real and Imaginary Parts of a Loop with Bridged Taps Including an HDSL Transformer

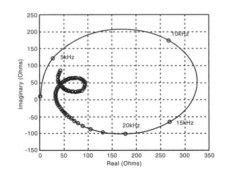

Figure 6.25 Input Impedance of a Twisted-Pair Loop with Bridged Taps

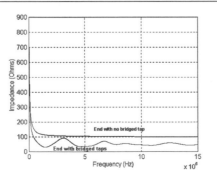

The echo path transfer function for the single-ended hybrid circuit can be calculated by letting $R_1 = 135 \; \Omega$ and $R_2 = Z_b = 1000 \; \Omega$ in conjunction with twisted-pair loop impedances with the inclusion of transformers. The echo path transfer function derived in section 6.1, "Single-Ended Hybrid Circuits," for the single-ended hybrid circuit can be simplified as follows:

$$H_{ec}^s(f) = \frac{1}{2} \frac{Z_i(f) - R_1^s}{Z_i(f) + R_1^s}$$

The superscript s denotes the transfer function and the resistor for the single-ended hybrid circuit to distinguish those of the differential hybrid circuits. Figure 6.26 shows the echo path transfer function for the twisted-pair loop with bridged taps and an HDSL transformer.

Figure 6.26   Echo Path Transfer Function for a Single-Ended Hybrid Circuit with a Twisted-Pair Loop of Bridged Taps and an HDSL Transformer

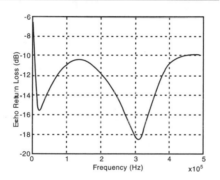

To enhance the echo return loss, Z_b can be implemented with an RC network.[2]

Note
An RC network can be used to emulate the frequency dependent input impedance of a twisted-pair telephone loop.

The RC balance network #1 in Figure 6.27 has a resistor in parallel with a serial RC network. The RC balance network #2 has a parallel RC network and a serial RC network in serial.

Figure 6.27 Two RC Balance Networks

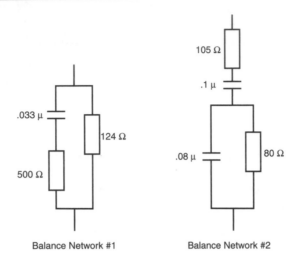

Balance Network #1   Balance Network #2

Figures 6.28 and 6.29 show echo path transfer functions with RC balance networks #1 and #2, respectively, in conjunction with an R_2 of 100 ohms. The use of a fixed RC balance network balance is not particularly effective against telephone subscriber loops with bridged taps.

Figure 6.28 Echo Path Transfer Function for a Single-Ended Hybrid Circuit with the RC Network #1

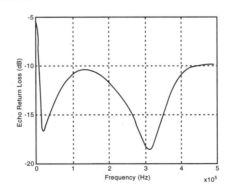

Figure 6.29 Echo Path Transfer Function for a Single-Ended Hybrid Circuit with the RC Network #2

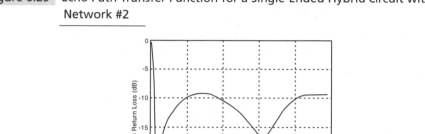

The echo path transfer function for the differential hybrid circuit can be calculated by letting $R_1 = R_2 = 67\ \Omega$ and $R_3 = 2R_4 = 2000\ \Omega$ also in conjunction with twisted-pair loop impedances with the inclusion of transformers. The echo path transfer function derived in section 6.2, "Differential Hybrid Circuits," for the differential hybrid circuit can be simplified as follows:

$$H_{ec}^d(f) = \frac{1}{3}\frac{2R_1^d - Z_i(f)}{2R_1^d + Z_i(f)}$$

The superscript d denotes the transfer function and the resistor for the differential hybrid circuit.

Figure 6.30 shows the echo path transfer function for the twisted-pair loop with bridged taps and an HDSL transformer.

Figure 6.30 Echo Path Transfer Function for a Differential Hybrid Circuit with a Twisted-Pair Loop of Bridged Taps

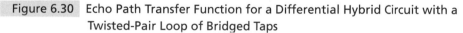

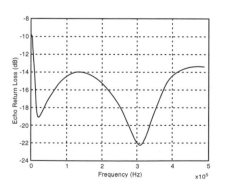

The transfer function has the same shape as that of a single-ended hybrid; the loss difference is due to the scaling factors of $1/2$ over $1/3$ when $R_1^s = 2R_1^d$. The loss difference is $20 \times \log_{10}(3/2) = 3.52 \text{ dB}$. The performance of a differential hybrid, however, is the same as that of a single-ended hybrid circuit because the received signal through a differential hybrid circuit also experiences 3.52 dB more loss.

End Notes

1. Midcom web page at **http://www.midcom-inc.com/technotes/tn17.html**.

2. W. Y. Chen, J. L. Dixon, and D. L. Waring, "HDSL Echo Cancellation," *IEEE JSAC*, vol. 9, no. 6 (August 1991): 848–860. G. S. Moschytz and S. V. Ahamed, "Transhybrid Loss with RC Balance Circuits for Primary-Rate ISDN Transmission Systems," *IEEE JSAC*, vol. 9, no. 6 (August 1991): 951–959.

7

Analog Front-End Precision

Some transmission systems can be realized with analog circuit technology only, such as transmit line driver, receiver amplifier, and threshold detector. The transmission potential cannot be fully realized, however, with the use of current analog circuit technology only. Digital processing techniques, such as adaptive channel equalization and adaptive echo cancellation, have played a very important role at maximizing the transmission efficiency of DSL systems.

On the other hand, the transmit signal still needs to be in analog format to fit the analog twisted-pair telephone loop better. Information after digital signal processing with limited precision is converted to analog format through a *Digital to Analog Converter* (DAC), and the received analog signal is converted through an *Analog to Digital Converter* (ADC) for further digital signal processing.

The precision of DAC and ADC should be fine enough to realize the potential of the analog telephone subscriber loop channel. In other words, the precision should be chosen such that the DAC and ADC quantization noise will not be a limiting factor for the transmission performance of DSL systems. The required DAC and ADC precision depends on the following:

- The transmit signal line code
- The transmit shaping filter
- The characteristics of the channel
- The attenuation of the echo path

There are baseband, passband single-carrier, and multiple-carrier line codes used for DSL systems. The four-level baseband line code, also called 2B1Q for 2 bits per quaternary, has been used for both the *Basic Rate Access ISDN channel* (also called DSL) and for HDSL.

A baseband line code usually consists of many parity symmetric and equally spaced signal levels. Passband single carrier line codes, such as *Quadrature Amplitude Modulation* (QAM) *and Carrierless AM/PM* (CAP), have also been proposed for DSL systems. A passband single carrier line code has a two-dimensional signal. The two-dimensional signal is divided into an in-phase channel and a quadrature channel implemented by the cosine and sine phases of the single carrier, respectively.

Parity symmetric and equally spaced multiple signal levels are used for both in-phase and quadrature channels. The *Discrete MultiTone* (DMT) line code is the standard for ADSL. A DMT line code consists of a multiple of single carriers implemented through the *Discrete Fourier Transform* (DFT). The number of carriers available to carry information is equal to, or slightly less than, half of the DFT size. Each carrier of a DMT line code has the same two-dimensional signal as that of a passband single carrier system.

Different line codes have different peak-to-average voltage ratios. The peak-to-average voltage ratio can also be affected by transmit shaping filters for a DAC and by the channel and the echo path for an ADC. This chapter discusses issues related to the determination of DAC and ADC precision requirements including the following:

- *Peak-to-average ratio (PAR) of line codes.* PARs are calculated for baseband multiple level, passband single carrier, and DMT multiple carrier line codes. Relationships of PARs to the number of signal levels, constellation size, and the number of carriers are derived. The effect of clipping for the DMT line code is also discussed.

- *Effects of transmit filter, channel, and echo path.* The use of a transmit filter generally leads to a higher PAR. The PAR can also be increased for a signal passing through the telephone subscriber loop channel. The echo path could produce the same effect.

- *Characteristics of ADC and DAC.* The effect of ADC and DAC quantization noise and its relationship to required PAR are discussed. The effect of ADC and DAC nonlinearity is compared with that of quantization noise.

- *ADC and DAC precision requirements.* Combining PARs of different line codes and the quantization noise of ADC and DAC, precision requirements are estimated for a few practical DSL system examples.

7.1   *Transmit Signal Peak-to-Average Voltage Ratio*

A binary baseband signal can have signal levels of –1 and +1. A four-level baseband signal can have signal levels of –3, –1, +1, and +3. Figure 7.1 shows the waveform of a baseband 2B1Q line code.

Figure 7.1   A Baseband 2B1Q Line Code

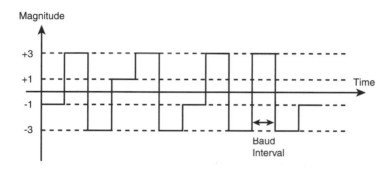

For the previous and following baseband signals, the distance between adjacent signal levels is maintained to be 2. In general, an *n* level baseband signal can have signal levels of *–n+1*, *–n+3*, ... *n–3*, *n–1*, for which *n* is an even number.

Assuming a load resistance of one, the average power for a binary signal is one. Using the same load resistance value assumption, the average power for a four-level signal is $\left(1^2 + 3^2\right)/2$. In general, the average power for an *n* level baseband signal is

$$\frac{2}{n}\left(1^2 + 3^2 + ...(n-1)^2 + (n-1)^2\right) = \frac{n^2-1}{3}$$

Assuming a load resistance of one, the average voltage of this *n* level baseband signal is

$$\sqrt{\frac{n^2-1}{3}}$$

Figure 7.2 shows average voltage levels for different levels of baseband signals assuming a voltage of two volts between adjacent signal levels.

Figure 7.2 Average Signal Magnitude of Baseband Signal

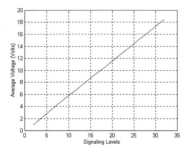

For a peak voltage level of $(n-1)$ volts, the peak-to-average voltage ratio of an n level baseband signal is

$$(n-1)\sqrt{\frac{3}{(n^2-1)}} = \sqrt{\frac{3(n-1)}{n+1}}$$

Figure 7.3 shows peak-to-average voltage ratio (PAR) for baseband signals with different numbers of signaling levels.

Figure 7.3 Peak-to-Average Voltage Ratio of Baseband Signal

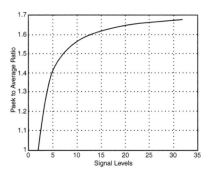

Figure 7.4 shows the same PAR in terms of dB.

Figure 7.4 Peak-to-Average Voltage Ratio (dB)

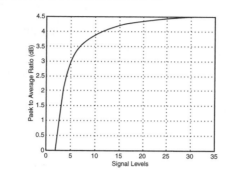

In practice, the peak transmit voltage is limited by the voltage level of a power supply. For a 5 volt power supply, the peak-to-peak voltage can be as high as 4.6 volts without introducing too much amplifier nonlinearity. Using a single-ended hybrid circuit, the peak signal level can be represented by a voltage level of 2.3 volts. Under the power supply voltage limited condition, the average transmit power for an n level baseband signal with a load resistance of 135 ohms is then

$$P_T = \frac{2.3^2}{135}\left(\frac{(n+1)}{3(n-1)}\right)$$

For an example of a four-level signal, the average transmit power is

$$P_T = \frac{2.3^2}{135}\left(\frac{5}{3 \times 3}\right) = 0.02177 \text{ Watts} = 13.38 \text{ dBm}$$

Because of the increased PAR, the average transmit power for a 32-level baseband signal with the same 5 volt power supply is 2 dB lower.

7.1.1 PAR of Passband Single Carrier Line Codes

A two-dimensional passband single carrier line code can be characterized by its constellation. A CAP line code is a little different compared with the QAM line code. The difference is explained in Chapter 8, "Channel Equalization." CAP and QAM line codes can, however, share the same constellation. A QAM with a constellation size of 4 is also called *Quadrature Phase Shift Keying* (QPSK) for its four phases of the same magnitude.

Assuming a two-dimensional constellation can be represented by multiple signal levels, similar to the baseband case, in each orthogonal dimension, a 4 CAP/QAM signal can have signal levels of –1 and +1 in each dimension, but only one magnitude of $\sqrt{2}$. A 16 CAP/QAM signal can have four signal levels, –3, –1, +1, or +3, in each orthogonal dimension. Possible magnitude values for a 16 CAP/QAM signal are $\sqrt{2}$, $\sqrt{10}$, and $3\sqrt{2}$. Figure 7.5 shows a 16 CAP/QAM constellation.

Figure 7.5 A 16 CAP/QAM Constellation

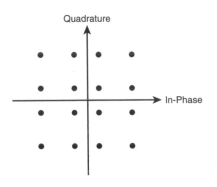

In general, a 2^{2n} CAP/QAM constellation can have magnitudes of the following:

$$\sqrt{2}, \sqrt{1+3^2}, \cdots, \sqrt{1+\left(2^n-1\right)^2}, \sqrt{3^2+1}, \sqrt{3^2+3^2}, \cdots, \sqrt{3^2+\left(2^n-1\right)^2}, \cdots,$$

$$\sqrt{\left(2^n-1\right)^2+1}, \cdots, \sqrt{\left(2^n-1\right)^2+\left(2^n-1\right)^2}$$

The value n is the constellation size index, which is the number of bits in each dimension.

For $n=1$, we have a 4 CAP/QAM constellation; for $n=2$, we have a 16 CAP/QAM constellation, and so forth.

Also, by assuming a load resistance of one, the average power for a 4 CAP/QAM signal is 2. Assuming the same load resistance value, the average power for a 16 CAP/QAM signal is

$$(4\times 2+8\times 10+4\times 18)/16 = 10$$

In general, the average power for a 2^{2n} CAP/QAM signal is

$$\left(\frac{4}{2^{2n}} \times \sum_{i=1}^{2^{n-1}} \sum_{j=1}^{2^{n-1}} \left((2i-1)^2 + (2j-1)^2\right)\right) = \frac{2}{3}(2^{2n} - 1)$$

The average voltage of a 2^{2n} CAP/QAM signal in conjunction with a 1 ohm load resistance is

$$\sqrt{\frac{2}{3}(2^{2n} - 1)}$$

Figure 7.6 shows average voltage levels for a passband signal with different constellation size indices.

Figure 7.6   Average Signal Magnitude of Passband Signal

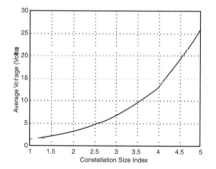

A passband sinusoidal signal also has a peak-to-mean square root voltage, which corresponds to the power ratio of $\sqrt{2}$. With the consideration of the sinusoidal peak value, the peak-to-average voltage ratio of a passband signal is

$$\sqrt{\frac{6(2^n - 1)}{2^n + 1}}$$

Figure 7.7 shows peak-to-average voltage ratio (PAR) for passband signals of different constellation size indices.

Figure 7.7 Peak-to-Average Voltage Ratio of Passband Signal

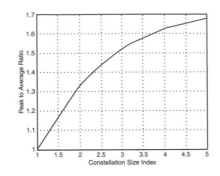

Figure 7.8 shows the same PAR in terms of dB.

Figure 7.8 Peak-to-Average Voltage Ratio in dB

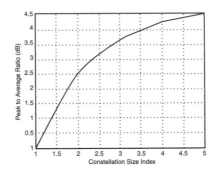

Using a 5 volt power supply and a single-ended hybrid circuit, the average transmit power for an n level passband signal in conjunction with a load resistance of 135 ohms is then

$$P_T = \frac{2.3^2}{135} \frac{2^n + 1}{6(2^n - 1)}$$

For an example of a 16 CAP/QAM signal, the average transmit power is

$$P_T = \frac{2.3^2}{135}\left(\frac{5}{6 \times 3}\right) = 0.01088 \text{ Watts} = 10.37 \text{ dBm}$$

Under the same power supply voltage, the average transmit power of a 16 CAP/QAM line code is about 3 dB less compared with a 2B1Q line code of the same transmission throughput under the same transmission bandwidth. The 3 dB power reduction of the 16 CAP/QAM line code is partially caused by the sinusoid peak-to-average ratio of $\sqrt{2}$.

7.1.2 PAR of DMT Line Codes

A Discrete MultiTone (DMT) system consists of multiple QAM constellations, each of which has a different carrier frequency. The total average power of a DMT system is the average power sum of each carrier as expressed in the following:

$$P_{DMT} = \sum_{i=1}^{m} P_{T_i}$$

The value P_{DMT} is the total average power, m is the number of carriers, and P_{sub_i} is the average power of ith carrier of a DMT system. If peaks of all carriers can be aligned, the peak voltage of a DMT system is the peak voltage sum of all carriers. Under this assumed condition and for the particular case where the average power of each carrier is the same, you have

$$PAR_{DMT} = \frac{V_p}{\sqrt{\dfrac{P_{DMT}}{R}}} = \frac{\displaystyle\sum_{i=1}^{m} V_{pi}}{\sqrt{\dfrac{\displaystyle\sum_{i=1}^{m} P_{sub_i}}{R}}} = \frac{\displaystyle\sum_{i=1}^{m} V_{pi}}{\sqrt{\dfrac{mP_{sub}}{R}}} = \frac{1}{\sqrt{m}} \sum_{i=1}^{m} \frac{V_{pi}}{\sqrt{\dfrac{P_{sub}}{R}}} = \frac{1}{\sqrt{m}} \sum_{i=1}^{m} PAR_i$$

The values are as follows:

V_p is the peak voltage of the DMT system.

V_{pi} is the peak voltage of ith carrier.

P_{sub} is the same average power for all carriers.

With the additional special condition of $PAR_i = PAR_{sub}$, for which PAR_{sub} is the same PAR for all carriers, you have

$$PAR_{DMT} = \sqrt{m}\, PAR_{sub}$$

Figure 7.9 shows the DMT PAR for different numbers of carriers, assuming the following: Peaks of all carriers can be aligned, average carrier powers are equal, and each carrier has constellation sizes of 16, 64, and 256, respectively.

Figure 7.9 Cosine Carrier Peak-to-Average Voltage Ratio

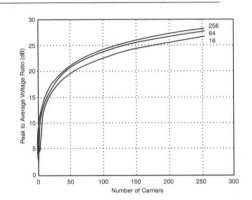

For a practical case where the peak of a DMT signal occurs when all carriers have the maximum amplitudes and 45 degree phase (that is, all carriers produce the top rightmost constellation point), we have

$$PAR_{DMT} = \frac{1}{\sqrt{m}} \sum_{i=1}^{m} k_i PAR_i = \frac{K_m}{\sqrt{m}} \sum_{i=1}^{m} PAR_i$$

for which k_is are modification factors associated with the addition of the next adjacent carrier, and K_ms are modification factors associated with the total number of carriers. Values of k_is and K_ms are obtained through computer simulation.

With the additional special condition of $PAR_i = PAR_{sub}$, we have

$$PAR_{DMT} = \frac{PAR_{sub}}{\sqrt{m}} \sum_{i=1}^{m} k_i = K_m \sqrt{m} PAR_{sub}$$

Figure 7.10 shows values of peak reduction factors, k_is.

Figure 7.10 Peak Reduction Factor, k_i

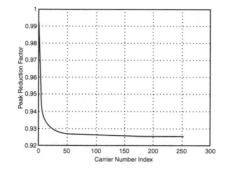

Figure 7.11 shows the DMT PAR for different numbers of carriers with modification factors, k_is, and assumes that average carrier powers are equal and each carrier has constellation sizes of 16, 64, and 256, respectively. The inclusion of peak reduction factor reduces the estimated DMT PAR by about 1 dB.

Figure 7.11 Peak-to-Average Voltage Ratio

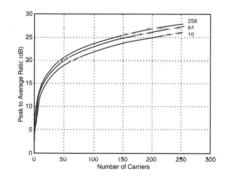

The DMT signal approaches a Gaussian distribution when the number of carriers is larger than 20. The representation of all DMT peak values might be necessary. In other words, the clipping of a DMT signal due to the limit of available voltage value might not degrade the performance of a DMT-based transmission system. The clipping noise spreads across all carriers. The clipping noise power level is usually low compared with signal power for a clipping-to-average voltage ratio of larger than 4. Figure 7.12 shows the clipping rate of a Gaussian-distributed signal with a limiting peak-to-average voltage ratio.

Figure 7.12 Clipping Rate of a Gaussian Signal

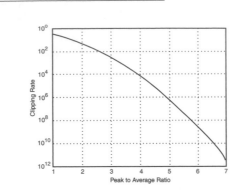

7.2 *Transmit Filter, Channel, and Echo Path Effects*

An analog or digital transmit filter is usually used to shape the spectrum of a DSL system. The transmit filter expands the PAR. The effect of a digital *Finite Impulse Response* (FIR) filter can be analyzed by calculating the mean, the variance, and the peak value of the FIR filter output with random data as the FIR filter input. Effects of the analog transmit filter, channel, and echo path are similar to that of the digital FIR filter.

The magnitude distribution of a multi-level signal after an FIR filter can be calculated as follows. We have the FIR filter output signal as

$$x(k) = \sum_{i}^{m} h_i a_{k-i}$$

The values are as follows:

h_is are FIR filter coefficients.

The FIR filter has a total of *m* coefficients.

a_is are *n*-level data symbols with magnitudes of $-(n-1), -(n-3), \ldots, -1, 1, \ldots, (n-3), (n-1)$.

The mean of the FIR filter output is

$$E[x(k)] = \sum_{i=1}^{m} E[h_i] E[a_{k-i}] = 0$$

for

$$E[a_{k-i}] = 0$$

The variance of the FIR filter output is

$$E[x^2(k)] = E\left[\left(\sum_{i=1}^{m} h_i a_{k-i}\right)^2\right] = \sum_{i=1}^{m} E[h_i^2]E[a_{k-i}^2] = mE[h_i^2]E[a_{k-i}^2]$$

$$= \frac{2\sum_{i=1}^{n/2}(2i-1)^2}{n}\sum_{i=1}^{m} h_i^2 = \frac{(n^2-1)\sum_{i=1}^{m} h_i^2}{3}$$

The mean square root voltage, assuming a load resistance of 1, is then

$$\sqrt{\frac{(n^2-1)\sum_{i=1}^{m} h_i^2}{3}}$$

The FIR filter output also has a peak magnitude of

$$x(k)_{MAX} = MAX(a_{k-i})\sum_{i=1}^{m} |h_i| = (n-1)\sum_{i=1}^{m} |h_i|$$

The filter output peak-to-average voltage ratio is

$$\sum_{i=1}^{m} |h_i| \sqrt{\frac{3(n-1)}{(n+1)\sum_{i=1}^{m} h_i^2}}$$

For a four-level signal, we have

$$\frac{3}{\sqrt{5}} \frac{\displaystyle\sum_{i=1}^{m} |h_i|}{\sqrt{\displaystyle\sum_{i=1}^{m} h_i^2}}$$

7.2.1 Baseband Square Root Nyquist Shaping Filters

For using a baseband square root Nyquist shaping filter, as shown in Figure 7.13, the peak-to-average ratio for a four-level signal after the filter is about 18 dB. The square root Nyquist shaping filter introduces the minimum signal distortion when used as a transmit and receive filter pair. The design of the square root Nyquist filter is discussed in more detail in Chapter 8 and Chapter 13, "ADSL (Asymmetrical Digital Subscriber Lines)."

Figure 7.13 A Baseband Square Root Nyquist Filter

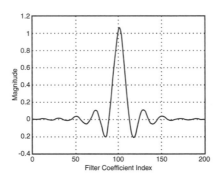

7.2.2 Passband Square Root Nyquist Shaping Filters

For using passband square root Nyquist shaping filters, as shown in Figure 7.14, the peak-to-average ratio for a 16 CAP/QAM signal after these filters is about 17 dB.

Figure 7.14   Passband Square Root Nyquist Filters

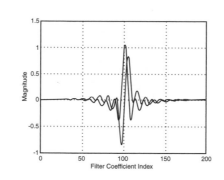

7.2.3   *Baseband Channel Impulse Response*

For a baseband signal using fourth order Butterworth transmit and receive filters with corner frequencies of 200 kHz over a 2 mile, 26-gauge twisted-pair loop, as shown in Figure 7.15, the peak-to-average ratio for a four-level signal after the equivalent channel is about 15.2 dB.

Figure 7.15   A Baseband Channel Impulse Response

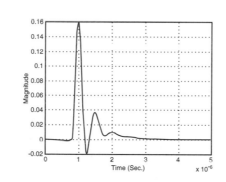

7.2.4   *Passband Channel Impulse Response*

For a passband equivalent channel defined by a passband Nyquist filter with a baud rate of 125 kHz and a center frequency of 83.33 kHz over a 2 mile, 26-gauge twisted-pair loop, as shown in Figure 7.16, the peak-to-average ratio for a four-level signal after the equivalent channel is about 18 dB.

Figure 7.16 Peak-to-Average Ratio for a Passband Channel

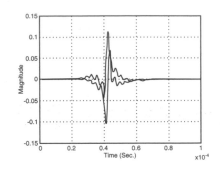

7.2.5 Baseband Echo Path

For a baseband echo path also using fourth order Butterworth transmit and receive filters with corner frequencies of 200 kHz in conjunction with a 2 mile, 26-gauge twisted-pair loop, as shown in Figure 7.17, the peak-to-average ratio for a four-level signal after the echo path is about 16.2 dB. The Baseband echo path is defined for each path with a baseband signal.

Figure 7.17 Echo Path Impulse Response

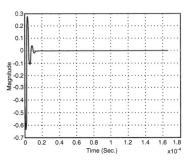

PARs after transmit filters are of concern for DACs while PARS after channel and echo path are of concern for ADCs.

7.3 ADC and DAC Characteristics

Data symbols are generated, received, and processed in a digital format while they are carried over a transmission channel in analog formats. Data symbols are converted to analog format in a transmitter with a Digital to Analog Converter (DAC). Data symbols are recovered in a receiver first through an Analog to Digital Converter (ADC). Figure 7.18

represents the ideal relationship between the digital input and analog output of a DAC. Discrete analog voltage levels are generated according to corresponding digital inputs.

Figure 7.18   Ideal Digital to Analog Conversion Relationship

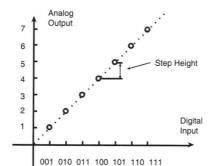

Conversely, Figure 7.19 represents the ideal relationship between the analog input and digital output of an ADC. A continuous analog input signal is quantified into discrete digital values.

Figure 7.19   Ideal Analog to Digital Conversion Relationship

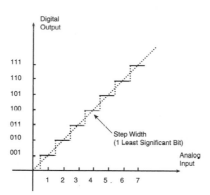

7.3.1   Calculation of Quantization Noise

Although quantization noise exists for a DAC device, the effect might not be obvious because the DAC takes digital input. On the other hand, the effect of quantization noise is always there for an ADC. The voltage difference between the analog input and corresponding digital output values acts as a quantization noise from an ADC, as shown in Figure 7.20.

Figure 7.20 Calculation of Quantization Noise

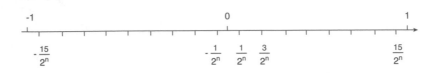

Figure 7.20 is a good reference to calculate the amount of quantization noise. An N bits ADC can represent a normalized voltage range of -1 to $+1$ with a step size of

$$\frac{1}{2^{N-1}}$$

An N bits ADC can have a quantization error whose magnitude range is

$$-\frac{1}{2^N} - \frac{1}{2^N}$$

The average quantization error power or quantization noise level is

$$e_q = \frac{1}{\frac{1}{2^N} - \left(-\frac{1}{2^N}\right)} \int_{-\frac{1}{2^N}}^{\frac{1}{2^N}} x^2 dx = \frac{2^{N-1}}{3} x^3 \Big|_{-\frac{1}{2^N}}^{\frac{1}{2^N}} = \frac{1}{3}\left[\frac{1}{2^N}\right]^2$$

Assuming the maximum value that an ADC or DAC can represent is 1 and the minimum is -1 (that is, the maximum magnitude is 0 dB), the quantization noise of an ADC is[1]

$$e_q = -10 \times \log_{10} 3 - 20 \times N \times \log_{10} 2 = -4.77 - 6.02N \, \text{dB}$$

About 6 dB of quantization noise level reduction is associated with every bit of resolution increase. For $N = 12$, we have

$$e_q = -4.77 - 6.02N = -77.01 \, \text{dB}$$

On the other hand, a signal with a peak-to-average voltage ratio of K can be represented with a signal level of

$$S_{PAR_K} = 20 \times \log_{10} \frac{1}{K}$$

For $K=5.75$, corresponding to a clipping rate of 10^{-8}, we have

$$S_{PAR_K} = 20 \times \log_{10} \frac{1}{5.8} = -15.27dB$$

Therefore, the maximum signal-to noise-ratio (SNR) represented by an N bits ADC with a PAR of 5.75 is then

$$SNR = S_{PAR_K} - e_q = -15.27 + 77.01 = 67.74dB$$

Table 7.1 lists the maximum representable SNR for other ADC resolutions and PAR values.

Table 7.1 Maximum SNR (dB)

	8 bits	9 bits	10 bits	11 bits	12 bits	13 bits	14 bits
PAR 1	52.93	58.95	64.97	70.99	77.01	83.03	89.05
PAR 2	46.91	52.93	58.95	64.97	70.99	77.01	83.03
PAR 3	43.39	49.41	55.43	61.45	67.47	73.49	79.51
PAR 4	40.89	46.91	52.93	58.95	64.97	70.99	77.01
PAR 5	38.95	44.97	50.99	57.01	63.03	69.05	75.07
PAR 6	37.37	43.39	49.41	55.43	61.45	67.47	73.49

7.3.2 ADC and DAC Nonlinearity

In practice, input and output values of a DAC or ADC do not always match. For an ADC, the range of analog input corresponding to a particular digital output might be bigger or smaller than desired or offset a little. For a DAC, the analog output corresponding to a particular digital input might be off-set a little. *Nonlinearity* is the term that refers to these input/output value deviations. For a DAC or ADC with many bits, the offset can be greater than 1 bit. The effect of the nonlinearity is the reduction of DAC or ADC effective resolution. Figure 7.21 shows the best straight line linearity error for which the overall linearity errors are minimized.

Figure 7.21 Best Straight Line Linearity Error

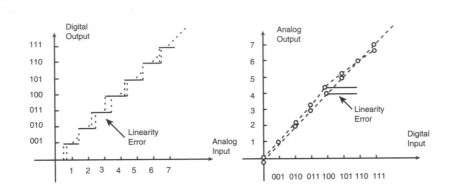

Conversely, Figure 7.22 shows the end-point matched linearity error for which end points of input and output are matched. The best-straight-line and end-point linearity errors are defined through different calibration methods.

Figure 7.22 End Point Linearity Error

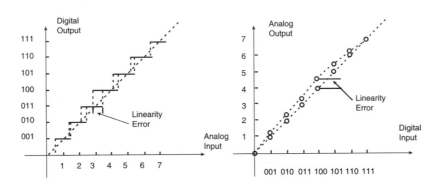

The effect of nonlinearity can also be characterized as additional quantization noise enhancement. The nonideal ADC quantization noise at ith step (between two adjacent digital outputs) can be described as

$$e_{q_i} = \cfrac{1}{\cfrac{1}{2^N} + \Delta_i - \left(-\cfrac{1}{2^N} + \Delta_{i-1}\right)} \int\limits_{-\frac{1}{2^N}+\Delta_{i-1}}^{\frac{1}{2^N}+\Delta_i} x^2 dx = \cfrac{1}{3\left(\cfrac{2}{2^N} + \Delta_i - \Delta_{i-1}\right)} x^3 \Big|_{-\frac{1}{2^N}+\Delta_{i-1}}^{\frac{1}{2^N}+\Delta_i}$$

$$= \cfrac{1}{3\left(\cfrac{2}{2^N} + \Delta_i - \Delta_{i-1}\right)} \left(\left(\cfrac{1}{2^N} + \Delta_i\right)^3 + \left(\cfrac{1}{2^N} - \Delta_{i-1}\right)^3\right)$$

in which Δ_i and Δ_{i-1} are amounts of deviations at the high end and low end of the analog input range. For the special case of

$$e_{q_i} = e_{q_n}$$

(that is, the ADC nonlinearity is represented by its nonlinearity at the ith step) and

$$\Delta_i = \Delta_{i-1} = \Delta$$

we have

$$e_{q_n} = \frac{2^{N-1}}{3}\left(2\left(\frac{1}{2^N}\right)^3 + 6\frac{1}{2^N}\Delta^2\right) = \frac{1}{3}\left(\frac{1}{2^N}\right)^2 + \Delta^2$$

The ratio of quantization noise with nonlinearity to that of ideal is

$$\frac{e_{q_n}}{e_q} = \frac{\cfrac{1}{3}\left(\cfrac{1}{2^N}\right)^2 + \Delta^2}{\cfrac{1}{3}\left(\cfrac{1}{2^N}\right)^2} = 1 + 3 \times 2^{2N}\Delta^2$$

These ratios of nonlinearity quantization noise enhancement are summarized in Table 7.2 for different values of Δ.

Table 7.2 Nonlinearity Noise Level (dB)

Δ	2^{-N-1}	$2^{-N-0.5}$	2^{-N}	$2^{-N+0.5}$	2^{-N+1}	$2^{-N+1.5}$	2^{-N+2}
e_{q_n}/e_q	11.14	8.45	6.02	3.98	2.43	1.38	0.75

A nonlinearity of 1/4 bit can cause a quantization noise enhancement of 2.43 dB while a nonlinearity of 1/2 bit can cause a quantization noise enhancement of 6.02 dB, which is equivalent to the loss of one effective bit. In practice, the worst case nonlinearity decides the available ADC or DAC resolution.

7.4 DAC and ADC Dynamic Range Requirements

The dynamic range of a DAC or an ADC defined by their precision should be comparable with that required by the line code, error rate, and the channel condition of a DSL system. The required DAC precision can be different for different digital transmit filters and line codes. The required ADC precision is further affected by the twisted-pair loop channel and the echo path.

7.4.1 DAC Resolution Requirements for Baseband Transmitters

For a baseband transmitter without digital filters, the required resolution for a DAC is the same as that for the baseband line signal. For example, a four-level baseband signal needs only a DAC of 2 bits, while an eight-level baseband signal needs only a DAC of 3 bits. Additional signal spectrum shaping is carried out by analog filters after the DAC.

For a baseband transmitter with digital shaping filters, the required resolution for a DAC is determined by the following factors:

- The number of line signal levels

- The desired signal-to-noise ratio or error rate

- The peak-to-average voltage ratio of digital shaping filters

The average signal power is expressed as

$$\frac{n^2 - 1}{3}$$

The value n is the number of signal levels. For using a voltage difference of 2 between adjacent signal levels, the probability of error is

$$P_e = \frac{2}{\sqrt{2\pi}\sigma} \int\limits_{1}^{\infty} e^{-\frac{y^2}{2\sigma^2}} dy$$

The value σ^2 is the variance of the noise. This can also be expressed as

$$P_e = \frac{2}{\sqrt{2\pi}} \int\limits_{\frac{1}{\sigma}}^{\infty} e^{-\frac{y^2}{2}} dy = Q\left(\frac{1}{\sigma}\right)$$

$Q(x)$ is defined for this error probability function. The inverse of the noise power is the inverse function of the error probability, as expressed in the following equation:

$$\frac{1}{\sigma^2} = \left(Q^{-1}(P_e)\right)^2$$

The required SNR is

$$\frac{n^2 - 1}{3} = \left(Q^{-1}(P_e)\right)^2$$

Table 7.3 shows the required SNRs for baseband signals with different numbers of signal levels and different error rates.

Table 7.3   Required SNRs (dB)

Error Rate	Number of Signal Levels				
	4	8	16	32	64
10^{-6}	20.7	26.9	33.0	39.0	45.1
10^{-7}	21.6	27.8	33.9	39.9	46.0
10^{-8}	22.2	28.4	34.5	40.5	46.6

The results in Table 7.3 indicate that doubling the number of signal levels (equivalent to adding one more bit) for a baseband system costs approximately 6 dB of SNR.

Table 7.4 shows the required DAC resolution for a different number of signal levels and different error rates for a Nyquist shaping filter with a peak-to-average voltage ratio of 18 dB.

Table 7.4 Required DAC Resolution

Error Rate	Number of Signal Levels				
	4	8	16	32	64
10^{-6}	6	7	8	9	10
10^{-7}	6	7	8	9	10
10^{-8}	6	7	8	9	10

One or two extra bits might be necessary to allow the inclusion of other noise sources while meeting the same SNR objective. Results in Table 7.4 are obtained by equating the sum of SNR and PAR to the negative dB of the quantization noise level, as follows:

$$SNR + PAR = -e_q = 4.77 + 6.02N$$

The required number of bits is expressed as

$$N = \frac{1}{6.02}(SNR + PAR - 4.77)$$

7.4.2 DAC Resolution Requirements for Passband Transmitters

For a passband transmitter with digital shaping filters, the required resolution for a DAC is determined by the following factors:

- The constellation size
- The desired signal-to-noise ratio or error rate
- The peak-to-average voltage ratio of digital shaping filters

The average signal power is expressed as

$$\frac{2(2^{2n} - 1)}{3}$$

The value n is the constellation size index or number of bits per dimension. The probability of error is

$$P_e = \frac{2}{\sqrt{\pi}\sigma} \int_1^\infty e^{-\frac{y^2}{\sigma^2}} dy$$

The value σ^2 is the variance of the noise. This also can be expressed as

$$P_e = \frac{2}{\sqrt{2\pi}} \int_{\frac{\sqrt{2}}{\sigma}}^\infty e^{-\frac{y^2}{2}} dy = Q\left(\frac{\sqrt{2}}{\sigma}\right)$$

The inverse of the noise power is the inverse function of the error probability, as shown in the following expressions:

$$\frac{2}{\sigma^2} = Q^{-1}(P_e)$$

or

$$\frac{1}{\sigma^2} = \frac{Q^{-1}(P_e)}{2}$$

The required SNR for a passband signal with a constellation size of 2^{2n} is

$$\frac{2^{2n}-1}{3}\left(Q^{-1}(P_e)\right)^2$$

Table 7.5 shows the required SNRs for different constellation sizes and different error rates.

Table 7.6 shows the required DAC resolution for different constellation sizes and different error rates for a Nyquist shaping filter with a peak-to-average ratio of 17 dB.

Table 7.5 Required SNRs (dB)

Error Rate	Constellation size				
	4	16	64	256	1024
10^{-6}	13.7	20.7	26.9	33.0	39.0
10^{-7}	14.6	21.6	27.8	33.9	39.9
10^{-8}	15.2	22.2	28.4	34.5	40.5

Table 7.6 Required DAC Resolution

Error Rate	Number of Signal Levels				
	4	16	64	256	1024
10^{-6}	5	6	7	8	9
10^{-7}	5	6	7	8	9
10^{-8}	5	6	7	8	9

Again, one or two extra bits might be necessary for a better quantization noise margin.

7.4.3 DAC Resolution Requirements for DMT Transmitters

For a DMT transmitter with 256 carriers and a maximum constellation size of 1,024, the PAR is around 28 dB, the required SNR is about 40 dB, and the required DAC resolution is as follows:

$$N = \frac{1}{6.02}(SNR + PAR - 4.77) = (40 + 28 - 4.77)\big/6.02 = 105 \approx 11 bits$$

We might need a few extra bits to minimize the effect of quantization noise compared with other transmission impairments.[2] Therefore, a DMT transmitter might need a DAC resolution of 11 to 14 bits if no clipping is allowed.

The required DAC resolution of a DMT system can be relaxed significantly if clipping is allowed.[3] The power of the clipping noise can be expressed as

$$P_{clip} = 2 \int_{A_{clip}}^{\infty} \left(x - A_{clip}\right)^2 \frac{e^{-\frac{x^2}{2\sigma^2}}}{\sqrt{2\pi}\sigma} dx \approx \sqrt{\frac{8}{\pi}} \frac{\sigma^2}{\mu^3 e^{\frac{\mu^2}{2}}}$$

in which

$$\mu = \frac{A_{clip}}{\sigma} \text{ is the clipping ratio and}$$

$$\frac{\sigma^2}{P_{clip}} \approx \sqrt{\frac{\pi}{8}} \mu^3 e^{\frac{\mu^2}{2}} \text{ is the signal-to-clipping-noise power ratio.}$$

For $\mu = 5.35$ or 15 dB, corresponding to a clipping rate of 10^{-7}, we have

$$\frac{\sigma^2}{P_{clip}} \approx 82 \text{ dB}$$

These calculations show that a DMT transmitter can be designed with a PAR of only 15 dB without much performance degradation. This could result in a reduction of about 2 bits in the DAC resolution requirement. Therefore with clipping, the required DAC resolution for a DMT transmitter is between 9 to 12 bits.

7.4.4 The Effect of ADC Quantization Noise

If a transmission channel has only a flat loss, the receiver ADC needs at least the same resolution as that of transmitter DAC. To minimize the effect of receiver ADC quantization noise under a certain receiver front-end noise level, we need a quantization noise level that is lower than that of the receiver front-end noise. The overall receiver front-end signal-to-noise ratio after the ADC is expressed as

$$SNR = \frac{P_{signal}}{\sigma_n^2 + \sigma_{ADC}^2} = \frac{P_{signal}}{\sigma_n^2} \frac{1}{1 + \frac{\sigma_{ADC}^2}{\sigma_n^2}} = SNR_n \frac{1}{1 + \frac{\sigma_{ADC}^2}{\sigma_n^2}}$$

The values are as follows:

P_{signal} is the received signal power.

σ_n^2 is the receiver front-end noise power.

σ_{ADC}^2 is the ADC quantization noise power.

For the quantization noise limited case, σ_n^2 represents the DAC quantization noise power. We can let $\sigma_n^2 = \sigma_{ADC}^2$. For this assumption, σ_n^2 and σ_{ADC}^2 each need to be 3 dB lower compared to that calculated for ADC alone to meet the same *SNR* objective.

For the receiver front-end noise limited case, σ_n^2 represents the receiver front-end noise power. The noise enhancement introduced by the receiver ADC quantization is

$$1 + \frac{\sigma_{ADC}^2}{\sigma_n^2}$$

Figure 7.23 shows the relationship between the noise enhancement and the quantization to the receiver front-end noise ratio. A ratio of one or 0 dB will increase the noise level by 3 dB, while a ratio of 0.25 or –6 dB will only produce a noise enhancement of 1 dB. This corresponds to one extra bit than the required number of bits calculated in Tables 7.4 and 7.6 and that calculated for the DMT transmitter.

Figure 7.23 Degree of Noise Enhancement

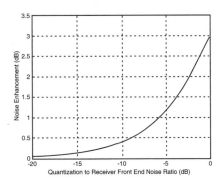

7.4.5 ADC Precision Requirements Considering Channel Loss

At the receiver front end, a twisted-pair loop channel can introduce a loss difference of as much as 40 dB within a signaling band; however, a portion of the channel with heavy signal losses can also tolerate a relatively high quantization noise level. In other words, the signal-to-noise power density ratio at the high-frequency end, where heavy channel loss occurs, can be less than that required by a particular line code.

The use of an adaptive channel equalizer could automatically compensate the low signal-to-noise ratio at a certain frequency region. Figure 7.24 shows relationships between the received signal level, the average received signal level, and the receiver front-end noise level for a 2 mile, 26-gauge twisted-pair loop.

Figure 7.24   Received Signal and Noise Power Level

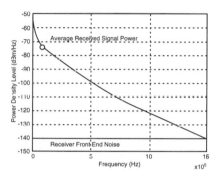

The required ADC resolution to recover all information delivered by this twisted-pair loop channel can be calculated as

$$(-75.2 + 140 + 20 - 4.77)/6.02 \approx 14 \text{ bits}$$

The values are as follows:

–75.2 dBm/Hz is the average received signal power density level.

–140 dBm/Hz is the receiver front-end noise power level.

The desired SNR is the average received signal power density minus the receiver front-end noise power density.

20 dB is for the received signal PAR.

If the received signal only uses a frequency spectrum of 200 kHz, such as the signal spectrum of HDSL, the average received signal level is –66.9 dBm/Hz, and the loss difference for a bandwidth of 200 kHz is about 30 dB. The required ADC resolution for this 200 kHz band with a four-level signal can be calculated as

$$(21.4 + 30 + 15 - 4.77)/6.02 \approx 11 \text{ bits}$$

The values are as follows:

21.4 dB is the required SNR for a four-level signal.

30 dB is the channel loss difference.

The desired SNR is the SNR for a four-level signal plus the channel loss difference.

15 dB is for the received signal PAR.

Figure 7.25 shows relationships between the received signal level, the average received signal level, and the receiver front-end noise level for a 3 mile, 26-gauge twisted-pair loop.

Figure 7.25 Received Signal and Noise Power Level

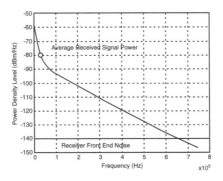

The required ADC resolution to recover all information delivered by this twisted-pair loop channel can be calculated as

$$(-79 + 140 + 20 - 4.77)/6.02 \approx 13 \text{ bits}$$

The values are as follows:

–79 dBm/Hz is the average received signal power density level.

–140 dBm/Hz is the receiver front-end noise power level.

The desired SNR is the average received signal power density minus the receiver front-end noise power density.

20 dB is for the received signal PAR.

If the received signal uses a frequency spectrum of only 40 kHz, such as the spectrum of the Basic Access Rate ISDN channel, the average received signal level is –66.5 dBm/Hz, and the loss difference for a bandwidth of 40 kHz is about 26 dB. The required ADC resolution for this 40 kHz band with a four-level signal can be calculated as

$$(21.4 + 26 + 15 - 4.77)/6.02 \approx 10 \text{ bits}$$

The values are as follows:

21.4 dB is the required SNR for a four-level signal.

26 dB is the channel loss difference.

The desired SNR is the SNR for the four level signal plus the channel loss difference.

15 dB is for the received signal PAR.

7.4.6 *ADC Precision Requirements Considering Echo Path*

The echo level is usually much higher compared with the received signal level. The echo is attenuated by the hybrid circuit and bandpass filters in the case of a *Frequency Division Duplex* (FDD) system. For cases in which the transmit signal and received signal are further separated with the help of a digital echo canceller, a higher resolution ADC becomes necessary. For an assumed echo return loss of 15 dB, required ADC resolutions are calculated for the examples in section 7.4.5, "ADC Precision Requirements Considering Channel Loss."

The required ADC resolution to recover all information delivered by a 2 mile, 26-gauge twisted-pair loop channel can be calculated as

$$(-55 + 140 + 16 - 4.77)/6.02 \approx 16 \text{ bits}$$

The values are as follows:

–55 dBm/Hz is the average echo mixed with the received signal power density level.

–140 dBm/Hz is the receiver front-end noise power level.

The desired SNR is the average echo power density minus the average receiver front-end noise power density.

16 dB is for the echo mixed with the received signal PAR.

If the received signal uses a frequency spectrum of only 200 kHz, such as the signal spectrum of HDSL, the desired signal-to-noise ratio is increased by –55–(–66.9)=11.9 dB. The required ADC resolution for this 200 kHz band with a four-level signal can be calculated as

$$(21.4 + 11.9 + 30 + 16 - 4.77)/6.02 \approx 13 \text{ bits}$$

The values are as follows:

21.4 dB is the required SNR for a four-level signal.

11.9 dB accounts for the stronger echo level.

30 dB is the channel loss difference.

The desired SNR is the sum of the required SNR for a four-level signal, the stronger echo level, and the channel loss difference.

16 dB is for the received signal PAR.

The required ADC resolution to recover all information delivered by a 3 mile, 26-gauge twisted-pair loop channel can be calculated as

$$(-55 + 140 + 16 - 4.77)/6.02 \approx 16 \text{ bits}$$

The values are as follows:

−55 dBm/Hz is the average echo mixed with the received signal power density level.

−140 dBm/Hz is the receiver front-end noise power level.

The desired SNR is the average echo power density minus the average receiver front-end noise power density.

16 dB is for the echo mixed with the received signal PAR.

If the received signal use a frequency spectrum of only 40 kHz, such as the signal spectrum of the Basic Rate Access ISDN channel, the required signal-to-noise ratio is increased by −55−(−66.5)=115 dB. The required ADC resolution for this 40 kHz band with a four-level signal can be calculated as

$$(21.4 + 11.5 + 26 + 16 - 4.77)/6.02 \approx 12 \text{ bits}$$

The values are as follows:

21.4 dB is the required SNR for a four-level signal.

11.5 dB accounts for the stronger echo level.

26 dB is the channel loss difference.

The desired SNR is the sum of the required SNR for a four-level signal, the stronger echo level, and the channel loss difference.

16 dB is for the received signal PAR.

End Notes

1. W. Y. Chen, "The Distribution of Echo Signal and Required A/D Precision," *IEEE ISCAS '92.*

2. N. Al-Dhahir and J. M. Cioffi, "On the Uniform ADC Bit Precision and Clip Level Computation for a Gaussian Signal," *IEEE Trans. on Signal Processing,* vol. 44, no. 2 (February 1998): 434–438.

3. D. J. G. Mestdagh, P. Spruyt, and B. Biran, "Analysis of Clipping Effect in DMT-Based ADSL System," *Alcatel T1E1 Contribution,* T1E1.4/93-129 (May 10, 1993).

CHAPTER 8

Channel Equalization

The usable bandwidth of a twisted-pair telephone subscriber loop is much wider than the voice band telephony channel; however, the channel distortion is also more severe for using the full available bandwidth. Specifically, amplitude attenuation and phase delay could be very different at different frequency regions within the available bandwidth. A transmitting signal could become unrecognizable after going through a telephone subscriber loop because of the amplitude and phase distortion. The channel capacity estimation in the frequency domain only indicates the transmission potential of the telephone subscriber loop— but does not reveal any method of achieving that.

An information bit stream is usually converted into a sequence of data symbols. The transmission throughput is the product of the symbol rate and the number of bits carried by every data symbol. The faster the symbol rate, the higher the transmission throughput; however, the symbol rate is limited by the channel amplitude and phase distortion. Specifically, the channel distortion causes the data symbols to spread. Therefore, there are certain limitations to how close symbols can be lined up next to each other without the use of any channel distortion compensation technique.

The effect of channel distortion can be minimized using a channel equalizer, which can be used to control the spread of the data symbol after going through the channel. Dividing the available bandwidth into many smaller frequency regions where channel distortion becomes relatively insignificant also can minimize the effect of channel distortion. A channel equalizer also can be very useful even for the bandwidth divided DSL systems.

In theory, an equalizer should have a frequency response that is the inverse of the channel. In practice, a channel equalizer is normally implemented with a digital adaptive filter. An adaptive channel equalizer can be further categorized as linear or decision feedback, baud rate or fractionally spaced, baseband or passband (depending on performance requirement), signal processing capability, and system architecture.

The development of the adaptive channel equalization technique has helped the evolution of the voice band modem technology. The adaptive channel equalization technique has also been successfully used for DSL systems to realize the transmission throughput potential available over the telephone subscriber loops. Equalizer coefficients and equalizer output signal-to-noise ratio (SNR) can characterize the implementation requirement and the effectiveness of an adaptive channel equalizer. Equalizer coefficients and output SNR can be obtained iteratively through the simulation of the adaptation process or directly through some matrix calculation in conjunction with channel and noise models.

This chapter addresses issues related to the determination of equalizer coefficients and equalizer output SNR, based on the matrix calculation method. Detailed results are derived for the following equalizer configurations:

- *Adaptive Linear Channel Equalizer.* Concepts of channel equalization and adaptive filtering are discussed. Baud rate and fractionally spaced linear equalizer coefficients and equalizer output SNRs are calculated. The issue of noise enhancement is also addressed.

- *Decision Feedback Channel Equalizer (DFE).* DFE equalizer coefficients and equalizer output SNRs are calculated for baud rate and fractionally spaced *feed forward filters* (FFF). The Tomlinson/Harashima precoding method is also introduced.

- *Passband Equalizer and Carrierless AM/PM (CAP).* Equalizer coefficients and output SNRs are calculated for the passband *Quadrature Amplitude Modulation* (QAM) system. A linear equalizer or the FFF of a DFE can be placed before or after the demodulation process. Linear equalizer and DFE structures for a CAP system are derived. Equalizer coefficients and equalizer output SNRs are also calculated for a CAP system.

- *Equalizer for Discrete MultiTone (DMT) Systems.* The concept of *intersymbol interference* for a DMT system is introduced. Equalizer coefficients and equalizer output SNRs are calculated for a DMT system based on the *Minimum Mean Square Error* (MMSE) criteria.

8.1   *Adaptive Linear Channel Equalization*

A channel equalizer can be used to minimize the effect of channel distortion; however, every twisted-pair loop has its own unique transmission characteristics due to the composition and the configuration of that particular loop. Furthermore, the transmission characteristics of a twisted-pair loop is slightly time varying and temperature dependent.

An adaptation process is used to identify the optimal channel equalizer coefficients and keep tracking possible variation of the channel characteristics. A linear equalizer is usually implemented with a digital *Finite Impulse Response* (FIR) filter. The output of a linear equalizer depends only on the received signal versus that of a DFE whose output depends on estimated data symbols.

Although there is enough signal-to-noise ratio to carry a signal over the twisted-pair loop channel, the channel distortion to the transmitted signal is very severe. At signaling rates of higher than a few hundred kHz, the received signal has a disbursing many times that of the signaling interval.

Figure 8.1 shows normalized impulse responses after 1, 2, and 3 miles of 26-gauge twisted-pair loops. Signaling intervals, or baud periods, are 12.5, 2.5, and 1 microseconds for signaling baud rates of 80 kHz, 400 kHz, and 1 mHz, respectively. Even for the 1 mile loop, the impulse response lasts more than 30 microseconds. The tail of the impulse response can interfere with the next baud signal if the baud period is shorter than that of the tail. This is called *channel intersymbol interference*.

Figure 8.1 Impulse Responses for Twisted-Pair Loops of Different Lengths

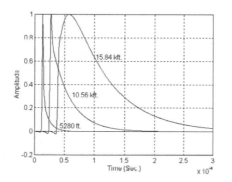

8.1.1 *Compensating for Channel Distortion*

In theory, the channel distortion can be compensated if you use a filter, with a frequency response that is the inverse of that of the twisted-pair loop channel, in front of the receiver. We let

$$H_F(f) = \frac{1}{H(f)}$$

$H_F(f)$ is the transfer function of the compensation filter.

$H(f)$ is the transfer function of the channel.

This channel compensation filter cannot be realized in analog format, however, because the *Fourier transform* of the inverse channel does not exit. For the simplified channel model of

$$H(d,f) = e^{-d\left(k_1\sqrt{f}+k_2 f\right)} e^{-jdk_3 f}$$

the transfer function for the compensation filter is expressed as

$$H_F(d,f) = e^{d\left(k_1\sqrt{f}+k_2 f\right)} e^{jdk_3 f}$$

The Fourier transform of this transfer function does not exist because $H_F(d,f) \to \infty$ when $f \to \infty$. On the other hand, the channel compensation can be realized in the sampled digital domain. The frequency response of the channel in the sampled digital domain is expressed as

$$H_s(f) = \frac{1}{T}\sum_{i=-\infty}^{\infty} H\left(f - \frac{i}{T}\right)$$

The frequency response of the compensation filter, also in the sampled digital domain, is expressed as

$$H_{s,F}(f) = \frac{1}{\dfrac{1}{T}\displaystyle\sum_{i=-\infty}^{\infty} H\left(f - \dfrac{i}{T}\right)}$$

The discrete frequency domain version of this compensation filter is expressed as

$$H_{s,F}(k) = H_{s,F}(k\Delta f) = \frac{1}{\dfrac{1}{T}\displaystyle\sum_{i=-\infty}^{\infty} H\left(k\Delta f - \dfrac{i}{T}\right)}$$

Filter coefficients of this digital compensation filter exist and can be obtained through the discrete Fourier transform using the following expression:

$$h_{s,F}(n) = h_{s,F}(n\Delta t) = \frac{1}{T}\sum_{k=0}^{n-1} H_{s,F}(k)e^{j2\pi kn\frac{\Delta t}{T}}$$

Filter coefficients of this digital compensation filter also can be obtained directly in the discrete time domain. It is preferable to have the combined output of the channel and compensation filter be zeros all the time except at one particular sampling instance, l:

$$\sum_i h(i)h_{s,F}(j-i) = 0, \ j \neq l$$

$$\sum_i h(i)h_{s,F}(j-i) = 1, \ j = l$$

Because data symbols are transmitted in sequence, every sampling instance can be made unique, corresponding to a particular data symbol. The received signal detected from this sequence of sampling instances can be made free of channel distortion. This condition can be expressed in a matrix format. An example of channel and filter lengths both being equal to 5 is expressed as

$$\begin{bmatrix} h(1) & 0 & 0 & 0 & 0 \\ h(2) & h(1) & 0 & 0 & 0 \\ h(3) & h(2) & h(1) & 0 & 0 \\ h(4) & h(3) & h(2) & h(1) & 0 \\ h(5) & h(4) & h(3) & h(2) & h(1) \\ 0 & h(5) & h(4) & h(3) & h(2) \\ 0 & 0 & h(5) & h(4) & h(3) \\ 0 & 0 & 0 & h(5) & h(4) \\ 0 & 0 & 0 & 0 & h(5) \end{bmatrix} \begin{bmatrix} h_{s,F}(1) \\ h_{s,F}(2) \\ h_{s,F}(3) \\ h_{s,F}(4) \\ h_{s,F}(5) \end{bmatrix} = \begin{matrix} 0 \\ 0 \\ 0 \\ 0 \\ 1 \\ 0 \\ 0 \\ 0 \\ 0 \end{matrix}$$

These compensation filter coefficient values can be obtained by solving the above set of overly specified linear equations. In general, the unit response does not need to be exactly in the middle of the convolution span. The previous matrix relationship can be described in a simplified notation, as follows:

$$\overline{H}\overline{h}_{s,F} = \overline{p}$$

Because $\overline{H}$ is not a square matrix, the solution is expressed as

$$\overline{h}_{s,F} = \left(\overline{H}^T\overline{H}\right)^{-1}\overline{H}^T\overline{p}$$

Figures 8.2, 8.3, and 8.4 show normalized filter coefficients of compensation filters as well as original and compensated channel impulse responses for 1, 2, and 3 miles of 26-gauge twisted-pair loops, respectively. Because the channel impulse response is normalized, and compensation filter coefficients and compensated channel impulse response all have similar magnitudes, they are organized together in all three figures for the comparison of different shapes.

Figure 8.2 Channel and Compensation Filter for a 1 Mile, 26-Gauge Loop

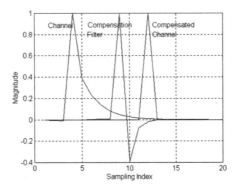

This digital compensation filter is called a *linear channel equalizer* because the equalizer output is a linear combination of the received signal.[1] Equalizer coefficients obtained according to the previous matrix relationship results in what is called a *zero forcing channel equalizer*, which works well in a noiseless or low-noise environment.

Figure 8.3   Channel and Compensation Filter for a 2 Mile, 26-Gauge Loop

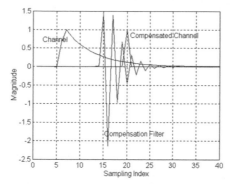

Figure 8.4   Channel and Compensation Filter for a 3 Mile, 26-Gauge Loop

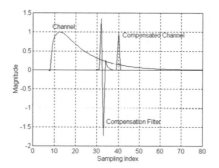

8.1.2   *Obtaining Optimal Equalizer Coefficients*

For a twisted-pair channel with crosstalk and background noise, optimal equalizer coefficients are obtained through minimizing the mean square error between the desired unit response and the channel and equalizer combined output. The frequency domain derivation of this Minimum Mean Square Error equalizer is equivalent to the *Wiener Filter.*[2]

The received signal contains information of the current as well as past and future data symbols. The ideal equalizer output should only contain the current data symbol. The difference between the current data symbol and the output of the equalizer contains the error of the current data symbol estimation and residual channel distortion. Based on the assumption that the received signal and the error between the unit response and the equalizer output should not be correlated, we have

$$E\left\{\left[a(t) - \int_{-\infty}^{\infty} x(t-\alpha)q(\alpha)d\alpha\right]x(t-\tau)\right\} = 0$$

The values are as follows:

$a(t)$ is the transmit signal.

$x(t)$ is the received signal.

$q(t)$ is the equalizer.

This expectation yields the relationship between the correlation of the transmitted signal and the received signal and the autocorrelation of the received signal:

$$R_{ax}(\tau) = \int_{-\infty}^{\infty} R_{xx}(\tau-\alpha)q(\alpha)d\alpha$$

The values are as follows:

$R_{ax}(t)$ is the correlation between the transmitted signal and the received signal.

$R_{xx}(t)$ is the autocorrelation of the received signal.

This can be equivalently expressed in frequency domain as

$$S_{ax} = (\omega) = S_{xx}(\omega)Q(\omega)$$

Therefore, the minimum mean square equalizer solution in frequency domain is

$$Q(\omega) = \frac{S_{ax}(\omega)}{S_{xx}(\omega)}$$

You can derive the discrete Minimum Mean Square Error equalizer solution directly in the discrete time domain. The instantaneous error between the desired data symbol and the equalizer output is expressed as

$$e_k = a_{k-d} - X_k^T Q_k$$

a_{k-d} is the desired data symbol after a channel delay of d signaling periods.

$X_k^T = \begin{bmatrix} x_k & x_{k-1} & \cdots & x_{x-n+1} \end{bmatrix}$ is the received signal vector for an equalizer length of n.

$Q_k^T = \begin{bmatrix} q_{1k} & q_{2k} & \cdots & q_{nk} \end{bmatrix}$ is the equalizer coefficient vector.

e_k is the error between the desired signal and the equalizer output.

We further expand the received signal as the convolution of the transmitted signal and the twisted-pair loop channel impulse response as

$$x_k = \sum_{i=1}^{l} a_{k-i+1}h(i) = \begin{bmatrix} a_k & a_{k-1} & \cdots & a_{k-l+1} \end{bmatrix} \begin{bmatrix} h(1) \\ h(2) \\ \cdots \\ h(l) \end{bmatrix} + n_k = A_k^T \overline{h} + n_k$$

The channel impulse response, which has a duration of l and n_k, is the sampled receiver front-end noise.[3] The received signal vector can be expressed as

$$X_k^T = \begin{bmatrix} a_k & a_{k-1} & \cdots & a_{k-l-n+2} \end{bmatrix} \begin{bmatrix} h(1) & 0 & 0 & 0 \\ h(2) & h(1) & 0 & 0 \\ h(3) & h(2) & 0 & 0 \\ \cdots & \cdots & \cdots & h(1) \\ h(l) & h(l-1) & 0 & h(2) \\ 0 & h(l) & 0 & h(3) \\ 0 & 0 & 0 & \cdots \\ 0 & 0 & 0 & h(l) \end{bmatrix} + \begin{bmatrix} n_k & n_{k-1} & \cdots & n_{k-n+1} \end{bmatrix} = A_k^{nT}\overline{H} + N_k^T$$

$\overline{H}$ has a dimension of $l+n-1$ by n, and the data vector A_k^{nT} has a length of $l+n-1$. The expected value of the squared error, or mean squared error, for a particular equalizer Q is

$$E[e_k^2] = E\left[(a_{k-d} - X_k^T Q)^2\right]$$

The derivative of the mean squared error with respect to the equalizer coefficient vector, Q, is

$$\frac{\partial\left(E\left[e_k^2\right]\right)}{\partial Q} = -2E\left[\left(a_{k-d} - X_k^T Q\right)X_k^T\right]$$

By setting the derivative equal to zero, we obtain the optimal equalizer coefficient vector, Q_{opt}, for the minimum mean squared error as

$$Q_{opt}^T E\left[X_k X_k^T\right] = E\left[a_{k-d} X_k^T\right]$$

$$Q_{opt}^T = \left(E\left[X_k X_k^T\right]\right)^{-1} E\left[a_{k-d} X_k^T\right]$$

When the channel noise is set to zero, the Minimum Mean Square Error equalizer solution becomes the zero forcing equalizer solution:

$$Q_{opt} = \left(\overline{H}^T \overline{H}\right)^{-1} \overline{H}^T p$$

Figures 8.5, 8.6, and 8.7 show Minimum Mean Square Error equalizer coefficients for 1, 2, and 3 miles of 26-gauge twisted-pair loops, respectively, under different white background noise levels. The results in Figures 8.6 and 8.7 indicate that a balance exists between the degree of channel equalization and the amount of noise enhancement. Under a lower noise level, a better channel equalization can be realized.

Figure 8.5 Channel Equalizer for a 1 Mile, 26-Gauge Loop with Different Noise Levels

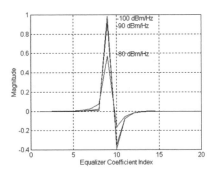

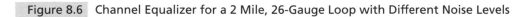

Figure 8.6 Channel Equalizer for a 2 Mile, 26-Gauge Loop with Different Noise Levels

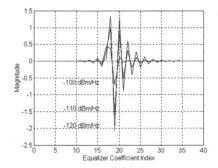

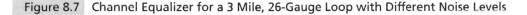

Figure 8.7 Channel Equalizer for a 3 Mile, 26-Gauge Loop with Different Noise Levels

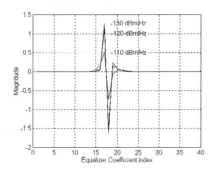

In a hardware implementation, equalizer coefficient values are identified iteratively most often with the LMS algorithm[4]

$$Q_{k+1} = Q_k + \mu X_k \left(a_{k-d} - X_k^T Q_k \right)$$

for which the adjustment step size should satisfy the following condition:

$$\mu < \frac{1}{trE\left[X_k X_k^T \right]}$$

The value $trE\left[X_k X_k^T \right]$ refers to the sum of the diagonal elements of the matrix $E\left[X_k X_k^T \right]$.

If the received signal is properly normalized, that is, $E[x_k^2] = 1$ through receiver front-end amplification, the result will be

$$\mu < \frac{1}{n}$$

in which n is the length of the channel equalizer.

The expression

$$\xi_{min} = E[a_{k-d}^2] - E[a_{k-d} X_k^T]Q_{op}$$

describes the Minimum Mean Square Error (MMSE) between the desired signal and the output of an optimal equalizer, which is determined by the receiver front-end noise level, the twisted-pair loop channel, and the length of the equalizer.

A 26-gauge, 10,560 foot loop with receiver front-end noise power density levels of –110 dBm/Hz, –120 dBm/Hz, and –130 dBm/Hz, for example, has MMSE levels of –18.3 dB, –27.9 dB, and –36.6 dB, respectively.

The actual mean square error between the desired signal and the output of an optimal equalizer is slightly higher than the MMSE by the amount of excessive MMSE due to the use of a finite adjustment step size. The amount of excessive MMSE is proportional to the adjustment step size and is described by the following expression:

$$excess\ \xi_{min} \approx \mu \xi_{min} trE[X_k X_k^T]$$

For a simple example of $E[x_k^2] = 1$ with an adjustment step size of $\mu = 1/80$, the amount of excessive MMSE is then

$$excess\ \xi_{min} \approx 0.5\xi_{min}$$

The total mean square error between the desired signal and the output of an optimal equalizer is

$$\xi = excess\ \xi_{min} + \xi_{min} \approx 1.5\xi_{min}$$

This effect of a 50 percent addition is equivalent to raising the mean square error by the amount of 1.76 dB. Figure 8.8 shows convergence of the mean square error for adjustment step sizes of 1/200, 1/300, and 1/400 for a 1 mile, 26-gauge twisted-pair loop. The middle curve has an adjustment step size of 1/300. A slightly lower mean square error level can be observed for a step size of 1/300 compared with that for a step size of 1/200.

Figure 8.8 Convergence of an Adaptive Channel Equalizer

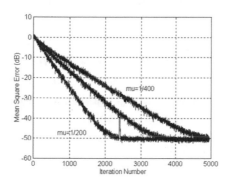

8.1.3 *Baud Rate Equalizer Performance*

The preceding derived equalizer operates at the signaling baud rate and, therefore, is also called the *baud rate equalizer.* It also can be called the *symbol rate* or the *symbol spaced equalizer.* The performance of a baud rate equalizer is very sensitive to the sampling timing phase because the sampled signal strength could be different relative to the background noise. Figure 8.9 shows the MMSE values for a 2 mile, 26-gauge twisted-pair loop with different sampling timing phases. These MMSE values can differ by as much as 9 dB at different timing phases. Ten sample points were taken for a phase rotation of 2π in Figure 8.9.

Figure 8.9 Equalizer Output Signal-to-Noise Ratio Versus Timing Phase

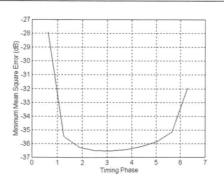

The effective bandwidth is half of the sampling rate or baud rate for this special baud rate equalizer case. Nyquist frequency is often used to describe the bandwidth defined by the half sampling frequency. The analog channel, including channel attenuation and receiver front-end noise, is folded along the Nyquist frequency due to the sampling process.

The interference caused by sampling images is often referred to as the *aliasing effect*. An analog filter with a Nyquist corner frequency is usually used to minimize the effect of aliasing. The performance of a baud rate equalizer also suffers from aliasing at the region near the half of the sampling frequency.

8.1.4 *Fractionally Spaced Equalizer Performance*

The alternative to the baud rate equalizer is the *fractionally spaced equalizer*.[5] A fractionally spaced equalizer has a data input rate a few times of the baud rate while maintaining the equalizer output rate at the baud rate. Figure 8.10 shows the structure of the fractionally spaced equalizer and its multiple baud rate equalizer equivalence. For example, a three times over sampled fractionally spaced equalizer can be considered as consisting of 3 baud rate equalizers, each of which has a third number of equalizer coefficients.

Figure 8.10 Multiple Equalizer Equivalence of a Fractionally Spaced Equalizer

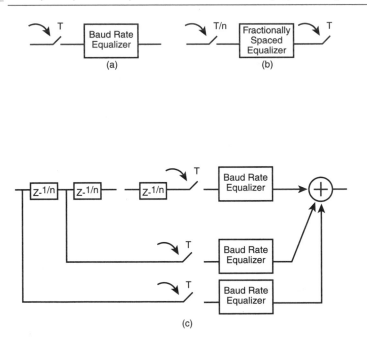

The optimal fractionally spaced equalizer coefficients also can be derived from the discrete time domain. Given a two times over-sampled case, dividing the fractionally spaced equalizer into a phase 1 part and a phase 2 part, the instantaneous error between the desired signal and the output of a fractionally spaced equalizer is

$$e_k = a_{k-d} - X_k^{1T} Q_k^1 - X_k^{2T} Q_k^2$$

a_{k-d} is the desired data symbol after the channel delay of d signaling periods.

$X_k^{1T} = \begin{bmatrix} x_k & x_{k-2} & \cdots & x_{x-n} \end{bmatrix}$ and $X_k^{2T} = \begin{bmatrix} x_{k-1} & x_{k-3} & \cdots & x_{x-n+1} \end{bmatrix}$ are received signal vectors.

$Q_k^{1T} = \begin{bmatrix} q_{1k} & q_{3k} & \cdots & q_{(n-1)k} \end{bmatrix}$ is the equalizer coefficient vector for the phase 1 part of the fractionally spaced equalizer.

$Q_k^{2T} = \begin{bmatrix} q_{2k} & q_{4k} & \cdots & q_{nk} \end{bmatrix}$ is for the phase 2 part.

e_k is the error between the desired signal and the equalizer output.

Notice that both phase 1 and phase 2 equalizers have a length of $n/2$. We also have

$$x_k = \sum_{i=1}^{l/2} a_{k-i+1} h(1+2(i-1)) = \begin{bmatrix} a_k & a_{k-1} & \cdots & a_{k-l/2+1} \end{bmatrix} \begin{bmatrix} h(1) \\ h(3) \\ \cdots \\ h(l-1) \end{bmatrix} + n_k$$

for odd k and

$$x_k = \sum_{i=1}^{l/2} a_{k-i+1} h(2i) = \begin{bmatrix} a_k & a_{k-1} & \cdots & a_{k-l/2+1} \end{bmatrix} \begin{bmatrix} h(2) \\ h(4) \\ \cdots \\ h(l) \end{bmatrix} + n_k$$

for even k. We further have

$$X_k^{1T} = \begin{bmatrix} a_k & a_{k-1} & \cdots & a_{k-n/2-l/2+2} \end{bmatrix} \begin{bmatrix} h(1) & 0 & 0 & 0 \\ h(3) & h(1) & 0 & 0 \\ h(5) & h(3) & 0 & 0 \\ \cdots & \cdots & \cdots & h(1) \\ h(l-1) & h(l-3) & 0 & h(3) \\ 0 & h(l-1) & 0 & h(5) \\ 0 & 0 & 0 & \cdots \\ 0 & 0 & 0 & h(l-1) \end{bmatrix} + \begin{bmatrix} n_k & n_{k-2} & \cdots & n_{k-n/2} \end{bmatrix}$$

$$X_k^{2T} = \begin{bmatrix} a_k & a_{k-1} & \cdots & a_{k-n/2-l/2+2} \end{bmatrix} \begin{bmatrix} h(2) & 0 & 0 & 0 \\ h(4) & h(2) & 0 & 0 \\ h(6) & h(4) & 0 & 0 \\ \cdots & \cdots & \cdots & h(2) \\ h(l) & h(l-2) & 0 & h(4) \\ 0 & h(l) & 0 & h(6) \\ 0 & 0 & 0 & \cdots \\ 0 & 0 & 0 & h(l) \end{bmatrix} + \begin{bmatrix} n_{k-1} & n_{k-3} & \cdots & n_{k-n/2+1} \end{bmatrix}$$

With two baud spaced received signal vector defined as X_k^{1T} and X_k^{2T}, the expected value of the square error, or mean square error, for a particular equalizer vector, Q, is

$$E\left[e_k^2\right] = E\left[\left(a_{k-d} - X_k^{1T}Q^1 - X_k^{2T}Q^2\right)^2\right]$$

Q^1 and Q^2 represent the first and second sampling phase of the equalizer, Q, respectively. The derivative of the mean squared error with respect to the equalizer coefficient vectors Q^1 and Q^2 are

$$\frac{\partial\left(E\left[e_k^2\right]\right)}{\partial Q^1} = -2E\left[\left(a_{k-d} - X_k^{1T}Q^1 - X_k^{2T}Q^2\right)X_k^{1T}\right]$$

$$\frac{\partial\left(E\left[e_k^2\right]\right)}{\partial Q^2} = -2E\left[\left(a_{k-d} - X_k^{1T}Q^1 - X_k^{2T}Q^2\right)X_k^{2T}\right]$$

To obtain the optimal equalizer coefficient vector Q_{opt}, set the derivative equal to zero, as shown in the following expressions:

$$Q^{1T}E\left[X_k^1 X_k^{1T}\right] + Q^{2T}E\left[X_k^1 X_k^{2T}\right] = E\left[a_{k-d}X_k^{1T}\right]$$

$$Q^{1T}E\left[X_k^2 X_k^{1T}\right] + Q^{2T}E\left[X_k^2 X_k^{2T}\right] = E\left[a_{k-d}X_k^{2T}\right]$$

You also can use these expressions in an arranged matrix form as

$$\begin{bmatrix} E\left[X_k^1 X_k^{1T}\right] & E\left[X_k^1 X_k^{2T}\right] \\ E\left[X_k^2 X_k^{1T}\right] & E\left[X_k^2 X_k^{2T}\right] \end{bmatrix} \begin{bmatrix} Q^1 \\ Q^2 \end{bmatrix} = E\left[a_{k-d} \begin{bmatrix} X_k^1 \\ X_k^2 \end{bmatrix} \right]$$

The optimal equalizer solution is as follows:

$$\begin{bmatrix} Q_{opt}^1 \\ Q_{opt}^2 \end{bmatrix} = \left(\begin{bmatrix} E\left[X_k^1 X_k^{1T}\right] & E\left[X_k^1 X_k^{2T}\right] \\ E\left[X_k^2 X_k^{1T}\right] & E\left[X_k^2 X_k^{2T}\right] \end{bmatrix} \right)^{-1} E\left[a_{k-d} \begin{bmatrix} X_k^1 \\ X_k^2 \end{bmatrix} \right]$$

The matrix inverse exists as long as there is receiver front-end noise. Figures 8.11, 8.12, and 8.13 show normalized, fractionally spaced equalizer coefficients as well as baud rate equalizer coefficients, in little circles, as a comparison for 1, 2, and 3 miles of 26-gauge twisted-pair loops, respectively.

Figure 8.11   Fractionally Spaced Equalizers for a 1 Mile, 26-Gauge Loop

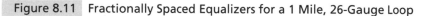

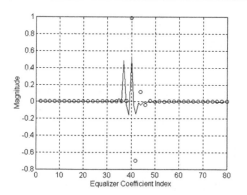

Figure 8.12 Fractionally Spaced Equalizers for a 2 Mile, 26-Gauge Loop

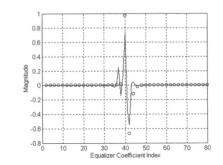

Figure 8.13 Fractionally Spaced Equalizers for a 3 Mile, 26-Gauge Loop

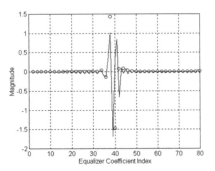

The expression

$$\xi_{min} = E\left[a_{k-d}^2\right] - E\left[a_{k-d}\begin{bmatrix}X_k^1\\X_k^2\end{bmatrix}^T\right]\begin{bmatrix}Q_{opt}^1\\Q_{opt}^2\end{bmatrix}$$

describes the MMSE between the desired signal and the output of a fractionally spaced equalizer, which is also determined by receiver front-end noise, the twisted-pair loop channel, and the length of the channel equalizer.

For the same simple example of a 26-gauge, 10,560 foot loop with receiver front-end noise power density levels of –110 dBm/Hz, –120 dBm/Hz, and –130 dBm/Hz, we have MMSE levels of –20.1 dB, –30 dB, and –39.6 dB, respectively.

The equalizer coefficients of a fractionally spaced equalizer are also identified iteratively with the LMS algorithm and updated at the signaling baud rate, but not at the sampling rate.

The LMS algorithm for the updating of a two times over sampled equalizer coefficients is expressed as

$$
\begin{bmatrix} Q_{k+1}^1 \\ Q_{k+1}^2 \end{bmatrix} = \begin{bmatrix} Q_k^1 \\ Q_k^2 \end{bmatrix} + \mu \begin{bmatrix} X_k^1 \\ X_k^2 \end{bmatrix} \left(a_{k-d} - \begin{bmatrix} Q_k^1 \\ Q_k^2 \end{bmatrix}^T \begin{bmatrix} X_k^1 \\ X_k^2 \end{bmatrix} \right)
$$

In a finite bit resolution hardware implementation, the fractionally spaced equalizer can become unstable when coefficient values exceed the hardware limitation. A tap leakage algorithm[6] is usually required for the adaptation of fractionally spaced equalizer coefficients, as expressed in the following:

$$
\begin{bmatrix} Q_{k+1}^1 \\ Q_{k+1}^2 \end{bmatrix} = (1 - \alpha) \begin{bmatrix} Q_k^1 \\ Q_k^2 \end{bmatrix} + \mu \begin{bmatrix} X_k^1 \\ X_k^2 \end{bmatrix} \left(a_{k-d} - \begin{bmatrix} Q_k^1 \\ Q_k^2 \end{bmatrix}^T \begin{bmatrix} X_k^1 \\ X_k^2 \end{bmatrix} \right)
$$

The value α is usually smaller than 0.1.

8.1.5 *Noise Power After Equalization*

The effect of intersymbol interference is minimized by the equalizer, and the energy of the received signal is concentrated on to a single baud interval sampling point; however, because of the concentration effect of the equalizer, the noise power is also amplified. Assuming the noise component has a power of σ^2 at every sampling point, the noise power after the equalization is then

$$
\sigma^2 \sum_{i=1}^{m} q_i^2
$$

The signal-to-noise ratio after equalization is

$$
SNR_{eq} = \frac{1}{\sigma^2 \displaystyle\sum_{i=1}^{m} q_i^2}
$$

The signal-to-noise ratio at a receiver front end with n sampling point is

$$SNR_{rf} = \frac{\sum_{i=1}^{n} h^2(i)}{n\sigma^2}$$

The relationship between receiver front-end signal-to-noise ratio and equalizer output signal-to-noise ratio is expressed as

$$SNR_{eq} = SNR_{rf} \frac{n}{\sum_{i=1}^{n} h^2(i) \sum_{i=1}^{m} q_j^2}$$

The noise enhancement introduced by the equalization is[7]

$$\frac{\sum_{i=1}^{n} h^2(i) \sum_{i=1}^{m} q_j^2}{n}$$

The receiver front-end peak signal-to-noise ratio is also defined as

$$SNR_{rf} = \frac{Max[h^2(i)]}{\sigma^2}$$

The relationship between receiver front-end peak signal-to-noise ratio and equalizer output signal-to-noise ratio is

$$SNR_{eq} = SNR_{rf} \frac{1}{Max[h^2(i)] \sum_{i=1}^{m} q_j^2}$$

The corresponding noise enhancement is

$$Max[h^2(i)] \sum_{i=1}^{m} q_j^2$$

For an example of a 2 mile, 26-gauge twisted-pair loop, the noise enhancement is 1.34 and 1.05 for baud rate and fractionally spaced equalizers, respectively, compared with receiver front-end maximum signal-to-noise ratio.

8.2 Decision Feedback Channel Equalization

The amount of noise enhancement discussed in section 8.1.4, "Fractionally Spaced Equalizer Performance," can be reduced by minimizing the required number of equalizer coefficients while still achieving the desired equalization effect. Using a *Decision Feedback Equalizer* (DFE) enables the realization of this less noise enhancement objective.[8,9,10] Figure 8.14 shows a DFE, which consists of a *FeedForward Filter* (FFF) and a *FeedBack Filter* (FBF). The FFF also can be fractionally spaced, as depicted in part b of Figure 8.14.

Figure 8.14 The Structure of a Decision Feedback Equalizer

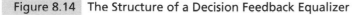

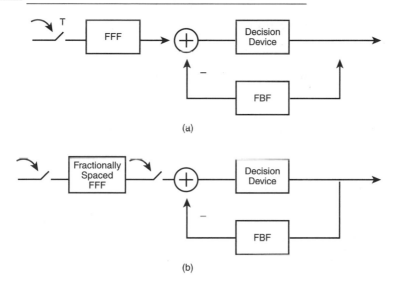

The received signal is only used by the FFF while the estimated signal is used by the FBF. An FFF filtered version of the tail portion of the channel impulse response is canceled by the FBF weighted estimated signals. The noise enhancement of a DFE is only caused by the equalization of the remaining much smaller portion of the channel impulse response.

8.2.1 Determining DFE Coefficients

The DFE equalizer coefficients also can be derived in the discrete time domain. The instantaneous error between the desired signal and the DFE output is

$$e_k = a_{k-d} - X_k^T Q^f + A_{k-d-1}^T Q^b$$

a_{k-d} is the desired data symbol after d symbol intervals of channel delay.

$X_k^T = \begin{bmatrix} x_k & x_{k-1} & \cdots & x_{x-n+1} \end{bmatrix}$ is the received signal vector.

$Q^{fT} = \begin{bmatrix} q_1^f & q_2^f & \cdots & q_n^f \end{bmatrix}$ is the FFF coefficient vector.

$A_{k-d-1}^T = \begin{bmatrix} a_{k-d-1} & a_{k-d-2} & \cdots & a_{x-d-m} \end{bmatrix}$ is the estimated data symbol vector for previous m data symbols.

$Q^{bT} = \begin{bmatrix} q_1^b & q_2^b & \cdots & q_m^b \end{bmatrix}$ is the FBF coefficient vector.

e_k is the error between the desired signal and the decision feedback equalizer output.

The expected value of the square error or mean squared error for a particular set of equalizer coefficient vectors Q^f and Q^b is

$$E\left[e_k^2 \right] = E\left[\left(a_{k-d} - X_k^T Q^f + A_{k-d-1}^T Q^b \right)^2 \right]$$

Derivatives of the mean square error with respect to the equalizer coefficient vectors Q^f and Q^b are

$$\frac{\partial \left(E\left[e_k^2 \right] \right)}{\partial Q^f} = -2E\left[\left(a_{k-d} - X_k^T Q^f + A_{k-d-1}^T Q^b \right) X_k^T \right]$$

$$\frac{\partial \left(E\left[e_k^2 \right] \right)}{\partial Q^b} = -2E\left[\left(a_{k-d} - X_k^T Q^f + A_{k-d-1}^T Q^b \right) A_{k-d-1}^T \right]$$

By setting derivatives equal to zero, we obtain the optimal equalizer coefficient vectors Q_{opt}^f and Q_{opt}^b for the minimum mean squared error as

$$Q_{opt}^{fT} E\left[X_k X_k^T \right] - Q_{opt}^{bT} E\left[A_{k-d-1} X_k^T \right] = E\left[a_{k-d} X_k^T \right]$$

$$Q_{opt}^{fT} E\left[X_k A_{k-d-1}^T \right] - Q_{opt}^{bT} E\left[A_{k-d-1} A_{k-d-1}^T \right] = E\left[a_{k-d} A_{k-d-1}^T \right]$$

or

$$Q_{opt}^{fT} = \left(E[X_k X_k^T] - E[X_k A_{k-d-1}^T] E[A_{k-d-1} X_k^T] \right)^{-1} E[a_{k-d} X_k^T]$$

$$Q_{opt}^{bT} = Q_{opt}^{fT} E[X_k A_{k-1}^T]$$

This solution also can be written in matrix form as

$$\begin{bmatrix} Q_{opt}^f \\ Q_{opt}^b \end{bmatrix} = \begin{bmatrix} R_{XX} & R_{XA} \\ R_{XA}^T & I \end{bmatrix}^{-1} \begin{bmatrix} R_{Xa} \\ 0 \end{bmatrix}$$

in which

$$R_{XX} = E[X_k X_k^T]$$

$$R_{Xa} = E[X_k a_{k-d}]$$

and

$$R_{XA} = E[X_k A_{k-d-1}^T] = \overline{H}^T E \left[\begin{bmatrix} a_k \\ a_{k-1} \\ \cdots \\ a_{k-n-m+2} \end{bmatrix} \begin{bmatrix} a_{k-d-1} & a_{k-d-2} & \cdots & a_{k-d-m} \end{bmatrix} \right]$$

$$= \overline{H}^T E \begin{bmatrix} a_k a_{k-d-1} & \cdots & \cdots & a_k a_{k-d-m} \\ a_{k-1} a_{k-d-1} & \cdots & \cdots & a_{k-1} a_{k-d-m} \\ \cdots & \cdots & \cdots & \cdots \\ a_{k-d-1} a_{k-d-1} & \cdots & \cdots & \cdots \\ \cdots & \cdots & \cdots & \cdots \\ \cdots & \cdots & \cdots & a_{k-d-m} a_{k-d-m} \\ \cdots & \cdots & \cdots & \cdots \\ 0 a_{k-n-m+2} a_{k-d-1} & \cdots & \cdots & a_{k-n-m+2} a_{k-d-m} \end{bmatrix} = \overline{H}^T \begin{bmatrix} 0 & \cdots & \cdots & 0 \\ 0 & \cdots & \cdots & 0 \\ \cdots & \cdots & \cdots & \cdots \\ 1 & \cdots & \cdots & \cdots \\ \cdots & 1 & \cdots & \cdots \\ \cdots & \cdots & \cdots & 1 \\ \cdots & \cdots & \cdots & \cdots \\ 0 & \cdots & \cdots & 0 \end{bmatrix} = \overline{H}^T P$$

Notice that the DFE solution also can be obtained by expanding the received signal vector to include transmitting data symbols. Assume a super received signal vector to be

$$\tilde{X}_k^T = \begin{bmatrix} X_k^T & A_{k-d-1}^T \end{bmatrix} = \begin{bmatrix} x_k & x_{k-1} & \cdots & x_{k-n+1} & a_{k-d-1} & a_{k-d-2} & \cdots & a_{k-d-m} \end{bmatrix}$$

$$\tilde{X}_k^T = \begin{bmatrix} a_k & a_{k-1} & \cdots & a_{k-n-m+2} \end{bmatrix} \begin{bmatrix} h(1) & 0 & \cdots & 0 & 0 & \cdots & 0 & 0 \\ h(2) & h(1) & \cdots & 0 & 0 & \cdots & 0 & 0 \\ \cdots & \cdots & \cdots & \cdots & \cdots & \cdots & \cdots & \cdots \\ \cdots & \cdots & \cdots & \cdots & 1 & \cdots & 0 & 0 \\ \cdots & \cdots & \cdots & \cdots & \cdots & \cdots & 1 & 0 \\ 0 & \cdots & \cdots & \cdots & 0 & \cdots & 0 & 1 \\ \cdots & \cdots & \cdots & \cdots & \cdots & \cdots & \cdots & \cdots \\ 0 & 0 & \cdots & h(n) & 0 & \cdots & 0 & 0 \end{bmatrix}$$

$$+ \begin{bmatrix} n_k & n_{k-1} & \cdots & n_{k-n+1} & 0 & \cdots & 0 \end{bmatrix} = \tilde{A}_k^T \tilde{H} + \tilde{N}_k^T$$

$$R_{\tilde{X}\tilde{X}} = E\begin{bmatrix} \tilde{X}_k \tilde{X}_k^T \end{bmatrix} = \begin{bmatrix} \tilde{H}^T \tilde{H} \end{bmatrix} + E\begin{bmatrix} \tilde{N}_k \tilde{N}_k^T \end{bmatrix} = \begin{bmatrix} H^T H & H^T P \\ (H^T P)^T & I \end{bmatrix} + \begin{bmatrix} E[N_k N_k^T] & 0 \\ 0 & 0 \end{bmatrix} = \begin{bmatrix} R_{XX} & R_{XA} \\ (R_{XA})^T & I \end{bmatrix}$$

We can use this method to derive equalizer coefficient vectors for the DFE with a fractionally spaced FFF. For example, we set two super received signal vectors for two sampling phases of the received signal

$$\left(\tilde{X}_k^1\right)^T = \begin{bmatrix} \left(X_k^1\right)^T & \begin{bmatrix} 0 & 0 & \cdots & 0 \end{bmatrix}^T \end{bmatrix}$$

and

$$\left(\tilde{X}_k^2\right)^T = \begin{bmatrix} \left(X_k^2\right)^T & \left(A_{k-d-1}^m\right)^T \end{bmatrix}$$

Replacing these super received signal vectors into the solution for the fractionally spaced equalizer, we then have

$$
\begin{bmatrix} \tilde{Q}^1_{opt} \\ \tilde{Q}^2_{opt} \end{bmatrix} = \left(\begin{bmatrix} E\left[\tilde{X}^1_k \tilde{X}^{1T}_k \right] & E\left[\tilde{X}^1_k \tilde{X}^{2T}_k \right] \\ E\left[\tilde{X}^2_k \tilde{X}^{1T}_k \right] & E\left[\tilde{X}^2_k \tilde{X}^{2T}_k \right] \end{bmatrix} \right)^{-1} E\left[a_{k-d} \begin{bmatrix} \tilde{X}^1_k \\ \tilde{X}^2_k \end{bmatrix} \right]
$$

$$
= \left(\begin{bmatrix} E\left[X^1_k X^{1T}_k \right] & 0 & E\left[X^1_k X^{2T}_k \right] & E\left[X^1_k \left(A^m_{k-d-1}\right)^T \right] \\ 0 & 0 & 0 & 0 \\ E\left[X^2_k X^{1T}_k \right] & 0 & E\left[X^2_k X^{2T}_k \right] & E\left[X^2_k \left(A^m_{k-d-1}\right)^T \right] \\ E\left[A^m_{k-d-1}\left(X^1_k\right)^T \right] & 0 & E\left[A^m_{k-d-1}\left(X^2_k\right)^T \right] & I \end{bmatrix} \right)^{-1} \left(E\left[a_{k-d} \begin{bmatrix} X^1_k \\ 0 \\ X^1_k \\ A^m_{k-d-1} \end{bmatrix} \right] \right) = \begin{bmatrix} Q^1_{opt} \\ 0 \\ Q^2_{opt} \\ Q^b_{opt} \end{bmatrix}
$$

By eliminating the second zero row and the second zero column, we obtain the equalizer coefficient solution for the DFE with a fractionally spaced FFF as

$$
\begin{bmatrix} Q^1_{opt} \\ Q^2_{opt} \\ Q^b_{opt} \end{bmatrix} = \left(\begin{bmatrix} E\left[X^1_k X^{1T}_k \right] & E\left[X^1_k X^{2T}_k \right] & E\left[X^1_k \left(A^m_{k-d-1}\right)^T \right] \\ E\left[X^2_k X^{1T}_k \right] & E\left[X^2_k X^{2T}_k \right] & E\left[X^2_k \left(A^m_{k-d-1}\right)^T \right] \\ E\left[A^m_{k-d-1}\left(X^1_k\right)^T \right] & E\left[A^m_{k-d-1}\left(X^2_k\right)^T \right] & I \end{bmatrix} \right)^{-1} = E\left[a_{k-d} \begin{bmatrix} X^1_k \\ X^2_k \\ A^m_{k-d-1} \end{bmatrix} \right]
$$

This fractionally spaced FFF DFE solution also can be obtained from that for the baud rate DFE by using

$$
R_{XX} = E \begin{bmatrix} X^1_k X^{1T}_k & X^1_k X^{2T}_k \\ X^2_k X^{1T}_k & X^2_k X^{2T}_k \end{bmatrix}
$$

$$
R_{XA} = E \begin{bmatrix} X^1_k \left(A^m_{k-d-1}\right)^T \\ X^2_k \left(A^m_{k-d-1}\right)^T \end{bmatrix}
$$

$$
R_{Xa} = E \begin{bmatrix} X^1_k a_{k-d} \\ X^2_k a_{k-d} \end{bmatrix} \quad \text{and}
$$

$$
Q^f_{opt} = \begin{bmatrix} Q^{f1}_{opt} \\ Q^{f2}_{opt} \end{bmatrix}
$$

Figures 8.15, 8.16, and 8.17 show normalized baud rate FFF and FBF coefficients as well as baud rate linear equalizer coefficients, as a comparison, for 1, 2, and 3 miles of 26-gauge twisted-pair loops, respectively. Again, the channel impulse response is normalized to produce compensation filter coefficients and compensated channel impulse response of the similar magnitudes for easy comparison.

Figure 8.15 Channel Equalizers for a 1 Mile, 26-Gauge Loop

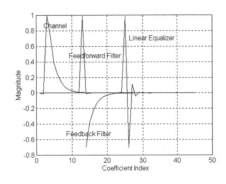

Figure 8.16 Channel Equalizers for a 2 Mile, 26-Gauge Loop

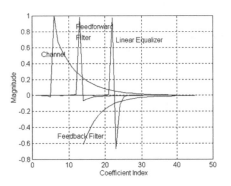

8.2.2 DFE MMSE Levels

The MMSE between the desired signal and the output of a DFE is also determined by receiver front-end noise, the twisted-pair loop channel, and the structure of a DFE. However, the amount of MMSE is only related to the FFF due to the fact that the FBF does not contribute to the noise enhancement. The expression

$$\xi_{min} = E\left[a_k^2\right] - R_{Xa}^T Q_{opt}^f$$

describes the MMSE between the desired signal and the output of a DFE.

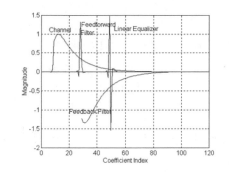

For the simple example of a 26-gauge, 10,560 foot loop with receiver front-end noise power-er density levels of –110 dBm/Hz, –120 dBm/Hz, and –130 dBm/Hz, we have MMSE levels of –18.38 dB, –28.3 dB, and –38 dB, respectively. A DFE with a fractionally spaced FFF can produce lower MMSE levels. The performance of an equalizer also is often judged by the SNR at the equalizer output. We have

$$SNR \approx \frac{1}{\xi_{min}}$$

Table 8.1 summarizes equalizer output SNRs for different equalizer structures as well as the receiver front-end peak signal-to-noise ratio for similar transmission conditions. A 2 mile, 26-gauge twisted-pair loop is used for receiver front-end noise density levels of –110 dBm/Hz, –120 dBm/Hz, and –130 dBm/Hz. SNR estimates in Table 8.1 do not include the effect of finite precision implementation of channel equalizers. The sampling rate is 300 kHz for a bandwidth of 150 kHz.

Table 8.1 Receiver Front-End and Equalizer Output SNRs

Noise Level	Receiver Front	Linear	Fraction Linear	DFE	Fraction DFE
–110 dBm/Hz	20.9	18.3	20.1	18.4	22.72
–120 dBm/Hz	30.9	27.9	30.0	28.3	32.7
–130 dBm/Hz	40.9	36.0	39.6	38.0	42.7

8.2.3 DFE Error Propagation and Precoding

As indicated by results of Table 8.1, a DFE has a better performance compared with a linear equalizer. Also, a DFE with a fractionally spaced FFF has the best performance. The drawback of a DFE, however, is the error propagation problem.[11]

Because the tail cancellation signal from the FBF is generated according to the estimated signal, a wrong estimation of the signal could reduce the chance of correct estimation of subsequent signals. In fact, for a channel with severe intersymbol interference, which can be characterized by a channel impulse response with a long tail or a long FBF with significant magnitudes, multiple errors do occur because of the phenomenon of error propagation. It might take many symbol intervals for a DFE to recover from the error propagation.

The Tomlinson[12]/Harashima[13] precoding method can be used to avoid the DFE error propagation problem. In this precoding method, the FBF (depicted in part (a) of Figure 8.18) is moved into the transmitter to filter the original data symbols (depicted in part (b) of Figure 8.18).

Figure 8.18 Comparison Between a DFE System and a Tomlinson Precoding System

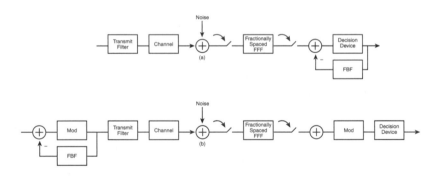

In addition, a modulo operation, *Mod*, is used in the feedback loop to make the operation stable. Without this modulo operation, the FBF would behave like a recursive filter, which could become unstable depending on values of filter coefficients. Another modulo operation is used after the FFF in the receiver to recover the original signal magnitude. The modulo operation is designed to contain the output signal to be in the same magnitude range as that of the input signal after the loopback of FBF. For a line code with M equally spaced signal levels, the modulo operation is implemented as

$$y(t) = remain\left(\frac{x(t) + (2n+1)M}{2M}\right) - M$$

for $y(t) > M$ or $y(t) < -M$ in which $n = 0, 1, 2...$ is chosen such that $x(t) + (2n + 1)M > 0$.

In a normal DFE, the FBF does not form a feedback loop by itself, but through a decision device. As long as decisions are correct, the FBF is equivalent to an FIR filter with data symbols as its input. Even when the decision device makes wrong decisions, the magnitude of the equalizer output is still limited by the decision device. Therefore, a DFE is always stable as an FIR filter.

FBF filter coefficients for a straight twisted-pair loop can be approximated by

$$h_{FBF}(k) = Ae^{-Bk}$$

B is larger than zero. The z transformation of this FIR filter is

$$H_{FBF}(z) = A\frac{z}{z - e^{-B}}$$

and is always stable because $e^{-B} < 1$. When this FBF is used in a Tomlinson/Harashima transmitter without a modulo operation, we have

$$y(k) = x(k) - y(k-1)h(1) - y(k-2)h(2) - ...$$

This relationship in z domain is

$$Y(z) = X(z)\frac{1}{1 + z^{-1}H_{FBF}(z)}$$

The z transformation of the FBF in a transmitter is

$$H'_{FBF}(z) = \frac{1}{1 + \dfrac{A}{z - e^{-B}}} = \frac{z - e^{-B}}{z - (e^{-B} - A)}$$

The feedback loop becomes unstable when $e^{-B} - A$ is close to 1 for a pole near the unit circle. A twisted-pair loop usually consists of many different sections and with bridged taps. There are many possible loop configurations where the FBF used in a Tomlinson/Harashima transmitter could become unstable.

You can examine the effect of modulo operations by assuming that the FFF normalizes received signal level and equalizes part of the channel distortion such that the remaining channel distortion can be completely compensated by the FBF. In other words, the equivalent channel transfer function after FFF can be described as

$$H_{channel}(z) = 1 + z^{-1}H_{FBF}(z)$$

$H_{FBF}(z)$ is the transfer function of the FBF. The $z^{-1}H_{FBF}(z)$ part of the equivalent channel causes the expansion of the received signal.[14] The received signal expansion is similar to the PAR increase caused by a filter or a channel. In a conventional DFE, the received signal magnitude expansion caused by the channel is compensated by FBF before a decision device.

In a Tomlinson/Harashima transceiver, the signal magnitude expansion at the transmitter is limited by the modulo operation. However, the signal magnitude expansion caused by the channel remains because of the mission of a FBF. A modulo operation is used instead to map the received signal to the original signal constellation.

Figure 8.19 shows the following:

- The effect of modulo operation after FBF feedback loop, $Mod_N(x - a)$

- The effect of channel, $Mod_N(x - a) + a$

- The modulo operation in the receiver, $Mod_N(Mod_N(x - a) + a)$

- The identity of $Mod_N(x) = Mod_N(Mod_N(x - a) + a)$

The duo-modulo operation makes the modulo operation transparent under the channel-distortion-only condition; however, the received signal before a decision device does not have to be confined by maximum and minimum levels of a particular line code. The receiver front-end additive noise also can cause the received signal to exceed signal maximum or minimum levels. This slight signal magnitude expansion should be preserved for making correct data symbol estimate decisions; otherwise, *data-flipping* will occur.[15]

When data-flipping occurs, a data symbol corresponding to the maximum signal level can be mistaken as the data symbol with the minimum signal level because an additive noise caused the received signal to exceed the maximum level and the modulo operation to bring it down to near the minimum signal level, as shown in Figure 8.20.

Figure 8.19 Effects of Modulo Operations

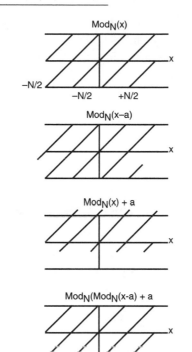

Figure 8.20 The Data-Flipping Effect of a Tomlinson/Harashima System

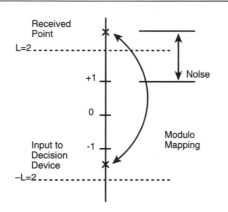

The effect of data-flipping can be minimized by using a slightly larger allowed signal magnitude range for the receiver modulo operation. The additional allowed magnitude range is related to the receiver front-end noise level and the degree of channel distortion.

8.3 Passband Equalization and Carrierless AM/PM

The direct application of data symbols of different magnitudes creates a baseband signal spectrum. Spectrum shaping of a baseband signal can be realized using transmit filters that correlate to adjacent data symbols. Modulating data symbols with a carrier of a particular frequency can generate a passband signal.

A Quadrature Amplitude Modulation (QAM) line code is realized by modulating the cosine phase and sine phase of a particular carrier with independent data sequences. A Carrierless AM/PM (CAP) line code can be considered as a variation of the QAM line code with the omission of a phase rotator in the transmitter and a phase derotator in the receiver. Transmitter shaping filters are used by passband line codes for the control of signal bandwidth.

8.3.1 QAM Baseband and Passband Implementation

A passband Quadrature Amplitude Modulation (QAM) signal is usually generated with a pair of transmitter shaping filters and a carrier modulator consisting of a cosine phase and a sine phase. A QAM signal after shaping filter and modulation can be described as

$$f(t) = \sum_{i=-\infty}^{\infty} a_i g(t - iT) \cos \omega_c t - \sum_{i=-\infty}^{\infty} b_i g(t - iT) \sin \omega_c t$$

The values are as follows:

a_is are in-phase channel data symbols.

b_is are quadrature channel data symbols.

$g(t)$ is the baseband shaping filter.

Denoting a complex data symbol as $C_i = a_i + jb_i$ results in

$$f(t) = \text{Re}\left[\sum_{i=-\infty}^{\infty} C_i g(t - iT) e^{j\omega_c t} \right]$$

This can be rearranged to

$$f(t) = \text{Re}\left[\sum_{i=-\infty}^{\infty} C_i e^{j\omega_c iT} g(t - iT) e^{j\omega_c (t - iT)} \right]$$

or in another format as

$$f(t) = \sum_{i=-\infty}^{\infty} \left(a_i \cos \overline{\omega}_c iT - b_i \sin \omega_c iT\right) g(t - iT) \cos \omega_c (t - iT)$$

$$- \sum_{i=-\infty}^{\infty} \left(a_i \sin \omega_c iT + b_i \cos \omega_c iT\right) g(t - iT) \sin \omega_c (t - iT)$$

The preceding expression describes an alternative QAM signal generation process (see Figure 8.22) in which the data symbols are phase rotated first and then convolved with a pair of passband shaping filters. The in-phase channel passband shaping filter is the product of the baseband shaping filter and the cosine phase of the carrier. The quadrature channel passband shaping filter is the product of the baseband shaping filter and the sine phase of the carrier.

For an ideal channel, data symbols carried by a QAM signal are usually recovered first through demodulation and then through lowpass filtering, as depicted in Figure 8.21.

Figure 8.21   A Conventional QAM Transceiver Pair

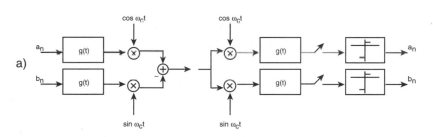

The in-phase channel signal is demodulated by the cosine phase of the carrier, and the quadrature channel signal is demodulated by the sine phase of the carrier. There is a lowpass filter for each channel. The transmission characteristics of the lowpass filter could be the same as those of the transmitter shaping filter. The demodulation and lowpass filtering process for the recovery of data symbols is expressed as

$$\hat{a}_k + j\hat{b}_k = \left[\left(f(t)e^{-j\omega_c t}\right) * g(t)\right]_{t=kT}$$

By changing the order of demodulation and lowpass filtering, data symbols carried by a QAM signal also can be recovered first by in-phase and quadrature bandpass filtering and then followed by a phase derotating process similar to the alternative approach of QAM transmitter implementation, as shown in Figure 8.22. The passband filtering and phase derotation process for the recovery of data symbols is expressed as

$$\hat{a}_k + j\hat{b}_k = \left[\left(f(t) * \left(g(t)e^{j\omega_c t}\right)\right)e^{-j\omega_c t}\right]_{t=kT}$$

Figure 8.22 An Alternative QAM Implementation with a Phase Modulator and a Phase Demodulator

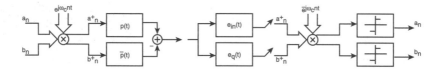

Linear channel equalizers might be necessary to compensate for the channel distortion in a practical implementation. A linear channel equalizer can be placed after these lowpass filters. The demodulation, lowpass filtering, and linear equalization process for the recovery of data symbols is expressed as

$$\hat{a}_k + j\hat{b}_k = \left[\left(f(t)e^{-j\omega_c t}\right) * g(t) * Q_{IQ}(t)\right]_{t=kT}$$

The linear equalizer consists of a real part, in-phase equalizer, and an imaginary part, cross-coupled equalizer, expressed as

$$Q_{IQ}(t) = Q_I(t) + jQ_Q(t)$$

Similar to the lowpass filter case, we can move the position of the channel equalizer around at different positions. Replacing the received signal, $f(t)$, with

$$\left(\operatorname{Re}\left(\left(C_i * g(t)\right)e^{j\omega_c t}\right)\right) * h(t)$$

The value $h(t)$ is the channel impulse response; the received signal in the front of a channel equalizer is

$$\left(\left(\left(\operatorname{Re}\left(\left(C_i * g(t)\right)e^{j\omega_c t}\right)\right) * h(t)\right)e^{-j w_c t}\right) * g(t)$$

By changing the order of multiplication and convolution, we obtain

$$\left(\mathrm{Re}\!\left((C_i * g(t)) e^{j\omega_c t} \right) * h(t) \right) e^{-j\omega_c t} = \left(\mathrm{Re}\!\left((C_i * g(t)) e^{j\omega_c t} \right) e^{-j\omega_c t} \right) * h(t) e^{-j\omega_c t}$$

In particular, we have

$$\mathrm{Re}\!\left((C_i * g(t)) e^{j\omega_c t} \right) e^{-j\omega_c t} = \left((a_k * g(t)) \frac{e^{j\omega_c t} + e^{-j\omega_c t}}{2} - (b_k * g(t)) \frac{e^{j\omega_c t} - e^{-j\omega_c t}}{2j} \right) e^{-j\omega_c t}$$

$$= \frac{a_k * g(t)}{2} + j\frac{b_k * g(t)}{2} + F\!\left(e^{-j2\omega_c t} \right)$$

Using the preceding relationships, the received signal in the front of a channel equalizer also can be described as

$$\left(\left(\left(\mathrm{Re}\!\left((C_i * g(t)) e^{j\omega_c t} \right) \right) * h(t) \right) e^{-j\omega_c t} \right) * g(t)$$

$$= \left(\frac{a_k * g(t)}{2} + j\frac{b_k * g(t)}{2} \right) * \left(h(t)\cos\omega_c t - jh(t)\sin\omega_c t \right) * g(t)$$

$$= \frac{1}{2}\left(\begin{array}{l} a_k * g(t) * h(t)\cos\omega_c t + b_k * g(t) * h(t)\sin\omega_c t \\ + j(b_k * g(t) * h(t)\cos\omega_c t - a_k * g(t) * h(t)\sin\omega_c t) \end{array} \right) * g(t)$$

The previous expressions assume that the high frequency components $F\!\left(e^{-j2\omega_c t} \right)$ were eliminated by the lowpass filter $g(t)$. We therefore identify the QAM in-phase passband equivalent channel as

$$h_I = g(t) * h(t)\cos\varpi_c t * g(t) - jg(t) * h(t)\sin\omega_c t * g(t) = h_{REAL}(t) - jh_{IMAG}(t)$$

and the QAM quadrature passband equivalent channel as

$$h_Q = g(t) * h(t)\cos\varpi_c t * g(t) + jg(t) * h(t)\sin\omega_c t * g(t) = h_{REAL}(t) + jh_{IMAG}(t)$$

We further call

$$h_{REAL}(t) = g(t) * h(t)\cos\varpi_c t * g(t)$$

the real passband equivalent channel and

$$h_{IMAG}(t) = g(t) * h(t)\sin\omega_c t * g(t)$$

the imaginary passband equivalent channel.

8.3.2 Calculation of QAM Linear Equalizer

Equalizer coefficients for a QAM transceiver can be similarly calculated. For the in-phase passband equivalent channel, we have the relationship between the desired data symbol and in-phase and cross-coupled equalizer combined output as

$$e_k = a_{k-d} - X_k^T Q_I - Y_k^T Q_Q$$

a_{k-d} is the desired data symbol after d baud rate intervals of channel delay.

$X_k^T = \begin{bmatrix} x_k & x_{k-1} & \cdots & x_{x-n+1} \end{bmatrix}$ is the received signal vector from the real part of the passband equivalent channel.

$Y_k^T = \begin{bmatrix} y_k & y_{k-1} & \cdots & y_{x-n+1} \end{bmatrix}$ is the received signal vector from the imaginary part.

$Q_I^T = \begin{bmatrix} q_{1I} & q_{2I} & \cdots & q_{nI} \end{bmatrix}$ is the in-phase equalization coefficient vector.

$Q_Q^T = \begin{bmatrix} q_{1Q} & q_{2Q} & \cdots & q_{nQ} \end{bmatrix}$ is the cross-coupled equalizer coefficient vectors.

e_k is the error between the desired signal and the combined equalizer output.

We can further express the received signal as a result of data symbols convolved with equivalent channels plus noise. We thus have

$$x_k = \sum_{i=1}^{l} a_{k-i+1} h_{REAL}(i) + \sum_{i=1}^{l} b_{k-i+1} h_{IMAG}(i) + n_{I,k}$$

$$= \begin{bmatrix} a_k & a_{k-1} & \cdots & a_{k-l+1} \end{bmatrix} \begin{bmatrix} h_{REAL}(1) \\ h_{REAL}(2) \\ \cdots \\ h_{REAL}(l) \end{bmatrix} + \begin{bmatrix} b_k & b_{k-1} & \cdots & b_{k-l+1} \end{bmatrix} \begin{bmatrix} h_{IMAG}(1) \\ h_{IMAG}(2) \\ \cdots \\ h_{IMAG}(l) \end{bmatrix} + n_{I,k}$$

and

$$y_k = \sum_{i=1}^{l} b_{k-i+1} h_{REAL}(i) - \sum_{i=1}^{l} a_{k-i+1} h_{IMAG}(i) + n_{Q,k}$$

$$= \begin{bmatrix} b_k & b_{k-1} & \cdots & b_{k-l+1} \end{bmatrix} \begin{bmatrix} h_{REAL}(1) \\ h_{REAL}(2) \\ \cdots \\ h_{REAL}(l) \end{bmatrix} - \begin{bmatrix} a_k & a_{k-1} & \cdots & a_{k-l+1} \end{bmatrix} \begin{bmatrix} h_{IMAG}(1) \\ h_{IMAG}(2) \\ \cdots \\ h_{IMAG}(l) \end{bmatrix} + n_{Q,k}$$

We further have

$$X_k^T = \begin{bmatrix} a_k & a_{k-1} & \cdots & a_{k-l-n+2} \end{bmatrix} \begin{bmatrix} h_{REAL}(1) & 0 & 0 & 0 \\ h_{REAL}(2) & h_{REAL}(1) & 0 & 0 \\ h_{REAL}(3) & h_{REAL}(2) & 0 & 0 \\ \cdots & \cdots & \cdots & h_{REAL}(1) \\ h_{REAL}(l) & h_{REAL}(l-1) & 0 & h_{REAL}(2) \\ 0 & h_{REAL}(l) & 0 & h_{REAL}(5) \\ 0 & 0 & 0 & \cdots \\ 0 & 0 & 0 & h_{REAL}(l) \end{bmatrix}$$

$$+ \begin{bmatrix} b_k & b_{k-1} & \cdots & b_{k-l-n+2} \end{bmatrix} \begin{bmatrix} h_{IMAG}(1) & 0 & 0 & 0 \\ h_{IMAG}(2) & h_{IMAG}(1) & 0 & 0 \\ h_{IMAG}(3) & h_{IMAG}(2) & 0 & 0 \\ \cdots & \cdots & \cdots & h_{IMAG}(1) \\ h_{IMAG}(l) & h_{IMAG}(l-1) & 0 & h_{IMAG}(2) \\ 0 & h_{IMAG}(l) & 0 & h_{IMAG}(5) \\ 0 & 0 & 0 & \cdots \\ 0 & 0 & 0 & h_{IMAG}(l) \end{bmatrix} + \begin{bmatrix} n_{Q,k} & n_{Q,k-1} & \cdots & n_{Q,k-n+1} \end{bmatrix}$$

$$= \tilde{A}_k^T \overline{H}_{REAL} + \tilde{B}_k^T \overline{H}_{IMAG} + N_{I,k}$$

$$Y_k^T = \begin{bmatrix} b_k & b_{k-1} & \cdots & b_{k-l-n+2} \end{bmatrix} \begin{bmatrix} h_{REAL}(1) & 0 & 0 & 0 \\ h_{REAL}(2) & h_{REAL}(1) & 0 & 0 \\ h_{REAL}(3) & h_{REAL}(2) & 0 & 0 \\ \cdots & \cdots & \cdots & h_{REAL}(1) \\ h_{REAL}(l) & h_{REAL}(l-1) & 0 & h_{REAL}(2) \\ 0 & h_{REAL}(l) & 0 & h_{REAL}(5) \\ 0 & 0 & 0 & \cdots \\ 0 & 0 & 0 & h_{REAL}(l) \end{bmatrix}$$

$$-\begin{bmatrix} a_k & a_{k-1} & \cdots & a_{k-l-n+2} \end{bmatrix} \begin{bmatrix} h_{IMAG}(1) & 0 & 0 & 0 \\ h_{IMAG}(2) & h_{IMAG}(1) & 0 & 0 \\ h_{IMAG}(3) & h_{IMAG}(2) & 0 & 0 \\ \cdots & \cdots & \cdots & h_{IMAG}(1) \\ h_{IMAG}(l) & h_{IMAG}(l-1) & 0 & h_{IMAG}(2) \\ 0 & h_{IMAG}(l) & 0 & h_{IMAG}(5) \\ 0 & 0 & 0 & \cdots \\ 0 & 0 & 0 & h_{IMAG}(l) \end{bmatrix} + \begin{bmatrix} n_{Q,k} & n_{Q,k-2} & \cdots & n_{Q,k-n+1} \end{bmatrix}$$

$$= \tilde{B}_k^T \overline{H}_{REAL} - \tilde{A}_k^T \overline{H}_{IMAG} + N_{Q,k}$$

The expected value of the squared error, or mean squared error, for a particular Q is

$$E[e_k^2] = E\left[\left(a_{k-d} - X_k^T Q_I - Y_k^T Q_Q \right)^2 \right]$$

The derivative of the mean squared error with respect to the equalizer coefficient vectors Q_I and Q_Q are as follows:

$$\frac{\partial \left(E[e_k^2] \right)}{\partial Q_I} = -2E\left[\left(a_{k-d} - X_k^T Q_I - Y_k^T Q_Q \right) X_k^T \right]$$

$$\frac{\partial \left(E[e_k^2] \right)}{\partial Q_Q} = -2E\left[\left(a_{k-d} - X_k^T Q_I - Y_k^T Q^2 \right) Y_k^T \right]$$

To obtain the optimal equalizer coefficient vector, Q_{opt}, set the derivative equal to zero, as follows:

$$Q_{I,opt}^T E\left[X_k X_k^T\right] + Q_{Q,opt}^T E\left[X_k Y_k^T\right] = E\left[a_{k-d} X_k^T\right]$$

$$Q_{I,opt}^T E\left[Y_k X_k^T\right] + Q_{Q,opt}^T E\left[Y_k Y_k^T\right] = E\left[a_{k-d} Y_k^T\right]$$

Or in another form as

$$\begin{bmatrix} E\left[X_k X_k^T\right] & E\left[X_k Y_k^T\right] \\ E\left[Y_k X_k^T\right] & E\left[Y_k Y_k^T\right] \end{bmatrix} \begin{bmatrix} Q_{I,opt} \\ Q_{Q,opt} \end{bmatrix} = E\left[a_{k-d} \begin{bmatrix} X_k \\ Y_k \end{bmatrix}\right]$$

The QAM linear equalizer solution is

$$\begin{bmatrix} Q_{I,opt} \\ Q_{Q,opt} \end{bmatrix} = \left(\begin{bmatrix} R_{XX} & R_{XY} \\ R_{YX} & R_{YY} \end{bmatrix}\right)^{-1} \begin{bmatrix} R_{aX} \\ R_{aY} \end{bmatrix}$$

in which

$$R_{XX} = E\left[X_k X_k^T\right] = \overline{H}_{REAL}^T \overline{H}_{REAL} + \overline{H}_{IMAG}^T \overline{H}_{IMAG} + \sigma_{N,I}^2 I$$

$$R_{YY} = E\left[Y_k Y_k^T\right] = \overline{H}_{REAL}^T \overline{H}_{REAL} + \overline{H}_{IMAG}^T \overline{H}_{IMAG} + \sigma_{N,Q}^2 I$$

$$R_{XY} = R_{YX}^T = E\left[X_k Y_k^T\right] = \overline{H}_{REAL}^T \overline{H}_{IMAG} + \overline{H}_{IMAG}^T \overline{H}_{REAL}$$

$$R_{aX} = \left(\overline{H}_{REAL}^T - \overline{H}_{IMAG}^T\right) p$$

$$R_{aY} = \left(\overline{H}_{REAL}^T + \overline{H}_{IMAG}^T\right) p$$

Denoting, $\sigma_{N,I}^2$ and $\sigma_{N,Q}^2$ as noise powers for the in-phase and quadrature channels respectively, we have $\sigma_{N,I}^2 = \sigma_{N,Q}^2$ and $R_{XX} = R_{YY}$ in the normal condition.

Figure 8.24 shows real and imaginary channel impulse response for the 2 mile, 26-gauge twisted-pair loop with a carrier frequency of 200 kHz and a 150 kHz 20 percent excessive bandwidth squared root Nyquist filter $g(t)$. The impulse response of $g(t)$ is expressed as

$$g(t) = \frac{\sin\left[\pi(1-\alpha)t'\right] + 4\alpha t' \cos\left[\pi(1+\alpha)t'\right]}{\pi t'\left[1-(4\alpha t')^2\right]}$$

when $t \neq 0$ and $g(0) = (1-\alpha) + \dfrac{4\alpha}{\pi}$. Figure 8.23 shows the impulse response of the transmit shaping filter with 200 filter coefficients. Real and imaginary impulse responses can be different for using a different shaping filter $g(t)$.

Figure 8.23 Impulse Response of Squared Root Nyquist Filter

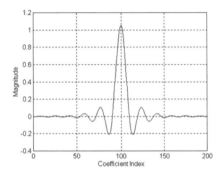

Figure 8.24 Real and Imaginary Channel Impulse Response

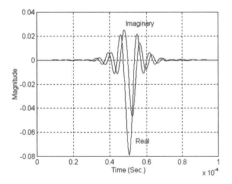

Figures 8.25 through 8.27 show QAM in-phase and cross-coupled equalizer coefficient values for 1, 2, and 3 miles of 26-gauge twisted-pair loops, respectively. The length of the passband equalizer is also dependent on the length of the channel impulse response. Required numbers of equalizer coefficients are 15, 20, and 60 for 1, 2, and 3 miles of 26-gauge twisted-pair loops, respectively.

Figure 8.25 Channel Equalizers for a 1 Mile, 26-Gauge Loop

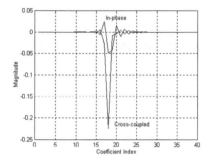

Figure 8.26 Channel Equalizers for a 2 Mile, 26-Gauge Loop

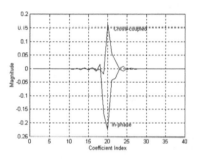

Figure 8.27 Channel Equalizers for a 3 Mile, 26-Gauge Loop

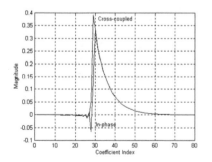

The MMSE at the output of a QAM equalizer is related to the twisted-pair loop channel characteristics, the receiver front-end noise level, and the length of equalizers, and is expressed as

$$\xi_{min} = E\left[a_k^2\right] - \begin{bmatrix} R_{Xa}^T & R_{Xb}^T \end{bmatrix} \begin{bmatrix} Q_{I,opt} \\ Q_{Q,opt} \end{bmatrix}$$

For the simple example of a 26-gauge, 10,560 foot loop with receiver front-end noise power density levels of −110 dBm/Hz, −120 dBm/Hz, and −130 dBm/Hz, we have MMSE levels of −20.1 dB, −30 dB, and −39.6 dB, respectively.

8.3.3 Calculation of QAM DFE

A QAM equalizer also can have a DFE structure consisting of two in-phase FFFs, two cross-coupled FFFs, two in-phase FBFs, and two cross-coupled FBFs, as shown in Figure 8.28. Equalizers for the in-phase and quadrature channels are identical.

Figure 8.28 The Structure of a QAM DFE

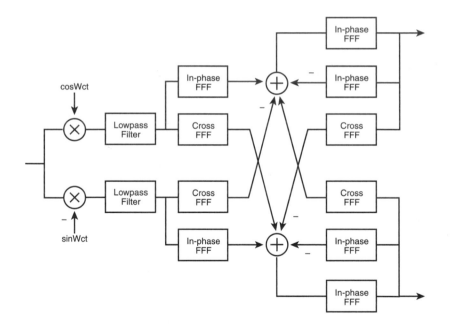

Based on the equalizer solution derived for a linear QAM equalizer, we let

$$\left(\tilde{X}_k\right)^T = \begin{bmatrix} X_k^T & A_{k-d-1}^T \end{bmatrix}$$

and

$$\left(\tilde{Y}_k\right)^T = \begin{bmatrix} Y_k^T & B_{k-d-1}^T \end{bmatrix}$$

to obtain the DFE solution as

$$
\begin{bmatrix} Q_{I,opt}^f \\ Q_{Q,opt}^f \\ Q_{I,opt}^b \\ Q_{Q,opt}^b \end{bmatrix} = \begin{bmatrix} R_{XX} & R_{XY} & R_{XA} & R_{XB} \\ R_{YX} & R_{YY} & R_{YA} & R_{YB} \\ R_{XA}^T & R_{YA}^T & I & 0 \\ R_{XB}^T & R_{YB}^T & 0 & I \end{bmatrix}^{-1} \begin{bmatrix} R_{aX} \\ R_{aY} \\ 0 \\ 0 \end{bmatrix}
$$

$Q_{I,opt}^f$ is the in-phase FFF.

$Q_{Q,opt}^f$ is the cross-coupled FFF.

$Q_{I,opt}^b$ is the in-phase FBF.

$Q_{Q,opt}^b$ is the cross-coupled FBF.

Figures 8.29 through 8.31 show QAM DFE in-phase and cross-coupled FFF and FBF coefficient values for 1, 2, and 3 miles of 26-gauge twisted-pair loops, respectively.

Figure 8.29   Channel Equalizers for a 1 Mile, 26-Gauge Loop

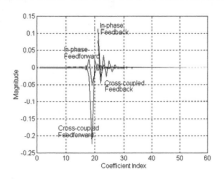

Figure 8.30   Channel Equalizers for a 2 Mile, 26-Gauge Loop

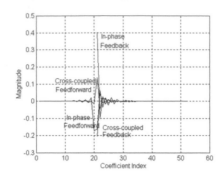

Figure 8.31   Channel Equalizers for a 3 Mile, 26-Gauge Loop

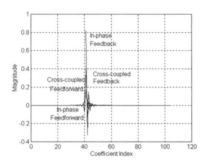

The MMSE at the output of a QAM DFE equalizer is related to the twisted-pair loop channel characteristics, the receiver front-end noise level, and only the length of in-phase and cross-coupled FFFs, and is expressed as

$$\xi_{min} = E\left[a_k^2\right] - \begin{bmatrix} R_{Xa}^T & R_{Xb}^T \end{bmatrix} \begin{bmatrix} Q_{I,opt}^f \\ Q_{Q,opt}^f \end{bmatrix}$$

A QAM equalizer also can have fractionally spaced linear equalizer or fractionally spaced FFF. Equalizer solutions can be derived based on those of baud rate linear equalizer and baud rate DFE by replacing the single-phase, received-signal vectors with multiple-phased, received-signal vectors.

8.3.4 *From QAM to CAP*

The order of demodulation and lowpass filtering also can be exchanged in the case of using channel equalizers for a QAM system resulting to a pair of passband filters followed by a phase derotator, as depicted in Figure 8.32. A fractionally spaced QAM equalizer is required after the phase derotator.

Figure 8.32 QAM Demodulation After Passband Filtering

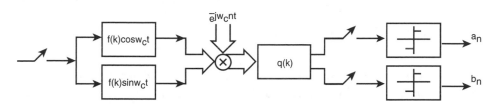

The passband filtering, demodulation, and linear equalization process for the recovery of data symbols are expressed as

$$\hat{a}_i + j\hat{b}_i = \left(f(t) * \left(g(t) e^{j\omega_c t} \right) \right) e^{-j\omega_c t} * Q_{IQ}(t)$$

By again changing the order of filtering and convolution and its mathematical equivalence, we can derive a QAM transceiver with passband equalizers, as shown in Figure 8.33. The passband filtering, passband equalization, and phase derotation process for the recovery of data symbols is expressed as

$$\hat{a}_i + j\hat{b}_i = \left[f(t) * \left(g(t) e^{j\omega_c t} \right) * Q_{IQ}(t) e^{j\omega_c t} \right] e^{-j\omega_c t}$$

Figure 8.33 A QAM Receiver with Passband Equalizers

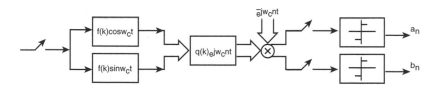

We recognize that the received signal is first filtered by a pair of passband filters and then by a pair of passband equalizers. Therefore, the function of passband filtering and passband equalization can be further combined in the following expression:

$$\hat{a}_i + j\hat{b}_i = [f(t) * Q(t)]e^{-j\omega_c t}$$

The combined equalizers are the result of the convolution of filters and equalizers. Specifically, a pair of in-phase and quadrature passband equalizers can be used in place of a pair of passband filters followed by passband channel equalizers, as follows:

$$Q(t) = \left(g(t)e^{j\omega_c t}\right) * \left(Q_{IQ}(t)e^{j\omega_c t}\right) = Q_{in}(t) + jQ_{qu}(t)$$

This passband equalization structure has been studied and implemented for many practical QAM systems.[16,17,18]

A Carrierless AM/PM (CAP) system is the result of removing the phase rotator and the phase derotator from a QAM system with passband transmitter filters and passband receiver filters or passband equalizers. A CAP transmit signal is generated with a pair of passband shaping filters whose impulse response is the product of a baseband shaping filter and the in-phase or quadrature phase of the center frequency. The passband shaping filtering process for the generation of a CAP line signal is expressed as

$$f(t) = \text{Re}\left[C_i g(t - iT)e^{j\omega_c(t - iT)}\right]$$

For a distortionless channel, the data symbols can be recovered with the same pair of passband shaping filters. The passband filter process for the recovery of data symbols carried by a CAP line code is expressed as

$$\hat{a}_i + j\hat{b}_i = \left(f(t) * \left(g(t)e^{j\omega_c t}\right)\right)$$

The receiver passband shaping filters need to be replaced with a pair of in-phase and quadrature passband equalizers for a twisted-pair loop channel, as shown in Figure 8.34. The equalizers are the same as those in a direct passband-implemented QAM system. The passband equalization process for the recovery of data symbols carried by a CAP line code is expressed as

$$\hat{a}_i + j\hat{b}_i = [f(t) * Q(t)]$$

Figure 8.34   A CAP Transceiver Pair Resulting from the Removal of Phase Modulator and Demodulator

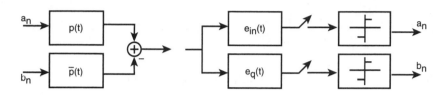

8.3.5   *Calculation of CAP Linear Equalizer*

CAP equalizer solutions are derived for a three times over-sampled implementation as an example. Instantaneous errors between desired in-phase and quadrature data symbols and outputs from a pair of in-phase and quadrature passband equalizers are

$$e_{ik} = a_{k-d} - X_k^{1T} Q_i^1 - X_k^{2T} Q_i^2 - X_k^{3T} Q_i^3$$

$$e_{qk} = b_{k-d} - X_k^{1T} Q_q^1 - X_k^{2T} Q_q^2 - X_k^{3T} Q_q^3$$

The values are as follows:

a_{k-d} is the desired in-phase data symbol after d baud intervals of channel delay

$a_{k-d} b_k$ is the desired quadrature data symbol also after d baud intervals of channel delay.

$X_k^{1T} = \begin{bmatrix} x_k & x_{k-3} & \cdots & x_{k-n+3} \end{bmatrix}$ is the first phase of the received-signal vector.

$X_k^{2T} = \begin{bmatrix} x_{k-1} & x_{k-3-1} & \cdots & x_{x-n+2} \end{bmatrix}$ is the second phase of the received signal vector.

$X_k^{3T} = \begin{bmatrix} x_{k-2} & x_{k-3-2} & \cdots & x_{x-n+1} \end{bmatrix}$ is the third phase of the received-signal vector.

$Q_i^{1T} = \begin{bmatrix} q_{i1} & a_{i4} & \cdots & a_{i(n-2)} \end{bmatrix}$ is the first phase of the in-phase channel equalizer filter coefficient vector.

$Q_i^{2T} = \begin{bmatrix} q_{i2} & a_{i5} & \cdots & a_{i(n-1)} \end{bmatrix}$ is the second phase of the in-phase channel equalizer filter coefficient vector.

$Q_i^{3T} = \begin{bmatrix} q_{i3} & a_{i6} & \cdots & a_{in} \end{bmatrix}$ is the third phase of the in-phase channel equalizer filter coefficient vector.

$Q_q^{1T} = \begin{bmatrix} q_{q1} & a_{i4} & \cdots & a_{q(n-2)} \end{bmatrix}$ is the first phase of the quadrature channel equalizer filter coefficient vector.

$Q_q^{2T} = \begin{bmatrix} q_{q2} & a_{q5} & \cdots & a_{q(n-1)} \end{bmatrix}$ is the second phase of the quadrature channel equalizer filter coefficient vector.

$Q_q^{3T} = \begin{bmatrix} q_{q3} & a_{q6} & \cdots & a_{qn} \end{bmatrix}$ is the third phase of the quadrature channel equalizer filter coefficient vector.

e_{ik} is the error between the desired in-phase data symbol and the in-phase channel equalizer output.

e_{qk} is the error between the desired quadrature data symbol and the quadrature channel equalizer output.

The received signal can be expressed as

$$x_k = \sum_{i=1}^{l} a_{k-i+1} h_I \big(1+3(i-1)\big) + \sum_{i=1}^{l} b_{k-i+1} h_Q \big(1+3(i-1)\big) + n_{I,k}$$

$$= \begin{bmatrix} a_k & a_{k-1} & \cdots & a_{k-l+1} \end{bmatrix} \begin{bmatrix} h_I(1) \\ h_I(4) \\ \cdots \\ h_I(l-2) \end{bmatrix} + \begin{bmatrix} b_k & b_{k-1} & \cdots & b_{k-l+1} \end{bmatrix} \begin{bmatrix} h_Q(1) \\ h_Q(4) \\ \cdots \\ h_Q(l-2) \end{bmatrix} + n_{I,k}$$

for $k=1, 4, 7\ldots$

$$x_k = \sum_{i=1}^{l} a_{k-i+1} h_I \big(2+3(i-1)\big) + \sum_{i=1}^{l} b_{k-i+1} h_Q \big(2+3(i-1)\big) + n_{I,k}$$

$$= \begin{bmatrix} a_k & a_{k-1} & \cdots & a_{k-l+1} \end{bmatrix} \begin{bmatrix} h_I(2) \\ h_I(5) \\ \cdots \\ h_I(l-1) \end{bmatrix} + \begin{bmatrix} b_k & b_{k-1} & \cdots & b_{k-l+1} \end{bmatrix} \begin{bmatrix} h_Q(2) \\ h_Q(5) \\ \cdots \\ h_Q(l-1) \end{bmatrix} + n_{I,k}$$

for $k=2, 5, 8\ldots$

$$x_k = \sum_{i=1}^{l} a_{k-i+1} h_I \big(3+3(i-1)\big) + \sum_{i=1}^{l} b_{k-i+1} h_Q \big(3+3(i-1)\big) + n_{I,k}$$

$$= \begin{bmatrix} a_k & a_{k-1} & \cdots & a_{k-l+1} \end{bmatrix} \begin{bmatrix} h_I(3) \\ h_I(6) \\ \cdots \\ h_I(l) \end{bmatrix} + \begin{bmatrix} b_k & b_{k-1} & \cdots & b_{k-l+1} \end{bmatrix} \begin{bmatrix} h_Q(3) \\ h_Q(6) \\ \cdots \\ h_Q(l) \end{bmatrix} + n_{I,k}$$

for $k=3, 6, 9\ldots$ in which

$$h_I(t) = \big(g(t)\cos\varpi_c t\big) * h(t)$$

and

$$h_Q(t) = \big(g(t)\sin\varpi_c t\big) * h(t)$$

The three phases of received signal vectors are expressed as

$$X_k^{1T} = \tilde{A}_k^T \overline{H}_I^1 + \tilde{B}_k^T \overline{H}_Q^1 + N_k$$

$$X_k^{2T} = \tilde{A}_k^T \overline{H}_I^2 + \tilde{B}_k^T \overline{H}_Q^2 + N_k$$

$$X_k^{3T} = \tilde{A}_k^T \overline{H}_I^3 + \tilde{B}_k^T \overline{H}_Q^3 + N_k$$

for which

$$\overline{H}_I^1 = \begin{bmatrix} h_I(1) & 0 & 0 & 0 \\ h_I(4) & h_I(1) & 0 & 0 \\ h_I(7) & h_I(4) & 0 & 0 \\ \cdots & \cdots & \cdots & h_I(1) \\ h_I(l-2) & h_I(l-5) & 0 & h_I(4) \\ 0 & h_I(l-2) & 0 & h_I(7) \\ 0 & 0 & 0 & \cdots \\ 0 & 0 & 0 & h_I(l-2) \end{bmatrix}$$

$$\overline{H}_I^2 = \begin{bmatrix} h_I(2) & 0 & 0 & 0 \\ h_I(5) & h_I(2) & 0 & 0 \\ h_I(8) & h_I(5) & 0 & 0 \\ \cdots & \cdots & \cdots & h_I(2) \\ h_I(l-1) & h_I(l-4) & 0 & h_I(5) \\ 0 & h_I(l-1) & 0 & h_I(8) \\ 0 & 0 & 0 & \cdots \\ 0 & 0 & 0 & h_I(l-1) \end{bmatrix}$$

$$\overline{H}_I^3 = \begin{bmatrix} h_I(3) & 0 & 0 & 0 \\ h_I(6) & h_I(3) & 0 & 0 \\ h_I(9) & h_I(6) & 0 & 0 \\ \cdots & \cdots & \cdots & h_I(3) \\ h_I(l) & h_I(l-3) & 0 & h_I(6) \\ 0 & h_I(l) & 0 & h_I(9) \\ 0 & 0 & 0 & \cdots \\ 0 & 0 & 0 & h_I(l) \end{bmatrix}$$

$$
\overline{H}_Q^1 =
\begin{bmatrix}
h_Q(1) & 0 & 0 & 0 \\
h_Q(4) & h_Q(1) & 0 & 0 \\
h_I(7) & h_Q(4) & 0 & 0 \\
\cdots & \cdots & \cdots & h_Q(1) \\
h_Q(l-2) & h_Q(l-5) & 0 & h_Q(4) \\
0 & h_Q(l-2) & 0 & h_Q(7) \\
0 & 0 & 0 & \cdots \\
0 & 0 & 0 & h_Q(l-2)
\end{bmatrix}
$$

$$
\overline{H}_Q^2 =
\begin{bmatrix}
h_Q(2) & 0 & 0 & 0 \\
h_Q(5) & h_Q(2) & 0 & 0 \\
h_Q(8) & h_Q(5) & 0 & 0 \\
\cdots & \cdots & \cdots & h_Q(2) \\
h_Q(l-1) & h_Q(l-4) & 0 & h_Q(5) \\
0 & h_Q(l-1) & 0 & h_Q(8) \\
0 & 0 & 0 & \cdots \\
0 & 0 & 0 & h_Q(l-1)
\end{bmatrix}
$$

$$
\overline{H}_Q^3 =
\begin{bmatrix}
h_Q(3) & 0 & 0 & 0 \\
h_Q(6) & h_Q(3) & 0 & 0 \\
h_Q(9) & h_Q(6) & 0 & 0 \\
\cdots & \cdots & \cdots & h_Q(3) \\
h_Q(l) & h_Q(l-3) & 0 & h_Q(6) \\
0 & h_Q(l) & 0 & h_Q(9) \\
0 & 0 & 0 & \cdots \\
0 & 0 & 0 & h_Q(l)
\end{bmatrix}
$$

The expected value of square errors or mean square errors for a particular set of equalizer coefficient vectors, Q_i and Q_q, are as follows:

$$E\left[e_{ik}^2\right] = E\left[\left(a_{k-d} - X_k^{1T}Q_i^1 - X_k^{2T}Q_i^2 - X_k^{1T}Q_i^3\right)^2\right]$$

$$E\left[e_{qk}^2\right] = E\left[\left(b_{k-d} - X_k^{1T}Q_q^1 - X_k^{2T}Q_q^2 - X_k^{1T}Q_q^3\right)^2\right]$$

Derivatives of the mean square error with respect to the equalizer coefficient vectors Q_i^1, Q_i^2, Q_i^3, Q_q^1, Q_q^2, and Q_q^3 are

$$\frac{\partial\left(E\left[e_{ik}^2\right]\right)}{\partial Q_i^1} = -2E\left[\left(a_{k-d} - X_k^{1T}Q_i^1 - X_k^{2T}Q_i^2 - X_k^{3T}Q_i^3\right)X_k^{1T}\right]$$

$$\frac{\partial\left(E\left[e_{ik}^2\right]\right)}{\partial Q_i^2} = -2E\left[\left(a_{k-d} - X_k^{1T}Q_i^1 - X_k^{2T}Q_i^2 - X_k^{3T}Q_i^3\right)X_k^{2T}\right]$$

$$\frac{\partial\left(E\left[e_{ik}^2\right]\right)}{\partial Q_i^3} = -2E\left[\left(a_{k-d} - X_k^{1T}Q_i^1 - X_k^{2T}Q_i^2 - X_k^{3T}Q_i^3\right)X_k^{3T}\right]$$

$$\frac{\partial\left(E\left[e_{qk}^2\right]\right)}{\partial Q_q^1} = -2E\left[\left(b_{k-d} - X_k^{1T}Q_q^1 - X_k^{2T}Q_q^2 - X_k^{3T}Q_q^3\right)X_k^{1T}\right]$$

$$\frac{\partial\left(E\left[e_{qk}^2\right]\right)}{\partial Q_q^2} = -2E\left[\left(b_{k-d} - X_k^{1T}Q_q^1 - X_k^{2T}Q_q^2 - X_k^{3T}Q_q^3\right)X_k^{2T}\right]$$

$$\frac{\partial\left(E\left[e_{qk}^2\right]\right)}{\partial Q_q^3} = -2E\left[\left(b_{k-d} - X_k^{1T}Q_q^1 - X_k^{2T}Q_q^2 - X_k^{3T}Q_q^3\right)X_k^{3T}\right]$$

Setting derivatives equal to zero, we obtain the optimal equalizer coefficient vectors Q_i^1, Q_i^2, Q_i^3, Q_q^1, Q_q^2, and Q_q^3 for Minimum Mean Square Errors, as

$$Q_{i,opt} = \begin{bmatrix} Q_{i,opt}^1 \\ Q_{i,opt}^2 \\ Q_{i,opt}^3 \end{bmatrix} = \begin{bmatrix} R_{XX}^{11} & R_{XX}^{12} & R_{XX}^{13} \\ R_{XX}^{21} & R_{XX}^{22} & R_{XX}^{23} \\ R_{XX}^{31} & R_{XX}^{32} & R_{XX}^{33} \end{bmatrix}^{-1} \begin{bmatrix} R_{Xa}^1 \\ R_{Xa}^2 \\ R_{Xa}^3 \end{bmatrix} = \left(R_{XX} \right)^{-1} R_{Xa}$$

$$Q_{q,opt} = \begin{bmatrix} Q_{q,opt}^1 \\ Q_{q,opt}^2 \\ Q_{q,opt}^3 \end{bmatrix} = \begin{bmatrix} R_{XX}^{11} & R_{XX}^{12} & R_{XX}^{13} \\ R_{XX}^{21} & R_{XX}^{22} & R_{XX}^{23} \\ R_{XX}^{31} & R_{XX}^{32} & R_{XX}^{33} \end{bmatrix}^{-1} \begin{bmatrix} R_{Xb}^1 \\ R_{Xb}^2 \\ R_{Xb}^3 \end{bmatrix} = \left(R_{XX} \right)^{-1} R_{Xb}$$

for which

$$R_{XX}^{11} = E\left[X_k^1 X_k^{1T} \right]$$

$$R_{XX}^{22} = E\left[X_k^2 X_k^{2T} \right]$$

$$R_{XX}^{33} = E\left[X_k^3 X_k^{3T} \right]$$

$$R_{XX}^{12} = \left(R_{XX}^{21} \right)^T = E\left[X_k^1 X_k^{2T} \right]$$

$$R_{XX}^{13} = \left(R_{XX}^{31} \right)^T = E\left[X_k^1 X_k^{3T} \right]$$

$$R_{Xa}^1 = E\left[a_k X_k^1 \right]$$

$$R_{Xa}^2 = E\left[a_k X_k^2 \right]$$

$$R_{Xa}^3 = E\left[a_k X_k^3 \right]$$

$$R_{Xb}^1 = E\left[b_k X_k^1 \right]$$

$$R_{Xb}^2 = E\left[b_k X_k^2 \right]$$

$$R_{Xb}^3 = E\left[b_k X_k^3 \right]$$

Figure 8.35 shows CAP in-phase and quadrature passband shaping filter impulse responses for a center frequency of 166.67 kHz, a baud rate of 250 kHz, and an excessive bandwidth of 20 percent.

Figure 8.35 In-Phase and Quadrature Transmit Filter Coefficients

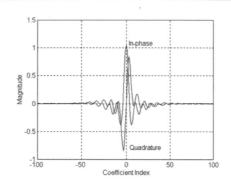

Figure 8.36 shows possible in-phase and quadrature channel impulse responses for a twisted-pair loop.

Figure 8.36 In-Phase and Quadrature Channel Impulse Responses

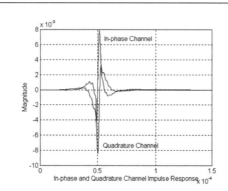

Figures 8.37 through 8.39 show fractionally spaced CAP equalizer coefficient values with three times of oversampling for 1, 2, and 3 miles, respectively, of 26-gauge twisted-pair loops.

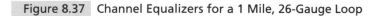

Figure 8.37   Channel Equalizers for a 1 Mile, 26-Gauge Loop

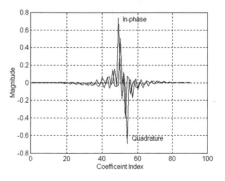

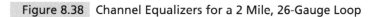

Figure 8.38   Channel Equalizers for a 2 Mile, 26-Gauge Loop

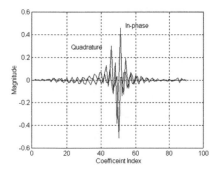

Figure 8.39   Channel Equalizers for a 3 Mile, 26-Gauge Loop

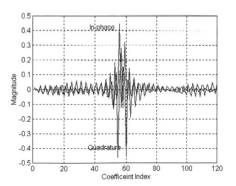

The MMSE at the output of a CAP linear equalizer is related to the twisted-pair loop channel characteristics, the receiver front-end noise level, and the length of equalizers. In-phase and Quadrature MMSEs are expressed separately as

$$\xi_{iin,min} = E\left[a_k^2\right] - \begin{bmatrix} R_{Xa}^{1T} & R_{Xa}^{2T} & R_{Xa}^{3T} \end{bmatrix} \begin{bmatrix} Q_{i,opt}^1 \\ Q_{i,opt}^2 \\ Q_{i,opt}^3 \end{bmatrix}$$

$$\xi_{qu,min} = E\left[b_k^2\right] - \begin{bmatrix} R_{Xb}^{1T} & R_{Xb}^{2T} & R_{Xb}^{3T} \end{bmatrix} \begin{bmatrix} Q_{q,opt}^1 \\ Q_{q,opt}^2 \\ Q_{q,opt}^3 \end{bmatrix}$$

8.3.6 Calculation of CAP DFE

You can derive CAP DFE equalizer coefficients as well as its structure by expanding the length of received-signal vectors and let one phase of the expanded portion of the data vector contain the estimated data symbols and expanded portions of two other received signal vectors filled with zeros. For an example of using a phase to contain the estimated data symbols, we have

$$\left(\tilde{X}_k^1\right)^T = \left[\left(X_k^1\right)^T \quad \begin{bmatrix} 0 & 0 & \cdots & 0 \end{bmatrix}^T\right]$$

$$\left(\tilde{X}_k^2\right)^T = \left[\left(X_k^2\right)^T \quad \begin{bmatrix} 0 & 0 & \cdots & 0 \end{bmatrix}^T\right]$$

and

$$\left(\tilde{X}_k^3\right)^T = \left[\left(X_k^3\right)^T \quad A_{k-d-1}^T\right]$$

or

$$\left(\tilde{X}_k^3\right)^T = \left[\left(X_k^3\right)^T \quad B_{k-d-1}^T\right]$$

We have the CAP DFE equalizer solution as

$$
\begin{bmatrix} Q^1_{i,opt} \\ Q^2_{i,opt} \\ Q^3_{i,opt} \\ Q^b_{i,opt} \end{bmatrix} = \left(\begin{bmatrix} E[X^1_k X^{1T}_k] & E[X^1_k X^{2T}_k] & E[X^1_k X^{3T}_k] & E\left[X^1_k \left(A^m_{k-d-1}\right)^T\right] \\ E[X^2_k X^{1T}_k] & E[X^2_k X^{2T}_k] & E[X^2_k X^{3T}_k] & E\left[X^2_k \left(A^m_{k-d-1}\right)^T\right] \\ E[X^3_k X^{1T}_k] & E[X^3_k X^{2T}_k] & E[X^3_k X^{3T}_k] & E\left[X^3_k \left(A^m_{k-d-1}\right)^T\right] \\ E\left[A^m_{k-d-1}\left(X^1_k\right)^T\right] & E\left[A^m_{k-d-1}\left(X^2_k\right)^T\right] & E\left[A^m_{k-d-1}\left(X^3_k\right)^T\right] & I \end{bmatrix} \right)^{-1} E\left[a_{k-d} \begin{bmatrix} X^1_k \\ X^2_k \\ X^3_k \\ 0 \end{bmatrix} \right]
$$

$$
\begin{bmatrix} Q^1_{i,opt} \\ Q^2_{q,opt} \\ Q^3_{q,opt} \\ Q^b_{q,opt} \end{bmatrix} = \left(\begin{bmatrix} E[X^1_k X^{1T}_k] & E[X^1_k X^{2T}_k] & E[X^1_k X^{3T}_k] & E\left[X^1_k \left(B^m_{k-d-1}\right)^T\right] \\ E[X^2_k X^{1T}_k] & E[X^2_k X^{2T}_k] & E[X^2_k X^{3T}_k] & E\left[X^2_k \left(B^m_{k-d-1}\right)^T\right] \\ E[X^3_k X^{1T}_k] & E[X^3_k X^{2T}_k] & E[X^3_k X^{3T}_k] & E\left[X^3_k \left(B^m_{k-d-1}\right)^T\right] \\ E\left[B^m_{k-d-1}\left(X^1_k\right)^T\right] & E\left[B^m_{k-d-1}\left(X^2_k\right)^T\right] & E\left[B^m_{k-d-1}\left(X^3_k\right)^T\right] & I \end{bmatrix} \right)^{-1} E\left[b_{k-d} \begin{bmatrix} X^1_k \\ X^2_k \\ X^3_k \\ 0 \end{bmatrix} \right]
$$

A CAP DFE consists of two, in-phase and quadrature, separate DFEs, as shown in Figure 8.40. Cross-coupled FBFs are not necessary. The orthogonality between in-phase and quadrature channels is maintained in the transmitter by these passband shaping filters.

Figure 8.40 The Structure of a CAP DFE

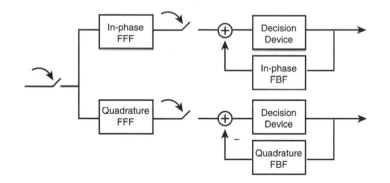

Figures 8.41 through 8.43 show CAP DFE equalizer coefficients for 1, 2, and 3 miles, respectively, of 26-gauge twisted-pair loops.

Figure 8.41 Channel Equalizers for a 1 Mile, 26-Gauge Loop

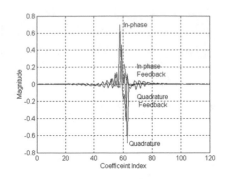

Figure 8.42 Channel Equalizers for a 2 Mile, 26-Gauge Loop

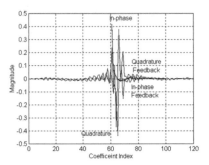

Figure 8.43 Channel Equalizers for a 3 Mile, 26-Gauge Loop

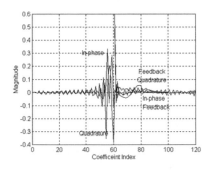

Because FBFs does not contribute to the noise enhancement, MMSEs for a CAP DFE system are the same as those described for the CAP linear equalizer system. The additional performance improvement comes from a different set of CAP FFF filter coefficients:

$$\xi_{iin,min} = E[a_k^2] - \begin{bmatrix} R_{Xa}^{1T} & R_{Xa}^{2T} & R_{Xa}^{3T} \end{bmatrix} \begin{bmatrix} Q_{i,opt}^1 \\ Q_{i,opt}^2 \\ Q_{i,opt}^3 \end{bmatrix}$$

$$\xi_{qu,min} = E[b_k^2] - \begin{bmatrix} R_{Xb}^{1T} & R_{Xb}^{2T} & R_{Xb}^{3T} \end{bmatrix} \begin{bmatrix} Q_{q,opt}^1 \\ Q_{q,opt}^2 \\ Q_{q,opt}^3 \end{bmatrix}$$

Equalizer output SNRs for QAM and CAP systems are summarized in Table 8.2 for different equalizer structures under different receiver front-end noise power density levels for the 2 mile, 26-gauge twisted-pair loop. Results show that DFE performance is only slightly better for the passband system. However, a QAM equalizer with a fractionally spaced FFF could make performance robustness irrelevant to the sample timing phase.

Performances of a QAM system and a CAP system with fractionally spaced FFFs should be about the same. The difference in the table is caused by the sample timing phase of the channel because the QAM system used a two times over-sampled FFF and the CAP system used a three times over-sampled FFF.

Table 8.2 Passband Equalizer Output SNRs

Noise Level	QAM Linear	QAM DFE	Fractional QAM Linear	CAP Linear	CAP DFE
−110 dBm/Hz	22.0	22.2	25	26.0	26.8
−120 dBm/Hz	32.0	32.2	35	36.0	36.8
−130 dBm/Hz	42.0	42.2	45	45.9	46.7

8.4 Equalizers for Discrete Multitone Systems

The severe channel intersymbol interference of a twisted-pair loop also can be avoided by signaling at a lower baud rate while letting each baud carry many bits of information. For a 1 mile, 26-gauge twisted-pair loop, the tail of the impulse response is about 30 microseconds. To make the intersymbol interference negligible, the signaling baud interval can be chosen as 100 times that of the tail. This results in a signaling baud rate of 333 Hz.

Data can be carried in this long baud interval with many waveforms of different frequencies. In other words, bits of information are encoded in the frequency domain. This information encoding process can be carried out with the *Inverse Discrete Fourier Transform* (IDFT). Bits of information are recovered in a receiver with the *Discrete Fourier Transform* (DFT). This approach has been called *Discrete MultiTone* (DMT) line code for the use of multiple numbers of carriers. QAM and CAP are called *single-carrier systems*.

A slower baud rate can lead to less intersymbol interference. On the other hand, a slower baud rate requires a higher number of carriers for certain desired transmission throughputs. This in turn results in a bigger IDFT/DFT size. The implementation of a large size IDFT/DFT requires more buffering memories and a longer process delay time.

As an alternative for DMT-based systems, a higher baud rate can be used also, thus lowering the size of the IDFT/DFT requirement. The intersymbol interference at a particular baud rate also can be minimized by the introduction of a guard period where repetitive information is encoded.[19] Figure 8.44 shows the relationship between a long duration baud interval and the tail of the impulse response.

Figure 8.44   Baud Interval Pulse and Residual Tail

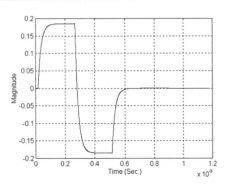

Incidentally, the duration of the impulse response tail also can be reduced using the general channel equalization technique. The idea is to use a linear channel equalizer in the receiver front end of a DMT system to minimize the MMSE between the linear equalizer output and an unknown channel with a desired impulse response tail. The solution of this DMT time-domain equalizer has been examined by many studies[20,21] and for other receiver structures.[22,23]

The DMT time-domain equalizer solution also can be derived in the discrete time domain. We assume that the equalized unknown channel is the convolution of the channel and the equalizer and can be expressed as

$$h_{equ}(k) = h(k) * Q(k)$$

To constrain the length of the equalized unknown channel, for an example of an original channel length of 5, an equalizer length of 5, and a equalized channel length of 3, we need to have

$$
\begin{bmatrix}
h(1) & 0 & 0 & 0 & 0 \\
h(2) & h(1) & 0 & 0 & 0 \\
h(3) & h(2) & h(1) & 0 & 0 \\
h(4) & h(3) & h(2) & h(1) & 0 \\
h(5) & h(4) & h(3) & h(2) & h(1) \\
0 & h(5) & h(4) & h(3) & h(2) \\
0 & 0 & h(5) & h(4) & h(3) \\
0 & 0 & 0 & h(5) & h(4) \\
0 & 0 & 0 & 0 & h(5)
\end{bmatrix}
\begin{bmatrix}
q_1 \\ q_2 \\ q_3 \\ q_4 \\ q_5
\end{bmatrix}
=
\begin{bmatrix}
0 \\ 0 \\ 0 \\ h_{equ}(1) \\ h_{equ}(2) \\ h_{equ}(3) \\ 0 \\ 0 \\ 0
\end{bmatrix}
$$

In general, the equalized unknown channel can have an infinite number of solutions. The optimal equalizer solution is called the target channel, which produces the MMSE in conjunction with the equalized channel. Figure 8.45 illustrates the mean square error between the output of a DMT time domain linear channel equalizer and the unknown target channel. The size of the target channel of a DMT system is usually defined by the guard period of the DMT system, and that is normally part of the design parameters.

Figure 8.45 **Equalizer and Target Channel**

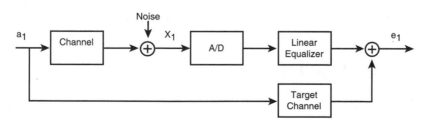

For the special case of a casual target channel, the solution to this mean square error minimization problem is the decision feedback channel equalizer. Therefore, the linear equalizer and the target channel for this special case can be solved as

$$\begin{bmatrix} Q_{opt} \\ \overline{h}_{equ} \end{bmatrix} = \begin{bmatrix} R_{XX} & R_{XA} \\ R_{XA}^T & I \end{bmatrix}^{-1} \begin{bmatrix} R_{Xa} \\ 0 \end{bmatrix}$$

The values are as follows:

$$R_{XX} = E\left[X_k X_k^T\right]$$

$$R_{XA} = E\left[X_k A_{k-d-1}^T\right]$$

$$R_{Xa} = E\left[X_k a_{k-d}\right]$$

For the general case of a DMT time-domain linear channel equalizer, we remove the constraint of a casual target channel. Therefore, the data symbol vector can have the following form:

$$A_{k-i}^T = \begin{bmatrix} a_{k-i} & \cdots & a_{k-d+1} & a_{k-d-1} & \cdots & a_{k-i-l+1} \end{bmatrix}$$

The data symbol vector can have data symbols before or after, but not include the currently desired data symbol within a certain time window. The mean square error between the output of a DMT time-domain linear equalizer and the target channel is

$$\xi_{\min} = E\left[a_k^2\right] - R_{XA}^T Q_{opt}^i$$

Q_{opt}^i stands for the equalizer solution corresponding to the symbol vector A_{k-i}^T.

The optimal DMT time-domain linear channel equalizer solution is chosen such that its corresponding mean square error is minimal:

$$\underset{i}{Min}\left(\xi_{\min}\right) = \underset{i}{Min}\left(E\left[a_k^2\right] - R_{Xa}^T Q_{opt}^i\right)$$

for $d - l < i < d + 1$ among different A_{k-i}^Ts.

Figures 8.46 through 8.51 show MMSEs corresponding to different A_{k-i}^Ts, the optimal DMT time-domain linear equalizer coefficients, and the target channel impulse responses for 1, 2, and 3 miles, respectively, of 26-gauge twisted-pair loops.

Figure 8.46   Mean Square Errors for a 1 Mile, 26-Gauge Loop

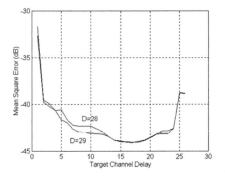

Figure 8.47   Equalizer Coefficient and Target Channel Impulse Response

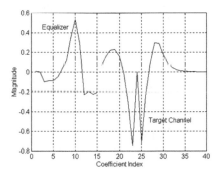

Figure 8.48   Mean Square Errors for a 2 Mile, 26-Gauge Loop

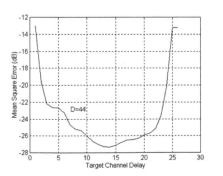

Figure 8.49 Equalizer Coefficient and Target Channel Impulse Response

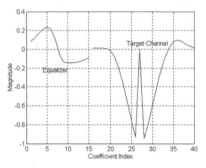

Figure 8.50 Mean Square Errors for a 3 Mile, 26-Gauge Loop

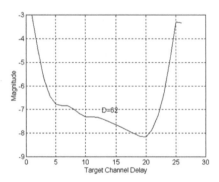

Figure 8.51 Equalizer Coefficient and Target Channel Impulse Response

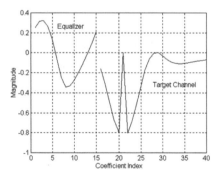

It should be pointed out that the optimal DMT time-domain linear equalizer is not necessarily obtained based on this MMSE criteria. An optimal DMT linear channel equalizer can

be defined to maximize the transmission throughput under certain error rate requirements in conjunction with a given channel and noise environment.[24]

End Notes

1. R. W. Lucky, "Automatic Equalization for Digital Communication," *B.S.T.J.*, vol. 44, no. X (April 1965): 547–588.

2. A. Papoulis, *Signal Analysis* (McGraw-Hill Book Company, 1977).

3. D. W. Lin, "MMSE Echo Cancellation and Equalization for Digital Subscriber Line Transmission: Part I—Theory and Computation," *IEEE Trans. on Commun.*, vol. 38, no. 1 (January 1990): 31–38.

4. B. Widrow and S. D. Stearns, *Adaptive Signal Processing* (Prentice-Hall 1985).

5. R. D. Gitlin and S. B. Weinstein, "Fractionally-Spaced Equalization: An Improved Digital Transversal Equalizer," *B.S.T.J.*, vol. 60, no. 2 (February 1981): 275–296.

6. R. D. Gitlin, H. C. Meadors, Jr., and S. B. Weinstein, "The Tap-Leakage Algorithm: An Algorithm for the Stable Operation of a Digitally Implemented, Fractionally Spaced Adaptive Equalizer," *B.S.T.J.*, vol. 61, no. 8 (October 1982).

7. E. A. Lee and D. G. Messerschmitt, *Digital Communication* (Kluwer Academic Publishers, 1988).

8. M. E. Austin, *Decision Feedback Equalization for Digital Communication Over Dispersive Channels* (M.I.T. Lincoln Laboratory, August 1967).

9. J. Salz, "Optimum Mean-Square Decision Feedback Equalizer," *B.S.T.J.*, vol. 52 (October 1973): 1341–1373.

10. C. A. Belfiore and J. H. Park, "Decision Feedback Equalization," *Proceedings of the IEEE*, vol. 67, no. 8 (August 1979).

11. D. L. Duttweiler, J. E. Mazo, and D. G. Messerschmitt, "Error Propagation in Decision Feedback Equalizer," *IEEE Trans. On Information Theory*, vol. IT-20 (July 1974): 490–497.

12. M. Tomlinson, "New Automatic Equalizer Employing Modulo Arithmetic," *Electron, Lett.*, vol. 7 (March 1971): 138–139.

13. H. Harashima and H. Miyakawa, "Matched-Transmission Technique for Channels with Intersymbol Interference," *IEEE Trans. on Comm. Tech.*, vol. COM-20 (August 1972): 774–780.

14. N. J. Lynch-Aird, "Tomlinson Precoding and DFE PAM: An Analytical Comparison for Recursive and Non-Recursive Equalizers," *BTL T1E1 Contribution*, T1E1.4/90-146 (September 1990).

15. A. K. Aman, R. L. Cupo, and N. A. Zervos, "Combined Trellis Coding and DFE Through Tomlinson Precoding," *IEEE JSAC*, vol. 9, no. 6 (August 1991): 876–884.

16. K. H. Mueller and J. J. Werner, "A Hardware Efficient Passband Equalizer Structure for Data Transmission," *IEEE Trans. Commun.*, vol. COM-30 (March 1982): 538–541.

17. G. H. Im and C. K. Un, "A Reduced Structure for the Passband Fractionally Spaced Equalizer," *Proc. IEEE*, vol. 75 (June 1987): 847–849.

18. F. Ling and S. U. H. Qureshi, "Convergence and Steady-State Behavior of a Phase-Splitting Fractionally Spaced Equalizer," *IEEE Trans. On Commun.*, vol. 38, no. 4 (April 1990): 418–425.

19. S. B. Weistein, "Data Transmission by Frequency-Division Multiplexing Using the Discrete Fourier Transform," *IEEE Trans. on Commun.*, vol. COM-19, no. 5 (October 1971): 628–634.

20. J. S. Chow and J. M. Cioffi, "A Cost-Effective Maximum Likelihood Receiver for Multicarrier System," *Proc. IEEE ICC '92* (June 1992): 948–952.

21. J. S. Chow, J. M. Cioffi, and J. A. C. Bingham, "Equalizer Training Algorithms for Multicarrier Modulation Systems," *Proc. IEEE ICC '93* (June 1993): 761–765.

22. D. D. Falconer and F. R. Magee, Jr., "Adaptive Channel Memory Truncation for Maximum Likelihood Sequence Estimation," *B.S.T.J.*, vol. 52 (November 1973): 1541–1562.

23. D. G. Messerschmitt, "Design of a Finite Impulse Response for the Viterbi Algorithm and Decision Feedback Equalizer," *Proc. IEEE ICC '74* (June 1974): 37D.1–37D.5.

24. N. Al-Dhahir and J. M. Cioffi, "Optimum Finite-Length Equalization for Multicarrier Transceivers," *IEEE Trans. On Commun.*, vol. 44, no. 1 (January 1996): 56–64.

CHAPTER 9

Echo Cancellation

For the voice application, a certain amount of echo was considered a positive feedback for telephone conversations until the satellite link was used for long distance calls. The long delay introduced by the satellite link makes echo an unpleasant experience. Voice echo cancellers are usually installed in COs to significantly reduce the magnitude of the echo. The echo cancellation level for voice applications is between 20 to 30 dB. For data communication, full-duplex transmission over a single pair of twisted-pair telephone loops can be realized using the echo cancellation technique.

The echo for DSL systems occurs at the hybrid circuit where the transmit path and the receiving path are joined together and connected to the twisted-pair telephone loop. An adaptive echo canceller is usually an integrated part of a DSL transceiver. To maintain a low residual echo level compared with the weak received signal, the required echo cancellation level can be as high as 60 dB.

The Basic Rate Access ISDN channel (also called DSL) and HDSL both use echo cancellation for the full-duplex transmission over a single pair of telephone loops using the same frequency band for opposite directions. The DMT ADSL has an option to use echo cancellation for an improved transmission throughput in the downstream direction (from a CO to a telephone subscriber). The echo cancellation for DMT ADSL is asymmetrical because signal bandwidths are different at opposite directions.

The general echo cancellation technique also can be used to reduce the crosstalk noise level if information and signal processing can be shared between DSL transceivers connected to different pairs of telephone loops.

This chapter discusses issues related to the requirements of echo cancellation, implementation of baseband and asymmetrical echo cancellers, and the feasibility of crosstalk cancellation as follows:

- *Echo cancellation requirements*. The echo path model is analyzed for the determination of required echo cancellation level and the length of an echo canceller. This chapter discusses the effect of line coupling transformer primary inductance.

- *Echo canceller requirements*. Based on the *Least Means Square* (LMS) algorithm, required adaptation step sizes are derived for half-duplex and full-duplex echo cancellation operations. This chapter analyzes the echo canceller convergence behavior and explains how to derive echo canceller implementation precision requirements for the full-duplex adaptation condition.

- *Asymmetrical cancellation*. This chapter introduces the concept of asymmetrical echo cancellation and discusses alternatives for efficient asymmetrical echo canceller implementation.

- *Crosstalk cancellation*. This chapter illustrates how to derive the crosstalk transfer function model as well as discusses the benefit and the general architecture of multiple-input and multiple-output crosstalk noise cancellation.

9.1   Echo Cancellation Requirements

A hybrid circuit can provide only limited echo attenuation due to the uncertain twisted-pair loop impedance for a wide range of frequency band. Echo needs to be filtered out for the case of a frequency division duplex system, or digitally reduced for the case of an echo cancellation based system. Bandpass filters that reject echo can be put in serial with the echo path because the desired signal does not share the same spectrum as the echo.

Digital adaptive echo cancellers, on the other hand, need to be in parallel with the echo path. Figure 9.1 shows the general application of a digital adaptive echo canceller in conjunction with a hybrid circuit. An echo canceller synthesizes the echo path including the DAC, the transmit filter, the hybrid circuit, the receiver filter, and the ADC. An echo canceller can produce an echo replica with the same transmitting data, but with reversed sign to cancel the real echo.

Figure 9.1   Adaptive Echo Cancellation

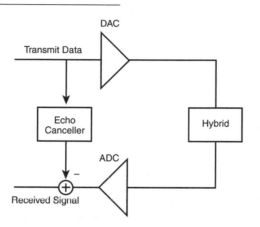

9.1.1   *Echo Path Transfer Function and Impulse Response*

Figure 9.2 shows the echo path transfer function for a twisted-pair loop with bridged taps. The varying echo attenuation values are caused by the variation of the loop input impedance that is related to bridged taps. The relatively low echo return loss at the low-frequency region is due to the higher impedance of the twisted-pair loop. The relatively low echo return loss at the high-frequency region is due to the leakage inductance of the transformer.

Figure 9.2   Echo Path Transfer Function

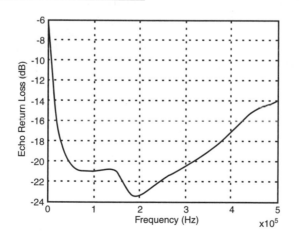

We define the echo return loss as the signal attenuation level of the echo path. The average echo return loss can be calculated as

$$K_{ep} = \frac{1}{f_c} \int_0^{f_c} |H_{ec}(f)|^2 \, df$$

$H_{ec}(f)$ is the transfer function of the echo path.

f_c is the corner frequency representing the bandwidth of interest.

The average echo return loss for this twisted-pair loop is 18.5 dB for $f_c = 500kHz$ with the worst echo return loss at only about 6 dB.

The echo return loss with a particular bandwidth constrained by transmit and receive filters could be slightly different compared with the echo return loss without these filters. We have

$$K_{ec} = \frac{1}{f_c} \int_0^{f_c} |G_t(f)H_{ec}(f)G_r(f)|^2 \, df$$

$G_t(f)$ is the frequency response of the transmit filter.

$G_r(f)$ is the frequency response of the receiver filter.

The average echo return loss for the same twisted-pair loop includes additional fourth order Butterworth transmit and receive filters with corner frequencies of 200 kHz and 17 dB.

Although echo path impulse responses are different, they generally consist of a rapidly changing initial portion and a slowly decaying tail portion, as shown in Figure 9.3. In general, the rapidly changing initial portion is due to reflections generated at terminal impedance mismatch and bridged tap locations, and the tail portion is mainly related to the primary inductance of the line transformer.

Figure 9.3   Echo Path Impulse Response

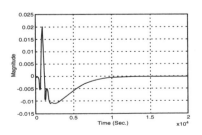

The reflections should die out in a relatively short period compared with the duration of the echo tail. Assuming they become negligible beyond the first round trip across the twisted-pair loop, reflections should not last more than the round trip delay of the longest twisted-pair loop. For an 18 kft, twisted-pair loop, the round trip delay is about 40 µs.

9.1.2 The Effect of Transformer and Bandpass Filtering

To see the effect of the primary inductance value on the echo tail, we can derive a simplified echo path model by using the RC network model (see Figure 9.4) in place of the loop impedance Z_i and the primary inductance L_{pri} alone in place of the line transformer equivalent circuit.

Figure 9.4 A Model Twisted-Pair Loop Impedance

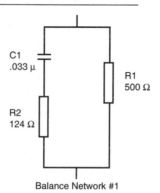

C1
.033 µ

R1
500 Ω

R2
124 Ω

Balance Network #1

For the resistor-only balance network, the simplified echo path model is

$$H(s)_{ec} = \frac{R_{12}}{Z_o + R_{12}} \frac{s(s+\omega_1)}{s^2 + 2\alpha + \omega_0^2} - \frac{1}{2}$$

for which

$$R_{12} = \frac{R_1 R_2}{R_1 + R_2}$$

$$\omega_1 = \frac{1}{R_2 C_1}$$

$$\omega_o^2 = \frac{1}{L_{pri}C_1} \frac{\dfrac{R_1 Z_0}{R_1 + Z_0}}{\dfrac{R_1 Z_0}{R_1 + Z_0} + R_2}$$

$$\alpha = \frac{1}{2}\left(\frac{1}{C_1\left(\dfrac{Z_o R_1}{Z_o + R_1} + R_2\right)} + \frac{Z_o R_1 R_2}{(R_1 R_2 + Z_o R_2 + Z_o R_1)L_{pri}} \right)$$

The simplified echo path is a typical overdamped RLC network with a resonant frequency of ω_o and a damping ratio of α.

Figure 9.5 shows that the duration of the echo tail is directly related to the primary inductance of the line transformer. We can use a line transformer with a low primary inductance to reduce the length of the echo tail, as long as we satisfy the transformer efficiency, linearity, and system bandwidth requirements.

Figure 9.5   A Baseband Echo Path Impulse Response Model

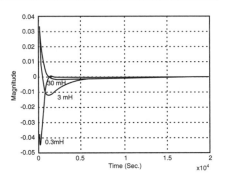

A passband system has a significantly shorter echo tail due to the avoidance of heavy, low-frequency phase and magnitude distortions. The effect of a passband signal on the echo tail is demonstrated by passing the echo path impulse response of the simplified model through a highpass filter with a corner frequency of 20 kHz, as shown in Figure 9.6.

Figure 9.6   A Passband Echo Path Impulse Response Model

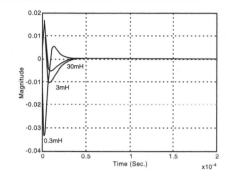

The echo tail disappears at around 100 μs. Similarly, a simple digital highpass filter of $H(z) = 1 - z^{-1}$ also can effectively shorten the echo tail.

Note
Attention also should be paid to the overall system low-frequency performance when using a highpass filter. In general, the removal of low-frequency energy will shorten the echo tail and ease implementation at the expense of some loss in overall system performance in a NEXT dominated environment.[1]

9.1.3 *Required Echo Cancellation Level and Length of Echo Canceller*

Assuming a white residual echo, the required echo cancellation level, K_{EC}, can be calculated according to

$$K_{EC} = SNR + K_{ch} - K_{ep}$$

The values are described as follows:

K_{ch} is the average channel loss.

K_{ep} is the average echo path loss.

SNR is the required average signal-to-residual noise floor ratio.

For the twisted-pair loop depicted in Figure 9.1, we have $K_{ep} = 17\,\text{dB}$ and $K_{ch} = 23\,\text{dB}$, and for an $SNR = 44\,\text{dB}$, the required echo cancellation level, K_{EC}, is about 60 dB. An SNR of 44 dB, here, corresponds to a noise floor of –40–23–44=–107 dBm/Hz, assuming a transmit signal power level of –40 dBm/Hz. With this required echo cancellation level, we can find the required echo cancellation time span through integration by setting the following:

$$K_{EC} = -10\log_{10}\left(\frac{\int_{t_s}^{\infty} h_{ec}^2(t)dt}{\int_{0}^{\infty} h_{ec}^2(t)dt}\right)$$

For an echo canceller size of 128 taps with an input/output rate of 400 kHz, we need to have a $t_s \leq 320$ μs.

For a self-NEXT dominant environment, where the NEXT noise level is much higher than the background noise or receiver front-end noise level, in conjunction with certain line code, the desired noise floor might not need to be that low. For using a baseband four-level line code, the desired SNR at the equalizer output is about 27.5 dB, including a performance margin of 6 dB for an error rate of 10^{-7}. For this case, a receiver front-end SNR of about 35 dB might be sufficient.

9.2 Echo Canceller Requirements

An adaptive echo canceller is a typical application of the digital adaptive FIR filter. Figure 9.7 shows the structure of a conventional FIR data driven echo canceller. Transmit data symbols, denoted by $x(k)$, are input to the adaptive filter. The output of this digital adaptive FIR filter is used as an echo replica to cancel the echo, denoted by $y(k)$, coming back from the hybrid circuit. The adaptation of filter coefficients is based on the error between the echo and its replica and the values of the data symbols.

9.2.1 Adaptation Step Size

Echo canceller filter coefficients (denoted by vector h_{ik}s) are estimated and updated iteratively according to the LMS algorithm[2]

$$H_{k+1} = H_k + \mu A_k \left(y(k) - H_k^T A_k \right)$$

for which

$$H_k = \begin{bmatrix} h_1 \\ h_2 \\ \dots \\ h_m \end{bmatrix}_2 \qquad A_k = \begin{bmatrix} a_k \\ a_{k-1} \\ \dots \\ a_{k-m+1} \end{bmatrix}$$

a_k is the current signal symbol, and $y(k)$ is the echo. To have a fast initial convergence, the echo canceller needs to be trained in half-duplex mode at startup. The optimal convergence step size under the half-duplex mode can be calculated as

$$\mu_{opt} \le \frac{1}{mE[a_k^2]} \mu_{opt} \le \frac{1}{(m+1)E[a_k^2]}$$

Figure 9.7   The Structure of an Echo Canceller

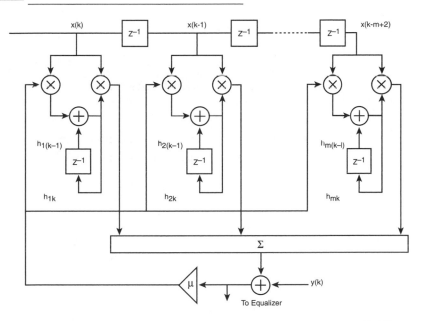

The value m is the number of filter coefficients. For $m = 128$ and $E[a_k^2] = 1$, we have $\mu_{opt} \le 0.007752$.

The convergence behavior of an echo canceller can be studied through its learning curve, which relates the mean square error to eigenvalues of the input data symbol autocorrelation matrix and the echo path impulse response. We have

$$\xi_k = \xi_{min} + \sum_{n=1}^{m} h_n^2 \lambda_n (1 - 2\mu\lambda_n)^{2k}$$

for which eigenvalues are obtained through

$$\det\left[E[A_k A_k^T] - \lambda I \right] = 0$$

For a normalized white data symbol, we have $E\left[A_k A_k^T\right] = I$.

The preceding expression becomes $(1-\lambda)^m = 0$.

An echo canceller has m equal eigenvalues. For the normalized data symbol case, all eigenvalues are equal to 1. For this equal eigenvalue case, the learning curve can be simplified as follows:

$$\xi_{k=}\xi_{\min} + (1-2\mu)^{2k}\sum_{n=1}^{m} h_n^2$$

Note
Because all eigenvalues are the same, it is possible to use the previous expression to accurately predict the real-time convergence behavior of data-driven echo cancellers.

Assuming $\xi_{\min}$ is negligible, we can estimate the number of iterations required to reach a certain echo cancellation level based on the simplified learning curve. We have

$$\frac{\xi_0}{\xi_k} = (1-2\mu)^{-2k}$$

For $\xi_0 / \xi_k = 10^6$, we have

$$k = -\frac{3}{\log_{10}(1-2\mu)}$$

It will take an echo canceller at least 688 iterations to converge to a −60 dB residual echo level for a step size of $\mu = 0.005$. The real attainable convergence time is usually two to three times the estimation for using an LMS algorithm.

The convergence step size, μ, should be significantly reduced during full-duplex operation to maintain a low level of residual echo while tracking echo path transfer function variations. The attainable echo cancellation ratio is[3]

$$K_{EC} \approx \frac{(2 - \mu_{full} m)K_{ch}}{\mu_{full} m}$$

K_{EC} and K_{ch} are expressed in power ratio. Therefore, we have

$$\mu_{full} \approx 2\frac{K_{ch}}{m\left(K_{EC} + K_{ch}\right)} = \frac{2}{m\left(1 + \dfrac{K_{EC}}{K_{ch}}\right)}$$

For $\dfrac{K_{EC}}{K_{ch}} = \dfrac{60}{23} = 37\,\text{dB}$ or 0.000199, we have $\mu_{full} = 0.0000031$ for $m=128$.

If the required K_{EC} is 50 dB, we have $\mu_{full} = 0.000031$ for the same m.

9.2.2 Echo Canceller Precision Requirements

There could be two precision requirements for echo canceller coefficients:

- Matching the FIR filter output quantization error to the available ADC precision

- Enabling the filter coefficient adaptation process when the step size is small during full-duplex operation

The first precision requirement applies to the half-duplex operation. For an ADC device of n bits, the quantization noise is uniformly distributed between $-\dfrac{1}{2^n}$ and $\dfrac{1}{2^n}$. To fully utilize the available bits of the ADC device, the echo replica from the echo canceller also will have n bits with the same or less quantization noise level. If the echo canceller has only one filter coefficient, the required coefficient precision is n bits.

For an echo canceller with more than one filter coefficient, the quantization noise will not be uniformly distributed, but approaches Gaussian as the number of coefficients increases. The filter output quantization noise is required to have the same or a smaller variance as that of an ADC device.

The variance for an ADC device of N bits is $\sigma^2_{A/D} = \dfrac{1}{3}\dfrac{1}{2^{2N}}$.

N is the A/D resolution, and the variance of the echo replica from an echo canceller of length m with a resolution of M bits for filter coefficients is $\sigma^2_{filter} = m\dfrac{1}{3}\dfrac{1}{2^{2M}}$.

By setting $\sigma^2_{A/D} = \sigma^2_{filter}$, we have $M = N + \dfrac{1}{2}\log_2 m$.

To make the echo canceller quantization noise equal to, or smaller than, that of an ADC, we need the following:

$$M \geq N + \frac{1}{2}\log_2 m$$

For a 12-bit A/D device, the precision required for a 128 filter coefficient echo canceller is 16 bits. The filter coefficient precision requirements are 17 bits and 18 bits for 13-bit and 14-bit A/D converters, respectively.

To update them adaptively usually requires a higher precision for filter coefficients when a small step size is required for the full-duplex operation. We need to have[4]

$$M \geq -\log_2\left(\mu_{full}10^{-\frac{K_{EC}}{20}}\right)$$

K_{EC} is expressed in units of dB. Therefore, to keep 60 dB of echo cancellation in full-duplex operation, we have

$$M \geq -\log_2\left(10^{-\frac{60}{20}}\right) - \log_2\left(\mu_{full}\right) = 9.66 + \log_2\frac{1}{\mu_{full}}$$

For $\mu_{full} = 0.0000031$, we have $M \geq 9.66 + \log_2\dfrac{1}{0.0000031} = 9.96 + 18.30 = 28.26$ bits.

For $\mu_{full} = 0.000031$, we have $M \geq 9.96 + \log_2\dfrac{1}{0.000031} = 9.96 + 14.98 = 24.94$ bits.

9.3 Asymmetrical Echo Cancellation

Transmission throughputs in opposite directions of a twisted-pair loop do not need to be equal. Under this asymmetrical throughput condition, transmit spectra and sampling rates in opposite directions might be very different. At the high-rate transmit and low-rate receive end of a system based on twisted-pair loops, echo is caused by the high-rate data and is digitized at the low sampling rate of the low-rate receiver. At the low-rate transmit and high-rate receive end, echo is caused by the low-rate data and is digitized by the high sampling rate.

Figure 9.8 shows the general transceiver structure and associated echo cancellation task for the cancellation of higher bandwidth echo.[5] This configuration is associated with the high-rate transmit end where the transmit baud rate is higher than the receive sampling rate. The echo canceller can operate at the high baud rate while having its output decimated to the low sampling rate; however, this requires a high speed echo canceller with many adaptive filter coefficients.

Figure 9.8   Higher Bandwidth Echo Cancellation

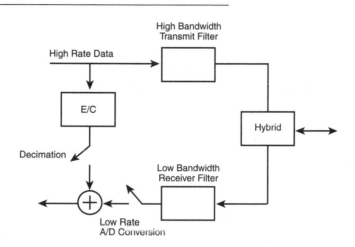

Figure 9.9 shows the general transceiver structure and associated echo cancellation task for the cancellation of lower bandwidth echo. This configuration is associated with the low bit rate transmit end where the transmit baud rate is much lower than the receive sampling rate. The echo canceller can operate at the high sampling rate while having its input interpolated from the low baud rate. The interpolation process can be accomplished by inserting zeros at sampling instances between low-rate sampling points, as well as other methods. However, this also requires a high-speed echo canceller with many adaptive filter coefficients.

Finding the minimum hardware configuration for this asymmetrical adaptive echo cancellation problem involves an understanding of the general topic of multirate signal processing.[6] Cancellation of higher bandwidth echo involves a *decimation* process. Cancellation of lower bandwidth echo involves an *interpolation* process.

For a conventional data-driven echo canceller for which the symbol rate is the same as the sampling rate, the echo path can be represented by a *discrete time domain* model with a delay interval the inverse of the symbol/sampling rate. Hence, a digital echo canceller with the same discrete time delay interval can be constructed, emulating the echo path, to generate an echo replica.

Figure 9.9 Lower Bandwidth Echo Cancellation

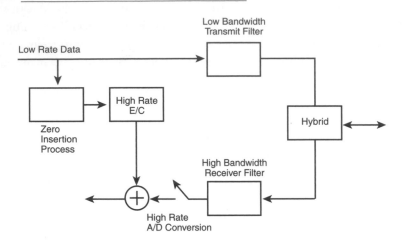

When the symbol rate and the sampling rate are different, the delay time interval of the discrete echo path model is the inverse of the higher rate among the symbol and sampling rates. This leads to a high processing speed echo canceller.

9.3.1 High Bandwidth Echo Cancellation

For the case of higher bandwidth echo cancellation, the effective symbol rate through the echo path can be reduced by using a high-order, lowpass filter before or after the receiver lowpass filter. A corresponding digital lowpass filter followed by a decimation process should be used to reduce the effective symbol rate to the digital echo canceller. Thus, a lower processing rate echo canceller can be utilized, as shown in Figure 9.10. This also will result in a much shorter echo canceller time span; however, the data input to the echo canceller is no longer a four-level signal, but of high precision.

Furthermore, the time domain spread of the transmit signal by the lowpass filter will cause an eigenvalue spread of the autocorrelation matrix associated with the adaptive echo canceller. This in turn will slow down the echo canceller initial convergence time.

Because there is always some leakage in the stopband of a practical lowpass filter, the processing rate of the adaptive echo canceller should be at least twice the sampling rate to have a better attenuation of the stopband signal while maintaining a smooth response on the passband signal. Leakage energy from both lowpass filters will appear as residual echo. Furthermore, leakage energy as noise will affect the adaptation process. When using the LMS algorithm, the adjustment step size should be accordingly reduced to minimize the excessive residual noise level.

Figure 9.10   Low-Rate, Higher-Bandwidth Echo Cancellation

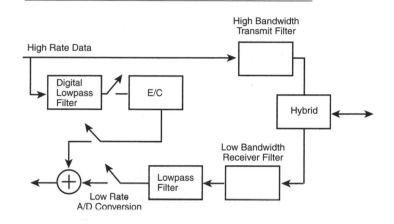

9.3.2   *Low Bandwidth Echo Cancellation*

For the case of lower bandwidth echo cancellation, the minimum sampling rate for the purpose of echo cancellation also can be reduced by using a high-order, lowpass filter before or after the transmit lowpass filter. Thus, a lower processing rate echo canceller would be sufficient to generate echo replica for the purpose of echo cancellation.

The corresponding high sampling rate echo replica is generated with an interpolation process with the same lowpass filter as used in the transmit path, as shown in Figure 9.11. This configuration will result also in a much shorter echo canceller time span. To provide some excessive bandwidth for the low throughput channel and to avoid an additional interpolation process, the stopband edge of the high-order, lowpass filter should be twice that of the –3dB bandwidth of the low throughput channel.

Under this configuration, the operation rate of the echo canceller can be reduced to twice that of the low sampling rate. We simply insert zeros between each of the low-rate transmit data samples to provide data input for the echo canceller. The error signal also will be sampled twice for every low-rate baud interval.

The interpolation lowpass filter will take the output of the echo canceller as its input with zeros filling these missing high sampling data points. Proper time delay should be considered to compensate delays caused by these high-order, lowpass filters. Because the data input to the echo canceller is still white, these echo canceller coefficients can be effectively identified by the LMS algorithm.

Figure 9.11 Lower-Rate, Lower-Bandwidth Echo Cancellation

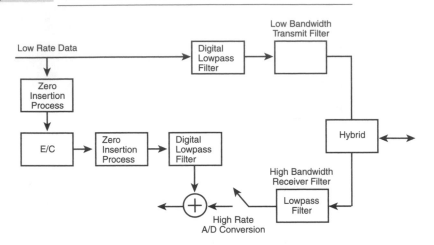

Asymmetrical echo cancellation can be applied to an asymmetrical throughput twisted-pair loop system to yield efficient all digital implementations. Asymmetrical echo cancellation with low processing rate echo cancellers is possible with proper higher-order, lowpass filtering. Additional decimation or interpolation processes are involved. While the hardware savings are very significant for cancellation of lower bandwidth echo with a low-rate echo canceller, additional cost on analog and digital lowpass filtering might be significant.

Modest hardware savings also can be realized for the cancellation of higher bandwidth echo with a low-rate echo canceller. However, the resulting initial convergence time might be slow, and the residual echo level might be high if the LMS algorithm is used.

9.4 Crosstalk Cancellation

Echo cancellation can be used to realize the full-duplex transmission in the same frequency bandwidth for opposite directions. The same adaptive signal processing technique can be used also to cancel the crosstalk to reduce the noise level, consequently improving the transmission throughput. The differences for crosstalk cancellation are the need for signal processing across different transceivers and the required signal processing power to handle such a multiple-input and multiple-output problem.

To cancel an interference, such as an echo, we need access to the original disturber signal, such as data symbols, to generate echo replica in conjunction with a simulated echo path. If we have access to data symbols generating crosstalk and we can identify and simulate the crosstalk transfer function, we can avoid the effect of crosstalk by performing crosstalk noise cancellation. The access of crosstalk-generating data symbols is possible given a cable with a small number of twisted pairs all sharing the same transceiver electronics.

9.4.1 Derivation of the Crosstalk Impulse Response

The crosstalk transfer function can be estimated by examining the fundamental mechanism of crosstalk. It has been shown that crosstalk is caused by the unbalance of coupling capacitances between twisted pairs, as depicted in Figure 9.12.[7] We can have four coupling capacitors between two pairs of twisted-pair loops at a particular location.

Figure 9.12 Crosstalk Caused by Coupling Capacitors

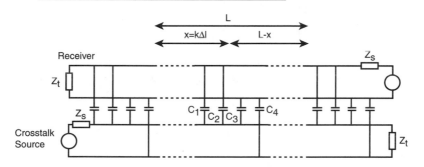

There are many such distributed coupling mechanisms along pairs of twisted pair loops. The overall coupling effects of crosstalk can be obtained by the summation of each individual coupling mechanism at all locations. The effect of an individual coupling mechanism can be examined by using the equivalent two-port network circuit, as shown in Figure 9.13. Transmission characteristics of each two-port network are described by its ABCD parameters.

Figure 9.13 A Two-Port Network Equivalent Circuit for Crosstalk

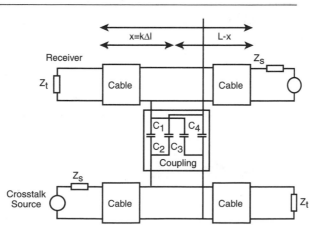

For the analysis of NEXT, the twisted-pair loop sections beyond the coupling point can be simplified to parallel impedances similar to bridged taps. The simplified two-port network circuit for the analysis of NEXT has two two-port networks representing two cable sections, including parallel twisted-pair loop impedances and one two-port network representing the capacitor coupling mechanism. The ABCD parameters for the crosstalk originating cable section are as follows:

$$
\begin{bmatrix} A_O & B_O \\ C_O & D_O \end{bmatrix} = \begin{bmatrix} A_N & B_N \\ C_N & D_N \end{bmatrix} \begin{bmatrix} 1 & 0 \\ \dfrac{1}{C_F Z_t + D_F} & 1 \\ A_F Z_t + B_F \end{bmatrix} = \begin{bmatrix} A_N + B_N \dfrac{C_F Z_t + D_F}{A_F Z_t + B_F} & B_N \\ C_N + D_N \dfrac{C_F Z_t + D_F}{A_F Z_t + B_F} & D_N \end{bmatrix}
$$

Subscript N denotes the near-end section of the cable and subscript F denotes the far end section of the cable in reference to the location of the crosstalk source and the receiver. The ABCD parameters for the crosstalk receiving cable section are defined as

$$
\begin{bmatrix} A_R & B_R \\ C_R & D_R \end{bmatrix} = \begin{bmatrix} 1 & 0 \\ \dfrac{1}{C_F Z_t + D_F} & 1 \\ A_F Z_t + B_F \end{bmatrix} \begin{bmatrix} A_N & B_N \\ C_N & D_N \end{bmatrix} = \begin{bmatrix} A_N & B_N \\ A_N \dfrac{C_F Z_t + D_F}{A_F Z_t + B_F} + C_N & B_N \dfrac{C_F Z_t + D_F}{A_F Z_t + B_F} + D_N \end{bmatrix}
$$

The ABCD parameters for the capacitor coupling mechanism can be developed by splitting these four coupling capacitors into two two-port networks in parallel, as depicted in Figure 9.14.

Figure 9.14 Equivalence of the Coupling Two-Port Network

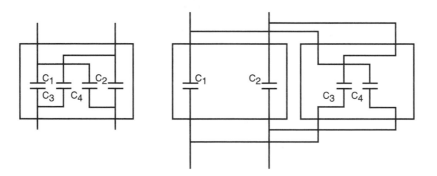

Then for network A at left (refer to Figure 9.14), we have

$$\begin{bmatrix} A_A & B_A \\ C_A & D_A \end{bmatrix} = \begin{bmatrix} 1 & \dfrac{1}{j\omega(C_1 + C_2)} \\ 0 & 1 \end{bmatrix}$$

And for network B at right (refer to Figure 9.14), we have

$$\begin{bmatrix} A_B & B_B \\ C_B & D_B \end{bmatrix} = -\begin{bmatrix} 1 & \dfrac{1}{j\omega(C_3 + C_4)} \\ 0 & 1 \end{bmatrix}$$

The ABCD parameters for the capacitor coupling mechanism are as follows:

$$\begin{bmatrix} A_C & B_C \\ C_C & D_C \end{bmatrix} = \begin{bmatrix} 1 & \dfrac{1}{j\omega(C_1 + C_2 - C_3 - C_4)} \\ 0 & 1 \end{bmatrix} = \begin{bmatrix} 1 & \dfrac{1}{j\omega C_{coup}} \\ 0 & 1 \end{bmatrix}$$

Therefore, the coupling mechanism can be further simplified to one capacitor with the possibility of having negative capacitance, as illustrated in Figure 9.15.

Figure 9.15 A Simplified Two-Port Network Circuit for Crosstalk

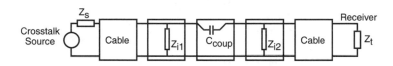

The ABCD parameters for the NEXT transfer function due to a particular value of C_{coup} at a particular location of $x = k\Delta l$ are

$$\begin{bmatrix} A_k & B_k \\ C_k & D_k \end{bmatrix} = \begin{bmatrix} A_O & B_O \\ C_O & D_O \end{bmatrix}\Bigg|_{x=k\Delta l} \begin{bmatrix} A_C & B_C \\ C_C & D_C \end{bmatrix}\begin{bmatrix} A_R & B_R \\ C_R & D_R \end{bmatrix}\Bigg|_{x=k\Delta l}$$

in which the twisted-pair loop has been divided into n sections of equal distance Δl. For a fixed length twisted-pair loop with no bridged taps, the crosstalk at a particular frequency is

$$H_{cross}(\omega_i) = \sum_{k=1}^{n} H_k(\omega_i) H_{cross}(\varpi_i) = \sum_{k=1}^{n} H_k(\varpi_i)$$

We have

$$H_k(\omega_i) = \frac{Z_t}{Z_s \big(C_k(\omega_i) Z_t + D_k(\omega_i) \big) + A_k(\omega_i) Z_t + B_k(\omega_i)}$$

$$H_k(\varpi_i) = \frac{Z_t}{Z_s \big(C_k(\varpi_i) Z_t + D_k(\varpi_i) \big) + A_k(\varpi_i) Z_t + B_k(\varpi_i)}$$

The transfer function of NEXT can be constructed by evaluating $H_{cross}(\omega_i) H_{cross}(\varpi_i)$ for an interested frequency band of $\omega_i \varpi_i$s. Figure 9.16 shows the estimated NEXT transfer function in conjunction with a 26-gauge, 9 kft twisted-pair loop with source and terminal impedances of 100 ohms using uniformly distributed random-coupling capacitances between −3 to 3 pF and $\Delta l = 9$ ft.

Figure 9.16 Estimated NEXT Transfer Function

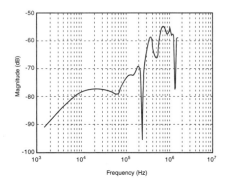

Figure 9.17 shows corresponding impulse response with and without two 200 kHz fourth order Butterworth transmit and receive filters. The impulse response is smoother with filters.

For the NEXT dominant case, in which the NEXT noise level is much higher than background noise, any reduction of NEXT noise level will improve the transmission performance in terms of a higher transmission throughput or a lower error rate. The background noise level can be 30 dB lower than the NEXT noise level. Under this assumption, a NEXT canceller with 30 dB of NEXT noise cancellation can suppress the effect of NEXT.

Figure 9.17   Estimated NEXT Impulse Response

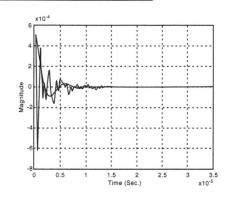

The time span of a NEXT impulse response lasts only about 20 μs. Because there is not much low-frequency content, the NEXT impulse response is relatively short. With a sampling rate of 400 kHz, the NEXT impulse response can be emulated with only 8 taps.

9.4.2   NEXT Cancellation Architecture

Figure 9.18 shows the general architecture of the application of NEXT cancellers for two pairs of two-pair transceivers; $n2$ NEXT cancellers are necessary for n transceiver pairs.

Figure 9.18   The Configuration of the NEXT Cancellation

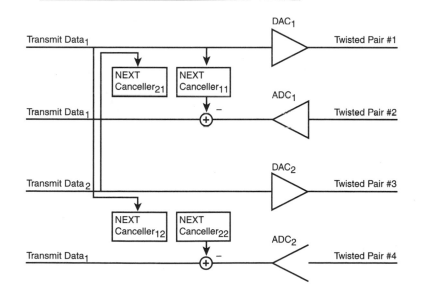

The NEXT cancellation requires multiple-input and multiple-output adaptive signal processing. Although the required signal processing is very extensive, it might become feasible depending on the development of semiconductor technology.

End Notes

1. W. Y. Chen, "Echo Cancellation for Passband and Passband Systems," *Bellcore T1E1 Contribution,* T1E1.4/90-181 (September 1990).

2. B. Widrow, *Adaptive Signal Processing* (Prentice-Hall, 1995).

3. K. H. Mueller, "A New, Fast-Converging Mean-Square Algorithm for Adaptive Equalizers with Partial Response Signaling," *B.S.T.J.,* vol. 54 (January 1975): 143–153.

4. R. D. Gitlin and S. B. Weinstein, "On the Required Tap-Weight Precision for Digitally Implemented, Adaptive, Mean-Squared Equalizers," *B.S.T.J.,* vol. 58, no. 2 (February 1979): 301–321.

5. W. Y. Chen, "Asymmetrical Echo Cancellation for a Baseband ADSL," *Bellcore T1E1 Contribution,* T1E1.4/92-156 (August 1992).

6. R. E. Crochiere and L. R. Rabiner, *Multirate Digital Signal Processing* (Prentice Hall, 1993).

7. "Dr. Campbell's Memoranda of 1907 and 1912," *Bell Systems Technical Journal,* vol. 14, no. 4 (October 1935): 552–572.

CHAPTER 10

Error Correction and Trellis Coding

The selection of a proper line code according to the transmission condition in conjunction with the use of an adaptive channel equalizer can maximize the transmission potential for a particular channel environment. Transmission error will occur, however, due to the random nature of the channel noise. Error correction coding can be used to reduce the transmission error rate by introducing certain transmission redundancy. The transmission redundancy can be allocated at either the bit level (such as the Reed-Solomon code) or embedded at the bit-to symbol conversion level (such as the Trellis coded modulation).

There are many methods for the allocation of bit-level redundancy. A simple and effective approach is parity checking. A simple parity check can be used to identify whether an error has occurred. With multiple applications of parity checking, a certain amount of errors can be automatically corrected. Depending on the size of the code, there could be many different ways of applying parity checking. With a few rules of guidance, efficient codes have been identified by computer searching.

Besides the coding efficiency, the simplicity of encoder and decoder implementation is also a very important concern. Reed-Solomon code has been used for ADSL as well as many other transmission systems for its coding efficiency and relative implementation simplicity.

For a bandwidth-limited transmission environment, the direct application of coding overhead at bit level might result in a negative coding gain because of the necessary signal level or constellation size increase to accommodate the additional transmission throughput. Under the bandwidth limited condition, the Trellis coded modulation has been very effective at providing a reasonably high coding gain depending on the code complexity.

For a Trellis code, the net signal-to-noise ratio decrease due to the increase of signal level or constellation size has been avoided by systematically interrelating possible occurrences of adjacent symbols. In other words, a random sequence of data is purposely encoded into allowed sequences of symbols. The correlation between adjacent symbols effectively improves the signal-to-noise ratio, therefore providing a coding gain.

This chapter reviews fundamental knowledge and design parameters of coding techniques related to DSL systems, including:

- *Parity check codes.* General concepts of parity check and error syndrome for transmission error identification and correction are discussed. Corresponding matrix representation and manipulation are introduced with calculation examples. Galois field-based polynomial representation also is introduced. Algebra manipulation of the polynomial representation is discussed with numerical examples.

- *Reed-Solomon codes.* The Reed-Solomon code is introduced as a non-binary BCH code. The generation polynomial of the Reed-Solomon code is discussed with numerical examples. Possible Reed-Solomon encoder and decoder implementations are discussed. The use of the Reed-Solomon code for the application of ADSL is discussed with reference to some simulation results.

- *Convolution codes.* The general structure of a convolution encode is introduced, and its generation matrix is defined. Concepts of transition, tree, and Trellis diagrams are discussed. The Viterbi decoder in conjunction with the convolution code is described with numerical examples for both hard and soft decision devices.

- *Trellis code modulation.* The rationale for using Trellis coded modulation for bandwidth-limited transmission systems is explored. Trellis codes and corresponding signal level and constellation mappings are discussed for baseband and passband line codes, respectively.

Both feedforward and feedback implementation of Trellis codes are described with examples. The analytical representation is also discussed with a numerical example. Examples of linear and non-linear phase invariant Trellis codes for passband line codes are listed.

10.1 Parity Check Codes

When transmitting a binary sequence, the received sequence might be a little different than the original sequence due to the channel uncertainty caused by additive noise and so forth. We cannot tell from the received sequence itself if it is correct unless some redundancy is involved. We can repeat the transmission of the same sequence and compare sequences from each repetition to decide if the received sequence is correct and/or what the correct value should be based on a majority decision if the repetition occurs more than twice.

To check for just the possible occurrence of errors, we also can count the number of 1s or 0s in the sequence, and use a parity check bit to indicate whether it is an even or odd number.[1,2] We then send this check bit along with the original sequence. At the receiver side, a new parity bit is generated according to the received sequence and compared with the received one to decide whether an error or errors have occurred.

To increase the reliability of error-checking, we can divide the sequence into a number of exclusive groups and put a parity check bit for each group. The number of bits in each group can be as small as two. Furthermore, we can define redundant groups—a bit can belong to a number of different groups. Through this redundancy, not only can errors be detected through the parity check bits, but they also can be corrected by cross examining different groups to which these bits belong.

For a binary sequence, the parity checking can be performed through the exclusive-or operation. By denoting $\oplus$ for the exclusive-or operation, the results between two binary digits are as follows:

$$0 \oplus 0 = 0$$
$$0 \oplus 1 = 1$$
$$1 \oplus 0 = 1$$
$$1 \oplus 1 = 0$$

We can, for example, send a sequence of two information bits together with a parity check bit. The receiver will generate its own parity bit and compare it with the received one to detect an error in the received information bits. This is called a $\left(N, k, d_{min}^{H} \right)$ parity check code. All possible combinations of information bits and associated parity check bits are called as code words. For this example, we have

- The code word dimension, the length of code words, of $N=3$;

- The information bit sequence of dimension, the length of information sequence, $k=2$;

- The shortest Hamming distance, the minimum distance or the number of different bits between code words, of $d_{min}^{H} = 2$;

- The code rate, the ratio of information bit sequence dimension over code word dimension, is $R_{c} = \dfrac{k}{N} = \dfrac{2}{3}$. This code can be used for error detection, but not error correction.

Code words for this example are (000), (011), (101), and (110). In general,

$$t = \left[\frac{d_{min}^{H} - 1}{2} \right] \text{ errors}$$

can be corrected for a code of d_{min}^{H}.

10.1.1 *Achieving Error Correction*

To achieve error correction, we can combine two of the code words for this example with more parity check bits. For every two (3,2,2) code words, we generate three more parity bits based on three two-bit groups across these two code words. For two original code words,

$$\left(i_1, i_2, p_1 \right) \text{and} \left(i_3, i_4, p_2 \right)$$

in which

$$p_1 = i_1 \oplus i_2 \text{ and } p_2 = i_3 \oplus i_4$$

we have the new code word

$$\left(i_1, i_2, p_1, i_3, i_4, p_2, p_3, p_4, p_5 \right)$$

in which

$$p_3 = i_1 \oplus i_3$$
$$p_4 = i_2 \oplus i_4$$
$$p_5 = p_3 \oplus p_4$$

This combination is a (9, 4, 4) parity check code and has a code rate of 4/9. This code can be used to detect one error: (4−1)/2. The position of an error can be identified by cross two-parity check bits that indicate errors.

In general, the position of errors can be identified using a syndrome vector. The elements of the syndrome vector are the parity check of these parity bits and their corresponding information bits. For example, given a (6,3,3) code, we have

$$p_1 = i_1 \oplus i_2$$
$$p_2 = i_2 \oplus i_3$$
$$p_3 = i_1 \oplus i_3$$

For a syndrome vector $s = (s_1, s_2, s_3)$, we have

$$s_1 = i_1 \oplus i_2 \oplus p_1$$
$$s_2 = i_2 \oplus i_3 \oplus p_2$$
$$s_3 = i_1 \oplus i_3 \oplus p_3$$

A look up table can be constructed to relate the value of the syndrome vector to a particular error pattern. The look up table can be implemented in either a memory or logic-based circuit.

A code vector also can be described in the following matrix format. A code vector, c, is a product of the message vector, m, and the generator matrix, G. We have $c = mG$. For a systematic code, where the first k components of any code vector are the components of message vector, m, the generator matrix can be further divided as follows:

$$G - \begin{bmatrix} I_k & P \end{bmatrix}$$

I_k is the $k \times k$ dimensional identity matrix and P is the $k \times r$ dimensional parity check array in which $r = N - k$. For the (3,2,2) parity check code example, we have the following:

$$G = \begin{bmatrix} 1 & 0 & 1 \\ 0 & 1 & 1 \end{bmatrix}$$

These code words are expressed as the following:

$$\begin{bmatrix} 0 & 0 \end{bmatrix} \begin{bmatrix} 1 & 0 & 1 \\ 0 & 1 & 1 \end{bmatrix} = \begin{bmatrix} 0 & 0 & 0 \end{bmatrix}$$

$$\begin{bmatrix} 0 & 1 \end{bmatrix} \begin{bmatrix} 1 & 0 & 1 \\ 0 & 1 & 1 \end{bmatrix} = \begin{bmatrix} 0 & 1 & 1 \end{bmatrix}$$

$$\begin{bmatrix} 1 & 0 \end{bmatrix} \begin{bmatrix} 1 & 0 & 1 \\ 0 & 1 & 1 \end{bmatrix} = \begin{bmatrix} 1 & 0 & 1 \end{bmatrix}$$

$$\begin{bmatrix} 1 & 1 \end{bmatrix} \begin{bmatrix} 1 & 0 & 1 \\ 0 & 1 & 1 \end{bmatrix} = \begin{bmatrix} 1 & 1 & 0 \end{bmatrix}$$

The addition of matrix elements also is performed with exclusive-or.

For the (6,3,3) parity check code example, we have the following:

$$G = \begin{bmatrix} 1 & 0 & 0 & 1 & 0 & 1 \\ 0 & 1 & 0 & 1 & 1 & 0 \\ 0 & 0 & 1 & 0 & 1 & 1 \end{bmatrix}$$

These code words are expressed as

$$\begin{bmatrix} 0 & 0 & 0 \end{bmatrix} \begin{bmatrix} 1 & 0 & 0 & 1 & 0 & 1 \\ 0 & 1 & 0 & 1 & 1 & 0 \\ 0 & 0 & 1 & 0 & 1 & 1 \end{bmatrix} = \begin{bmatrix} 0 & 0 & 0 & 0 & 0 & 0 \end{bmatrix}$$

$$\begin{bmatrix} 0 & 0 & 1 \end{bmatrix} \begin{bmatrix} 1 & 0 & 0 & 1 & 0 & 1 \\ 0 & 1 & 0 & 1 & 1 & 0 \\ 0 & 0 & 1 & 0 & 1 & 1 \end{bmatrix} = \begin{bmatrix} 0 & 0 & 1 & 0 & 1 & 1 \end{bmatrix}$$

$$\begin{bmatrix} 0 & 1 & 0 \end{bmatrix} \begin{bmatrix} 1 & 0 & 0 & 1 & 0 & 1 \\ 0 & 1 & 0 & 1 & 1 & 0 \\ 0 & 0 & 1 & 0 & 1 & 1 \end{bmatrix} = \begin{bmatrix} 0 & 1 & 0 & 1 & 1 & 0 \end{bmatrix}$$

$$\begin{bmatrix} 0 & 1 & 1 \end{bmatrix} \begin{bmatrix} 1 & 0 & 0 & 1 & 0 & 1 \\ 0 & 1 & 0 & 1 & 1 & 0 \\ 0 & 0 & 1 & 0 & 1 & 1 \end{bmatrix} = \begin{bmatrix} 0 & 1 & 1 & 1 & 0 & 1 \end{bmatrix}$$

$$\begin{bmatrix} 1 & 0 & 0 \end{bmatrix} \begin{bmatrix} 1 & 0 & 0 & 1 & 0 & 1 \\ 0 & 1 & 0 & 1 & 1 & 0 \\ 0 & 0 & 1 & 0 & 1 & 1 \end{bmatrix} = \begin{bmatrix} 1 & 0 & 0 & 1 & 0 & 1 \end{bmatrix}$$

$$\begin{bmatrix} 1 & 0 & 1 \end{bmatrix} \begin{bmatrix} 1 & 0 & 0 & 1 & 0 & 1 \\ 0 & 1 & 0 & 1 & 1 & 0 \\ 0 & 0 & 1 & 0 & 1 & 1 \end{bmatrix} = \begin{bmatrix} 1 & 0 & 1 & 1 & 1 & 0 \end{bmatrix}$$

$$\begin{bmatrix} 1 & 1 & 0 \end{bmatrix} \begin{bmatrix} 1 & 0 & 0 & 1 & 0 & 1 \\ 0 & 1 & 0 & 1 & 1 & 0 \\ 0 & 0 & 1 & 0 & 1 & 1 \end{bmatrix} = \begin{bmatrix} 1 & 1 & 0 & 0 & 1 & 1 \end{bmatrix}$$

$$\begin{bmatrix} 1 & 1 & 1 \end{bmatrix} \begin{bmatrix} 1 & 0 & 0 & 1 & 0 & 1 \\ 0 & 1 & 0 & 1 & 1 & 0 \\ 0 & 0 & 1 & 0 & 1 & 1 \end{bmatrix} = \begin{bmatrix} 1 & 1 & 1 & 0 & 0 & 0 \end{bmatrix}$$

A syndrome vector also can be described in the following matrix format. A syndrome vector, s, is a product of the received code vector, y, and the parity check matrix, H. We have $s = yH^T$. Also for a systematic code, the parity check matrix can be further divided as follows:

$$H = \begin{bmatrix} P^T & I_r \end{bmatrix}$$

I_r is the $r \times r$ dimensional identity matrix, and P is the same $k \times r$ dimensional parity check array. For the (3,2,2) parity check code example, we have $H=[1\ 1\ 1]$. For the (6,3,3) parity check example, we have the following:

$$H = \begin{bmatrix} 1 & 1 & 0 & 1 & 0 & 0 \\ 0 & 1 & 1 & 0 & 1 & 0 \\ 1 & 0 & 1 & 0 & 0 & 1 \end{bmatrix}$$

$$G = \begin{bmatrix} 1 & 0 & 0 & 1 & 0 & 1 \\ 0 & 1 & 0 & 1 & 1 & 0 \\ 0 & 0 & 1 & 0 & 1 & 1 \end{bmatrix}$$

We always have the orthogonal property of

$$GH^T = \begin{bmatrix} 1 & 0 & 1 \\ 0 & 1 & 1 \end{bmatrix} \begin{bmatrix} 1 \\ 1 \\ 1 \end{bmatrix} = 0$$

If the received code vector has no error (that is, $y=c$), we have

$$s = cH^T = mGH^T = 0$$

If it contains errors, we represent the received code vector as the sum of code vector and the error vector. We have

$$s = yH^T = (c+e)H^T = cH^T + eH^T = eH^T$$

The dimension of s is r, while the dimension of e is $k+r$ There are 2^k error vectors, es, satisfying above r linear equations. For a Binary Symmetrical Channel, we choose the one that has the minimum non-zero digits as the error vector, e, so that the vector corresponds to the least number of errors, and the probability of receiving a sequence with the least number of errors is higher than the probability of receiving a sequence with more errors. For the (6,3,3) parity check code example, we let

$$y = \begin{bmatrix} 1 & 1 & 1 & 0 & 0 & 1 \end{bmatrix}$$

We have the syndrome

$$s = yH^T = \begin{bmatrix} 1 & 1 & 1 & 0 & 0 & 1 \end{bmatrix} \begin{bmatrix} 1 & 0 & 1 \\ 1 & 1 & 0 \\ 0 & 1 & 1 \\ 1 & 0 & 0 \\ 0 & 1 & 0 \\ 0 & 0 & 1 \end{bmatrix} = \begin{bmatrix} 0 & 0 & 1 \end{bmatrix}$$

We have following $2^3 = 8$ error vectors, es, satisfying $s = eH^T = \begin{bmatrix} 0 & 0 & 1 \end{bmatrix}$:

$\begin{bmatrix} 0 & 0 & 0 & 0 & 0 & 1 \end{bmatrix}$

$\begin{bmatrix} 0 & 0 & 1 & 0 & 1 & 0 \end{bmatrix}$

$\begin{bmatrix} 0 & 1 & 0 & 1 & 1 & 1 \end{bmatrix}$

$\begin{bmatrix} 0 & 1 & 1 & 1 & 0 & 0 \end{bmatrix}$

$\begin{bmatrix} 1 & 0 & 0 & 1 & 0 & 0 \end{bmatrix}$

$\begin{bmatrix} 1 & 0 & 1 & 1 & 1 & 1 \end{bmatrix}$

$\begin{bmatrix} 1 & 1 & 0 & 0 & 1 & 0 \end{bmatrix}$

$\begin{bmatrix} 1 & 1 & 1 & 0 & 0 & 1 \end{bmatrix}$

We choose $\begin{bmatrix} 0 & 0 & 0 & 0 & 0 & 1 \end{bmatrix}$ as the error vector because it has only one non-zero digit. The corresponding code vector is $\begin{bmatrix} 1 & 1 & 1 & 0 & 0 & 0 \end{bmatrix}$.

10.1.2   Cyclic Codes

An important subclass of a linear code is called a cyclic code, in which every cyclic shift of a code vector is also a code vector. The encoding and syndrome computation of cyclic codes can be implemented with shift registers, and the decoding can be handled effectively with its algebraic structure. We can treat components of a message or a code vector

$$m = \begin{bmatrix} i_1 & i_2 & \cdots & i_k \end{bmatrix}$$

as coefficients of a polynomial, as follows:

$$m(x) = i_1 + i_2 x + \ldots + i_k x^{k-1}$$

Code polynomials, corresponding to code vectors, can be generated as products of message polynomials and a generator polynomial. Table 10.1 shows a (6,3,3) cyclic code that is generated with three-bit message polynomials and a generator polynomial, $1 + x^3$.

Table 10.1 A (6,3,3) Cyclic Code

Messages	Code Vectors	Code Polynomial
$[0 \ 0 \ 0]$	$[0 \ 0 \ 0 \ 0 \ 0 \ 0]$	$0(1 + x^3) = 0$
$[0 \ 0 \ 1]$	$[0 \ 0 \ 1 \ 0 \ 0 \ 1]$	$x^2(1 + x^3) = x^2 + x^5$
$[0 \ 1 \ 0]$	$[0 \ 1 \ 0 \ 0 \ 1 \ 0]$	$x(1 + x^3) = x + x^4$
$[0 \ 1 \ 1]$	$[0 \ 1 \ 1 \ 0 \ 1 \ 1]$	$(x + x^2)(1 + x^3) = x + x^2 + x^4 + x^5$
$[1 \ 0 \ 0]$	$[1 \ 0 \ 0 \ 1 \ 0 \ 0]$	$1(1 + x^3) = 1 + x^3$
$[1 \ 0 \ 1]$	$[1 \ 0 \ 1 \ 1 \ 0 \ 1]$	$(1 + x^2)(1 + x^3) = 1 + x^2 + x^3 + x^5$
$[1 \ 1 \ 0]$	$[1 \ 1 \ 0 \ 1 \ 1 \ 0]$	$(1 + x)(1 + x^3) = 1 + x + x^3 + x^4$
$[1 \ 1 \ 1]$	$[1 \ 1 \ 1 \ 1 \ 1 \ 1]$	$(1 + x + x^2)(1 + x^3) = 1 + x + x^2 + x^3 + x^4 + x^5$

10.1.3 Galois Field Arithmetic

In dealing with these vector and polynomial manipulations, we have used some algebraic properties of a binary *Galois field, GF(2)*. In general, for a sequence of length m with q values for each bit, there could be q^m different vectors. For q a prime number, we can have a field ranging from 0 to $q-1$ different elements (values). We sometimes call this a Galois field of q elements—GF(q).

Elements of the field can be manipulated through addition and multiplication operations; however, because we are dealing with a finite field, these operations are defined in a modular sense. The binary exclusive-or operation is actually a modular addition in GF(2). For an example of GF(3), we have the following for addition and multiplication:

Addition	Multiplication
$0 + 0 = 0$	$0 \times 0 = 0$
$0 + 1 = 1$	$0 \times 1 = 1$
$0 + 2 = 2$	$0 \times 2 = 2$

$$1+0=1 \qquad 1\times 0 = 0$$
$$1+1=2 \qquad 1\times 1 = 1$$
$$1+2=0 \qquad 1\times 2 = 2$$
$$2+0=2 \qquad 2\times 0 = 0$$
$$2+1=0 \qquad 2+1 = 2$$
$$2+2=1 \qquad 2\times 2 = 1$$

10.1.4 *Extended Galois Field Arithmetic*

It is sometimes more convenient to consider binary information sequences and corresponding parity check bits in 2^m base as those we often used for binary representation of octal or hexadecimal numbers in computer and electronics circuits. We call GF(2^m) an extension field of the binary Galois field, GF(2). Similar to the binary representation of octal numbers, any element in GF(2^3) can be represented by a sequence of three binary digits, a_0, a_1, and a_2, for example. These are coefficients of a base 2 polynomial. We have the following:

$$b = a + a\times 2 + a\times 2^2 = 1+0\times 2+1\times 2^2 = 5$$

The corresponding binary representation is (1 0 1). The presentation can be dramatically simplified for long binary information sequences. For an example of a binary information sequence of 128 bits, we need only a binary sequence of seven bits for presentation. In other words, the same information of a 128-bit binary sequence can be represented using seven bits based on a base 2 polynomial notation.

The modular addition between elements of a $GF(2^m)$ is defined as the binary modular coefficient addition of the same power. The following is an example:

$$(1 \quad 0 \quad 1)+(1 \quad 1 \quad 0)=\left(1+0\times 2+1\times 2^2\right)+\left(1+1\times 2+0\times 2^2\right)=\left(0+1\times 2+1\times 2^2\right)=(0 \quad 1 \quad 1)$$

The modular multiplication between elements of a $GF(2^m)$ is defined as element-to-element modular multiplication of two polynomials. Each element-to-element modular multiplication is carried out by the summation of powers of multiplicands. We need to associate each element with a power representation to carry out the multiplication (see Table 10.2).

Table 10.2 Power Representation for the Elements of GF(2^3)

Power	Polynomial	Binary
0	0	(0 0 0)
1	1	(1 0 0)
α	α	(0 1 0)
α^2	α^2	(0 0 1)
α^3	$1+\alpha$	(1 1 0)
α^4	$\alpha+\alpha^2$	(0 1 1)
α^5	$1+\alpha+\alpha^2$	(1 1 1)
α^6	$1+\alpha^2$	(1 0 1)

For this example, we can still associate α with 2^1 and α^2 with 2^2, but not α^i to 2^i for $i > 2$. In fact, α^3 is calculated based on the primitive polynomial for *m=3*. A primitive polynomial of *m*, $p(X)$, divides $X^n + 1$ for $n = 2^m - 1$. The primitive polynomial for *m=3* is

$$p(X) = 1 + X + X^3$$

By setting $p(\alpha) = 1 + \alpha + \alpha^3 = 0$, we can obtain a representation of α^3 in terms of α. We have

$$1 + \alpha + \alpha^3 + 1 + \alpha = 1 + \alpha$$
$$\alpha^3 = 1 + \alpha$$

According to Table 10.2, we have

$$\left(1+\alpha^2\right)\left(1+\alpha\right) = 1 + \alpha + \alpha^2 + \alpha^3 = 1 + \alpha + \alpha^2 + 1 + \alpha = \alpha^2$$

Division between two polynomials is better handled by their power presentation, for example

$$\frac{1+\alpha^2}{1+\alpha} = \frac{\alpha^6}{\alpha^3} = \alpha^3 = 1+\alpha$$

With these defined operations between polynomials, the encoding and decoding can be reduced to algebra operations and solving for the solution of a set of linear equations.

Table 10.3 lists primitive polynomials for the construction of power representations for $m=4, 5, 6, 7$, and 8.

Table 10.3   Primitive Polynomials

m	Primitive Polynomial
4	$1 + X + X^4$
5	$1 + X^2 + X^5$
6	$1 + X + X^6$
7	$1 + X^3 + X^7$
8	$1 + X^2 + X^3 + X^4 + X^8$

10.2   *Reed-Solomon Codes*

Reed-Solomon[3] codes are non-binary Bose, Chaudhuri, and Hocquenghem (BCH) codes. Bose, Chaudhuri, and Hocquenghem published two papers defining basic properties of the BCH cyclic code.[4,5] A code word can be generated by multiplying a message polynomial by a generator polynomial. The specification of the generator polynomial for BCH codes is relatively simple. A BCH code can be designed on the desired code size and code distance.

The generator polynomial of a t-error-correcting BCH code of length $2^m - 1$ can be found through the least common multiple of minimum polynomials of roots α^i, for $1 \le i \le 2t$, where α^i s are elements of GF(2^m). A minimal polynomial of α^i has the smallest degree of a polynomial whose coefficient is in GF(2). Minimal polynomials for α, α^3, and α^5 are $1 + X + X^4$, $1 + X + X^2 + X^3 + X^4$, and $1 + X + X^2$, respectively.

The generator polynomial for the two-error-correcting BCH code of length $n = 2^4 - 1 = 15$ is

$$g(x) = \left(1 + X + X^4\right)\left(1 + X + X^2 + X^3 + X^4\right) = 1 + X^4 + X^6 + X^7 + X^8$$

The generator polynomial for the three-error-correcting BCH code, also of length $n = 2^4 - 1 = 15$, is

$$g(x) = (1 + X + X^4)(1 + X + X^2 + X^3 + X^4)(1 + X + X^2) = 1 + X + X^2 + X^4 + X^5 + X^8 + X^{10}$$

Reed-Solomon codes are used to encode symbols consisting of m binary digits into blocks consisting of $n_s = 2^m - 1$ symbols (or $n_b = m(2^m - 1)$ binary digits). For $m=8$ $m=8$, the symbol block size is $n_s = 255$ and the total number of bits in each block is $n_b = 8 \times 255 = 2040$. For Reed-Solomon codes, the degree of generator polynomial is $r=n-k$ $r=n-k$ and the code word minimum distance is $d_{min} = r+1$, where n is the code word size and k is the message sequence size. The number of errors that can be corrected is defined by

$$t = \frac{d-1}{2} = \frac{r}{2}$$

Shorter than n_s or n_b Reed-Solomon codes can be derived also by using only a subset of the full size code. We can pre-define the last portion of the message as 0s. Therefore, these 0s can be automatically added at the receiver end without transmission of a full size code word. In other words, the code word size becomes $n' = n - k_z$ when the message size is $k - k_z$ by specifying k_z zeros at the end of the message. These k_z zeros need not be included in code words.

10.2.1 Generating Reed-Solomon Code Words

Reed-Solomon code words can be generated based on message sequences—$m(x)$, using generator polynomials—$g(x)$. In general, the generator polynomial of a BCH code is the lowest common multiple of minimum polynomials. For a Reed-Solomon code, the minimum polynomials of elements, α^is, of GF(2^m) all have the degree of 1. The Reed-Solomon generator polynomial has the following form:

$$g(x) = (x - \alpha)(x - \alpha^2)(x - \alpha^3)...(x - \alpha^{d-1})$$

For an example of a binary representation with $d = 3$ in GF(4), we have

$$g(x) = (x - \alpha)(x - \alpha^2) = x^2 - (a + \alpha^2)x + \alpha^3 = x^2 + x + 1$$

for

$$-(\alpha + \alpha^2) = \alpha + \alpha^2 = \alpha(1 + \alpha) = \alpha\alpha^2 = \alpha^3 = 1 \text{ (see Table 10.4)}$$

because we always have $\alpha^{2^m - 1} = 1$ for $GF(2^m)$.

Table 10.4 Power Representation

Power	Polynomial	Binary
0	0	$(0 \quad 0)$
1	1	$(1 \quad 0)$
α	α	$(0 \quad 1)$
α^2	$1+\alpha$	$(1 \quad 1)$

For another example of a byte-based Reed-Solomon code with $d=3$ in GF(2^8), we have the following:

$$g(x) = (x - \beta)(x - \beta^2) = x^2 + (\beta + \beta^2)x + \beta^3 = x^2 + (\alpha^7 + \alpha^{14})x + \alpha^{21} = x^2 + \alpha^{119}x + \alpha^{21}$$

$\beta = \alpha^7$ and $\alpha^7 + \alpha^{14} = \alpha^{119}$ according to the GF(256) power representation in Table 10.4.

In practice, a systematic form cyclic code, including the Reed-Solomon code, $c(x)$, is generated in three steps:

1. Pre-multiply the message $m(x)$ by x^d.

2. Obtain the remainder, $r(x)$, by dividing $x^d m(x)$ by the generator polynomial $g(x)$.

3. Combine $r(x)$ and $x^d m(x)$.

We have

$$c(x) = r(x) + x^d m(x) = \text{Re } m\left[x^d m(x)/g(x)\right] + x^d m(x)$$

It is interesting to note that the code-generating method of

$$c(x) = \text{Re } m\left[x^d m(x)/g(x)\right] + x^d m(x)$$

is not the same as multiplying the message polynomial with the generator polynomial, $m(x)g(x)$. For an example of $m(x) = 1 + x + x^2$ and $g(x) = 1 + x + x^3$ in GF(2^4) with $d = 3$, we have

$$m(x)g(x) = (1 + x + x^2)(1 + x + x^3) = 1 + x + x^3 + x + x^2 + x^4 + x^2 + x^3 + x^5 = 1 + x^4 + x^5$$

and

$$\mathrm{Rem}\left[\frac{x^3+x^4+x^5}{1+x+x^3}\right]+x^3+x^4+x^5=\mathrm{Rem}\left[x^2+x+\frac{x}{1+x+x^3}\right]+x^3+x^4+x^5=x+x^3+x^4+x^5$$

10.2.2 *Reed-Solomon Encoder Implementation*

The encoder circuit for the code-generating method

$$c(x)=\mathrm{Re}\ m\left[x^d m(x)/g(x)\right]+x^d m(x)$$

can be conveniently implemented with a division circuit using shift registers, adders, and multipliers, as shown in Figure 10.1. The division circuits can be implemented in any number of bits or bytes, for example.

Figure 10.1 A Systematic Reed-Solomon Encoder

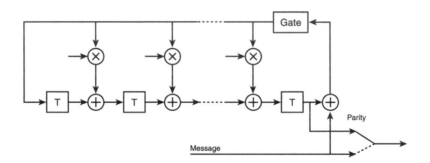

The encoding process is as follows:

1. With the gate turned on, the *k* information bytes are shifted into the circuit and simultaneously into the communications channel. Shifting the message *m(x)* into the circuit from the front is equivalent to pre-multiplying *m(x)* by x^d.

2. As soon as the complete message has entered the circuit, the *n-k* bytes in the register form the remainder and are thus the parity check bytes. The gate is then blocked.

3. The parity check bytes are shifted out to the channel.

10.2.3 *Decoding of Reed-Solomon Code*

The decoding of cyclic codes consists of three steps:

1. Syndrome computation

2. Association of the syndrome to an error pattern

3. Error correction

The syndrome computation for cyclic codes can be accomplished with a division circuit whose complexity is linearly proportional to the number of parity check digits.

The association of the syndrome to an error pattern can be completely specified by a decoding table. A straightforward approach to the design of a decoding circuit is via a combinational logic circuit that implements the table-lookup procedure. The limit to this approach, however, is that the complexity of the decoding circuit tends to grow exponentially with the code length and the number of errors that we intend to correct.

The error correction step for the binary code case is simply adding (modulo-2) the error pattern to the receiver vector. For the Reed-Solomon code, we need the additional calculation of error values.

Syndrome Computation

The first step of decoding the syndrome computation, corresponding to the previously described encoder circuit, can be accomplished with another division circuit, but with the received polynomial as the input, as shown in Figure 10.2.

Figure 10.2 A Syndrome Computation Circuit

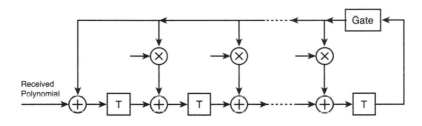

The received polynomial is shifted into the register with all stages initially set to 0. As soon as the entire received polynomial is shifted into the register, the contents in the register form the syndrome.

The syndrome computation can be obtained also by substituting the field elements α, $\alpha^2, \ldots \alpha^d$ into the received polynomial $v(x)=c(x)+e(x)$. For software implementation, substituting α^i into $v(x)$ is best accomplished in the following manner:

$$S_i = v(\alpha^i) = v_{n-1}(\alpha^i)^{n-1} + v_{n-2}(\alpha^i)^{n-2} + \ldots + v_1\alpha^i + v_0$$

$$= \left(\ldots\left((v_{n-1}\alpha^i + v_{n-2})\alpha^i + v_{n-3}\right)\alpha^i + \ldots + v_1\right)\alpha^i + v_0$$

The value n is the code word size. This computation takes $n–1$ addition and $n–1$ multiplication. It requires about $d(n–1)$ additions and nd multiplication to calculate all syndrome components, in which d is the minimum distance and equals the size of the parity check plus 1.

Syndrome/Error Pattern Association

In the second step of decoding, the error-location polynomial, $\sigma(x)$, is defined. We can rewrite the components of syndrome as

$$S_1 = \alpha^{j1}\alpha^{j2}+...+\alpha^{jv}$$
$$S_2 = \left(\alpha^{j1}\right)^2 +\left(\alpha^{j2}\right)^2+...+\left(\alpha^{jv}\right)^2$$
$$S_3 = \left(\alpha^{j1}\right)^3 +\left(\alpha^{j2}\right)^3+...+\left(\alpha^{jv}\right)^3$$

$$\cdot$$

$$\cdot$$

$$S_d = \left(\alpha^{j1}\right)^d +\left(\alpha^{j2}\right)^d+...+\left(\alpha^{jv}\right)^d$$

in which

$$0 \le j1 < j2 <...< jv < n$$

and v is the number of errors.

Let

$$\beta_l = \alpha^{jl}$$

and the preceding expressions become

$$S_1 = \beta_1 + \beta_2+...+\beta_v$$
$$S_2 = \beta_1^2 + \beta_2^2+...+\beta_v^2$$
$$S_3 = \beta_1^3 + \beta_2^3+...+\beta_v^3$$

$$\cdot$$

$$\cdot$$

$$S_d = \beta_1^d + \beta_2^d+...+\beta_v^d$$

We call $\beta_l = \alpha^{jl}$ error location numbers because they tell us the locations of the errors. Now we define the following error location polynomial:

$$\sigma(x) = (1 + \beta_1 x)(1 + \beta_2 x)\ldots(1 + \beta_v x)$$
$$= \sigma_0 + \sigma_1 x + \sigma_2 x^2 + \ldots + \sigma_v x^v$$

The roots of $\sigma(x)$ are β_1^{-1}, β_2^{-1}, ..., β_v^{-1}, which are the inverse of the error location numbers. The coefficients of $\sigma(x)$ and the error location numbers are related by the following equations:

$$S_1 + \sigma_1 = 0$$
$$S_2 + \sigma_1 S_1 + 2\sigma_2 = 0$$
$$S_3 + \sigma_1 S_2 + \sigma_2 S_1 + 3\sigma_3 = 0$$

.

.

$$S_v + \sigma_1 S_{v-1} + \ldots + \sigma_{v-1} S_1 + v\sigma_v = 0$$
$$S_{v+1} + \sigma_1 S_v + \ldots + \sigma_{v-1} S_2 + \sigma_v S_1 = 0$$

It requires about $2(d/2)^2$ addition and multiplication procedures to find $\sigma(x)$.

Error Correction

The third step of decoding is to determine the error location numbers by finding the roots of $\sigma(x)$ and to correct the errors in $v(x)$. The roots of $\sigma(x)$ can be found simply by substituting $1, \alpha, \alpha^2 \ldots \alpha^{n-1}$ into $\sigma(x)$. If α^l is a root of $\sigma(x)$, α^{n-l} is an error location number, and the received digit is an erroneous digit. This could be up to 2^m evaluations of d multiplication and addition procedures each, for which 2^m is the base of the Galois field.

For the Reed-Solomon code, we need one additional step of error value calculations—we form another polynomial:

$$z(x) = 1 + (S_1 + \sigma_1)x + (S_2 + \sigma_1 S_1 + \sigma_2)x^2 + (S_v + \sigma_1 S_{v-1} + \ldots + \sigma_{v-1} S_1 + \sigma_v)x^v$$

The error value at location $\beta_l = \alpha^{jl}$ is given by the following:

$$e_{jl} = \frac{z\left(\beta_l^{-1}\right)}{\displaystyle\prod_{\substack{i=1 \\ i\neq l}}^{v}\left(1+\beta_i\beta_l^{-1}\right)}$$

Note

The preceding analysis assumes that modular or Galois field arithmetic operations are available.

10.2.4 DSL Applications of Reed-Solomon Codes

Reed-Solomon coded twisted-pair-based transmission systems have an SNR loss[6,7] relative to uncoded systems because of a higher signaling rate, therefore, a wider bandwidth where the portion of the expanded bandwidth usually has a lower SNR. For using eight bits per symbol in GF(2^8), the symbol error rate is $P_s = 1-\left(1-P_e\right)^8$, in which P_e is the bit error rate without coding. The bit error rate (BER) at the output of the (n,k) Reed-Solomon decoder is closely approximated by the following:[8]

$$BER = \frac{n-k+1}{2n}\sum\binom{n}{i}P_S^i\left(1-P_S\right)^{n-i},$$

Figure 10.3 shows the BER at the output of a Reed-Solomon decoder with 10 percent redundancy, or coding overhead, based on a 16 QAM line code twisted-pair-based transmission system. These curves correspond to single, double, triple, and quadruple error corrections.

Coding overhead-caused SNR losses are included also. The coding loss for 10 percent overhead is about 0.83 dB for this particular twisted-pair loop environment. Table 10.5 summarizes coding losses for differing amounts of overhead.

Table 10.5 Coding Overhead SNR Loss

Percentage Redundancy	SNR Loss (dB)
2%	0.17
5%	0.42
10%	0.83
15%	1.15
20%	1.58

Figure 10.3   BER for 10 Percent Redundancy Reed-Solomon Code (Reproduced from *Bellcore T1E1.4/92-153 Contribution*)

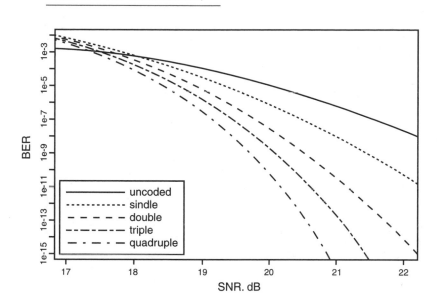

Figure 10.4 shows BERs at the output of a double-byte error correcting Reed-Solomon decoder with different redundancies also based on the 16 QAM line code twisted-pair-based transmission system. Respective coding overhead SNR losses for different amounts of redundancies are included also.

10.3   *Convolution Codes*

In contrast to the block code, a convolution code does not have a clean boundary between information bits and redundancy bits. In fact, the encoder runs like a sliding window across an information bit stream. A general binary convolution encoder can have a memory size of M with $M-1$ delay elements. k information bits are inputted to the encoder during every clock cycle. n outputs are generated every clock cycle based on modulo combinations of bit groups derived from k input information bits of different delays.

Encoder inputs and outputs are driven by the same synchronized clock. The ratio of the input information bit rate to the encoded output bit rate, k/n, is the coding rate. Figure 10.5 shows the general structure of a convolution encoder.

Figure 10.4 BER for Double-Error Correcting Reed-Solomon Code (Reproduced from *Bellcore T1E1.4/92-153 Contribution*)

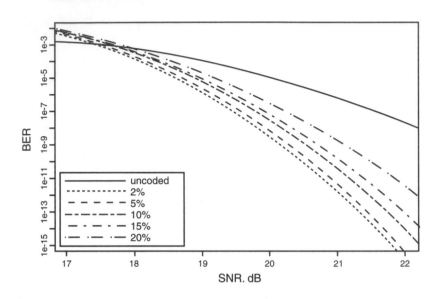

Figure 10.5 A Generic Convolution Encoder

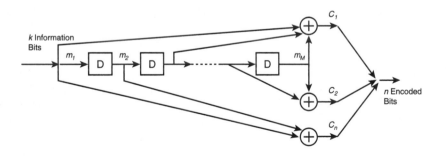

Each encoded output bit is the exclusive-or combination of a selected number of input information bits with up to M clock cycle delays. We have

$$c_i = m_{11}g_{i11} \oplus m_{12}g_{i12} \oplus \ldots \oplus m_{1k}g_{i1k} \oplus m_{21}g_{i21} \oplus m_{22}g_{i22} \oplus \ldots \oplus m_{2k}g_{i2k} \oplus \ldots$$
$$\oplus m_{M1}g_{iM1} \oplus m_{M2}g_{iM2} \oplus \ldots \oplus m_{Mk}g_{iMk}$$

$$= \begin{bmatrix} m_1 & m_2 & \ldots & m_M \end{bmatrix} \begin{bmatrix} g_{i1} \\ g_{i2} \\ \ldots \\ g_{iM} \end{bmatrix} = mg_i$$

in which

$$m_i = \begin{bmatrix} m_{i1} & m_{i2} & \ldots & m_{ik} \end{bmatrix}$$
$$g_{ij} = \begin{bmatrix} g_{ij1} & g_{ij2} & \ldots & g_{ijk} \end{bmatrix}$$

In other words, m is a row vector of dimension $M \times k$, and g_i is a column vector of the same dimension.

For the steady state case (all delay stages are filled with information bits), the encoder output can be represented by

$$c = m \oplus g$$

in which

$$m = \begin{bmatrix} m_1 & m_2 & \ldots & m_M \end{bmatrix}$$
$$g = \begin{bmatrix} g_1 & g_2 & \ldots & g_n \end{bmatrix}$$
$$c = \begin{bmatrix} c_1 & c_2 & \ldots & c_n \end{bmatrix}$$

There are k input information bits and n encoded output bits for every clock cycle. Because $m_i = D^{i-1}m_1$ where $D^{i-1}m_1$ means $i-1$ clock cycle delayed version of m_1, we have $m = m_1\Gamma$, for which

$$\Gamma = \begin{bmatrix} 1 & 0 & 0 & 0 & D & 0 & 0 & 0 & & D^{M-1} & 0 & 0 & 0 \\ 0 & 1 & 0 & 0 & 0 & D & 0 & 0 & & 0 & D^{M-1} & 0 & 0 \\ & & \ldots & & & \ldots & & \ldots & & & & \ldots & \\ 0 & 0 & 0 & 1 & 0 & 0 & 0 & D & & 0 & 0 & 0 & D^{M-1} \end{bmatrix}$$

Consequently, we have $c = m_1\Gamma g$ or $c = m_1 g(D)$, for which

$$g(D) = \begin{bmatrix} g_{111} + g_{121}D + \ldots + g_{1M1}D^{M-1} & g_{211} + g_{221}D + \ldots + g_{2M1}D^{M-1} & g_{n11} + g_{n21}D + \ldots + g_{nM1}D^{M-1} \\ g_{112} + g_{122}D + \ldots + g_{1M2}D^{M-1} & g_{212} + g_{222}D + \ldots + g_{2M2}D^{M-1} & g_{n12} + g_{n22}D + \ldots + g_{nM2}D^{M-1} \\ & \cdots & \\ g_{11k} + g_{12k}D + \ldots + g_{1Mk}D^{M-1} & g_{21k} + g_{22k}D + \ldots + g_{2Mk}D^{M-1} & g_{n1k} + g_{n2k}D + \ldots + g_{nMk}D^{M-1} \end{bmatrix}$$

Many elements of $g(D)$ are zeros. A convolution code is generally characterized as an (n,k,M) convolution code. Figure 10.6 shows a simple example of a $(4,2,3)$ convolution code.

Figure 10.6 An Example of a (4,2,3) Convolution Code

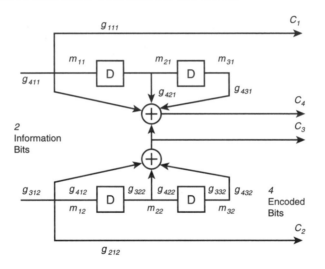

As represented in Figure 10.6:

m_{ij} denotes the jth information bit with $i-1$ delay.

g_{kij} denotes the weight for the kth encoded bit from m_{ij}.

The generator matrix for this convolution encoder is the following:

$$g = \begin{bmatrix} 1 & 0 & 0 & 1 \\ 0 & 1 & 1 & 1 \\ 0 & 0 & 0 & 1 \\ 0 & 0 & 1 & 1 \\ 0 & 0 & 0 & 1 \\ 0 & 0 & 1 & 1 \end{bmatrix} \text{ or } g(D) = \begin{bmatrix} 1 & 0 & 0 & 1+D+D^2 \\ 0 & 1 & 1+D+D^2 & 1+D+D^2 \end{bmatrix}$$

In analogy to parity check code, the matrix of g or $g(D)$ is in systematic format also.

10.3.1   Convolution Encoder State

We can characterize a convolution encoder also as a finite state machine. The operating condition of a finite state machine can be defined by its input signal vector, its state, and its output signal vector. For the preceding example with four memory elements, we could have a total of 16 distinguishable states. For easy demonstration, we simplify the sample circuit by eliminating two delay elements and one output bit (see Figure 10.7).

Figure 10.7   A (3,2,2) Convolution Encoder

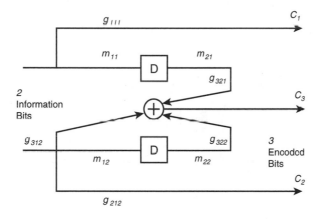

The generator matrix for this simplified convolution encoder is

$$g = \begin{bmatrix} 1 & 0 & 0 \\ 0 & 1 & 1 \\ 0 & 0 & 1 \\ 0 & 0 & 1 \end{bmatrix} \text{ or } g(D) = \begin{bmatrix} 1 & 0 & D \\ 0 & 1 & 1+D \end{bmatrix}$$

There are four states for this simplified encoder:

S_0 for $m_2 = 00$
S_1 for $m_2 = 01$
S_2 for $m_2 = 10$
S_3 for $m_2 = 11$

Figure 10.8 shows the state transition diagram of the simplified example of a (3,2,2) encoder. For a transition label of xx/yyy, xx represents the input and yyy represents the output.

Figure 10.8 State Transition Diagram for a (3,2,2) Encoder

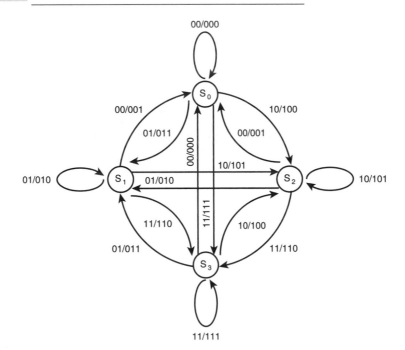

Starting from the zero state, possible state transitions and output signal vectors also can be demonstrated with a tree diagram, as shown in Figure 10.9. For a branch label of yyy(zz), yyy represents the output and zz represents the state.

Figure 10.9   Tree Diagram for the (3,2,2) Encoder

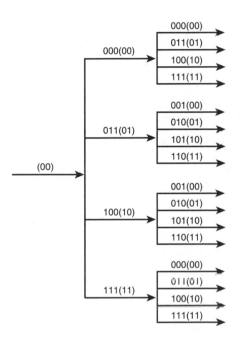

The information contained in a tree diagram also can be displayed with a Trellis diagram of less complexity, as shown in Figure 10.10 for the (3,2,2) convolution encoder.

The encoder output is labeled on the branch from the current state to the next state, as follows:

- Outputs from the first state, S_0, to other states are labeled between the first stage and the second stage.

- Outputs from the second state, S_1, to other states are labeled between the second stage and the third stage.

- Outputs from the third state, S_2, to other states are labeled between the third stage and the fourth stage.

- Outputs from the fourth state, S_3, to other states are labeled between the fourth stage and the fifth stage.

Figure 10.10 Trellis Diagram of a (3,2,2) Convolution Encoder

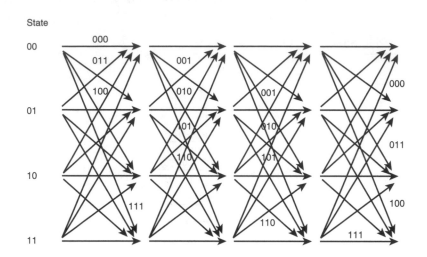

Corresponding input is defined by the encoder matrix or the state transition diagram. Figure 10.11 shows the Trellis for an input sequence of m=(01 10 00 11) from zero state. The output encoded sequence is the combination of all bit sequences labeled on branches—c=(011 101 001 111). For this systematic encoder, the first two bits of the output are the same as the input bits.

Figure 10.11 Trellis of a Message Sequence

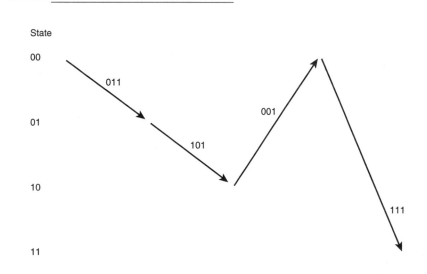

Because of the state machine mechanism of the convolution encoder, the encoded bits as well as their sequences are very much related to the state and input information bits, which happened to be the same for this simple example. The information bits are recovered at a decoder based not only on received bits, which might be erroneous due to channel noise, but also on the likelihood of reconstruction of the state transition sequence or of the Trellis.

10.3.2 *Viterbi Decoding*

Assuming an origin from a known state, the maximum likelihood detection[9] or Viterbi[10] algorithm calculates distances—the total code differences—between the received code and codes leading to next possible states. After the accumulation of a certain number of calculations, the Viterbi algorithm then selects the sequence that has the minimal total distances as the right one. The information bits are then recovered based on the sequence, states it traveled through, and its corresponding input bits. The assumed known state can be identified once in awhile when all sequences pass the same state. In other words, a selection of the right sequence can be made when different sequences converge at a certain state.

Specifically, the Viterbi algorithm for the convolution code decoding can be described in the following steps:

1. For every group of received encoded bits $\left(r_1 \quad r_2 \quad \ldots \quad r_n \right)$ during each clock cycle, we calculate branch metrics from surviving states to all possible next states:

$$B_M^{jl} = \sum_{i=1}^{n} r_i \oplus \beta_i^{jl}$$

B_M^{jl} is the branch metric from the surviving j state to the next l state.
$\left(\beta_1^{jl} \quad \beta_2^{jl} \quad \ldots \quad \beta_n^{jl} \right)$ are right convolution encoder output bits switching from the j state to the next l state.

2. All surviving path metrics are updated as

$$P_M^l = P_M^j + B_M^{jl}$$

3. A small number of paths that have the lowest path metric values are kept for the next iteration. When a path with a significantly lower path metric value is identified or a maximum number of iterations is reached, the path that has the lowest metric value is selected as the right encoded sequence.

4. Original information bits are recovered according to the input bits, state, and output bits relationship.

The performance of the Viterbi algorithm can be improved if the received encoded bits are not quantized before the metric evaluation algorithm. The branch metric is then evaluated according to

$$B_M^{jl} = \sum_{i=1}^{n} \left(r_i - \beta_i^{jl} \right)^2$$

Assuming the received information is
$r = (0.2, 1.4, 0.7 \quad 0.4, -0.3, 1.6 \quad -0.2, 0.2, 1.1 \quad 1.3, 0.9, 0.8)$ for the previous example,
we have $\ddot{r} = (011 \quad 001 \quad 001 \quad 111)$ after quantization. Figure 10.12 shows branch and path metric values starting from a zero state.

Figure 10.12 Viterbi Decoding with Quantized Input

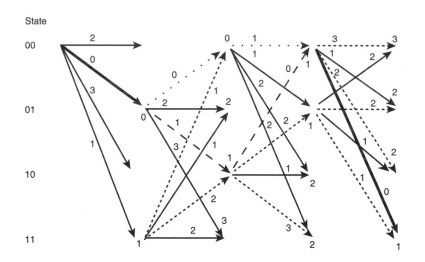

These regular dashed lines represent paths with a higher path metric value compared with those of alternative lines. The bold lines represent paths with the lowest path metric values. We can identify the lowest valued path metric at the end. There are, however, two paths producing the same lowest path metric value. In Figure 10.12, the two paths that produce the same lowest path metric values are shown in a dotted line and in a thick dashed line during the second and third stage of the Trellis diagram. Figure 10.13 shows calculations of branch and path metric values with non-quantized received information.

Figure 10.13   Viterbi Decoding with Soft Input

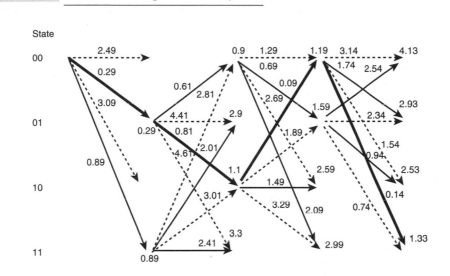

The right path, bold solid lines, is properly identified according to the lowest path metric value at the end.

10.4   *Trellis Code Modulation*

We have observed that the block codes, such as Reed-Solomon codes, can be used on a twisted-pair-loop channel for reducing the transmission error rate. The coding overhead due to parity check bits of a block code will increase the required transmission throughput. The additional transmission throughput requirement can be satisfied by either increasing the transmission bandwidth for a faster signaling rate or expanding the number of symbols for a denser constellation size.

For a non-bandwidth limited case, the transmission bandwidth can be increased for a slight reduction of signal-to-noise ratio of up to 1.58 dB, as for the Reed-Solomon code example. The resulting coding gain measured as a reduction of error rate or an equivalent SNR improvement could still be significant.

For the bandwidth limited case, however, the expansion of the number of symbols could cause a minimum of 3 or 6 dB of signal-to-noise ratio reduction for passband and baseband systems, respectively. Trellis code modulation is an effective coding method that can be used to produce significant coding gain for bandwidth limited cases.[11,12] Trellis code modulation combines a specially selected convolution code with a particular line symbol mapping to be discussed in more detail in this section. The effective coding gain of a Trellis code modulation system can be in the range of between 3 to 6 dB, depending on the convolution encoder memory size.

The performance of a general purpose convolution code in its binary format is evaluated according to its minimum Hamming distance between code symbols. The direct application of a convolution code in conjunction with a particular baseband or passband system has two problems:

- A soft Viterbi algorithm instead of the conventional DFE is necessary to avoid the loss of information after the encoded information is received.

- There is no direct correlation between the minimum Hamming distance and the Euclidean distance that is crucial for the proper operation of the Viterbi algorithm.

Note

The minimum Hamming distance is related to the binary structure of a convolution code, while the Euclidean distance is related to the constellation structure of a line code.

For a simple $(3,2,2)$ convolution code example of Figure 10.8, the minimum free distance, d_{free}, is 2, which is obtained by examining the corresponding state transition diagram and identifying the minimum weight of all paths that diverge from, and remerge with, the all-zero state, S_0. The asymptotic (or the maximum achievable) coding gain, when SNR is very high, is

$$\gamma = 10\log_{10}\frac{Rd_{free}}{2} = 10\log_{10}\frac{2\times 2}{2} = 3dB$$

R denotes the number of bits per symbol.

The average power for an n-level baseband signal with a voltage difference of 2 between adjacent signal levels is

$$P = \frac{n^2 - 1}{3}$$

For a normalized signal power, the voltage difference between adjacent signal levels for an n-level baseband system is

$$V_{diff} = 2\sqrt{\frac{3}{n^2-1}}$$

The normalized SNR for an n-level baseband system is

$$SNR = \frac{1}{\sigma^2}$$

The bit error rate for an n-level baseband system is

$$P_e = \frac{2}{\sqrt{2\pi}\sigma}\int_{\frac{V_{diff}}{2}}^{\infty} e^{-\frac{y^2}{2\sigma^2}}\,dy = \frac{2}{\sqrt{2\pi}}\int_{\frac{V_{diff}}{2\sigma}}^{\infty} e^{-\frac{x^2}{2}}\,dx = \frac{2}{\sqrt{2\pi}}\int_{\sqrt{\frac{3SNR}{n^2-1}}}^{\infty} e^{-\frac{x^2}{2}}\,dx$$

For a four-level baseband system, the SNR requirement for an error rate of 10^{-7} is about 21.5 dB. The error rate is about 9.3×10^{-3} under the same 21.5 dB SNR, but with a three-bit per symbol, eight-level baseband system to accommodate the extra bit generated by the convolution encoder. The simple convolution code, however, is not powerful enough to reduce the error rate from 9.3×10^{-3} to 10^{-7}. Therefore, the net coding gain is negative, and the asymptotic coding can never be realized.

10.4.1 Achieving Significant Trellis Coding Gain

Some special convolution codes have been identified to generate significant Trellis coding gain.[13] Figure 10.14 shows a good two-bit/three-bit or four-level/eight-level (3,2,2) convolution encoder.

Figure 10.14 A 2/3 Convolution Encoder

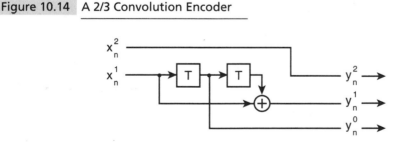

The generator matrix of this $(3,2,2)$ convolution code to be used in a Trellis code modulation system is

$$g = \begin{bmatrix} 1 & 0 & 0 \\ 0 & 1 & 0 \\ 0 & 0 & 0 \\ 0 & 0 & 1 \\ 0 & 0 & 0 \\ 0 & 1 & 0 \end{bmatrix}$$

or

$$g(D) = \begin{bmatrix} 1 & 0 & 0 \\ 0 & 1+D^{-2} & D^{-1} \end{bmatrix}$$

The corresponding eight signal levels should be mapped according to Figure 10.15, assuming the bits are arranged as $(y_2\, y_1\, y_0)$.

Figure 10.15 Eight-Level Bit-to-Signal Mapping

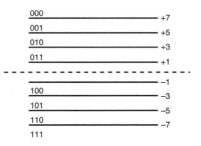

Asymptotic coding gain of about 3.3 dB can be realized by combining the specially selected convolution code and the eight-level bit-to-signal level mapping in conjunction with a soft Viterbi receiver.

The mapping is designed such that y_0 divides the eight-level line code into two four-level line code with wider distance between signal levels, y_1 further divides each four-level line code into two two-level line code, and y_2 selects the signal level among these two-level line codes.

The parity check matrix of this convolution code is

$$H(D) = \begin{bmatrix} 0 & D & 1+D^2 \end{bmatrix}$$

We have the orthogonality of

$$GH^T = \begin{bmatrix} 1 & 0 & 0 \\ 0 & 1+D^2 & D \end{bmatrix} \begin{bmatrix} 0 \\ D \\ 1+D^2 \end{bmatrix} = \begin{bmatrix} 0 \\ D+D^3+D+D^3 \end{bmatrix} = \begin{bmatrix} 0 \\ 0 \end{bmatrix}$$

This parity matrix also leads to a systematic format implementation of the same encoder. Denote encoded bits as $\begin{pmatrix} y_2^i & y_1^i & y_0^i \end{pmatrix}$, where superscripts indicate the time index. We have

$$\begin{pmatrix} y_2^i & y_1^i & y_0^i \end{pmatrix} H^T = \begin{pmatrix} y_2^i & y_1^i & y_0^i \end{pmatrix} \begin{bmatrix} 0 \\ D \\ 1+D^2 \end{bmatrix} = y_1^{i-1} \oplus y_0^i \oplus y_0^{i-2} = 0$$

or

$$y_0^i = y_0^{i-2} \oplus y_1^{i-1}$$

Figure 10.16 shows the corresponding systematic or feedback format encoder.

Figure 10.16 The Systematic Format Implementation of a Convolution Encoder

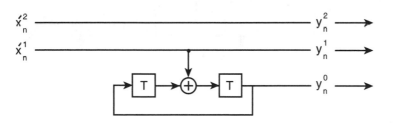

Figure 10.17 shows the general case of systematic format implementation of a convolution encoder with one extra coding bit.[14]

Figure 10.17 Systematic Convolution Encoder Structure

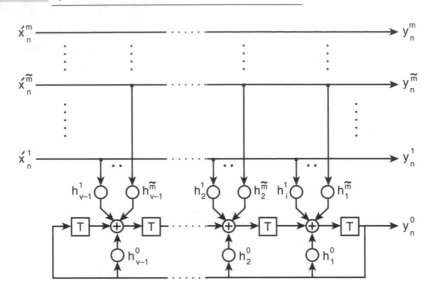

Other convolution encoders with more memory stage can provide even higher coding gains. For three memory stages, the parity check matrix for a convolution code capable of 3.7 dB of coding gain is

$$H(D) = \begin{bmatrix} 0 & D^2 & 1 + D^2 + D^3 \end{bmatrix}$$

The corresponding coding relationship is

$$\begin{pmatrix} y_2^i & y_1^i & y_0^i \end{pmatrix} H^T = \begin{pmatrix} y_2^i & y_1^i & y_0^i \end{pmatrix} \begin{bmatrix} 0 \\ D^2 \\ 1 + D^2 + D^3 \end{bmatrix} = y_1^{i-2} \oplus y_0^i \oplus y_0^{i-2} \oplus y_0^{i-3} = 0$$

or

$$y_0^i = y_0^{i-2} \oplus y_0^{i-3} \oplus y_1^{i-2}$$

For four memory stages, the parity check matrix for a convolution code capable of 4.1 dB of coding gain is as follows:

$$H(D) = \begin{bmatrix} 0 & D^2 & 1 + D + D^2 + D^4 \end{bmatrix}$$

The corresponding coding relationship is

$$\begin{pmatrix} y_2^i & y_1^i & y_0^i \end{pmatrix} H^T = \begin{pmatrix} y_2^i & y_1^i & y_0^i \end{pmatrix} \begin{bmatrix} 0 \\ D^2 \\ 1+D+D^2+D^4 \end{bmatrix} = y_1^{i-2} \oplus y_0^i \oplus y_0^{i-1} \oplus y_{0,}^{i-2} \oplus y_0^{i-4} = 0$$

or

$$y_0^i = y_0^{i-1} \oplus y_0^{i-2} \oplus y_0^{i-4} \oplus y_1^{i-2}$$

For five memory stages, the parity check matrix for a convolution code capable of 4.5 dB of coding gain is as follows:

$$H(D) = \begin{bmatrix} 0 & D+D^4 & 1+D^2+D^3+D^5 \end{bmatrix}$$

The corresponding coding relationship is

$$\begin{pmatrix} y_2^i & y_1^i & y_0^i \end{pmatrix} H^T = \begin{pmatrix} y_2^i & y_1^i & y_0^i \end{pmatrix} \begin{bmatrix} 0 \\ D+D^4 \\ 1+D^2+D^3+D^5 \end{bmatrix} = y_1^{i-1} \oplus y_1^{i-4} \oplus y_0^i \oplus y_0^{i-2} \oplus y_0^{i-3} \oplus y_0^{i-5} = 0$$

or

$$y_0^i = y_0^{i-2} \oplus y_0^{i-3} \oplus y_0^{i-5} \oplus y_1^{i-1} \oplus y_1^{i-4}$$

For six memory stages, the parity check matrix for a convolution code capable of 4.9 dB of coding gain is as follows:

$$H(D) = \begin{bmatrix} 0 & D^3+D^4 & 1+D+D^2+D^5+D^6 \end{bmatrix}$$

The corresponding coding relationship is

$$\begin{pmatrix} y_2^i & y_1^i & y_0^i \end{pmatrix} H^T = \begin{pmatrix} y_2^i & y_1^i & y_0^i \end{pmatrix} \begin{bmatrix} 0 \\ D^3+D^4 \\ 1+D+D^2+D^5+D^6 \end{bmatrix} = y_1^{i-3} \oplus y_1^{i-4} \oplus y_0^i \oplus y_0^{i-1} \oplus y_0^{i-2} \oplus y_0^{i-5} \oplus y_0^{i-6} = 0$$

or

$$y_0^i = y_0^{i-1} \oplus y_0^{i-2} \oplus y_0^{i-5} \oplus y_0^{i-6} \oplus y_1^{i-3} \oplus y_1^{i-4}$$

For seven memory stages, the parity check matrix for a convolution code capable of 5.2 dB of coding gain is as follows:

$$H(D) = \begin{bmatrix} 0 & D + D^2 + D^3 + D^4 + D^5 + D^6 & 1 + D + D^3 + D^5 + D^6 + D^7 \end{bmatrix}$$

The corresponding coding relationship is

$$\left(y_2^i \quad y_1^i \quad y_0^i \right) H^T = \left(y_2^i \quad y_1^i \quad y_0^i \right) \begin{bmatrix} 0 \\ D + D^2 + D^3 + D^4 + D^5 + D^6 \\ 1 + D + D^3 + D^5 + D^6 + D^7 \end{bmatrix}$$

$$= y_1^{i-1} \oplus y_1^{i-2} \oplus y_1^{i-3} \oplus y_1^{i-4} \oplus y_1^{i-5} \oplus y_1^{i-6} \oplus y_0^i \oplus y_0^{i-1} \oplus y_0^{i-3} \oplus y_0^{i-5} \oplus y_0^{i-6} \oplus y_0^{i-7} = 0$$

or

$$y_0^i = y_0^{i-1} \oplus y_0^{i-3} \oplus y_0^{i-5} \oplus y_0^{i-6} \oplus y_0^{i-7} \oplus y_1^{i-1} \oplus y_1^{i-2} \oplus y_1^{i-3} \oplus y_1^{i-4} \oplus y_1^{i-5} \oplus y_1^{i-6}$$

Figure 10.18 shows the realizable coding gains of a four-level to eight-level Trellis coded baseband system: PAM stands for *Pulse Amplitude Modulation* for the conventional baseband line code.

10.4.2 *Feedback/Feedforward Implementations*

For each systematic or feedback implementation of a convolution encoder, we can find a corresponding feedforward implementation of the same convolution encoder by deriving the generator matrix, $G(D)$, from the parity check matrix, $H(D)$, according to $G(D)H^T(D) = 0$.[15] Some special techniques of finding feedforward implementation formats might be necessary for multistage convolution codes.[16]

Some convolution codes suitable for two-dimensional Trellis coded modulation are shown in feedforward and feedback implementation formats in Figures 10.19 and 10.20, respectively.

Figure 10.18   PAM Trellis Coding Gain[13]

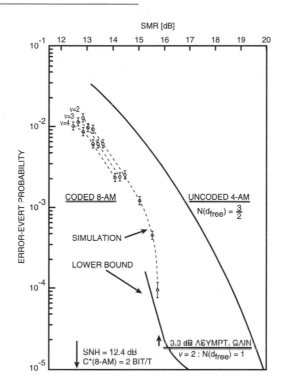

Figure 10.21 shows a 16 QAM (or 16 QASK, for Quadrature Amplitude Shift Keying, as labeled in the figure) constellation mapping division example.

The mapping is such designed that y^0 divides the 16-point constellation into two eight-point constellations with wider distance between adjacent constellation points, y^1 further divides each eight-point constellation into two four-point constellations, y^2 again divides each four point constellation into two two-point constellations, and y^3 selects the constellation point among these two-point constellations.

Figure 10.22 shows realizable coding gains of a 8 PSK (Phase Shift Keying) or 8 AMPM (Amplitude and Phase Modulation) to 16 QAM (or 16 QASK as labeled in the figure) Trellis coded passband system.

Figure 10.19 Feedforward Convolution Encoder for Trellis Code Modulation

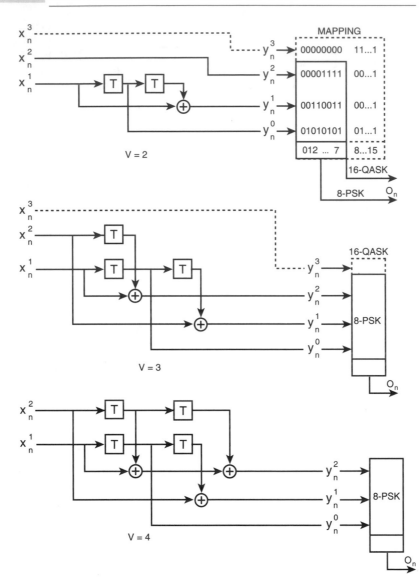

Figure 10.20 Feedback Convolution Encoder for Trellis Code Modulation

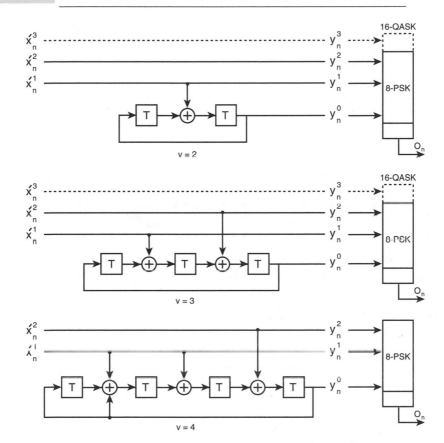

10.4.3 An Analytical Trellis Encoder Description

A Trellis encoder that includes the convolution encoder and the signal mapping also can be described in the analytical format.[17] For an example of the two memory stage four level to eight-level Trellis encoder of Figure 10.14, we let the mapping output be a nonlinear function of input bits and state variables, as follows:

$$f\left(x_1^1 \quad x_0^1 \quad x_0^2 \quad x_0^3\right) = d_0 + d_1 x_1^1 + d_2 x_0^1 + d_3 x_0^2 + d_4 x_0^3 + d_{12} x_1^1 x_0^1 + d_{13} x_1^1 x_0^2 + d_{14} x_1^1 x_0^3 + d_{23} x_0^1 x_0^2$$

$$+ d_{24} x_0^1 x_0^3 + d_{34} x_0^2 x_0^3 + d_{123} x_1^1 x_0^1 x_0^2 + d_{124} x_1^1 x_0^1 x_0^3 + d_{134} x_1^1 x_0^2 x_0^3 + d_{234} x_0^1 x_0^2 x_0^3 + d_{1234} x_1^1 x_0^1 x_0^2 x_0^3$$

Figure 10.21 16 QAM Constellation Set Partitioning

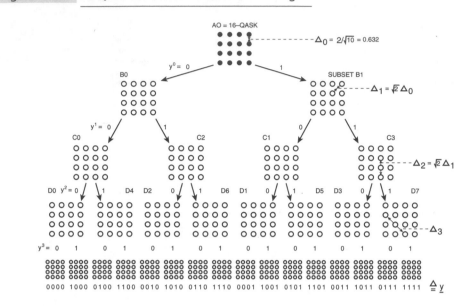

Figure 10.22 16 QAM Trellis Coding Gain[13]

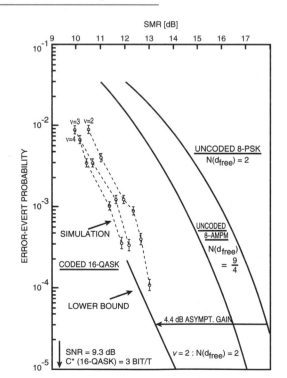

The value x_1^1 corresponds to the input bit of x_n^2 in Figure 10.14, x_0^1 corresponds to the input bit of x_n^1 also in Figure 10.14, x_0^2 is the one stage delay version of x_0^1, and x_0^3 is the two stage delayed version of x_0^1. For the general case, we have the following:

$$d = \frac{1}{2^n} B^T f$$

With the example of $n=4$, we have

$$d = \begin{bmatrix} d_0 & d_1 & d_2 & d_3 & d_4 & d_{12} & d_{13} & d_{14} & d_{23} & d_{24} & d_{34} & d_{123} & d_{124} & d_{134} & d_{234} & d_{1234} \end{bmatrix}$$

$$f = \begin{bmatrix} f_1 \\ f_2 \\ \cdots \\ f_{2^n} \end{bmatrix} = \begin{bmatrix} f_1 \\ f_2 \\ \cdots \\ f_{2^4} \end{bmatrix} \qquad B = \begin{bmatrix} B_1 \\ B_2 \\ \cdots \\ B_{2^n} \end{bmatrix} = \begin{bmatrix} B_1 \\ B_2 \\ \cdots \\ B_{2^4} \end{bmatrix}$$

f_i is related to B_i as

$$f_i = f\begin{pmatrix} x_1^1 & x_0^1 & x_0^2 & x_0^3 \end{pmatrix}$$

for

$$x_1^1 = a_j^1, \; x_0^1 = a_k^1, \; x_0^2 = a_k^2$$

and

$$x_0^3 = a_k^3$$

when

$$B_i = \begin{bmatrix} 0 & x_1^1 & x_0^1 & x_0^2 & x_0^3 & x_1^1 x_0^1 & x_1^1 x_0^2 & x_1^1 x_0^3 & x_0^1 x_0^2 & x_0^1 x_0^3 & x_0^2 x_0^3 & x_1^1 x_0^1 x_0^2 & x_1^1 x_0^1 x_0^3 & x_1^1 x_0^2 x_0^3 & x_0^1 x_0^2 x_0^3 & x_1^1 x_0^1 x_0^2 x_0^3 \end{bmatrix}$$

also for

$$x_1^1 = a_j^1, \; x_0^1 = a_k^1, \; x_0^2 = a_k^2, \; x_0^3 = a_k^3$$

According to the preceding relationship, we have the following for the example in Figure 10.14:

$$f_1 = f(1 \quad 1 \quad 1 \quad 1) = -3 \qquad f_9 = f(1 \quad 1 \quad 1 \quad -1) = -7$$
$$f_2 = f(-1 \quad 1 \quad 1 \quad 1) = 5 \qquad f_{10} = f(-1 \quad 1 \quad 1 \quad -1) = 1$$
$$f_3 = f(1 \quad -1 \quad 1 \quad 1) = -7 \qquad f_{11} = f(1 \quad -1 \quad 1 \quad -1) = -3$$
$$f_4 = f(-1 \quad -1 \quad 1 \quad 1) = 1 \qquad f_{12} = f(-1 \quad -1 \quad 1 \quad -1) = 5$$
$$f_5 = f(1 \quad 1 \quad -1 \quad 1) = -1 \qquad f_{13} = f(1 \quad 1 \quad -1 \quad -1) = -5$$
$$f_6 = f(-1 \quad 1 \quad -1 \quad 1) = 7 \qquad f_{14} = f(-1 \quad 1 \quad -1 \quad -1) = 3$$
$$f_7 = f(1 \quad -1 \quad -1 \quad 1) = -5 \qquad f_{15} = f(1 \quad -1 \quad -1 \quad -1) = -1$$
$$f_8 = f(-1 \quad -1 \quad -1 \quad 1) = 3 \qquad f_{16} = f(-1 \quad -1 \quad -1 \quad -1) = 7$$

This is equivalent to

$$f = \begin{bmatrix} -3 & 5 & -7 & 1 & -1 & 7 & -5 & 3 & -7 & 1 & -3 & 5 & -5 & 3 & -1 & 7 \end{bmatrix}^T$$

The corresponding B matrix is

$$B = \begin{bmatrix}
0 & 1 & 1 & 1 & 1 & 1 & 1 & 1 & 1 & 1 & 1 & 1 & 1 & 1 & 1 & 1 \\
0 & -1 & 1 & 1 & 1 & -1 & -1 & -1 & 1 & 1 & 1 & -1 & -1 & -1 & 1 & -1 \\
0 & 1 & -1 & 1 & 1 & -1 & 1 & 1 & -1 & -1 & 1 & -1 & -1 & 1 & -1 & -1 \\
0 & -1 & -1 & 1 & 1 & 1 & -1 & -1 & -1 & -1 & 1 & 1 & 1 & -1 & -1 & 1 \\
0 & 1 & 1 & -1 & 1 & 1 & -1 & 1 & -1 & 1 & -1 & -1 & 1 & -1 & -1 & -1 \\
0 & -1 & 1 & -1 & 1 & -1 & 1 & -1 & -1 & 1 & -1 & 1 & -1 & 1 & -1 & 1 \\
0 & 1 & -1 & -1 & 1 & -1 & -1 & 1 & 1 & -1 & -1 & 1 & -1 & -1 & 1 & 1 \\
0 & -1 & -1 & -1 & 1 & 1 & 1 & -1 & 1 & -1 & -1 & -1 & 1 & 1 & 1 & -1 \\
0 & 1 & 1 & 1 & -1 & 1 & 1 & -1 & 1 & -1 & -1 & 1 & -1 & -1 & -1 & -1 \\
0 & -1 & 1 & 1 & -1 & -1 & -1 & 1 & 1 & -1 & -1 & -1 & 1 & 1 & -1 & 1 \\
0 & 1 & -1 & 1 & -1 & -1 & 1 & -1 & -1 & 1 & -1 & -1 & 1 & -1 & 1 & 1 \\
0 & -1 & -1 & 1 & -1 & 1 & -1 & 1 & -1 & 1 & -1 & 1 & -1 & 1 & 1 & -1 \\
0 & 1 & 1 & -1 & -1 & 1 & -1 & -1 & -1 & -1 & 1 & -1 & -1 & 1 & 1 & 1 \\
0 & -1 & 1 & -1 & -1 & -1 & 1 & 1 & -1 & -1 & 1 & 1 & 1 & -1 & 1 & -1 \\
0 & 1 & -1 & -1 & -1 & -1 & -1 & -1 & 1 & 1 & 1 & 1 & 1 & 1 & -1 & -1 \\
0 & -1 & -1 & -1 & -1 & 1 & 1 & 1 & 1 & 1 & 1 & -1 & -1 & -1 & -1 & 1
\end{bmatrix}$$

We obtain

$$d = \frac{1}{16}\begin{bmatrix} 0 & 64 & 0 & -16 & 0 & 0 & 0 & 0 & 0 & 32 & 0 & 0 & 0 & 0 & 0 & 0 \end{bmatrix}$$

Therefore, the (3,2,2) four-level to eight-level Trellis encoder can be described in the analytical form as follows:

$$f\left(x_1^1 \quad x_0^1 \quad x_0^2 \quad x_0^3\right) = 4x_1^1 - x_0^2 + 2x_0^1 x_0^3$$

The analytical format has the advantage of describing the Trellis encoder and corresponding signal level or constellation mapping in a single expression.

10.4.4   *Phase Invariant Trellis Encoders*

For a two-dimensional constellation, such as that of a 16 QAM, the parity of recovered information bits is related to the phase of the carrier in the receiver. The correct carrier phase is usually identified in the initialization process through the use of a known training sequence. Without the reference of the carrier phase, the 16 QAM constellation could become 90° phase invariant.

Note
The automatic recovery of the correct phase is important during a temporary transmission disconnect when the normal training process involving the use of the training sequence is avoided to minimize the recovery time.

Note
180° phase invariant Trellis encoders can be realized with a combination of a one-bit differential encoder, a convolution encoder, and a specially designed bit to symbol mapping.[18] Figures 10.23 and 10.24 show the encoder structure and corresponding constellation mapping for a four-state, 180° phase invariant Trellis encoder.

Figures 10.25 and 10.26 show the encoder structure and corresponding constellation mapping for an alternative four-state, 180° phase invariant Trellis encoder.

180° phase invariant Trellis encoders also can be realized with a combination of a one-bit differential encoder, a convolution encoder in the feedback format, and a specially designed bit-to-symbol mapping in feedback format. Figures 10.27 and 10.28 show the feedback implemented encoder structure and corresponding constellation mapping also for a four-state, 180° phase invariant Trellis encoder.

Figure 10.23 A Four-State 180° Phase Invariant Trellis Encoder

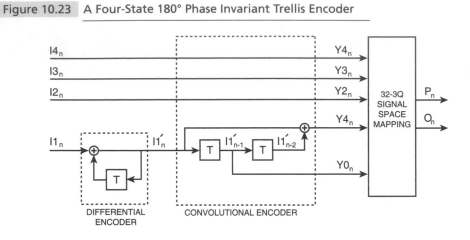

Figure 10.24 A Four-State 180° Phase Invariant Constellation Mapping

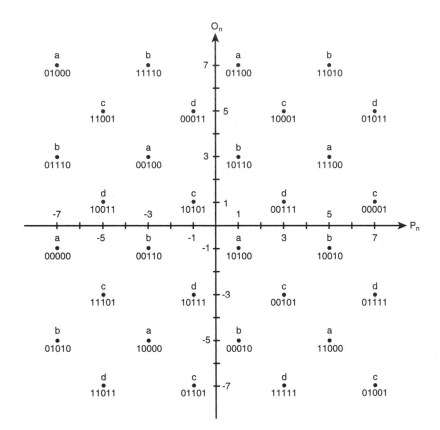

Figure 10.25 Another Four-State 180° Phase Invariant Encoder

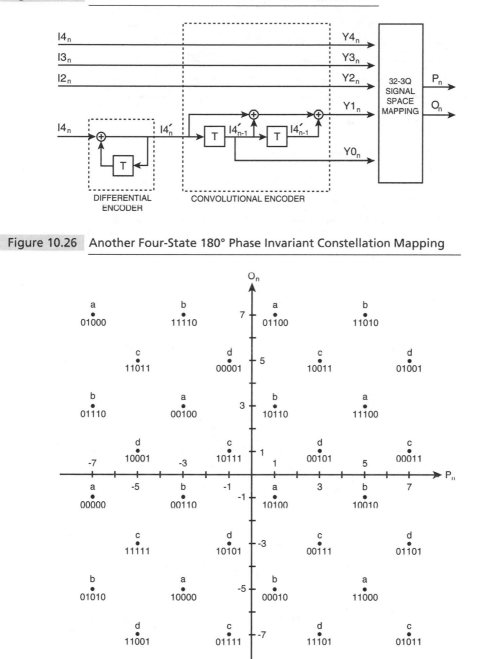

Figure 10.26 Another Four-State 180° Phase Invariant Constellation Mapping

Figure 10.27 A Four-State 180° Feedback Phase Invariant Trellis Encoder

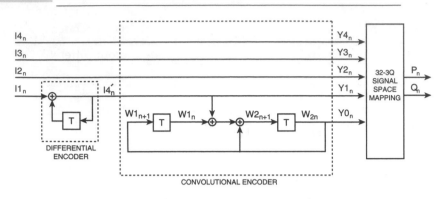

Figure 10.28 A Four-State 180° Feedback Phase Invariant Constellation Mapping

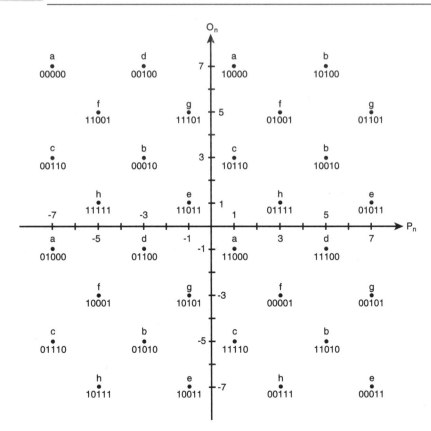

For the feedback implemented Trellis encoder, the differential encoder can sometimes be eliminated. The encoder structure shown in Figure 10.29 in conjunction with the bit mapping of Figure 10.28 also is a four-state, 180° phase invariant Trellis encoder.

Figure 10.29 A 180° Phase Invariant Feedback Trellis Encoder Without Differential Encoding

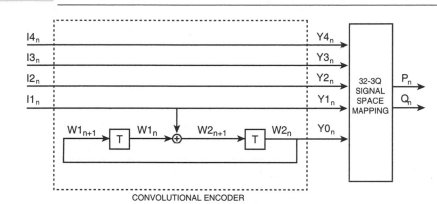

It has been shown that the 90° phase invariant Trellis encoder does not exist;[19] 90° phase invariant Trellis encoders can be realized, however, with non-linear Trellis code.[20] Figures 10.30 and 10.31 show the encoder structure and the constellation mapping of a 90° phase invariant non-linear Trellis encoder.

Figure 10.30 A 90° Phase Invariant Non-Linear Trellis Encoder

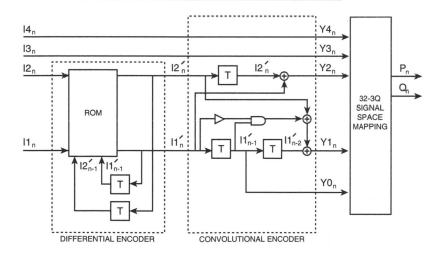

Figure 10.31 A 90° Phase Invariant Non-Linear Trellis Constellation Mapping

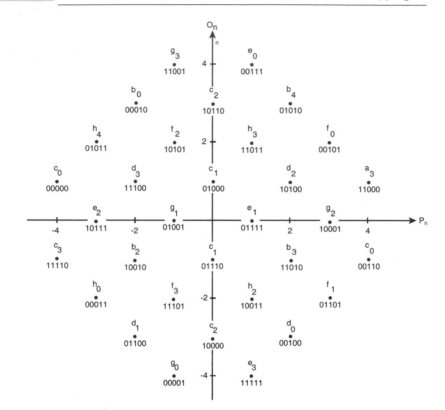

The relationship between two input bits

$$I1'_n \text{ and } I2'_n$$

and three state variables

$$I1'_{n-1}, I1'_{n-2}, \text{ and } I2'_{n-1}$$

and three encoder output bits

$$Y0_n, Y1_n, \text{ and } Y2_n$$

are not linear. For example, for

$$I_{k1} = \begin{bmatrix} I1'_{k1} & I1'_{k1-1} & I1'_{k1-2} & I2'_{k1} & I2'_{k1-1} \end{bmatrix} = \begin{bmatrix} 1 & 0 & 0 & 1 & 1 \end{bmatrix}$$

we have

$$Y_{k1} = \begin{bmatrix} Y2_{k1} & Y1_{k1} & Y0_{k1} \end{bmatrix} = \begin{bmatrix} 0 & 1 & 0 \end{bmatrix}$$

and for

$$I_{k2} = \begin{bmatrix} I1'_{k2} & I1'_{k2-1} & I1'_{k2-2} & I2'_{k2} & I2'_{k2-1} \end{bmatrix} = \begin{bmatrix} 0 & 1 & 0 & 0 & 0 \end{bmatrix}$$

we have

$$Y_{k2} = \begin{bmatrix} Y2_{k2} & Y1_{k2} & Y0_{k2} \end{bmatrix} = \begin{bmatrix} 0 & 1 & 1 \end{bmatrix}$$

However, if we combine I_{k1} and I_{k2} together as the input vector, $I_{k1} \oplus I_{k2} = \begin{bmatrix} 1 & 1 & 0 & 1 & 1 \end{bmatrix}$, the output is $\begin{bmatrix} 0 & 1 & 1 \end{bmatrix}$, which is not the combination of output vectors, $Y_{k1} \oplus Y_{k2} = \begin{bmatrix} 0 & 1 & 0 \end{bmatrix} \oplus \begin{bmatrix} 0 & 1 & 1 \end{bmatrix} = \begin{bmatrix} 0 & 0 & 1 \end{bmatrix}$, due to each individual input vector.

10.4.5   *Multidimensional Trellis Codes*

Multidimensional Trellis codes[21] also can be realized by Trellis encoding of a *multidimensional constellation*. A multidimensional constellation can be realized by combining a multiple of one- or two-dimensional data symbols. For an example, a four-dimensional constellation can be formed by combining two two-dimensional data symbols. If only one extra Trellis coding bit is introduced for a multidimensional constellation, the amount of SNR reduction can be relatively low. The discovery and the definition of a multidimensional Trellis encoder could be quite involved, however.

End Notes

1. S. Lin and D. J. Costello, Jr., *Error Control Coding: Fundamentals and Applications* (Prentice-Hall, 1983).

2. E. Biglieri, D. Divslar, P. J. McLane, and M. K. Simon, *Introduction to Trellis-Coded Modulation with Applications* (Macmillan Publishing Company, 1991).

3. I. S. Reed and G. Solomon, "Polynomial Codes Over Certain Finite Fields," *J. Soc. Ind. Appl. Math.*, 9 (June 1960): 300–304.

4. A. Hocquenghem, "Codes corecteurs d'erreurs," *Chiffres*, 2 (1959): 147–156.

5. R. C. Bose and D. K. Ray-Chaudhuri, "On a Class of Error Correcting Binary Group Codes," *Inf. Control*, 3 (March 1960): 68–79.

6. K. J. Kerpez, "Forward Error Correction for Asymmetric Digital Subscriber Lines (ADSL)," *Bellcore Globecom '91 Proceedings* (November 1991).

7. K. J. Kerpez, "Coding for ADSL," *Bellcore T1E1 Contribution*, T1E1.4/92-153 (August 1992).

8. R. H. Deng and D. J. Costello, "High Rate Concatenated Coding Systems Using Bandwidth Efficient Trellis Inner Codes," *IEEE Trans. Commun.*, vol. 37 (May 1989): 420-427.

9. G. D. Forney, Jr., "Maximum Likelihood Sequence Estimation of Digital Sequences in the Presence of Intersymbol Interference," *IEEE Trans. Inf. Theory*, IT-18 (May 1972): 363–378.

10. A. J. Viterbi, "Error Bounds for Convolutional Codes and an Asymptotically Optimum Decoding Algorithm," *IEEE Trans. Inf. Theory*, IT-13 (April 1967): 260–269.

11. G. Ungerboeck, "Trellis-Coded Modulation with Redundant Signal Sets, Part I: Introduction," *IEEE Communication Magazine*, vol. 25 (February 1987): 5–11.

12. G. Ungerboeck, "Trellis-Coded Modulation with Redundant Signal Sets, Part I: State of The Art," *IEEE Communication Magazine*, vol. 25 (February 1987): 12–21.

13. G. Ungerboeck, "Channel Coding with Multi-Level/Phase Signals," *IEEE Trans. Information Theory*, vol. IT-28 (January 1982): 55–67.

14. G. D. Forney, Jr., "Convolution Codes I: Algebraic Structure," *IEEE Trans. Information Theory*, IT-16 (November 1970): 720–738.

15. E. Biglieri, D. Divsalar, P. J. McLane, and M. K. Simon, *Introduction to Trellis-Coded Modulation with Applications* (Macmillan, 1991).

16. J. E. Porath, "Algorithms for Converting Convolution Codes from Feedback to Feedforward Form and Vice Versa," *Electron. Lett.* (July 1989).

17. A.R. Calderbank and N.J.A. Sloane, "New Trellis Codes Based on Lattices and Cosets," *IEEE Trans. Information Theory*, vol. IT-33 (1987): 177–195.

18. L. F. Wei, "Rotationally Invariant Convolutional Channel Coding with Expanded Signal Space, Part I: 180°," *IEEE JSAC*, vol. SAC-2, no. 5 (September 1984): 659–671.

19. IBM Europe, "Trellis-Coded Modulation Schemes for Use in Data Modems Transmitting 3–7 Bits per Modulation Interval," *CCITT SG XVII Contribution COM XVII*, no. D114 (April 1983).

20. L. F. Wei, "Rotationally Invariant Convolutional Channel Coding with Expanded Signal Space, Part II: Nonlinear Codes," *IEEE JSAC*, vol. SAC-2, no. 5 (September 1984): 672–686.

21. L.F. Wei, "Trellis Coded Modulation with Multi-Dimensional Constellations," *IEEE Trans. Information Theory*, vol. IT-33 (1987): 483–501.

PART II

DSL Systems: System and Transceiver Architectures

DSL (Digital Subscriber Lines)

Digital Subscriber Lines as a transmission technology was originally developed for the *ISDN (Integrated Services Digital Network) Basic Rate Access channel*. The name *DSL* has been used to describe the transmission technology or physical layer for the ISDN Basic Rate Access channel. Most recently, DSL, as well as xDSL, has been used as a generic name to describe any DSL system. The DSL transmission technology for the ISDN Basic Rate Access channel is sometimes referred to as IDSL. In this chapter, we use *DSL* to describe the physical layer for the ISDN Basic Rate Access channel. In contrast, we use *DSL system* as a generic name in this book.

DSL for the ISDN Basic Rate Access channel is the first bandwidth efficient telephone loop transmission system relying on advanced digital signal processing techniques. The development of DSL has involved the extensive examination of up-to-date advanced signal-processing algorithms in conjunction with the evaluation of capable semiconductor technologies. Specifically, the development of DSL went through initial line code proposal, transmission performance simulation study, and hardware prototype testing stages. Similar stages have been repeated by the development of other DSL systems.

This chapter covers the development history, transmission performance, and interface standards of Digital Subscriber Lines, including:

- *DSL technology development*. This section reviews the development history of DSL. It also discusses different duplex methods, including *Frequency Division Multiplex* (FDM), *Time Compressed Multiplex* (TCM), and *echo cancellation*. You also will have the opportunity to study *candidate line codes* and their transmission characteristics.

- *Transceiver structure and line code.* This section discusses general transceiver architecture and transmission characteristics of the *2B1Q DSL line code.* DSL equalizer and echo canceller requirements are calculated. DSL semiconductor technologies and implementation alternatives are reviewed.

- *Performance objectives.* DSL test loop configurations and corresponding transfer functions as well as NEXT models are presented. DSL transmission performances are simulated for these test loops under the self-NEXT noise condition.

- *Network interfaces.* Possible CO as well as *Digital Loop Carrier* (DLC) interfaces for DSL are discussed. The customer end S and T interfaces, including the framing structure, are also described.

- *DSL standards.* Key features of the ANSI 2B1Q DSL standard, including bit-to-symbol encoding, pulse mask, power spectrum mask, test configuration, frame structure, scrambler, and startup timing sequence, are revealed.

11.1 DSL Technology Development

A Digital Subscriber Line (DSL), as defined for ISDN Basic Access,[1,2] provides transmission capability for a single ISDN Basic Access customer over a nonloaded, two-wire telephone loop.[3,4] The DSL has a transmission throughput of 160 kbps that consists of a payload throughput of 144 kbps and an overhead throughput of 16 kbps. The payload throughput is divided into two B channels, each of which is 64 kbps, and one D channel of 16 kbps. The B channel was designed for digital telephony, and the D channel was designed for signaling and packet applications.

The transmission throughput of DSL is symmetrical in downstream (from a CO to a subscriber) and upstream (from a subscriber to a CO) directions. The DSL technology was developed at the ANSI working group T1D1.3, mainly during 1985 and 1986. An initial version of the standard document for DSL was delivered during 1988.[5]

In the early standardization process, four-wire transmission was ruled out because of the large plant cost that it could incur. There are basically three approaches for the two-wire, full-duplex transmission:

- Frequency Division Multiplex (FDM)

- Time Compression Multiplex (TCM)

- Echo cancellation (EC)

The debate on the choice between TCM and EC approaches to DSL provision has been in progress for some time. The central issues in the comparison of these two approaches were transmission loss, echo level, compatibility with other systems, and system complexity. In summary, the TCM system has the advantage of not requiring an echo canceller, as the separation of the different transmission directions occurs in time. This advantage diminishes as economically realized echo cancellers are made available by advances in *Very Large Scale Integrated-Circuits* (VLSI) technology. The EC system, while potentially more complex, uses less than 50 percent of the transmission bandwidth of its TCM counterparts.

The engineering trade-off between these competing technologies resulted in a decision by the ANSI T1D1.3 working group in favor of the adoption of the echo cancellation technique as the DSL transmission technology standard. One of the major reasons why TCM was not chosen as a standard in the U.S. had to do with synchronization. ISDN signals originating from different COs could share the same twisted-pair cable. This requires different COs to be synchronized for all DSL systems, which was not considered feasible in the U.S. telephone network. However, synchronization was feasible in Japan, and TCM was used for a Japanese version of DSL.

11.1.1   FDM Transmission for DSL

Figure 11.1 shows the block diagram of an FDM transceiver. With FDM, the two directions of transmission are assigned to different frequency bands. With the same line code and, therefore, symmetrical bandwidth, the range of the system was thus determined by the range of the lossier high frequency band. It was considered then that the FDM had a heavy range penalty and, therefore, the FDM was ruled out for the DSL. FDM for DSL systems is also sometimes called FDD for *Frequency Division Duplex.*

Figure 11.1   FDM Transceiver Block Diagram

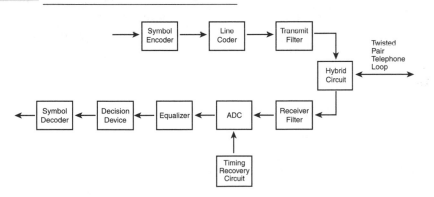

11.1.2 TCM Transmission for DSL

Figure 11.2 shows the block diagram of a TCM transceiver. In TCM, the two directions of transmission are separated in time. With TCM, data transmission actually occurs in half-duplex mode, though to the user it appears to be full-duplex because the gap is smoothed with buffers.

The quiescent period between bursts must be long enough to allow for slight errors in synchronization between opposite ends of the transmission path and to permit transients to die down sufficiently. This requires that the baud rate be approximately 2.25 times that which is required by the throughput for a particular line code. TCM for DSL systems is also sometimes called TDD for *Time Division Duplex*.

Figure 11.2 TCM Transceiver Block Diagram

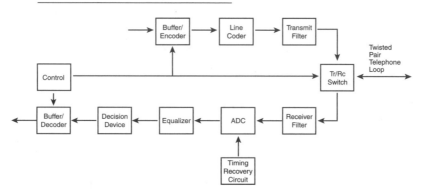

Bursts of transmission alternate between the transmitters on opposite ends of the line, as shown in Figure 11.3. The first row represents continuous data to be transmitted from a CO to a subscriber. The compressed CO-to-subscriber data is shown in the third row. The second row represents continuous data to be transmitted from a subscriber to a CO. The compressed subscriber-to-CO data is shown in the third row. The fourth row is the decompressed CO-to-subscriber data arrived at the subscriber end. The fifth row is the decompressed subscriber-to-CO data arriving at the CO end.

11.1.3 EC-Based Transmission for DSL

Figure 1.4 shows the block diagram of an echo-canceller-based transceiver. The two directions of transmission are separated by a hybrid circuit and the echo canceller. The hybrid circuit can usually provide only about 15 dB of separation. An echo cancellation level of about 60 dB by the echo canceller is required to remove the residual echo. In other words,

75 dB of combined echo-path attenuation is required to make the residual echo level much lower than the weak received signal level over a long telephone subscriber loop.

Figure 11.3 TCM Burst Principle

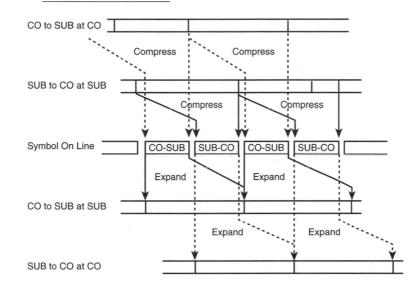

The echo canceller is based on a relatively stable transmit/receive clock. Otherwise, the adaptation of echo canceller coefficients might not be fast enough under the full-duplex operation. The transmit clock and the receiver clock can be locked using loop timing, usually at the customer end.

Figure 11.4 Echo Canceller Transceiver Block Diagram

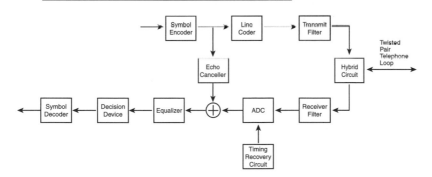

11.1.4 Candidate DSL Line Code Characteristics

There are two general characteristics of line codes that are determinants of their transmission performance: the transmit symbol pulse shape and the logic bit encoding of the symbol. Both symbol pulse shape and logic bit encoding affect the spectrum of a code. Codes considered in the ANSI T1D1.3 working group included the following:

- *2B1Q*.[6] Converts blocks of two consecutive signal bits into a single, four-level pulse. The signaling baud rate is half of the information rate.

- *3B2T*.[7,8] Maps the eight possible combinations of three bits of information into the nine possible combinations of two ternary symbols. This code has lower baud compression than 2B1Q.

- *4B3T*. Maps 16 possible combinations of four bits of information into the 27 possible combinations of three ternary symbols. This block code has less baud rate reduction than 3B2T.

- *AMI (Alternate Mark Inversion)*. Reverses the polarity of a one or mark from that of the previous mark. The baud rate of AMI equals the information rate.

- *MDB (Modified Duobinary)*. Baud rate is the same as the bit rate; however, every baud symbol of the MDB code is repeated with the opposite sign after a baud interval.

- *Manchester*. Also referred to as *Biphase code*, the Manchester code consists of a positive pulse and a negative pulse within a baud. The bandwidth of the Manchester code is twice that of AMI.

Figure 11.5 shows the pulse shapes of these different line codes.

Figure 11.5 Base Pulse Shape of Different Line Codes

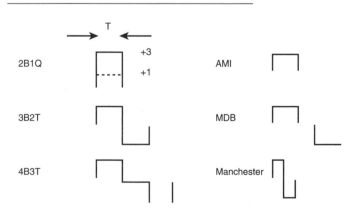

MMS43,[9,10,11,12] which was given the most attention at T1D1.3, is also a 4B3T code with three code books. One of the books contains code words that are biased toward positive polarity, one contains words that are negatively biased, and a third is neutral. In addition, the algebraic sum of recently transmitted symbols determines which code book is used.

Note

A code book defines a mapping between bit patterns of input and output for an encoder.

Interleaving is another method of reducing bandwidth. Interleaving involves splitting the transmission sequence into separate, independently encoded sequences and then adding them. The DI43 code, also considered by T1E1.3, is an interleaved code.[13] The U88 code,[14] invented by J. H. W. Unger, is an 8B8T code designed to give spectra properties that would provide good crosstalk and intersymbol interference performance on subscriber loops.

Note

Name interleaving is also used in conjunction with error correction coding for ADSL discussed in Chapter 13, "ADSL (Asymmetrical Digital Subscriber Lines)."

11.1.5   Candidate DSL Line Code Transmission Performance

The power spectrum of a line code is shaped by both the pulse shape and the coding of the amplitude sequence.[15] In particular, we have the line code power spectral density

$$S_s(f) = \frac{1}{T} S_d(f) |P(f)|^2$$

$S_d(f)$ is the power spectral density of the amplitude level sequence.

$|P(f)|^2$ is the power spectral density of the signaling pulse.

For the rectangular pulse, we have

$$|P(f)|^2 = T^2 \left[\frac{\sin \pi f T}{\pi f T} \right]^2$$

For the 2B1Q line code, we have

$$S_d(f) = \frac{5}{9}$$

$$|P(f)|^2 = T^2 \left[\frac{\sin \pi f T}{\pi f T} \right]^2$$

$$S_{2B1Q}(f) = \frac{5}{9} T' \left[\frac{\sin \pi f T'}{\pi f T'} \right]^2$$

T' is the 2B1Q baud rate, which is half of the bit rate.

For the 3B2T line code, we have the following:

$$S_d(f) = 1$$

$$|P(f)|^2 = T^2 \left[\frac{\sin 2\pi f T}{2\pi f T} \right]^2 + T^2 \left[\frac{\sin \pi f T}{\pi f T} \right]^2 \sin^2(\pi f T) + \frac{1}{2} T^2 \left[\frac{\sin \pi f T}{\pi f T} \right]^2$$

$$S_{3B2T} = T \left[\frac{\sin 2\pi f T}{2\pi f T} \right]^2 + T \left[\frac{\sin \pi f T}{\pi f T} \right]^2 \sin^2(\pi f T) + \frac{1}{2} T \left[\frac{\sin \pi f T}{\pi f T} \right]^2$$

T is the 3B2T baud rate, which is 2/3 of the bit rate.

For the 4B3T line code, the power spectrum density can be calculated depending on the selection of a particular code book. Because of the 16 information bits to 27 different ternary codes ratio, there are multiple choices of code books.

For the AMI line code, we have

$$S_d(f) = \sin^2(\pi f T)$$

$$|P(f)|^2 = T^2 \left[\frac{\sin 2\pi f T}{2\pi f T} \right]^2$$

$$S_{AMI}(f) = T\sin^2(\pi fT)\left[\frac{\sin \pi fT}{\pi fT}\right]^2$$

For the Manchester or Biphase code, we have

$$S_m(f) = T\frac{\sin^4(\pi fT/2)}{(\pi fT/2)}$$

For the MDB code, we have

$$S_d(f) = 1$$

$$|P(f)|^2 = 4T^2\sin^2(2\pi fT)\left[\frac{\sin \pi fT}{\pi fT}\right]^2$$

$$S_{MDB}(f) = 4T\sin^2(2\pi fT)\left[\frac{\sin \pi fT}{\pi fT}\right]^2$$

Figure 11.6 illustrates the power spectrum density for the different line codes.

Figure 11.6   Power Spectrum Density of Different Line Codes

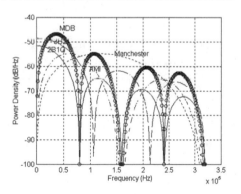

Performances of different line codes for the application of DSL were compared,[16,17,18,19,20,21,22] and it was found that the 2B1Q line code was the most favorable

for its higher performance margin. The performance margin is defined as the difference between the signal-to-noise ratio of a particular line code under the selected loop and noise condition and that desired for the defined error rate. The choice of line code was also considered for system cost[23,24,25,26,27,28,29] and VLSI implementation issues.[30,31,32,33,34,35] Table 11.1 illustrates the relative performance parameters of the different DSL line codes.

Table 11.1 DSL Line Codes and Relative Performance Parameters

Code	Input	Output	Bit/Symbol	Redundancy	Margin
2B1Q	2 bits	1 quaternary	2	0	12 dB
3B2T	3 bits	2 ternary	3/2	1/9	9–10 dB
4B3T	4 bits	3 ternary	4/3	11/27	9–10 dB
AMI	1 bit	1 ternary	1	1/3	6–8 dB
MDB	1 bit	1 ternary	1	1/3	6–8 dB
Manchester	1 bit	1 bit	1	0	2–4 dB

11.2   *DSL Transceiver Structure and Line Code*

Figure 11.7 shows the general architecture of a DSL transceiver. The data is first scrambled to prevent long streams of zeros or ones. Every two bits of transmit signal are encoded into a symbol through the 2B1Q encoder. The symbol or baud rate is therefore one-half of the bit rate. The symbol is sent to the line encoder, which can be a Digital to Analog Converter (DAC) with or without a digital pulse shaping function.

A second-order Butterworth lowpass filter is used for the transmit filter and receiver filter. The transmit filter reduces the out-of-band energy. The receiver filter minimizes the out-of-band noise. Before using the Analog to Digital Converter (ADC) for analog to digital conversion, a preamplifier is necessary to bring the received signal to the proper voltage level. The ADC is synchronized to the timing recovery circuits.

These same 2B1Q data symbols also are sent to the echo canceller—which resembles the equivalence of the echo path, including transmit filter, hybrid circuits, receiver filter, and ADC at the ADC sampling rate. The 2B1Q encoder's sampling clock is also synchronized to the ADC sampling clock to maintain a stable echo path transfer function. The digitized and echo-canceled received signal is further filtered by the decision feedback channel equalizer before being sent to the *decision device.*

Figure 11.7   A General DSL Transceiver Structure

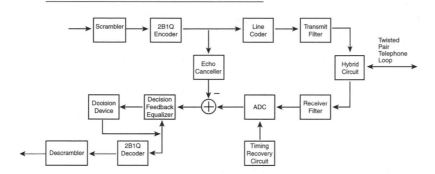

The decision device is a four-level threshold detector corresponding to the 2B1Q line code. Received symbols generated from the decision device are converted back to information bits through the 2B1Q decoder. The binary bit information is descrambled to obtain the original data stream.

11.2.1   DSL 2B1Q Line Code Parameters

Table 11.2 shows the general transceiver parameters.

Table 11.2   DSL Transceiver Parameters

Line code	2B1Q
Bandwidth (3 dB)	40 kHz
Baud rate	80 kHz
Line rate	160 kbps
Transmit power	12.99 dBm (135 Ohms)

The receiver sampling rate as well as the baud rate is 80 kHz, resulting in a 3 dB transmission bandwidth of 40 kHz. For the 2B1Q line code, each baud carries two bits of information. Therefore, the transmission throughput is 160 kbps. Assuming a power supply of 5 volts and a utilization efficiency of 88 percent, the maximum transmit output voltage is 2.2 volts. For a line impedance of 135 ohms, the total transmit power delivered on the telephone loop is expressed as follows:

$$P = \frac{1}{2}\left(2.2^2 + \left(\frac{2.2}{3}\right)^2\right)\frac{1}{135} = \frac{4.84}{2 \times 135}\left(1 + \frac{1}{9}\right) = \frac{4.84 \times 10}{2 \times 135 \times 9} = 0.01992\,Watts = 12.99\,dBm$$

The DSL transmit power density is expressed as

$$PSD = \frac{0.01992}{40 \times 10^3} = 4.98 \times 10^{-7} \, Watts \, / \, Hz = -33.0 dBm \, / \, Hz$$

11.2.2 DSL Equalizer Requirements

The length of the decision feedback equalizer should be long enough to cover the duration of the equivalent channel impulse response. The equivalent channel response is the combination of the transmit filter, the transmit transformer, the twisted-pair loop channel, the receiver transformer, and the receiver filter. Figure 11.8 shows the impulse response of the 15 kft, 26-gauge loop.

Figure 11.8 Impulse Response of the 15 kft, 26-Gauge Loop

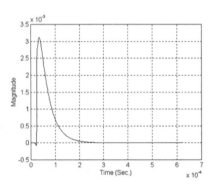

Figure 11.9 shows the impulse response of a second-order Butterworth lowpass filter that was recommended for the transmit/receiver filter.

Figure 11.9 Impulse Response of the Second-Order Butterworth Lowpass Filter

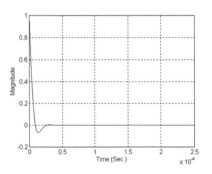

Figure 11.10 shows the impulse response of the equivalent channel that includes two second-order lowpass filters and the 15 kft, 26-gauge twisted-pair loop in cascade assuming the transmission characteristics of transformers are almost ideal.

Figure 11.10 Impulse Response of the Equivalent Channel

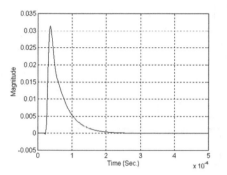

The equivalent channel impulse response approaches zero at about 300 microseconds. Considering 30 microseconds of peak delay, the feedback filter should last about 270 microseconds. For a baud sampling rate of 80 kHz, the time between each sample is 12.5 microseconds. Therefore we need about 22 (the round up of 270/12.5=21.6) feedback filter taps. The feedforward filter should have sufficient length to cover the equivalent channel impulse response up to the peak. The required number of feedforward filter taps is therefore three (the round up of 30/12.5=2.4).

11.2.3 DSL Echo Canceller Requirements

The length of the echo canceller should be long enough to cover the duration of the equivalent echo path impulse response. The equivalent echo path response is the combination of the transmit filter, the echo path, and the receiver filter. Assuming for an ideal transformer, the echo path transfer function for the hybrid circuit of Figure 11.11 can be described as:

$$H_{ec}(s) = \frac{RZ_i(s) - RR_b}{(Z(s) + R)(R_b + R)}$$

$Z_i(s)$ is the input impedance of the subscriber loop.

Figure 11.11 A Simplified Echo Path Circuit

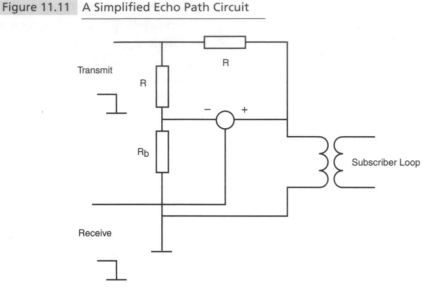

Figure 11.12 shows the impulse response of the echo path in conjunction with a 15 kft, 26-gauge loop.

Figure 11.12 The Impulse Response of an Echo Path

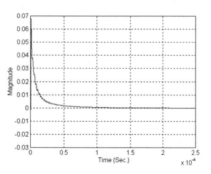

Figure 11.13 shows the impulse response of the equivalent echo path, which includes two second-order lowpass filters and the echo path, in conjunction with a 15 kft, 26-gauge twisted-pair loop in cascade, assuming the transmission characteristics of transformers are almost ideal.

The echo path impulse response approaches zero at about 150 microseconds. Therefore, we need about 150/12.5=12 filter taps for the echo canceller.

The performance of DSL is limited by self-NEXT for long loops. Figure 11.14 depicts the signal-to-NEXT noise ratio from about 65 dB at near DC to about 0 dB at about 135 kHz. The 49 disturber NEXT model is used.

Figure 11.13 The Impulse Response of the Equivalent Echo Path

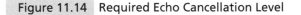

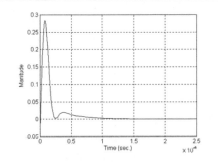

Figure 11.14 Required Echo Cancellation Level

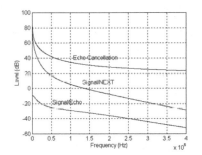

On the other hand, we also see from Figure 11.14 that the signal-to-echo ratio is negative at all frequencies because the echo path return loss is always smaller than the channel loss. Figure 11.14 also shows the required echo cancellation level, which is the difference between the signal-to-noise ratio and the signal-to-echo ratio. The required echo cancellation level, which ranges from 80 dB at near DC to 30 dB at about 135 kHz, is expressed as follows:

$$K_{ec}(f) = \frac{\dfrac{|H(f)|^2}{NEXT(f)}}{\dfrac{|H(f)|^2}{|H_{ec}(f)|^2}} = \frac{|H_{ec}(f)|^2}{NEXT(f)}$$

$H(f)$ is the channel transfer function.

$H_{ec}(f)$ is the echo path transfer function.

$NEXT(f)$ is the NEXT power coupling function.

The required average echo cancellation level is

$$\overline{K}_{ec} = \frac{1}{f_{max}} \int_0^{f_{max}} K_{ec}(f)df = 68dB$$

in which $f_{max} = 135kHz$. Although the main energy of DSL is concentrated at below 40 kHz, the signal spectrum of DSL extends above 100 kHz due to its side lopes and a low order transmit filter. The required echo cancellation level for an echo canceller implementation can be relaxed a little because the larger than 60 dB signal to residual echo ratio at low frequencies might not be necessary due to hardware quantization noises.

11.2.4 DSL Timing Recovery Circuits

The timing recovery circuit of a DSL transceiver can be implemented with the spectral line method.[36] Figure 11.15 shows the block diagram of the timing recovery circuit using the spectral line method.

Figure 11.15 A Spectral Line Timing Recovery Circuit

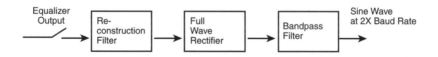

The input of the timing recovery circuit is connected to the output of the decision feedback channel equalizer. The timing recovery circuit consists of the following components:

- *Reconstruction filter.* Generates an analog version of the equalized and echo-canceled signal. The frequency characteristics of the reconstruction filter can be optimized to minimize the timing jitter.

- *Full wave rectifier.* Generates harmonics of the received signal. A square operation can sometimes be used instead of the rectifying operation for the same purpose of harmonics generation.

- *Bandpass filter.* Selects the desired sampling frequency. The bandwidth of the bandpass filter is usually relatively narrow, and the Q relatively high.

The timing recovery circuit can be implemented with digital circuits with a sampling rate that is at least three to four times the baud rate.

The timing recovery circuit of a DSL transceiver can also be implemented with the baud rate sampling techniques.[37] Figure 11.16 illustrates a block diagram of the timing recovery circuit using the baud rate sampling method in conjunction with a decision feedback channel equalizer.

Figure 11.16 A Baud Rate Sampling Timing Recovery Circuit

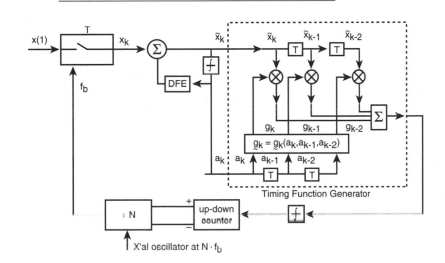

The timing function generator functional block uses both the equalized and echo-canceled signal and the estimated data symbol to generate the timing information to drive an up-down counter. The function g_k can be chosen as simple as

$$g_k = a_k x_{k-1} - a_{k-1} x_k$$

The output of the timing function generator is used to control the up-down counter. We obtain the nominal sampling clock rate by dividing a master clock by a nominal N. The up count action will increase the value of N and subsequently reduce the sampling rate. A down count action will decrease the value of N and subsequently increase the sampling rate. The timing recovery circuit can be implemented with digital circuits operating at the baud rate.

11.3 DSL Semiconductor Technologies

The capability of semiconductor technology has been a primary consideration during the development of DSL. The economic feasibility of DSL was studied based on the cost structure of VLSI technologies. The performance and integration requirements in turn pushed the state of the art of related semiconductor technologies. The adaptive echo cancellation for DSL was quite a challenge for semiconductor digital signal processing circuits operating at a sampling rate of 160 kHz compared with that of voice band modem at only 8 kHz at that time. At such a high sampling rate, the implementation of ADC and DAC also demanded some special analog circuit techniques.

Overall, the partitioning of different functions among digital and analog semiconductor circuits was itself an interesting task. To reduce system cost, the amount of discrete components in addition to the semiconductor chips was minimized. A single-chip solution that included both analog and digital circuits also was part of the cost minimization objective.

11.3.1 A COM DSL Analog Front-End Chip from Siemens

The analog front-end part of a DSL chip set was implemented using the 2 μm double-metal CMOS technology. It consists of about 58,000 transistors for a chip size of 8.2 by 7.3 mm². The power consumption of this analog front-end chip is about 125 mW.[38] Figure 11.17 shows the functional block diagram of this analog front-end chip, which has four major functional blocks: pulse shaper, line driver, wake up signal detector, and A/D converter.

Figure 11.17 Block Diagram of a Transceiver

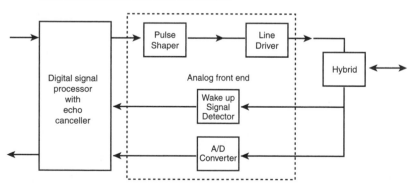

Figure 11.18 shows the functional circuit diagram of the transmit direction for a 2B1Q-coded signal with levels of +3, +1, −1, and −3. At the pulse shaper, positive or negative pulses are formed using charge redistribution between an array of six switched capacitors C_1 to C_6 and the capacitor C_{i1} in the feedback loop of an operational amplifier V_1. To get a fully

differential approach, a second set of six switched capacitors, not shown in Figure 11.18, and the capacitor C_{i2} are implemented at the positive input of V_1. A reset pulse R is used to close switches across C_{i1} and C_{i2}, thereby setting a voltage $V_s=0$ at the differential outputs of V_1 at an appropriate time.

Figure 11.18 Transmit Part

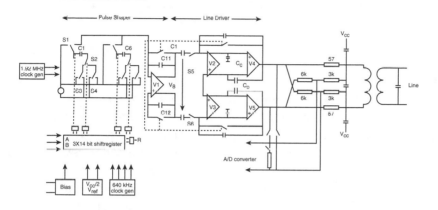

The line driver is built up by two stages of push-pull power amplifiers: V_2, V_3, V_4, and V_5. The gain of the power amplifiers is set to 1.2, corresponding to a capacitor feedback with $C_A=3$ pF and $C_B=2.5$ pF. By using a capacitor feedback, there are no common-mode signals at the input of the line drivers. The hybrid function of the interface is performed with six external resistors if the switches S are nonconducting. With zero output impedance of the line driver and a 150 Ω load, they act as a bridge circuit with high echo return loss to the input of the A/D converter. The amplitude of a single +3 pulse at the load is 2 volts.

The capacitors in the external coupling circuit are part of a low pass filter. The filter is used to smooth the staircase of the transmit pulses. The capacitors connected to Vcc avoid oscillation of the line driver at high frequencies. For testing the transceiver, the transmit pulse can be looped back in the receive direction. To do this, the switches S, realized as low-impedance MOS transistors, are put in a conducting state. The resistor in series with one of the switches together with other switches build a voltage divider to prevent overloading of the A/D converter in the loopback mode.

Figure 11.19 shows a simplified schematic for a second-order sigma-delta modulator.[39] Two integrators in the forward path, two 1-bit DACs in the feedback path, and a 1-bit ADC (a comparator) are used. An over-sampling frequency of 15.36 MHz and a second-order noise shaping filter guarantee an adequate accuracy, which is independent of capacitor or resistor ratio. The quantization noise is less than −65 dB at the output of a following digital filter with 120 kHz bandwidth, which is implemented in the digital part of the transceiver.

Figure 11.19 A Second-Order Sigma-Delta Modulator

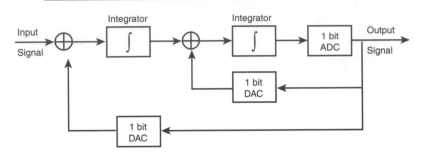

Figure 11.20 shows a functional circuit schematic of the realized sigma-delta modulator. Switched-capacitor integrators in a fully differential configuration are used in the forward path. The operational amplifiers are folded cascade amplifiers with dynamic common-mode feedback. To ensure proper settling in the switched-capacitor integrators working with a clock rate of 15 mHz requires operational amplifiers with bandwidth above 100 mHz. The 1-bit ADC following these two integrators consists of a clocked comparator and a subsequently added RS flip-flop. Using a four-phase clock in the switched-capacitor circuitry minimizes nonlinearities caused by feedthrough.[40]

Figure 11.20 Receiver Part

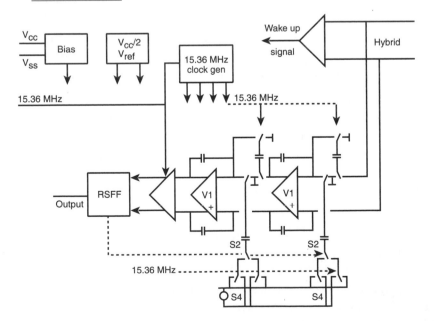

11.3.2   A DSL Analog and Digital Chip Set from AT&T

Another DSL chip set, the AT&T ISDN Chip Set (see Figure 11.21), has a digital *Algorithm Specific Signal* (ASSP) part implemented using the 1.75 μm double-poly CMOS technology and an analog front-end (AFE) part implemented using the 1.25 μm double-metal CMOS technology with chip sizes of 14.5 mm² and 47 mm², respectively.[41] The ASSP consists of *Decision Feedback Equalizer* (DFE), *RECeiver filter* (REC), *Timing Recovery* (TR), *Automatic Gain Control* (AGC), *Nonlinear Echo Canceller* (NEC), *Linear Echo Canceller* (LEC), *DECimation* (DEC), and *TEST functional blocks.* The AFE consists of 2B1Q encoder, sample and hold, transmitter filter, line driver, sigma-delta A to D converter, and D to A converter in conjunction with the *Voltage Controlled Crystal Oscillator* (VCXO).

Figure 11.21   The Functional Block Diagram of the AT&T ISDN Chip Set

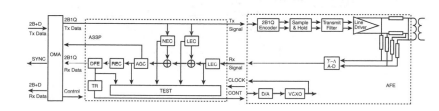

11.3.3   A Single-Chip DSL Solution from Mitel Semiconductor

A single-chip DSL solution was also implemented using a 2 μm single-metal CMOS technology.[42] The single-chip solution DSL chip consists of about 60,000 transistors with chip size of 65.5 mm². Figure 11.22 shows the functional block diagram of this *Digital Subscriber Line Integrated Circuit* (DSLIC). At the encoder, the data stream is scrambled, a 12-bit CRC is calculated, and a nine-symbol synchronization word is inserted before the stream is converted into a two-bit parallel word at 80 kbaud/s. A four-level encoding sampled-analog finite impulse response (FIR) transmit filter, smoothing filter, and dual line drivers are used to differentially drive the line through a transformer.

On the receiver side, analog-to-digital conversion is performed by an over-sampled, second-order delta-sigma converter running at 10.24 mHz master clock rate. All echo cancellation and equalization is then performed in the digital domain using dedicated baud-rate sampling DSP hardware. After frame and superframe recovery, decoding, and descrambling, the data stream is recovered. An on-chip PLA state machine implements a training sequence generator to control the adaptive structures and perform the ANSI network-termination (NT)/line-termination (LT) activation/deactivation procedures. Clock recovery is accomplished by digital phase-locked loops within the DSP and interface, driven by timing decisions derived from the received 2B1Q line signal.

Figure 11.22 DSLIC Block Diagram

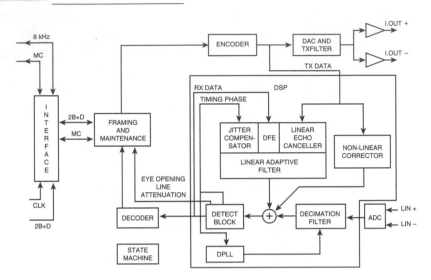

The *Linear Adaptive Filter* (LAF) implements the transceiver's *Linear Echo Canceller* (LEC) and DFE. For both functions, the processing in each line symbol interval consists of

- A convolution of recent quaternary data values with the tap weights of a FIR fitter, generating a linear correction to be applied to the received signal

- An update of tap weights using the clipped LMS algorithm

The LAF is implemented in three main sections:

- A block of three-transistor DRAM for storage of 58 LEC, JC (jitter compensator), DFE, taps, and 58 corresponding transmit and receive data values

- A data path far convolution

- A data path for update

Each data path has an associated controller implemented in random logic. The RAM is addressed cyclically with each tap weight, and its corresponding data value, being both read and written once per line symbol interval. Figure 11.23 shows the functional block diagram of the Linear Adaptive Filter.

Figure 11.23   Linear Adaptive Filter Block Diagram

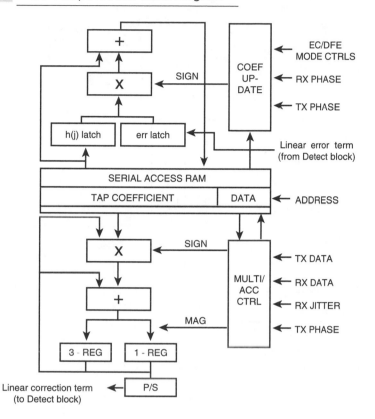

The *Nonlinear Corrector* (NLC) implements a modular RAM-based table look-up adaptive filter. Each NLC module maintains 16 values in a look-up table. Each value is the correction to be applied when one of 16 possible pairs of successive transmit data values is transmitted. The NLC models nondispersive and dispersive nonlinearity is caused by the interaction between two successive transmit symbols. This structure was chosen because the dominant nonlinearity is in the analog transmit circuitry, where pulses overlap about 60 percent of the time due to two successive transmit symbols.

Each NLC module, as shown in Figure 11.24, consists of a block of three-transistor DRAM of size 16 words×24 bits, address/refresh logic, a PISO/SIPO, and a serial adder.

Figure 11.24 Nonlinear Corrector Module Block Diagram

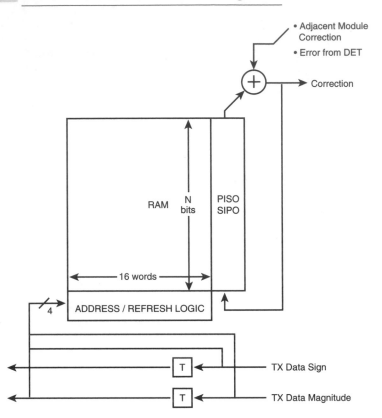

In each line symbol interval, the RAM is accessed three times in the following sequence:

1. The chosen data value is read, serialized, and added to values from other NLC modules to form an overall nonlinear correction.

2. The same value is read again, serialized, and added to an error value, generating the updated value.

3. The updated value is converted to parallel form and written back to RAM. When not in use for read/write access, the address/refresh logic carries out a cyclical refresh of the RAM.

The performance requirements of the ADC can be determined by analyzing the variation, in input level, and required echo cancellation, as one varies the loop length (attenuation) of the transmission system. Due to the strong presence of the near-end component, the input range varies only by some 10 dB, while the highest SNR is required at the lowest signal level because the far end is so heavily attenuated.

A total SNR of approximately 70 dB was found to be necessary to achieve the desired margin. A second-order delta-sigma modulator with an over-sampling ratio of 128 (master clock to decimated output clock) was chosen due to its capability to meet the requirements, its suitability for MOS integration, and after consideration of the inherent tradeoffs between silicon area and design time.

Figure 11.25 illustrates a block diagram of the ADC. Nondelaying integrators were chosen because they result in lower output levels and reduced slew requirements in the operational amplifiers. Time-domain simulations, with sinusoidal inputs, of this structure predict an SNR of 84 dB for a 40 kHz bandwidth (brickwall filter) and 71 dB for an 80 kHz bandwidth. The actual decimation filter used results in an effective bandwidth between these two extremes.

Figure 11.25   Block Diagram of Second-Order Delta-Sigma Modulator

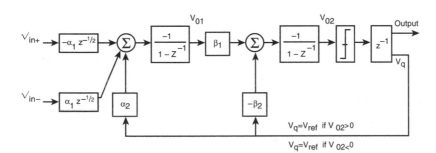

11.3.4   A Single-Chip DSL Solution from National Semiconductor

Another single-chip DSL solution was implemented using a 1.5 μm double-metal CMOS technology.[43] This single-chip solution DSL chip has a chip size of 77 mm². Analog signal processing preconditions the signal by maximizing the dynamic range utilization of the 13-bit A/D converter. The digital signal processor performs the high-pass filtering, precursor equalization, linear echo cancellation, far-end signal equalization, and timing recovery functions. The analog signal preconditioning technique enables the entire DSP section to be designed without a single dedicated multiplier.

As shown by Figure 11.26, there are three main functional sections:

- The digital interface on the left of the diagram

- The digital signal processor (DSP) at the center

- The analog front end at the right

Figure 11.26 Transceiver Block Diagram

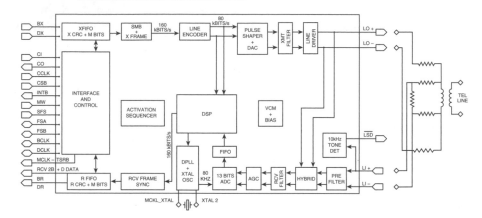

The digital interface adapts the data rate from 144 to 160 kbps, formats the transmit data, and inserts cyclic redundancy check (CRC) and maintenance bits. The resulting data stream is then scrambled, and 18-b synchronization words are inserted.

The analog front end (AFE) of the DSL transceiver is tailored completely to improving the far-end signal-to-echo ratio, band-limiting this composite signal to achieve higher immunity to noise and to enable baud-rate sampling. As shown by Figure 11.27, the AFE contains the following circuit functions:

- A pulse-density-modulation (PDM) 2B1Q signal generator and line driver

- An adaptive echo precanceller or hybrid balance filter

- An antialiasing filter

- A lowpass receiver filter

- An adaptive gain control (AGC) circuit

- An Analog to Digital Converter (ADC)

The *Digital Signal Processor* (DSP) completes the echo cancellation task and performs far-end signal equalization and timing recovery utilizing a sampled signal strongly preconditioned by the AFE. Figure 11.28 shows the major circuit blocks in the DSP section, which include a highpass filter, a precursor equalizer, an adaptive echo canceller, an adaptive decision feedback equalizer, and the timing recovery function.

Figure 11.27 Analog Front-End Block Diagram

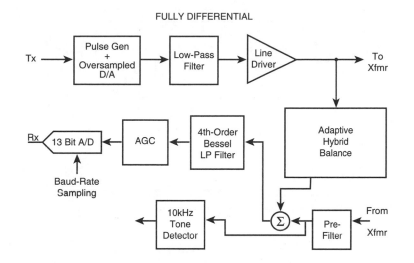

Figure 11.28 DSP Functional Block Diagram

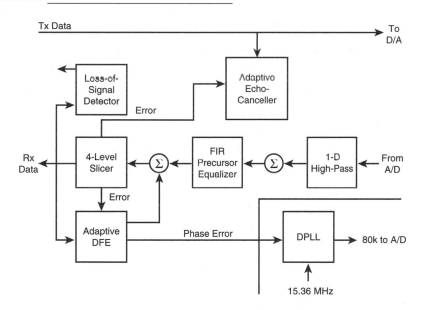

As shown in Figure 11.29, the DSP computation tasks were divided between two identical arithmetical and logical units—ALU1 and ALU2—each of which operated at 7.68 mHz.

Figure 11.29 DSP Architecture

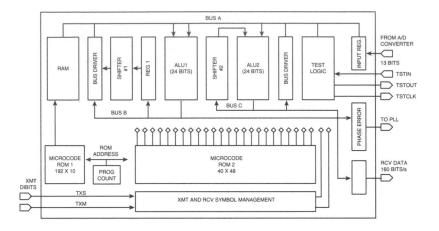

The instruction set executed by each of the two ALUs was limited to addition, subtraction, pass-through (data transfer), shift one location left (X2), and shift two locations left (X4). Rather than dedicating one ALU to each of the filtering tasks, it was more economical to share ALU2 between both the EC and DFE convolutions, while ALU1 performs the EC and DFE coefficient updating. This architecture minimizes busing by enabling the two ALUs to share the same input bus *A*. A shorter bus *B* returns the updated coefficients to the RAM, and transfers the phase error information to the main phaselocked loop.

The 80-word RAM stores the 34 EC and the 34 DFE coefficients, as well as several intermediary variables. During each cycle of the 7.68 mHz clock, one coefficient is read from the RAM, while the previous updated coefficient is returned to the RAM. The RAM address is provided by ROM1. Another microcode ROM, ROM2, generates the commands for the two ALUs and for the data-path registers and shifters.

11.4   DSL Performance Objectives

The performance of the DSL system is decided by the transmission characteristics of the twisted-pair telephone loop, the receiver front-end noise level, and the structure of the DSL transceiver. Figures 11.30, 11.32, and 11.34 show configurations of 15 selected DSL test loops.[44] The transmission characteristics of these loops are representative for the 10 percent worst nonloaded resistance design loops.

As indicated by their transfer functions, the first five loops have the most transmission losses (see Figure 11.31), the next five loops have fewer losses (see Figure 11.33), and the last five loops have the least losses (see Figure 11.35). These transfer functions are characterized by a 15 dB loss at about 1 kHz, and about a 35 to 45 dB loss at about 50 kHz. Bridged taps cause nulls at different frequencies.

Figure 11.30   Test Loops 1–5

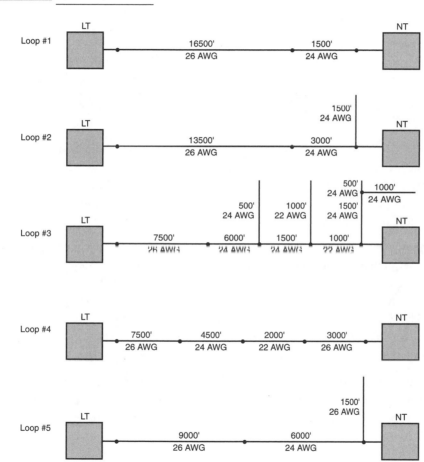

Figure 11.31 Transfer Functions of ISDN Test Loops 1–5

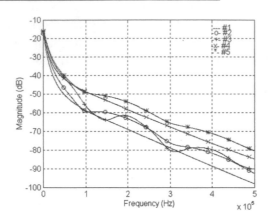

Because of the use of the echo-cancellation-based full-duplex method, the dominant noise component at the receiver front end is the self Near End Crosstalk (NEXT). The self-NEXT is induced by neighboring DSL transmitters. The NEXT noise level depends on the transmit signal level and the NEXT loss. Figure 11.36 shows the DSL NEXT loss model derived from the 1 percent, 49-disturber NEXT loss model.

The performance of a DSL transceiver can be estimated through computer simulation. A white binary sequence is generated and encoded as a random data symbol sequence. The binary sequence is generated at the data transmission rate and 2B1Q encoded into the symbol rate. Meanwhile, a white Gaussian sequence is also generated to drive the NEXT filter. The white Gaussian sequence is generated at the simulation sampling rate. The simulation sampling rate is usually 5 to 10 times that of the baud rate to emulate the channel covering excessive bandwidth signal energy and to show the effect of sampling phase.

The performance of a DSL transceiver is simulated using the virtual DSL system, as shown in Figure 11.37, assuming that the residual echo level is insignificant and, therefore, can be ignored. The received signal is the combination of the data symbol after the equivalent channel and the white Gaussian sequence after the equivalent NEXT coupling function.

The equivalent channel consists of the transmit filter, the channel, and the receiver filter. The equivalent NEXT coupling function consists of the transmit filter, the NEXT filter, and the receiver filter. Both transmit and receiver filters are second-order Butterworth filters with a 3 dB corner frequency of 40 kHz. The channel models are 15 selected DSL test loops. The NEXT filter is an FIR filter designed according to the DSL NEXT loss model.

Figure 11.32 Test Loops 6–10

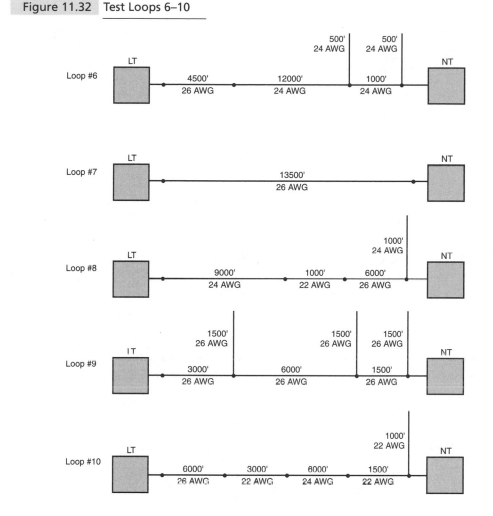

Figure 11.38 shows the impulse response of the NEXT FIR filter, and Figure 11.39 shows the transfer function of the NEXT FIR filter. For the simplicity of computer simulation, the effect of the analog transmit shaping filter is also included in this NEXT filter.

Figure 11.33 Transfer Functions of ISDN Test Loops 6–10

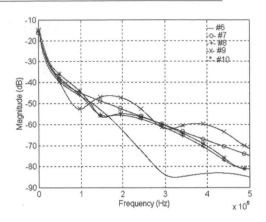

Table 11.3 shows simulated DEF output SNR for the 15 test loops. The required SNR is 21.5 dB for an error rate of 10^{-7}. A 6 dB measured performance margin is required for DSL test loops 5 through 15. The 6 dB of performance margin on test loops 1 through 4 is difficult to reach, even for simulation results in which timing error and some other hardware tolerance have not been accounted for.

The simulation results in Table 11.3 are based on a baud rate DFE with 5 FFF and 32 FBF coefficients. Results might be different for different DFE size and other hardware parameter assumptions.

Table 11.3 Simulated Performance on 15 DSL Test Loops

Test Loop Number	SNR	Margin
1	23.6	2.1
2	20.5	−1.0
3	25.8	4.3
4	23.4	1.9
5	32	10.5
6	32.9	11.4
7	33.2	11.7
8	32.5	11.0
9	30.4	8.9
10	32.0	10.5

Test Loop Number	SNR	Margin
11	34.6	13.1
12	35.5	14.0
13	34.1	12.6
14	40.2	18.7
15	37.5	16.0

Figure 11.34 Test Loops 11–15

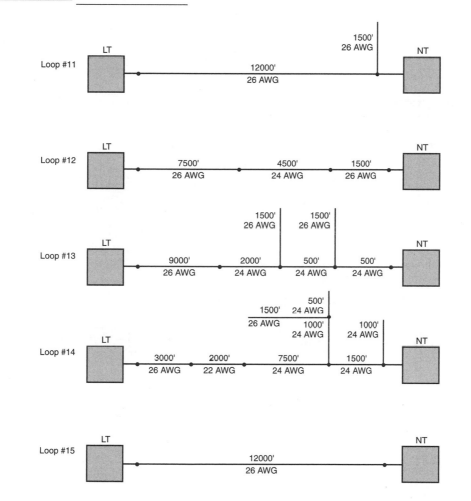

Figure 11.35 Transfer Functions of ISDN Test Loops 11–15

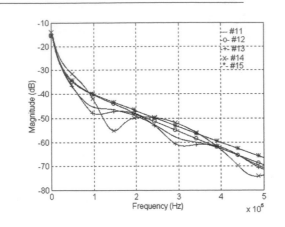

Figure 11.36 NEXT Model

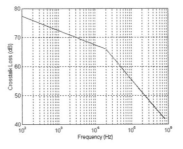

Figure 11.37 The Generation of DSL Received Signal

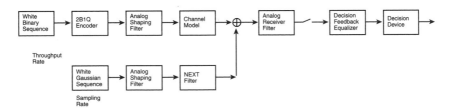

Figure 11.38 Impulse Response of the NEXT Filter

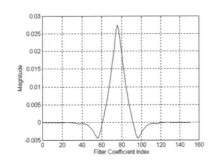

Figure 11.39 Transfer Function of the NEXT Filter

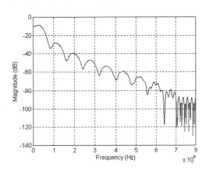

11.5 DSL Network Interfaces

The concept of the Integrated Service Digital Network (ISDN) was gradually formed from aspects of end-to-end digitization of telephony services, data users, integration of services, Intelligent Network Architecture (INA), and the improvement of traffic efficiency.[45]

It was discovered that the digital technology can be used to improve telephone equipment efficiency during these telephone service expansion days. Now, Central Offices and the network connections in between them are all digital. Today, the digitization of POTS happens right at its local connecting Central Office. Major corporations are early data users to interconnect their own computer networks. Small businesses become important data users when their productivity depends on the access of commercial data networks. Individual data users work at home either during or after regular hours to reach their business data networks.

With digitization of all applications, services with different rates and different transmission requirements can all be processed with the same switch and network equipment. Features and capabilities of different services can be all realized at user end equipment with the help of properly defined communication protocols. The concept of INA is based on the coordination of trunk, network, service, and management capabilities. With the concentration of switch and transmission capabilities, the equipment efficiency is increased and the service quality is improved.

The concept of ISDN is to have integrated access—which is defined as a single point of access to multiple networks and to different kinds of networks—for all digitized services. Access interfaces of ISDN are defined as Basic Rate Access with two B channels and one D channel, Primary Rate Access with 23 B channels and one D channel, and Multiple Access. The throughput of Multiple Access can be H0 of 384 kbps or H1 of 1.536 Mbps.

DSL was developed for the Basic Rate Access ISDN interface with two B channels and one D channel. The total transmission throughput for two B channels and one D channel is 144 kbps, while the transmission throughput of DSL is 160 kbps. The difference of 16 kbps is allocated for the overhead channel. The D channel can be used to send switching signals, such as SS7, for the connection of these B channels. Depending on the user terminal type, B channels can be used for either POTS or data applications.

Two B channels can be reverse multiplexed to provide a digital link between end users with a transmission throughput of 128 kbps. The D channel can also be used for packet-oriented applications, via X.25, for example, by itself. The overhead channel connects DSL transceivers at both ends after the initialization of the DSL link. The overhead channel consists of timing and framing information, consuming a throughput of 12 kbps, and networking operation information, consuming a throughput of 4 kbps.

A DSL can be used to connect an ISDN capable CO, a *remote terminal* (RT), which is extended from an ISDN capable CO via a Digital Loop Carrier (DLC), or a serving CO that is extended from an ISDN capable CO via an integrated interoffice digital carrier to an end Basic Rate Access ISDN user, as shown in Figure 11.40.

A DSL is designed to provide Basic Access Rate ISDN connections between an ISDN capable Central Office and subscriber ISDN terminal equipment. Figure 11.41 illustrates the components of the DSL link between the CO and the telephone subscriber.

Figure 11.40 Architecture for ISDN Basic Rate Access

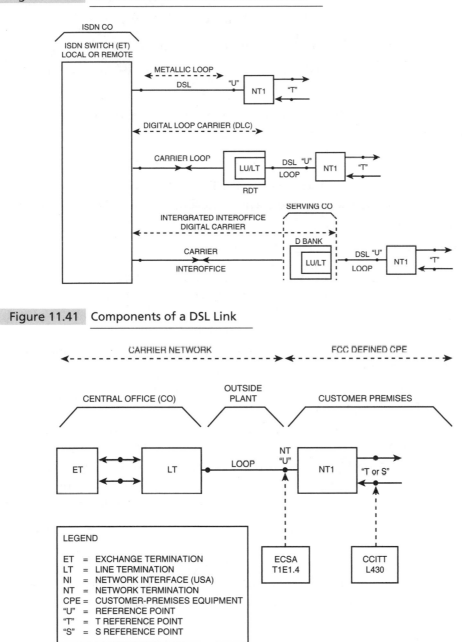

Figure 11.41 Components of a DSL Link

The definition and functions of the DSL link components are as follows:

- *Line Termination (LT)*. The DSL transceiver at the Central Office side.

- *Network Termination 1 (NT1)*. The DSL transceiver at the subscriber side.

- *U interface*. The connection between a DSL transceiver and the twisted-pair loop for both LT and NT1.

- *T interface*. The connection between an NT1 and subscriber terminal equipment (TE), which only specifies network layer 1 multiplexing and maintenance functions.

- *Network Termination 2 (NT2)*. Can be placed between an NT1 and a TE.

- *S interface*. The connection between a NT2 and a TE, which specifies network layers 2 and 3 protocol handling, switching, and maintenance functions. The S interface is more suitable for PBX connections.

- *Exchange Termination (ET)*. Connects the telephone network to an LT.

The Basic Rate Access provided by a DSL is available to subscriber ISDN terminal equipment through the T or S interfaces. Typical ISDN telephony terminal equipment as originally defined has the capability of 2 POTS lines and a data port of 16 kbps corresponding to these two B channels and one D channel. The T interface can be implemented as a bus with two pairs of twisted pairs, enabling multiple ISDN terminal equipment to be connected to the same T interface. A simpler ISDN telephony terminal could have the capability of only one POTS channel supported by the choice of either of these two B channels plus the access to the D channel for switch signaling.

An ISDN-to-POTS Converter (IPC) can also be used to connect a conventional telephone set, a conventional FAX machine, or a voice band modem to the ISDN line. The IPC also could have a serial port or an Ethernet interface for computer networking. The IPC can have either a U interface or a T interface for the ISDN line, and it should carry out the A/D and D/A conversion and the signaling and power supply functions for the POTS line.

For the application of computer networking, the IPC should also include the *router function*. With some built-in intelligence, the IPC should also be able to perform some data/voice multiplexing functions. The multiplexing can be implemented within two B channels or within each B channel if packetized applications are available. A variety of applications can be realized with the combination of an NT1 and a multiple function IPC, as illustrated by Figure 11.42.

Figure 11.42 An ISDN-to-POTS Converter

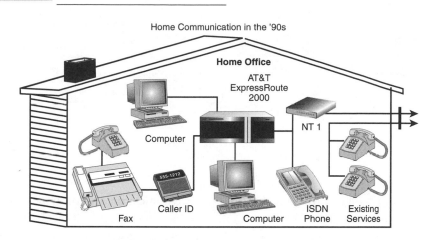

11.5.1 DSL T Interfaces

The T interface is defined[46] based on a two-pair, twisted-pair wiring system. The twisted-pair cable can be either *Category 3* or *Category 5*. Category 3 and Category 5 twisted-pair cables are designed for data transmission applications. Transmission characteristics of Category 5 cable are better than those of Category 3 cable. One twisted-pair is for the transmission from the NT1 to terminal equipment (TE) and the other pair is for the transmission from TE to the NT1, as illustrated in Figure 11.43.

In the case of only one TE, a point-to-point configuration is realized. Two twisted pairs connect the NT1 and the TE. In the case of multiple TE installations, a point-to-multipoint configuration is realized. For this late case, two twisted pairs start from the NT1 and end at a location of physical convenience. A TE at the other end of twisted pairs is not necessary; however, termination resistors at the other end of twisted pairs are always required. TE can be connected to twisted pairs anywhere between the NT1 and the end of the twisted pairs. Twisted pairs are connected to the NT1 and TE via the RJ45 plugs.

Binary rectangle pulse of zero-to-peak amplitude 750 mV is used for the transmission on these twisted pairs. The nominal pulse width is 5.21 µs, resulting to a signaling rate of about 192 kHz. The additional transmission overhead is necessary for the implementation of the T interface frame, which enables the access of multiple TE installations at different locations. The nominal T interface terminal impedance is 100 ohms.

Figure 11.43 Reference Customer Premises Configuration

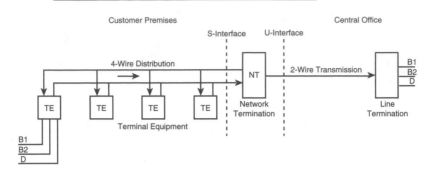

Specifically, as illustrated by Figure 11.44, a T interface frame has a length of 48 bits in 250 μs. The frame starts with a frame bit of value +1 and is followed by a DC balance bit of value −1. There are two bytes each for two B channels for a total of four B channel bytes.

In the NT-to-TE direction, each B channel byte is followed by an E bit, which is the repetition of the last D bit from the TE-to-NT direction. The E bit is followed by the D bit. The D bit is followed by an A, M, S, or L bit for B byte number 1, 2, 3, and 4, respectively. The A bit is used for activation, M is the multiframe bit, S is the S-channel bit, and L is the DC balancing bit. In the TE-to-NT direction, the E bit is replaced by an L bit.

> **Note**
> There are an F_A bit and an N bit following the A bit and before the second B byte. The F_A bit is an auxiliary framing bit, and the N bit has the negative value of the F_A bit.

Figure 11.44 Frame Structure at S Interface

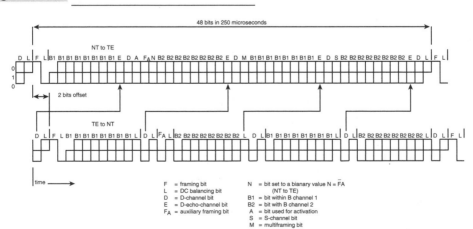

There is a two-bit offset between NT-to-TE and TE-to-NT frames. Because the transmission delay is relatively small, the two-bit offset can be approximately maintained among the NT and all TE. There could be up to eight TE installations sharing the same T interface; however, not all eight TE installations can be active if multiplexing of B bytes in the T interface is not implemented.

There is a contention resolution procedure for the TE-to-NT D bit positions. The contention can be detected by monitoring values of E bits. In the case of contention, retransmission will be necessary. To avoid further contention, a random wait will be necessary for TE. The contention of the B channel is totally avoided if the connection of the B channel is established through the D channel with a proper protocol.

The S interface defines some additional signaling protocols between an NT and TE installations for advanced functions, as required by a PBX with the T interface as the physical transmission layer. The U interface is defined as between the twisted-pair telephone loop and a DSL transceiver. The transmission physical layer of a DSL transceiver is also called the U interface.

11.6   DSL Standards

The T1.601-1992[47] addresses interface details for the 2B1Q DSL line code. Specifics covered include the following:

- Transmission methods, which include
  - Pulse shape
  - Transmit power spectrum
  - Transmitter linearity
  - Test loops
  - Test procedures
- Functional characteristics, which include
  - Frame structure
  - Superframe
  - Scrambling method
  - Startup sequence

- M-channel bit functions, which include

  - Cyclic Redundancy Check (CRC)

  - Overhead bits

  - Embedded operation channel (eoc)

Primary constants of typical telephone cables are also included in Annex G of T1.601-1992.

11.6.1 Bit-to-Symbol Encoders

The 2B1Q line code uses the gray code to encode every two bits into a quaternary symbol, as detailed in Table 11.4. A quaternary symbol can have four different possibilities designated by its magnitude for this baseband case.

Table 11.4 The DSL Gray Encoder

First Bit (Sign)	Second Bit (Magnitude)	Quaternary Symbol (Quat)
1	0	+3
1	1	+1
0	1	−1
0	0	−3

11.6.2 DSL Pulse Mask

The DSL line signal from a transmitter should confirm the pulse mask defined in the time domain, as depicted in Figure 11.45. The compliance can be achieved by choosing the proper combination of a transmitter filter and a hybrid circuit. The transmit pulse shape can be measured in real time using either a single pulse or a known pulse sequence with some signal processing. Labels A through H are used for easy reference of any pulse mask violation.

11.6.3 DSL Transmit Power Mask

The upper boundary of the average power spectral density of the transmit signal is shown by Figure 11.46, which can be summarized as that the power density should be −30 dBm/Hz from 0 Hz to 50 kHz, −50 dB/decade attenuation from −30 dBm/Hz at 50 kHz to −80 dBm/Hz at 500 kHz, and −80 dBm/Hz above 500 kHz.

Figure 11.45   DSL Pulse Mask

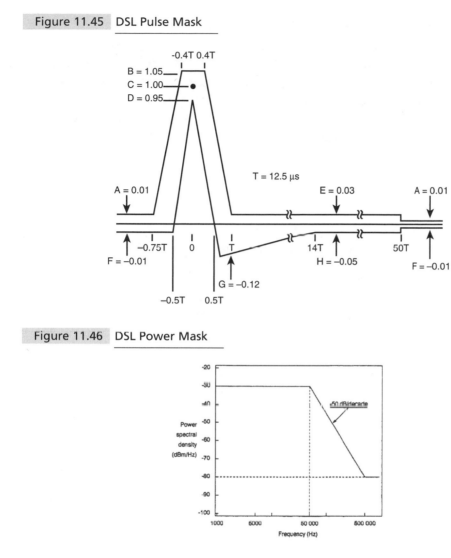

Figure 11.46   DSL Power Mask

The –50 dB/decade attenuation slope can be obtained with a second-order Butterworth lowpass transmit filter in conjunction with the natural decay of the transmit power above one-half of the baud rate. The total power of the transmit signal is between 13 dBm and 14 dBm over the frequency band between 0 Hz–80 kHz.

11.6.4 Nonlinearity Measurements

The transmitted and received signals should have sufficient linearity so that the residual noise caused by nonlinearity is at least 36 dB below the signal power. The measurement of the transmitter linearity can be performed using a test set up, as illustrated by Figure 11.47. The adaptive linear filter identifies the combination of the 2B1Q transmitter, anti-alias filter, sampler, and A/D converter. The nonlinear noise is obtained by subtracting adaptive filter output from those from the A/D converter.

Figure 11.47 Measurement of Nonlinearity

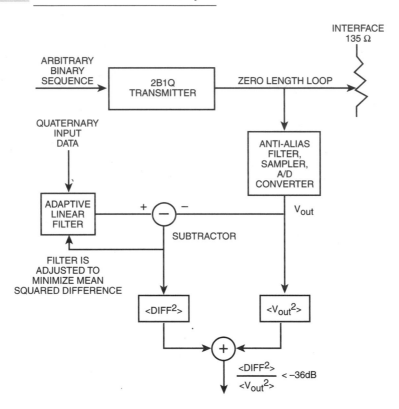

11.6.5 DSL Transmission Performance Measurement

Figure 11.48 shows a general test setup for the measurement of error rates for a pair of DSL transceivers under certain performance margins. The DSL transceivers are made active in both directions, while the bit error rate of only one direction is measured at a time. Real loops or loop emulators can be used for these test loops. Simulated NEXT noise as well as power related noise are applied to the receiver front end through high-impedance coupling circuits.

Figure 11.48   Test Environment

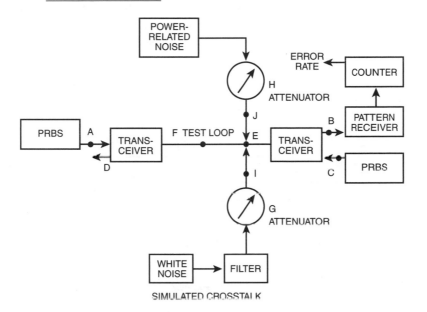

Figure 11.49 shows the transfer function of the NEXT emulation filter—which combines the power spectrum of the DSL transmitter, including the second-order Butterworth transmitter filter and the NEXT coupling function.

Figure 11.49   NEXT Generation Filter Spectrum

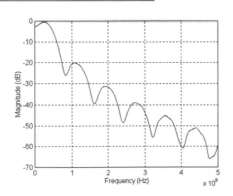

11.6.6 The DSL Frame Structure

A DSL frame has 120 quats with a length of 1.5 milliseconds. Figure 11.50 illustrates a DSL frame that starts with a Synchronization Word (SW) of 9 quats, followed by 108 of information payload quats, which consist of 12 groups of two B channel bytes and two D channel bits (shown in Figure 11.51), and ends with 3 quats of M bits.

Figure 11.50 DSL Frame Structure

← 1.5 milliseconds →

FRAME	SW/ISW	12x(2B+D)	M
Function	Sync word	2B+D	Overhead
# Quats	9	108	3
Quat positions	1-9	10-117	118-120
# Bits	18	216	6
Bit Positions	1-18	19-234	235-240

Frames in the NT-to-network direction are offset from frames in the network-to-NT direction by 60 ± 2 quats.

Figure 11.51 2B1Q Encoding of 2B+D Bit Fields

Time →

Data	B_1				B_2				D
Bit pairs	$b_{11}b_{12}$	$b_{13}b_{14}$	$b_{15}b_{16}$	$b_{17}b_{18}$	$b_{21}b_{22}$	$b_{23}b_{24}$	$b_{25}b_{26}$	$b_{27}b_{28}$	d_1d_2
Quat # (relative)	q_1	q_2	q_3	q_4	q_5	q_6	q_7	q_8	q_9
# Bits	8				8				2
# Quats	4				4				1

11.6.7 The DSL Super Frame Structure

A super frame consists of eight frames. The super frame is identified by the first frame whose SW is inverted. The normal SW is +3 +3 –3 –3 –3 +3 –3 +3 +3, and the inverted SW (ISW) is –3 –3 +3 +3 +3 –3 +3 –3 –3. The super frame consists of the following:

- 24 eoc bits
- 12 crc bits
- one far-end block error (febe) bit
- one turn-off (dea) (network to NT) bit
- one startup (act) (network to NT and NT to network) bit
- two power-status (ps) (NT to network) bits

- one NT-in-test-mode (ntm) (NT to network) bit

- one cold-start-only (cso) (NT to network) bit

- one U-interface-only activation (uoa) (network to NT) bit

- one S/T interface activity indicator (sai) (NT to network) bit

- one alarm indicator bit (aib) (network to NT) bit

- three reserved bits

The total is 48 M-bits, which are distributed through the superframe structure, as illustrated in Figure 11.52.

Figure 11.52 DSL Superframe Structure

		FRAMING	2B+D	Overhead Bits (M_1–M_6)					
	Quat positions	1-9	10-117	118s	118m	119s	119m	120s	120m
	Bit positions	1-18	19-234	235	236	237	238	239	240
Superframe #	Basic frame #	Sync word	2B+D	M_1	M_2	M_3	M_4	M_5	M_6
A	1	ISW	2B+D	eoc_{a1}	eoc_{a2}	eoc_{a3}	act	1	1
	2	SW	2B+D	eoc_{dm}	eoc_{i1}	eoc_{i2}	dea	1	febe
	3	SW	2B+D	eoc_{i3}	eoc_{i4}	eoc_{i5}	1	crc_1	crc_2
	4	SW	2B+D	eoc_{i6}	eoc_{i7}	eoc_{i6}	1	crc_3	crc_4
	5	SW	2B+D	eoc_{a1}	eoc_{a2}	eoc_{a3}	1	crc_5	crc_6
	6	SW	2B+D	eoc_{dm}	eoc_{i1}	eoc_{i2}	1	crc_7	crc_8
	7	SW	2B+D	eoc_{i3}	eoc_{i4}	eoc_{i5}	uoa	crc_9	crc_{10}
	8	SW	2B+D	eoc_{i6}	eoc_{i7}	eoc_{i6}	aib	crc_{11}	crc_{12}
B, C, ...									

a) Network ⟶ NT

		FRAMING	2B+D	Overhead Bits (M_1–M_6)					
	Quat positions	1-9	10-117	118s	118m	119s	119m	120s	120m
	Bit positions	1-18	19-234	235	236	237	238	239	240
Superframe #	Basic frame #	Sync word	2B+D	M_1	M_2	M_3	M_4	M_5	M_6
1	1	ISW	2B+D	eoc_{a1}	eoc_{a2}	eoc_{a3}	act	1	1
	2	SW	2B+D	eoc_{dm}	eoc_{i1}	eoc_{i2}	ps_1	1	febe
	3	SW	2B+D	eoc_{i3}	eoc_{i4}	eoc_{i5}	ps_2	crc_1	crc_2
	4	SW	2B+D	eoc_{i6}	eoc_{i7}	eoc_{i6}	ntm	crc_3	crc_4
	5	SW	2B+D	eoc_{a1}	eoc_{a2}	eoc_{a3}	cso	crc_5	crc_6
	6	SW	2B+D	eoc_{dm}	eoc_{i1}	eoc_{i2}	1	crc_7	crc_8
	7	SW	2B+D	eoc_{i3}	eoc_{i4}	eoc_{i5}	sai	crc_9	crc_{10}
	8	SW	2B+D	eoc_{i6}	eoc_{i7}	eoc_{i6}	1'	crc_{11}	crc_{12}
2,3, ...									

b) NT ⟶ Network

11.6.8 DSL Scrambler/Descrambler

All data bits, except the Synchronization Words (SW), are scrambled with a 23rd-order polynomial prior to the 2B1Q encoder. In the NT-to-network direction, the polynomial is

$$x^{-23} \oplus x^{-18} \oplus 1$$

In the network-to-NT direction, the polynomial is

$$x^{-23} \oplus x^{-5} \oplus 1$$

in which $\oplus$ denotes a modular 2 addition. The scramblers and descramblers are self synchronized, as illustrated in Figure 11.53.

Figure 11.53 Scrambler and Descrambler

NT transmit scrambler (NT to LT):

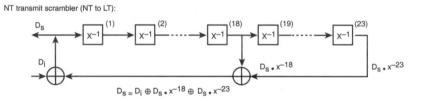

$$D_s = D_i \oplus D_s \cdot x^{-18} \oplus D_s \cdot x^{-23}$$

LT transmit scrambler (LT to NT):

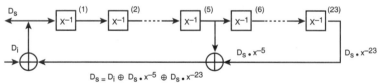

$$D_s = D_i \oplus D_s \cdot x^{-5} \oplus D_s \cdot x^{-23}$$

LT receive descrambler (NT to LT):

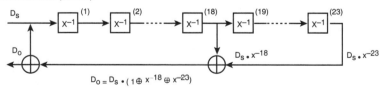

$$D_o = D_s \cdot (1 \oplus x^{-18} \oplus x^{-23})$$

NT receive descrambler (LT to NT):

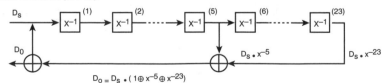

$$D_o = D_s \cdot (1 \oplus x^{-5} \oplus x^{-23})$$

11.6.9   The DSL Startup Sequence

The startup sequence involving the network and the NT lasts less than 15 seconds. Figure 11.54 illustrates the timing relationship of the startup sequence.

Figure 11.54   DSL Startup Sequence

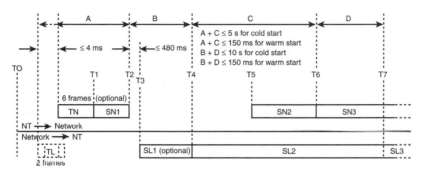

The startup is initiated by a wake up tone: either TL (network to NT) or TN (NT to network). The signals TN and TL are 10 kHz tones generated by repeating the following unscrambled and unframed symbol pattern: ... +3 +3 +3 +3 −3 −3 −3 −3.... Six frames after TN, optional SN1 can be applied from NT to network. The contents of different segments are described as follows:

- SN1 and SN2 are scrambled 1s with SW, but no ISW and with 1s for M bits.

- SN3 is scrambled 1s with SW and ISW and normal M bits.

- SL1 is scrambled 1s with SW, but no ISW and with 1s for M bits.

- SL2 and SL3 are scrambled 0s with SW and ISW and normal M bits.

The periods during SN1 and SL1 can be used to train echo cancellers at NT and network ends, respectively. With echo levels, reduced channel equalizers can be trained quickly under the full-duplex mode.

More detailed descriptions and explanations of the standard DSL interface can be found in the ANSI T1.601 standards document at **http://web.ansi.org/**.

End Notes

1. "Integrated Service Digital Network (ISDN): Basic Access Interface for Use on Metallic Loops for Application on the Network Side of the NT-Layer 1 Specification," ANSI T1.601-1992.

2. "ISDN Basic Access Digital Subscriber Lines," *Bellcore Technical Reference*, TR-TSY-000393, Issue 1 (May 1988).

3. N. S. Lin and C-P. J. Tzeng, "Full-Duplex Data Over Local Loops," *IEEE Communication Magazine*, vol. 26, no. 1 (February 1988): 31–42.

4. D. T. Huang and C. F. Valenti, "Digital Subscriber Lines: Network Considerations for ISDN Basic Access Standard," *Proc. IEEE*, vol. 79, no. 2 (February 1991): 125–144.

5. "Integrated Service Digital Network (ISDN): Basic Access Interface for Use on Metallic Loops for Application on the Network Side of the NT-Layer 1 Specification," ANSI T1.601-1988.

6. British Telecom Research Laboratories, "2B1Q Measurement Results," *ECSA Contribution* T1D1.3/86-177.

7. Siemens Communication Systems, "A Comparison of 4B3T and 3B2T Proposals for the Interface at the Network Side of the NT1," *ECSA Contribution* T1D1.3/86-036 (January 1986).

8. J. W. Lechleider, "A Comparison of Crosstalk Performance of Dicode, PR-4 and 3B2T: Using Decision Feedback Equalization," *ECSA Contribution* T1D1.3/86-005 (January 1986).

9. Siemens Communication Systems, Inc., "Some Characteristics of the MMS43 Line Code," *ECSA Contribution* T1D1.3/85-133.

10. J. W. Lechleider, "Estimated Coverage of the Population of Non-Loaded Loops in the 1983 Survey Using AMI, U88, MMS43, and DI43 Line Codes," *ECSA Contribution* T1D1.3/85-154.

11. C. F. Valenti, "Calculation of RMS Loop Insertion Loss for AMI, U88, MMS43, and DI43 Codes for Loops in the 1983 Loop Survey," *ECSA Contribution* T1D1.3/85-159 (August 15, 1985).

12. L. Wu and K. Laker, "Cost Estimates for AMI and MMS43," *ECSA Contribution* T1D1.3/86-007.

13. P. Fleischer and L. Wu, "The DI43 Code and Its Spectral Properties," *ECSA Contribution* T1D1.3/85-154.

14. J. Lechleider, "A Block Code for ISDN Access Studies," *ECSA Contribution* T1D1.3/85-157.

15. R. D. Gitlin, J. F. Hayes, and S. B. Weinstein, *Data Communication Principles* (New York: Plenum Press, 1992).

16. J. Lechleider, "Line Codes for Digital Subscriber Lines," *IEEE Communications Magazine,* vol.9 (September 1989).

17. J. W. Lechleider and R. A. McDonald, "Capability of the Telephone Loop Plant for ISDN Basic Access," *IEEE Int'l Symp. Subs. Loops Serv.* (1986): 156–161.

18. G. Brand, et al., "Comparison of Line Codes with Optimal DFE Design and Bridged Taps," *ECSA Contribution* T1D1.3/86-018.

19. Bell Communications Research, Inc., "The Calculated Performance of Reference Configurations of AMI, MDB, and MMS43 Are Compared," *ECSA Contribution* T1D1.3/86-155.

20. J. W. Lechleider, "DSLs for Use with Correlated Line Codes," *IEEE Trans. On Comm.,* vol. COM-35, no. 10 (October 1987): 1029–1036.

21. Bell Communications Research, Inc., "The DI43 Line Code and Its Spectral Properties," *ECSA Contribution* T1D1.3/85-154.

22. Bell Communications Research, Inc., "Simulation of 2B1Q Performance," *ECSA Contribution* T1D1.3/86-210.

23. AT&T Technology, Inc., "ISDN Access Cost Model," *ECSA Contribution* T1D1.3/86-081.

24. Bellcore, "Sensitivity of LT Line Card Cost to Transceiver Line Code Selection," *ECSA Contribution* T1D1.3/86-008.

25. ITT Europe, "Cost and Complexity of Various Line Codes," *ECSA Contribution* T1D1.3/85-205 (September 1985).

26. BellSouth Services, "Cost, Complexity, and Risk Versus Reach and Coverage for U-Interface Technology," *ECSA Contribution* T1D1.3/85-191 (October 1986).

27. Pacific Bell, "Economic Considerations for Evaluating the Line Code at the U Reference Point," *ECSA Contribution* T1D1.3/85-225 (September 1985).

28. D. V. Batorsky, D. T. Huang, and R. A. McDonald, "Economic Model for Line Code Selection for Digital Subscriber Lines," *ECSA Contribution* T1D1.3/85-230.

29. D. V. Batorsky, "Summary of Line Code Performance and Hardware Costs Supporting Selection of a Block Code as a Standard Line Code," *ECSA Contribution* T1D1.3/86-009 (January 1986).

30. National Semiconductor Corporation, "Cost/Performance Comparison of Various Echo-Cancellation Systems for Digital Loop Transmission," *ECSA Contribution* T1D1.3/85-171.

31. Intel Corporation, "Cost, Performance, and Complexity Comparison of Various Line Codes for Basic Access on the Network Side of NT1," *ECSA Contribution* T1D1.3/85-171.

32. AT&T Technology, Inc., "Estimates of Impact of Chip Area on IC Price," *ECSA Contribution* T1D1.3/86-079.

33. Intel Corporation, "Die Size Versus Price Estimates," *ECSA Contribution* T1D1.3/86-009 (April 7, 1986).

34. ITT Telecom, "Comparison of Die Size Estimates for Implementation of Systems Based on 4B3T and AMI-Dicode (1+D)," *ECSA Contribution* T1D1.3/86-012 (June 1986).

35. D. V. Batorsky and M. L. Liou, "Comparison of Chip Complexity," *ECSA Contribution* T1D1.3/86-109.

36. L. E. Franks and J. P. Bubrouski, "Statistics Properties of Timing Jitter in a PAM Timing Recovery Scheme," *IEEE Trans. Commun.*, vol. COM-22, no. 7 (July 1974): 913–920.

37. J. Tzeng, D.A. Hodges, and D.G. Messerschmitt, "Timing Recovery in Digital Subscriber Loops Using Baud Rate Sampling," *IEEE Trans. on Selected Areas in Communications* (November 1986).

38. B. Roessler and E. Wolter, "CMOS Analog Front End of a Transceiver with Digital Echo Cancellation for ISDN," *IEEE Journal on Solid State Circuits,* vol. 23, no. 2 (April 1988): 311–317.

39. J. C. Candy, "A Use of Double Integration in Sigma-Delta-Modulation," *IEEE Trans. Commun.*, vol. COM-33, no. 3 (1985): 249–258.

40. D. G. Haigh and B. Singh, "A Switching Scheme for Switched Capacitor Filters Which Reduces the Effect of Parasitic Capacitances Associated with Switch Control Terminals," *Proc. ISCAS 1983*: 586–589.

41. H. Khorramabadi, et al., "An ANSI Standard ISDN Transceiver Chip Set," *IEEE ISSCC '89*: 256–257.

42. R. P. Colbeck, et al., "A Single-Chip 2B1Q U-Interface Transceiver," *IEEE Journal on Solid State Circuits,* vol. SC-24, no. 6 (December 1989): 1614–1624.

43. R. Batruni, et al., "Mixed Digital/Analog Signal Processing for a Single-Chip 2B1Q U-Interface Transceiver," *IEEE Journal on Solid State Circuits,* vol. SC-25, no. 6 (December 1990): 1414–1425.

44. "ISDN Basic Access Digital Subscriber Lines," *Bellcore Tech. Ref.* TR-TSY-000393, issue 1 (May 1988).

45. P. Verma, *ISDN Systems* (Prentice-Hall, 1990).

46. American National Standards Institute, Inc., "Integrated Services Digital Network (ISDN) Basic Access Interface for Use on Metallic Loops for Application on the Network Side of the NT (Layer 1 Specification)," ANSI T1.605-1992.

47. American National Standards Institute, Inc., "Integrated Services Digital Network (ISDN): Basic Access Interface for Use on Metallic Loops for Application on the Network Side of the NT (Layer 1 Specification)," ANSI T1.601-1992.

CHAPTER 12

HDSL (High-Bit-Rate Digital Subscriber Lines)

The capability of a digital subscriber line system depends on a particularly defined telephone loop plant transmission environment and also on the required signal processing power supported by current semiconductor technologies. HDSL is simply a technological extension of DSL based on the same 2B1Q baseband line code and the same echo cancellation method.

An HDSL transceiver operates at five times that of DSL. The required signal processing power, however, could be 25 times more because channel and echo path impulse responses become five times longer under the five times higher sampling rate. The transmission throughput improvement of HDSL over DSL is due to the shorter CSA operation range instead of that defined by all non-loaded loops.

T1 lines can provide a transmission throughput of about 1.544 Mbps. T1 lines can be used to provide a high-speed digital link between a CO and a customer through the existing telephone loop plant. The provisioning of the T1 line, however, involves the removal of bridged taps and the installation of repeaters with the traditional T1 technology developed during the early 1960s.

HDSL has been successfully used as the repeaterless T1 technology, achieving a huge provisioning cost savings. With HDSL, the T1 service can be provided whenever transceivers can be installed at both ends of a twisted-pair loop, which is much simpler compared with bridged tap removal and repeater installation. HDSL technology can also be used to provide high-speed data links in a campus or business environment over previously installed twisted-pair cables.

This chapter covers development activities, transmission performance, and interface standards of High-bit-rate Digital Subscriber Lines, including the following:

- *HDSL technology development.* Technical discussions leading to the development of HDSL are reviewed. Early performance measurements on prototype HDSL systems and corresponding transmit power levels are presented.

- *Transceiver structures and line codes.* The general HDSL transceiver architecture and major transmission parameters are discussed. HDSL equalizer and echo canceller requirements are calculated. A symbol rate timing recovery circuit for the application of HDSL is also discussed. HDSL semiconductor technologies and implementation alternatives are reviewed.

- *Performance objectives.* HDSL test loop configurations and corresponding transfer functions as well as NEXT models are presented. HDSL transmission performances are simulated for these test loops under the self-NEXT noise condition. The effect of transceiver termination resistance to the transmission performance of HDSL is studied. Options for dealing with the slight difference in transmission throughputs in opposite directions are discussed.

- *Network interfaces.* Network interface for using HDSL as a dual-duplex repeaterless T1 technology is defined. The HDSL frame structure is reviewed. Possibilities of line powering HDSL transceivers are also discussed.

- *HDSL technical report.* Key features of the ANSI HDSL technical report, including bit-to-symbol encoding, pulse mask, power spectrum mask, additional test loops, performance test configuration, crosstalk coupling circuit, error rate measurement procedures, scrambler, and startup sequence, are revealed. Key features of CAP HDSL are also discussed.

12.1   HDSL Technology Development

The development of HDSL can be summarized as initial system definition discussions, followed by simulation studies, and concludes with prototype performance measurements. In this section, many technical discussions and study results are briefly mentioned for background and historical reasons. Some details are further discussed in later sections of this chapter and other details can be found through referenced T1E1.4 contribution documents.

12.1.1   The Initial Definition of HDSL

T1E1.4 initiated a study project for HDSL with a data rate of 1.544 Mbps in 1988.[1] Early in the study, it was suggested that there were a number of issues that required further study before an HDSL could be implemented,[2] including the following:

- A/D conversion

- Timing

- Signal processing (including exploiting NEXT cyclostationarity)

- Echo cancellation

- Viterbi receivers

- Adaptive transmitters

- Wire center and customer premises wiring characteristics

- Impulse noise

- Other services sharing the same cable sheath as the HDSL

- Architecture issues

In the following year, 1989, it was also pointed out that the technical feasibility and the type of service to be offered would have a bearing on the desirability of establishing a new stan dard for HDSL.[3] For example, if HDSL is used for ISDN primary access transport, no new standard would be required. The assumptions used in the Bellcore studies of HDSL were presented in an effort to gain a common frame of performance reference.[4]

The critical issues were that the required performance would include a bit error ratio of 10^{-7}, and that the margin used in theoretical and simulation studies would be 12 dB, while the margin on a measured piece of equipment need only be 6 dB. The crosstalk model has a NEXT loss of about 57 dB at 80 kHz and decreases at about 15 dB per decade for frequencies above about 20 kHz. Plant models were taken from the 1983 loop survey, and impulse noise data was taken from a survey of impulse noise by the NYNEX Corporation, the results of which were used in basic access studies. The issue of defining a 6 dB margin was further discussed.[5,6]

12.1.2 Studies on Baseband 2B1Q Line Code

Early study results indicated that at DS1 rate (1.544 Mbps), *single-pair HDSLs* using modified basic access technology would have a range of about a mile, or 5.3 kft.[7] It was also pointed out that HDSLs using modified basic access technology, but operating at 800 kbps, would perform satisfactorily on most Carrier Serving Area (CSA) loops, but would have a theoretical margin of about 6 dB on the lossiest loop in a population of CSA loops.[8]

A study of using Trellis coded modulation to make up an extra 4 dB of performance improvement was also reported.[9] The Shannon capacity of subscriber loops using a simple crosstalk model and identical signal spectra in the two directions of transmission was studied.[10] It was found that the capacity of subscriber loops far exceeds the DS1 rate.

Some possible enhancements[11] to basic access technology can achieve performance that is acceptable on a large percentage of loops. This contention was later supported by data on the distribution of losses in a CSA.[12] The performance of a Decision Feedback Equalizer (DFE) with an infinitely long feedback filter on a population of CSA loops was also calculated.[13] It was found that performance is not enhanced by increasing the length of the feedforward filter in the DFE to more than nine taps, with baud-rate sampling.

12.1.3   *Studies on Passband QAM Line Code with Coding*

Coded Quadrature Amplitude Modulation (QAM) was proposed as the line code for the HDSL.[14] It was suggested that two-wire transmission at DS1 rates was feasible in a CSA. It was also pointed out that because QAM is a passband code, it could be used above the voice band.

Calculations of the theoretical performance of the 64 QAM HDSL line code[15] were based on a bandwidth of 257.33 kHz and a Trellis coding gain of 4 dB. These theoretical results showed that performance was adequate for the crosstalk model used, which was less conservative than the Bellcore model. In addition, there was no margin. Performances of four-wire simplex and duplex transmission were compared.[16] It was pointed out that the range penalty was suffered by the simplex approach. Further analysis was pursued for the simplex/duplex issue, noting that the best line code used in these two cases might be different.[17]

12.1.4   *Studies Toward an HDSL Technical Report*

A technical report for the study of the HDSL project was proposed.[18] Cable models for the HDSL study were proposed.[19,20] The performances of HDSL under other common types of systems, such as ISDN and T1 NEXT, were studied.[21,22] The CSA cable loss at 200 kHz was studied.[23] The benefit of coding for band limited channel was discussed.[24] The performance of a combined coding and precoding approach was studied.[25,26] The idea of Tomlinson precoding was also discussed in more detail.[27] A tutorial on the Carrierless AM/PM was also given.[28]

Performances of baseband and passband systems on a 9 kft, 26-gauge loop and on a 12 kft, 24-gauge loop were compared.[29] It was found that self-NEXT, baseband, and passband systems have roughly the same performance, and that signaling at two bits per dimension leads to better performance than signaling at three.

Another result was that baseband systems perform better in the presence of interference from ISDN basic access systems in the same cable. The reason for this is that interference from basic access systems is very low at frequencies below 20 kHz so that the low-frequency portion of the HDSL band is a good place to put power to mitigate the effects of basic access interference. These comparison results were generally confirmed on a large population of CSA loops by another Bellcore study.[30]

Impulse noise wave forms were presented for the HDSL performance study.[31] Comparative study results of impulse noise performance for 2BIQ PAM systems and QAM systems were also reported.[32] In an effort to narrow the possibilities for consideration for HDSL implementation, it was suggested that HDSL configurations to be considered in further study be limited to repeaterless DS1 applications in CSA.[33]

It was discovered that there might be complications with HDSLs that are connected to DS1 lines that have slight frequency or baud offsets.[34] Techniques used in voice band modems to overcome this asynchronous problem were discussed.[35] Further discussions revealed that the asynchronous problem could be avoided by the use of a variable frame.[36] Other variable frame formats were also proposed.[37,38] Performances for different variable frame proposals were compared and the idea of a Double Barker code was introduced.[39]

12.1.5 Performance Measurements of HDSL Prototypes

The measurements of experimental HDSLs were first reported.[40] A margin of 3.7 dB on a 12 kft, 24-gauge loop for a full-duplex 772 kbps system that uses the 2B1Q line code was achieved. The measurements of a Carrierless AM/PM HDSL system were also reported.[41] Margins of greater than 6 dB on some CSA loops for a half DS1 rate two-pair simplex system with simulated crosstalk noise were achieved.

Measurements of the performance of a 3B1O (3 Bits per Octal symbol) system were also reported.[42] An operating margin of 3.8 dB in a 49-disturber simulated NEXT environment was achieved. Although the number of Pulse Amplitude Modulation (PAM) levels that achieve optimal performance in a self-NEXT environment is between five and six, the eight-level code was used for simplicity of implementation.

A plan for the laboratory testing of proposed HDSL systems in a normalized environment was proposed,[43] which was similar to that used for the testing of ISDN basic access transceivers. A loop emulator testbed that permits the rapid emulation of a large number of loop configurations for the testing of proposed HDSL architectures was also discussed.[44]

The loop emulator testbed consists of twisted-pair cable sections of different lengths and sizes and mechanical relays. A particular loop configuration can be established through a convenient PC user interface. A collection of eight CSA loop configurations that are representative of the population and may be used for simulation studies of HDSL architecture was presented.[45]

A 6B+D HDSL using the 2B1P (two bits per Penternary [5 level] symbol) line code that was being studied for use in Europe was also reported[46] along with a framing structure for the system.[47] DMT was proposed for HDSL.[48,49] The effect of terminal impedance was further examined for PAM and QAM systems.[50] A 2B1Q HDSL VLSI solution was discussed.[51] The performance of a decision feedback equalizer-based 2B1Q HDSL was further studied.[52] The effect of impulse noise on baseband and passband HDSL systems was further analyzed.[53] The ISDN test loop #12 was also proposed to be used for stretched HDSL performance testing.[54] The adoption of a variable frame format for HDSL was gradually finalized.[55,56,57]

The possibility of including a POTS channel with an HDSL was discussed.[58] The HDSL frame structure was further discussed.[59,60] A VLSI chip for the implementation of an HDSL transceiver was discussed.[61] The effect of temperature variation on the subscriber loop transmission characteristics was reported.[62] HDSL transceiver performance test results were published for units from British Telecom Research Laboratories,[63] Bell-Northern Research,[64] AT&T,[65] Tellabs,[66] and PairGain Technologies.[67] After sharing these test results, it was generally agreed that a dual-duplex 2B1Q HDSL system will be defined mainly as a repeaterless T1 technology[68] with the Carrierless AM/PM system as an alternative line code.[69]

Table 12.1 summarizes results of NEXT margin performance tests for different HDSL transceivers. While performance margins are generally consistent for the 2B1Q line code, the higher terminal impedance seems to help the performance. CAP line code is only used by AT&T's HDSL transceiver.

Table 12.2 shows HDSL transceiver transmit power levels. Signal[1] represents the transmitter power measured with a spectrum analyzer. Signal[2] represents the transmitter power measured with a wide-band meter. NEXT is the calculated NEXT level at 0 dB margin. The CAP HDSL transmitter power and the NEXT power are relatively lower compared with other HDSL systems.

Table 12.1 NEXT Performance Margin Measurements (dB)

Loop #	BT Labs. 110 ohms		Bell Northern Research 110 ohms		120 ohms		AT&T 110 ohms		Tellabs 110 ohms		120 ohms		PairGain 110 ohms	
	For.	Rev.	For.	Rev.	For.	Rev.	For.	Rev.	For.	Rev.	For.	Rev.	For.	Rev.
1	4.5	4.5	5.0	5.0	7.0	7.0	8.5	9.0	4.0	4.0	5.0	5.0	5.0	5.5
2	4.0	3.5			7.0	5.5	9.5	5.5		1.5		2.0	5.5	3.5
3	3.0	3.0	4.0	4.5	6.0	6.0	6.5	7.0	3.0	3.5	3.5	3.5	4.0	4.0
4	3.0	3.5	2.5	3.0	4.0	5.0	5.0	6.0	0.5	2.0	-0.5	3.0	3.0	3.5
5	3.0	3.0	3.5	4.5	6.0	6.5	7.0	7.5	3.5	3.5	4.0	4.0	4.5	5.0
6	1.5		3.5		5.5		7.0		3.5		3.5		4.0	
7	4.0	4.0	9.0	5.0	11.0	7.5	14.0	9.0	5.0	5.0	6.5	5.0	9.0	5.5
8	3.5		6.5		8.5		10.5		6.5		6.5		7.0	

Table 12.2 HDSL Transmit and NEXT Power Level (dBm)

	BT Labs. 110 ohms	Bell Northern Research 110 ohms	120 ohms	AT&T 110 ohms	Tellabs 110 ohms	120 ohms	PairGain 110 ohms
Signal[1]	12.1	13.4	13.4	-1.1	13.9	13.9	14.1
Signal[2]	12.4	13.5	13.5	-1.0	14.0	14.0	14.3
NEXT	-45.8	-40.2	-40.2	-53.5	-40.3	-40.3	-40.7

12.2 HDSL Transceiver Structures and Line Codes

A pair of HDSL transceivers is required at both ends of a subscriber loop to form an HDSL link. A pair of HDSL links is necessary for a dual-duplex repeaterless T1 line. In other words, two HDSL links, each of which has a data rate of 784 kbps, are required to form a T1 line. Figure 12.1 shows the general architecture of an HDSL transceiver. Detailed descriptions of HDSL transceiver components and processes follow.

Figure 12.1 A General HDSL Transceiver Structure

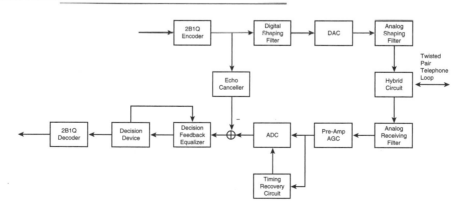

Every two bits of transmit signal are encoded into a symbol through the 2B1Q encoder. The symbol or baud rate is therefore one-half of the bit rate. The symbol is sent to the Digital to Analog Converter (DAC) with an optional digital transmit shaping filter. A fourth order Butterworth lowpass filter is usually sufficient for the transmit analog shaping filter. The purpose of the transmit shaping filter is to control the out-of-band energy. The use of the optional transmit digital shaping filter could reduce the overall transceiver component count.

The filtered transmit signal is connected to the twisted-pair telephone subscriber loop through a hybrid circuit, which has two unidirectional ports (one for transmitting and one for receiving) and one bi-directional port. The bi-directional port is connected to the subscriber loop. If the impedance of the subscriber loop matches the design impedance of the hybrid, there will be a perfect isolation between the transmitting port and the receiving port. For this ideal case, the hybrid return loss is infinity. In reality, the loop impedance is a variable of frequency and is very different for different loops. Therefore, even a well-designed hybrid can sometimes provide a return loss as low as 15 dB at certain frequencies.

A fourth-order Butterworth lowpass filter can also be used for the analog receiver filter. The function of the receiver filter is mainly to minimize out-of-band noise. The preamplifier is necessary to bring the received signal level to that close to the normal transmit signal level for subsequent digital signal processing. A preamplifier gain of about 35 dB might be necessary to compensate for the average CSA loop loss at a frequency of around 200 kHz.

The preamplifier gain should be adjustable to 0 dB for short loops. The gain of the preamplifier should be controlled by the digital signal processing function of the HDSL transceiver. The Analog to Digital Converter is synchronized to the timing recovery circuits. The timing recovery circuits derive the timing information based on the receiver signal after the preamplifier.

These same transmit data symbols are also sent to the echo canceller. The echo canceller resembles the equivalence of the echo path, including transmit shaping filters, DAC, hybrid circuits, analog receiver filter, preamplifier, and ADC at the ADC sampling rate. The DAC's sampling clock is also synchronized to the ADC sampling clock to maintain a stable echo path transfer function. Possible phase jitter between transmit signal and received signal is handled with bit stuffing defined by the HDSL frame structure. The echo path transfer function is identified with an adaptive signal processing algorithm.

The digitized and echo-canceled received signal is further filtered by the decision feedback channel equalizer before being sent to the decision device. A decision feedback equalizer consists of a feedforward filter and a feedback filter. The feedforward filter equalizes the precursor of the subscriber loop channel impulse response, while the feedback filter cancels the effect of the post-cursor of the channel impulse response.

The decision feedback equalizer is necessary for an HDSL transceiver to maintain a minimal noise enhancement during the channel equalization process. The decision device is a four level threshold detector corresponding to the 2B1Q line code. Received symbols generated from the decision device are converted back to original signal bits through the 2B1Q decoder.

12.2.1 HDSL Transceiver Parameters

Table 12.3 shows the general HDSL transceiver parameters.

Table 12.3   HDSL Transceiver Parameters

Line code	2B1Q
Bandwidth (3 dB)	200 kHz
Baud rate	400 kHz
Throughput	800 kbps
Transmit power	13.38 dBm (135 ohms)

The receiver is based on a baud rate decision feedback channel equalizer. The receiver sampling rate (as well as the baud rate) is 400 kHz, resulting in a 3 dB transmission bandwidth of 200 kHz. For the 2B1Q line code, each baud carries two bits of information. Therefore, the transmission throughput is 800 kbps. Assuming a power supply of five volts and a utilization efficiency of 92 percent, the maximum transmit output voltage is $Z_r(f)2.3$ volts. For a line impedance of 135 ohms, the total transmit power delivered on the telephone loop is as follows:

$$P = \frac{1}{2}\left(2.3^2 + \left(\frac{2.3}{3}\right)^2\right)\frac{1}{135} = \frac{5.29}{2\times135}\left(1+\frac{1}{9}\right)$$

$$= \frac{5.29\times10}{2\times135\times9} = 0.02177 \text{ Watts} = 13.38 dBm$$

The HDSL transmit power spectral density is defined as follows:

$$PSD = \frac{0.02177}{200\times10^3} = 1.08\times10^{-7} \text{ Watts/} Hz = -39.7 dBm/Hz$$

12.2.2 HDSL Channel Equalizer Requirements

The length of the decision feedback equalizer should be sufficiently long compared with the equivalent channel impulse response. The equivalent channel response represents the combination of the transmit filter, the transmit transformer, the twisted-pair loop channel, the receiver transformer, and the receiver filter. Assuming that the transmit and the receiver transformers are the same and that the transmit and receiver filters are also the same, the equivalent channel impulse response is the convolution of the twisted-pair loop impulse response twice convolved with the impulse response of the transformer and twice convolved with the transmit/receiver filter.

Figure 12.2 shows the impulse response of the 9 kft, 26-gauge CSA loop.

Figure 12.2 Impulse Response of the 9 kft, 26-Gauge Loop

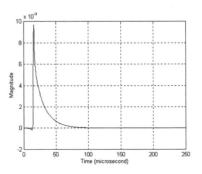

An HDSL transformer should be designed to have an almost flat frequency response from DC (direct current) to about 200 kHz; however, the transmission of low-frequency energy near DC could lead to excessive requirements on the DFE and echo canceller. In practice, the frequency components near DC occur only with a very low probability. The effective minimum frequency occurs when n consecutive baud symbols are of the same sign. For $n=30$ corresponding to an occurrence probability of $p=0.5^{30}=9.313\times10^{-10}$, the effective minimum frequency is as follows:

$$f_{em} = \frac{200\times10^3}{30} = 6.667kHz$$

For a loop impedance of 100 ohms, the transformer primary impedance is

$$L_{pri} = \frac{R}{2\pi f_{em}} 2.387mH$$

Figure 12.4 shows the impulse response of a transformer with an equivalent circuit illustrated in Figure 12.3.

Figure 12.3 A Transformer Equivalent Circuit

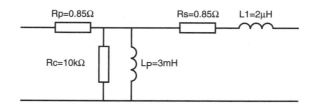

Rp=0.85Ω   Rs=0.85Ω   L1=2µH

Rc=10kΩ   Lp=3mH

Figure 12.4 Impulse Response of the Transformer

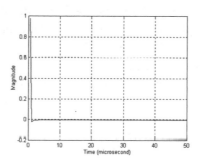

Figure 12.5 shows the impulse response of a fourth-order Butterworth filter, which was recommended for the transmit/receiver filter.

Figure 12.5 Impulse Response of the Fourth-Order Butterworth Lowpass Filter

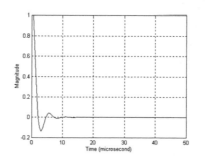

Figure 12.6 shows the impulse response of the equivalent channel, which includes two transformers, two Butterworth lowpass filters, and the twisted-pair loop in cascade.

Figure 12.6 Impulse Response of the Equivalent Channel

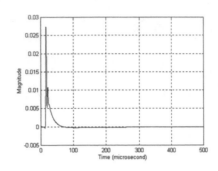

The equivalent channel impulse response approaches zero at about 300 microseconds. Considering 20 microseconds of peak delay, the feedback filter should last about 280 microseconds. For a baud sampling rate of 400 kHz, the time between each sample is 2.5 microseconds. Therefore, we need about 280/2.5=122 feedback filter taps, assuming the feedforward filter does not affect the length of the feedback filter too much. The feedforward filter should have a sufficient length to cover the equivalent channel impulse response up to the peak. The required number of feedforward filter taps is therefore 20/2.5=8.

12.2.3 HDSL Echo Canceller Requirements

The echo path transfer function can be calculated according to the following expression:[70]

$$H_{ec}(f) = H_{ec0}(f) \frac{1 + \dfrac{Z_n(f)}{Z_i(f)}}{1 + \dfrac{Z_d(f)}{Z_i(f)}}$$

The values are as follows:

$$H_{ec0}(f) = \frac{1}{2} - \frac{R_p + R_c \mathbin{/\!/} j2\pi f L_p}{100 + R_p + R_c \mathbin{/\!/} j2\pi f L_p}$$

$$Z_d(f) = R_p + R_c \mathbin{/\!/} j2\pi f L_p \mathbin{/\!/} Z_1(f)$$

$$Z_n(f) = R_p + R_c \mathbin{/\!/} j2\pi f L_p \mathbin{/\!/} Z_2(f)$$

$$Z_1(f) = j2\pi f L_l + R_s + 90.9$$

$$Z_2(f) = j2\pi f L_l + R_s - 1053$$

Further, $Z_i(f)$ is the impedance of the twisted-pair loop. This expression for $H_{ec}(f)$ is for the single-ended hybrid circuit. For the 9 kft, 26-gauge CSA loop, the echo path transfer function is shown by Figure 12.7, and the echo path impulse response is shown by Figure 12.8.

Figure 12.7   Echo Path Transfer Function for the 9 kft, 26-Gauge Loop

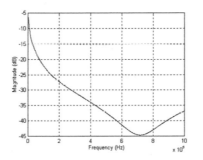

Figure 12.8   Echo Path Impulse Response for the 9 kft, 26-Gauge Loop

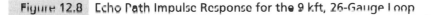
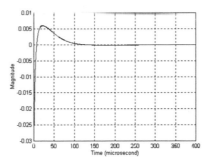

The echo path impulse response approaches zero at about 280 microseconds. Echo path impulse responses for other loops exhibit a similar duration. Therefore, we need about 280/2.5=122 filter taps for the echo canceller.

The performance of HDSL is limited by self-NEXT. Figure 12.9 defines the Signal-to-NEXT-Noise ratio from about 65 dB at near DC to about 0 dB at about 400 kHz. This figure also shows the required echo cancellation level, which is the difference between the signal-to-noise ratio and the signal-to-echo ratio.

Figure 12.9 Required Echo Cancellation Level

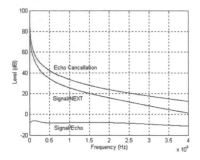

On the other hand, Figure 12.9 also shows that the signal-to-echo ratio is negative at all frequencies because the echo path return loss is always smaller than the channel loss. The required echo cancellation level, which ranges from 80 dB at near DC to 13 dB at about 400 kHz, is expressed as

$$K_{ec}(f) = \frac{\dfrac{|H(f)|^2}{NEXT(f)}}{\dfrac{|H(f)|^2}{|H_{ec}(f)|^2}} = \frac{|H_{ec}(f)|^2}{NEXT(f)}$$

in which

$H(f)$ is the channel transfer function.

$H_{ec}(f)$ is the echo path transfer function.

$NEXT(f)$ is the NEXT power coupling function.

The required average echo cancellation level is defined by

$$K_{ec} = \frac{1}{f_{max}} \int_0^{f_{max}} K_{ec}(f)df = 3.09 \times 10^6 = 64.9 dB$$

$F_{max} = 400 \text{ kHz}.$

12.2.4   HDSL Timing Recovery Circuits

The Decision Feedback channel Equalizer (DFE) and the Echo Canceller (EC) of an HDSL transceiver operate on baud sampled signals generated from the receiver's front-end Analog to Digital Converter (ADC). Sampling frequencies of HDSL transceivers at each end of a telephone subscriber loop should be synchronized. Using crystal oscillators, the baud frequency difference between transceivers at each end of the loop can be kept within a few parts per million. However, the accumulation of the frequency difference in a short period of operation could result in a huge sampling frequency discrepancy if a proper synchronization mechanism is not in place.

Among a pair of HDSL transceivers at both ends of a loop, one can use its own crystal to generate the baud frequency driving its digital signal processing circuits, while the other should recover the baud frequency from the received signal. The HDSL transceiver that recovers the baud frequency from the received signal is said to be in *loop timing mode* of operation.

A timing recovery circuit should be used by the loop timing HDSL transceiver to synchronize its digital signal processing to those of the transmitter at the other end of the loop. The timing recovery circuit is usually used to select the optimal sampling phase in conjunction with a particular receiver. The performance of a baud rate DFE is very sensitive to the sampling phase of an ADC. The optimal sampling phase enables the realization of the whole performance potential of a baud-rate-based DFE.

Because the received signal is available at the baud rate, only baud-rate-based timing recovery circuits can be used if additional higher sampling rate ADC is not used. Mueller and Muller proposed an effective baud rate timing recovery circuit architecture in 1976.[71] A timing function can be constructed using a few sampling points around the optimal sample point of a Nyquist channel impulse response. The first proposed timing function is

$$f_1(\tau) = \frac{1}{2}\big(h(\tau+T) - h(\tau-T)\big)$$

$h(t)$ is the channel impulse response.

τ is the sampling instance.

T is the baud interval.

For a Nyquist channel, we have

$$f_1(\tau) = \frac{1}{2} \frac{\sin \pi \left(\frac{\tau+T}{T} \right)}{\pi \left(\frac{\tau+T}{T} \right)} \frac{\cos \alpha \pi \left(\frac{\tau+T}{T} \right)}{1 - 4\alpha^2 \left(\frac{\tau+T}{T} \right)^2} - \frac{1}{2} \frac{\sin \pi \left(\frac{\tau-T}{T} \right)}{\pi \left(\frac{\tau+T}{T} \right)} \frac{\cos \alpha \pi \left(\frac{\tau-T}{T} \right)}{1 - 4\alpha^2 \left(\frac{\tau+T}{T} \right)^2}$$

The value α is the excessive bandwidth. For $\alpha = 0$, we have

$$f_1(\tau) = \frac{1}{\pi} \frac{\sin \pi \frac{\tau}{T}}{\frac{\tau^2}{T^2} - 1}$$

The second proposed timing function is

$$f_2(\tau) = h(\tau + T)$$

For a Nyquist channel, we have

$$f_2(\tau) = \frac{1}{2} \frac{\sin \pi \left(\frac{\tau+T}{T} \right)}{\pi \left(\frac{\tau+T}{T} \right)} \frac{\cos \alpha \pi \left(\frac{\tau+T}{T} \right)}{1 - 4\alpha^2 \left(\frac{\tau+T}{T} \right)^2}$$

which is just a one-baud shifted version of the Nyquist channel impulse response. For $\alpha = 0$, we have the one-baud shifted version of the sine function:

$$f_2(\tau) = \frac{\sin \pi \left(\frac{\tau+T}{T} \right)}{\pi \frac{\tau+T}{T}}$$

Figure 12.10 illustrates the sensitivities of these timing functions in relationship to the duration of the baud interval.

Figure 12.10   Timing Function Versus Timing Phase

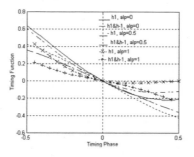

Such a channel impulse response-based timing function can be derived based on received signal and corresponding data symbols. Data symbols can be recovered from the received data through a threshold decision device for the case of the Nyquist channel. We can define a timing function

$$F\big(\bar{x}_k(\tau), \bar{a}_k(\tau)\big)$$

such that

$$E\big\{F\big(\bar{x}_k(\tau), \bar{a}_k(\tau)\big)\big\} = f(\tau)$$

in which

$$\bar{x}_k(\tau) = \big[x_{k-m+1}(\tau), x_{k-m+2}(\tau), ..., x_k(\tau)\big]^T$$

is the received signal vector and

$$\bar{a}_k(\tau) = \big[a_{k-m+1}(\tau), a_{k-m+2}(\tau), ..., a_k(\tau)\big]^T$$

is the data symbol vector. Figure 12.11 illustrates the general structure of such a timing recovery circuit.

Figure 12.11 The General Structure of the Baud Rate Timing Recovery Circuit

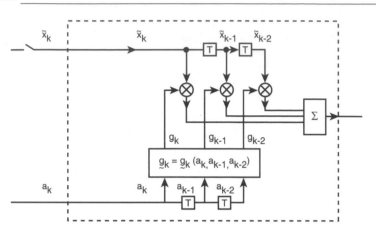

Specifically, we can have a simple

$$F_1\big(\bar{x}_k(\tau),\bar{a}_k(\tau)\big) = \frac{1}{2}\big(x_k(\tau)a_{k-1}(\tau) - x_{k-1}(\tau)a_k(\tau)\big)/E\big\{a_k^2(\tau)\big\}$$

as illustrated in Figure 12.12 for $f_1(\tau)$ in which $E\big\{a_k^2(\tau)\big\}$ is available through the automatic gain control circuits, and a simple

$$F_2\big(\bar{x}_k(\tau),\bar{a}_k(\tau)\big) = a_{k-1}(\tau)\big(x_k(\tau) - a_k(\tau)h_0(\tau)\big)/E\big\{a_k^2(\tau)\big\}$$

as illustrated in Figure 12.13 for $f_2(\tau)$ in which $h_0(\tau)$ is also available through the received signal strength.

Figure 12.12 A Simple Timing Circuit for Even Channel Impulse Response

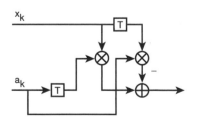

Figure 12.13   A Simple Timing Circuit for Odd Channel Impulse Response

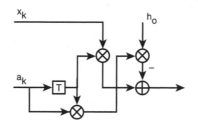

With proper recognition of

$$f_1(\tau) = \frac{1}{2}\big(h(\tau + T) - h(\tau - T)\big)$$

that is, the selection of received signal samples in relation to corresponding estimated data symbol, this timing recovery technique can also be applied to a general twisted-pair telephone subscriber loop channel, including transmitter and receiver filters. With proper delay, Figure 12.14 shows the timing function for a zero-length loop with a fourth-order Butterworth transmit filter, a fourth-order receiver filter, and a 9 kft, 26-gauge loop with and without transmit and receiver filters in comparison with that of a Nyquist channel.

Figure 12.14   Timing Function on Twisted-Pair Loops

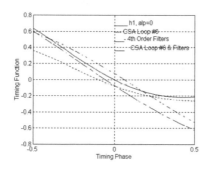

Due to the extensive channel intersymbol interference distortion, the estimation of the data symbols required in the timing function can only be obtained after the decision feedback channel equalization. Figure 12.15 shows the general structure of an HDSL timing recovery circuit.

Figure 12.15 An HDSL Timing Recovery Circuit

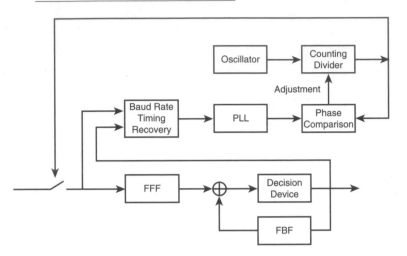

The operation of this timing recovery circuit is based on the assumption that the frequency difference between the transmit clock and the receiver clock is so close (< 30 PPM) that the convergence of the equalizer can be realized even without the timing recovery circuit.

The main purposes of the timing recovery circuit are to obtain the optimal sampling phase and to avoid long-term frequency/phase shift between transmit and receiver clocks. There could be some jitter from the original baud rate timing recovery circuit. The inclusion of a Phase Locked Loop (PLL) should help improve the overall timing recovery performance. A PLL consists of a very narrow bandpass filter, which only allows the desired frequency to pass through.

12.2.5 HDSL DFE/EC Semiconductor Technologies

Two major signal processing functions of an HDSL transceiver are the adaptive Decision Feedback channel Equalizer (DFE) and the adaptive Echo Canceller (EC). The DFE consists of a *Feedforward Filter* (FFF) and a *Feedback Filter* (FBF). The FFF is an adaptive *Finite Impulse Response* (FIR) filter with eight taps and 12 bits, corresponding to the ADC precision, in the data path. The FBF and EC are both adaptive FIR filters with about 128 taps. The data path for both FFF and EC is two bits for the 2B1Q four level signal.

Either the FBF or EC function can be effectively implemented with an *Application Specific Integrated Circuit* (ASIC) of the same structure. A possible ASIC chip implementation with a 64-tap cascading taps is explained in the following paragraphs.[72] Figure 12.16 shows a simplified block diagram of the EC/DFE ASIC chip.

Figure 12.16   Simplified Block Diagram of EC/DFE Chip

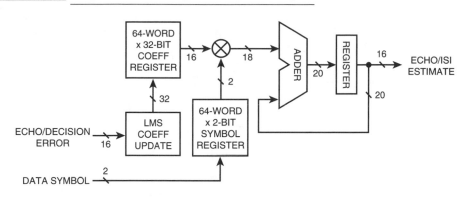

The coefficients of the adaptive FIR filter are updated using a sign-LMS update equation given by

$$C_k(n+1) = C_k(n) + \mu e(n)\,\mathrm{sgn}\big(x(n-k)\big)$$

for $k = 1, 2,...64$. The sign algorithm and the true LMS update algorithm have virtually identical performance in a 2BIQ system. This is due to the fact that $x(n–k)$ is a two-bit signal $(+3, +1, -1, -3)$ and, therefore, quantizing $x(n\ k)$ to 1 bit $(+1, -1)$ has virtually no effect on the convergence of the algorithm. This modification does, however, result in a very simple multiplierless hardware implementation when power-of-two step-sizes are used.

The FBF and EC update equations have the same form. In an EC application, $x(n)$ represents the transmit symbol sequence and $e(n)$ represents the residual uncancelled echo error. In an FBF application, $x(n)$ represents the receive symbol decisions and $e(n)$ represents the slicer decision error. Figure 12.17 shows an overview of the EC/DFE chip architecture.

The EC/DFE chip accepts a two-bit data symbol, $x(n)$, and a 16-bit error input, $e(n)$, and produces a 16-bit echo estimate (for EC applications) or equalized signal (for DFE applications), $y(n)$, during each symbol period. In addition, all filter coefficients are updated in every symbol period using a sign-LMS algorithm. The 16-bit error input is either the residual echo error (for EC applications) or the decision error (for DFE applications). The FIR filter coefficients are updated and stored with 32 bits of precision, and the filter computations are performed to 20 bits of accuracy.

For applications requiring filters longer than 64 taps, the EC/DFE chip can be cascaded to implement adaptive FIR filters of arbitrary length. Figure 12.18 illustrates how to interconnect several EC/DFE chips.

Figure 12.17 Overview of EC/DFE Chip Architecture

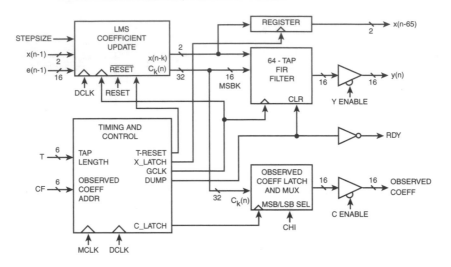

Figure 12.18 Interconnections Required for Cascading EC/DFE Chips

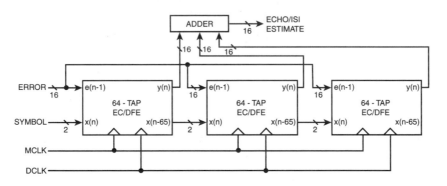

The EC/DFE chip consists of four main sections:

- An FIR filter section

- An LMS coefficient update section

- A register block

- A control section

The chip floor plan exploits the regular nature of these elements by using a parallel datapath approach. Figure 12.19 shows the floorplan of the EC/DFE chip.

Figure 12.19 Floor Plan of EC/DFE Chip

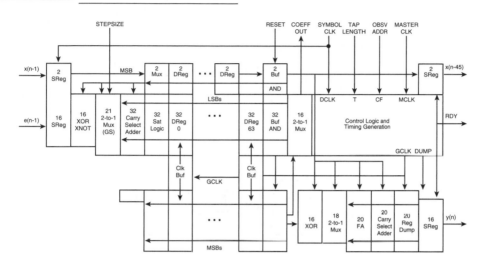

The data flow is primarily in one direction, as follows:

1. The error input is accepted on the left side of the EC/DFE chip and is routed directly to the LMS coefficient update section.

2. The updated coefficients are then directly routed to the input of the register block.

3. The input symbol data is also routed directly to the register block.

4. The filter coefficients and symbol data at the output of the register block are then delivered to the FIR filter section.

5. The final filter output is delivered to the output pads on the right side of the chip.

The FIR Filter Section

The FIR filter section is essentially a multiply-accumulate block that operates at the master clock rate and implements the following equation:

$$y(n) = \sum C_k x(n-k)$$

Figure 12.20 shows a block diagram of the FIR filter section.

Figure 12.20 FIR Filter Section Block Diagram

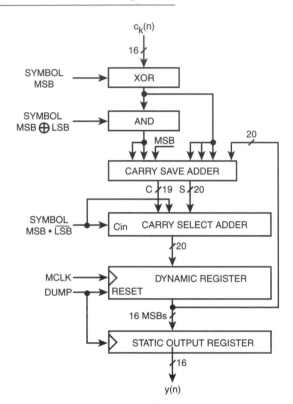

The two major logic blocks in the FIR filter are the *multiplier* and the *accumulator*. However, since the symbol word length is only two bits, the multiplier simplifies to a shift-and-add block. To achieve the speed goals, the multiplier was implemented using a carry-save adder and the accumulator was implemented using a carry-select adder.[73] This arrangement minimizes the delay through the FIR block since only one 20-bit carry-propagate addition is needed per multiply-accumulate cycle.

The LMS Coefficient Update Section

The LMS coefficient update section implements the sign-LMS algorithm as specified by

$$C_k(n+1) = C_k(n) + \mu e(n-1)\text{sgn}[x(n-k-1)]$$

The coefficient update equation can be mapped into a straightforward bit-slice architecture, as shown in Figure 12.21.

Figure 12.21   LMS Update Section Block Diagram

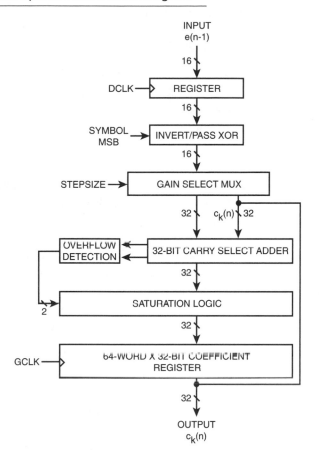

The input error signal *e(n – 1)* is clocked into a static register at the symbol rate. The multiplication by the sign of the data symbol is achieved with an invert-or-pass circuit (an array of XORs), and the multiplication by the power-of-two step-size μ is achieved by a hardwired shift. The value of μ is user selectable to either of two values through the use of a two-to-one multiplexer.

Finally, a 32-bit carry-select adder is used to sum the update term $\mu e(n-1)\text{sgn}[x(n-k-1)]$ with the old coefficient value, with the result being stored in the register block. After all 64 coefficients have been updated, a new error input is received and the cycle is repeated.

The Register Block

The register block consists of a 64-word by 34-bit wide shift register stack. Thirty-two bits of each word are allocated for coefficient storage, and two bits are allocated for symbol data storage. A dynamic master-slave, eight-transistor clocked-CMOS (C^2MOS) shift register cell design[74] was used to achieve high-speed operation. The design has the drawback, however, of drawing much more power than a conventional RAM-based implementation because all data is shifted on every clock cycle.

If a RAM design were used, only one column of 34-bit data would be accessed and written to in each clock cycle. In spite of this drawback, the shift register design was implemented in the EC/DFE chip because speed and robustness were more important design criteria than power dissipation for this demonstration chip.

Note
Dynamic RAM cell designs have the potential for significantly reducing the area and power consumption of the register block, although meeting the speed goals will be more difficult.

The filter coefficients that are stored in the register block are delivered to the LMS coefficient update section, where they are updated and circulated back into the register block. Because undefined states are initially present in the register stack (after power-up), a means of resetting the coefficients and symbol data is provided. Regardless of the desired tap length of the FIR filter, all coefficients and symbol data are cycled through the register block.

The Control Section

The control section generates the internal system clock and various control signals for the FIR filter section, the LMS coefficient update section, and the register block. The control section also generates the necessary control signals to accommodate variable tap lengths and to allow complete coefficient observability.

For tap length programmability, the desired tap length of the FIR filter is input to the EC/DFE chip as a six-bit address. For coefficient observability, a 6-bit address is input to the EC/DFE chip to select the appropriate 32-bit coefficient, and a 1-bit select signal determines whether the 16 *Most Significant Bits* (MSB) or 16 *Least Significant Bits* (LSB) of the coefficient are delivered to the 16-bit output bus.

12.3 *Performance Objectives*

The performance of HDSL is primarily determined by the selected loop population and corresponding transceiver architecture. The value of termination impedance also has a slight influence on the performance of HDSL. The issue of the slight transmission throughput difference in opposite directions for HDSL also needs a practical solution.

12.3.1 General HDSL Performance Objectives

The performance of the HDSL system is primarily determined by the following factors:

- Transmission characteristics of the twisted-pair telephone loop

- The receiver front-end noise level

- The structure of the HDSL transceiver

Figure 12.22 shows configurations of eight selected *Carrier Serving Area* (CSA) test loops[75] that have been used in the engineering process of the HDSL system.

Figure 12.22   CSA Test Loops

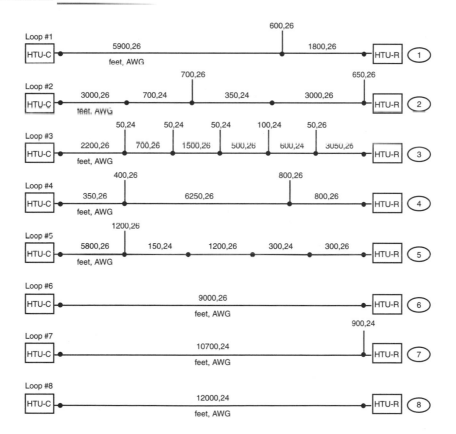

The transmission characteristics of these CSA loops have been used in a computer simulation study, incorporated into the test procedure,[76] and duplicated by test equipment.[77,78] The worst-case CSA loops are typically defined by a straight 9 kft, 26-gauge loop or a straight 12 kft, 24-gauge loop. For loops with bridge taps, the total length including bridge taps should be less than 9 kft or 12 kft, depending on the cable gauge.

Figures 12.23a and 12.23b show the transfer functions of the eight CSA test loops. These transfer functions are characterized by a 10 dB loss at about 1 kHz and about 35 dB loss at about 200 kHz. Bridged taps cause nulls at different frequencies.

Figure 12.23a   Transfer Function of CSA Loops 1–4

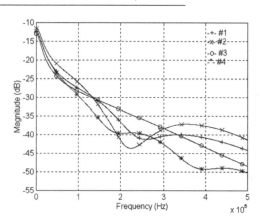

Figure 12.23b   Transfer Function of CSA Loops 5–8

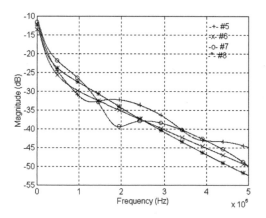

Because of the use of an echo-cancellation-based full-duplex method, the dominant noise component at the receiver front end is the self Near End Crosstalk, self-NEXT. Self-NEXT is induced by neighboring HDSL transmitters. The self-NEXT noise level depends on the transmit signal level and the NEXT loss. Figure 12.24 shows the NEXT loss model for three different numbers of disturbers and one simplified NEXT model for 49 disturbers. For HDSL simulation studies and the performance test environment, the simplified 49-disturber NEXT model is used. The 49 disturber is the worst-case scenario, while the use of a straight line extension at low frequencies introduces little performance difference.

Figure 12.24 NEXT Model

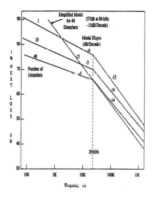

The performance of an HDSL transceiver can be judged by the SNR of its decision feedback channel equalizer output. The SNR in turn can be expressed by the mean squared error of the decision feedback channel equalizer as

$$SNR = \frac{1 - E\left[e_k^2\right]}{E\left[e_k^2\right]} \approx \frac{1}{E\left[e_k^2\right]}$$

The mean squared error of the HDSL decision feedback channel equalizer is

$$E\left[e_k^2\right] = E\left[\left(d_k - X_k^T A_{opt} + D_{k-1}^T B_{opt}\right)^2\right]$$

The values are as follows:

d_k is the desired data symbol.

$X_k^T = \begin{bmatrix} x_k & x_{k-1} & \cdots & x_{x-n+1} \end{bmatrix}$ is the received signal vector.

$A_{opt}^T = \begin{bmatrix} a_1 & a_2 & \cdots & a_n \end{bmatrix}_{opt}$ is the feedforward filter coefficient vector.

$D_{k-1}^T = \begin{bmatrix} d_{k-1} & d_{k-2} & \cdots & d_{x-m} \end{bmatrix}$ is the estimated data symbol vector.

$B_{opt}^T = \begin{bmatrix} b_1 & b_2 & \cdots & b_m \end{bmatrix}_{opt}$ is the feedback filter coefficient vector.

e_k is the error between the desired signal and the decision feedback equalizer output.

A_{opt}^T and B_{opt}^T are defined as

$$A_{opt}^T = \left(E\left[X_k X_k^T\right] - E\left[X_k D_{k-1}^T\right] E\left[D_{k-1} X_k^T\right] \right)^{-1} E\left[d_k X_k^T\right]$$

$$B_{opt}^T = A_{opt}^T E\left[X_k D_{k-1}^T\right]$$

The performance of an HDSL transceiver can be estimated through computer simulation based on a pseudo-random signal generated according to the configuration, as illustrated in Figure 12.25.

Figure 12.25 The Generation of an HDSL Received Signal

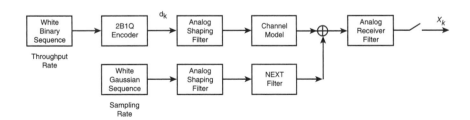

A white binary sequence is generated and encoded as a random data symbol sequence. The binary sequence is generated at the data transmission rate and encoded into the symbol rate. Meanwhile, a white Gaussian sequence is also generated to drive the NEXT filter. The white Gaussian sequence is generated at the simulation sampling rate. The simulation sampling rate is usually 5 to 10 times that of the baud rate to emulate the channel covering excessive bandwidth signal energy and to show the effect of sampling phase.

The performance of an HDSL transceiver is characterized by the relationship between the received signal vector, X_k, and the transmit data symbol vector, D_k. The data symbol vector, D_k, is directly available after the 2B1Q encoder. The received signal vector is the combination of the data symbol after the filtering of the equivalent channel consisting of the transmit filter, the channel, and the receiver filter, and the white Gaussian sequence after the filtering of the equivalent NEXT coupling function consisting of the transmit filter, the NEXT filter, and the receiver filter.

Both transmit and receiver filters are fourth-order Butterworth filters with a 3 dB corner frequency of 200 kHz. The channel models are these eight selected CSA loops. The NEXT filter is an FIR filter designed according to the simplified 49-disturber NEXT model. Figure 12.26 shows the impulse response of the NEXT FIR filter.

Figure 12.26   Impulse Response of the NEXT Filter

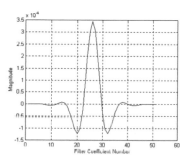

Figure 12.27 shows the transfer function of the NEXT FIR filter.

Figure 12.27   Transfer Function of the NEXT Filter

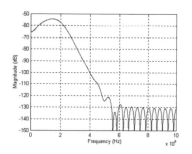

Table 12.4 shows simulated DEF output SNR for these eight test loops. The required SNR is 21.5 dB for an error rate of 10^{-7}. A 6 dB measured performance margin is required for all

HDSL test loops. The simulation results in Table 12.4 are based on a baud rate DFE with 16 FFF and 128 FBF coefficients. Results might be different for different DFE sizes and other hardware parameter assumptions.

Table 12.4 Simulated Performance on Eight HDSL Test Loops

Test Loop Number	SNR	Margin
1	30.6	9.1
2	30.1	8.6
3	27.8	6.3
4	29.4	7.9
5	30.9	9.4
6	29.2	7.7
7	31.1	9.6
8	30.1	8.6

12.3.2 *The Effect of Termination Resistance Value*

The subscriber loop terminal resistor value has some effect on the performance of an HDSL transceiver. Traditionally, the terminal resistor value can be chosen to maximize the front-end received signal power as in some analog receivers. For the case of a receiver with an ideal DFE, variation in performance due to the terminal resistor could disappear because of the matching filter effect. In practice, the HDSL terminal resistor value can be adjusted to further improve the overall system performance when a baud rate DFE is utilized, as shown in Figure 12.28.

Figure 12.28 Terminal Resistance Optimization

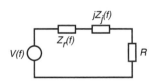

For a frequency variable voltage source with a frequency-dependent source impedance, $Z(f) = Z_r(f) + jZ_j(f)$, we would like to find the optimal load resistor value to maximize the total power delivered from the source to the load.[79] We have the total power:

$$P = \int_0^\infty P_r(f)df = \int_0^\infty |I_r(f)|^2 R df = \int \frac{V^2(f)R}{\left(Z_r(f)+R\right)^2 + Z_j^2(f)} df$$

The values are as follows:

$V(f)$ is the frequency variable voltage.

$Z_r(f)$ is the real part of the frequency-dependent source impedance.

$Z_j(f)$ is the imaginary part of the frequency-dependent source impedance.

R is the load resistor.

Setting

$$\frac{dP}{dR} = 0$$

we get

$$\int \frac{\left(\left(Z_r(f)+R\right)^2 + Z_j^2(f)\right)V^2(f) - 2R\left(Z_r(f)+R\right)V^2(f)}{\left(\left(Z_r(f)+R\right)^2 + Z_j^2(f)\right)^2} df = 0$$

We can write the preceding expression as

$$\int_0^\infty \frac{\left(Z_r^2(f)+Z_j^2(f)\right)V^2(f)}{\left(\left(Z_r(f)+R\right)^2 + Z_j^2(f)\right)^2} df = R^2 \int_0^\infty \frac{V^2(f)}{\left(\left(Z_r(f)+R\right)^2 + Z_j^2(f)\right)^2} df$$

We can solve for R iteratively using the following:

$$R_{i+1}^2 = \frac{\displaystyle\int_0^\infty \frac{\left(Z_r^2(f)+Z_j^2(f)\right)V^2(f)}{\left(\left(Z_r(f)+R_i\right)^2 + Z_j^2(f)\right)^2} df}{\displaystyle\int_0^\infty \frac{V^2(f)}{\left(\left(Z_r(f)+R_i\right)^2 + Z_j^2(f)\right)^2} df}$$

For the HDSL system, we let $V^2(f) = P_5(f)$ in which

$$P_5(f) = K \frac{1}{f_0} \cdot \frac{\sin^2\left(\frac{\pi f}{f_0}\right)}{\left(\frac{\pi f}{f_0}\right)^2} \cdot \frac{1}{1 + \left(\frac{f}{f_h}\right)^4} \cdot \frac{1}{1 + \left(\frac{f_l}{f}\right)^4}$$

for

$f_0 = 400kHz$

$f_h = 256kHz$

$f_l = 5kHz$

$Z_r(f)$ and $Z_j(f)$ equal to the input impedance of a 9 kft, 26-gauge loop.

We find that $R_{opt} = 120\Omega$.

Computer simulations are carried out based on the 9 kft, 26-gauge loop and the 49-disturber self-NEXT model for the HDSL system. Figure 12.29 summarizes computer simulation results in terms of SNRs as functions of terminal resistor value R and lowpass filter frequency responses. The fourth and eighth labels in Figure 12.29 represent the orders of receiver filters.

Figure 12.29 DFE Output SNR Versus R for HDSL

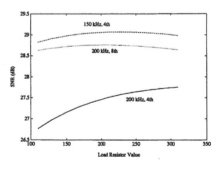

The front-end received signal power can be maximized by adjusting the load resistor value; however, the SNR at the receiver detection point is not a direct function of the front-end signal power. The SNR is affected by terminal resistor value, receiver lowpass filter frequency response, and the structure of the DFE. The effect of varying the terminal resistor value becomes small when the excessive crosstalk power due to the sampling image is suppressed by the receiver lowpass filter. A 135 ohms terminal resistor value, the same value as that for DSL, is therefore adopted for HDSL.

12.3.3   Measures to Handle the Slight Data Rate Difference in Opposite Directions

It has been reported that at least for some private point-to-point DS1 circuits, it is not necessary that the line have network timing or that the Customer Premises Equipment (CPE) at the ends be loop-timed.[80] For instance, a customer can lease a DS1 line between two locations and attach his own digital channel banks equipped with voice channel units at the ends. The channel bank transmitter at each end will control the receiver frequency at the far end.

If only voice services are transported, neither channel bank needs to be loop-timed to the other. The free-running clock frequency accuracy requirement is between 50 bps (32 parts/million) and 200 bps (130 parts/million) for DS1 line output. As a result, the DS1 line frequency for such non-loop-timed circuits might be offset from each other by as much as 400 bps.

Another possible application for HDSL is to interconnect local area networks (LANs) through gateway or bridge devices. IEEE 802 LAN requirements for frequency accuracy and stability are less stringent than DS1 requirements. IEEE 802.3 for CSMA/CD LANs (such as ethernet) and IEEE 802.4 for token bus LANs require origination stations to have 100 parts/million frequency accuracy and repeating stations on 150 parts/million.

At DS1 rates, these requirements translate to 154 bps at best and 232 bps at worst. In the case that the loop-timing is not implemented, the throughput difference between each direction could be as much as 434 bps. In addition, there might also be a synchronization problem between a private digital network and a local exchange carrier.[81]

The asynchronous throughput in each direction poses a problem for the adaptive echo cancellation technique, which requires certain stability between transmitted and received data. While there have been some phase shifting insensitive echo cancellation techniques proposed in the past,[82,83] their performance under the dual-duplex HDSL asynchronous environment requires further study. In particular, the problem of missing bits or the occurrence of extra random bits should be addressed.

The same asynchronous problem has been in existence for the voice band modem for some time. A simple analog solution[84] is to perform ADC first for echo cancellation on the transmitting clock. The echo-removed signal is converted back to analog form with a Digital to Analog Converter. The echo-removed analog signal is then converted to digital for the equalizer using the recovered receiver clock. The extra DAC and ADC operation can be saved by using a digital technique,[85] especially in the form of a Finite Impulse Response (FIR) digital filter.[86]

Both the analog double A to D conversion and the digital FIR filter solutions are studied in the context of a dual-duplex HDSL application.[87] Figure 12.30 shows the structure of the double A to D conversion solution.

Figure 12.30 Double ADC Approach

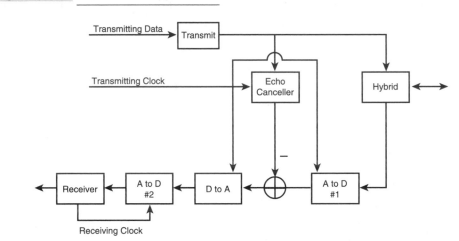

The required number of bits of the first A to D converter is related to the required echo cancellation level. The required number of bits of the second A to D converter is only related to the required signal-to-noise ratio of the DFE-based receiver. The echo cancellation level could be as high as 60 dB. In comparison, the required SNR corresponding to a 10^{-7} error rate for the 2B1Q signal is only about 30 dB. Hence, the cost of the second A to D converter is significantly less than the first one.

Rate Conversion Filters

To understand the operation of the rate conversion filter, let us first consider the case where the transmitting clock and the receiving clock have the same frequency but with a phase delay of αT, for which $-0.5 < \alpha < 0.5$. We can use an FIR filter with $N\alpha$ dependent filter coefficients to reconstruct the original signal in place of the combination of a D to A converter and an A to D converter. The output of the D to A converter has an ideal Nyquist pulse shape, and the output of the following A to D converter is then a sampled version of that Nyquist pulse (see Figure 12.31).

Figure 12.31 The D to A and A to D Equivalence of a Rate Conversion Filter

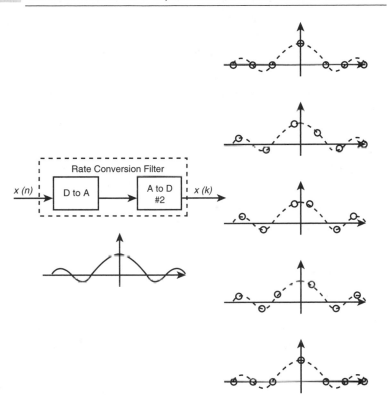

Possible digital Nyquist filters of different sampling phases are shown at the right side of Figure 12.31. We denote the FIR filter coefficient vector as

$$C(\alpha)^T = \begin{bmatrix} c(\alpha)_0 & c(\alpha)_1 & \cdots & c(\alpha)_{n-1} \end{bmatrix}$$

To realize any $C(\alpha)$ for $-0.5 < \alpha < 0.5$, however, we need an infinite number of $C(\alpha)$s. On the other hand, because $C(\alpha)$ is a function of α, we can implement each $c(\alpha)_l$ as a polynomial function of α, that is, we let

$$c(\alpha)_i = c_{i,0} + c_{i,1}\alpha + c_{i,2}\alpha^2 + \ldots$$

Therefore, for a third-degree polynomial fitting of a length N FIR filter, we only need to store $4N$ values for any $C(\alpha)$, with this polynomial approach.

For the general asynchronous clock case, the assumption of a fixed delay between two clocks is not valid. The rate conversion FIR filter can still function well, however, if we let the filter coefficients be functions of instantaneous phase, $\alpha(k)$, that is

$$c(\alpha)^T = \left[c(\alpha(k))_0 \quad c(\alpha(k-1))_1 \quad c(\alpha(k-N+1))_{n-1} \right]$$

No additional computations are introduced if the filter output is generated according to

$$y_m = \sum_n x(n)c_{n,m}$$

$$z(k,m) = \sum \alpha(k)^m y_m$$

The index n corresponds to the transmitting clock, while k corresponds to the receiving clock. The $\alpha(k)$ is defined as

$$\alpha(k) = \operatorname{Re} m\left(\frac{nT_t - kT_r}{T_r} \right)$$

T_t is the period of the transmitting clock and T_r is of the receiving clock. If $\alpha(k)$ overflows, two new $x(n)$s are shifted into the delay line; if $\alpha(k)$ underflows, then no $x(n)$s are shifted in. Figure 12.32 shows the filter implementation.

This rate conversion filter can avoid the loss and the occurrence of extra bits. Because the length of the FIR filter and also the degree of polynomial are both limited, there are small errors introduced by this filter. In practice, for a sufficiently high degree of polynomial, $c_{i,j}$ are chosen offline to minimize the mean squared error according to

$$\int\int \left| \sum\sum \alpha^m C_{n,m} e^{jn\omega T} - e^{j\omega\alpha T} \right|^2 d\omega d\alpha$$

Figure 12.32   The Structure of the Rate Conversion Filter

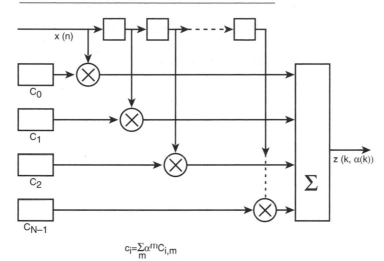

$$c_i = \sum_m \alpha^m c_{i,m}$$

Table 12.5 shows a set of possible $c_{n,m}$ values corresponding to a baseband dual-duplex DSL with 50 percent excessive bandwidth and a sampling rate of 800 kilo-samples per second.

Table 12.5   A Possible Set of Rate Conversion Filter Coefficients

n	m			
	0	1	2	3
0	-0.005569	0.000732	0.022278	-0.00293
1	0.017471	-0.003174	-0.069885	0.012695
2	-0.040802	0.0103	0.163208	-0.041199
3	0.085114	-0.03157	-0.340454	0.126282
4	-0.183044	0.11792	0.732178	-0.47168
5	0.626038	-1.24646	-0.50412	0.98584
6	0.626038	1.24646	-0.50412	-0.98584
7	-0.183044	-0.11792	0.732178	0.47168
8	0.085114	0.03157	-0.340454	-0.126282
9	-0.040802	-0.0103	0.163208	0.041199
10	0.017471	0.003174	-0.069885	-0.012695
11	-0.005569	-0.000732	0.022278	0.00293

Variable Frame Approaches

The other approach to overcome the asynchronous clock problem is to introduce a variable frame structure. The clock difference between each direction can then be compensated through *bit stuffing*. Bit stuffing is used to expand the length of a frame by inserting some dummy bits at some defined location. A method should be defined for the transmitter to decide when bit stuffing is required. The method should also allow the receiver to recognize stuffed bits to remove them. Two different variable frame formats have been proposed by Tellabs and PairGain[88] and Northern Telecom, Inc.[89]

Tellabs' and PairGain's Variable Frame Proposal

Tellabs' proposal starts with a 7-quats (or 14 bits, for each quat contains two bits) Barker code sync word. There are three bit-stuffing control bits evenly distributed between DS1 data blocks, indicating whether there is 0 or 2 quats stuffing at the end of an HDSL frame. The bit error rate is assumed to be $P_e = \eta$ for the following analysis.

A majority decision, two out of three, is made based on these three control bits. The probability of a wrong indication is as follows:

$$P_W = P_e(c_1)P_e(c_2) + P_e(c_1)P_e(c_3) + P_e(c_2)P_e(c_3) - 2P_e(c_1)P_e(c_2)P_e(c_3) = 3\eta^2 - 2\eta^3 = \eta^2(3 - 2\eta)$$

A sync word is considered recognized only when there is no error in any of its quats. The probability of receiving a bad sync word is as follows:

$$P_{bsw} = 1 - (1 - \eta)^{14}$$

A bad frame is declared when both the sync word and control bits are in error. The probability for a bad frame is as follows:

$$P_{w\&bsw} = P_W P_{bsw} = \eta^2 \left(1 - (1 - \eta)^{14}\right)(3 - 2\eta)$$

For a frame repetition rate of 6 milliseconds, the expected bad frames per day is as follows:

$$E(Badframes / day) = P_{w\&bsw} \frac{24 \times 3600}{6 \times 10^{-3}}$$

Table 12.6 provides the performance estimation for the Tellabs variable frame structure proposal, assuming the preceding expressions are true. In Table 12.6, CFA stands for *Certainty of Frame Acquisition*, as will be examined shortly.

Table 12.6 Performance Estimation for Tellabs' Proposal

η	1×10^{-3}	1×10^{-4}	1×10^{-5}	1×10^{-6}	1×10^{-7}
P_w	2.998×10^{-6}	3.000×10^{-8}	3.000×10^{-10}	3.000×10^{-12}	3.000×10^{-14}
E(B.F./D.)	6.005×10^{-1}	6.043×10^{-4}	6.048×10^{-7}	6.048×10^{-10}	6.048×10^{-13}
CFA	95.51%	98.04%	98.19%	98.21%	98.21%

Because the sync word is only searched for at two places as suggested by the proposal, the framing will be hard to recover for two bad frames in a row. In this sense, the performance is more closely related to the expected number of bad frames than the probability of the loss of 6 sync words in a row as is commonly used in fixed frame formats.

The probability of misdetecting a sync word in n quats of random data is

$$P_{se(n-6)} = 1-\left(1-\frac{2}{4^7}\right)^{n-6}$$

The first sync word could occur equally likely between the first 7-quats position and the 2,346th 7-quats position. We have the probability of detecting a sync word for a frame length of N quats as

$$P_{se} = 1-\left(1-\frac{2}{4^7}\right)^{\frac{N-1}{2}}$$

using a mean random data length of

$$\frac{N-1}{2}$$

before the real sync word as the position where the frame search begins.

There are three cases in which the frame acquisition, two consecutive detections of two sync words, can be completed in three frames.[90] The first one is when there is no misdetection of a sync word before the successful detection of two consecutive sync words. The second case is for successful detection of two sync words after a misdetection of one sync word. The third case is when there is also no misdetection, but one missed real sync word before the successful detection of two sync words. Naming probabilities corresponding to these cases as P_1, P_2, and P_3, respectively, the probability of frame acquisition within the first three frames is

$$P_{3f} = P_1 + P_2 + P_3$$

We have the following (see Figure 12.33):

$$P_1 = (1 - P_{se})(1 - P_{bsw})(1 - P_{bsw})$$

Figure 12.33 Calculation of P_1

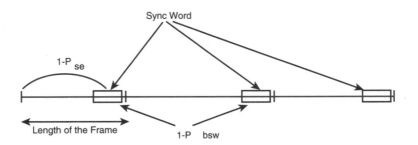

We also have the following (see Figure 12.34):

$$P_2 = P_{se}(1 - P_{se2})(1 - P_{se})(1 - P_{bsw})(1 - P_{bsw})$$

Figure 12.34 Calculation of P_2

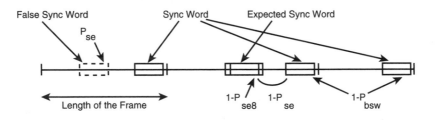

Finally, we have the following (see Figure 12.35):

$$P_3 = (1 - P_{se})P_{bsw}(1 - P_{se})(1 - P_{bsw})(1 - P_{bsw})$$

Figure 12.35  Calculation of P_3

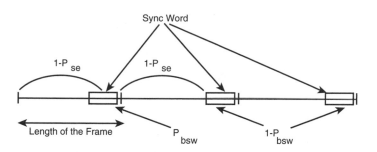

Given these probability calculations, we thus have

$$P_{3f} = \left(1 - P_{bsw}\right)^2 \left(1 - P_{se}\right)\left(1 + P_{se}\left(1 - P_{se2}\right)\right) + \left(1 - P_{se}\right)P_{bsw}\right)$$

The probability of frame acquisition in three frames is shown earlier in this section in Table 12.6 as CFA.

Although a 7-bit Barker code is used, the property of the Barker code is never utilized. In other words, the performance of the proposal will be exactly the same if the Barker code is replaced by any other bit pattern. Hence, through examining P_W, P_{bsw}, and $P_{w\&psw}$, the performance of the proposal depends primarily on P_W.

Northern Telecom's Variable Frame Proposal

Northern's proposal starts with an 11-bit Barker code sync word appearing as sign-only information in the first 11 quats of a frame. Stuffing occurs immediately prior to the sync word, in other words, at the end of an HDSL frame. The stuffing is a single quat plus or minus one quat. The deframer calculates correlation for three possible sync word windows. The window with the highest correlation is considered to contain the sync word. Considering the scenario for which the sync word is at the normal position, correlation for the advanced, normal, and delayed windows for zero bit error are 0, 11, and 0, respectively, assuming the following:

$$Corr(1,1) = Corr(0,0) = 1$$
$$Corr(1,0) = Corr(0,1) = -1$$
$$Corr(1,x) = Corr(0,x) = Corr(x,0) = Corr(x,0) = 0 \text{ (see Figure 12.36)}$$

Figure 12.36 Calculation of P_E

```
11100010010        Corr+=0
11100010010        Corr=11
11100010010        Corr-=0
```

Corr(1,1)=Corr(0,0)=1
Corr(1,0)=Corr(0,1)=-1

Any bit error will reduce the correlation of the normal window by the amount equal to two times the number of errors. The correlation of the advanced or the delayed window will either be decreased or increased depending on error positions. The misdetection of the sync word position could happen only when the number of errors is larger than two. Hence, the probability of detecting a wrong sync word window is as follows:

$$P_E = \sum_{3}^{11} P(BitErrorNumber = i)\left[P(Corr+ > 11-i)\big|_c + P(Corr- > 11-i)\big|_c \right]$$

$$= \sum_{3}^{11} C_{11}^i P_e^i (1-P_e)^{11-i}\left[P(Corr+ > 11-i)\big|_c + P(Corr- > 11-i)\big|_c \right]$$

The values are as follows:

c means that the condition of $P_E = \sum_{3}^{11} P(BitErrorNumber = i) \, P_e \eta$ is the bit error probability.

Corr + means the correlation of the third window.

Corr − means the correlation of the first window.

For

$$P_e \leq 10^{-3}$$

we have

$$P_E \approx C_{11}^3 P_e^3 (1-P_e)^8 \left[P(Corr+ > 5)\big|_c + P(Corr- > 5)\big|_c \right]$$

From Figure 12.36, there are five bit positions where an error will cause an increase in *Corr+* or *Corr−*. There are C_5^3 ways the 3-bit errors can be arranged in these five positions. There are C_{11}^3 ways the 3-bit error can be arranged in the entire sync word.

Therefore, we have

$$P(Corr+>5)\big|_c = P\left(Corr->5\big|_c\right) = \frac{C_5^3}{C_{11}^3} = \frac{10}{165}$$

Hence, we have

$$P_E \approx C_{11}^3 P_e^3 \left(1-P_e\right)^8 2\frac{C_5^3}{C_{11}^3} = 20\eta^3\left(1-\eta\right)^8$$

For a frame repetition rate of 6 milliseconds, the expected bad frames per day is

$$E(badframes\,/\,day) = P_E\,\frac{24\times3600}{6\times10^{-3}}$$

Table 12.7 lists the performance estimation, assuming the preceding expressions are true.

Table 12.7   Performance Estimation for Northern's Proposal

η	1×10^{-3}	1×10^{-4}	1×10^{-5}	1×10^{-6}	1×10^{-7}
P_E	1.984×10^{-8}	1.998×10^{-11}	2.000×10^{-14}	2.000×10^{-17}	2.000×10^{-20}
E(B.F./D.)	2.856×10^{-1}	2.878×10^{-4}	2.880×10^{-7}	6.048×10^{-10}	2.880×10^{-13}
CFA	52.25%	53.20%	53.29%	53.30%	53.30%

The detection of the first sync word is assumed to be a perfect match:

$$P_{ds} = \left(1-\eta\right)^{11}$$

The probability of misdetecting a sync word in n quats of random data is

$$P'_{se(n-10)} = 1-\left(1-\frac{2}{2^{11}}\right)^{n-10}$$

The probability of misdetecting a first sync word for a frame of length N is

$$P'_{se} = 1-\left(1-\frac{2}{2^{11}}\right)^{\frac{N-1}{2}}$$

The confirmation of the second sync word requires a perfect match in one of three possible windows. The probability of a match, assuming we know which window to look at, is P_{ds}. The probability of the sync word being in one of the three positions equals one. Therefore

$$P_{cs} = (1-\eta)^{11}$$

The possibility of misdetecting a second sync word has been omitted because we assume the framing circuitry knows where to "look" for the second sync word. Again, for three possible cases in which frame acquisition can be accomplished in the first three frames, we have

$$P_1 = (1 - P'_{se}) P_{ds} P_{cs}$$

$$P_2 = P'_{se} (1 - P'_{se3})(1 - P'_{se}) P_{ds} P_{cs}$$

$$P_3 = (1 - P'_{se})(1 - P'_{ds})(1 - P'_{se}) P_{ds} P_{cs}$$

This leads to

$$P'_{3f} = P_{ds} P_{cs} (1 - P'_{se})(1 + P'_{se}(1 - P'_{se3}) + (1 - P'_{se})(1 - P_{ds}))$$

Assuming the preceding expressions, the performance estimation is also listed in Table 12.7 as CFA. The initial acquisition performance is much poorer than that of Tellabs' proposal due to usage of the magnitude bits for other purposes. As a result, Northern Telecom's proposal might not be considered adequate for the HDSL application.

Performance of Fixed Frame as a Reference

The performance of a traditional fixed frame format, where bad frames are declared for six consecutive bad sync words and an initial frame acquisition is declared after two perfect detections of the sync word, is also estimated for comparison. Both a 7-quat sync word and an 11-bit sync word are assumed for fixed frames. For the fixed frame, the probability of six consecutive bad sync words is as follows:

$$P_{sl} = (1 - (1-\eta)^j)^6$$

The probabilities for detection and confirmation of the sync word are both

$$P_d(1-\eta)^j$$

The probability of misdetecting a sync word in n quats of random data is

$$P_{s(n-j+1)} = 1 - \left(1 - \frac{2}{2^j}\right)^{(n-j+1)}$$

The probability of misdetecting a first sync word is

$$P_s = 1 - \left(1 - \frac{2}{2^j}\right)^{\frac{N-1}{2}}$$

The value j is 14 for the 7-quat sync word and 11 for the 11-bit sync word. The probability for frame acquisition in the first three frames is

$$P''_{3f} = (1 - P_s)P_d^2 + P_s(1 - P_{s1})(1 - P_s)P_d^2 + (1 - P_s)(1 - P_d)(1 - P_s)P_d^2$$

Table 12.8 lists the probabilities for the 7-quat sync word. Table 12.9 lists the probabilities for the 11-bit sync word. After achieving frame synchronization, the exact location of the sync word is known. The probability of detecting a valid sync word in 6 tries is very high. This phenomenon is known as *flywheel*.

Table 12.8 Performance Estimation for a 7-Quat Fixed Frame

η	1×10^{-3}	1×10^{-4}	1×10^{-5}	1×10^{-6}	1×10^{-7}
P_{s1}	7.242×10^{-12}	7.500×10^{-18}	7.527×10^{-24}	7.529×10^{-30}	7.530×10^{-36}
E(B.F./D.)	6.258×10^{-4}	6.480×10^{-10}	6.504×10^{-16}	6.504×10^{-22}	6.504×10^{-28}
CFA	95.51%	98.04%	98.19%	98.21%	98.21%

Table 12.9 Performance Estimation for an 11-Bit Fixed Frame

η	1×10^{-3}	1×10^{-4}	1×10^{-5}	1×10^{-6}	1×10^{-7}
P_{s1}	1.719×10^{-12}	1.766×10^{-18}	1.771×10^{-24}	1.772×10^{-30}	1.772×10^{-36}
E(B.F./D.)	1.484×10^{-4}	1.526×10^{-10}	1.531×10^{-16}	1.531×10^{-22}	1.531×10^{-28}
CFA	52.29%	53.24%	53.33%	53.34%	53.34%

The Double-Barker Code Variable Frame Approach

Analysis shows that while normal operation performances—expected bad frames per day—of both proposals are close to each other, their performance is not as good compared with that of a fixed frame format. On the other hand, the initial acquisition performance—certainty of frame acquisition in the first three frames—of the Tellabs proposal is much better than the Northern Telecom proposal. Based on Tellabs' and Northern Telecom's proposals, a double-coded 7-quat Barker code for the variable frame format is proposed (see Figure 12.37).[91]

Figure 12.37	Calculation of P_E

```
        11 11 11 00 00 11 00      Corr = 14
     11 11 11 00 00 11 00         Corr+ = 2

        Corr(1,1)=Corr(0,0)=1
        Corr(1,0)=Corr(0,1)=-1
```

A two-window with autocorrelation detection scheme is used, with either 0 or 2 quats of bit stuffing at the end of each frame. The probability of detecting a wrong sync word window is as follows:

$$P_E = \frac{1}{16} \sum_{i=3}^{14} P(BitErrorNumber = i) P(Corr+ \geq 14 - 2i)\big|_c$$

$$+ \frac{10}{16} \sum_{i=4}^{14} P(BitErrorNunber = i) P(Corr+ \geq 14 - 2i)\big|_c$$

$$\frac{1}{4} \sum_{i=5}^{14} P(BitErrorNumber = i) P(Corr+ \geq 14 - 2i)\big|_c$$

$$\approx \frac{1}{16} C_{14}^3 P_e^3 (1 - P_e)^{11} P(Corr+ \geq 8)\big|_c$$

for

$$P(Corr+ \geq 6)\big|_c = \frac{C_6^3}{C_{14}^3} = \frac{20}{C_{14}^3}$$

and

$$P_e = \eta$$

As a result, we have

$$P_E \approx \frac{5}{4}\eta^3(1-\eta)^{11}$$

Table 12.10 summarizes the performance estimation for a 7-quat double-Barker code.

Table 12.10   Performance Estimation for a 7-Quat Double-Barker Code

η	1×10^{-3}	1×10^{-4}	1×10^{-5}	1×10^{-6}	1×10^{-7}
P_E	1.236×10^{-9}	1.249×10^{-12}	1.250×10^{-15}	1.250×10^{-18}	1.250×10^{-21}
E(B.F./D.)	1.780×10^{-2}	1.780×10^{-5}	1.780×10^{-8}	1.800×10^{-11}	1.800×10^{-14}
CFA	95.51%	98.04%	98.19%	98.21%	98.21%

The certainty of frame acquisition in the first three frames is the same as the Tellabs proposal. The 7-quat double-Barker code can be coded as [+3 +3 +3 −1 −1 +3 −1] following the conventional gray code or as [+3 +3 +3 −3 −3 +3 −3] in conjunction with a special autocorrelation decoder. Table 12.11 summarizes the performance of using an 11-quat double-Barker code, which is also estimated according to similar expressions.

Table 12.11   Performance Estimation for an 11-Quat Double-Barker Code

η	1×10^{-3}	1×10^{-4}	1×10^{-5}	1×10^{-6}	1×10^{-7}
P_E	1.548×10^{-14}	1.572×10^{-19}	1.575×10^{-24}	1.575×10^{-29}	1.575×10^{-34}
E(B.F./D.)	2.229×10^{-7}	2.264×10^{-12}	2.268×10^{-17}	2.268×10^{-22}	2.268×10^{-27}
CFA	97.77%	99.77%	99.98%	100.00%	100.00%

Figure 12.38 illustrates the performance comparison (in expected bad frames per day) between a 7-quat double-Barker code and an 11-quat double-Barker code.

Figure 12.39 illustrates the performance comparison (in initial frame acquisition) between a 7-quat double-Barker code and an 11-quat double-Barker code.

The proposed double-Barker code variable frame format has performance closer to that of a fixed frame format. The 7-quat double-Barker code variable frame format requires three less bits compared with Tellabs' proposal and needs an autocorrelation operation only 3 bits longer than Northern's proposal. The 7-quat double-Barker code frame format is therefore adopted for the HDSL variable frame application. The performance of this double-Barker code variable frame format is also very robust under impulse noise.[92]

Figure 12.38 Expected Bad Frames per Day

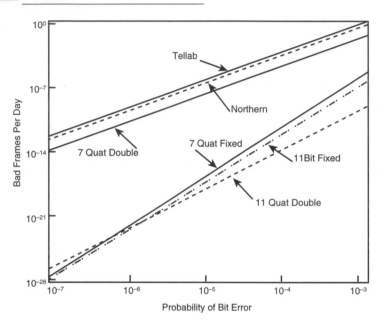

12.4 HDSL Network Interfaces

The dual-duplex HDSL is designed to be a cost-effective repeaterless T1 transceiver. A T1 transceiver is generally used to carry the DS1 traffic for the Public Switch Telephone Network (PSTN). The DS1, which stands for Digital Signal 1, is the first level of the North American digital hierarchy with a nominal rate of 1.544 Mbps. A specific implementation of DS1 is further referred to as DSX-1. ANSI T1.107[93] defines the DS1 bit rate and format.

ANSI T1.102[94] defines the DS1 electrical interconnection requirements for frequency accuracy and frequency stability, line code, impedance, and pulse shape for DSX-1 cross-connect points. ANSI T1.403[95] and T1.408[96] define the requirements for DS1 signals for network-customer interfaces.

Figure 12.39 Initial Certainty of Frame Acquisition

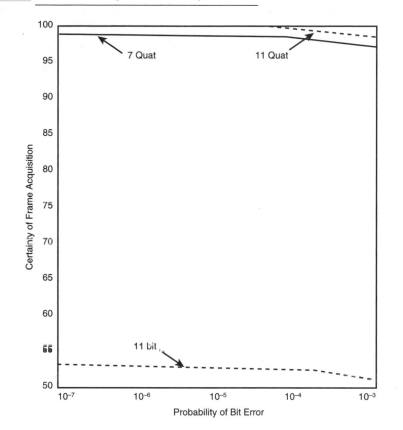

12.4.1 The DS1 Infrastructure

For most network applications, the DS1 signal has a 125 μsec frame structure (see T1.107) with 192 payload bits and one framing/overhead bit. The first bit is the DS1 frame bit, called the *F* bit. The F frame channel is composed entirely of framing information, as in the Superframe format, or made up of a framing pattern, a data link, and a 6-bit cyclic redundancy check code, as in the Extended Superframe format. The framed DS1 payload is thus 1536 kbps (192 bits/125 μsec) with an overhead of 8 kbps (1 bit/125 μsec).

Most applications define the 192 bits in a frame as 24 8-bit DS0 channels of 64 kbps each. These 8-bit time slots are called bytes. These DS0 channels traditionally carried digitally encoded telephony voice signals, but they can be any 64 kbps signal.

The DSX-1 signal is a bipolar signal where binary one levels alternate in polarity and have a peak magnitude ranging from 2.4 to 3.6 volts. A zero binary level is represented by zero volts. Time wave shape templates are specified for the binary one pulses. This bipolar signal line code is also called *Alternate Mark Inversion* (AMI). A variation on the bipolar line code is *bipolar with 8-zero substitution* (B8ZS). A B8ZS transmitter replaces strings of eight consecutive zeros by a specific eight-symbol pattern that violates the alternating polarity rule.

The receiver detects the pattern and restores the original eight-zero-bit string. The B8ZS encoding ensures sufficient pulse density for older line regenerators to derive timing from the incoming signal. At the network side, the DSX-1 wiring is connected by wire wrap pins on the back plane of the frame containing the device. At the customer side, the DSX-1 wiring is connected via a standard RJ-48C jack and also by screw-down strips.

A T1 transceiver is a transmission system designed to transport bi-directional 1.544 Mbps signals over twisted-pair loops. Each direction is transmitted on a separate twisted-pair loop with a transmitter at one end and a receiver at the other end. Line repeaters are placed in the outside plant at intervals, typically between 3 and 6 kft, determined by the wire gauge and the number of other T1 systems sharing the cable. Bridged taps are not allowed. They are removed during the T1 line installation from conventional telephone subscriber loops.

With the use of many repeaters, a range of 100 miles is possible. While DS1 signals have many options for framing or nonframing, and many possibilities exist for multiplexing the DS1 payload, HDSL is intended to be independent of the details beyond the 1.544 Mbps and the +−3 volt bipolar line encoding, just as a T1 line repeater is.

HDSL DS1 Interface

Dual-duplex HDSL systems could have transported DS1 signals by multiplexing the signal onto the two HDSL transceiver-loop sub-systems on a bit-by-bit, a byte-by-byte, or a group-by-group basis or other schemes. One concern is to minimize end-to-end transmission delay. Another consideration is possibly taking advantage of the DS1 service transport with only one loop operation.

A bit-by-bit mapping would make the remaining payload virtually unusable. The Group 1 and Group 2 multiplexing scheme proposed in the standards committee report appears to be a reasonable compromise solution, adding about 63 μsec (half a DS1 frame) more delay than the minimum, but providing contiguous DS0s in one loop operation.

For transport via a dual-duplex HDSL system, the DS1 signals are disassembled into three components:

- The DS1 framing (F) bits (if present)

- The Group 1 bytes (1 through 12)

- The Group 2 bytes (13 through 24)

The DS1 framing bit occurs at every 0-th bit position in each 125 μsec DS1 signal frame at a nominal bandwidth of 8 kbps. A DS0 time slot is made up of eight bits (one byte) in each 125-microsecond frame and has a nominal bandwidth of 64 kbps. Specifically, it was defined that the DS1 framing F bits, if present, shall be transported via both HDSL transceivers over two loops and that the HDSL system shall have a default option to detect B8ZS line encoding on the incoming DS1 bitstream and recreate B8ZS on the outgoing DS1 bitstream.

DS1 components of the HDSL payload for each transceiver require 12×64=768 kbps nominal bandwidth. The 8 kbps of DS1 F bit overhead will be added to both transceiver pairs. The composite HDSL payload through each transceiver and on each loop is thus a nominal 768+8=776 kbps. For an unframed DS1 signal, the HDSL shall choose a bit to represent the F bit position and count bytes relative to the chosen bit to represent the Group 1 and Group 2 bytes.

The dual-duplex HDSL system should accommodate differences in total length (working length plus the sum of bridged tap lengths) between two loops as large as 1 kilometer (3.3 kft). The HDSL system also should accommodate DS1 signals when the two directions have frequency offsets relative to each other or to the network or to the HDSL timing averaging as much as +−130 PPM.

Figure 12.40 shows the detailed DS1-to-HDSL-to-DS1 signal conversion process.

Figure 12.41 shows the HDSL framing structure during the normal operation after the initialization.

The HDSL frame starts with a seven-symbol synchronization word followed by 1 quat of other HDSL overhead. Here, a quat consists of two bits and occupies one symbol interval. The synchronization word is a 7-quat Barker code (+3 +3 +3 −3 −3 +3 −3) in one direction and the time reverse (−3 +3 −3 −3 +3 +3 +3) of the same Barker code in the other direction. This double assignment of the code word binary value is referred to as a *double-Barker code*.

The double-Barker code has been shown to have superior autocorrelation properties in the presence of noise. To further enhance the SNR in the initialization process, the double-Barker code is coded with 11 for +3 and 00 for −3 instead of the gray code used during the normal transmission.

Figure 12.40 The HDSL-DS1 Payload Interface

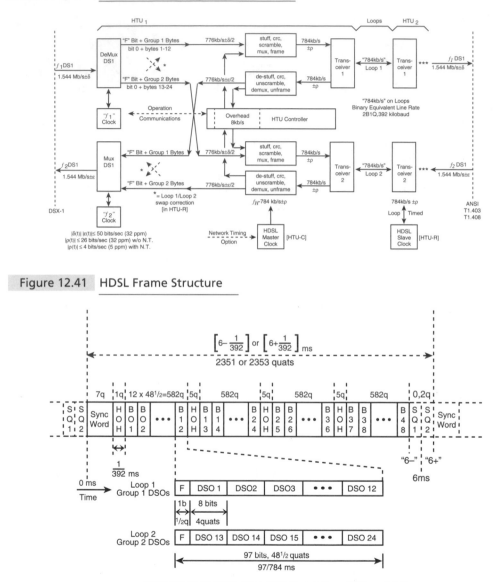

Figure 12.41 HDSL Frame Structure

HDSL DS1 Payload Block (48 per HDSL Frame): Group 1 & Group 2 Split

After the overhead quat, there are four groups of HDSL payloads. Each of the first three HDSL payload groups has 581 payload quats and five overhead quats. The last HDSL payload group has only 581 payload quats. At the end of the HDSL frame there could be two stuffing quats. The total length of an HDSL frame is either 2,351 or 2,353 quats corresponding to 6–1/392 ms or 6+1/392 ms. Each HDSL payload group is further divided into 12 DS1 blocks. Each DS1 block is composed of a DS1 framing bit, F (if present, or an HDSL-chosen substitute), and 12 bytes of DS0 data, for a total of 97 bits encoded to 481/2 quats.

Used as a dual-duplex T1 transceiver, each HDSL frame covers four DS1 frames. With a total HDSL overhead of 24 quats or 48 bits plus 24 duplicated F bits per frame, the HDSL binary equivalent line rate is 784 kbps for a single pair or 1.568 Mbps for two pairs.

HDSL Line Powering Options

An HDSL Terminal Unit-Remote (HTU-R) can be powered through a central office, as indicated by Figure 12.42.

Figure 12.42 Dual-Loop HDSL Loop Powering

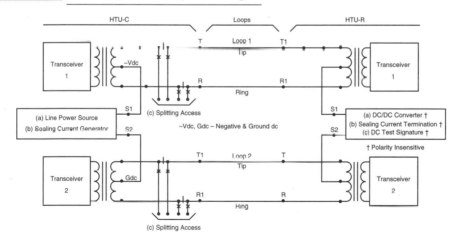

One pair is used as ground while the other pair is used to supply the necessary voltage. The HTU-R should have a DC-DC converter to re-generate a proper and stable voltage level suitable for the HDSL transceiver. The HTU-R can also be powered through a single loop, as indicated by Figure 12.43.

Figure 12.43 Single-Loop HDSL Loop Powering

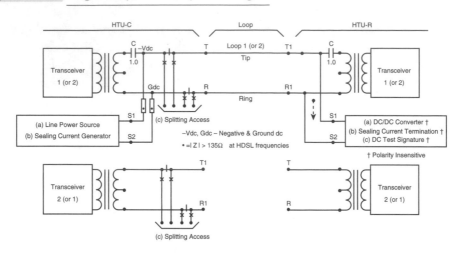

In the single-loop case, capacitors need to be inserted between line transformers and the loop to prevent the short circuit of the power supply.

12.5 HDSL Technical Report

The draft T1E1.4 HDSL technical report[97] addresses interface details for the 2B1Q line code as well as for the alternative CAP HDSL line code. Specifics for the 2B1Q line code covered are pulse shaped and transmit power spectrum, test loops, test procedures, frame structure, scrambling method, start-up and training, and jitter requirement, as well as Operation, Administration, Maintenance (OAM), and provisioning and Embedded Operations Channels (EOC). Specifics for the CAP line code covered are transmit power spectrum, scrambling method, frame structure, and start-up procedure.

12.5.1 2B1Q Bit-to-Symbol Encoding

The 2B1Q line code uses the gray code to encode every two bits into a quaternary symbol, as shown in Table 12.12.

Table 12.12 The HDSL Gray Encode

First Bit (Sign)	Second Bit (Magnitude)	Quaternary Symbol (Quat)
1	0	+3
1	1	+1

First Bit (Sign)	Second Bit (Magnitude)	Quaternary Symbol (Quat)
0	1	−1
0	0	−3

12.5.2 *Transmit Signal Pulse Mask*

The HDSL line signal from a transmitter should confirm the pulse mask defined in the time domain (see Figure 12.44).

Figure 12.44 HDSL Transmit Signal Pulse Mask

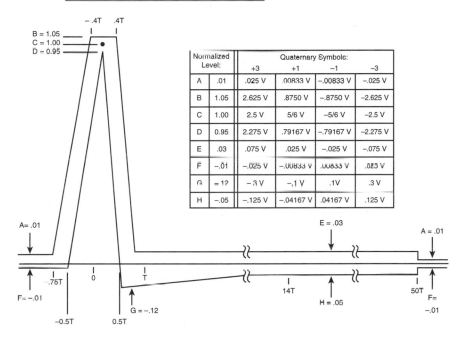

Normalized Level:		Quaternary Symbols:			
		+3	+1	−1	−3
A	.01	.025 V	.00833 V	−.00833 V	−.025 V
B	1.05	2.625 V	.8750 V	−.8750 V	−2.625 V
C	1.00	2.5 V	5/6 V	−5/6 V	−2.5 V
D	0.95	2.275 V	.79167 V	−.79167 V	−2.275 V
E	.03	.075 V	.025 V	−.025 V	−.075 V
F	−.01	−.025 V	−.00833 V	.00833 V	.025 V
G	−.12	−.3 V	−.1 V	.1V	.3 V
H	−.05	−.125 V	−.04167 V	.04167 V	.125 V

The compliance of the transmit signal in the time domain can be achieved by choosing the proper combination of a transmitter filter and a hybrid circuit. The transmit pulse shape can be measured in real time using either a single pulse or a known pulse sequence with some signal processing.

12.5.3 Transmit Signal Power Mask

Figure 12.45 shows the upper bound of the average power spectral density of the transmit signal, which can be summarized as that the power density should be –38 dBm/Hz from 0 Hz to 196 kHz, –80 dB/decade attenuation from –38 dBm/Hz at 196 kHz to –118 dBm/Hz at 1.96 MHz, and –118 dBm/Hz above 1.96 MHz.

Figure 12.45 HDSL Transmit Signal Power Mask

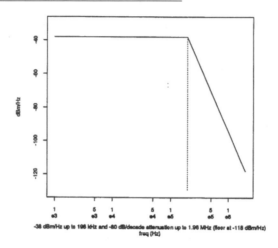

-38 dBm/Hz up to 196 kHz and -80 dB/decade attenuation up to 1.96 MHz (floor at -118 dBm/Hz)
freq (Hz)

The –80 dB/decade attenuation slope can be obtained with a fourth-order Chebychev low-pass transmit filter. The total power of the transmit signal is between 13 dBm and 14 dBm over the frequency band between 0 Hz to 784 kHz. The power consumption of the line driver can be made less than 100 mW for using a 5-volt power supply. The worst case power consumption on the loop is $2.5^2/135 = 46.3$ mW. Therefore, the power consumption of a line driver can be 92.6 mW for an circuit efficiency of 50 percent.

12.5.4 HDSL Test Loops

In addition to the eight CSA loops used for the simulation study, a zero-length loop and two extended (longer than) CSA loops also are used for the HDSL transceiver test. They are named CSA test loop –0, –9, and –10, respectively, for a total of 11 CSA test loops. The 49-disturber 1 percent worst-case self-NEXT is the test noise environment. A performance margin of at, or better than, 6 dB at an error rate of 10^{-7} is expected for these eight CSA test loops. No margin objectives are provided for these two extended CSA loops (see Figure 12.46).

Figure 12.46   Additional Two CSA Test Loops

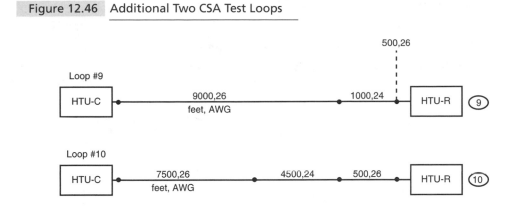

12.5.5   HDSL Performance Test Configuration

Figure 12.47 shows a general HDSL performance test configuration

Figure 12.47   The Test Environment

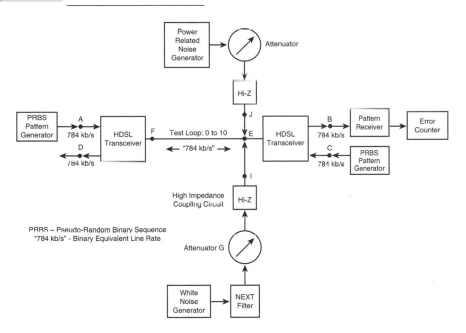

The HDSL transceivers are made active in both directions, while the bit error rate of only one direction is measured at a time. Real loops or a loop emulator can be used for these test

loops. Simulated NEXT noise as well as impulse noise wave forms are applied to the receiver front end through high-impedance coupling circuits (see Figure 12.48). During the NEXT performance margin test, impulse noise wave forms are not injected.

Figure 12.48 An Implementation of the NEXT Noise Coupling Circuit

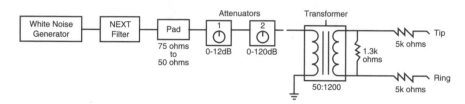

A particular implementation[98] of the NEXT noise emulation circuit has a two-stage adjustable attenuator, a 1:24 ratio transformer, and a coupling impedance of about 10 kilo-ohms. The NEXT filter has a transfer function, which is the combination of the 2B1Q transmit signal spectrum, the fourth-order Chebychev transmit lowpass filter, and the simplified 49-disturber 1 percent worst-case NEXT coupling function.

Figure 12.49 shows the transfer function of a possible NEXT filter. Due to the limited power of the white noise generator, the net loss of this NEXT filter should be limited to less than 15 dB.[99]

Figure 12.49 Transfer Function of a NEXT Filter

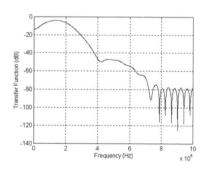

Figure 12.50 shows the impulse response of this NEXT filter.

Figure 12.50   Impulse Response of the NEXT Filter

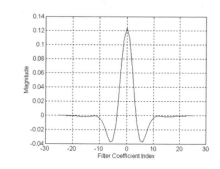

12.5.6   *Measurement Calibration Procedures*

The transmit signal power, the emulated NEXT noise power, and the relative strength between the signal and noise power all need to be measured and calibrated before a meaningful error rate measurement can be performed. The transmit power spectral density (PSD) is first measured. The transmit PSD is then multiplied by the transfer function of the simplified 49-disturber 1 percent worst-case crosstalk loss model to obtain the PSD of the expected NEXT noise. The total expected NEXT power is computed by integrating the PSD of the NEXT noise.

The total power of the emulated NEXT measured at the output of a high-impedance coupling circuit, terminated in half of the nominal loop impedance, is adjusted (by adding attenuation) until the power is 3 dB higher than the total power calculated for the expected NEXT noise. This power level of the emulated NEXT is the *reference level* (also called the *point of 0 dB margin*). The shape of the PSD for the emulated NEXT measured at the output of the coupling circuit is also compared with the shape of the calculated PSD of the expected NEXT to certify the correctness of the NEXT filter. The difference between the two curves should be less than 2 dB at any frequency.

To find the performance margin level at an error rate of 10^{-7}, the attenuation of the NEXT power is removed repeatedly in 1 dB steps, and the errors are counted for at least two minutes at each attenuation setting until a total of 10 errors are counted in any two-minute interval. The corresponding error rate is

$$\frac{10}{2 \times 60 \times \dfrac{1.544 \times 10^6}{2}} = \frac{10 \times 10^{-7}}{6 \times 1.544} \approx 1 \times 10^{-7}$$

The two-minute observation interval is necessary to have a high enough confidence level on the determination of the error rate. For an error rate of η, the probability of observing an error at a particular independent sampling point is η, while the probability of not observing an error at a particular sampling point is $1 - \eta$. Therefore, the probability of not observing any error for n independent sampling points is

$$\bar{\gamma}_n = (1 - \eta)^n$$

Similarly, the probability of observing any error for n independent sampling points is

$$\gamma_n = 1 - (1 - \eta)^n$$

For $\eta = 1 \times 10^{-7}$, we have γ_n calculated in Table 12.13 for different values of window size n.

Table 12.13 The Probabilities of Window Sizes

n	$\bar{\gamma}_n = (1 - \eta)^n$	$\gamma_n = 1 - (1 - \eta)^n$
1×10^7	0.3678794229711	0.6321205770289
2×10^7	0.1353352698456	0.8646647301544
3×10^7	0.04978706097842	0.9502129390216
5×10^7	0.006737945332332	0.9932620546677
1×10^8	4.539990730149e-5	0.9999546000927

According to results in Table 12.13, a choice of selecting a window size to capture only one error will have only a 63-percent chance of observing any error, while a choice of selecting a window size to capture 10 errors will have a 99.99-percent chance of observing errors. The window of capturing 10 errors can also be viewed as averaging a few windows with higher than 95-percent chance of capturing errors. Therefore, with the absence of the error occurrence statistics, a window size of capturing 10 errors is considered adequate.

12.5.7 *Scambler and Descrambler*

All data bits, except the 14 bits for the double-Barker code and stuff quart bits, is scrambled with a 23rd-order polynomial prior to the 2B1Q encoder. In the upstream direction, the polynomial is

$$x^{-23} \oplus x^{-18} \oplus 1$$

In the downstream direction, the polynomial is

$$x^{-23} \oplus x^{-5} \oplus 1$$

The symbol $\oplus$ denotes a modular 2 addition. The scramblers and descramblers are self synchronized, as shown in Figure 12.51.

Figure 12.51 Scrambler and Descrambler

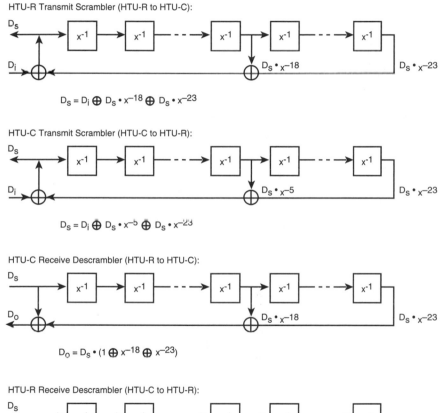

HTU-R Transmit Scrambler (HTU-R to HTU-C):

$$D_s = D_i \oplus D_s \cdot x^{-18} \oplus D_s \cdot x^{-23}$$

HTU-C Transmit Scrambler (HTU-C to HTU-R):

$$D_s = D_i \oplus D_s \cdot x^{-5} \oplus D_s \cdot x^{-23}$$

HTU-C Receive Descrambler (HTU-R to HTU-C):

$$D_o = D_s \cdot (1 \oplus x^{-18} \oplus x^{-23})$$

HTU-R Receive Descrambler (HTU-C to HTU-R):

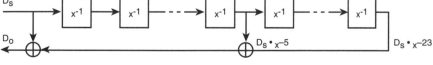

$$D_o = D_s \cdot (1 \oplus x^{-5} \oplus x^{-23})$$

12.5.8 HDSL Initialization Procedure

At installation, following power failures or after temporarily disconnecting an HTU or switching off its power, the HDSL system must synchronize transmission between the two ends. In these situations, the HDSL system utilizes a specific startup sequence in order to achieve proper operation. Also, in the event that synchronization is lost for an extended period, it may be necessary to retrain the transceivers to restore proper operation.

States

There are seven states defined for the operation of both HDSL Terminal Unit-Central Office (HTU-C) and HTU-R:

- *Inactive*. The HTU-C/R is inactive.

- *Activating*. The HTU-C/R is becoming active.

- *Active-Tx*. The HTU-C/R is transmitting.

- *Active-Rx*. The HTU-C/R is receiving.

- *Active-Tx/Rx*. The HTU-C/R is transmitting and receiving.

- *Pending De-Activation*. The HTU-C/R is becoming deactivated.

- *De-Activated*. The HTU-C/R is deactivated.

Line Signals

Two level signals, RS0 and CS0, are used in the early stage of the startup procedure. Four level signals, RS1 and CS1, are used in the late stage of the startup procedure. Two level signals, RS0 and CS0, are derived from the scrambling of a bit stream with all 1s. Only the sign of the output quat is used to determine whether the transmit symbol should be +3 or −3.

Synchronization words are periodically inserted into RS0 and CS0. RS0 is used by the HTU-R transmitter and CS0 is used by the HTU-C transmitter. The four level signals, RS1 and CS1, include normal framing synchronization words. The overhead channel and stuffing quats are all included in RS1 and CS1. A portion of the HDSL payload is filled with scrambled 1s. RS1 is used by the HTU-R transmitter, and CS1 is used by the HTU-C transmitter.

Indication Bits and Registers

One indication bit, bit #3536, is used to indicate that a receiver is ready for receiving data. The indication bit is used by the HTU-R as INDR and by the HTU-C as INDC. The INDR is set to 1 when the HTU-R receiver is ready, and the INDC is set to 1 when the HTU-C receiver is ready.

There are two registers, LOS and LOST, used for both HTU-C and HTU-R for the purpose of received signal detection. The LOS register is set to 1 when the received signal is not detected and set to 0 when the received signal is detected. The LOST register is set to 1 when LOS=1 for 1 second. The LOST register is set to 0 when the received signal is detected.

There are two registers, LOSW and LOSWT; two major states, OUT OF SYNC and IN SYNC; and six transition states used for both HTU-C and HTU-R for the purpose of tracking the detection of the synchronization word, Double Barker Code. The LOSWT register is set to 1 when a synchronization word is missed during a period. The LOSWT register is set to 0 when a synchronization word is detected during a period. The LOSW register is set to 1 when synchronization is lost, which is denoted by the OUT OF SYNC state. The LOSW register is set to 0 when synchronization is regained, which is denoted by the IN SYNC state.

From the OUT OF SYNC state, it takes two consecutive successful detections of the synchronization word to get into the IN SYNC state. The state after the first successful detection of a synchronization word is state 0. From the IN SYNC state, it takes six consecutive losses of the synchronization word to get into the OUT OF SYNC state. There are state 1, state 2, state 3, state 4, and state 5 after the first, second, third, fourth, and fifth losses of the synchronization word, respectively.

Startup Sequence

When powered on, the HTU-C is initially in the Inactive State. If the activation request signal ACTREQ is set to 1, which is normally the default when powering on, the HTU-C proceeds immediately to the Activating State. In the Activating State, the HTU-C executes the startup procedure.

The startup procedure covers the Activating State, Active-Tx State, and Active-Rx State. Initially, the startup procedure is started after both units have been powered on and any self-tests completed. When the HTU-C starts the startup procedure, it automatically begins to transmit. When the HTU-R starts the startup procedure, it automatically remains silent and waits to detect signal power from the HTU-C. The 30-second Activation Timers at the HTUs start at the beginning of the startup procedure.

At the startup, the HTU-C begins to transmit a two-level signal, CS0. During the first T2 seconds (2.0 +/–0.1 seconds), the HTU-R remains silent. At the end of this time the HTU-R begins to transmit a two-level signal, RS0. Within T4=4 seconds of beginning transmission, the timing recovery loop within the HTU-R should have reached a stable timing phase. Since the HTU-R is loop timed, this implies that the HTU-R transmitter has reached a stable transmit phase at this point as well.

The HTU-C will switch from two-level transmission to four-level transmission T1 seconds after the end of T2, providing that the HTU-C has detected signal power from the HTU-R at a point T2 seconds from the beginning of the startup procedure. The value of T1 can range from 5 to 10 seconds. If no signal power is detected from the HTU-R at the end of T2, the HTU-C will continue in CS0 until the 30-second Activation Timer forces it to leave the Activating State. If signal power is detected from the HTU-R after T2 seconds but before the 30-second Activation Timer expires, the HTU-C will reset the 30-second Activation Timer at this occurrence for a point two seconds into the startup procedure to correspond to the point at the end of T2 in the startup procedure.

Within T3 seconds from the time the HTU-C changes from CS0 to CS1 and the four-level signal is detected at the HTIJ-R, the HTU-R must switch to a four-level signal, RS1. The T3 interval can range from zero to four seconds; the precise duration is under control of the HTU-R.

Within 30 seconds from the start of the timeline, the HTUs should be transporting normal 2BIQ data. With a successful startup, the switch to normal data is accomplished after frame synchronization is acquired—either by signaling via indicator bits in the overhead channel or by the expiration of the 30-second Activation Timer.

If the activation process fails, then the Activation Timer expires 30 seconds after the start of the timeline and the unit moves to the De-Activated State.

After entering the De-Activated State, either due to a period of synchronization word loss (LOSWT=1) or due to expiration of the 30-second Activation Timer, the HTU-C transmitter goes silent and the HTU-C begins to look for a loss of signal power from the HTU-R. When LOS=1 for one second, the timer LOST is set to 1 and the unit moves to the Inactive State. If (or when) ACTREQ=1, the unit will proceed once again to the Activating State, and another attempt is made at the startup process.

After entering the De-Activated State, the HTU-R transmitter goes silent and the HTU-R begins to look for a loss of signal power from the HTU-C. When a loss of signal power is detected (LOS=1), the unit moves immediately to the Inactive State. When signal power is detected from the HTU-C (LOS=0), the unit will proceed once again to the Activating State, and another attempt is made at the startup process.

An HTU receiving a signal to go to QUIET mode will make the transition to the De-Activated State. The signal for QUIET mode can be generated from a network command, the front panel, or by some other means.

12.5.9   Key Features of the Optional CAP HDSL

Figure 12.52 shows a functional block diagram of an HDSL transceiver using the optional CAP line code.

Figure 12.52   CAP HDSL Functional Block Diagram

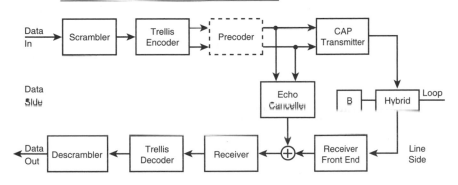

Bits to be transmitted are scrambled and passed to the bit-to-symbol mapper and Trellis encoder, which generates two multi-level symbols (in-phase and quadrature) during each symbol period. These symbols, represented by digital numbers, are passed through a Tomlinson precoder. The symbols are then passed to the CAP transmitter, which has two filters with the same passband amplitude response, but with phase responses that differ by 90 degrees. The outputs of the two filters (in-phase and quadrature) are summed, filtered, and passed to a hybrid circuit. This hybrid circuit passes the transmitted signal to the twisted-pair subscriber line while taking the received signal from the other end of the subscriber line and passing it to the receiver. Additionally, there is a balance circuit (B) that maximizes hybrid (echo path) loss.

The received signal is passed from the hybrid circuit through the receive front end. The receive front end generally has a filter to band limit the noise, as well as a programmable gain amplifier and a converter to produce the digital words from the analog received signal.

Next, a replica of the transmitted echo is subtracted from the digital signal, and the remaining signal is passed to the receiver. The receiver performs the necessary equalization as well as Viterbi decoding of the received signal. Finally, the signal is descrambled and passed on as the received bits.

The bit rate on each subscriber line is 784 kbps. The line format is Trellis-coded 64-CAP with Tomlinson precoding. A 2D (two-dimensional), eight-state Trellis code is used; however, the use of an optional 4D (four-dimensional), 16-state Trellis code is permitted. In the 2D, eight-state Trellis code, of the six bits per symbol, five are information bits, and one bit of redundancy is added by the 2D, eight-state Trellis code.

The symbol rate is 784/5 or 156.9 kbauds for the 2D, eight-state Trellis code. In the 4D, 16-state Trellis code, of the six bits per symbol, 5.5 are information bits, and 0.5 bits of redundancy are added by the 4D, 16-state Trellis code. The symbol rate is 784/5.5 or 142.54 kbauds for the 4D, 16-state Trellis code.

CAP Transmit Power Mask

Figures 12.53 and 12.54 provide templates for the CAP HDSL transmit signal spectrum. These power mask templates define the passband section and the upper and lower stop band sections of the spectrum.

Figure 12.53 CAP HDSL Transmit Signal Spectrum for the 4D, 16-State Trellis Code

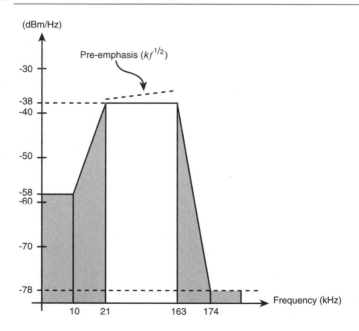

Figure 12.54 CAP HDSL Transmit Signal Spectrum for the 2D, Eight-State Trellis Code

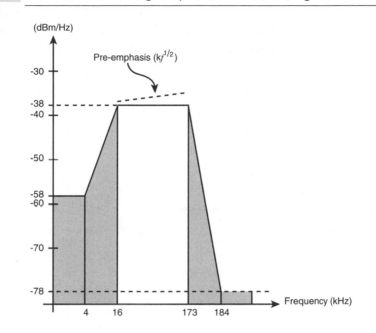

Figure 12.53 shows the transmit signal spectrum for the CAP HDSL transmitter using the 4D, 16-state Trellis code, while Figure 12.54 shows the transmit signal spectrum when using the 2D, eight-state Trellis code. The nominal shape of the transmit signal spectrum is that of the square root of a raised-cosine shape with a nominal 15-percent excess bandwidth.

The passband for any CAP implementation using the 4D, 16-state Trellis code lies in the frequency band between 20 kHz and 165 kHz, not including the excess bandwidth. The nominal −3 dB frequencies are approximately 21 kHz and 163 kHz. The spectrum is centered around a frequency of 91.96 kHz. Ripple within the passband is less than 0.5 dB. The passband for any CAP implementation using the 2D, eight-state Trellis code lies in the frequency band between 15 kHz and 175 kHz, not including the excess bandwidth. The nominal −3 dB frequencies are approximately 16 kHz and 173 kHz. The spectrum is centered around a frequency of 94.16 kHz. Ripple within the passband is less than 0.5 dB.

The signal amplitude at frequencies in the lower stop band is at least 20 dB below the nominal signal amplitude at frequencies in the passband. The lower stop band includes those frequencies below the 15-percent excess bandwidth portion shown in Figures 12.53 and 12.54. This lower stop band is not below 10 kHz. The signal amplitude at frequencies in the upper stop band is at least 40 dB below the nominal signal amplitude at frequencies in the passband. The upper stop band includes those frequencies above the 15-percent excess bandwidth portion shown in Figures 12.53 and 12.54. For the 4D, 16-state Trellis code, this upper stop band does not exceed 174 kHz. For the 2D, eight-state Trellis code, this upper stop band does not exceed 184 kHz.

The transmit signal might incorporate some pre-emphasis in its signal spectrum to provide compromise equalization. Within the passband, the nominal spectrum might include a signal gain bound by a curve that increases at the rate shown by the dashed curve in Figures 12.53 and 12.54. The scaling factor k in the pre-emphasis is to be determined such that the overall signal power is 13.5 dBm nominal.

The average transmit power at the transmitter output is between 13.0 and 14.0 dBm into a 110 ohm termination impedance.

CAP Scambler and Descrambler

The scrambler and descrambler included in each transceiver are different for the two directions of transmission. The generating polynomials are

$$1 + x^{-18} + x^{-23}$$

for the customer premises transceiver and

$$1 + x^{-5} + x^{-23}$$

for the Central Office transceiver.

During startup, the scramblers and descramblers operate in self-synchronizing mode. During data transfer, the scramblers are locked, and the scrambled sequence is added at the transmitter and subtracted (modulo 2) at the receiver. The transfer from self-synchronizing mode to locked mode occurs with the transmit data being all 1s. Note that all bits are scrambled including the overhead bits, frame alignment word, and stuff/delete bits.

CAP Frame Structure

Figure 12.55 shows the frame format structure. The basic structure is a frame of 6 milliseconds duration that is divided into four payload data blocks (PD1–PD4) and five overhead framing blocks (F1–F5). Each 6 ms frame contains 4,704 bits, which corresponds to a nominal line bit rate of 784 kbps in each loop. Both loops have the same frame structure, but have different identifiers.

Figure 12.55 The CAP HDSL Frame Structure

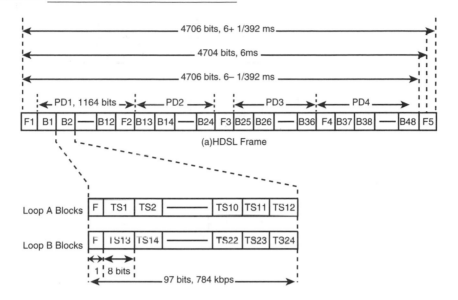

(a)HDSL Frame

Within each payload data block are twelve 97-bit sub-blocks. Each frame contains 48 sub-blocks labeled B1–B48. Figure 12.55 also shows the sub-block data structure with the corresponding DS1 payload bits. The sub-blocks in the loop A frame contain DS0s 1–12 plus the DS1 frame (F) bit. Likewise, the sub-blocks in the loop B frame contain DS0s 13–24 plus the DS1 F bit. Note that the DS1 F bit is transmitted in both loops. Figure 12.56 shows the structure of the overhead framing blocks.

The bit definitions are described as follows:

- *Block F1.* Contains a 14-bit Frame Alignment Word (FAW) or sync word for identifying the beginning of the frame, one loss-of-line signal indicator bit (losd), and one bit indicating far-end block error (febe). Loops A and B (refer to Figure 12.55) each have a unique 14-bit FAW.

- *Block F2.* Contains four embedded operations channel bits (eoc1–eoc4), two crc-6 bits (crc1–crc2), power status bits 1 and 2 (ps 1 and ps 2), one bipolar violation bit (bpv), and one additional eoc bit (eoc5).

- *Block F3.* Contains four eoc bits (eoc6–eoc9), two crc-6 bits (crc3–cro4), one regenerator present bit (hrp), one regenerator remote block error (rrbe), one regenerator central block error (rcbe), and one regenerator alarm bit (rega).

Figure 12.56 Frame Sub-Blocks

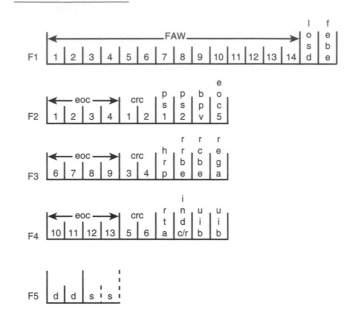

- *Block F4.* Contains the remaining four eoc bits (eoc10–wc13), the remaining two crc-6 bits (crc5–crc6), one remote terminal alarm bit (rta), one ready-to-receive bit (indelindr), and two undefined bits (uib).

- *Block F5.* Contains either zero, two, or four stuff bits.

CAP HDSL Startup

The startup procedure for CAP HDSL transceivers consists of four phases (as illustrated in Figure 12.57):

1. Alerting

2. Front-end training

3. Echo canceller and equalizer training

4. Tomlinson coefficient exchange

Figure 12.57 CAP HDSL Startup Sequences

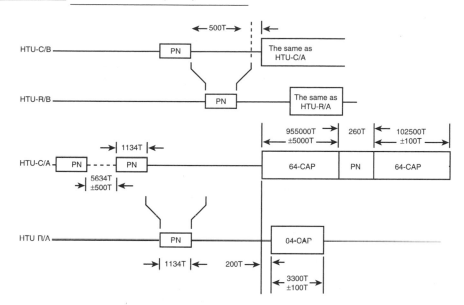

Details of the CAP HDSL startup sequence can be found in the ANSI HDSL technical report.

Relying on extensive decision feedback equalization and echo cancellation, HDSL can provide a transmission throughput of 800 kbps at a signal spectral bandwidth of 200 kHz over CSA loops. As lately discovered during the study of Asymmetric Digital Subscriber Lines (ADSL), the frequency band above 200 kHz can be very useful if the NEXT can be avoided through Frequency Division Multiplex (FDM).

The use of FDM can achieve a higher transmission throughput potential while saving the signal processing of digital adaptive echo cancellation. The development of single-pair HDSL, also called *HDSL2* or *next generation HDSL,* has explored the benefit of minimizing the effect of NEXT in conjunction with the use of some advanced Trellis coding techniques.

End Notes

1. J. W. Lechleider, "The Feasibility and Advisability of a DSL Operating at Substantially Higher Information Rates Than That of the Basic Access DSL Should Be Studied," *Bellcore T1E1 Contribution,* T1E1.4/88-038 (1988).

2. J. W. Lechleider, "Some Areas for Further Study for HDSL," *Bellcore T1E1 Contribution*, T1E1.4/88-144 (July 25, 1988).

3. R. A. McDonald, "Suggestions for the Study of the HDSL," *Bellcore T1E1 Contribution*, T1E1.4/89-065 (1989).

4. R. A. McDonald and C. F. Valenti, "Assumptions for Bellcore HDSL Studies," *Bellcore T1E1 Contribution*, T1E1.4/89-066 (1989).

5. C. F. Valenti, "Margin Considerations for HDSL Studies," *Bellcore T1E1 Contribution*, T1E1.4/89-232 (1989).

6. P. Adams and J. Cook, "The Specification of NEXT Margin for a High Rate DSL," *BT Labs T1E1 Contribution*, T1E1.4/89-261 (1989).

7. J. W. Lechleider, "The Range of DSLs Using a Single Pair and Operating at 1.544 Mbps," *Bellcore T1E1 Contribution*, T1E1.4/89-070 (1989).

8. J. W. Lechleider, "The Performance of the 2B1Q Line Code at 800 kbps in a Carrier Serving Area," *Bellcore T1E1 Contribution*, T1E1.4/89-068 (July 25, 1989).

9. J. W. Lechleider, "The Application of Trellis Coded Modulation to a Population of Carrier Serving Area Loops," *Bellcore T1E1 Contribution*, T1E1.4/89-069 (1989).

10. V. B. Lawrence, J. J. Werner, and N. Zervos, "HRDSL Line Code: Fundamental Limits," *AT&T Bell Labs T1E1 Contribution*, T1E1.4/89-103 (1989).

11. E. Arnon, "High Rate DSL System Reach with Enhanced Feed Forward Filtering," *Northern Telecom T1E1 Contribution*, T1E1.4/89-085 (1989).

12. E. Arnon and E. Ehrlich, "Cable Loss Distribution in a Carrier Serving Area," *Northern Telecom T1E1 Contribution*, T1E1.4/89-085 (1989).

13. K. Sistanizadeh, "The Performance of an Ideal Decision Feedback Filter on HDSL," *Bellcore T1E1 Contribution*, T1E1.4/89-234 (1989).

14. G. E. Smith, "High Rate DSL Line Code: Proposal for Coded QAM," *AT&T Bell Labs T1E1 Contribution*, T1E1.4/89-151 (1989).

15. G. E. Smith, "Performance of Coded QAM in the HDSL Environment," *AT&T Bell Labs T1E1 Contribution*, T1E1.4/89-199 (1989).

16. C. F. Valenti and R. A. McDonald, "Two Pair Full-Duplex vs. Two Pair Simplex Loss and Range Consideration," *Bellcore T1E1 Contribution*, T1E1.4/89-233 (1989).

17. J. A. C. Bingham, "Duplex Systems and Signal Formats for HDSL," *Telebit T1E1 Contribution,* T1E1.4/89-242 (1989).

18. R. A. McDonald, "Technical Report: Study of the Feasibility and Advisability of Digital Subscriber Lines Operating at Rates Substantially in Excess of the Basic Access Rate," T1E1.4/90-002 (1990).

19. T. Starr and M. Bono, "Proposed HDSL Cable Models," *Ameritech T1E1 Contribution,* T1E1.4/89-243 (1989).

20. T. Starr and M. Bono, "Proposed HDSL Cable Models and Delay Limits," *Ameritech T1E1 Contribution,* T1E1.4/90-012 (1990).

21. N. Cole and N. Lynch-Aird, "Calculated NEXT-Limited Reach of a Simple 800 kbps HDSL System in the Presence of ISDN Basic Rate and T1 Interferes," *BT Labs T1E1 Contribution,* T1E1.4/89-262 (1989).

22. N. Cole and N. Lynch-Aird, "Re-calculated NEXT-Limited Reach for Simple 800 kbps HDSL Systems in the Presence of ISDN Basic Rate and T1 Interferes," *BT Labs T1E1 Contribution,* T1E1.4/90-027 (1990).

23. E. Anon, "Cable Loss Distribution in Carrier Serving Area," *Northern Telecom T1E1 Contribution,* T1E1.4/90-053 (1990).

24. G. Forney, Jr., "Coding for Band-Limited Channels," *Motorola Codex T1E1 Contribution,* T1E1.4/90-084 (1990).

25. M. V. Eyuboglu, G. Pottie, and L. Brown, "Combined Coding and Precoding for HDSL," *Motorola Codex T1E1 Contribution,* T1E1.4/90-059 (March 1990).

26. M. V. Eyuboglu, G. Pottie, and L. Brown, "Performance of Combined Coding: Precoding in the Presence of Channel Variations," *Motorola Codex T1E1 Contribution,* T1E1.4/90-085 (June 1990).

27. N. J. Lynch-Aird, "Tomlinson Precoding and DFE PAM: An Analytical Comparison for Recursive and Nonrecursive Equalizers," *BT Labs T1E1 Contribution,* T1E1.4/90-146 (1990).

28. M. Sorbara, J. J. Werner, and N. A. Zervos, "Carrierless AM/PM Tutorial," *AT&T Bell Labs T1E1 Contribution,* T1E1.4/90-154 (1990).

29. G. J. Pottie, "Comparison of Baseband vs. Passband Systems for HDSL," *Motorola Codex T1E1 Contribution,* T1E1.4/90-164 (1990).

30. K. Sistanizadeh, "Performance Evaluation Studies of QAM and PAM Schemes on a Sample of CSA Loops with an Ideal DFE," *Bellcore T1E1 Contribution*, T1E1.4/90-180 (1990).

31. E. Anon, "Impulse Noise Immunity of HDSL Systems," *Northern Telecom T1E1 Contribution*, T1E1.4/90-170 (1990).

32. K. J. Kerpez, "2B1Q and QAM Performance in the Presence of Impulse Noise," *Bellcore T1E1 Contribution*, T1E1.4/90-179 (1990).

33. D. L. Waring and K. Sistanizadeh, "Suggested Plan to Assess and Select HDSL Transmission Schemes for Further Study," *Bellcore T1E1 Contribution*, T1E1.4/90-109 (1990).

34. R. C. McConnell, "HDSL Applications with DS1 Lines Having Frequency Offsets Between Direction," *Bellcore T1E1 Contribution*, T1E1.4/90-110 (1990).

35. W. Y. Chen, "Analog and Digital Solutions for Asynchronous Clocks," *Bellcore T1E1 Contribution*, T1E1.4/91-029.

36. E. Arnon and E. Ehrlich, "A Frame Format and Overhead Channel for HDSL," *BNR T1E1 Contribution*, T1E1.4/90-114 (1990).

37. W. R. Murphy, "Alternative HDSL Framing Format and Overhead Channel," *Tellabs T1E1 Contribution*, T1E1.4/90-152 (1990).

38. H. Nicholas and H. Flagg, "HDSL Frame Format," *PairGain Technologies T1E1 Contribution*, T1E1.4/90-167 (1990).

39. W. Y. Chen, "A Double-Barker Code Variable Frame Format," *Bellcore T1E1 Contribution*, T1E1.4/91-109 (August 10, 1991).

40. E. Arnon and E. Ehrlich, "Measurement Results of an HDSL Transmission System," *BNR T1E1 Contribution*, T1E1.4/90-15X (1990).

41. R. Cupo and M. Sorbara, "Margin Performance of a Carrierless AM/PM HDSL System," *AT&T Bell Labs T1E1 Contribution*, T1E1.4/90-153 (1990).

42. K. T. Foster, "Crosstalk Margin Measurements for an Example 768 kbps HDSL Transmission System," *BT Labs T1E1 Contribution*, T1E1.4/90-165 (1990).

43. B. A. Blake, "Suggested Testing Plan for HDSL Prototype Transceivers," *Bellcore T1E1 Contribution*, T1E1.4/90-182 (1990).

44. B. A. Blake, "Description of a Loop Emulator Test Bed at Bellcore for Constructing Loops Out of Actual Cable in the Lab," *Bellcore T1E1 Contribution*, T1E1.4/90-183 (1990).

45. K. Sistanezadeh, "A Tentative CSA Loop Population for Preliminary Studies of HDSL Transmission Schemes," *Bellcore T1E1 Contribution,* T1E1.4/90-184 (1990).

46. D. A. Fisher and D. R. Donovan, "Advantages of 448 kbps (6B+D) Modularity and the 2B1P Line Code," *STC Technology T1E1 Contribution,* T1E1.4/90-120 (1990).

47. D. A. Fisher and D. R. Donovan, "A Proposal for 448 kbps Framing Structure," *STC Technology T1E1 Contribution,* T1E1.4/90-121 (1990).

48. J. S. Chow, J. C. Tu, and J. M. Cioffi, "A Discrete Multitone Transceiver System for HDSL Application," *Stanford University T1E1 Contribution,* T1E1.4/90-209 (December 1990).

49. J. C. Tu, J. S. Chow, and J. M. Cioffi, "A Discrete Multitone Transceiver System for HDSL Application," *Stanford University T1E1 Contribution,* T1E1.4/90-210 (December 1990).

50. K. Sistanezadeh, "Performance Variation of QAM and PAM with Respect to Source and Load Terminations on HDSL," *Bellcore T1E1 Contribution,* T1E1.4/90-213 (December 1990).

51. H. Samueli, "Design and Implementation of a 64-Tap CMOS Echo Canceller/Decision-Feedback Equalizer for 2B1Q HDSL Transceivers," *UCLA T1E1 Contribution,* T1E1.4/90-218 (December 1990).

52. "Finite-Length Decision Feedback Equalizer for HDSL," *Motorola Codex T1E1 Contribution,* T1E1.4/90-225 (December 1990).

53. H. Y. Chang and M. Sorbara, "Effects of Impulse Noise on Baseband and Passband Transmission Schemes for HDSL," *AT&T Bell Labs T1E1 Contribution,* T1E1.4/90-224 (December 1990).

54. K. Sistanezadeh and B. Blake, "A Non-CSA Loop for HDSL Performance Evaluation Studies," *Bellcore T1E1 Contribution,* T1E1.4/90-215 (December 1990).

55. M. D. Martino and W. R. Murphy, "A Format for the HDSL Framing and Overhead Channel," *Tellabs T1E1 Contribution,* T1E1.4/90-220 (December 1990).

56. M. Sorbara, "Frame Format for a Passband HDSL," *AT&T Bell Labs T1E1 Contribution,* T1E1.4/90-223 (December 1990).

57. "HDSL Framing Overhead Ad Hoc Working Group Report," T1E1.4/90-238 (December 1990).

58. T. Starr, "Baseband Analog Voice Transmission for HDSL," *Ameritech T1E1.4 Contribution*, T1E1.4/91-013 (February 1991).

59. R. C. McConnel, "Example HDSL Framing and Overhead Structure," *Bellcore T1E1 Contribution*, T1E1.4/91-021 (February 1991).

60. H. Flagg, "Frame Structure for a High-Rate Digital Subscriber Line," *PairGain T1E1 Contribution*, T1E1.4/91-036 (February 1991).

61. D. Amrany and S. Gadot, "General Adaptive FIR Filter: a VLSI Chip for HDSL and ADSL," *AT&T Network Systems T1E1 Contribution*, T1E1.4/91-034 (February 1991).

62. R. Brackert and B. Itri, "Aerial Cable Performance on a 9 kft Loop: A Study of Environment Temperature Changes on an HDSL Transceiver," *PairGain Technologies T1E1 Contribution*, T1E1.4/91-061 (February 1991).

63. B. A. Blake, "NEXT Performance Margin Test Results for a 3B1O HDSL Transceiver Demonstration System from British Telecom Research Laboratories," *Bellcore T1E1 Contribution*, T1E1.4/91-023 (February 1991).

64. B. A. Blake, "NEXT Performance Margin Test Results for a 2B1Q HDSL Transceiver Prototype from Bell-Northern Research," *Bellcore T1E1 Contribution*, T1E1.4/91-024 (February 1991).

65. B. A. Blake, "NEXT Performance Margin Test Results for a Carrierless AM/PM HDSL Transceiver Prototype from AT&T," *Bellcore T1E1 Contribution*, T1E1.4/91-025 (February 1991).

66. B. A. Blake, "NEXT Performance Margin Test Results for a 2B1Q HDSL Transceiver Prototype from Tellabs," *Bellcore T1E1 Contribution*, T1E1.4/91-026 (February 1991).

67. B. A. Blake, "NEXT Performance Margin Test Results for a 2B1Q HDSL Transceiver Prototype from PairGain Technologies," *Bellcore T1E1 Contribution*, T1E1.4/91-027 (February 1991).

68. R. A. McConnel, "Proposal to Change the Name of HDSL Technical Report," *Bellcore T1E1 Contribution*, T1E1.4/91-033 (February 1991).

69. Ad Hoc Group on HDSL Framing and Overhead, "Ad Hoc Group Meeting on HDSL Framing and Overhead and Outline for Text on Alternative Transmission Techniques," T1E1.4/91-046 (February 1991).

70. W.Y.Chen, J.L.Dixon, and D.L.Waring, "HDSL Echo Cancellation," *IEEE JSAC*, vol. 9, no. 6 (August 1991): 848–860.

71. K. H. Mueller and M. Muller, "Timing Recovery in Digital Synchronous Data Receivers," *IEEE Trans. On Comm.*, vol. COM-24, no. 5 (May 1976): 516–531.

72. H. Samueli, B. Daneshrad, R. B. Joshi, B. C. Wong, and H. T. Nicholas, III, "A 64-Tap CMOS Echo Canceller/Decision Feedback Equalizer for 2B1Q HDSL Transceivers," *IEEE JSAC*, vol. 9, no. 6 (August 1991): 839–847.

73. K. Hwang, *Computer Arithmetic, Principles, Architecture, and Design* (New York: Wiley, 1979).

74. N. H. E. Weste and K. Eshraghian, *Principles of CMOS VLSI Design* (Reading, Mass.: Addison-Wesley, 1985).

75. K. Sistanizadeh, "A Tentative CSA Loop Population for Preliminary Studies of HDSL Transmission Schemes," *Bellcore T1E1 Contribution*, T1E1.4/90-184 (1990).

76. ANSI T1E1.4 Working Group on Digital Subscriber Lines, "A Technical Report on High-bit-rate Digital Subscriber Lines (HDSL)," T1E1.4/96-006 (April 22, 1996).

77. Test sets from TAS, **http://www.taskit.com/**.

78. Test sets from Consultronics, **http://www.consultronics.on.ca/**.

79. W. Y. Chen, "Choices of HDSL Load Resistor Values," *Bellcore T1E1 Contribution*, T1E1.4/91-078 (May 13, 1991).

80. R. C. McDonnel, "HDSL Application with DS1 Lines Having Frequency Offsets Between Directions," *Bellcore T1E1 Contribution*, T1E1.4/90-110 (June 18, 1990).

81. R. C. McDonnel, "Private Digital Network Frequency Synchronization with Local Exchange Carriers," *Bellcore T1E1 Contribution*, T1E1.4/90-217 (December 10, 1990.)

82. S. A. Cox, "Clock Sensitivity Reduction in Echo Cancellers," *Electron. Lett.*, vol. 21 (July 4, 1985).

83. D. G. Messerschmitt, "Asynchronous and Timing Jitter Insensitive Data Echo Cancellation," *IEEE Trans. Com,-nun.*, vol. COM-34, no. 12 (December 1986): 1209–1217.

84. J-J. Werner, "An Echo-Cancellation-Based 4800 Bit/s Full-Duplex DDD Modem," *IEEE Trans. JSAC*, vol. SAC-2, no. 5 (September 1984): 722–730.

85. J. C. Candy and 0. J. Benjamin, "A Circuit That Changes the Word Rate of Pulse Code Modulated Signals," *Bell System Tech. J.*, vol. 62, no. 4 (April 1983): 1161–1168.

86. C. W Farrow, "A Continuously Variable Digital Delay Element," *Proc. IEEE ISCAS '88* (1988): 2641–2645.

87. W. Y. Chen, "Analog and Digital Solutions for Asynchronous Clocks," *Bellcore T1E1 Contribution*, T1E1.4/91-029.

88. M. D. Martino, W. R. Murphy, and H. Flagg, "Proposed Format for the HDSL Framing and Overhead Channel," *Tellabs and PairGain Contribution*, T1E1.4/91-085 (May 13, 1991).

89. E. Arnon, "Frame Format for HDSL," *Northern Telecom Contribution*, T1E1.4/91-082 (May 13, 1991).

90. Conversation with Michael Martino of Tellabs.

91. W. Y. Chen, "A Double-Barker Code Variable Frame Format," *Bellcore T1E1 Contribution*, T1E1.4/91-109 (August 10, 1991).

92. W. Y. Chen, "The Performance of the Double-Barker Code Under Impulse Noise," *Bellcore T1E1 Contribution*, T1E1.4/91-110 (August 10, 1991).

93. *Digital Hierarchy-Formats Specifications*, ANSI T1.107-1988 (1988).

94. *Digital Hierarchy-Electrical Interfaces*, ANSI T1.102-1989 (1989).

95. *Carrier-to-Customer Installation: DS1 Metallic Interface*, ANSI T1.403-1989 (1989).

96. *ISDN Primary Rate: Customer Installation Metallic Interfaces Layer 1 Specification*, ANSI T1.408-1990 (1990).

97. T1E1.4 Working Group on Digital Subscriber Lines, R. C. McConnell and B. H. Soloway, Ed., "High-bit-rate Digital Subscriber Lines," Working Draft, *Technical Report Issue 2*, T1E1.4/96-006 (April 22, 1996).

98. B. A. Blake and W. Y. Chen, "Suggested Testing Plan for HDSL Prototype Transceivers," *Bellcore T1E1 Contribution*, T1E1.4/90-182 (September 26, 1990).

99. B. A. Blake and W. Y. Chen, "Amendment to Suggested Testing Plan for HDSL Prototype Transceivers," *Bellcore T1E1 Contribution*, T1E1.4/90-216 (December 10–14, 1990).

CHAPTER 13

ADSL (Asymmetrical Digital Subscriber Lines)

The desire for the further advancement of telephone subscriber loop-based DSL technology was very strong after the initial definition of the dual-duplex HDSL as a repeaterless T1 technology. The performance improvement of HDSL was partially due to its broader signaling bandwidth compared with that of DSL. Therefore, the next DSL technology after HDSL should utilize more bandwidth than that used by HDSL.

On the other hand, the NEXT noise could have made the telephone subscriber loop channel useless beyond the frequency band of HDSL even at CSA range. The only possibility to further expand the usable bandwidth is to avoid the NEXT noise by adopting one directional transmission among all telephone subscriber loops.

Consumer broadband services that could benefit from DSL technologies had been considered video oriented. Video telephony was a candidate, but its market potential was questionable based on previous attempts. The video-on-demand service had been considered as a telephone company's response to video rental and cable television pay-per-view markets. The video-on-demand service can be provided through a T1 rate (1.544 Mbps) DSL system in conjunction with a digital video compression technique, such as MPEG1 from a CO to a telephone subscriber. In the reverse direction, only a lower throughput channel is necessary to send ordering information as well as real-time control commands similar to that of a VCR.

Asymmetrical Digital Subscriber Lines (ADSL) were originally developed for such a video-on-demand service with a downstream (from a CO to a subscriber) transmission throughput of 1.544 Mbps and an upstream (from a subscriber to a CO) transmission throughput of between 16 and 64 kbps. With ADSL, one compressed video channel can be provided to all consumers connected with nonloaded telephone subscriber loops. At CSA range, up to four compressed video channels can be provided. Meanwhile, Trellis and forward error correction coding techniques had been introduced in conjunction with the Discrete MultiTone (DMT) line code to improve the transmission performance under the crosstalk and impulse noise environment.

Most recently, ADSL has been considered as the next-generation transmission technology for high-speed data access applications. The ever increasing population of home PCs and the widespread use of the Internet create a demand for a higher access speed than what a voice band modem can provide. Because of the random nature of data communication and corresponding transmission protocol, some ADSL transmission overhead designed for multiple video channels can be simplified. The adoption of an ATM-oriented transmission interface is another flexible approach to make ADSL technology suitable for different applications.

This chapter covers development activities, line codes, transmission performances, and interface standards of Asymmetrical Digital Subscriber Lines, including the following:

- *Development of ADSL technology.* Technical discussions leading to the development of ADSL are reviewed. Early performance measurements on prototype ADSL systems and in conjunction with a POTS service are presented.

- *ADSL transceiver structures and line codes.* For the ADSL standard defined by T1.413, the general ADSL transceiver architecture and issues, such as TEQ, FEQ, and sub-carrier SNR, are discussed. Transmission parameters for both downstream and upstream directions are summarized. ADSL specific techniques including Trellis coding, Reed-Solomon coding, interleaving, and asymmetric echo cancellation are reviewed.

  Implementation strategy, requirement, and complexity are addressed with respect to digital interface, digital signal processing, and analog interface functional blocks for both CO and subscriber side transceivers. Transceiver structures, transmission parameters, specifics of transmit filter and equalizer coefficients, and possible implementation approaches are also discussed for CAP line code ADSL.

- *ADSL performance objectives.* An additional six ADSL mid-CSA test loop configurations and corresponding transfer functions as well as three noise models with combined NEXT, FEXT, and AWG noises are presented. DMT ADSL transmission performances are simulated for three different ranges of test loops with associated noise conditions. Transmission performances of CAP ADSL are also estimated.

- *ADSL network and premises interfaces.* ADSL network interface at a CO or a RT for providing video on demand services is discussed. Associated ADSL multi-channel specifications are reviewed. ADSL network interface for providing data access services is also discussed. The function and the design of POTS splitter is addressed. Possible approaches of POTS splitter installation in conjunction with existing telephone in-house wiring are presented.

* *ADSL standards*. Key features of ADSL defined by ANSI T1.413, such as frame/super-frame structure, channelization, bit-to-constellation mapping, and initialization procedures, are discussed.

13.1   *Development of ADSL Technology*

The development of HDSL is relatively straightforward. Based on experience gained from DSL development, people involved felt that the same signal processing and *Very-Large-Scale Integrated circuit* (VLSI) technologies could be enhanced for a higher transmission throughput. The next logical step of higher throughput is the T1 rate: 24 B channels at a rate of 1.544 Mbps. Computer performance simulation studies indicated that two pairs of cables were required.

After the demonstration of the prototype VLSI chip, the echo cancellation-based 2B1Q line code was selected for HDSL. HDSL then found an application as the dual-duplex repeater-less T1 technology. To avoid the lengthy standardization process experience of DSL, it was decided that a technical report by the T1E1.4 working group would be sufficient to guide HDSL vendors for the compliance of interoperability.

During these performance studies, two other line codes—Carrierless AM/PM (CAP) and Discrete MultiTone (DMT)—were also proposed as alternatives. Due to the lack of understanding of these alternative line codes by the majority of standards activity participants, these line codes were not favored for HDSL. Due to persistent efforts of their proponents as well as the availability of corresponding tutorial material, however, the T1E1.4 working group recognized the potential of using CAP and DMT line codes for the next generation of higher throughput DSL systems. The early market acceptance of HDSL by the business community further enhanced the desire for the development of a higher throughput digital subscriber line system for the mass consumer market.

HDSL is somewhat restrictive for residential services.[1] The need for two pairs and the CSA range limitation may prove prohibitive in certain areas where a significant portion of customers are beyond 12 kft or where the number of pairs-per-living unit are less than two. Thus, the genesis for the next generation of high throughput DSL systems was to design a new transport access capability to provide economic wideband services directly to the residential customer. Objectives are to cover most of the nonloaded loop plant out to 18 kft, as is the case for Basic Rate Access. In addition, it is highly desirable to reduce the number of pairs required because pairs-per-living unit ratios can be as low as 1.3 in some areas.

Although intended for the residential market, the higher throughput DSL system under consideration then needed to co-exist with early developed DSL and HDSL systems. To be conservative, the co-existance with T1 lines using the traditional transceiver technology also needed to be considered. In other words, the system under consideration then needed to operate with DSL, HDSL, and T1 NEXT. The level of crosstalk noise depend on the number of disturbers. A point of contention is that in a residential environment, the number of deployed HDSLs might be smaller. According to Figure 13.1, the new system under development could have a transmit spectrum above that of HDSL to realize the full potential of the available bandwidth of the copper loop plant.

Figure 13.1 Noise Environment with DSL, HDSL, and T1

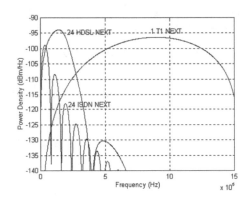

Observing that many services needed greater transmission rates from the central office to the customer than in the other direction, Dr. Joseph Lechleider proposed the idea of asymmetrical DSLs (ADSL).[2] Adding asymmetry to a DSL system opened a new dimension to be considered with system configuration. Lechleider mainly considered 18 kft range, 2B+D full duplex, and 1.544 Mbps downstream; CSA range, 2B+D full duplex, and 3.088 Mbps downstream; and 5 kft range, 1.544 Mbps upstream, and 6.176 Mbps downstream single pair as well as a few other dual-pair ADSL options.

For the first two options, Lechleider assumed a unilateral downstream channel occupying a frequency band above 75 kHz in addition to DSL. For the third option, Lechleider assumed a unilateral downstream channel occupying a frequency band above 425 kHz in addition to a double baud rate HDSL. The higher transmission throughput of unilateral channels are possible because they are limited only by effect of Far End Crosstalk (FEXT).

This concept of ADSL fits the concept of a video-on-demand service provided through the existing copper loop plant very well. The CCITT H.261 recommendation and the ISO Moving Picture Experts Group (MPEG) recommendation both provide full-motion video at rates of around 1.3 Mbps. The video, an audio channel, and associated overhead can be transmitted within a 1.5 Mbps signal. Users could signal the network, scan archives of programming, and receive video-on-demand. For this service, only a low transmission throughput upstream control channel is necessary to send back control signals for interactive commands, such as Pause and Play.

The concept of ADSL also fits applications, such as network computing where software and database records could be stored on network servers and retrieved at a speed equivalent to the CD-ROM and tele-education where a specialist can be shared with a large student population through downstream channels and individual feedback can be provided through upstream channels. It was realized that for residential applications, a POTS service—with which the traditional telephone service can be provided regardless of whether the ADSL was on or off—was more practical than the ISDN service.

After sharing ideas among Bellcore, regional Bell operating companies, and other industry and academic leading ADSL proponents, ADSL was proposed as having the traditional duplex POTS channels, occupying the frequency band between 300 Hz and 4 kHz, an upstream control channel of 16–64 kbps, occupying the frequency band between 10 kHz to 50 kHz, and a downstream channel of 1.544 Mbps, occupying the frequency band of 100 kHz–500 kHz. Figure 13.2 shows the initial frequency spectra for ADSL technology.

Figure 13.2 Initial ADSL Frequency Spectra

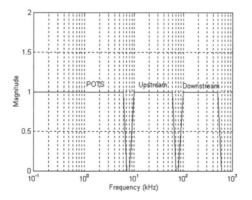

13.1.1 *Convergence of Initial Ideas on ADSL*

The discussion about ADSL at T1E1.4 working group was not started until after the proposal of a new study project about ADSL by U.S. West during the May 1991 meeting.[3] During the August 1991 T1E1.4 meeting, the performance of a QAM ADSL was studied in conjunction with DSL NEXT,[4,5] 18 test loops were proposed for ADSL,[6] the effect of impulse noise was examined,[7] and the performance of a multi-carrier system, DMT, was compared with that of a single-carrier system, QAM.[8]

During the November 1991 T1E1.4 meeting, performance of DMT was further discussed,[9,10,11] the nature of burst error was discussed,[12] the forward error correction code was proposed for ADSL,[13,14] the feasibility of an ADSL control channel was discussed,[15] and the use of Trellis code for ADSL was discussed.[16]

During the February 1992 T1E1.4 meeting, the similarity between CAP and QAM was explored,[17] and the performances of DMT and QAM were further studied.[18,19,20,21] During the May 1992 T1E1.4 meeting, ADSL system issues—ranging from interfaces to frame format—were discussed,[22,23,24,25,26,27,28] a QAM ADSL including a control channel was discussed for spectrum compatibility with other DSLs,[29,30] the ADSL Radio Frequency Interference (RFI) was discussed,[31] the POTS-generated impulse noise was discussed,[32] a performance test plan for ADSL "Olympics," was presented,[33] and the A/D precision issue was discussed.[34] The possibility of having an ADSL standard project was also discussed.[35,36]

During the August 1992 T1E1.4 meeting, the possibility of a baseband ADSL was discussed,[37] the idea of asymmetrical echo cancellation was discussed,[38] the idea of impulse noise cancellation was discussed,[39] the design issues of a CAP ADSL were discussed,[40,41] milestones of the ADSL standard were proposed,[42] possible ADSL interfaces were discussed,[43] the ADSL "Olympic" test plan was further discussed in more detail,[44,45,46] ADSL spectral compatibility was further discussed in more detail,[47,48] the possibility of an ADSL with embedded ISDN was discussed,[49] and ADSL coding and interleaving issues were further discussed.[50, 51,52,53]

During the December 1992 T1E1.4 meeting, test plans were further discussed,[54,55] Trellis coding and forward error correction coding for ADSL were discussed,[56,57,58,59] the issue of impulse noise was discussed, [60,61,62] the idea of an analytical testbed was proposed,[63] the design of a DMT transceiver was discussed,[64] the possibility of providing multiple 1.544 Mbps rates was discussed,[65,66,67] the DMT echo canceller structure was discussed,[68] the spectrum compatibility between ADSL and other DSLs was examined,[69,70] ADSL frame structure and maintenance issues were further discussed,[71,72] and possibilities of including POTS and ISDN were discussed.[73]

During the March 1993 T1E1.4 meeting, the issue of selecting forward error correction code was further discussed,[74,75,76] implementation details of the DMT ADSL were discussed,[77,78,79,80] inclusion and alternatives of providing 6 Mbps were discussed,[81,82] the effect of ADSL spectrum on T1 performance was discussed,[83] and performance measurements of ADSL prototypes were reported by Northern Telecom, Inc.[84] and Bellcore.[85,86,87,88] NTI measurements showed positive performance margins for self-FEXT (see Figure 13.3), 49-disturber ISDN NEXT (see Figure 13.4), and 24-disturber HDSL NEXT (see Figure 13.5). No error was observed when a POTS operation was performed on the same test loop.

Figure 13.3 NTI Self-FEXT Margin

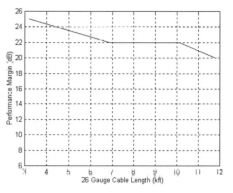

Figure 13.4 NTI 49 ISDN NEXT Margin

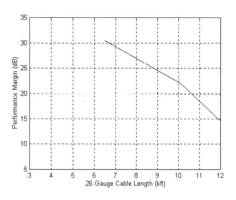

Figure 13.5 NTI 24 HDSL NEXT Margin

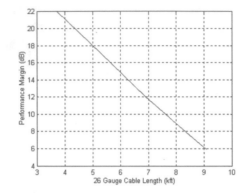

Bellcore ADSL "Olympic" test measurements, summarized in Table 13.1, showed Amati's ADSL prototype in the first place, Reliance/Bellcore's ADSL prototype in the second, and AT&T Paradyne's ADSL prototype in the third. The operation of the POTS sharing the same test loop also was verified for Reliance/Bellcore and Amati prototypes. Little disturbance was observed. Amati's ADSL prototype had forward error correction code. Based on these test measurements, DMT line code was selected as the ADSL standard also based on the fact that Amati's prototype could operate at 6 Mbps in addition to 1.5 Mbps.

Table 13.1 Bellcore ADSL "Olympic" Test Results

Loop Number	Distur- bers	Reliance/ Bellcore	Amati 21 dBm	Amati 16 dBm	AT&T
ADSL #4	24-DSL	−6	8	4	Not work
ADSL #6	24-DSL	<−8	7	3	Not work
ADSL #9	24-DSL	7	>16	>16	Not work
ADSL #17	24-DSL	1	15	10	Not work
CSA #2	24-HDSL	>11	>11	>11	<−8
CSA #6	24-HDSL	5	>11	>11	−8
CSA #7	24-HDSL	>11	>11	>11	−1
CSA #2	1-T1	7	>10	>10	<0
CSA #6	1-T1	2	>10	8	<0
CSA #7	1-T1	8	>10	>10	−2

13.1.2   Concerns for POTS Interference

The feasibility of ADSL with a POTS service was established by the aforementioned proto-type efforts and verified by laboratory measurements. The most obvious transmission challenge associated with the ADSL was the high level of signal loss at the extreme range of the nonloaded loop plant. Figure 13.6 shows the attenuation of an 18 kft, 24-gauge loop.

Figure 13.6   Attenuation of an 18 kft, 24-Gauge Loop

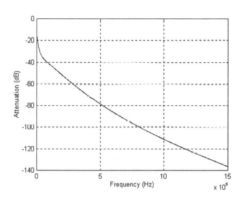

To fully realize the potential of a twisted-pair loop, the electronics front-end noise should be a few dBs below that of the twisted-pair loop plant. For an assumed twisted-pair loop plant noise power density level of –140 dBm/Hz, the RMS noise voltage for a bandwidth of 500 kHz is about 700 μV as calculated by the following expressions:

$$P = 10^{\frac{-140}{10}} \times 5 \times 10^{5} = 5 \times 10^{-9} \ \text{Watts}$$

$$0 \qquad\qquad k \qquad\qquad \mu V$$

P is the total noise power in a bandwidth of 500 kHz, and V_{rm} is the corresponding voltage level. Within a single ADSL system itself, there is the potential for interference between the three derived channels:

- The POTS channel

- The high throughput downstream channel

- The low throughput upstream channel

The POTS channel is separated by a POTS splitter, which consists of a lowpass filter and a highpass filter. The POTS splitter design and implementation are very challenging. Ringing voltage applied at the Central Office is 86 Vrms superimposed on –48 Vdc with a two seconds on/four seconds off pattern. When ringing is interrupted due to a telephone handset going off-hook (referred to as *ring trip*), a considerable transient can be induced in the line.

Other lower level transients are produced by dial pulsing and on-off hooks. Upstream and downstream channels can be separated by either frequency division using highpass and lowpass filters, echo cancellation, or a combination of frequency division and echo cancellation. Due to the combination of heavy channel attenuation and light echo path attenuation, a filter stop band attenuation or echo cancellation level of more than 60 dB is expected.

13.1.3 The Convergence of ADSL Standards

The first issue of ADSL standard, T1.413, was released during 1995 by the T1E1 committee. The concept of ADSL was also heavily promoted by professional technical conferences and the formation and activities of the ADSL Forum. The ADSL technology has been in technical and market trials since early 1994. The purpose of the technical trial was to verify the performance of ADSL technology in the real field. The purpose of the market trial was to get user feedback about the technology and its potential applications. Technical trials have established the viability of the ADSL technology. Market trials have likewise indicated strong user interest. Most recently, ADSL has been considered as an ideal vehicle for Internet access and telecommuniting applications.

13.2 Transceiver Structures and Line Codes

The DMT line code is a multi-carrier system. The spectrum of a DMT signal consists of many narrow bandwidth QAM-like carriers with different and equally distributed carrier frequencies. Information is attached in the transmitter and recovered in the receiver from these carriers through discrete versions of Fourier Transforms. The CAP line code, similar to QAM, is a single carrier system. Information is attached to and recovered from the single carrier through transmit filters and receiver channel equalizers. One similarity between DMT and CAP line codes is that there is no carrier modulation and demodulation required.

13.2.1 DMT Line Code

We can envision the DMT ADSL as a group of 256 voice band modems with their carrier frequencies ranging from a few kHz to near 1 MHz and with no guardband in between adjacent carriers. The need of guardband is eliminated due to the *orthogonolity* between all carriers. Similar to the voice band situation, each modem in this group can fall back to lower data rates by changing its constellation size. The capability of variable constellation size for each subcarrier is the DMT approach of dealing with a random channel with different Signal to Noise Ratios (SNRs) at different frequencies.

On the other hand, because frequency responses of all subchannels of this modem group are relatively flat, equalizers of the group of voice band modems are all omitted. The use of Trellis coding can still be applied. Because all the modems in this group can be synchronized, the transmit and receive filter functions can be combined and performed by an IFFT (Inverse Fast Fourier Transform) for all transmit filters, and an FFT (Fast Fourier Transform) for all receive filters.

On the line after the ADSL transmitter, we can imagine 256 different but synchronized signals each of which has its distinguishable carrier frequency and constellation size. The number of 256 subchannels corresponding to an IFFT/FFT size of 512 was chosen to maximize ADSL transceiver hardware efficiency while maintaining a tolerable IFFT/FFT processing delay time. A 512 real-to-complex FFT and a 512 complex-to-real IFFT were actually used.

Figure 13.7[89] shows a simplified DMT system. The major function of a DMT transmitter is the N (for which $N=512$) dimensional IFFT. The major function of a DMT receiver is the N-dimensional FFT.

Figure 13.7   Simplified Illustration of DMT Transceiver and Channel

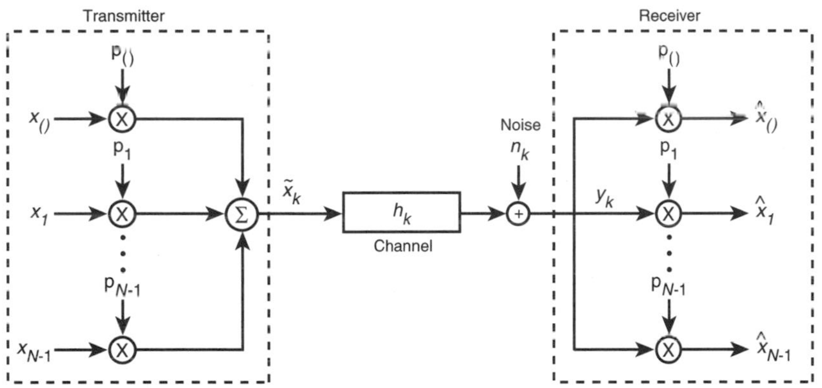

DMT ADSL Transmitters

The general transmitter illustrated in Figure 13.8 consists of bit parsing, buffering, coset-encoder, IFFT, cyclic prefix, parallel to serial conversion, Digital to Analog Conversion, (DAC), transmitter filter, and line interface functions.

Figure 13.8 Block Diagram of a DMT Transmitter

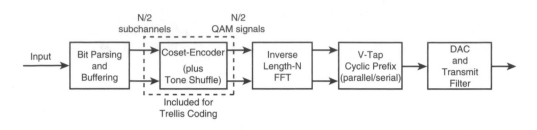

The serial bit stream is first converted into parallel data in the transmitter. The N-dimensional parallel data is then mapped into $N/2$ multibit subchannels according to a bit allocation algorithm. The coset-encoder implements the bit allocation algorithm. To achieve an efficient DFT implementation we need $N=2^i$, where i is a positive integer.

Each multibit subchannel can use a QAM signal constellation. The parallel time domain data after the IDFT is converted back to serial. A guard period stuffed with cyclic prefixes is introduced before the DAC function. The cyclic prefix is defined as the partial duplication and addition of the last v points in front of the N original data points, resulting in a total number of $v+N$ cyclic prefixed data points.

DMT ADSL Receivers

Figure 13.9 shows the general structure of a DMT receiver. The general receiver consists of a line interface, Analog to Digital Conversion (ADC), Time-Domain Equalizer (TEQ), serial to parallel conversion, FFT, Frequency-Domain Equalizer (FEQ), symbol decision, bit decision, and inverse bit parsing functions.

Figure 13.9 Block Diagram of a DMT Receiver

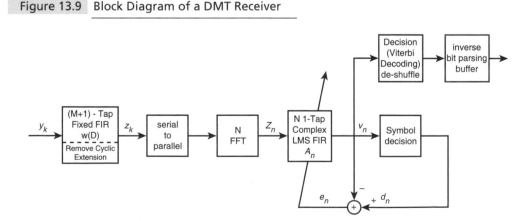

After ADC, the received signal is first filtered by the TEQ (the (M+1) tap fixed FIR filter, as illustrated in Figure 13.9. The samples corresponding to the guard period cyclic prefix are simply ignored. The rest of the samples are converted into parallel data for input to the DFT process. The FEQ (the N 1-tap complex FIR filter in Figure 13.9) is implemented by inverse target channel scaling. The target channel is the combination of channel and TEQ. FEQ is necessary to correct both magnitude and phase distortion of the equalized channel when using a single decision device for all subchannels.

Note

It is worthwhile to mention that the purpose of the TEQ is to contain the amount of channel distortion in the time domain. The use of guard periods is to avoid the residual inter-baud-symbol interference. Residual channel distortion, in the form of different magnitude attenuation and phase delay for each subcarrier, however, still exists for each baud symbol.

Combating Channel Distortion

In theory, the channel distortion can be avoided by a DMT system through the fine division of the available bandwidth into many subcarriers such that each subchannel is almost distortion free. The finer division in frequency domain is equivalent to further extension of the signaling baud period. The channel distortion can be considered negligible if the channel impulse response tail caused by channel distortion is negligible compared with the signaling baud period. Figure 13.10 shows the channel impulse response of the 9 kft, 26-gauge loop.

Figure 13.10   Channel Impulse Response of a 9 kft, 26-Gauge Loop

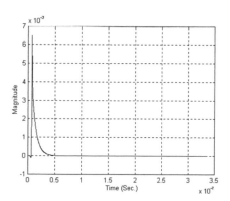

The tail length is about 2.77 microseconds at 1 percent of the peak amplitude. The signaling baud length can be chosen as 277 microseconds for a factor of 100 of the tail length. The baud rate is then 3.61 kHz. On the other hand, the overall delay time, which is about three times the baud length, should also be constrained according to the system requirement.

The channel distortion could cause inter-subchannel interference. The inter-subchannel interference is caused by amplitude attenuation and phase delay differences between subchannels. The total inter-subchannel interference for a particular subchannel can be calculated as follows:

$$10\log_{10}\sum_{\substack{k=1\\k\neq i}}^{N}\int_{0}^{T}\cos\left(2\pi i\frac{t}{T}-\theta_i\right)\cdot\frac{1-\Delta A_k}{1-\Delta A_i}\left(\cos\left(2\pi k\frac{t}{T}-\theta_k\right)+\sin\left(2\pi k\frac{t}{T}-\theta_k\right)\right)dt$$

The values are as follows:

ΔA_i and ΔA_k are the subchannel and interfering subchannel amplitude attenuations, respectively.

θ_i and θ_k are the subchannel and interfering subchannel phase delays, respectively.

The inter-subchannel interference can be minimized by selecting a lower baud rate or by using a channel equalizer.

Although the effect of the channel impulse response tail is minimized through the selection of a slow baud rate, the tail of one baud will extend to the next adjacent baud. This inter-baud interference is the DMT inter-symbol interference. The effect of DMT inter-symbol interference can be minimized by using a guard period or a cyclic prefix.[90] The length of a cyclic prefix is chosen such that the tail portion of one baud will die out before the next adjacent baud starts. The cyclic prefix repeats the last v time domain serial data points before the first serial data point, in which v is the length of the guard period. The length of the cyclic prefix can also be minimized by using a channel equalizer.

We have the following:

$$v=T_g f_s, \; N=T f_s, \; \text{or} f_s = \frac{N}{T}=\frac{v}{T_g}$$

The value f_s is the sampling frequency, and T_g is the guard period. The sampling frequency should be higher than twice that of the usable channel bandwidth.

A time domain channel equalizer is necessary for the DMT receiver to reduce the amount of channel distortion present in the subscriber loop environment. The channel equalizer reduces the length of the cyclic prefix.

Note

In theory, a linear equalizer can reduce the cyclic prefix to zero length; however, a linear equalizer operating on the sampling rate to reach that goal might not be practical to implement in hardware. Furthermore, such a linear equalizer could cause excessive noise enhancement.

A linear equalizer with a small number of taps can reduce the cyclic prefix length to less than 30 sampling points. The conventional channel equalizer optimizes the desired signal to noise ratio at a particular decision point; however, the channel equalizer in general can modify the channel response according to particular needs just as what an FIR filter is capable of. A DMT Time Domain Equalizer can modify the loop channel response to the target channel response, as shown in Figure 13.11. The desired target channel response has the minimum mean square error when compared with any other equalized channel response.

Figure 13.11 Analysis of DMT Time-Domain Equalizer

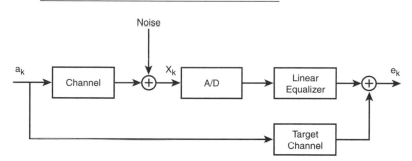

The pair of DMT Time-Domain Equalizers and the target channel is similar to the pair of feedforward and feedback filters of a Decision Feedback channel Equalizer (DFE), except the impulse response of the target channel does not have to be causal. The optimal DMT Time-Domain Equalizer coefficients can be calculated using the same matrix operation method used for the calculation for those of a DFE, but in several iterations. The target channel impulse response is calculated only for evaluation, but not for real-time filtering. In practice, DMT Time-Domain Equalizer coefficients are identified iteratively in real-time in frequency or time domain.[91,92]

To complete the received signal detection, a Frequency-Domain Equalizer is also required. Although the inter-symbol interference has been mainly avoided by utilizing a cyclic prefix, amplitude attenuation and phase delay differences still exist for different subchannels. We can imagine each DMT baud pulse consisting of 256 sinusoids of different frequencies. At the transmit side, all these sinusoids are synchronized by the IFFT operation; however, these sinusoids are not synchronized in phase after the FFT operation at the receiver due to the channel distortion.

The purpose of the Frequency-Domain Equalizer (FEQ) is to correct phase and amplitude distortion of each subchannel such that a unified symbol detection mechanism can be applied to all subchannels. The FEQ has one complex tap for each subchannel resulting to an N/two-dimensional equalizer coefficient vector. The FEQ coefficient vector has the inverse frequency response of the equivalent channel, including transmit and receiver filters and the Time-Domain Equalizer. FEQ is performed by multiplying the FFT output with the FEQ coefficient vector.

Bit Loading Algorithm

Based on the Signal to Noise Ratio (SNR) of each subchannel, the number of bits that can be transmitted through each subchannel for certain error probability can be calculated as follows:

$$b_j = \log_2\left(1 + \frac{SNR_j}{\Gamma}\right)$$

The $SNRj$ is expressed in power ratio. Γ for an error rate of 10^{-7} is 9.8 dB or 9.55 in terms of power ratio. Γ of 9.8 dB is the reference point for uncoded system with 0 dB performance margin. To achieve an additional SNR performance margin, the value of Γ should be adjusted accordingly. For the same error rate, but with a 6 dB performance margin, the value of Γ would be increased to 15.8 dB or 38.02 in terms of power ratio. The value of Γ should be adjusted accordingly if any coding gain is to be considered. To add a coding gain of 3 dB, Γ will be reduced to 12.8 dB or 19.05 in terms of power ratio.

Note
It should be noted that Γ is only used here for analytical purpose—not as a design parameter.

The computation for the number of bits that can be transmitted through each subchannel will result in a fractional number of bits for each subchannel. An integer number of bits for up to 11 bits per subchannel is expected if a simple two-dimensional QAM-like constellation is to be implemented; however, the use of an integer number of bits could reduce the transmission efficiency.

One way to improve the transmission efficiency with integer number of bits is to assign a different signal power for each subchannel. The other way to improve transmission efficiency is to use a multidimensional signal constellation.[93] Up to 1 dB of performance improvement can be achieved by using these advanced loading algorithms.

The overall transceiver throughput is the sum of the number of bits for all subchannels times the modified baud rate, that is, the inverse of the baud period plus the guard period.

The computation of the performance margin for a target throughput can be achieved using the following expression in several iterations:

$$R = \sum_{j=1}^{256} b_j \frac{1}{T + T_g}$$

In other words, we first choose a particular SNR margin and calculate corresponding transmission throughput. We then adjust the value of the SNR margin and repeat the transmission throughput calculation until the desired transmission throughput is obtained.

Pilot Tone for Timing Recovery

The clock synchronization between a DMT transmitter and a DMT receiver is maintained through a timing recovery circuit in at least one transmission direction. This synchronization is based on the configuration where the transmitter and the receiver at one end of an ADSL system use their own clock source, and the transmitter and receiver at the other end use the recovered clock.

The timing recovery circuit of a DMT system involves the transmission of a pilot tone at the clock source end and the recovery of the pilot tone at the other end. The pilot tone could have periodic phase shift to reduce its interference with other tones. The transmit power of the pilot tone is usually a little lower than other information bearing subcarriers. The recovered pilot tone is usually filtered with a phase locked loop to increase its stability. The transmit power of the pilot tone may actually be more than the nominal transmit power of the information bearing subcarriers, especially for longer loops.

Note

A pilot tone is a subcarrier dedicated only for the purpose of timing recovery. A pilot tone has a fixed amplitude and fixed or alternating phases.

DMT ADSL Transceiver Parameters

The transceiver parameters[94] of a DMT system are summarized in Table 13.2 for the downstream channel.

Table 13.2 DMT Downstream Parameters

Symbol rate	4 kHz
FFT size	512 samples
Cyclic prefix	32 samples
Synchronization	Average 8 samples/symbol
Sampling rate	2.208 MHz
Transmit power	20 dBm
Time-Domain Equalizer	16 taps
Highpass filter (without echo cancellation)	6th order elliptic, passband corner frequency 62.5 kHz, 1 dB passband ripple

With the parameters in Table 13.2, the downstream DMT subcarriers are spaced at 4.3125 kHz intervals. The lowest carrier available is at 64.6875 kHz or 12.938 kHz with echo cancellation. The highest carrier available is at 1099.6875 kHz. The transceiver parameters of a DMT system are summarized in Table 13.3 for the upstream channel.

Table 13.3 DMT Upstream Parameters

Symbol rate	4 kHz
FFT size	64 samples
Cyclic prefix	4 samples
Synchronization	Average 1 sample/symbol
Sampling rate	276 kHz
Transmit power	7 dBm
Time-Domain Equalizer	32 taps
Lowpass filter	6th order elliptic, passband corner frequency 43.875 kHz, 1 dB passband ripple

With the parameters in Table 13.3, the upstream DMT subcarriers are also spaced at 4.3125 kHz intervals (identical to the downstream direction). The lowest carrier available is at 11.25 kHz (leaving below 10 kHz for POTS), the highest carrier available is at 42.75 kHz or 271.6875 kHz with echo cancellation. In addition, we need to meet an error rate of 10^{-7} and have a POTS highpass filter with a corner frequency of higher than 4 kHz. The performance should be examined with a background noise level of -140 dBm/Hz as well as NEXT and FEXT noise.

DMT ADSL Trellis Coding

The use of Trellis-Coded Modulation (TCM) is an option for ADSL to either meet performance margin requirements for long loops or increase the transmission throughput under a certain performance margin. Wei's 16-state 4D code, which has emerged from ten years of study and development, was proposed for ADSL.[95] This code has a theoretical gain of 4.5 dB and a practical gain of 4.2 dB against background and crosstalk noise.

In the TCM decoder, maximum-likelihood decoding using the Viterbi algorithm is employed to estimate the transmitted sequence. The use of a four-dimensional code (compared with a two-dimensional code) has the advantage of a smaller constellation expansion, and hence a smaller peak-to-average power ratio. As a result, it is more immune to nonlinear distortion. With the same decoding complexity, the four-dimensional codes also give higher coding gains.

The proposed Wei's code uses a rate 2/3 (2 bit/3 bit) convolutional code with parity check matrix (D3+D2, D, D4+1). The number of bits in a four-dimensional symbol increases from the uncoded case of b bits to the coded case of b+1 bits. The 2^{b+1} points are partitioned into eight cosets. Two of the b message bits are fed into the convolutional encoder. The three output bits from the convolutional encoder are used to specify the coset. The other b-2 message bits determine which point in the coset should be transmitted. Figure 13.12 shows the structure of the convolutional encoder.

Figure 13.12   Structure of the Convolution Encoder

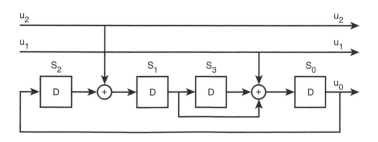

The minimum square Euclidean distance between points in the same coset is 4, with 24 neighbors. The minimum square Euclidean distance between coded coset sequences is 6. The fundamental coding gain of the code is determined by the smaller of the two, and is equal to

$$10\log_{10} 4 - 1/2 \ 10 \ \log_{10} 2 = 4.52 \ \text{dB}$$

The term $1/2 \ 10 \ \log_{10} 2$ is for the adjustment of constellation expansion per two dimensions. In the uncoded case, there are only eight nearest neighbors for each four-dimensional symbol. The factor of 3 increase in the number of nearest neighbors causes the coding gain to decrease from 4.52 dB to an effective value of 4.2 dB. Trellis coding and decoding are applied to each subcarrier individually.

DMT ADSL Forward Error Correction (FEC) Coding

To accommodate maximum flexibility for the providers and end users of ADSL services, it was recommended that FEC be selectively applied to 32 kbps increments of the composite data streams to, or from, the Central Office.[96] This permits FEC to be included or excluded selectively both on a call-by-call basis and within portions of the composite data stream.

As an example of mixed requirements for FEC in an ADSL service, consider transmitting a one-way DS1 stream from the Central Office to the remote terminal (CO to RT) along with a bi-directional basic rate ISDN channel. The end user may require high reliability on the one-way channel because the one-way channel might contain highly compressed data with no possibility for request for retransmission. For this portion of the ADSL signal, FEC is necessary. Voice services and duplex data services with their own embedded protocols will require minimum latency on the embedded ISDN channel. For this portion of the ADSL signal, FEC is optional.

FEC of ADSL employs Reed-Solomon codes based on symbols of 8 bits=1 byte (that is, a code over $GF(2^8)$). The maximum codeword length for such codes is 255, with varying error correction capabilities. Relatively long codeword lengths for a minimal redundancy of 8–10 percent were used. The redundancy and interleave depths chosen accomplish the following: correct for error bursts of up to $1/2$ ms of transmitted data and reduce the background bit error rate (BER) from 10^{-7} to 10^{-10}.

Tables 13.4–13.6 summarize the chosen encoding system. Table 13.4 specifies interleave depths (the number of codewords in the interleave matrix) and codeword lengths (specified in ms) for uncoded data rates ranging from 32 kbps to 7584 kbps. Table 13.4 aids in the calculation of the number of message bytes in a codeword for any uncoded data rate. Note that the interleave depth times the codeword length, which equals the interleave latency, is kept constant at 16 ms.

Table 13.4 Interleave Depth and Codeword Length Parameters

Data Rate (kbps)	Interleave Depth (codewords)	Codeword Length (ms)
32–64	1	16
96–224	2	8
256–448	4	4
480–928	8	2
960–1888	16	1
1920–3776	32	0.5
3808–7584	64	0.25

Table 13.5 and Table 13.6 specify the number of check bytes in a codeword for data rates below and at or above 256 kbps, respectively. For the flexibility offered, very few parameters must be stored in the ADSL unit to implement selectable FEC.

Table 13.5 Message Bytes and Check Bytes (Data Rates < 224 kbps)

Data Rate (kbps)	Message Length (bytes)	Redundancy Length (bytes)
32	64	8
64	128	16
96–128	96–128	12
160–192	160–192	16
224	224	20

Table 13.6 Message Bytes and Check Bytes (Data Rates > 224 kbps)

Message Length (bytes)	Redundancy Length (bytes)
128–147	12
148–175	14
176–207	16
208–237	18

As a simple example in the use of Tables 13.4–13.6, consider adding FEC to an uncoded data rate of 1568 kbps. Using Table 13.4, we see one codeword contains (1568 kbits/sec)×(1 msec/codeword)×(1 byte/8 bits)=196 message bytes. Using Table 13.6, we find that for a codeword of length 196 bytes, we need to add 16 check bytes to form a codeword of 212 bytes. The coded data rate, or line rate, is calculated as (212 bytes/codeword)×(1 codeword/1 msec)×(8 bits/byte)=1696 kbps.

Interleaving for Reed-Solomon Coding

The combination of Reed-Solomon code with interleaving is effective at correcting errors caused by impulse noise in the subscriber loop plant. Some studies indicate that a burst error correction capability of 500 microseconds (μs)=1/2 ms should provide sufficient protection against the effects of nearly all impulses encountered for a well-designed ADSL system.[97] On average, the time between impulses was found to be 67 ms.[98] For redundancies in the range of 7–9 percent, the required end-to-end latency is about 16 ms to correct for 500 μs of data with errors. To correct for 1000 μs of data with errors would require double the latency or double the redundancy.[99]

Consider an uncoded transmission rate of 1600 kbps=200 kbyte/s. Adding 7 percent redundancy, at this data rate equal to 14 kbytes/s, results in a coded transmission rate of 214 kbytes/s. The impulse causes a burst of 1/2 ms=107 bytes coded data destroyed. Using a t=7 byte (2t=14 check bytes) error correction capability FEC code would require an interleave depth of at least 16 codewords to correct this burst of 107 bytes of data with errors.

At a coded data rate of 214 kbytes/s, a codeword of length 214 bytes would last 1 ms. The latency for an interleave depth of 16 codewords is thus 16 ms. Conventional block interleaving would require 16 ms for interleaving at the encoder and an additional 16 ms for deinterleaving at the decoder, but convolutional interleaving, as described later in this section, reduces the total delay to 16 ms.

Using a fixed latency of 16 ms for any data rate, you can achieve the same burst error correction capability with smaller codewords and proportionally larger interleave depths. For example, relatively short constituent codewords are used in the concatenated Reed-Solomon codes for compact discs. Longer codewords, however, allow for additional redundancy to be added for random bit error protection with little additional cost. Increasing the number of check bytes in the previous example from the minimum 2t=14 to 2t=16 adds only 1 percent additional redundancy and results in a background bit error rate (BER) improvement from 10^{-7} to 10^{-10}. This last result is found using the following formula. Assume the following parameters:

- A burst error destroys x bytes per codeword

- A background random bit error rate (not due to the burst) of p

- A codeword length of N

- A redundancy of $2t$ bytes per codeword

The bit error rate[100] after burst and random error correction is given approximately by

$$\frac{1}{2}\left(\frac{N-x}{t-x+1}\right)\frac{t+1}{N}(8p)^{t+1}\frac{1}{2}\left(\frac{n-x}{t-x+1}\right)\frac{t+1}{n}(8p)^{t+1}$$

Adding one byte error correction capability to that needed for burst error correction, we chose $t=x+1$. Substituting $p=10^{-7}$, you can confirm the background bit error rate is reduced to the order of 10^{-10} for the codeword lengths chosen.

Convolutional interleaving reduces the end-to-end latency incurred for burst error correction to half the latency incurred by block interleaving. This reduction is achieved by alternately reading and writing to the interleave matrix for each encoded byte. First, consider block interleaving. Figure 13.13 illustrates the block interleave matrix for a codeword length of $N=8$ bytes and an interleave depth $d=5$ codewords.[96]

Figure 13.13 Block Interleave/Deinterleave Matrix

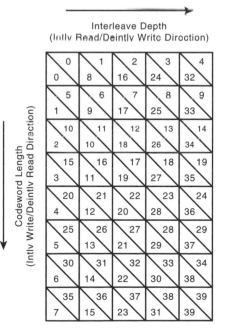

Block interleaving requires writing all positions in an entire interleave matrix prior to the first byte being read. The lower-left number x in each square in the matrix indicates the *time* index when writing into that location. The upper-right number y in each square in the matrix indicates the time index when reading from that location. Of course the entire matrix is written prior to any byte being read. Therefore, in actual implementation, two separate interleave matrices are used: one from which the current byte is read and one into which the current byte is written.

The same matrix describes deinterleaving, except the lower-left number in a square indicates the time index when reading from that location, while the upper-right number in a square indicates the time index when writing to that location. Deinterleaving adds a delay of $40+x-y$ bytes at the decoder end. The end-to-end delay with block interleaving for this example is thus 80 bytes. Note also that for correct decoding, the block deinterleaver must know the position of the beginning of the interleave matrix.

Now consider convolutional interleaving. As shown in Figure 13.14, in convolutional interleaving, after writing a byte into the interleave matrix, a previously written byte is read from the same interleave matrix. Only one interleave matrix is used for both reading and writing, so convolutional interleaving requires half the memory space of block interleaving.

Figure 13.14   Convolutional Interleave/Deinterleave Matrix

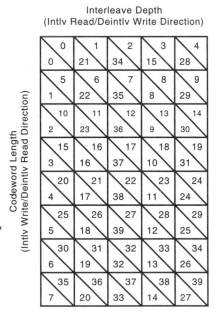

While the interleave matrix is read sequentially horizontally as with block interleaving, the matrix is written in a more complex manner, as shown by the numbers in the matrix. In general, the byte at the beginning of a codeword is written to, and read from, the same location. The remaining bytes in a codeword are written sequentially vertically within the same column as the first byte. For example, the first byte in a codeword experiences no delay (written and then read immediately thereafter).

At the decoder end, the same matrix describes deinterleaving except the bytes are now written sequentially horizontally and are now read in the more complex manner vertically. Thus, the first byte in a codeword incurs the minimum delay in the interleave matrix, but incurs maximum delay in the deinterleave matrix. The end-to-end total delay for this example is 40 bytes—exactly half the delay incurred by block interleaving.

Upon examining the interleave matrix, you should also note that the convolutional deinterleaver must know only the position of the beginning of a codeword to deinterleave correctly. Thus with convolutional interleaving, FEC synchronization need only search through a codeword depth rather than the entire interleave matrix. Note that for the entire interleave matrix to be used, the codeword length and interleave depth must be coprime. For ADSL, the interleave depths chosen are all powers of 2. Any odd codeword length will then be coprime to the interleave depth.

Convolutional interleaving incurs half the latency, requires half the memory, and needs less time for resynchronization compared with block interleaving. For this savings, convolutional interleaving requires a more complicated addressing scheme, needs alternate reading and writing of the interleave matrix, and requires an interleaving/deinterleaving codeword length coprime to the interleave depth. The convolution interleaving was selected for DMT ADSL.

DMT Asymmetrical Echo Cancellation

The asymmetrical echo cancellation technique can be used to improve the performance of an ADSL system. Although the upstream/downstream overlapped spectrum created by echo cancellation is NEXT limited, it still can provide a high enough SNR to be useful for transmission in both upstream and downstream directions. At the ADSL data rates, traditional time-domain and frequency-domain LMS echo cancellers can be prohibitively expensive to implement.

Mixed frequency and time-domain techniques are proposed to achieve low-complexity echo cancellation. The use of these techniques can achieve the required 70 dB of echo cancellation level.

A time-domain echo canceller needs to complete the discrete convolution process in the scale of the echo impulse response during every sampling interval. The echo impulse response could be as long as a few hundred sample points. For a sampling rate of about 1 MHz, a time-domain echo canceller would need a few hundred million multiplications and addition operations per second. On the other hand, if the echo cancellation is implemented in the frequency domain, assuming both echo path and data vectors are available in the frequency domain, the operations need to be completed only during each DMT baud interval. For 256 subcarriers and a baud rate of 4 kHz, the required operations are only a few million complex multiplication and addition operations per second.

For the mixed frequency and time-domain approach, most of the echo emulation is performed in the frequency domain. Because data vectors and therefore the echoes are not periodic, the time-domain convolution cannot be exactly duplicated in the frequency domain as a block multiplication. The circular nature of an echo block can be reinstalled by *tail cancellation* and *cyclic reconstruction*.[101,102]

Note

The tail cancellation is the subtraction of the tail caused by the previous data block, and the cyclic reconstruction is the replacement of a cyclic prefix corresponding to the current data block.

The combined process involves the convolution of an estimated echo path impulse response with portions of the current and the previous echo blocks.

Due to the asymmetrical transmission throughput nature, the sampling frequencies of transmission and receiving paths are different. Thus, a decimation, in the *Asymmetrical Terminal Unit-Central Office* (ATU-C), or an interpolation, in the ATU-R, process is necessary to match the rate of an analog to digital converter (ADC) to that of a digital to analog converter (DAC). Figure 13.15 shows a functional block diagram for an ATU-C DMT echo canceller. Figure 13.16 shows a functional block diagram for an ATU-R DMT echo canceller.

In the ATU-C, as illustrated in Figure 13.15, the ADSL upstream receiver has an FFT size of N. The ratio between the downstream DAC sampling rate and the upstream ADC sampling rate is k. Therefore, the ADSL downstream transmitter has an FFT size of kN. The echo has a tail of M sampling points in the transmitter sampling rate. The last $M-1$ previous and current data block points are combined through subtraction and used for tail cancellation and cyclic construction.

Figure 13.15   ATU-C DMT Echo Canceller

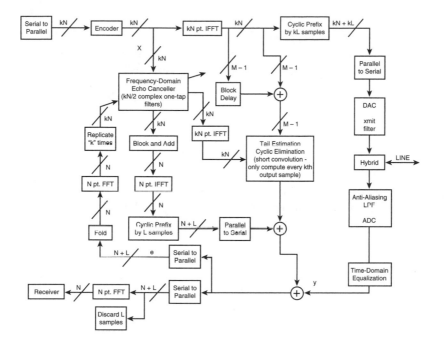

Figure 13.16   ATU-R DMT Echo Cancellation

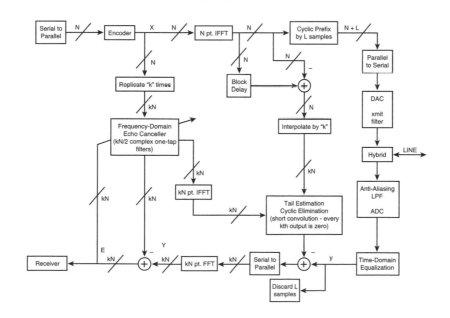

The estimated frequency-domain echo path is also transformed into time domain for the tail cancellation and cyclic construction purpose. The convolution output for tail cancellation and cyclic construction is only needed at the receiver sampling rate. The main echo duplication is generated in the frequency domain, decimated by a factor of k, and converted into time domain for echo cancellation. The main echo replica is generated in the frequency domain, but used in the time domain to avoid the out-off-band aliasing effect.

In ATU-R, transmitting data in both the frequency domain and the time domain is interpreted to the receiver sampling rate. The interpolated frequency-domain data is used for main frequency-domain echo replica generation. The interpolated previous and current data block points in time domain are combined through subtraction and used for tail cancellation and cyclic construction. The estimated frequency-domain echo path is transformed into time domain for the tail cancellation and cyclic construction purpose. The main echo replica is generated in the frequency domain and combined with FFT transformed received data for direct frequency-domain echo cancellation.

DMT ADSL Transceiver Implementation

As for other DSL systems, only if a transceiver can be implemented with a low-cost VLSI (Very-Large-Scale-Integrated) circuits solution will ADSL find its broad acceptance. Major functions that an ADSL transceiver needs to accomplish in the real time include complex FFT/IFFT, Time-Domain Equalizer, Frequency-Domain Equalizer, echo canceller, Reed-Solomon forward error correction, Trellis coding, timing recovery, digital interfaces of up to seven channels, and OAM.

ATU-C/ATU-R Transceivers

ATU-C and ATU-R transceivers can be divided into three major functional blocks: *Digital Interfaces* (DI), *Digital Signal Processing* (DSP), and *Analog Interfaces* (AI).[103] Figure 13.17 shows such a decomposition for ATU-C. Figure 13.18 shows such a decomposition for ATU-R.

Figure 13.17 ATU-C Functional Blocks

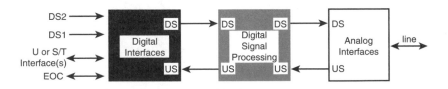

Figure 13.18   ATU-R Functional Blocks

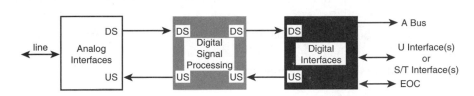

The DI includes the acquisition and generation of data and clocks that interface the Central-Office switch or remote-terminal applications module. The DI essentially formats and unformats data for convenient processing by the DSP. Modulation and demodulation of data from and to the discrete time modulated transmission signals is performed in the DSP Subsection. The digital signals are converted and conditioned to and from the line in the AI. Figure 13.19 shows the functional blocks of ATU-C DI.

Figure 13.19   ATU-C DI Functional Blocks

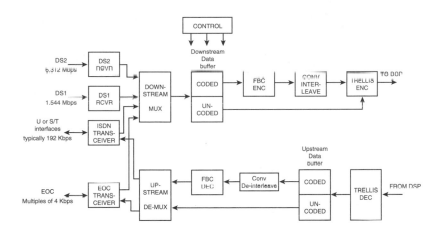

In the downstream direction, high-speed primary data at DS1 (1.544 Mbps) or DS2 (6.312 Mbps) rates, low-speed secondary data at multiples of 16 Kbps (typically 192 Kbps), and EOC data at small multiples of 4 Kbps are received, processed, and transferred to the DSP. The processing includes multiplexing the various received data streams into one data stream, which is then buffered and separated into two types. The first type of data will be FEC coded and interleaved for error protection. The second type of data will not be interleaved but might be FEC encoded because of its sensitivity to extra latency. The coded, interleaved data, together with the non-interleaved data, is then Trellis encoded before they are passed to the DSP.

In the upstream direction, only the secondary data and the EOC data are present. The data from the DSP is first Trellis decoded, then separated into FEC coded and uncoded data through the upstream buffer. The FEC coded data is then deinterleaved and FEC decoded. This decoded data, together with the uncoded data, are demultiplexed into the secondary data and the EOC data, which are then transferred to the transceivers. Table 13.7 summarizes the detailed semiconductor requirements:.

Table 13.7 DI Complexity Estimates

Functional Block	Random Logic	RAM	ROM
DS1 receiver	2000	N/A	N/A
DS2 receiver	2000	N/A	N/A
ISDN transceiver	2000	N/A	N/A
EOC transceiver	2000	N/A	N/A
Downstream multiplexer	1000	16	N/A
Downstream buffer	1000	512	N/A
FEC encoder	2000	18	128
Convolutional interleaver	1000	16 K	N/A
Trellis encoder	3000	192	1 K
Trellis decoder	15000	904	800
Upstream buffer	1000	512	N/A
Convolutional deinterleaver	1000	512	N/A
FEC decoder	7000	256	N/A
Upstream demultiplexer	1000	256	N/A
Control	8000	N/A	4 K×8
Total	49000	20 K	6 K

Figure 13.20 illustrates the ATU-C DSP functional blocks.

ATU-C DSP Functional Blocks Data symbols for each subchannel input are supplied by the Trellis encoder of the DI in 6-bit real and 6-bit imaginary parts. The downstream data symbols are modulated digitally by the 512 complex-to-real IFFT, and a 32-sample prefix is added to each block of time-domain samples at the DAC buffer, which is output to the AI at 2.208 Msamples/s.

Figure 13.20   ATU-C DSP Functional Blocks

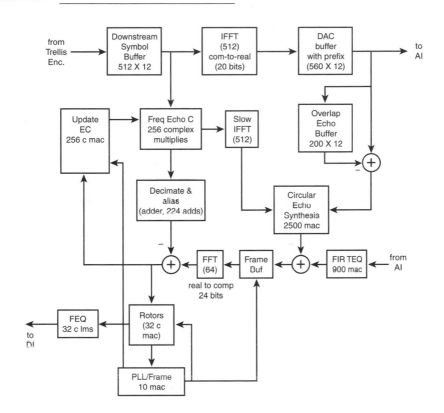

The echo canceller uses an overlap method to make the echo appear periodic so that a simple 1-tap per subchannel echo canceller will provide excellent cancellation range. The upstream ADC samples at 276 kHz are filtered by an FIR TEQ and followed by the circular echo adjustment, frame buffering, and demodulation by the 64-point real-to-complex FFT. A decimated frequency-domain echo is subtracted, timing is digitally interpolated in the frequency domain to the remote clock, and a 1-tap LMS gain/phase adjustment (FEQ) is made to each subchannel so that common decision boundaries can be used by the Trellis decoder in the DI. The ATU-C DSP requires about 67,000 gates, 12 K RAM, 6 K ROM, and 67 MIPS (Millions of Instructions Per Second). Figure 13.21 illustrates the ATU-C AI functional blocks.

Figure 13.21 ATU-C AI Functional Blocks

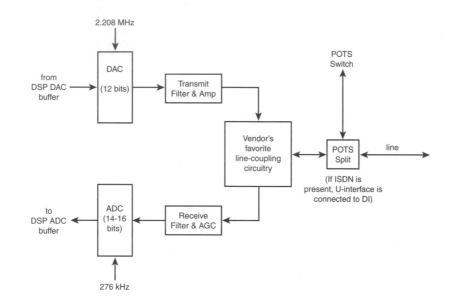

DAC precision is 12 bits at a sampling rate of 2.208 MHz, while ADC precision is 14–16 bits (good hybrids require 14, less sophisticated hybrids require 16) at a sampling rate of 276 kHz. The ADC clock is exactly eight times slower than the DAC clock, and both are run asynchronously with the CO clocks at a stable jitter-free crystal oscillator frequency. The jitter-free clocks are required for proper operation of the echo canceller in the DSP section. Interpolation and elastic queues in the DSP and DI sections realign clocks.

The ATU-R DI is very similar to the ATU-C DI. The main difference is that the decoder portion now runs at the downstream high data rate, while the encoder portion runs at the upstream low data rate. To save design effort, the basic computation modules (FEC encoder, FEC decoder, Trellis encoder, and Trellis decoder) are designed for both ATU-C and ATU-R DIs.

Figure 13.22 illustrates the functional blocks of an ATU-R DI.

In the upstream, low-speed secondary data at multiples of 16 Kbps (192 Kbps for example), and EOC data at small multiples of 4 Kbps are received, processed, and transferred to the Digital Signal Processor. The secondary data and EOC data are multiplexed, buffered, and separated into two types. The first type of data will be FEC coded and interleaved for error protection. The second type of data will not be interleaved because of its sensitivity to extra latency. The coded, interleaved data, together with the uncoded data, is then Trellis coded before they are passed to the DSP.

Figure 13.22   ATU-R DI Functional Blocks

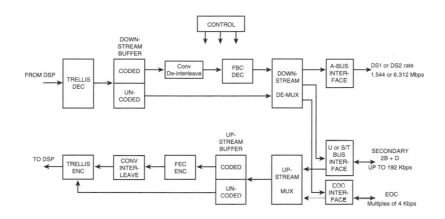

In the downstream direction, in addition to the secondary and EOC data, primary data at DS1 (1.544 Mbps) or DS2 (6.312 Mbps) rates are also present. The data from the DSP is first Trellis decoded, then separated into FEC coded and uncoded data through the downstream buffer. The FEC coded data is then deinterleaved and FEC decoded. This decoded data, together with the uncoded data, are demultiplexed into the primary and secondary data and the EOC data. The ATU-R DI also requires about 49,000 gates, 20 K RAM, and 6 K ROM. Figure 13.23 illustrates the functional blocks of an ATU-R DSP.

Data symbols for each subchannel input are supplied by the Trellis encoder of the DI in 6-bit real and 6-bit imaginary parts. The upstream data symbols are modulated digitally by the 64 complex-to-real IFFT and a 4-sample prefix is added to each block of time-domain samples at the DAC buffer, which is output to the AI at 276 ksamples/s. The echo canceller uses an overlap method to make the echo appear periodic so that a simple 1-tap per subchannel echo canceller will provide an excellent cancellation range.

The downstream ADC samples at 2.208 MHz are filtered by a 16-tap FIR TEQ and followed by the circular echo adjustment, frame buffering, and demodulation by the 512-point real-to-complex FFT. An interpolated polyphase frequency-domain echo is subtracted, timing is digitally interpolated in the frequency domain to the Central Office clock, and a 1-tap LMS gain/phase adjustment (FEQ) is made to each subchannel so that common decision boundaries can be used by the Trellis decoder in the DI. The ATU-R DSP requires about 72,000 gates, 12 K RAM, 4 K ROM, and 132 MIPS. Figure 13.24 illustrates the functional blocks of an ATU-R AI.

Figure 13.23 ATU-R Digital Signal Processing Functional Blocks

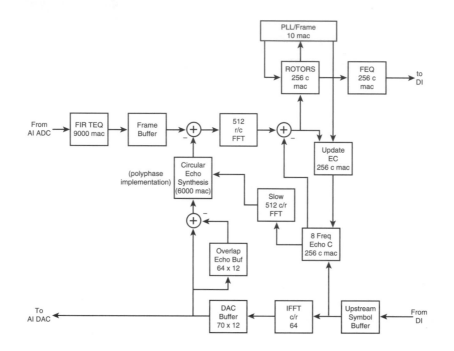

Figure 13.24 ATU-R AI Functional Blocks

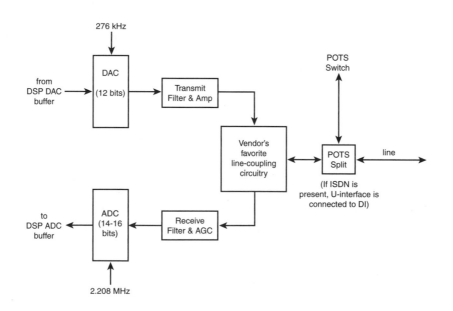

DAC precision is 12 bits at 276 kHz, while ADC precision is 14–16 bits (good hybrids require 14, less sophisticated hybrids require 16) at 2.208 MHz. The ADC clock is exactly eight times faster than the DAC clock and both are run asynchronously with the ATU-R data clocks at a stable jitter-free crystal oscillator frequency. The jitter-free clocks are required for proper operation of the echo canceller in the DSP section. Interpolation and elastic queues in the DSP and DI sections realign clocks.

13.2.2   CAP Line Code

A CAP (Carrierless AM/PM) ADSL system consists of an upstream channel and a downstream channel. There is a transmitter and receiver pair for each channel and for each transceiver. A CO-side CAP transceiver, ATU-C, has a downstream transmitter and an upstream receiver. A residential or remote side transceiver, ATU-R, has an upstream transmitter and a downstream receiver.

CAP Transmitter Structure and Functionality

A CAP transmitter should have a scrambler, an encoder, a pair of transmitter filters, a Digital to Analog converter (DAC), and a lowpass filter.[104] The encoder converts the scrambled data into an in-phase channel data and a quadrature channel data. The transmitter filters convert the data streams into passband line signal. The DAC puts the filtered signal into analog format. The lowpass after the DAC removes harmonic images of the transmit signal. The encoded signal arrives at the baud rate.

The filters operate three to four times the baud rate. The DAC usually has a higher internal operating rate. The lowpass filter could be in analog format. A transmitter clock, locked to network incoming data or to recovered data by the receiver, should be available to functional blocks of the transmitter. Figure 13.25 shows the structure of a CAP ADSL transmitter.

Figure 13.25   A CAP Transmitter

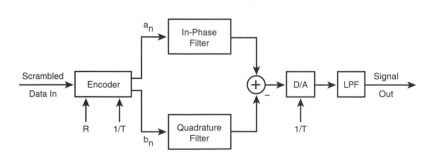

a) Transmitter Structure

CAP Receiver Structure and Functionality

A CAP receiver should have a clock recovery or timing generation circuit, an Analog to Digital Converter (ADC), a pair of adaptive channel equalizers, a symbol detection device, and a decoder. The clock/timing circuit is a very important part of the receiver and it can be independent or dependent of the receiver data path. The ADC transforms the received signal in digital format for further processing.

The data output rate of the ADC should be compatible with the operation rate of the pair of channel equalizers. The adaptive channel equalizers compensate for the signal distortion caused by channel intersymbol interference. The adaptive equalizers operate at a few times of the baud rate. The data output rate of the equalizer is the baud rate. The decision device converts the equalized signal to data symbols. The decoder converts the data symbol to the original bit stream. Figure 13.26 shows the structure of a CAP ADSL receiver with linear equalizers.

Figure 13.26 A CAP Receiver with Linear Equalizers

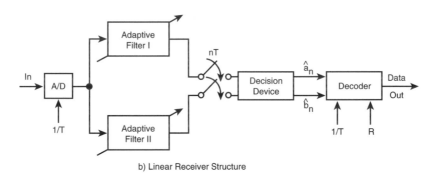

b) Linear Receiver Structure

The adaptive filters could be linear or decision feedback. The linear adaptive filters can also be used in conjunction with Tomlinson prefilters in the transmitter. The Tomlinson filter coefficients are usually identified with a decision feedback equalizer structure. To improve system performance, a DFE can be used instead of the linear equalizer in a CAP receiver. Figure 13.27 shows a CAP receiver with a conventional DFE.

The two feedforward filters of the CAP receiver, as shown in Figure 13.27, typically operate at a sampling rate of $3/T$ or $4/T$. Figure 13.28 shows a noise predictive DFE structure. The noise predictive CAP DFE might have a slight performance edge compared to that of a conventional CAP DFE.

Figure 13.27 A CAP Receiver with Traditional DFE

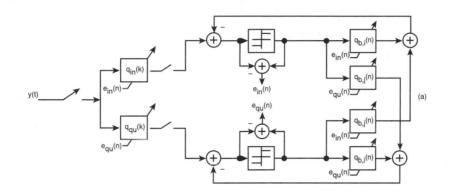

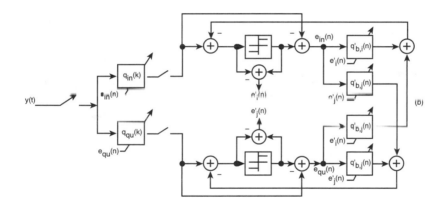

Figure 13.28 A CAP Receiver with Noise Predictive DFE

CAP Precoding Techniques

The Trellis coding does not work very well in conjunction with a DFE with long feedback filters. The DFE needs estimated signal symbols right after every decision point to drive the feedback filter. The Trellis coding, however, would not make a good decision until the probability of one possible tree is much higher than other possible alternatives. The decision needs to be made based on a past few baud intervals. Therefore, the correct decisions from a Trellis decode would be too late to be used by the feedback filter.

The Tomlinson precode approach[105] can be used to combine benefits of DFE and Trellis coding together. The idea is to move the feedback filter coefficients into the transmitter and prefilter the data symbols prior to transmission, therefore making the decision delay irrelevant. Because the modulation and the demodulation processes are transparent for the equivalent channel, the position of the feedback filter can be at either the transmitter or the receiver for a linear system.

One issue preventing the realization of this prefiltering approach is that the feedback filter used as a recursive filter in the transmitter might not be stable. Tomlinson proposed to use a modulo operation in the transmitter to stabilize the recursive feedback filter. Another modulo operation was also proposed in the receiver to recover the original data symbols. Figures 13.29 and 13.30 show a simplified DFE-based transceiver system and its Tomlinson precoding equivalent system, respectively.

Figure 13.29 A Simplified DFE System

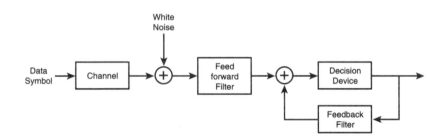

Figure 13.30 A Simplified Tomlinson Precoding System

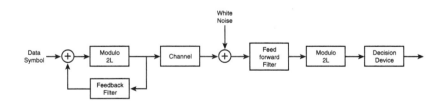

Figure 13.31 shows the transceiver structure for combining the CAP line code and the Tomlinson precoder together.

There are four modulo operations all together for both in-phase and quadrature channels. There are four feedback filters in the CAP transmitter. Filter coefficients of feedforward and feedback filters are calculated in the initialization phase. Feedback filter coefficients are transmitted from the transmitter to the receiver. At the minimum, feedforward filter coefficients need to be adaptively updated during the normal transmission phase.

Figure 13.31 CAP Transmitter with a Tomlinson Precoder

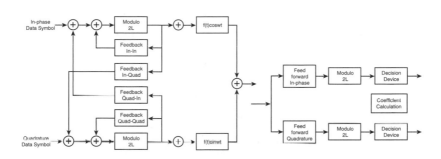

CAP Transceiver Characteristics and Timing Recovery

The CAP transceiver is derived from the traditional QAM transceiver. Transceivers at both ends of a QAM system need to be synchronized to make the channel equalizer and the rest of circuits work properly. The synchronization of a QAM system is achieved through carrier recovery and timing recovery circuits.

The carrier recovery of a QAM system is necessary for the demodulation process to generate a baseband signal and to maintain the orthogonality between in-phase and quadrature channels. In a digital implementation of a QAM system, the carrier frequency can be chosen to have a fixed relationship with the signaling baud rate. The synchronization between carrier frequency and baud rate can simplify the implementation of carrier recovery and timing recovery circuits.

For the digital implementation approach of a CAP transmitter, the center (carrier) frequency of a CAP system is always synchronized with the signaling baud rate. The orthogonality between in-phase and quadrature channels of a CAP system can be maintained through passband channel equalizers and the received signal is directly recovered by these passband equalizers. Therefore, the carrier recovery circuit is not necessary for a CAP system. A good timing recovery circuit is sufficient for a CAP receiver to synchronize with the CAP transmitter. Because CAP passband equalizers are fractionally spaced compared with the baud rate, the requirement for the accuracy of the timing phase of the timing recovery circuits can be relaxed.

Based on received signal without pilot tone, we can optimize the sampling timing phase based on the maximum likelihood estimation procedure. Through analysis, we can obtain the likelihood expression as follows:

$$l\left(\tilde{\tau}\right) \sim \sum_{n=0}^{N} q_n^{2}\left(\tilde{\tau}\right)$$

The values are as follows:

$q_n(\tilde{\tau})$ is the received signal after passing through a matched filter.

$\tilde{\tau}$ is the timing phase.

For a baseband system, the timing phase can be optimized through the practical circuit shown in Figure 13.32.

Figure 13.32 Square-Based Timing Recovery Circuit

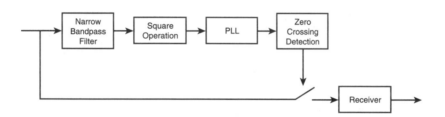

The narrow bandpass filter reduces the timing jitter, the squarer operation generates desired tones, and the Phase Locked Loop (PLL) selects the desired tone at 1/2T Hz. This circuit relies on the energy in the excess band (right outside of the signaling band) to make it work. Figure 13.33 shows a similar timing recovery circuit for a CAP transceiver.

Figure 13.33 CAP Timing Recovery Circuit

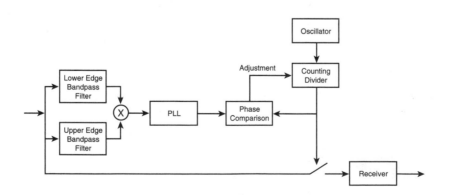

Instead of the squarer operation, the energy at the lower band edge and at the upper band edge is multiplied to generate desired tones. The timing information recovered by the PLL is compared with that of the local clock which drives the sampling circuit. If the local timing phase is tardy, the value in the counting divider is reduced to slightly increase the timing clock frequency; otherwise, the value is increased.

CAP ADSL Transceiver Parameters

Table 13.8 summarizes the transceiver parameters[106] of a CAP system. With the upstream channel transmit spectrum above 90 kHz, this CAP ADSL system can be deployed with either POTS or ISDN Basic Rate Access services. Transmit spectrum preshaping at 3 dB is implemented for this CAP ADSL also, resulting in power density levels of about –37 dBm/Hz at around 170 kHz and –40 dBm/Hz at around 410 kHz.

Table 13.8 CAP Transceiver Parameters

	Downstream	Upstream
Constellation size	64 CAP	16 CAP
Baud rate	266.667 kHz	6 kHz
Throughput	1.6 Mbps	24 kbps
Sampling rate	1.066667 MHz	
Transmit power	12.1 dBm (100 ohms)	–4.8 dBm (135 ohms)
Transmit spectrum	170 kHz–410 kHz	96 kHz–102 kHz

CAP Transmitter Filter and Equalizer Coefficients

The transmitter filters are usually designed based on the raised cosine or square root raised cosine function. The raised cosine function in the time domain is[104]

$$g(t) = \frac{\sin \pi t / T}{\pi t / T} \frac{\cos \alpha \pi t / T}{1 - (2\alpha t / T)^2}$$

The transfer function in the frequency domain is

$$G(f) = \left\{ \frac{T}{2} - \frac{T}{2} \sin \frac{\frac{T}{\pi T}}{\alpha} \left(f - \frac{1}{2T} \right) \quad \begin{array}{l} 0 \leq |f| \leq \frac{1}{2T}(1-\alpha) \\ \frac{1}{2T}(1-\alpha) < |f| \leq \frac{1}{2T}(1+\alpha) \end{array} \right.$$

The square root raised cosine function in the time domain is

$$g(t) = \frac{\sin[\pi(1-\alpha)t'] + 4\alpha t' \cos[\pi(1+\alpha)t']}{\pi t'[1-(4\alpha t')^2]}$$

The value $t' = t/T$ and its transfer function is

$$G(f) = \begin{cases} \dfrac{T}{\sqrt{2}}\sqrt{1-\sin\dfrac{\pi T}{\alpha}\left(f-\dfrac{1}{2T}\right)} & 0 \le |f| \le \dfrac{1}{2T}(1-\alpha) \\ & \dfrac{1}{2T}(1-\alpha) < |f| \le \dfrac{1}{2T}(1+\alpha) \end{cases}$$

Figure 13.34 shows the time domain raised cosine function.

Figure 13.34 Raised Cosine Function

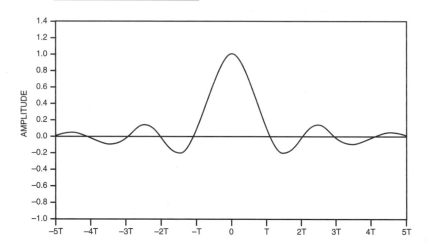

Figures 13.35 and 13.36 show the in-phase and quadrature transmitter filters, respectively, based on the raised cosine function.

Due to the dual functionality of equalization and baseband signal recovery, the linear channel equalizer still needs to cover both *pre-cursor* (before the peak) and *post-cursor* (after the peak) of the channel impulse response. Feedforward filter coefficient values are a little different compared with those of linear equalizers, due to the addition of the feedback filter. Figure 13.37 shows feedforward filter transfer functions for conventional DFE and noise predictive DFE (NPDFE). Figures 13.38 and 13.39 show corresponding real and imaginary feedback filter coefficients, respectively.

Figure 13.35   In-Phase Transmitter Filter

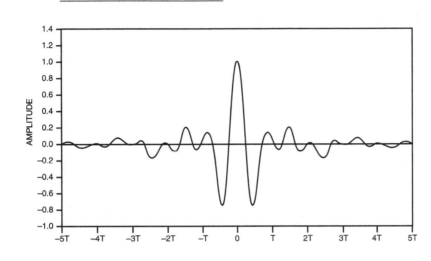

Figure 13.36   Quadrature Transmitter Filter

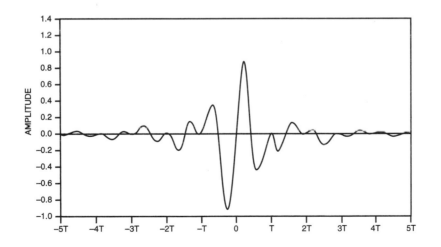

Figure 13.37 Transfer Function of Feedforward Filters

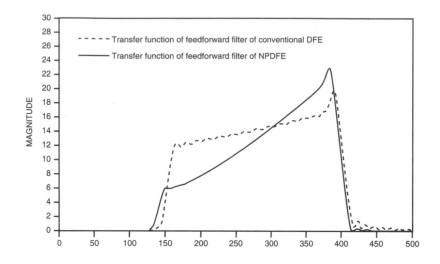

Figure 13.38 Real Feedback Filter Coefficients

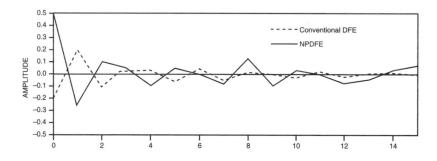

CAP Implementation on the VDT and GAFF Chipset

A CAP ADSL transceiver can be implemented with the General Adaptive FIR Filter (GAFF) chip.[107] A GAFF can provide the signal processing functions required for ADSL operations that include passband channel equalization and Tomlinson precoding. In addition to FIR operations, the GAFF chip also incorporates binary functions. Figure 13.40 depicts the system architecture using three GAFF chips in conjunction with a VDT (Viterbi Decoder, Data Interface, and Timing Recovery) chip, an analog front-end functional block, and a general-purpose DSP for an ADSL transceiver.

Figure 13.39 Imaginary Feedback Filter Coefficients

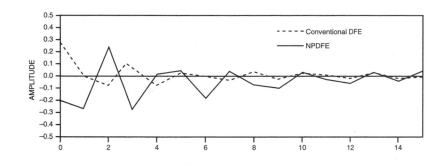

Figure 13.40 System Architecture for ADSL

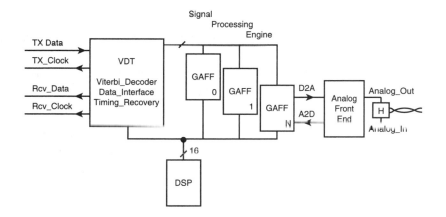

Three GAFF chips reside on a time division-multiplexed (TDM) bus, enabling the software to reconfigure system functions and interconnects. The GAFF chip is designed as a RAM-based, dual-processor engine consisting of an FIR processor and a binary processor. The FIR processor is a single-instruction, multiple-data processor. The binary processor is a simpler single controller with binary operations suitable for modem applications. Figure 13.41 shows the GAFF internal architecture.

The GAFF chip is composed of four circuit blocks:

- FIR processor (FP)

- FIR engines (FEs)

- binary processor (BP)

- external processors interface (XPI)

Figure 13.41 GAFF Functional Block Diagram

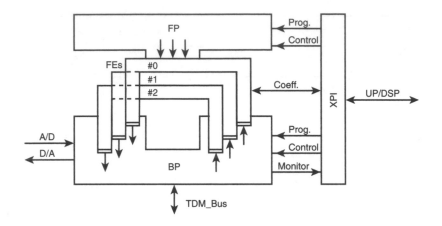

The FP contains a 128×32b program RAM that defines the signal processing operations. In addition to controlling its own program counter, the FP also controls the three FIR engines (FEs). The FP generates the coefficients and data address pointers, defines the signal-processing operations, and transfers results from the FEs to the output registers in the binary processor space.

The three FEs perform all operations in parallel, executing vector multiplications and coefficient updates concurrently. Each FE contains a multiplier, an accumulator, data multiplexors, and its own coefficients and data RAMS. The three FEs differ only by their data and coefficient values, not by the operations.

The binary processor (BP) is also fully programmable using a 128×32b program RAM that configures the FIR structure from the FEs' partial products. The BP performs basic binary operations (such as slicing) and defines system interconnectivity on the TDM Bus.

The external processor interface (XPI) supports the external bus interface to either a DSP or a microprocessor. The XPI permits code downloading, chip reconfiguration, and real-time control and monitoring.

The FP and BP are fully independent processors that are loosely coupled by input and output FIFO stages. The FP and BP program memories define the data and coefficient structures and their operations. The BP defines the input sources of the FEs, the output functions, and the error controls, while the FP defines the filter structures, the filtering operation, and the FIR outputs.

Each of the two program words is divided into subfields, enabling multiple operations (such as loop branch) to be performed in addition to control operations without any real-time penalties. Figure 13.42 shows the GAFF software model, illustrating data flow between the two processors and the external world. Many filter combinations are possible by independently programming the input content, filter structure, output functions, and error formats.

Figure 13.42   GAFF Software Model

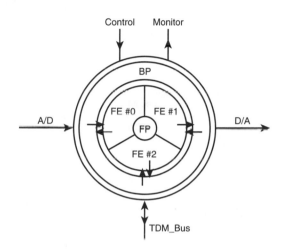

The 37.3 mm² device is packaged in an 84-pin PLCC and dissipates 750 mW at 33 MHz. The chip is designed in a 0.9 μm double-metal Complementary Metal Oxide Semiconductor (CMOS) technology, with a mixture of custom layout macros and the standard cell technology, for a total of 240 k transistors. The multiply/accumulate section is custom designed for minimum area and maximum speed. The six custom RAMs for data, coefficients, and programs are also designed using area-efficient custom-layout tools. The custom cells are integrated into a high-speed standard cell library.

At 33 MHz, the FP executes 100 M multiply/accumulate operations per second, while the BP section executes an additional 33 Mops, in addition to other program control operations that are executed in parallel. At a symbol rate of 1 Mbaud, the device can support a 99-tap transmitter filter.

13.3 Performance Objectives for Mid-CSA Test Loops

The 1.544 Mbps ADSL was proposed for resistance design loops. Test loops selected for DSL, as shown in Figures 11.30 through 11.35 in Chapter 11, "DSL (Digital Subscriber Lines)," are also used for simulation study and testing of this low throughput ADSL. CSA test loops, as shown in Figures 12.22 and 12.23 in Chapter 12, "HDSL (High-Bit-Rate Digital Subscriber Lines)," proposed for HDSL are used for simulation study and testing of high transmission throughput, 7 Mbps in the downstream ADSL. To verify the performance of the high throughput ADSL under T1 NEXT, six mid-CSA loops were also proposed.[108] Figure 13.43 shows configurations of these mid-CSA loops.

Figure 13.43 Mid-CSA Test Loops

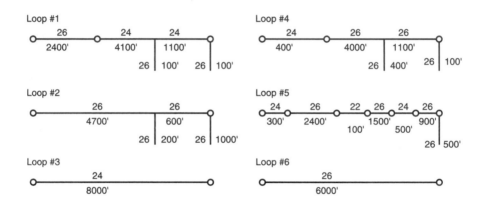

Figure 13.44 shows transfer functions of these mid-CSA test loops.

Figure 13.44 Transfer Functions of Mid-CSA Loops

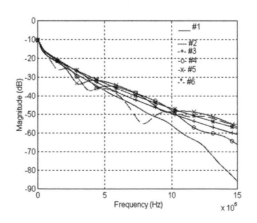

Figure 13.45 shows the transfer function of typical resistance design, CSA, and mid-CSA loops. The top mid-CSA loop has the least attenuation, and the bottom-resistance design loop has the most attenuation. For a maximum channel attenuation of 70 dB, useful channel bandwidths are 500 kHz, 1 MHz, and 1.5 MHz for resistance design, CSA, and mid-CSA loops, respectively.

Figure 13.45 Transfer Function of Resistance Design, CSA, and Mid-CSA Loops

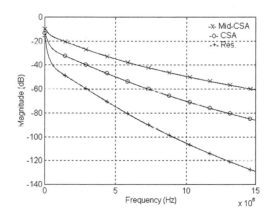

13.3.1 ADSL Noise Environments

Noise environments were proposed for simulation study and testing of resistance design, CSA, and mid-CSA loops. The parameters for the loops were as follows:

- *Resistance design loops.* 24 ISDN Basic Rate Access NEXT disturbers, 24 ADSL FEXT disturbers, and –140 dBm/Hz of white background noise (see Figure 13.46)

- *CSA loops.* 10 HDSL NEXT disturbers, 10 ADSL FEXT disturbers, and –140 dBm/Hz of white background noise (see Figure 13.47)

- *Mid-CSA loops.* 24 ISDN Basic Rate Access NEXT disturbers, 24 T1 NEXT disturbers in an adjacent binder group, and –140 dBm/Hz of white background noise (see Figure 13.48)

Figure 13.46 Noise Environment for Resistance Design Loops

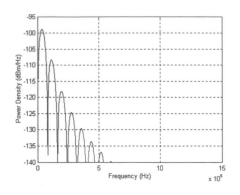

Figure 13.47 Noise Environment for CSA Loops

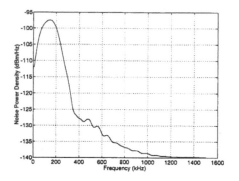

Figure 13.48 Noise Environment for Mid-CSA Loops

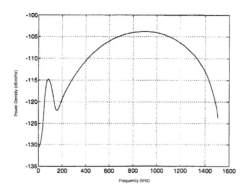

13.3.2   *DMT ADSL Transmission Throughput Estimation*

The transmission throughput of a DMT ADSL system can be estimated based on measured SNR of each subcarrier. The total transmission throughput, R, is the product of the prefix-modified baud rate and the number of bits each baud carries, as shown in the following expression:

$$R = \frac{1}{T} \sum_{i=1}^{256} \log_2 \left(1 + \frac{SNR_j}{9.55} \right)$$

The values are as follows:

$\Gamma = 9.55$ is chosen corresponding to an error rate of 10^{-7} without any coding gain.

SNR_j is the subcarrier-signal-to-noise-power ratio.

$1/T$ is the modified baud rate.

We have

$$\frac{1}{T} = \frac{2.2 \times 10^6}{512 + 32} = 4044 \, Hz$$

A flat transmit power spectrum density of –40 dBm/Hz is also assumed. The SNR_j is calculated according to transmit power density, loop attenuation, and noise power density. Figures 13.49 and 13.50 show performance margins of downstream ADSL with a transmission throughput of 1.544 Mbps for 15 resistance design DSL test loops with and without echo cancellation, respectively. The average performance difference between with and without echo cancellation is about 5 dB.

Figures 13.51 and 13.52 show performance margins of downstream ADSL with transmission throughput of 6.4 Mbps (DS2+C+BRA), 6.6 Mbps (DS2+C+H0), and 6.8 Mbps (DS2+C+H0+BRA) for eight CSA test loops with and without echo cancellation. The average performance difference between with and without echo cancellation is also about 5 dB.

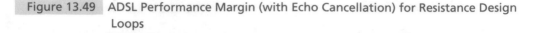

Figure 13.49 ADSL Performance Margin (with Echo Cancellation) for Resistance Design Loops

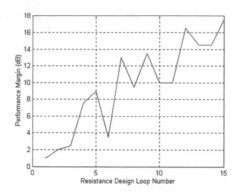

Figure 13.50 ADSL Performance Margin (without Echo Cancellation) for Resistance Design Loops

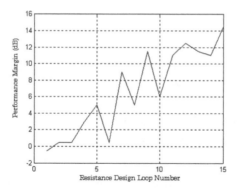

Figures 13.53 and 13.54 show performance margins of downstream ADSL with transmission throughput of 6.4 Mbps (DS2+C+BRA), 6.6 Mbps (DS2+C+H0), and 6.8 Mbps (DS2+C+H0+BRA) for six mid-CSA test loops with and without echo cancellation, respectively. The average performance difference between with and without echo cancellation again is also about 5 dB.

Figure 13.51   ADSL Performance Margin (with Echo Cancellation) for CSA Loops

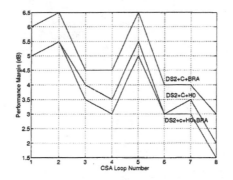

Figure 13.52   ADSL Performance Margin (without Echo Cancellation) for CSA Loops

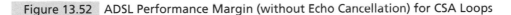

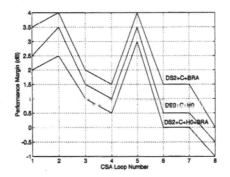

Figure 13.53   ADSL Performance Margin (with Echo Cancellation) for Mid-CSA Loops

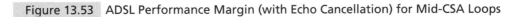

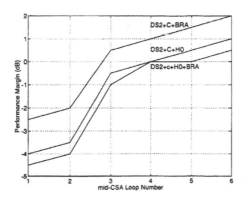

Figure 13.54 ADSL Performance Margin (without Echo Cancellation) for Mid-CSA Loops

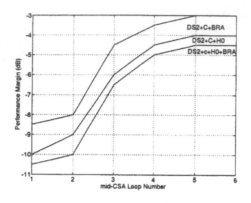

13.3.3 Estimating CAP ADSL Performance

The transmission throughput of a CAP ADSL depends on the combination of the baud rate and the constellation size. Assuming that the fractional level signaling is possible,[109] the transmission throughput can be optimized by selecting a particular baud rate and corresponding constellation size based on a target error rate performance requirement.[110] Similarly, the performance margin of CAP ADSL can also be optimized by selecting a particular baud rate and corresponding constellation size based on a target transmission throughput with a defined error rate.

The performance of a CAP ADSL can be estimated based on MMSE of a DFE assuming equalizers have sufficient number of filter coefficients. The MMSE of a DFE under the combination of FEXT and white background noise is

$$\varepsilon_{min} = \exp\left(\frac{1}{F_2 - F_1}\int_{F_1}^{F_2} \ln\left(1 + \frac{1}{8\times10^{-20}\,lf^2 + \dfrac{N}{S^2\left|H(f)\right|^2}}\right) df\right)$$

The values are as follows:

N is the background noise power.

l is the length of the loop.

$H(f)$ is the transfer function of the loop.

The integration bandwidth corresponds to the signaling baud rate—$\dfrac{1}{T} = F_2 - F_1$.

The corresponding SNR at the output of the DFE is

$$SNR = \frac{1 - \varepsilon_{\min}}{\varepsilon_{\min}} \approx \frac{1}{\varepsilon_{\min}}$$

On the other hand, the required constellation size, M, is related to the baud rate, $\dfrac{1}{T}$, and the target transmission throughput, R_b, according to

$$M = 2^{R_b T}$$

The required SNR_r for that M value under a defined error rate is

$$SNR_r = \frac{\sigma^2}{3}(M - 1) = \frac{\sigma^2}{3}\left(2^{R_b T} - 1\right)$$

The value σ^2 is related to the defined error rate. For a defined error rate of 10^{-7}, we can find the value of σ to be 5.333 according to the Gaussian distribution:

$$10^{-7} = \frac{2}{\sqrt{2\pi}} \int_{\sigma}^{\infty} e^{-\frac{x^2}{2}}\, dx$$

The performance margin is then the following:

$$SNR_m = SNR - SNR_r$$

13.4   Network and Premises Interfaces

ADSL was originally designed mainly for providing video-on-demand services. For this original application, an ATU-C accepts the 1.5 Mbps signal input and provides the low-speed control channel and the POTS channel. The POTS channel terminates on a conventional local switch. The 1.5 Mbps stream is provided by switched DS1 services. The low-speed control channel terminates on a packet handler, which in turn communicates with the DS1 switch and the Information Service Provider, as depicted in Figure 13.55.[111]

Figure 13.55 A Switch-Based Central Office ADSL Interface

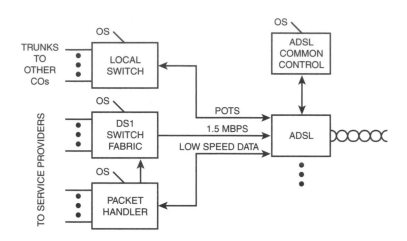

Figure 13.56 shows how the ADSL can be used with remote electronics.

Figure 13.56 A Switch-Based Remote Terminal ADSL Interface

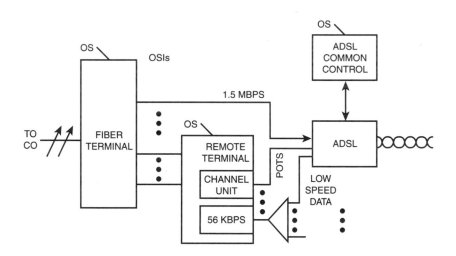

The POTS service terminates on a conventional plug-in in a digital loop carrier remote terminal. The 1.5 Mbps signal is carried over a spare DS1 channel on the fiber multiplexer that feeds the remote electronics site. The low-speed data channel terminates on a data channel unit in the remote terminal or perhaps a number of ADSL low-speed control channels are concentrated first before being transported over a 56 kbps data channel.

To enable the use of existing data protocols, it is desirable for the low speed control channel to be full duplex. At least two data formats were considered. The control channel could be implemented with an X.25 protocol, which could run at relatively low speeds, such as 9.6 kbps. The network transport is widely available for the X.25 protocol. The control channel could also be implemented through an ISDN Basic Rate D channel. The ISDN Basic Rate services are available from most Central Offices.

Figures 13.55 and 13.56 include an ADSL common controller that communicates with a number of ADSL office units. The office units in turn communicate with the remote units by way of an overhead channel. This overhead facilitates system synchronization and maintenance. Transmission performance and alarm conditions can be collected and forwarded to an operations system (OS). Eventually, many of the functions shown in Figures 13.55 and 13.56 can be integrated into one system, in which the ADSL office units become "line cards" in an advanced switch or remote terminal.

A DMT ATU-C can have an interface with up to seven different digital channels in addition to the POTS channel. This interface includes up to four asymmetrical channels, one control channel of 16 kbps or 64 kbps, one ISDN channel with 2B+D subchannels, and one H0 telephony channel that can be further divided into six B channels. Figure 13.57 depicts interfaces for a DMT ATU-C and an ATU-R. Most of these different digital channels can be handled by DS1 and ISDN interfaces for the video-on-demand and telephony services.

The low speed control channel can be either handled by the X.25 protocol or treated as a D channel. The POTS channel needs to be connected through the conventional switch. In short, the DMT ATU-C interface can be handled in a way similar to that of the 1.5 Mbps ADSL, but with a higher digital transmission throughput bandwidth.

Figure 13.57   DMT ATU-C and ATU-R Interfaces

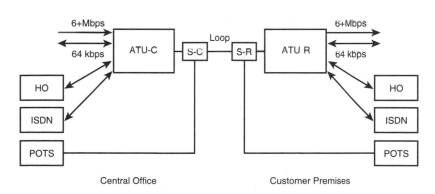

13.4.1 *Central Office Service Capabilities*

A Central Office number (the middle three digits of YYY as in a telephone number of (XXX) YYY-ZZZ) can have an average of about 5,000 subscribers. A Central Office with multiple CO numbers could have more subscribers. A Distribution Area (DA) can serve 200–600 subscribers. A Remote Terminal (RT) with Optical to Electrical (O/E) and Electrical to Optical (E/O) conversion and power supply equipment, can serve four to six DAs. In other words, an RT might need to serve about 3,000 subscribers; however, it is not likely that every subscriber will have ADSL service, especially at the early introductory stage. We call the ADSL service offering among all subscribers the *take rate* that could range from 5 to 25 percent initially.

Compared with the digitized voice service at 64 kbps, the throughput of a 1.72 Mbps ADSL, including overhead, is 26.875 times higher. The throughput of a 6.784 Mbps ADSL, also including overhead, is 106 times higher than digitized voice service. Considering a take rate of 10 percent, the required total throughput at a CO in the downstream direction will be 860 Mbps (5000×0.1×1.72) and 3.392 Gbps (5000×0.1×6.784). At an RT, the downstream will be 510 Mbps (3000×0.1×1.72) and 2.0352 Gbps (3000×0.1×6.784) for 1.72 Mbps and 6.784 Mbps ADSL systems, respectively. These calculations for the CO and RT represent a throughput upgrade of 2.6875 and 10.6 times, respectively.

On the other hand, the throughput upgrade can be much lower than the previous calculation for a CO and RT if only additional data traffic is considered, depending on delay and packet loss requirements. As a reference, the optical equipment that can be used to connect between multiple COs and between a CO and RTs have throughputs of 155.52 Mbps, OC-3, and 622.08 Mbps, OC-12, and so forth. Hence, depending on the RT size and the take rate, a number of OC-3 or OC-12 links is more than likely.

For ATM or TCP/IP-based data traffic, the dedicated digital interface might not be efficient and necessary. Therefore, all ADSL channels can be first statistically multiplexed through a Local Area Network (LAN) at the CO (see Figure 13.58) before being connected to the backbone digital network. A LAN interface is required for each ADSL transceiver. The traffic external to the LAN is connected to a public or private computer network through a router. The concentrated data traffic might or might not be connected to the computer network through a digital switch.

Because all ATU-Cs are close to each other and the LAN is only served as a traffic concentrator, the function of LAN and router can be combined to form a special-purpose ADSL ATU-C concentrator. This concentrator might evolve to a next-generation high-throughput digital switch if the ATM protocol can be implemented over the concentrator and over ADSL links.

Figure 13.58   Router and LAN Computer Connection

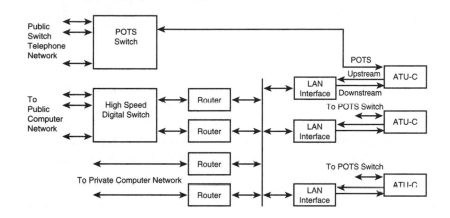

13.4.2   POTS Splitters

A POTS splitter separates the 300 Hz to 3,500 Hz voice channel from the upstream and downstream channels. In the voice passband, the POTS splitter should pass not only voice frequency signal with little distortion, but also dial tone, ringing, and on/off hook signals. For the voice frequency signal, the POTS splitter should maintain the original POTS impedance and return loss requirements. Otherwise, POTS automatic network test systems would have difficulty troubleshooting telephone subscriber loop and residential equipment problems. The POTS splitter interface also needs to pass high voltage and high current signals for ringing, on/off hook, and so forth.

The structure of a POTS splitter is similar for both ATU-C and ATU-R. A POTS splitter consists of mainly a lowpass filter for the POTS interface and a highpass filter for upstream and downstream channels. The lowpass filter removes the interference from upstream and downstream channels to the POTS channel. The POTS channel impedance, which is about 600 ohms, should not be affected by the impedance of upstream and downstream channels, which is about 100 ohms. The highpass filter removes the interference from the POTS channel to upstream and downstream channels. The harmonics of ringing and on/off hook signals should especially be prevented from entering upstream and downstream channels.

Figure 13.59 shows the circuit diagram of a POTS splitter.[112]

Figure 13.59 Circuit Diagram of a POTS Splitter

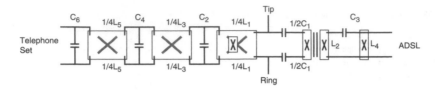

The inductors for the lowpass filter should have high Q for small signal attenuation and high current saturation levels to avoid generating harmonics under the heavy drive of high-intensity voltage or current. A stopband loss of 70 dB is required for both lowpass and highpass filters. Because of the narrow guard band, a slop of –60 dB per decade is also required. Figure 13.60 shows required lowpass and highpass frequency responses for a POTS splitter.

Figure 13.60 Desired Lowpass and Highpass Frequency Responses for a POTS Splitter

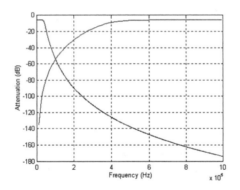

The highpass filter for ADSL is at the right side of the POTS input, and the lowpass filter for the telephone set is at the left side, as illustrated in Figure 13.59. Only POTS and telephone interfaces need balanced design. The highpass filter is a fourth-order filter with balanced input for the POTS line and unbalanced output for the ADSL transceiver. The lowpass filter is a seventh-order filter with balanced input and output ports. These filters can be first designed according to the conventional unbalanced structure.

The capacitance for the balanced part of the highpass filter is simply twice that calculated for the unbalanced structure. The inductance of the lowpass filter is a quarter of that calculated for the unbalanced structure, assuming a coupling coefficient of approximately one between two inductors sharing the same magnetic core.

The lowpass filter part of the POTS splitter is an LC ladder. Values for Ls and Cs can be calculated according to the following formula:

$$L_{2m-1} = \frac{2R_1 \sin\left(\dfrac{(4m-3)\pi}{2n}\right)}{\omega_c}$$

$$C_{2m} = \frac{2\sin\left(\dfrac{(4m-1)\pi}{2n}\right)}{R_1\omega_c}$$

For

$m=1,2,3$

$n=6$

$R_1=600$

$\omega c =2\ \pi 4$ kHz

we have

$L_1=2.06$ mH

$C_2=0.5627$ μF

$L_3=7.68$ mH

$C_4=0.768$ μF

$L_5=5.627$ mH

$C_6=0.206$ μF

These L and C values result to a Butterworth filter frequency response. A fourth-order low-pass filter can be first designed and then transformed to a highpass filter.

For

$m=1,2$

$n=4$

$R_1=100$

$\omega c =2\ \pi\ 40$ kHz

we have

$$L'_1 = 0.3045 \text{ mH}$$

$$C'_2 = 0.07352 \ \mu\text{F}$$

$$L'_3 = 0.7352 \text{ mH}$$

$$C'_4 = 0.03045 \ \mu\text{F}$$

The corresponding highpass filter component values are as follows:

$$C_1 = \frac{1}{\omega_c^3 L'_1} = 0.052 \text{ mF}$$

$$L_2 = \frac{1}{\omega_c^3 C'_2} = 0.21 \text{ mH}$$

$$C_3 = \frac{1}{\omega_c^3 L'_2} = 0.0215 \text{ mF}$$

$$L_4 = \frac{1}{\omega_c^3 C'_4} = 0.52 \text{ mH}$$

Values for Ls and Cs can also be calculated according to the following formula:

$$L_1 = \frac{2 R_1 \sin\left(\dfrac{\pi}{2n}\right)}{(\sinh a - \sinh \tilde{a})\omega_c}$$

$$L_{2m-1}C_{2m} = \frac{4 \sin \gamma_{4m-3} \sin \gamma_{4m-1}}{\omega_c^2 f_{2m-1}(\sinh a, \sinh \tilde{a})}$$

$$L_{2m+1}C_{2m} = \frac{4 \sin \gamma_{4m-1} \sin \gamma_{4m+1}}{\omega_c^2 f_{2m}(\sinh a, \sinh \tilde{a})}$$

in which

$$\gamma_m = \frac{m\pi}{2n}$$

$$\tilde{a} = \frac{1}{n} \sinh^{-1}\left(\frac{\sqrt{1 - K_n}}{\varepsilon}\right)$$

$$f_m(u,v) = u^2 + v^2 + \sin^2 \gamma_{2m} - 2uv \cos \gamma_{2m}$$

for a Chebyshev network.

13.4.3 *Application of POTS Splitter*

A POTS splitter could be included in an ATU-R, as shown in Figure 13.61.

Figure 13.61 An ATU-R with a Built-in POTS Splitter

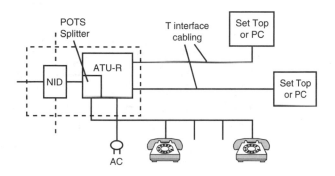

The ATU-R interfaces to the single loop pair on one side and demultiplexes POTS, control, and asymmetrical channels on the other side. The POTS channel is routed to the customer telephones, answering or facsimile machines, analog modems, and so forth, in the conventional fashion. Each asymmetrical channel should be connected to a service module.

The nature of the service module will vary from application to application. For example, the service module might include an MPEG video decoder, fast packet hardware, or CD-audio hardware. The output of the service module might be a baseband video signal, a packet protocol, or an audio signal. The low speed control channel must also be connected to all service modules. In computer-based applications, the service module functionality may reside on a card that plugs into a PC.

In Figure 13.61, NID stands for *Network Interface Device*, which is available for conventional POTS lines and is located at the phone wire entry point. Similar to the case of ISDN, ADSL T interfaces can be defined to connect an ATU-R to service modules. A POTS splitter also can be implemented external to an ATU-R (see Figure 13.62). This configuration provides the flexibility for the location of ATU-R, while avoiding the direct transmission of an ADSL signal over low-quality telephone in-house wiring. Low-quality in-house wiring with open bridge taps can easily damage the performance of an ADSL system.

Figure 13.62 An ATU-R with a Separate POTS Splitter

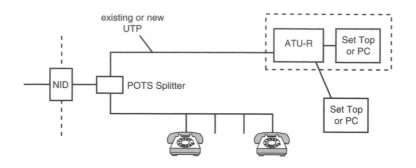

The definition of the ADSL T interface is not an easy task. While complexity is required for the acceptance of a consumer-oriented market, the ADSL T interface needs a combined transmission throughput of more than 7 Mbps with bi-directional multiple access points. For computer applications, the function of the T interface can be satisfied with a LAN, such as 10BaseT or 100BaseTX. To carry video or telephony—*isochronous traffic*—the concept of a high-throughput digital home network can be adapted to meet the demand of the ADSL T interface.

The high-throughput home network can be implemented with star topology data grade twisted-pair cable based on the transmission protocol of IEEE P1394.[113] The home network can also be shared with other network or local information resources. With a home network, a consumer does not have to struggle with deciding which terminal to be connected to which access network, as shown in Figure 13.63.

Figure 13.63 ADSL Connected to a Home Network

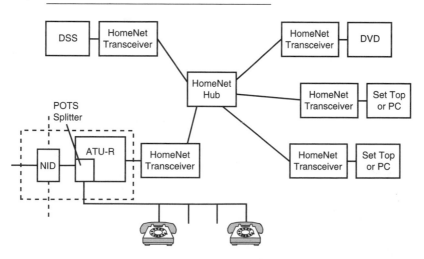

13.5 ADSL Standards (T1.413)

The main purpose of the T1.413 document is to describe interfaces of the DMT ADSL modem at the Central Office (CO) side and at the subscriber side. The extended interface covers not only pins and voltage levels, but also frame structure, coding, interleaving, channelization as well as initialization, bit loading, and online adaptation.

13.5.1 Frame Structure

The standard DMT ADSL was originally designed mainly for the video-on-demand application. It was observed that the minimum throughput for a compressed video channel is 1.544 Mbps (MPEG-I), and higher throughput (3 ~ 6 Mbps MPEG-II) might also be necessary to carry live programs. Bearing its name, ADSL mainly carries asymmetrical video-on-demand signals. For the video-on-demand application, the downstream throughput (from a CO to a subscriber) needs to be high (1.544 ~ 6.176 Mbps). Conversely, the upstream throughput requirement is to satisfy the need of control signals (16 ~ 64 kbps). For the need of high-throughput telephony applications, a symmetrical ISDN Basic Rate Access (128 kbps) channel and a symmetrical H0 (384 kbps) channel are also included.

To distinguish these channels for potential applications, a flexible frame structure with different options was defined. Due to the IFFT/FFT operation, the frame is only defined in retrieval sequence index for input/output interfaces, but has no real-time index as other systems do. For the downstream direction, a super frame is defined for every 68 IFFT/FFT operations. A synchronization frame is also created for every super frame. Therefore, there are 69 frames for every super frame. Because of the extra synchronization frame, in real time, every frame is not exactly aligned with every IFFT/FFT operation. In other words, a frame is not aligned with each IFFT/FFT operation.

In the downstream direction and for a baud rate of 4 kHz, the super frame has a time duration of 68/4000=17 milliseconds. Due to the added synchronization frame, the frame rate on the line becomes 69/68×4000. The sampling rate would have been 512×4000 Hz without cyclic prefix. With the addition of 40 prefix sampling points, the sampling rate is (512+40)×4000=2,208,000 Hz.

In practice, the prefix length is 32 and the reduction of eight sampling points every frame for 68 frames generates a synchronization frame of size 8×68=544 sampling points, which is the same size as a data frame with cyclic prefix. Therefore, we can also represent the sampling rate as (512+32)×69/68×4000=2,208,000 Hz.

Figure 13.64 shows the general structure of a frame as well as its relationship to the super frame.

Figure 13.64 DMT ADSL Frame Structure

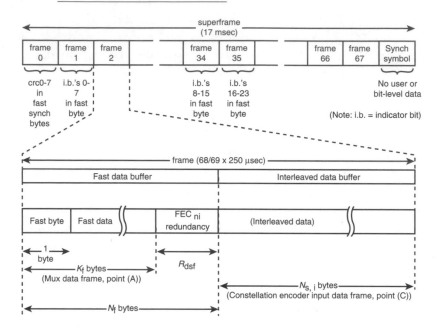

As shown in Figure 13.64, each frame consists of a fast data portion, for delay-sensitive applications, and an interleaved data portion, for video-on-demand applications. Depending on the transmission throughput, the number of data bytes for each frame can be different. On the other hand, the number of total bytes for each frame other than the synchronization frame is kept the same by inserting dummy bytes. The first byte of every frame is used for fast data, which could be for CRC bits, indication bits for OAM functions, *embedded operation channel* (eoc) bits, or synchronization control bits for fast data.

There are eight CRC bits, which are always located at the first byte of the first frame (frame 0), and 24 indicator bits, which are located at first bytes of frame 1, 34, and 35. The remaining first bytes of frames 2 to 33 and 36 to 67 are used for either eoc (embedded operation channel) or synchronization control. An eoc byte is indicated by a value 1 of bit 0. A synchronization control byte is indicated by a value 0 of bit 0. Both eoc and synchronization control bytes appear in a byte pair—an even byte followed by an odd byte.

Figure 13.65 indicates that FEC for interleaved data is appended at the end of a group of frames, and therefore the interleaved data logic frame where the channelization is defined does not share the frame boundary with that of IFFT/FFT frame. The size of the group for FEC is decided by the interleaving depth.

Figure 13.65   Frame Structure of Downstream Interleaved Data

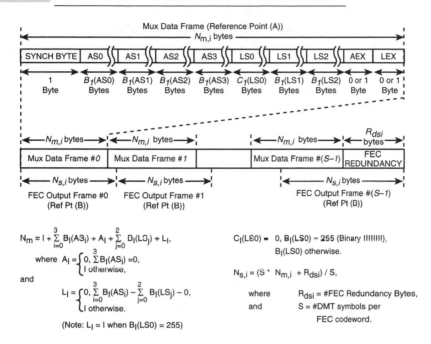

$$N_m = 1 + \sum_{i=0}^{3} B_I(AS_i) + A_I + \sum_{j=0}^{2} D_I(LS_j) + L_I,$$

$$\text{where } A_I = \begin{cases} 0, \sum B_I(AS_i) = 0, \\ I \text{ otherwise,} \end{cases}$$

and

$$L_I = \begin{cases} 0, \sum_{i=0}^{3} B_I(AS_i) - \sum_{j=0}^{2} B_I(LS_j) - 0, \\ I \text{ otherwise.} \end{cases}$$

(Note: $L_I = I$ when $B_I(LS0) = 255$)

$C_I(LS0) = 0$, $B_I(LS0) - 255$ (Binary IIIIIIII),
$B_I(LS0)$ otherwise.

$$N_{s,i} = (S * N_{m,i} + R_{dsi}) / S,$$

where R_{dsi} = #FEC Redundancy Bytes,
and S = #DMT symbols per
                FEC codeword.

For the interleaved data, the first byte is the SYNCH byte. The SYNCH byte of the first frame, frame 0, is for eight bits of CRC. The remaining SYNCH bytes are used either for synch control or aoc (ADSL overhead control). The synch control byte is valid as long as the interleave portion is occupied with data; otherwise, the aoc is presented. Both fast data and interleaved data portions can accommodate four asymmetrical and three symmetrical channels. At the end of fast data and interleaved data portions, there are stuffing AEX and LEX bytes for the synchronization control of each asymmetrical and symmetrical channel, respectively.

The channels, from AX0 through LX2, operate at rates that are multiples of the symbol rate. Therefore, the throughput of each channel might not be exactly the same as that of the backbone network. The AEX and LEX bytes regulate the minor throughput differences using the *bit stuffing technique*. That is, if the throughput of the channel is higher than that of the network, a dummy byte will be inserted/removed in the data stream. The ADSL standard also enables the deletion of a byte from the channel. The addition will match to a lower network throughput, while the deletion will match to a faster network throughput, but with the danger of losing data bytes.

For fast data buffers, the indication of which channel and the corresponding operation of bit insertion/deletion information is in the fast byte. For interleaved data buffer, the same information is in the synchronization byte. Both the fast byte and the synchronization byte offer the option of being used as an eoc frame and a ADSL overhead control channel, respectively.

ADSL can have up to four simplex channels (AS0, AS1, AS2, and AS3) that are causes of asymmetrical throughput, and three duplex channels (control channels LS0, LS1, and LS2). Depending on the class of operation—related to the transmission environment and the transceiver capacity—some of these channels can be activated in the initialization process with possibly a few different optional transmission throughputs. For an interface to the North America T digital hierarchy system, there could be four classes of channel and throughput combinations, as explained in the following list.

- *Class 1.* The maximum simplex throughput is 6.144 Mbps for up to four channels (AS0, AS1, AS2, AS3); the maximum duplex channel throughput is 640 kbps for up to two channels (LS1, LS2); and the control channel (LS0) throughput is 64 kbps.

- *Class 2.* The maximum simplex throughput is 4.608 Mbps for up to three channels (AS0, AS1, AS2); the maximum duplex channel throughput is 608 kbps for one channel (LS1 or LS2); and the control channel (LS0) throughput is 64 kbps.

- *Class 3.* The maximum simplex throughput is 3.072 Mbps for up to two channels (AS0, AS1); the maximum duplex channel throughput is 608 kbps for one channel (LS1 or LS2); and the control channel (LS0) throughput is also 64 kbps.

- *Class 4.* The simplex throughput is 1.536 Mbps for one channel (AS0); the duplex channel throughput is 160 kbps for one channel (LS1); and the control channel throughput is 16 kbps, which is not implemented in the control channel slot but through the synchronization overhead.

Multiplexing slots for both simplex and duplex channels are available in both fast and interleaved parts of every frame in a similar order, that is, starting with AS0 and followed by AS1, AS2, AS3, LS0, LS1, and LS2. The fast data buffer starts with a fast byte and ends with a few FEC redundancy bytes, as illustrated by Figure 13.66.

There also could be an AEX and/or LEX byte before FEC redundancy bytes. The interleaved data buffer starts with a synchronization byte and could end with AEX and/or LEX bytes. A group of FEC redundancy bytes for the interleaved buffer is attached at the end of the interleave frame, which has a number of frames equal to the interleaving depth.

Figure 13.66 Channelization of Downstream Fast Data

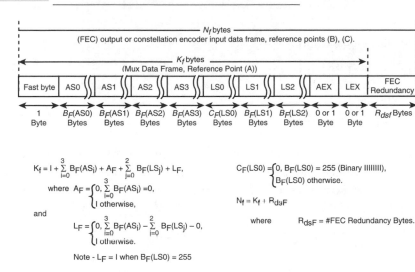

For class 1 transport, by default, both AS0 and AS1 channels should have 96 bytes each, the LS0 channel should have two bytes in the interleaved data buffer, the LS1 channel should have five bytes, and the LS2 channel should have 12 bytes in the fast data buffer.

For class 2 transport, by default, the AS0 channel should have 96 bytes, the AS1 channel should have 48 bytes, the LS0 channel should have two bytes in the interleaved data buffer, and the LS2 channel should have 12 bytes in the fast data buffer.

For class 3 transport, by default, both AS0 and AS1 channels should have 48 bytes each, the LS0 channel should have two bytes in the interleaved data buffer, and the LS2 channel should have 12 bytes in the fast data buffer.

For class 4 transport, by default, the AS0 channel should have 48 bytes in the interleaved data buffer and the LS1 channel should have five bytes in the fast data buffer.

A pair of bytes, B_I and B_F, is used for each channel, AS0 through LS2, in the third phase of the initialization process, which is discussed shortly. This byte pair indicates the number of bytes in either interleaved or fast data buffer. The allocation of each channel is exclusive, meaning that a channel can be either in fast data buffer or interleaved data buffer, but not in both. For the class 1 transport, the 16 kbps control channel can be either in interleaved or fast data buffer by designating either B_I=255 and B_F=0 or B_I=0 and B_F=255. For the default class 1 transport, we have the following byte pairs:

- $B_I(\text{AX0})=60$ and $B_F(\text{AX0})=00$

- $B_I(\text{AX1})=60$ and $B_F(\text{AX1})=00$

- $B_I(\text{AX2})=00$ and $B_F(\text{AX2})=00$

- $B_I(\text{AX3})=00$ and $B_F(\text{AX3})=00$

- $B_I(\text{LX0})=02$ and $B_F(\text{LX0})=00$

- $B_I(\text{LX1})=00$ and $B_F(\text{LX1})=05$

- $B_I(\text{LX2})=00$ and $B_F(\text{LX0})=0C$

In the upstream direction, there are no simplex channels and no AEX bytes. There could be a maximum of three channels and, therefore, three pairs of B_F and B_I bytes. Otherwise, the upstream super frame structure is similar to that of downstream, as illustrated in Figure 13.67.

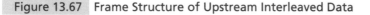

Figure 13.67 Frame Structure of Upstream Interleaved Data

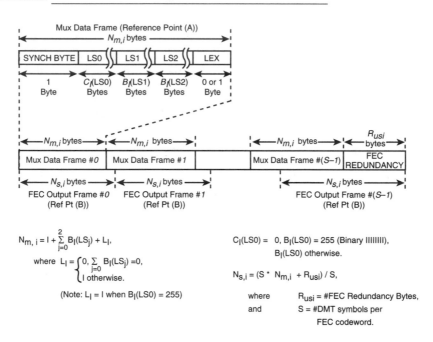

Figure 13.68 shows the channelization of upstream fast data. Similar to the downstream, the upstream fast data buffer starts with a fast byte and ends with a few FEC redundancy bytes.

Figure 13.68   Channelization of Upstream Fast Data

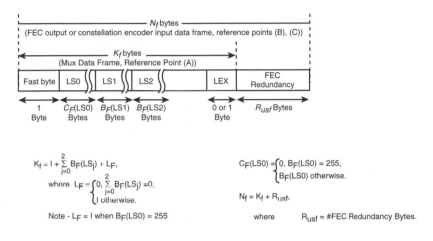

Although the upstream data baud rate is the same as that of the downstream data baud rate, the IFFT/FFT size is 64 and the sampling rate is correspondingly lower. In addition, due to the added synchronization frame, the frame rate on the line is 69/68×4000. The sampling rate would have been 64×4000 Hz without cyclic prefix. With the addition of five prefix sampling points, the sampling rate is (64+5)×4000=276,000 Hz. In practice, the prefix length is four and the reduction of one sampling point every frame for 68 frames generates a synchronization frame of size 68 sampling points, which is the same size as a data frame with cyclic prefix. Therefore, we can also represent the sampling rate as (64+4)×69/68×4000=276,000 Hz.

13.5.2   Interleaving

ADSL interleaving depths are 16, 32, and 64 FEC codewords for transport class 4, class 3, and classes 2 and 1, respectively. We also have the FEC message word size of 208, 212, 158, and 210 for transport class 4, class 3, class 2, and class 1, respectively. Therefore, the interleaving depths can also be described as follows:

- Class 4: 16×208=3,328 bytes

- Class 3: 32×212=6,784 bytes

- Class 2: 64×158=10,112 bytes

- Class 1: 64×210=13,448 bytes.

The interleaving can be implemented in a circular shift register or a dual port memory. For the shift register implementation, the first byte of every codeword should stay where it is and the rest bytes should be delayed by $(i-1) \times (N-1)$ bytes, in which i is the position of each byte, and N is the interleaving depth. For an interleaving depth of 64, the first byte of every codeword should have no delay, the second byte should be delayed by 63 bytes, the third byte should be delayed by 126 bytes, and so on.

13.5.3 Reed-Solomon Coding

The forward error correction (FEC) coding processes, using Reed-Solomon code, can be applied for both fast data and interleaved data. For fast data, there are four FEC redundancy bytes corresponding to 5 or 17 fast data bytes. For interleaved data, there could be 16 FEC redundancy bytes for 194 interleaved data bytes, 12 FEC redundancy bytes for 146 interleaved data bytes, 16 FEC redundancy bytes for 196 interleaved data bytes, or 16 FEC redundancy bytes for 192 interleaved data bytes. The code is based on the GF(256) Galois field arithmetic.

13.5.4 Bit Encoding

Each subchannel is designed for a maximum number of 15 bits corresponding to a 32,768 QAM constellation whenever the subchannel SNR permits. For an even number of bits, the constellation is square. Constellations are defined for n=2, 3 bits and a recursive procedure is also designed for n>3. The optional Wei's 16-state four-dimensional Trellis code can be used to improve the transmission performance.

Clipping, due to the limited precision of ADC and DAC, is most likely to cause errors on those tones that, in anticipation of higher received SNRs, have been assigned the largest number of bits (and therefore have the densest constellations). These occasional errors can be reliably corrected by the FEC coding if the tones with the largest number of bits have been assigned to the interleave buffer.

The *tone-ordered* encoding assigns the first B_F bytes from the symbol buffer to the tones with the smallest number of bits assigned to them, and the remaining B_I bytes to the remaining tones. The number of bits allowed for each tone information is used to construct a bit/tone order table. We round all tones with 0 bit allowed at the beginning of the order table, with 1 bit allowed next, and so on.

Data bytes from the DMT symbol buffer are extracted according to the ordered bit/tone allocation table by least significant bit first. The Trellis coding is based on a pair of adjacent tones, according to the ordered bit/tone table. The Trellis coding process generates one additional bit per pair of tones. Because the bit/tone parameter is pre-calculated, one fewer bit is extracted to make room for the extra coding bit. Figure 13.69 illustrates the tone ordering.

Figure 13.69 Tone Ordering

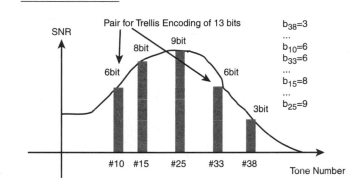

Bits extracted from the DMT symbol buffer are labeled as u_1, u_2,...u_{z-1}, u_z, and are encoded into w_0, w_1,...w_{y-1}, v_0, v_1,...v_{z-y}, for which $z=x+y-1$. x is the number of bits for one tone of the pair, and y is the number of bits for the other tone of the pair. We have $x+y-1$ bits coming into the encoder and $x+y$ bits going out from the encoder. The relationships between u_0, u_1, u_2, u_3, and w_0, w_1, v_0, v_1, are defined as

$$v_1 = u_1 \oplus u_3$$
$$v_0 = u_3$$
$$w_1 = u_0 \oplus u_1 \oplus u_2 \oplus u_3$$
$$w_0 = u_2 \oplus u_3$$

Figure 13.70 illustrates the DMT Trellis encoder.

For the Trellis coding, a minimum of two bits is used for each tone. For a pair of two tones, we have a minimum of four bits describing a four-dimensional space, which means there is only one position identified within that four-dimensional space by a group of four bits.

A two-dimensional Trellis encoder can be used to divide a two-dimensional space into four subsets. Within each subset, the space between each point is sufficient for the detection under a specific SNR. The function of the convolution encoder is such that the transition path of a signal sequence is made very distinctive from other possibilities due to possible misdetection of a particular signal point. By the same principle, ADSL uses a four-dimensional Trellis encoder to divide a four-dimensional space into eight subsets.

Figure 13.70 Trellis Encoding

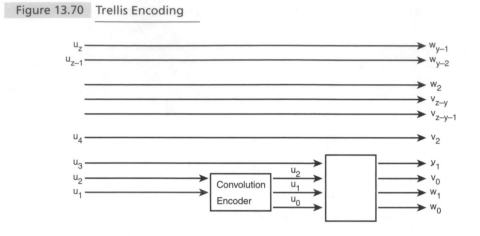

Each subcarrier can have its unique constellation depending on the SNR of that subcarrier. In general, a constellation with an even number of bits is square, and a constellation with an odd number of bits is almost square, but with corner points missing.

A minimum square constellation for even bits can be described with four numbers: 0, 1, 2, and 3. A square constellation with more than two bits can be generated recursively by replacing each label n by the 2×2 block of labels

$$4n+1 \qquad 4n+3$$
$$4n \qquad\quad 4n+2$$

Figure 13.71 illustrates an even bits constellation.

Figure 13.71 Even Bits Constellation

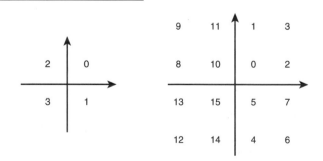

We can also describe a constellation by using b bits in digital or binary format. For $b=2$, we have 4QAM, for $b=4$, we have 16QAM, and so on. Coordinates of constellation points are $(v_{b-1}, v_{b-3}, \ldots v_1, 1)$ and $(v_{b-2}, v_{b-4}, \ldots v_0, 1)$ in binary format, for which v_{b-1} and v_{b-2} are sign bits with 1 for minus sign, and v_i can be either 0 or 1.

If b is odd and greater than 3, the 2 MSBs of X and the 2 MSBs of Y are determined by the 5 MSBs of b bits. Let $c=(b+1)/2$, the X and Y have the twos-complement binary representations $(X_c, X_{c-1}, v_{b-4}, v_{b-6}, \ldots v_3, v_1, 1)$ and $(Y_c, Y_{c-1}, v_{b-5}, v_{b-7}, v_{b-9}, \ldots v_2, v_0, 1)$ where Xc and Yc are the sign bits of X and Y, respectively. The same procedure can be used to construct the larger odd-bit constellation recursively. Figure 13.72 illustrates an odd bits constellation.

Figure 13.72   Odd Bits Constellation

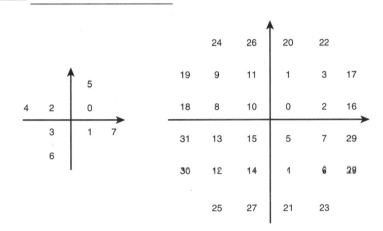

Because of the cyclic prefix, the frequency spacing between adjacent subcarriers is 4.3125 kHz instead of 4 kHz. The cyclic prefix has 32 sample points compared with the IFFT size of 512. Carrier #64, at 276 kHz, is a pilot tone for timing recovery purposes. The tone is generated by sending (0,0) to the carrier #64 of a constant magnitude. The carrier #256 at the Nyquist frequency is not used for the data transmission purpose. The magnitude of subcarrier from #51 to #256 can be uniformly raised by either 3 or 6 dB to combat T1 Near End Crosstalk (NEXT). A fine gain adjustment of -1.5 to $+1.5$ dB can also be used to fit the SNR of each subcarrier while keeping the overall transmit power level constant.

13.5.5   Scramblers

There are separate scramblers for fast data and interleaved data. The separate scramblers use the same algorithm. The operation of the scrambler can be described as

$$d_n' = d \oplus d_{n-18}' \oplus d_{n-23}'$$

The values are as follows:

d_n is the nth output from the fast or interleaved buffer.

d_n' is the nth output from the corresponding scrambler.

Figure 13.73 shows the structure of the scrambler used by the DMT ADSL.

Figure 13.73   Scrambler Structure

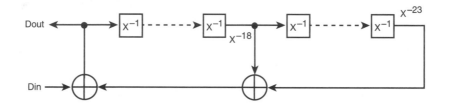

These scramblers shall be applied to the serial data stream without reference to any framing or symbol synchronization. The same expression is applied for both downstream and upstream directions.

13.5.6   Initialization

The whole initialization process takes about 24,000 symbols or, equivalently, six seconds of real-time. The initialization process has four phases:

1. *Activation and acknowledgment (384 symbols).* ATU-C and ATU-R detect each other and exchange information about timing and pilot tone options.

2. *Transceiver training (7,808 symbols).* Automatic gain adjustment, echo canceller, and channel equalizer training are performed.

3. *Channel analysis (18,186 symbols).* Rate options are indicated, and subchannel SNR analysis is performed.

4. *Exchange (about 200 symbols).* Exchange of information about loop attenuation, performance margin, and number of bits supported takes place. Bit loading selections are confirmed.

Activation and Acknowledgement Phase

Figure 13.74 illustrates phase one of initialization: activation and acknowledgment.

Figure 13.74 Activation and Acknowledgment Phase

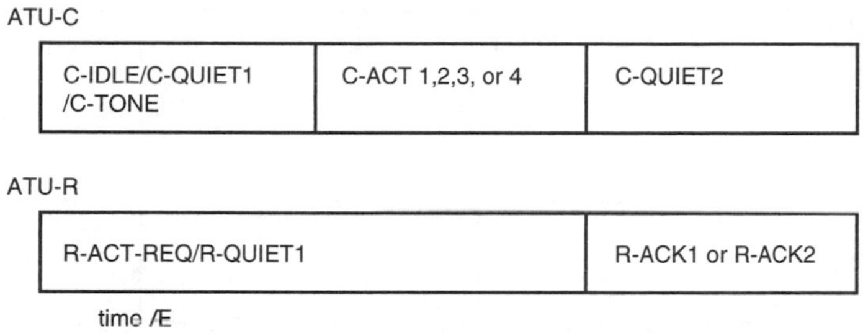

ATU-C

C-IDLE/C-QUIET1 /C-TONE	C-ACT 1,2,3, or 4	C-QUIET2

ATU-R

R-ACT-REQ/R-QUIET1	R-ACK1 or R-ACK2

time /E

R-ACT-REQ is a single sinusoid with a frequency of 34.5 kHz corresponding to upstream tone #8. The tone should be transmitted for 1024 symbols.

C-ACT1 is a single sinusoid with a frequency of 207 kHz corresponding to downstream tone #48. C-ACT2 is a single sinusoid with a frequency of 189.75 kHz corresponding to downstream tone #44. C-ACT3 is a single sinusoid with a frequency of 224.25 kHz corresponding to downstream tone #52. C-ACT4 is a single sinusoid with a frequency of 258.75 kHz corresponding to downstream tone #60. These C-ACTs should last for 128 symbols without a cyclic prefix.

R-ACK1 is a single sinusoid with a frequency of 43.125 kHz corresponding to upstream tone #10. R-ACK2 is a single sinusoid with a frequency of 34.5 kHz corresponding to upstream tone #12. R-ACK3 is a single sinusoid with a frequency of 60.375 kHz corresponding to upstream tone #14. R-ACK3 is still reserved for future initialization options. R-ACK should last 128 symbols.

Transceiver Training Phase

Figure 13.75 illustrates phase two of initialization: transceiver training.

C-REVEILLE is a sinusoid with a frequency of 241.5 kHz corresponding to downstream tone #56. C-REVEILLE lasts 128 symbols. The R-REVERB1 uses the same pseudo random sequence as that used for upstream synchronization symbol, but without cyclic prefix. The pseudo random sequence is repeated 64 times for a duration of 4096 symbols.

C-PILOT1 or C-PILOT2 is a sinusoid with a frequency of 276 kHz corresponding to downstream tone #64. C-PILOT1 or C-PILOT2 lasts at least 512 symbols. The C-REVERB1 uses the same pseudo random sequence as that used for downstream synchronization symbol but without cyclic prefix. The C-REVERB1 allows the ATU-R to adjust its gain control.

Figure 13.75 Transceiver Training Phase

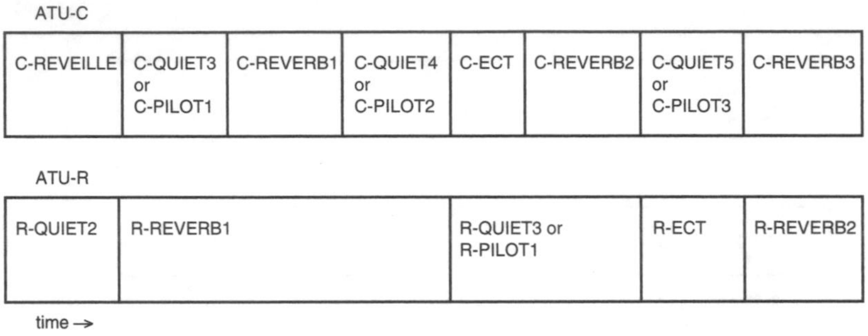

ATU-C

C-REVEILLE	C-QUIET3 or C-PILOT1	C-REVERB1	C-QUIET4 or C-PILOT2	C-ECT	C-REVERB2	C-QUIET5 or C-PILOT3	C-REVERB3

ATU-R

R-QUIET2	R-REVERB1		R-QUIET3 or R-PILOT1	R-ECT	R-REVERB2

time →

R-PILOT1 is a sinusoid with a frequency of 69 kHz corresponding to upstream tone #16. The R-PILOT1 should last 2048 symbols. C-ECT is a vendor-defined signal that is used by the echo canceller at ATU-C. The duration for C-ECT is 512 symbols. C-REVERB2 allows the ATU-R to perform synchronization and to train its equalizer. C-REVERB2 has the same signal format as C-REVERB1, but lasts for 1536 symbols.

C-PILOT3 is the same as C-PILOT1. C-REVERB3 is the same as C-REVERB2. C-REVERB3 allows the ATU-R to perform or maintain synchronization and to further train its equalizer. R-ECT is also a vendor-defined signal for training the echo canceller at ATU-R. R-ECT also has a duration of 512 symbols. R-REVERB2 is used by ATU-C to perform timing recovery and equalizer training. R-REVERB2 is the same as R-REVERB1, but lasts only 1024 symbols.

Channel Analysis Phase

Figure 13.76 illustrates phase three of initialization: channel analysis.

Figure 13.76 Channel Analysis Phase

ATU-C

C-SEGUE1	C-RATES1, C-CRC1, C-MSGS1, and C-CRC2	C-MEDLEY	C-REVERB4

ATU-R

R-SEGUE1	R-REVERB3	R-SEGUE2	R-RATES1, R-CRC1, R-MSGS1, and R-CRC2	R-MEDLEY	R-REVERB4

time →

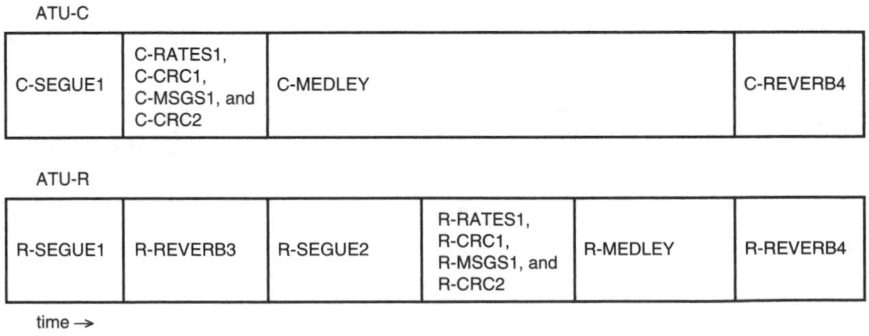

C-SEGUE1 is generated from a tone-by-tone 180 degree phase reversal of C-REVERB1. R-SEGUE1 is also generated from a tone-by-tone 180 degree reversal of R-REVERB1. C-RATES is the first ATU-C signal for which a cyclic prefix is used. The purpose of C-RATES1 is to transmit four options for data rates and formats to the ATU-R. The duration of C-RATES1 is 992 symbols. C-CRC1 is a cyclic redundancy code for the detection of errors in the reception of C-RATES1. The duration of C-CRC1 is 16 symbols.

C-MSGS1 transmits a 48-bit message signal to ATU-R. This message includes vendor identification, ATU-C transmit power level used, Trellis code option, echo cancellation option, and so on. The duration of C-MSGS1 is 48 symbols. C-CRC2 is a 16-bit cyclic redundancy code for the detection of errors in the reception of C-MSGS1. C-CRC2 also has a duration of 16 symbols. R-REVERB3 is similar to R-REVERB1, but with the addition of cyclic prefix. The duration of R-REVERB3 can have a maximum of 4000 symbols. R-REVERB3 should last 20 symbols longer than the C-CRC2.

C-MEDLEY is used by ATU-R for estimation of downstream SNR. C-MEDLEY uses the same pseudo random sequence as that used by C-REVERB1 except no 1s are filled at every 512 positions. Therefore, each subchannel sees a different signal from one symbol period to the next symbol period. C-MEDLEY lasts for 16,384 symbols. R-SEGUE2 is the same signal as R-SEGUE1 for 10 symbol periods.

Exchange Phase

Figure 13.77 illustrates phase four of initialization: exchange.

R-SEGUE3 is the same as R-SEGUE1. The duration of R-SEGUE3 is 10 symbol periods. R-MSGS2 transmits a 32-bit message signal to the ATU-C during a four symbol period. Two bits are encoded onto each of the sub-carriers numbered 6 through 9 using the 4QAM constellation. This message includes the total number of bits per symbol supported, the estimated upstream loop attenuation, and the performance margin with the selected rate option. R-CRC3 is a cyclic redundancy code for the detection of errors in the reception of R-MSGS2 by the ATU-C. R-CRC3 lasts two symbol periods.

R-RATES2 is the reply to C-RATES1, based on the results of the downstream channel analysis. The ATU-R sends back only the option number of the highest data rate that can be supported based on the measured SNR of the downstream channel. A total of eight bits are used for R-RATES2 in one symbol period. R-CRC4 is a cyclic redundancy code for the detection of errors in the reception of R-RATES2 at the ATU-C. R-CRC4 also lasts two symbol periods.

Figure 13.77 Exchange Phase

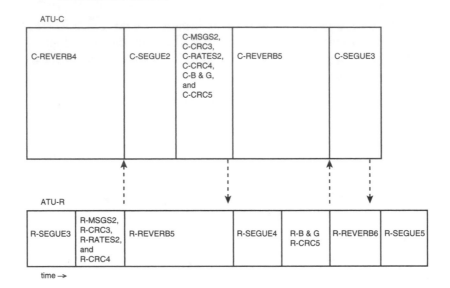

C-MSGS2 transmits a 32-bit message to the ATU-R. This message includes the total number of bits per symbol supported, the estimated upstream loop attenuation, and the performance margin with selected rate option. The C-MSGS2 lasts four symbol periods. C-CRC3 is a cyclic redundancy code for the detection of errors in the reception of C-MSGS2 for the ATU-R. The C-CRC3 lasts two symbol periods. C-RATES2 is the reply to R-RATES1.

C-RATES2 combines the downstream rate information contained in R-RATES2 with the option number of the highest upstream data rate that can be supported based on the measured SNR of the upstream channel. It thus transmits the final decision on the rates that will be used in both directions. It lasts one symbol period. C-CRC4 is the cyclic redundancy code for the detection of errors in the reception of C-RATES2 at the ATU-R. C-B&G transmits the bits and gains that are to be used on the upstream carriers to the ATU-R. A total of 62 bytes of bits and gains information is transmitted during 62 symbol periods. C-CRC5 is a cyclic redundancy code for the detection of errors in the reception of C-B&G at the ATU-R.

C-REVERB5 is the same as C-REVERB4. The ATU-C should transmit C-REVERB5 until it has received, checked the reliability of, and established the downstream bits and gain information contained in R-B&G. The purpose of R-B&G is to transmit the bits and gains information to be used on the downstream sub-carriers to the ATU-C. A total of 510 bytes of bits and gains information is transmitted during 510 symbol periods. R-CRC5 is a cyclic redundancy code for the detection of errors in the reception of R-B&G at the ATU-C.

R-REVERB6 is the same as R-REVERB3. The ATU-R transmits R-REVERB6 until it detects all ten symbols of C-SEGUE3. The maximum duration for R-REVERB6 is 4000 symbols. The ATU-C switches from sending C-REVERB5 to sending C-SEGUE3 after receiving, checking the reliability of, and establishing the downstream bits and gains information contained in R-B&G. C-SEGUE3 notifies the ATU-R that the ATU-C is about to enter the steady-state state C-SHOWTIME. The signal of C-SEGUE3 is the same as C-SEGUE1. The duration of C-SEGUE3 is 10 symbol periods. The ATU-R switches from sending R-REVERB6 to sending R-SEGUE5 after detecting 10 symbols of C-SEGUE3. The purpose of R-SEGUE5 is to notify the ATU-C that the ATU-R is about to enter the steady-state state of R-SHOWTIME. R-SEGUE5 lasts 10 symbol periods.

End Notes

1. D. L. Waring, "The Asymmetrical Digital Subscriber Line (ADSL): A New Transport Technology for Delivering Wideband Capacities to the Residence," *Proc. IEEE GLOBE-COM '91*: 1979–1986.

2. J. L. Lechleider, "Asymmetrical Digital Subscriber Lines," *Bellcore Internal Technical Memorandum* (September 4, 1989).

3. E. E. Manchester and L. D. Hofer, "T1 Standards Project Proposal for an Asymmetrical Digital Subscriber Line (ADSL)," T1E1.4/91-079 (May 13, 1991).

4. K. Sistanizadeh, "Proposed Spectrum Management Guide Lines for ADSL Deployment Using Single-Tone QAM," *Bellcore T1E1 Contribution*, T1E1.4/91-121 (August 1991).

5. K. Sistanizadeh, "Spectral Compatibility of Qam ADSl with Basic Rate DSL," *Bellcore T1E1 Contribution*, T1E1.4/91-118 (August 1991).

6. K. Sistanizadeh, "Proposed Canonical Loops for ADSL and Their Loss Characteristics," *Bellcore T1E1 Contribution*, T1E1.4/91-116 (August 1991).

7. K. J. Kerpez, "The Error Rate of ADSL in the Presence of Impulse Noise," *Bellcore T1E1 Contribution*, T1E1.4/91-122 (August 1991).

8. J. Cioffi and K. Maxwell, "A Comparison of Multi-Carrier and Single-Carrier Modulation for ADSL," *Amati T1E1 Contribution*, T1E1.4/91-123 (August 1991).

9. J. M. Cioffi, "A Multicarrier Primer," *Stanford University/Amati T1E1 Contribution*, T1E1.4/91-157 (November 1991).

10. J. Cioffi, P. Chow, and R. K. Maxwell, "Range Limits for Multicarrier DSL Systems," *Stanford University/Amati T1E1 Contribution*, T1E1.4/158 (November 1991).

11. P. S. Chow, J. Cioffi, and R. K. Maxwell, "Performance of Multicarrier with DSL Impulse Noise," *Stanford University/Amati T1E1 Contribution*, T1E1.4/158 (November 1991).

12. K. J. Kerpez, "A Model for the Probability Distribution of the Length of Burst Errors Caused by Impulse Noise," *Bellcore T1E1 Contribution*, T1E1.4/91-165 (November 1991).

13. K. J. Kerpez, "Forward Error Correction Codes for ADSL," *Bellcore T1E1 Contribution*, T1E1.4/91-166 (November 1991).

14. E. Arnon and E. J. Weldon, "Error Correction Codes in ADSL," *Northern Telecom T1E1 Contribution*, T1E1.4/91-179 (November 1991).

15. W. Y. Chen, "An ADSL Control Channel Architecture," *Bellcore T1E1 Contribution*, T1E1.4/91-164 (November 1991).

16. P. T. Tong, J. T. Aslanis, and J. M. Cioffi, "A Trellis-Code Proposal for ADSL Line Signals," *Amati T1E1 Contribution*, T1E1.4/91-176 (August 1992).

17. W. Y. Chen, "Carrierless Generation and Reception of Passband Signals for ADSL," *Bellcore T1E1 Contribution*, T1E1.4/92-024 (February 1992).

18. K. Sistanizadeh, "Discrete Multi-Tone Signaling (DMT) and Single-Tone Quadrature Amplitude Modulation (QAM) Performance for ADSL," *Bellcore T1E1 Contribution*, T1E1.4/92-026 (February 1992).

19. J. M. Cioffi, P. S. Chow, and R. K. Maxwell, "Multicarrier Range and Performance for ADSL-I (1.6 Mbps) and ADSL-II (4 Mbps)," *Amati T1E1 Contribution*, T1E1.4/92-007 (February 1992).

20. L. Ebringer, "Spectral Compatibility of QAM ADSL with HDSL and Basic Rate DSL," *Cambridge University T1E1 Contribution*, T1E1.4/92-027 (February 1992).

21. B. Daneshrad and H. Samueli, "Performance Analysis of a QAM Adaptive Receiver for 1.6 Mbps Digital Subscriber Line Transmission," *UCLA T1E1 Contribution*, T1E1.4/92-037 (February 1992).

22. M. Sorbara, "System Definition for ADSL," *AT&T T1E1 Contribution*, T1E1.4/92-066 (May 1992).

23. J. M. Cioffi and R. K. Maxwell, "A Programmable Protocol for ADSL Transceivers," *Amati T1E1 Contribution*, T1E1.4/92-076 (May 1992).

24. R.C. McConnell, "ADSL, ADSLII, and ADSLIII: Interfaces & Example Functional Architectures," *Bellcore T1E1 Contribution,* T1E1.4/92-083 (May 1992).

25. K. Swaminathan and M. R. Brown, "ADSL Operations Issues and Discussion Questions," *Bellcore T1E1 Contribution,* T1E1.4/92-084 (May 1992).

26. R.C. McConnell, "ADSL Overhead Function Bandwidth Allocations and Example Binary Equivalent Line Rates," *Bellcore T1E1 Contribution,* T1E1.4/92-085 (May 1992).

27. M. Sorbara, "ADSL Frame Format," *AT&T T1E1 Contribution,* T1E1.4/92-092 (May 1992).

28. K. R. Maxwell, "ADSL Service Options," *T1E1 Contribution,* T1E1.4/92-104 (May 1992).

29. K. Sistanizadeh, "A 16-QAM 16 kb/s Reverse ADSL Control Channel Spectrum Allocation and Performance," *Bellcore T1E1 Contribution,* T1E1.4/92-077 (May 1992).

30. K. Sistanizadeh, "Spectral Compatibility of a 16/64 QAM ADSL with Basic Rate DSL-Induced NEXT and AWGN," *Bellcore T1E1 Contribution,* T1E1.4/92-079 (May 1992).

31. M. Hoque, "Electromagnetic Interference Performance of QAM ADSL," *Bellcore T1E1 Contribution,* T1E1.4/92-080 (May 1992).

32. L. Baker, "Intra System Impulse Noise in ADSL/POTS System," *R-TEC T1E1 Contribution,* T1E1.4/92-070 (May 1992).

33. K. Sistanizadeh, "A Test Plan Proposal for Spectral Compatibility Evaluation of ADSL Transceiver Prototypes," *Bellcore T1E1 Contribution,* T1E1.4/92-081 (May 1992).

34. W. Y. Chen, "A Calculation of the Required A/D Precision for ADSL," *Bellcore T1E1 Contribution,* T1E1.4/92-082 (May 1992).

35. A. Hollbach, "Application and Service Drivers for an ADSL Standards Project in T1E1," *NTI T1E1 Contribution,* T1E1.4/92-107 (May 1992).

36. C. Valenti, "Standards Project Proposal: Interfaces Relating to Carrier to Customer Connection of Asymmetric Digital Subscriber Line (ADSL) Equipment," *Bellcore T1E1 Contribution,* T1E1.4/92-086 (May 1992).

37. K. J. Kerpez, "The Range of Baseband ADSLs as a Function of Nit Rate," *Bellcore T1E1 Contribution,* T1E1.4/91- (August 1991).

38. W. Y. Chen, "Asymmetrical Echo Cancellation for a Baseband ADSL," *Bellcore T1E1 Contribution,* T1E1.4/92-156 (August 1992).

39. J. Lechleider, "Impulse Noise Cancellation for ADSL," *Bellcore T1E1 Contribution,* T1E1.4/92-154 (August 1992).

40. W. Y. Chen, G. H. Im, and J. J. Werner, "Design of Digital Carrierless AM/PM Transceivers," *AT&T and Bellcore T1E1 Contribution,* T1E1.4/92-149 (August 1992).

41. H. Samueli, R. Joshi, and B. Daneshrad, "VLSI Complexity Comparison of a QAM vs. CAP ADSL Transceiver," *UCLA T1E1 Contribution,* T1E1.4/92-144 (August 1992).

42. C. Valenti, "Standards Project Proposal: Interfaces Relating to Carrier to Customer Connection of ADSL Equipment," *Bellcore T1E1 Contribution,* T1E1.4/92-086R2 (August 1992).

43. J. M. Cioffi, J. T. Aslanis, and J. A. C. Bingham, "A DMT Proposal for ADSL Transceiver Interfaces," *Amati T1E1 Contribution,* T1E1.4/92-174 (August 1992).

44. K. T. Foster and J. W. Cook, "A Symbolic Pulse for Impulsive Noise Testing," *BTL T1E1 Contribution,* T1E1.4/92-143 (August 1992).

45. B. A. Blake, "Generating Crosstalk Signals for Testing ADSL Systems," *Bellcore T1E1 Contribution,* T1E1.4/92-148 (August 1992).

46. D. L. Waring and K. Sistanizadeh, "Suggested Plan to Access and Select ADSL Transmission Schemes for Further Study," *Bellcore T1E1 Contribution,* T1E1.4/92-147 (August 1992).

47. E. Arnon and M. Elder, "ADSL, HDSL, and BRA Powers and Spectrum Compatibility," *NTI T1E1 Contribution,* T1E1.4/92-169 (August 1992).

48. E. Arnon and M. Elder, "BRA-ISDN and ADSL Signals on the Same Loop," *NTI T1E1 Contribution,* T1E1.4/92-170 (August 1992).

49. J. T. Aslanis, N. Al-Dhahir, and J. A. C. Bingham, "Performance of the Proposed DMT Line Code for ADSL with Embedded ISDN," *Amati T1E1 Contribution,* T1E1.4/92-178 (August 1992).

50. K. J. Kerpez, "Coding for ADSL," *Bellcore T1E1 Contribution,* T1E1.4/92-153 (August 1992).

51. P. T. Tong, J. T. Aslani, and J. M. Cioffi, "A Trellis-Code Proposal for ADSL Line Signals," *Amati T1E1 Contribution,* T1E1.4/92-176 (August 1992).

52. H. L. Lou, P. T. Tong, and J. M. Cioffi, "A Programmable VLSI Codec for Trellis-Coding," *Amati T1E1 Contribution,* T1E1.4/92-177 (August 1992).

53. J. T. Aslanis, P. T. Tong, and T. N. Zogakis, "An ADSL Proposal for Selectable Forward Error Correction with Convolution Interleaving," *Amati T1E1 Contribution*, T1E1.4/92-176 (August 1992).

54. D. L. Waring and K. Sistanizadeh, "A Revised Suggested Plan to Access ADSL Transmission Schemes for Further Study," *Bellcore T1E1 Contribution*, T1E1.4/92-147R2 (December 1992).

55. N. Epstein, R. Olshansky, and R. Gross, "ADSL Test Plan," *GTE T1E1 Contribution*, T1E1.4/92-217 (December 1992).

56. P. T. Tong, H. L. Lou, and P. H. Ang, "An Update on the Programmable Trellis Codes," *Amati and LSI Logic T1E1 Contribution*, T1E1.4/92-200 (December 1992).

57. T. N. Zogakis and J. T. Aslanis, "The Implementation of Selectable FEC for ADSL," *Amati T1E1 Contribution*, T1E1.4/92-202 (December 1992).

58. K. Manghani, "Availability of FEC and Related Chips for ADSL," *LSI Logic T1E1 Contribution*, T1E1.4/92-218 (December 1992).

59. K. Hohhof, "Forward Error Correction Proposal for ADSL," *Westell T1E1 Contribution*, T1E1.4/92-208 (December 1992).

60. G. Young, "Impulsive Noise in ADSL Systems," *B T Labs T1E1 Contribution*, T1E1.4/92-214 (December 1992).

61. J. S. Chow and R. R. Hunt, "Impulse Noise Measurements for DMT System," *Amati T1E1 Contribution*, T1E1.4/92-211 (December 1992).

62. K. J. Kerpez, "Minimum Mean Squared Error Impulse Noise Modeling," *Bellcore T1E1 Contribution*, T1E1.4/92-226 (December 1992).

63. W. Y. Chen, "An Analytical Test Bed for QAM/CAP ADSL Transceivers," *Bellcore T1E1 Contribution*, T1E1.4/92-224 (December 1992).

64. J. A. C. Bingham, "Design of Multitone Transceivers," *Amati T1E1 Contribution*, T1E1.4/92-198 (December 1992).

65. J. Cioffi, J. Aslanis, and M. Ho, "Performance of Enhanced (6 Mbps) ADSL," *Amati and Stanford University T1E1 Contribution*, T1E1.4/92-205 (December 1992).

66. T. Starr, "ADSL Bit Rates," *Ameritech T1E1 Contribution*, T1E1.4/92-231 (December 1992).

67. P. J. Kyees, "Suggestion to Remove Bit-Rate-Limit of Payload on Initial Work Outlined in ADSL Standards Project Proposal," *BellSouth Telecommunications T1E1 Contribution*, T1E1.4/92-246 (December 1992).

68. M. Ho, J. Cioffi, and J. A. C. Bingham, "An Echo Cancellation Method for DMT with DSLs," *Amati and Stanford University T1E1 Contribution,* T1E1.4/92-201 (December 1992).

69. H. Y. Chung, G. H. Im, M. Sorbara, and J. J. Werner, "Spectrum Compatibility Issues for DSLs," *AT&T T1E1 Contribution,* T1E1.4/92-233 (December 1992).

70. K. Sistanexadeh, "Spectral Compatibility of 2B1Q HDSL with 16-QAM ADSL Induced NEXT and AWGN," *Bellcore T1E1 Contribution,* T1E1.4/92-222 (December 1992).

71. J. Cioffi, "ADSL Maintenance with DMT," *Amati T1E1 Contribution,* T1E1.4/92-203 (December 1992).

72. K. Hohhof and R. Koval, "Frame Structure Proposal for ADSL," *Westell T1E1 Contribution,* T1E1.4/92-209 (December 1992).

73. J. Aslanis, J. Cioffi, and R. M. Adolf, "T1.601 Compatible Full ADSL Service with POTS," *Amati T1E1 Contribution,* T1E1.4/92-199 (December 1992).

74. K. J. Kerpez, "An Update on the Recommended Reed-Solomon Code for ADSL," *Bellcore T1E1 Contribution,* T1E1.4/93-035 (March 1993).

75. T. N. Zogakis, P. T. Tong, and J. Cioffi, "Performance Comparison of FEC/Interleave Choices with DMT for ADSL," *Amati T1E1 Contribution,* T1E1.4/93-091 (March 1993).

76. J. T. Aslanis, J. S. Chow, and P. T. Tong, "A Selective Error Correction Proposal for ADSL," *Amati T1E1 Contribution,* T1E1.4/93-023 (March 1993).

77. J. Cioffi and J. A. C. Bingham, "Echo Cancellation for ADSL," *Amati T1E1 Contribution,* T1E1.4/93-091 (March 1993).

78. J. Cioffi, "Revisiting Recommended DMT Line Code," *Amati T1E1 Contribution,* T1E1.4/93-021 (March 1993).

79. J. S. Chow and J. Cioffi, "DMT Initialization: Parameters Needed for Specification in a Standard," *Amati T1E1 Contribution,* T1E1.4/93-022 (March 1993).

80. J. Cioffi and P. T. Tong, "VLSI DMT Implementation for ADSL," *Amati T1E1 Contribution,* T1E1.4/93-025 (March 1993).

81. C. T. Throop, "Recommendation for the Inclusion of 6 Mbps Payload in the Initial Standard," *ECI Telecom, Inc., T1E1 Contribution,* T1E1.4/93-052 (March 1993).

82. L. M. Smith and M. Sorbara, "Alternative 6 Mbps ADSL Architectures: Advantages and Disadvantages," *AT&T T1E1 Contribution,* T1E1.4/93-055 (March 1993).

83. W. Y. Chen, "The Effect of ADSL Spectrum on T1 Performance," *Bellcore T1E1 Contribution,* T1E1.4/93-033 (March 1993).

84. E. Arnon and M. Elder, "Performance Measurement of ADSL System," *NTI T1E1 Contribution,* T1E1.4/93-064 (March 1993).

85. B. A. Blake, "Description of the Transmission Tests Performed on ADSL Transceiver Prototypes at Bellcore," *Bellcore T1E1 Contribution,* T1E1.4/93-029 (March 1993).

86. B. A. Blake, "Results of Transmission Tests on an ADSL Transceiver Prototype from Reliance COMM/TEC and Bellcore," *Bellcore T1E1 Contribution,* T1E1.4/93-030 (March 1993).

87. B. A. Blake, "Results of Transmission Tests on an ADSL Transceiver Prototype from Amati Communications Corp.," *Bellcore T1E1 Contribution,* T1E1.4/93 031 (March 1993).

88. B. A. Blake, "Results of Transmission Tests on an ADSL Transceiver Prototype from AT&T Paradyne," *Bellcore T1E1 Contribution,* T1E1.4/93-032 (March 1993).

89. J. S. Chow, J. C. Tu, and J. M. Cioffi, "A Discrete Multitone Transceiver System for HDSL Applications," *IEEE JSAC,* vol. 9, no. 6 (August 1991): 895–908.

90. S. B. Weistain and P. M. Ebert, "Data Transmission by Frequency-Division Multiplexing Using the Discrete Fourier Transform," *IEEE Trans. Commun. Tech.,* vol. COM-19 (October 1971): 628–634.

91. J. S. Chow and J. M. Cioffi, "A Cost-Effective Maximum Likelihood Receiver for Multicarrier Systems," *Proc. IEEE ICC '92* (June 1992): 948–952.

92. J. S. Chow, J. M. Cioffi, and J. A. C. Bingham, "Equalizer Training Algorithm for Multicarrier Modulation Systems," *Proc. IEEE ICC '93* (June 1993): 761–765.

93. J. C. Tu and J. M. Cioffi, "A Loading Algorithm for the Concatenation of Coset Codes with Multichannel Modulation Methods," *Proc. IEEE Globecom* (1990): 703.6.1–703.6.5.

94. J. T. Aslanis, N. Al-Dhahir, and J. A. C. Bingham, "Performance of the Proposed DMT Line Code for ADSL with Embedded ISDN," *Amati T1E1 Contribution,* T1E1.4/92-178 (August 1992).

95. P. T. Tong, J. T. Aslani, and J. M. Cioffi, "A Trellis-Code Proposal for ADSL Line Signals," *Amati T1E1 Contribution,* T1E1.4/92-176 (August 1992).

96. J. T. Aslanis, P. T. Tong, and T. N. Zogakis, "An ADSL Proposal for Selectable Forward Error Correction with Convolution Interleaving," *Amati T1E1 Contribution*, T1E1.4/ 92-180 (August 1992).

97. P. S. Chow, J. Cioffi, and R. K. Maxwell, "Performance of Multicarrier with DSL Impulse Noise," *Stanford University/Amati T1E1 Contribution*, T1E1.4/158 (November 1991).

98. K. J. Kerpez, "A Model for the Probability Distribution of the Length of Burst Errors Caused by Impulse Noise," *Bellcore T1E1 Contribution*, T1E1.4/91-165 (November 1991).

99. K. J. Kerpez, "Forward Error Correction Codes for ADSL," *Bellcore T1E1 Contribution*, T1E1.4/91-166 (November 1991).

100. S. Lin and D. J. Costello, Jr., *Error Control Coding: Fundamentals and Applications* (Prentice-Hall, 1983).

101. J. M. Cioffi and J. A. C. Bingham, "A Data-Driven Multitone Echo Canceller," *IEEE Trans. On Commun.*, vol. 42, no. 10 (October 1994): 2853–2869.

102. M. Ho, J. M. Cioffi, and J. A. C. Bingham, "Discrete Multitone Echo Cancellation," *IEEE Trans. On Commun.*, vol. 44, no. 7 (July 1996): 817–825.

103. J. Cioffi and P. T. Tong, "VLSI DMT Implementation for ADSL," *Amati T1E1 Contribution*, T1E1.4/93-025 (March 1993).

104. W. Y. Chen, G. H. Im, and J. J. Werner, "Design of Digital Carrierless AM/PM Transceivers," *AT&T and Bellcore T1E1 Contribution*, T1E1.4/92-149 (August 1992).

105. M. Tomlinson, "New Automatic Equalizer Employing Modulo Arithmatic," *Electron. Lett.*, vol. 7 (March 1971): 138–139.

106. B. A. Blake, "Results of Transmission Tests on an ADSL Transceiver Prototype from AT&T Paradyne," *Bellcore T1E1 Contribution*, T1E1.4/93-032 (March 1993).

107. D. Amrany, S. Gadot, and M. Dimyan, "A Programmable DSP Engine for High-Rate Modems," *Proc. IEEE ISSCC '92* (June 1992): 222–223.

108. W. Y. Chen and D. L. Waring, "ADSL Noise Environment and Potential Performance," *Bellcore Internal Technical Memorandum* (September 23, 1993).

109. J. C. Tu and J. M. Cioffi, "A Loading Algorithm for the Concatenation of Coset Codes with Multichannel Modulation Methods," *Proc. IEEE Globecom* (1990): 703.6.1–703.6.5.

110. W. Y. Chen, "Architecture and Performance Simulation of Single-Pair HDSL," *Proc. IEEE ICC '96* (June 1996).

111. D. L. Waring, "The Asymmetrical Digital Subscriber Line (ADSL): A New Transport Technology for Delivering Wideband Capacities to the Residence," *Proc. IEEE GLOBE-COM '91*: 1979–1986.

112. British Telecom Contribution.

113. IEEE P1394 standards.

SHDSL (Single-Pair High-Bit-Rate Digital Subscriber Lines)

The technical report of HDSL served the purpose of an industry standard interface for both equipment manufacturers and telephone companies. With additional effort on details of equipment interoperability, HDSL enjoyed a healthy market share as a dual-duplex repeaterless T1 technology. HDSL semiconductor chips with reliable performance are available from many vendors. Competition for the market share has lead to a higher level of semiconductor circuit integration and some technical innovations. It is expected that with more signal processing power plus the help of advanced coding techniques, the transmission throughput of HDSL can be realized on a single pair of CSA range loops.

At the June 1995 T1E1.4 meeting, Metalink made a proposal for a *single-pair HDSL* (SHDSL) study project.[1] It was argued that the single-pair HDSL had been offered as a product and a technical report should be generated to help the convergence of an industry standard. It was claimed that the 6 dB performance margin could be achieved on five CSA test loops and the 6 dB margin reaches were 10,800 feet for the 24-AWG loop and 7,800 feet for the 26-AWG loop.[2] The performance is achieved without any coding gain, but a proprietary Near Maximum Likelihood (NML) algorithm was used. The similar performance was also considered achievable by a CAP system with some coding gain.[3]

After that initial discussion, the single-pair HDSL (SHDSL) iteration has been an active discussion topic during subsequent T1E1.4 meetings. SHDSL is also referred as *HDSL2*. Most recently, the term *Next Generation HDSL* has been used for activities related to establishing an SHDSL standard. This chapter reviews major discussion topics related to T1E1.4 working group SHDSL activities. The current status of a possible SHDSL standard is also discussed. This chapter covers a myriad of SHDSL related topics including the following:

- *Performance improvements.* Measured and estimated performance margins as well as transmission throughputs on a single-pair CSA loop with or without coding are reviewed. Channel capacities of CSA loops are calculated in the context of SHDSL. The effect of the NEXT model and the issue of spectrum compatibility are addressed.

- *Coding gain.* Trellis codes with up to 1024 states are examined in conjunction with a Viterbi decoder or a sequential decoder based on the Fano algorithm. The applicability of Turbo codes is also discussed.

- *Minimizing NEXT with spectrum shaping.* Proposals of symmetrical and asymmetrical signal spectra and associated performance estimates are reviewed.

- *HDSL2 standard status.* The convergence of an SHDSL standard is discussed.

14.1   The Desired Performance Improvements

Metalink presented measurement results on CSA loops and 24-AWG and 26-AWG loops. For CSA loops #1, #4, #6, #7, and #8, the length of the longest section is made variable such that by reducing the variable section loop length, a performance margin (above the 10^{-7} bit error rate requirement) of 6 dB can be achieved. The percentage reach of the CSA loop is then calculated by dividing the total loop length (defined as the sum of lengths of fixed sections plus the length of the variable section) by the CSA loop length. The lengths of bridged taps are not included in the percentage calculation. Table 14.1 shows the CSA loop measurement results for both forward (from CO to subscriber) and reverse (Rev.) directions.

Table 14.1   Reach of a Single-Pair HDSL System

Loop	Variable Length (feet)	Total Loop Length (feet)	CSA Loop Length (feet)	Percentage of the CSA Loop
#1	5000	6900	7700	89
#1 Rev.	5000	6900	7700	89
#4	4550	5860	7600	77
#4 Rev.	4550	5810	7600	76
#6	7800	7800	9000	86
#7	10000	10000	10700	93
#7 Rev.	9200	9150	10700	86
#8	10600	10600	12000	88

Figures 14.1 and 14.2 show the performance results of a single-pair HDSL system on 24-AWG and 26-AWG loops, respectively.

Figure 14.1   Metalink Margin Over 24-AWG Loop

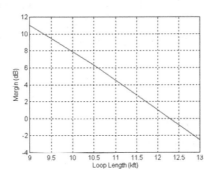

Figure 14.2   Metalink Margin Over 26-AWG Loop

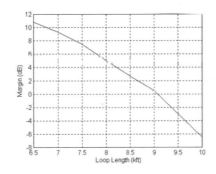

14.1.1   EC/FDM-Based CAP SHDSL Systems

Performances of an Echo Cancellation (EC)–based system and a Frequency Division Multiplexed (FDM)–based system were estimated by AT&T's contribution to the June 1995 T1E1.4 meeting. The EC-based system has a CAP 64 line code with a 3 dB bandwidth of 266 kHz and a 15-percent excessive bandwidth of 368 kHz. Because CAP is a passband system, the lower-corner frequency can be located at either 0 Hz or 35 kHz. For the latter case, a POTS channel can be made available simultaneously. The FDM system also has a CAP 64 line code. The upstream channel is located from 35 kHz to 403 kHz and the downstream channel is located from 580 kHz to 948 kHz. In the performance estimation, a 4 dB Trellis coding gain is assumed for both EC- and FDM-based systems.

The performance margin is about 1.5 dB for the EC system with 0 Hz lower-corner frequency on the 9 kft 26-AWG loop. The 6 dB performance margin reach is about 8 kft for the 26-AWG loop and 11.5 kft for the 24-AWG loop. When the lower-corner frequency is raised to 35 kHz, the performance margin is reduced to –1.1 dB on the 9 kft 26-AWG loop. The 6 dB performance margin reach is reduced to 7.3 kft for the 26-AWG loop and 10.3 kft for the 24-AWG loop. On the other hand, performance margins of the FDM-based system are estimated to be 11.3 dB and 13 dB on the 9 kft, 26-AWG loop and the 12 kft, 24-AWG loop, respectively.

14.1.2 DMT Line Code for SHDSL Systems

It is also possible to use the DMT[4] line code for the single-pair HDSL. The challenge for the DMT system is the delay constraint. To reduce the amount of *Inverse Fast Fourier Transform* (IFFT) and *Fast Fourier Transform* (FFT) delay, a small FFT size might be preferable. The percentage of cyclic prefix overhead, however, might increase unless a better time domain equalizer is adapted. The possible FFT sizes are 64 or 128 with a time domain equalizer length of up to 32 taps. Depending on the FFT size and bandwidth, a DMT-based single-pair HDSL could be realized with the assistance of coding gain.

14.1.3 Comparison of PAM and CAP/QAM Line Codes

ADTRAN's T1E1 contribution compares PAM and CAP/QAM line code performance in a single-pair HDSL system with a transmission throughput of 1.6 Mbps.[5] For this particular comparison study, the PAM family consists of 4, 8, and 16 level line codes. The best modulation type from the PAM family is determined to be coded 16-PAM, achieving reaches of up to 10,600 feet and 7,700 feet on 24-AWG and 26-AWG, respectively.

Coded 64-CAP is determined as the best modulation type from the CAP/QAM family, achieving reaches of up to 10,300 feet and 7,400 feet on 24-AWG and 26-AWG, respectively. Test results show that, when considering worst-case disturber types, coded 16-PAM has a loop reach up to 800 feet greater than coded 64-CAP. When considering only self-NEXT, coded 16-PAM and coded 64-CAP perform comparably. Tables 14.2 to 14.4 summarize performance simulation results for coded and uncoded PAM/CAP SHDSL systems with a 6 dB margin as well as performance margins at CSA loops.

AT&T's T1E1 contribution also compares CAP/QAM and PAM line code performance in SHDSL systems.[6] When deploying the transceiver without POTS, the results show that with the incorporation of Trellis coding and Tomlinson precoding in all transceivers, CAP/QAM and PAM can achieve essentially the same reach, assuming 4 dB of Trellis coding gain and that the CAP transmit spectrum starts at 0 Hz. An analysis of the following simulation results confirms that CAP/QAM and PAM achieve essentially the same loop reach.

Table 14.2   Summary of Uncoded PAM/CAP Results with a 6 dB Margin

	All Disturber		Self-NEXT	
	24 AWG	**26 AWG**	**24 AWG**	**26 AWG**
PAM Type (Uncoded)	8-PAM	8-PAM	4-PAM	4-PAM
PAM Loop Reach	9000	6500	9000	6700
CAP Type (Uncoded)	64-CAP	64-CAP	32-CAP	16-CAP
CAP Loop Reach	8600	6200	9000	6500

Table 14.3   Summary of Coded PAM/CAP Results with a 6 dB Margin

	All Disturber		Self-NEXT	
	24 AWG	**26 AWG**	**24 AWG**	**26 AWG**
PAM Type (Coded)	16-PAM	16-PAM	16-PAM	8-PAM
PAM Loop Reach	10600	7700	10600	7700
CAP Type (Coded)	128-CAP	128-CAP	64-CAP	64-CAP
CAP Loop Reach	10300	7400	10500	7700

Table 14.4   The Margin at CSA Loops

	All Disturber		Self-NEXT	
	12 kft, 24 AWG	**9 kft, 26 AWG**	**12 kft, 24 AWG**	**9 kft, 26 AWG**
Coded 16-PAM	2.6 dB	1.4 dB	2.6 dB	1.4 dB
Coded 64-CAP	1.1 dB	0.2 dB	2.2 dB	1.3 dB

On 24-gauge wire, coded 16-PAM shows a reach of 10.8 kft with 6 dB margin and coded 64-CAP has a reach of 10.7 kft with a 6.1 dB margin.

On 26-gauge wire, coded 8-PAM shows a reach of 7.8 kft with 6.2 dB margin and coded 64-CAP shows a reach of 7.8 kft with a 6.1 dB margin.

On CSA loop #8 (12 kft 24-AWG), coded 16-PAM shows 3.1 dB of margin and coded 64-CAP shows 2.9 dB of margin.

On CSA loop #6 (9 kft 26-AWG), both coded 64-CAP and 16-PAM show 1.9 dB of margin.

Tables 14.5 to 14.8 summarize the performance simulation results for reaches of 24-AWG and 26-AWG loops and performance margins for CSA loop #6 and #8, all with self-NEXT. The slight CAP performance difference from these two studies might be due to the difference in CAP lower-corner frequencies.

Table 14.5 The Reach with 6 dB Margin of 24-AWG and Self-NEXT

Line Code (w/TCM)	Distance (kft)	Margin (dB)
16-PAM	10.8	6.0
64-CAP	10.7	6.1
128-CAP	10.6	6.0
8-PAM	10.6	6.0
32-CAP	10.4	6.2
256-CAP	10.3	6.0

Table 14.6 The Reach with 6 dB Margin of 26-AWG and Self-NEXT

Line Code (w/TCM)	Distance (kft)	Margin (dB)
8-PAM	7.8	6.2
64-CAP	7.8	6.1
16-PAM	7.8	6.0
32-CAP	7.7	6.1
128-CAP	7.6	6.1
256-CAP	7.3	6.2

Table 14.7 The Margin on CSA #8 (12 kft, 24-AWG)

Line Code (w/TCM)	Margin (dB)
16-PAM	3.1
64-CAP	2.9
128-CAP	2.6
8-PAM	2.4
32-CAP	2.1
256-CAP	2.1

Table 14.8 The Margin on CSA #6 (9 kft, 26-AWG)

Line Code (w/ TCM)	Margin (dB)
64-PAM	1.9
16-CAP	1.9
8-PAM	1.9
32-CAP	1.5
128-CAP	1.4
256-CAP	0.7

Performances of different PAM line codes with or without coding are compared by Level One's T1E1 contribution.[7] It is concluded that in the presence of self-NEXT, 2B1Q (8-PAM) and 3B1O (16-PAM) perform about the same. In the presence of self-NEXT plus crosstalk from ADSL systems, however, coded 3B1O (16-PAM) achieves a higher performance than coded 2B1Q (8-PAM). In some cases, 3B1O outperforms 2B1Q by as much as 3 dB. Table 14.9 summarizes the performance margins for the 9 kft, 26-AWG loop.

Table 14.9 Performance Margins for the 9 kft, 26-AWG Loop

	24 Self-NEXT (dB)	49 Self-NEXT (dB)	24 Self-NEXT+25 (dB)	49 ADSL (dB)
2B1Q	0.2	−1.5	−2.6	−3.6
3B1O	0	−1.7	−1.8	−2.2
Coded 2B1Q	4	2.5	1.4	0.4
Coded 3B1O	4.2	2.3	2.2	1.8

14.1.4 Channel Capacity for SHDSL Systems

The channel capacity in the context of the SHDSL environment can be used as a reference for the searching of the desired transmission performance. The calculation of the channel capacity requires the knowledge of the channel transfer function, noise model, and specific representation of hardware impairments.

The self-NEXT channel capacity can be calculated using the following expression:[8]

$$C = \int_0^F \log_2 \left(1 + \frac{|H(f)|^2}{|X(f)|^2} \right) df$$

The values are as follows:

$H(f)$ is the loop transfer function.

$X(f)$ is the NEXT transfer function.

Figure 14.3 shows the channel capacity of the 9 kft, 26-AWG loop under the 49-disturber 1-percent worst-case scenario to be around 2.85 Mbps.

Figure 14.3 Channel Capacities for the 9 kft, 26-AWG Loop

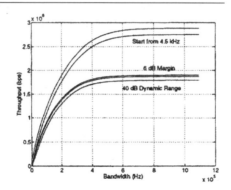

The capacity is reduced to around 2.75 Mbps if the frequency below 4.5 kHz is not used for the general case of using a line coupling transformer. The channel capacity with a 6 dB performance margin, emulated with a 6 dB of noise level increase, is about 1.9 Mbps. The 6 dB performance margin channel capacity is reduced a little if the frequency below 4.5 kHz is not used. The 6 dB performance margin channel capacity is further reduced to about 1.75 dB if the system dynamic range is limited to 40 dB.

The transmission throughput of a DFE-based transceiver can also be displayed as a function of the signaling bandwidth (half of the baud rate) using the following approximate expression:

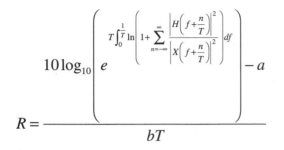

$$R = \frac{10\log_{10}\left(e^{T\int_0^{\frac{1}{T}}\ln\left(1+\sum_{n=-\infty}^{\infty}\frac{\left|H\left(f+\frac{n}{T}\right)\right|^2}{\left|X\left(f+\frac{n}{T}\right)\right|^2}\right)df} - a\right)}{bT}$$

The following are the values for an error rate of 10^{-7}:

$a = 9.5$

$b = 6$

The use of fractional number of bits per symbol is assumed possible.

Similarly, the transmission throughput of a matching filter-based transceiver can be displayed as a function of the signaling bandwidth using the following approximate expression:

$$R = \frac{10\log_{10}\left(\frac{\int_0^{\frac{1}{2T}}|H(f)|^2 df}{\int_0^{\frac{1}{2T}}|X(f)|^2 df} + 1\right) - a}{bT}$$

An ideal matching filter-based transceiver has a matching filter bank in front of the receiver to match any data symbol after the channel distortion. The performance of a matching filter-based transceiver is better because it does not cause much noise enhancement.

The achievable transmission throughput results are about 1.55 Mbps and 1.35 Mbps for a matching filter-based transceiver with a signaling bandwidth of 430 kHz and a DFE-based transceiver with a signaling bandwidth of 310 kHz, respectively, as shown in Figure 14.4. In other words, a coding gain of 6 dB is required for the matching filter-based transceiver with a 6 dB of performance margin and a larger than 6 dB of coding gain is required for a DFE-based transceiver with a 6 dB of performance margin. With only 3 dB of coding gain the achievable transmission throughput results are 1.2 Mbps and 1.1 Mbps, respectively. Transmission throughputs are below 900 kbps without any coding gain.

Figure 14.4 Channel Capacities for the 12 kft, 24-AWG Loop

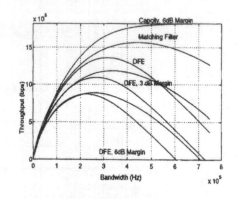

These estimations are very close to other study and measurement results (from referenced T1E1 contributions), as shown in Figure 14.5.

Figure 14.5 Receiver Performances Compared to the Channel Capacity

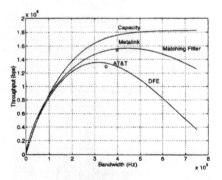

On the other hand, only on shorter than CSA loops—8 kft, 26-AWG and 11 kft, 24-AWG loops—a coding gain of a little higher 6 dB can be used in conjunction with a DFE-based transceiver to achieve a transmission throughput of 1.544 Mbps, as shown in Figure 14.6.

Figure 14.6   Receiver Performances on Shorter Loops

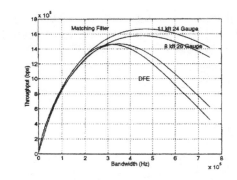

14.1.5   Modifying the NEXT Model to Improve Performance

The T1E1 contribution from ADTRAN[9] discusses the possibility of modifying the simplified crosstalk model and including the coupling transformer in the crosstalk model to obtain a simulated performance improvement of 0.8 dB. Specifically, the Unger (New) 49-disturber NEXT model should have a slope of –14 dB/decade instead of –15 dB/decade at frequencies above 20 kHz, as shown in Figure 14.7.

Figure 14.7   Unger and the Simplified NEXT Models

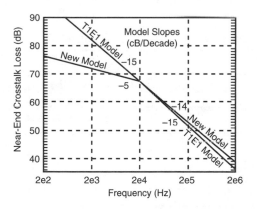

PairGain's T1E1 contribution[10] summarizes that the performance margins are about –2 dB with the simplified NEXT model and about –1 dB with the Unger NEXT model for uncoded systems. The Unger NEXT model has less crosstalk at lower frequencies, as shown in Figure 14.7. Table 14.10 summarizes SHDSL performance margins under different NEXT models.

Table 14.10 Performance Margin Summary on CSA Loop #6

Modulation	ADTRAN (Simplified/ Unger)	Level One (Unger)	AT&T (Simplified)	PairGain (Unger)
4-PAM	−2.6	−1.5	−2.1	−1.1
16-CAP	−3.1		−2.5	
32-CAP	−2.7		−2.1	−0.8 (5/2 PAM)
8-PAM	−2.6/−1.3	−1.7	−2.1	−1.3
64-CAP	−3.3		−2.6	

14.1.6 Spectrum Compatibility

A T1E1 contribution from AT&T studies the spectrum compatibility between SHDSL and ADSL.[11] CAP/QAM and PAM line codes are used for SHDSL. ADSL of 1.5 Mbps uses the 64-CAP line code and ADSL of 6 Mbps uses the DMT line code. Table 14.11 summarizes the results of SHDSL NEXT to the performance of a 1.5 Mbps ADSL. Table 14.12 summarizes the results of 1.5 Mbps CAP ADSL NEXT to the performance of an SHDSL. Table 14.13 summarizes the results of SHDSL NEXT to the performance of a 6 Mbps DMT ADSL. Results are expressed as ADSL or HDSL performance margins (above the SNR required for the 10^{-7} bit error rate).

Table 14.11 CAP ADSL Performance Margin Under SHDSL NEXT

HDSL Interferer	ADSL Margin (dB) (12 kft 24 AWG)	
	Ideal Spectrum	Practical Spectrum
64-CAP	8.9	6.9
128-CAP	18.0	14.8
8-PAM		-6.3
16-PAM	9.3	2.4

Table 14.12   SHDSL Performance Margin Under CAP ADSL NEXT

HDSL System	HDSL Margin (dB) for 9 kft, 26-AWG
64-CAP	15.1
128-CAP	18.6
8-PAM (no coding)	7.4
16-PAM	18.5
8-PAM	11.4

Table 14.13   DMT ADSL Performance Margin Under SHDSL NEXT

HDSL Interferer	ADSL Margin (dB) (12 kft 24 AWG)	
	Ideal Spectrum	Practical Spectrum
128-CAP	10.6	9.8
64-CAP	7.8	6.6
16-PAM	7.5	1.6

14.2   Searching for the Required Coding Gain

Many performance estimation studies for SHDSL have assumed a coding gain of about 4 dB. To meet the 6 dB performance margin requirement on CSA loops, a coding gain of about 6 dB is required. The requirement of such a high coding gain is a challenge both for the selection of a proper code and its implementation complexity.

14.2.1   Trellis Codes

A simple eight-state Trellis code can provide a coding gain of about 4 dB in conjunction with either 128-CAP or 16-PAM line codes. Trellis codes generally require a Tomlinson precoder and an adaptive transmitter instead of a Decision Feedback Equalizer (DFE).

Note
A Reed-Solomon code would also yield a 4 dB coding gain, but the resulting delay is too high.[12]

Figure 14.8 shows a single-pair HDSL (SHDSL) transceiver structure with Trellis coding.[13]

Figure 14.8 Trellis-Coded SHDSL Transceiver Block Diagram

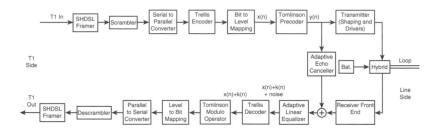

In the top transmitter path for the Trellis-coded SHDSL system, the process is as follows:

1. The SHDSL framer converts from the 1.544 Mbps T1 format to the 1.552 Mbps SHDSL serial data format.

2. The scrambler randomizes the incoming data stream.

3. The serial-to-parallel converter produces three information bits per symbol time.

4. The Trellis encoder adds redundancy in the form of a Trellis bit, resulting in a total of four coded bits per symbol.

5. The bit-to-level mapper maps the four bits of output from the Trellis encoder to one of 16 levels in a one-dimensional PAM constellation.

6. The constellation symbols are passed through a Tomlinson precoder to counter the effect of the loop intersymbol interference.

In the bottom receiver path for the Trellis-coded SHDSL system, the process is as follows:

1. The adaptive linear equalizer suppresses channel precursors and whitens the noise.

2. The Trellis decoder picks the most likely received constellation sequence.

3. The Tomlinson modulo operator removes the modulo sequence added by the transmitter's Tomlinson precoder.

4. The level-to-bit mapper maps each of the 16 possible constellation points to a unique 4-bit number, then discards the Trellis bit leaving the 3-tuple information sequence.

5. The parallel-to-serial converter serializes the 3-tuple sequence.

6. The descrambler removes the randomizing sequence, leaving the original 1.552 Mbps sequence.

7. The SHDSL framer converts from the 1.552 Mbps SHDSL format to the 1.544 Mbps T1 format.

There is also an adaptive echo canceller connected in between the output of the Tomlinson precoder and the input of the adaptive linear equalizer for the separation of the receive path from the transmit signal.

Figure 14.9 shows an eight-state Trellis encoder with an asymptotic coding gain of 4 dB in the systematic feedback form.

Figure 14.9 An Eight-State Trellis Encoder in Systematic Feedback Form

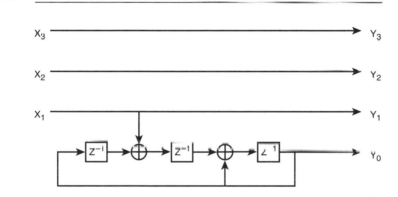

The effective coding gain is approximately 3.2 dB. The three input bits are passed directly to the output, and the Trellis bit becomes the least significant bit of the four output bits.

Tomlinson Precoding

Figure 14.10 shows the Tomlinson precoder.

Figure 14.10 Tomlinson Precoder

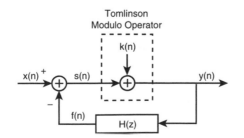

The Tomlinson precoder consists of a feedback filter, H(z), which is the replica of the feedback filter of the DFE, and a Tomlinson modulo operator. The input to the Tomlinson precoder is the 16-PAM signal, 8-PAM with the additional bit generated from the Trellis coding. The output of the Tomlinson precoder is the modulo remainder of the input sequence plus the feedback signal. The output of the Tomlinson precoder is also bounded between –16 and +16, assuming signal levels of –15, –13, ...–1, 1, ...13, 15.

Coefficient values of the feedback filter are obtained during the startup training by the receiver using a random uncoded PAM sequence. These coefficients are sent to the transmitter at the other end of the twisted-pair loop to be used in the Tomlinson precoder prior to the regular data transmission. Compared with the regular data transmission, the feedback filter during the startup is in place of the Trellis decoder and Tomlinson modulo operator. Figure 14.11 illustrates the startup mode functional block diagram of an SHDSL transceiver.

Figure 14.11 Startup Mode Functional Block Diagram

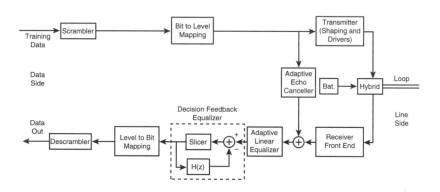

14.2.2   *Viterbi Decoding*

A sophisticated coding scheme is needed to achieve a reasonable NEXT performance margin on all CSA test loops for SHDSL. A high coding gain usually requires a more complicated Trellis decoder. Table 14.4 summarizes a comparison of complexities of rate 3/4 (three bits to four bits) Viterbi decoders of various numbers of states.[14]

Table 14.14   Rate 3/4 Viterbi Decoder's Relative Complexity

Number of States	Relative Complexity	Relative Memory
8	0.08	0.07
16	0.16	0.17
32	0.30	0.41

Number of States	Relative Complexity	Relative Memory
64	0.60	0.96
128	1.18	2.18
256	2.36	4.89
512	4.71	10.82
1024	9.40	23.74

A Viterbi decoder with its number of states between 64 and 128 has the same complexity as the combination of the echo canceller and the equalizer in a regular HDSL transceiver. In other words, a rate 3/4 Viterbi decoder with 64 or 128 states and an asymptotic coding gain of 4.94 dB or 5.01 dB at the error rate of 10^{-6} is economically feasible in a current (1997) CMOS (Complementary Metal Oxide Semiconductor) technology.

14.2.3   *Sequential Decoding*

The primary characteristic of the sequential decoding algorithm is that its complexity is essentially independent of the number of states in the encoder, but rather is dependent on the signal-to-noise ratio.[15]

PairGain's T1E1 contribution studied the possibility of using sequential decoding for Trellis codes to obtain a performance margin of 6 dB for SHDSL.[16] A real coding gain of at least 5.6 dB can be obtained at an error rate of 10^{-7} using the long constraint length rate 2/3 (two bits to three bits) codes with the sequential decoder whose buffer size is dictated by the 1 ms HDSL delay requirement. The computational requirements of a sequential decoder are substantially less than what would be required for a Viterbi decoder.

For a general Trellis-coded modulation system, the effective code rate of $k/(k+1)$ is established by using a rate $m/(m+1)$ convolution encoder, $m \leq k$, in conjunction with $k-m$ uncoded bits, where the convolutional encoder selects one of 2^{m+1} partitioned subsets, each consisting of 2^{k-m} constellation points. The $k-m$ uncoded bits are used to select the subset point.

Figure 14.12 shows the Trellis encoder part of a rate $k/(k+1)$ Trellis-coded modulation system.

Figure 14.12 Encoder and Channel

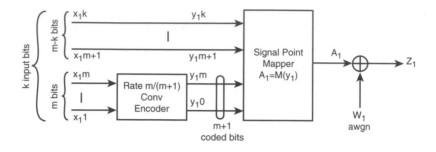

Figure 14.13 shows the sequential decoder part of a Trellis-coded modulation system.

Figure 14.13 Decoder Function

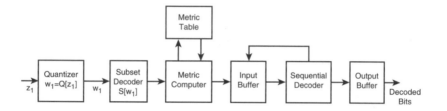

Fano Algorithm

The Fano algorithm[17] can be used for the sequential decoder. The Fano algorithm examines only one path of the code Trellis at any time, resulting in substantially reduced memory requirements and metric computations. A sequence of metric thresholds spaced at intervals of a basic increment threshold offset of Δ is used to determine if the correct path is being followed by the decoder. If the metric computed by the decoder is increasing sufficiently on a forward search, the threshold is tightened (incremented) by Δ. During backward searches, the threshold is relaxed (lowered). The search is implemented in a way that prevents any node in the trellis from being searched forward twice with the same threshold setting.

The Fano algorithm employs a metric that is optimal in the sense that the path of maximum Fano metric is the most likely path explored so far. For Trellis Coded Modulation (TCM), the metric computed for each new branch in the path is given by[18]

$$M_B(A_1, z_1) = \log_2 \frac{Kp\{z_1|A_1\}}{\sum_{i=0}^{K-1}\{z_1|A_1\}} - k$$

$$= \log_2 \frac{\exp\left(-|z_1 - A_1|^2/2\sigma^2\right)}{\sum_{i=0}^{K-1}\exp\left(-|z_1 - A_i|^2/2\sigma^2\right)} + n(1-R)$$

The values are as follows:

$n = m+1$ and $R = n/m = m/(m+1)$ so that $n(1-R) = 1$.

z_l is the received signal sample.

A_l is the branch label associated with the branch being extended.

The denominator is the summation of the probability that the sample z_l is received given A_i in the constellation. In practice, some method of recovery from buffer overflow must be implemented. The recovery method is necessary because, for the powerful codes under consideration, the dominant source of decoder errors becomes the overflow of the receiver symbol buffer. Data is framed for sequential decoding to ensure re-synchronization in a reasonable period of time.

The performance of a constraint length $v = 13$ corresponding to 8192-state code according to the code-combining approach of Porath and Aulin[19] was examined. The code parity check vectors are h⁰=20310, h¹=11002, and h²=04404 all in octal representation. Figure 14.14 shows the correlation between parity check bits and encoder structure.

For a 16-QAM system, the coding gain for this $v = 13$ code is about 5.6 dB in conjunction with a 256-symbol buffer and a backsearch depth of 128 symbols. Similar coding gain has also been confirmed for the 64-QAM system.[20] When compared to Viterbi decoding of $v = 6$ rate 2/3 Ungerboeck code, the computational requirements for the sequential decoder are trivial.

Figure 14.14 Systematic Encoder with Feedback

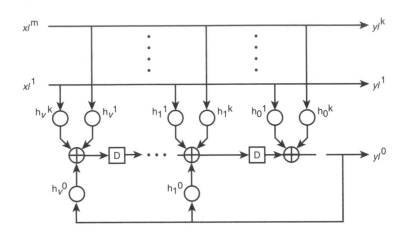

The ADTRAN T1E1 contribution also examined the performance of a 64-QAM SHDSL with Trellis coding and a sequence decoder.[21] The code parity check vectors for a rate 2/3 v = 13 code according to Pottie and Taylor[22] are h^0=020311, h^1=011002, and h^2=004404 all in octal representation. Figure 14.15 shows the correlation between parity check bits and the encoder structure. Figure 14.16 illustrates the decoder.

Because the computational load of the Fano algorithm is a random variable from symbol to symbol, input and output queues are used to produce a constant bit stream at the output. The input and output queues are complementary, such that when one is full, the other is empty, and such that the sum of their depths is a constant. The coset slicer rounds the received signal plus noise to the closest point in each of the eight cosets of the rate 2/3 code. The branch metric calculator computes the Euclidean distance between each of the points from the coset slicer and the received signal, then applies each distance to the Fano metric.

The backsearch buffer of size BS symbol holds the past BS symbol duration worth of branch metrics and slicer outputs. When a new element is placed in the buffer, the Fano algorithm moves backward and forward through this buffer until a path can be found through the Trellis that will include this new element and the previous BS-1 elements. The output of the backsearch buffer is the most likely slicer output corresponding to the oldest element in the backsearch buffer.

Figure 14.15   **The Structure of a Rate 3/4 Trellis Encoder**

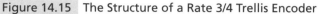

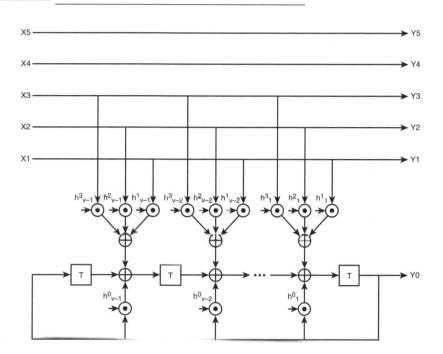

Figure 14.16   **Block Diagram of the Sequential Decoder**

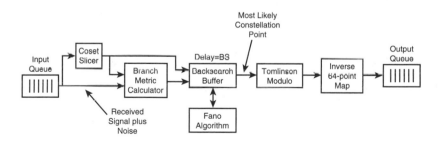

Figure 14.17 illustrates a block diagram of the Fano algorithm.

The variables for the Fano algorithm are as follows:

- The threshold T

- The cumulative path metric M

- The cumulative path metric after looking forward M_F

- The cumulative path metric after looking backward M_B

- The threshold offset Δ.

Figure 14.17 Block Diagram of the Fano Algorithm

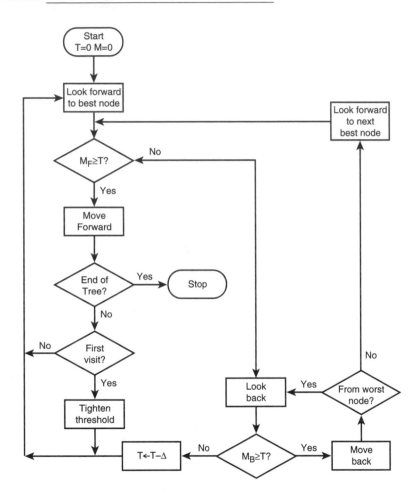

A coding gain of 5.1 dB has been observed and a degradation of 0.3 dB in coding gain can be caused by a constellation slicer compared with a slicer of infinite resolution. Similar coding gain can also be obtained for a 16-QAM Trellis-coded system with a similar sequential decoder.[23]

PairGain's T1E1 contribution also indicates that the maximum coding gain achievable with a rate 2/3 code using 64-QAM line code is 6.0 dB.[24] However, smaller speed factors, defined as the number of decoder operations per symbol interval, coupled with smaller input buffer and backsearch memory sizes, increase the probability of frame loss. The performance simulation results of a 64-QAM with Trellis coding and a sequence decoder show coding gain degradation of 0.7, 0.9, and 1.2 dB for speed factors of 128, 64, and 32, respectively. The code parity check vectors for this rate $2/3$ $v = 17$ code according to Wang and Costello[25] are $h^0=0627325$, $h^1=0275752$, and $h^2=0007350$, all in octal representation.

Figure 14.18 shows the structure of the simulated sequential decoder with an input queue after the metric operation.

Figure 14.18   Another Implementation of the Sequential Decoder

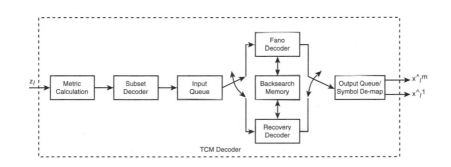

Further performance optimization can be obtained through the fine tuning of the decoder implementation.[26] The performance of a Trellis code transmission system with sequential decoder was also verified under the influence of typical channel impulse noise wave forms.[27]

Computational Cutoff Rates

The number of computations per unit time in a sequence decoder is a random variable. The peak number of computations is unbounded. The average number of computations increases as the SNR decreases and becomes unbounded at the SNR at which the computational cutoff rate, R_o^*,[28] falls below the information rate, R.

Table 14.15 summarizes computational cutoff rates for different line codes in addition to illustrating the difference between the computational cutoff rate SNR and the SNR for uncoded 10^{-7} error probability. This difference is not *coding gain* in the traditional sense because, given infinite memory, the sequential decoder does not make errors. The SNR difference does, however, provide a reference for achievable coding gain with limited memory size and computation power.

Table 14.15   Computational Cutoff Rates

Line Code	SNR (dB) where $R_o*<R$	SNR (dB) at 10^{-7} BER	SNR Difference
8-PAM	14.5	21.5	7.0
16-PAM	21.0	27.7	6.7
32-PAM	27.1	33.6	6.5
16-QAM	11.1	18.5	7.4
64-QAM	17.8	24.7	6.9
256-QAM	24.1	30.8	6.7

Turbo Codes for SHDSL

The communication within 1 dB of Shannon lemma (channel capacity) has been reported[29] with the use of *Turbo codes*. Turbo codes are also called *parallel concatenated codes*. An encoder of a Turbo code consists of parallel concatenation of two convolution codes with a random interleaver at the input of each encoder.

There are also proposals for *low latency Turbo codes*[30] and *Turbo-Trellis-Coded Modulation*.[31] An example of 4 bits/sec/Hz QAM was shown to achieve better than 10^{-5} BER at between 7.4 and 7.6 dB Eb/No, suggesting a coding gain of between 7.8 and 8 dB. The gain of such a code would be sufficient for SHDSL. Figure 14.19 shows the general structure of the encoder.

At a smaller latency of about 90 symbols, the encoder can only generate an equivalent coding gain of about 5.5 dB at 10^{-7} BER.[32] Preliminary study results show that the performance of Turbo code is inferior to the more mature sequential decoding technique under the condition of low latency and low BER. Such techniques[33,34] as using structured interleaver instead of random interleaver might be able to make the Turbo code more suitable for the application of SHDSL.

14.2.4   Coding Gain and Latency

Table 14.16 summarizes coding gain estimates and corresponding latencies for different line codes and from different resources.[35]

Figure 14.19 Parallel Concatenated Trellis-Coded Modulation

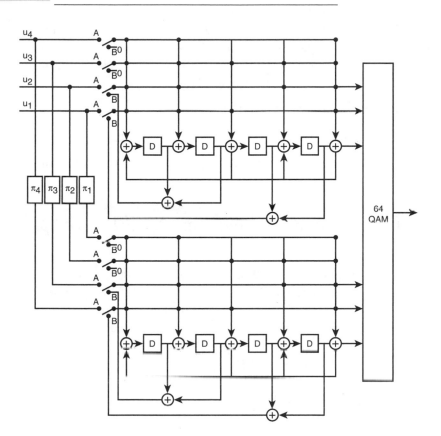

Table 14.16 Summary of FEC Techniques for SHDSL

Technique	Source	Line Code	Latency	Coding Gain (dB)
RS Block code	Metalink	2B1Q	300 us–1.5 ms	1.25–2.25
TCM	ADTRAN	16-PAM	25 us	3.20
TCM/sequential	PairGain	16-QAM	1 ms	5.60
TCM/sequential	Level One/ Heegard	64-QAM	483 us	5.50
TCM/sequential	ADTRAN	64-QAM	500 us–500 us	5.40–5.10
Turbo coding	PairGain	64-QAM	464 us–21 ms	4.50–7.50
Turbo coding	Globespan	64-QAM	324 us–469 us	5.00–5.20
			639 us–834 us	5.30–5.50

The results of Table 14.16 indicate that coding gains of up to 5.2 dB are achievable if the 500 ms system latency is met. The code proposed by Level-One/Heegard with a coding gain of 5.5 dB and a delay of 483 μs is a little too close to the delay requirement. Coding gains of up to 5.5 dB are achievable if the system latency can be relaxed to more than 500 μs. The advantages of using long constraint length convolution codes decodable via sequential decoding for SHDSL can be summarized as follows:[36]

- Currently achievable gains exceeding 5 dB

- Potential for gains of 6 dB and greater with future increases in VLSI speed or density

- Flexibility for multiple applications without specifying additional codes within the standard

14.3 Minimizing Self and Foreign NEXT with Spectrum Shaping

Most SHDSL proposals are echo cancellation based. The Bellcore T1E1 contribution also studied the possibility of a Frequency Division Multiplex (FDM) approach SHDSL.[37] Both echo cancellation and FDM approaches fell short of the desired performance margin on CSA test loops, even with about 5 dB of coding gain. The echo cancellation–based systems are self-NEXT limited. On the other hand, the FDM systems have no self-NEXT, but are limited by NEXT from previously defined DSL systems.

14.3.1 POET-PAM Systems

The ADTRAN T1E1 contribution proposed a Partially Overlapped Echo-Canceled Transmission (POET) approach to further enhance the performance of SHDSL.[38,39,40] The POET proposal uses the combination of non-symmetric baud rates and spectral shaping of the transmitter PSDs to achieve both spectral compatibility and CSA reach performance requirements.

For a POET-PAM system, a coded 2B1Q line code is used. A 2D Trellis code can be used, resulting in a coding overhead of 0.5 and an information rate of 1.5 bits per symbol. The downstream baud rate is 1.0347 MHz, resulting in a non-filtered 3 dB corner frequency of 517.35 kHz. A shaping filter is used to reduce the transmit power density level further by 10 dB at above 375 kHz, resulting in a power spectrum density as shown in Figure 14.20. The total downstream transmit power is 9.7 dBm.

Figure 14.20   POET-PAM Downstream Power Spectrum Density

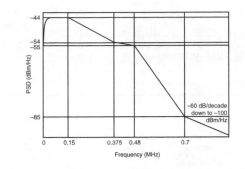

A coded 3B1O line code is used in the upstream direction. A 2D Trellis code can also be used, resulting in a coding overhead of 0.5 and an information rate of 2.5 bits per symbol. The upstream baud rate is 620.8 kHz, resulting in a non-filtered 3 dB corner frequency of 310.4 kHz. A gradual power spectrum density reduction of about 6 dB is created at 275 kHz by using a shaping filter. Figure 14.21 shows the upstream transmit power spectrum density. The total upstream transmit power is 14.7 dBm.

Figure 14.21   POET-PAM Upstream Power Spectrum Density

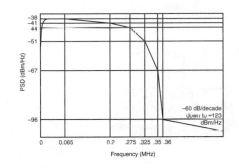

Simulations of Trellis-coded modulation techniques suitable for sequential decoding show that the 10^{-7} error rate can be achieved at an SNR of 13.4 dB for the downstream receiver and 19.6 dB for the upstream receiver. Table 14.17 summarizes the performance margins above those required. Notice that 5 dB of coded margin is achieved on CSA loop 6, and 6 dB of coded margin is achieved for both loops for all interferers except the EC ADSL.

Table 14.17 The SHDSL Performance Margin (dB)

Interferes	CSA Loop 6		CSA Loop 4	
	(US)	(DS)	(US)	(DS)
39 Self NEXT/FEXT	9.7	10.1	8.5	8.8
39 EC-ADSL NEXT/FEXT	5.0	16.5	3.9	16.2
49 HDSL NEXT	8.6	12.3	7.4	10.5
25 T1 NEXT	19.6	8.7	18.4	7.6
49 FDM-ADSLD NEXT, 49 ADSLU FEXT	10.3	15.9	9.0	15.6
49 CAP/QAM RADSL NEXT/FEXT	23.6	16.2	22.4	15.5
49 DSL NEXT	24.4	23.5	23.2	21.6

The performance of the POET system was examined for multiple type interference cases.[41] Figure 14.22 compares the transmit power spectra of T1 and different DSLs.

Figure 14.22 Comparison of Transmit Power Spectra

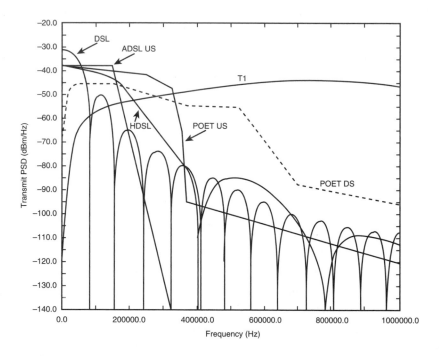

It was found that the coexistence of T1 and SHDSL could make the performance of POET very poor in the downstream direction, as indicated in Table 14.18.

Table 14.18   The HDSL2 Performance Margin (dB)

Interferers	CSA Loop 6		CSA Loop 4	
	(US)	**(DS)**	**(US)**	**(DS)**
39 Self NEXT/FEXT	4.9	4.9	3.7	3.7
39 EC-ADSL NEXT/FEXT	0.1	11.0	-1.0	10.8
49 HDSL NEXT	3.7	7.0	2.4	5.3
39 Self NEXT/FEXT +10 T1 NEXT	4.9	-5.6	3.7	-6.7

14.3.2   TCSFDM Systems

The PairGain Technologies T1E1 contribution proposes a Trellis Coded Staggered FDM (TCSFDM) in conjunction with a 64-QAM line code.[42] The total transmit power for both upstream and downstream is 16.8 dBm. Table 14.19 lists the starting, ending, and center frequencies.

Table 14.19   TCSFDM Spectral Placement

	Frequency (kHz)		
Direction	**Starting**	**Ending**	**Center**
Upstream	0	356.96	178.5
Downstream	131.52	441.92	310.0

Figure 14.23 shows the downstream transmit power spectrum.

Figure 14.23   Downstream Transmit Power Spectrum

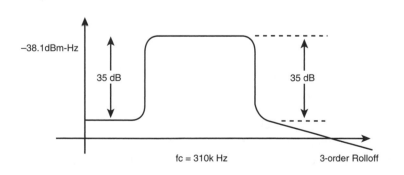

The downstream transceiver uses a square root–raised cosine spectrum with 15 percent excess bandwidth. At the first null of the square root–raised cosine, the attenuation flattens at 35 dB down, on the lower band edge. On the upper frequency band, there is a third-order lowpass filter. The rolloff frequency is 511 kHz.

Figure 14.24 shows the upstream transmit power spectrum.

Figure 14.24 Upstream Transmit Power Spectrum

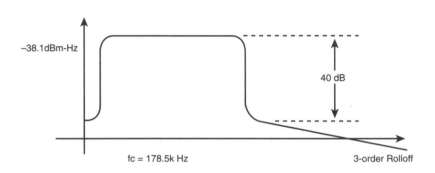

Like the downstream transceiver, the upstream transceiver also uses a square root–raised cosine spectrum with 15 percent excess bandwidth. Here, the attenuation following the first null is masked at 40 dB down. On the upper frequency band, there is, same as in the downstream case, a third-order lowpass filter. The corner frequency is 389.6 kHz.

Table 14.20 summarizes the performance estimate of this TCSFDM system. With 5.1 dB coding gain, minimum performance margin is expected to be 4.6 dB.

Table 14.20 Performance Estimate

Interferer	DFE SNR Margin
49 ADSL	–5.07
25 T1	1.22
39 Self-NEXT/FEXT	–0.384

14.3.3 OverCAPped Systems

PairGain Technologies modified their original TCSFDM proposal with asymmetric spectrum shaping similar to that of POET-PAM.[43] Table 14.21 summarizes the transmit power spectrum characteristics of the modified system, also called OverCAPped.[44]

Table 14.21   Transmit Power Spectrum Characteristics

	Upstream	Downstream
Transmit Power	16 dBm	11 dBm
Maximum PSD	−38.1 dBm/Hz	−43.1 dBm/Hz

It was believed that a passband line code could avoid signal losses at the near DC region. The line code still has a 64-point constellation size, including one coding overhead bit. Figure 14.25 shows the downstream transmit power spectrum.

Figure 14.25   Downstream Transmit Power Spectrum

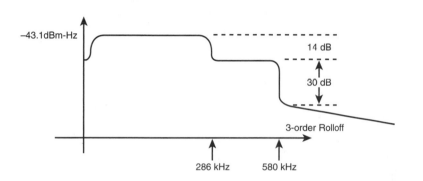

On the lower frequency band, the downstream transceiver might use a square root–raised cosine spectrum with 15 percent excess bandwidth with 3 dB frequency at 25 kHz. On the upper frequency band, a third-order lowpass filter is used and the corner frequency is 580 kHz.

Figure 14.26 shows the upstream transmit power spectrum.

On the lower frequency band, the upstream transceiver might use a square root–raised cosine spectrum with 15 percent excess bandwidth with 3 dB frequency at 25 kHz. On the upper frequency band, there is, same as in the downstream case, a third-order lowpass filter with a corner frequency of 356 kHz.

Uncoded performance margins are estimated for the two most difficult CSA loops. Table 14.22 lists the results of these uncoded performance margin estimates.

Figure 14.26 Upstream Transmit Power Spectrum

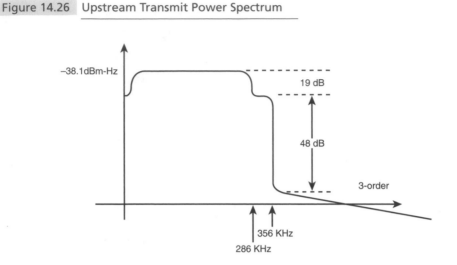

Table 14.22 The SHDSL Performance Margin (dB)

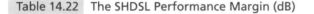

Interferes	CSA Loop 6		CSA Loop 4	
	(US)	(DS)	(US)	(DS)
39 Self NEXT/FEXT	4.05	3.68	3.14	2.64
39 EC-ADSL NEXT/FEXT	0.50	9.85	-0.38	10.2
49 EC-ADSL NEXT/FEXT	-0.06	9.26	-0.94	9.66
49 HDSL NEXT	4.05	3.68	3.14	2.64
25 T1 NEXT	16.80	11.65	15.88	10.72

The OverCAPped transmit spectrum is very similar to that of POET-PAM for both upstream and downstream. Figures 14.27 and 14.28 reveal the differences between OverCAPped and POET-PAM upstream and downstream power spectra, respectively.

Table 14.23 compares the difference in performance between OverCAPped and POET-PAM SHDSL systems, both without coding gain.

Figure 14.27   Upstream Transmit Power Spectra

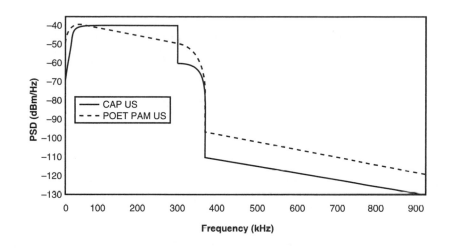

Figure 14.28   Downstream Upstream Transmit Power Spectra

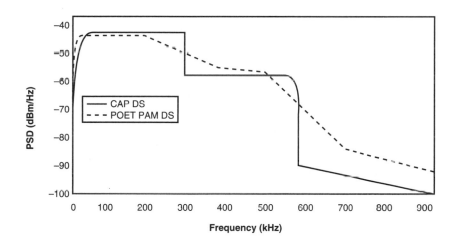

Table 14.23 SHDSL Performance Margin (dB)

Interferes	CSA Loop 4 Upstream		CSA Loop 4 Downstream	
	POET PAM	OverCAPped	POET PAM	OverCAPped
39 Self NEXT/FEXT	3.28	2.58	3.99	4.85
39 EC-ADSL NEXT/FEXT	-1.55	-0.94	11.26	9.32
49 EC-ADSL NEXT/FEXT	-2.10	-1.45	10.69	8.74
49 HDSL NEXT	2.10	2.18	5.47	2.21
25 T1 NEXT	13.49	13.85	1.85	9.17
49 FDM-ADSL NEXT/FEXT	2.70	3.35	10.70	8.76

14.3.4   SST Systems

The Level One Communications T1E1 contribution proposes a symmetric spectrum echo canceled system, called Spectral Shaped Passband Transmission (SST).[45] The baud rate for both upstream and downstream is 310.4 kHz with a coded 64-QAM/CAP line code. The total transmit power is 16.8 dBm. The transmit power density is raised to –35.2 dBm/Hz at around 30 kHz while the remaining power spectrum density, starting at 65 kHz, is –38.1 dBm/Hz, as illustrated in Figure 14.29.

Figure 14.29   SST Transmit Power Spectrum

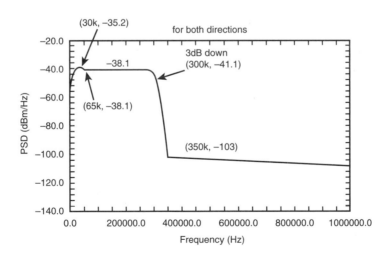

The increased power density will not cause harm to any existing DSL systems because the raised portion matches that of ISDN Basic Rate Access lines. Table 14.24 summarizes the estimated performance of the SST SHDSL for different interferer conditions. The SST system has a 3.2 dB performance margin on CSA loop 4 and a 4.3 dB margin on CSA loop 6 considering a coding gain of 5 dB.

Table 14.24 The SHDSL Performance Margin (dB)

Interferers	CSA Loop 6		CSA Loop 4	
	(US)	(DS)	(US)	(DS)
39 Self NEXT/FEXT	4.3	4.3	3.2	3.2
39 EC-ADSL NEXT/FEXT	7.0	20.4	5.9	20
49 HDSL NEXT	10.7	10.7	9.5	9.5
39 Self NEXT/FEXT +10 T1 NEXT	4.7	4.7	3.5	3.5

14.4 Status of the HDSL2 Standard

The agreement of key transceiver parameters among major proponents is a strong signal of the convergence of a possible SHDSL, also called HDSL2, standard. During the December 1997 T1E1.4 meeting, the basics of an SHDSL standard were agreed upon by co-authors from ADC Telecommunications, ADTRAN, Level One Communications, PairGain Technologies, and Siemens EZM of a joint T1E1.4 contribution.[46]

This contribution recommends the following items for SHDSL:

- A performance margin of 5 dB on all CSA loops

- A programmable encoder for rate 3/4 Trellis codes with 512 states

- The OPTIS (Overlapped PAM Transmission with Interlocking Spectra) asymmetrical transmit power spectral shapes

- The standards project name of Next Generation HDSL for SHDSL

14.4.1 The Rationale for a 5 dB Performance Margin

With the 16-PAM, 512-state, Trellis-coded modulation and the OPTIS transmit spectral shape, 6 dB of performance margin can be achieved on all CSA loops according to computer performance simulation except for one particular loop and noise combination. Table 14.25 summarizes the estimated uncoded OPTIS performance margins for the two worst CSA loops, loops #4 and #6, under different crosstalk noise conditions.[47]

Table 14.25 The OPTIS Uncoded Performance Margin (dB)

	CSA #4 Downstream	CSA #4 Upstream	CSA #6 Downstream	CSA #6 Upstream
39 SELF	9.8	1.7	9.8	2.7
49 HDSL	10.0	1.6	11.4	2.7
25 T1	15.9	18.8	16.6	19.8
49 FDM ADSL	16.1	8.0	14.2	8.9
39 EC ADSL	14.6	1.4	14.2	2.4
24 SELF + 24 T1	1.1	3.8	1.8	4.9
24 FDM ADSL +24 HDSL	9.9	0.8	10.2	1.9

For CSA loop #4 with 24 FDM ADSL and 24 HDSL, the performance margin is only 0.1 dB short considering a Trellis coding gain of 5.1 dB. On the other hand, the required 5 dB performance margin can provide enough room for hardware implementation tolerance.

14.4.2 The Programmable Encoder and 512-State Trellis Codes

The 512-state, 16-PAM, Trellis-coded modulation proposed by PairGain has been considered as a primary encoder for achieving the required 5.1 dB coding gain.[48] Figure 14.30 shows the structure of this 512-state convolution encoder.

Figure 14.30 Encoder Block Diagram

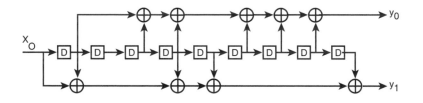

Figure 14.31 shows the structure of this Trellis encoder.

Figure 14.31 512-State Feedforward Convolutional Encoder

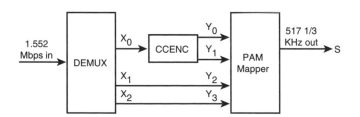

Figure 14.32 shows the bit-to-symbol mapping for the 16-PAM line code.

Figure 14.32 16-PAM Bit-to-Symbol Mapping

	-15	-13	-11	-9	-7	-5	-3	-1	1	3	5	7	9	11	13	15	
	0	1	0	1	0	1	0	1	0	1	0	1	0	1	0	1	y_0
	0	0	1	1	0	0	1	1	0	0	1	1	0	0	1	1	y_1
	0	0	0	0	1	1	1	1	1	1	1	1	0	0	0	0	y_2
	0	0	0	0	0	0	0	0	1	1	1	1	1	1	1	1	y_3

Assuming Tomlison precoding, this 16-PAM line code can achieve a coding gain of 5.1 dB with a latency of 217 ms. The generator polynomial for bit y_0 is denoted (in octal numbers) as g_0=0556. The generator polynomial for bit y_1 is denoted as g_1=1461. The corresponding generator matrix of this code is

$$
g = \begin{bmatrix} g_0 & g_1 & g_2 & g_3 \end{bmatrix} =
\begin{bmatrix}
0 & 1 & 0 & 0 \\
0 & 0 & 1 & 0 \\
0 & 0 & 0 & 1 \\
1 & 1 & 0 & 0 \\
0 & 0 & 0 & 0 \\
1 & 0 & 0 & 0 \\
1 & 1 & 0 & 0 \\
0 & 1 & 0 & 0 \\
1 & 0 & 0 & 0 \\
1 & 0 & 0 & 0 \\
1 & 0 & 0 & 0 \\
0 & 1 & 0 & 0
\end{bmatrix}
$$

or

$$
g(D) =
\begin{bmatrix}
D + D^3 + D^4 + D^6 + D^7 + D^8 & 1 + D + D^4 + D^5 + D^9 & 0 & 0 \\
0 & 0 & 1 & 0 \\
0 & 0 & 0 & 1
\end{bmatrix}
$$

This Trellis code can also be implemented in a feedback format. Figure 14.33 shows the general structure of a programmable encoder in the feedback format.

Figure 14.33 Block Diagram of a Programmable Encoder

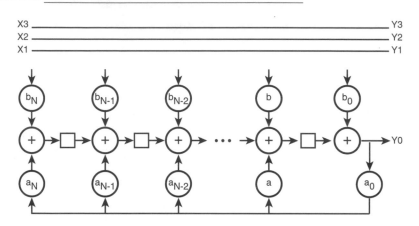

It has also been observed that many different codes can provide similar performance.[49] The adoption of a programmable encoder is proposed by ADTRAN[50] for accommodating a variety of coding schemes allowing differentiation and innovation among different vendors.

14.4.3 The OPTIS Transmit Spectra

Figure 14.34 shows the transmit power spectral density of the OPTIS line code in the downstream direction.

The downstream power spectrum consists of the base spectrum and a part of its mirror image. The bandwidth of the base spectrum is about 256 kHz. The mirror image extends the downstream bandwidth further to about 400 kHz. The power density of the mirror image is about 3 dB higher compared with that of the base spectrum. Figure 14.35 shows the transmit power spectral density of the OPTIS line code in the upstream direction.

The upstream power spectrum has only its base spectrum; however, the power spectrum density is enhanced by about 6 dB between 210 kHz and 245 kHz.

The downstream power spectrum can be implemented with two methods:

- Zero insertion and extension

- Expansion of single sideband

Figure 14.34 OPTIS Downstream Mask

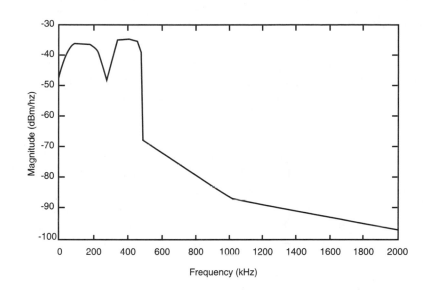

Figure 14.35 OPTIS Upstream Mask

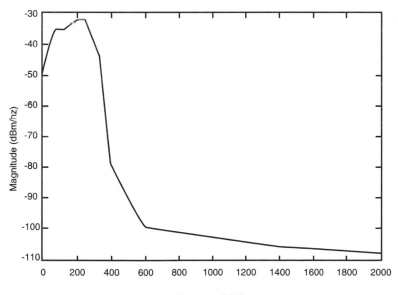

Figure 14.36 shows the functional block diagram of the zero insertion and extension approach.

Figure 14.36 Implementation with Zero Insertion and Extension

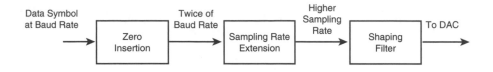

In Figure 14.36, a zero is inserted after every data symbol to double the baud rate. A higher sampling rate for spectral shaping filter is then obtained by extending symbol as well as zero points through sample and hold. For example, assuming a symbol sequence of [−15, 5, −5, 1], the sequence becomes [−15, 0, 5, 0, −5, 0, 1, 0] after zero insertion and becomes [−15, −15, 0, 0, 5, 5, 0, 0, −5, −5, 0, 0, 1, 1, 0, 0] after sampling rate extension. Figure 14.37 shows the functional block diagram of the single sideband approach.

Figure 14.37 Implementation with the Single Sideband Approach

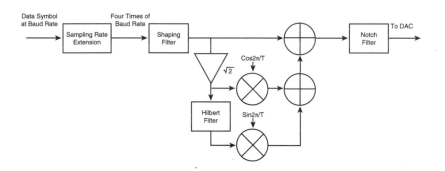

In Figure 14.37, data symbols are first extended to sampling rate through sample and hold. A shaping filter is used to control the excessive bandwidth and the energy of sidelopes. The partial mirror image is added through the single sideband modulation based on the digital Hilbert filter. The specific design of the digital Hilbert filter can control the mirror bandwidth. A notch filter creates the null between the base spectrum and the mirror image defined by the downstream power spectral density mask.

14.4.4 Analyzing SHDSL Transceiver Complexity

Figure 14.38 shows major functional blocks of an SHDSL transceiver.[51]

Figure 14.38 SHDSL Block Diagram

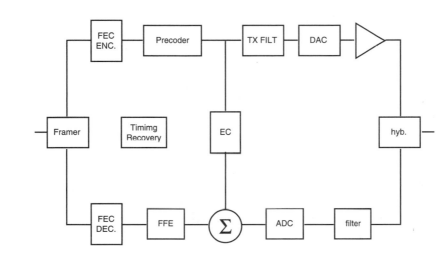

The implementation complexity of an SHDSL transceiver can be estimated by examining its digital computation intensity and analog front-end dynamic range and sampling rate requirements in comparison to those of an HDSL transceiver.

HDSL Transceiver Complexity

The digital computation requirements for an HDSL transceiver can be estimated as follows. Major computations are for the DFE and the echo canceller. The feedback filters (FBF) of a DFE and echo canceller are similar in terms of a low data resolution, 2-bit, adaptive filter with 128 filter coefficients.

The required calculation per second for a DFE or an echo canceller is described as

$$2 \times 128 \times 400 \text{ kHz} = 102.4 \text{ MIPS}$$

The value 400 kHz is the HDSL baud rate, 128 is the length of the adaptive filter, the number 2 accounts for both filtering and coefficient adapting operations, and MIPS stands for Millions of Instructions Per Second. The FBF and echo canceller combined calculation requirement is described as follows:

$$2 \times 102.4 = 204.8 \text{ MIPS}$$

In addition, the coefficient number for the feedforward filter (FFF) of DFE is about 8 and the data path resolution is about 12 bits. The FFF calculation requirement is described as follows:

$$2 \times 8 \times 400 \text{ kHz} = 6.4 \text{ MIPS}$$

This is equivalent to

$$6.4 \times 12 / 2 = 38.4 \text{ MIPS}$$

of 2-bit resolution filtering. The total computation requirement for an HDSL transceiver (in terms of 2-bit resolution filtering) is as follows:

$$204.8 + 38.4 = 243.2 \text{ MIPS}$$

The sampling rate of HDSL is 400 kHz. The peak-to-average ratio for a DAC without digital filtering is about 3.8 dB requiring a DAC resolution of only two bits. The required DAC resolution is seven bits even with a transmit filter. The ADC for an HDSL transceiver is about 13 bits as calculated in section 7.4.5, "ADC Precision Requirements Considering Channel Loss," in Chapter 7, "Analog Front-End Precision."

SHDSL Transceiver Complexity

The digital computation requirements for an SHDSL transceiver can be estimated as follows. Major computations are for the fractionally spaced equalizer (similar to FFF of a DFE), the Tomlinson precoder (similar to FBF of a DFE), the Viterbi decoder, and the echo canceller. The feedback filter (FBF) of a DFE and echo canceller are similar in terms of a low data resolution, 2-bit, adaptive filter with 128 filter coefficients.

For the same CSA loop channel, the Tomlinson precoder and echo canceller length is increased to

$$128 \times 517.3 / 400 = 165 \text{ taps}$$

due to a higher baud rate, assuming echo cancellation is performed at the baud rate.

The required calculation per second for a Tomlinson precoder is described as

$$165 \times 517.3 \text{ kHz} = 85.35 \text{ MIPS}$$

assuming the real-time updating is not necessary for the Tomlinson precoder.

The required calculation per second for an echo canceller (assuming real-time echo canceller coefficient adaptation) is described as follows:

$$2 \times 165 \times 517.3 \text{ kHz} = 170.7 \text{ MIPS}$$

In addition, the coefficient number for the fractionally spaced equalizer is about 20 due to the higher sampling rate and $T/2$ fractional operation. The fractionally spaced equalizer calculation requirement is described as follows:

$$2 \times 20 \times 1034.6 \text{ kHz} = 41.384 \text{ MIPS}$$

Because of the Tomlinson precoder, all these calculations require a full data resolution of between 12 bits (for filtering) and 14 bits (for echo cancellation). The total computation requirement for the combined equalization and echo cancellation operation (in terms of full resolution filtering) is

$$85.35 + 170.7 + 41.384 = 297.43 \text{ MIPS}$$

The computational complexity of a rate 3/4 Viterbi decoder depends on the state number of the encoder.[52] Table 14.26 summarizes Viterbi decoder complexities for convolutional encoders of 64 to 512 states in comparison to that required by the combined equalization and echo cancellation operation of an SHDSL transceiver.

Table 14.26 Rate 3/4 Viterbi Decoder Complexity

States	Computation	Storage
64	0.6	0.96
128	1.18	2.18
256	2.36	4.89
512	4.71	10.82

The complexity of a 512-state Viterbi decoder is about 4.7 times that required by the combined equalization and echo cancellation operation. The total computation requirement for an SHDSL transceiver (in terms of full resolution filtering) is about

$$297.43 \times 5.71 = 1698.348 \text{ MIPS}$$

The sampling rate of SHDSL is 1034.6 kHz. The peak-to-average ratio for a DAC is about 18 dB, requiring a DAC resolution of about eight bits. The ADC for an SHDSL transceiver is about 14 bits because of the 16-PAM line code and a wider signal bandwidth.

SHDSL-to-HDSL Computation Complexity Ratio

The SHDSL-to-HDSL MIPS requirements ratio is

$$1698.348 / 243.2 = 6.983$$

The implementation complexity can be seven to eight times higher than this ratio because of the filtering data path resolution factor of between 12/2=6 and 14/2=7. The combined ratio is between 40 and 50.

On the other hand, the VLSI technology advances according to Moor's law that the complexity of the semiconductor circuit doubles every 18 months. Since the development of the HDSL chip from 1990 to 1998, we have an elapsed time of about five 18-month periods. Therefore, the advance of semiconductor technology can absorb a complexity increase of $2^5 = 32$ times. With that semiconductor technology advance, the development of an SHDSL chip can still be as challenging as the development of an HDSL chip about eight years ago.

Table 14.27 summarizes the SHDSL VLSI complexity estimate in comparison to that of HDSL by Level One Communications and PairGain Technologies.

Table 14.27 VLSI Complexity Comparison

	Framer	FEC	DFE	FFF	EC	MISC	Tot. Digi.	AFE
HDSL	2	NA	1.0	0.93	1.15	1.9	6.98	1.0
HDSL2	2	9.3	2.2	2.0	6.4	6.5	28.4	3.85

The estimate is based on estimated gate count of digital semiconductor circuits and the layout size of analog semiconductor circuits.

End Notes

1. A. Kliger, "Proposal for Consideration of a Single-Pair HDSL Standard Project," *Metalink T1E1 Contribution*, T1E1.4/95-067 (June 1995).

2. A. Kliger, "Report on Measurements of a 1.568 Mbps Single-Pair HDSL System," *Metalink T1E1 Contribution*, T1E1.4/95-068 (June 1995).

3. G. H. Im, E. Langberg, and M. Sorbara, "Performance of 64-CAP–Based Single-Pair HDSL," *AT&T Network Systems T1E1 Contribution*, T1E1.4/95-076 (June 1995).

4. J. Cioffi, J. Chow, P. Chow, and K. Jacobsen, "Single-Duplex HDSL Range/Rate Projections," *Amati T1E1 Contribution*, T1E1.4/95-089 (August 1995).

5. R. Goodson, K. Schneider, and M. Turner, "Single Loop HDSL CAP/PAM Comparison," *ADTRAN T1E1 Contribution*, T1E1.4/95-107 (August 18, 1995).

6. M. Sorbara, "Performance of CAP and PAM for Single-Pair HDSL in Presence of SNEXT," *AT&T Network Systems T1E1 Contribution*, T1E1.4/95-106 (August 1995).

7. H. Takatori and N. Cole, "Performance of 2B1Q, Coded 2B1Q, 3B1O & Coded 3B1O for Single-Pair T1 HDSL," *Level One T1E1 Contribution*, T1E1.4/96-046 (January 22, 1996).

8. W. Y. Chen, "Approaches to a Single-Pair HDSL," *Bellcore T1E1 Contribution*, T1E1.4/95-108 (August 18, 1995).

9. R. Goodson and K. Schneider, "Effect of NEXT Models on SHDSL," *ADTRAN T1E1 Contribution*, T1E1.4/96-036 (January 22, 1996).

10. G. Zimmerman, "Approaches to CSA-Reach Single-Pair HDSL Transmission," *PairGain T1E1 Contribution*, T1E1.4/96-063 (April 22, 1996).

11. M. Sorbara, "Single-Pair T1 HDSL: Spectral Compatibility with ADSL & Implementation Issues," *AT&T Network Systems T1E1 Contribution*, T1E1.4/96-038 (January 1996).

12. K. Kerpez and R. McConnel, "Full-Duplex Trellis-Coded 128-CAP or 16-PAM Single-Pair HDSL," *Bellcore T1E1 Contribution*, T1E1.4/96-024 (January 23, 1996).

13. R. Goodson and K. Schneider, "Proposal for Single-Loop HDSL Using Simple Coded PAM," *ADTRAN T1E1 Contribution*, T1E1.4/96-037 (January 22, 1996).

14. S. Lin, "Relative Complexity of VLSI Viterbi Decoders in HDSL Transceivers," *PairGain Technologies T1E1 Contribution*, T1E1.4/96-064 (April 22, 1996).

15. R. Goodson, "Sequential Decoding and Trellis Coded Modulation for SHDSL," *ADTRAN T1E1 Contribution*, T1E1.4/96-131 (April 22, 1996).

16. R. M. Grayson, "Complexity and Achievable Gain of Sequential Decoding for Large Trellis Codes," *PairGain Technologies T1E1 Contribution*, T1E1.4/96-065 (April 22, 1996).

17. A. Viterbi and J. Omura, *Principles of Digital Communication and Coding* (McGraw-Hill, 1979).

18. F. Wang and D. J. Costello, "Erasure-Free Sequential Decoding of Trellis Codes," *IEEE Trans. Information Theory*, vol. IT-40 (December 1994): 1803–1817.

19. J. Porath and T. Aulin, "Algorithmic Construction of Trellis Codes," *IEEE Trans. Comm.*, vol. COM-41 (May 1993): 649–654.

20. R. M. Grayson, "Further Results on Sequential Decoding of TCM: The Performance of Coded 64-QAM with HDSL Delay Restrictions," *PairGain Technologies T1E1 Contribution*, T1E1.4/96-255 (September 4, 1996).

21. R. Goodson, "Simulation Results for Sequential Decoding of 2D Codes," *ADTRAN T1E1 Contribution*, T1E1.4/96-319 (November 11, 1996).

22. G. J. Pottie and D. P. Taylor, "A Comparison of Reduced Complexity Decoding Algorithms for Trellis Codes," *IEEE JSAC*, vol. 7, no. 9 (December 1989): 1369–1380.

23. R. Goodson, "Sequential Decoding of Coded 16-Point and 64-Point 2D TCM," *ADTRAN T1E1 Contribution*, T1E1.4/97-072 (February 3, 1997).

24. S. Ling, "Performance of HDSL2, Part II Coded System," *Level One Communications T1E1 Contribution*, T1E1.4/96-224 (July 22, 1996).

25. F. Wang and D. J. Costello, "Probabilistic Construction of Large Constraint Length Trellis Codes for Sequential Decoding," *IEEE Trans. Comm.*, vol. COM-43 (September 1995).

26. S. Ling and C. Heegard, "Updated Simulation Results of Sequential Decoding for HDSL2," *Level One Communications T1E1 Contribution*, T1E1.4/96-343 (November 11, 1996).

27. S. Ling and C. Heegard, "Performance of Error Control Coding in an Impulse Noise/ WGN Environment," *Level One Communications T1E1 Contribution*, T1E1.4/96-344 (November 11, 1996).

28. F. Q. Wang, "Efficient Sequential Decoding of Trellis Codes," Ph.D. Dissertation, University of Notre Dame (1993).

29. C. Berrou, A. Glavieux, and P. Thitimajshima, "Near Shannon Limit Error Correcting Coding and Decoding: Turbo-Codes," *Proc. of the ICC '93*, Geneva, Switzerland, (May 1993): 1064–1070.

30. D. Divsalar and F. Pollara, "Turbo Codes for PCS Applications," *Proc. of IEEE ICC '95*, Seattle, Washington (June 1995).

31. D. Divsalar and F. Pollara, "On the Design of Turbo Codes," *JPL TDA Progress Report 42-123* (November 15, 1995).

32. G. Zimmerman, "Turbo Codes for Band Limited Channels: Potential and State-of-the-Technology," *PairGain Technologies T1E1 Contribution*, T1E1.4/96-067 (July 22, 1996).

33. H. Herzberg, "Multilevel Turbo Coding for Single-Pair HDSL Using CAP," *Globespan Technologies T1E1 Contribution*, T1E1.4/96-322 (November 1996).

34. H. Herzberg, "A Structure Interleaver Embedded in Multilevel Turbo Codes for Single-Pair HDSL Using CAP," *Globespan Technologies T1E1 Contribution*, T1E1.4/97-024 (February 1997).

35. S. Ling and C. Heegard, "A Comparison of FEC Techniques for HDSL2," *Level One Communications T1E1 Contribution*, T1E1.4/97-057 (February 3, 1997).

36. G. Zimmerman, "Advantages of Sequential Decoding for HDSL2," *PairGain Technologies T1E1 Contribution*, T1E1.4/97-054 (February 3, 1997).

37. W. Y. Chen, "Architecture and Performance Simulation of Single-Pair HDSL," *Bellcore T1E1 Contribution*, T1E1.4/96-133 (April 19, 1996).

38. K. Schneider, "A Modulation Technique for CSA HDSL2," *ADTRAN T1E1 Contribution*, T1E1.4/97-073 (February 3, 1997).

39. K. Schneider, "Latency Estimate for POET-PAM Transmit Filters," *ADTRAN T1E1 Contribution*, T1E1.4/97-195 (May 12, 1997).

40. K. Schneider, "Effect of Noise Floor Level on POET-PAM Performance Margins," *ADTRAN T1E1 Contribution*, T1E1.4/97-197 (May 12, 1997).

41. H. Takatori, "Evaluation of the Performance of the POET System," *Level One Communications T1E1 Contribution*, T1E1.4/97-191 (May 12, 1997).

42. Jack Liu, "Proposal for HDSL2 Transmission: Spectra, Line Code and Coding," *PairGain Technologies T1E1 Contribution*, T1E1.4/97-074 (February 3, 1997).

43. Jack Liu, "HDSL2 Transmit Spectra," *PairGain Technologies T1E1 Contribution*, T1E1.4/97-178 (May 15, 1997).

44. G. Zimmerman, "Performance and Spectral Compatibility of POET PAM and Over-CAPped Transmission for HDSL2," *PairGain Technologies T1E1 Contribution*, T1E1.4/97-179 (May 15, 1997).

45. H. Takatori, "Spectral Shaped Transmission for HDSL2," *Level One Communications T1E1 Contribution*, T1E1.4/97-192 (May 12, 1997).

46. M. Rude, et al.,"Basis for HDSL2 Standard," *Joint T1E1 Contribution from ADC Telecommunications, ADTRAN, Level One Communications, PairGain Technologies, and Siemens EZM*, T1E1.4/97-471 (December 1997).

47. J. Girardeau, H. Takatori, M. Rude, and G. Zimmerman, "OPTIS PSD Mask and Power Specification for HDSL2," *Level One Communications and PairGain Technologies joint T1E1 Contribution*, T1E1.4/97-320 (September 1997).

48. M. Tu and J. Liu, "A 512-State PAM TCM Code for HDSL2," *PairGain T1E1 Contribution*, T1E1.4/97-300 (September 1997).

49. R. Goodson, "Performance and Characteristics of One-Dimensional Codes for HDSL2," *ADTRAN T1E1 Contribution*, T1E1.4/97-337 (September 1997).

50. R. Goodson, "Motivation for a Programmable Encoder for HDSL2," *ADTRAN T1E1 Contribution*, T1E1.4/97-442 (December 1997).

51. J. Camagna, S. Lin, and A. Gattani, "OPTIS Complexity Estimation," *Level One Communications and PairGain Technologies Joint T1E1 Contributions*, T1E1.4/97-343 (September 1997).

52. S. Lin, "Relative Complexity of VLSI Viterbi Decoders in HDSL Transceivers," *PairGain Technologies T1E1 Contribution*, T1E1.4/96-064 (April 1996).

15

VDSL (Very-High-Bit-Rate Digital Subscriber Lines)

If SHDL is the next generation HDSL, VDSL can also be considered as the next generation ADSL to some extent. The transmission throughput of VDSL is much higher than that of ADSL. The potential of a higher transmission throughput is achieved by expanding the signal bandwidth to the region of 10 to 30 MHz. At such a high frequency, a usable channel can only be realized on short twisted-pair telephone subscriber loops.

VDSL also has asymmetrical transmission throughput, although the symmetrical throughput could be an option. Due to a very high transmission bandwidth, which causes a very high sampling rate, the attempt of approaching the channel capacity has not been a top priority concern in related standard activities.

The idea of signaling at a very high rate has been explored during the early 1990s.[1] Prototype *fiber-to-the-curb* (FTTC) systems with a physical layer similar to a VDSL system have been used in conjunction with a broadband optical distribution network for field tests. The Digital Audio-Visual Council (DAVIC) has referenced such an FTTC system.[2]

Since 1995, VDSL has been a regular discussion topic at ANSI T1E1.4 working group meetings. A VDSL system requirement document[3] and a living list have been updated during these meetings. The European standards group, European Telecommunications Standardization Institute (ETSI), also addresses issues related to VDSL at its regular meetings. An ETSI VDSL system requirement document has also been created.[4]

VDSL is a natural extension of the evolving telecommunication network to the consumer market partially based on an existing loop plant infrastructure. The high transmission throughput telephone optical network can be initially terminated at the *Distribution Area* level and can be connected to end users through the VDSL technology.

The high throughput VDSL is easier to be made compatible with SONET and ATM-based services. VDSL can be used to interconnect business customers within a concentrated area through leased telephone lines for high-speed intranet use. VDSL can also be used in an enterprise or campus environment for providing high-speed digital transmission connections.

This chapter covers many topics related to VDSL, including the following:

- *Transmission environment.* Usable transmission bandwidths are examined for short telephone subscriber loops. Bases for slightly different high-frequency crosstalk models are reviewed. Behaviors of radio frequency ingress and egress through twisted pairs are studied.

- *General system architecture.* Channel capacities in conjunction with self-FEXT and background noise are calculated for short loops. Possible transmit power density levels are reviewed.

- *System proposals.* Key features of CAP/QAM and DMT VDSL line code proposals are reviewed.

- *Twisted-pair primary constants for VDSL.* Simplified primary parameter tables for different types of twisted pairs are provided for easy reference.

15.1   Transmission Environment for VDSL

I anticipate that the evolution of the existing telephone loop plant will bring more fiber links to telephone subscriber loops. Bigger portions of subscriber loops near a CO will be replaced by fiber links. The fiber link of a subscriber loop will be getting longer while the copper link will be getting shorter.

The size of a Distribution Area, where the distribution point can be connected to a CO through fiber links, will be shrinking from about 500 subscribers to a few dozen subscribers. The optical transceiver at the distribution point, also called the *Optical Network Unit* (ONU), can still be connected with remaining twisted-pair distribution cables and drop wires to utilize existing loop plant infrastructure.

Remaining copper twisted-pair loops from an ONU to a telephone subscriber are expected to be less than 5 kft. Consequently, a wider bandwidth becomes available for shorter twisted-pair loops. Primary parameters of twisted-pair cables, especially at higher frequencies, have been recently published[5,6,7,8] to facilitate the feasibility studies of a Very-high-bit-rate Digital Subscriber Line (VDSL) on an emerging short-distance copper twisted-pair telephone loop plant.

15.1.1   *VDSL Channel Model*

According to transmission characteristics defined by the recently published primary parameters of twisted-pair cables that make VDSL feasible on an emerging short-distance copper twisted-pair telephone loop plant, the 70 dB loss channel bandwidths are about 6.25 MHz, 14 MHz, and larger than 30 MHz for the 24-gauge 4500, 3000, and 1500 ft. twisted-pair loops,[9] respectively, as shown in Figure 15.1.

Figure 15.1   Insertion Loss of 24-Gauge Twisted-Pair Loop

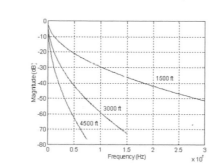

The transmit signal with a power density level of –60 dBm/Hz can maintain a signal-to-noise ratio of about 10 dB with respect to a receiver front-end background noise of –140 dBm/Hz at the 70 dB channel loss frequency point. The 70 dB loss channel bandwidths are 4 MHz, 9 MHz, and larger than 30 MHz for the 26-gauge 1500, 3000, and 4500 ft. twisted-pair loops, respectively, as shown in Figure 15.2.

Figure 15.2   Insertion Loss of 26-Gauge Twisted-Pair Loop

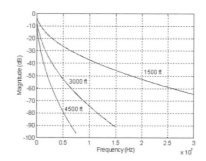

It has been observed that short bridged taps can cause deep notches for VDSL length loops.[10] Figure 15.3 shows the effect of different lengths of bridged taps at the middle of a

2 kft, 26-gauge twisted-pair loop. Bridged tap lengths range from 8 ft. to 128 ft. The shortest bridged tap of 8 ft. causes the deepest frequency null at about 20 MHz.

Figure 15.3 The Effect of Bridged Taps on Short Twisted-Pair Loops

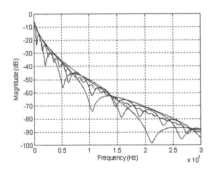

Figure 15.4 shows the effect of different lengths of bridged taps at the middle of a 1 kft, 24-gauge twisted-pair loop. Bridged tap lengths also range from 8 ft. to 128 ft. The notches could be as deep as 25 dB.

Figure 15.4 The Effect of Bridged Taps on Short Twisted-Pair Loops

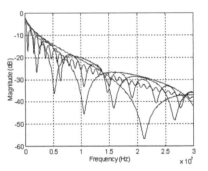

15.1.2 VDSL Crosstalk Model

Recent measurements of 24-AWG PIC aerial distribution cables have indicated some slight differences compared with the 15 dB per decade simplified Unger model.[11] The NEXT power sum transfer function can still be described by

$$\left| H_{NEXT}(f) \right|^2 = \chi_n f^n$$

At the frequency range of 1.5 to 30 MHz, however, we have

$$x_{24} = 1.41 \times 10^{-13} \text{ and } n = 1.37$$

instead of

$$x_{24} = 5.937 \times 10^{-13} \text{ and } n = 1.5$$

as defined previously. The difference between coupling coefficients, x_{24}s, is about 6.24 dB while the loss differences are more than 5 dB.

The FEXT power sum transfer function is generally described by

$$\left| H_{FEXT}(f) \right|^2 = \left| H_{channel}(f) \right|^2 \times k \times l \times f^2$$

The values are as follows:

$H_{channel}(f)$ is the channel transfer function.

k is the coupling constant.

l is the twisted-pair length.

f is the frequency.

For $l = 1000$ ft. and at the frequency range of 1.5 to 30 MHz, we have

$$k = 4.33 \times 10^{-19} \text{ and } n = 1.82$$

instead of

$$k = 5.21 \times 10^{-20} \text{ and } n = 2.0$$

as defined previously. The maximum loss difference is about 4 dB.

15.1.3 Radio Frequency Interference

For VDSL, the usable bandwidth is between 4 MHz and 30 MHz, depending on loop length and the twisted-pair cable type. Under such wide a bandwidth, there could be some interference between VDSL transceivers and traditional radio receivers. There are many Amplitude Modulated (AM) Medium Wave (MW) radio stations in the frequency band of between 550 kHz and 1700 kHz. Short Wave (SW) AM radio stations are located within a few frequency bands from 1.7 MHz and 30 MHz, as shown in Figure 15.5.

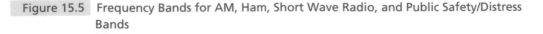

Figure 15.5 Frequency Bands for AM, Ham, Short Wave Radio, and Public Safety/Distress Bands

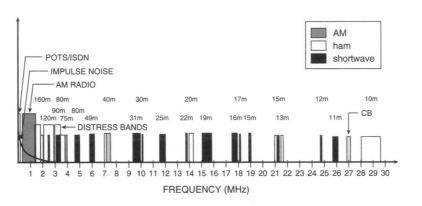

There are also amateur short wave frequency bands distributed in the same frequency range, as shown in Figure 15.5, and further summarized in Table 15.1. In addition, there are also some other specific-purpose radio transceivers.

Table 15.1 Amateur Ham Radio Frequency Bands

Wave Length (Meters)	Frequency Band (MHz)
180	1.8–2.0
80	3.5–4.0
40	7.0–7.3
30	10.10–10.15
20	14.00–14.35
17	18.068–18.168
15	21.00–21.45
12	24.89–24.99
10	28.00–29.70

The transmit power of AM MW radio stations is normally between 300 kW–500 kW. The high-power AM MW radio station, however, can have a transmit power of up to 5 MW.[12] The transmit power of AM SW radio stations is also normally between 300 kW and 500 kW. On the other hand, the transmit power of SW amateur radios is normally below 400 W or 1500 W, depending on local regulations.

The incident power at a location of distance d away from a transmit antenna of unit gain can be expressed as follows:[13]

$$P_{inc} = \frac{P_{trans}}{\pi d^2} |A_s|^2$$

in which

$$|A_s| = \frac{2 + 0.3p}{2 + p + 0.6p^2} - \sqrt{\frac{p}{2}} e^{-0.6p} \sin b$$

for

$$p \approx \frac{k_0 d \omega \varepsilon_0}{2\sigma}$$

$$b \approx \tan^{-1} \frac{\kappa' \omega \varepsilon_0}{\sigma}$$

With

$$\frac{\sigma}{\omega \varepsilon_0} = \frac{1.8 \times 10^4 \sigma}{f|_{MHz}}$$

we have

$$p \approx \frac{2.78 \times 10^{-5} k_0 d f|_{MHz}}{\sigma}, \quad b \approx \tan^{-1} \frac{5.56 \times 10^{-5} \kappa' f|_{MHz}}{\sigma}$$

The dielectric constant κ' is usually in the range of 10 to 15. We usually have

$$\sigma = 10^{-2} S/m \text{ and } k_0 = \frac{2\pi}{\lambda_0}$$

The wavelength λ_0 can be calculated as follows:

$$\lambda_0 = \frac{3 \times 10^2}{f|_{MHz}}$$

Assuming $\kappa' = 10$, we therefore have

$$p \approx 5.82 \times 10^{-5} d \left(f|_{MHz} \right)^2$$

$$b \approx \tan^{-1}\left(5.56 \times 10^{-2} f|_{MHz} \right)$$

The radio electromagnetic field strength, in the unit of $\mu V / m$, is related to the incident power, in the unit of W / m^2, through the intrinsic impedance

$$Z_0 = \sqrt{\frac{\mu_0}{\varepsilon_0}} = 377\Omega$$

of the free space by

$$\frac{|E|^2}{2Z_0} = P_{inc}$$

For a dipole antenna with matched antenna and terminal impedance of R_a, we have

$$R_a = \frac{Z_0}{1.64\pi}$$

and

$$|E| = \sqrt{3.28\pi R_a P_{inc}}$$

With some transmission and coupling losses, these radio signals appear as noise interference at the front end of a VDSL transceiver. The VDSL noise power density level has been expressed in the unit of *dBm/Hz*, which is 1 milliwatt per Hertz. On the other hand, the strength of radio electromagnetic field is expressed in the unit of *dBμV/m* , which is 1 microvolt per meter.

For a particular frequency band, a certain measuring distance, and a matched antenna and terminal impedance of 75 ohms, the equal power conversion factor between *dBm* and *dBμV* is the following:

$$0 dBm = 10 \times \log_{10} \frac{V^2}{100} \times \frac{1}{0.001} - > 0.2739 \text{ volts } -$$

$$> 20 \times \log_{10} \frac{0.2739}{0.000001} = 108.75 dB\mu V$$

For using a particular type of antenna, the antenna gain should also be included in the conversion factor. At 10 MHz, an isotropic antenna has an antenna gain of −5 dB.[14] For the isotropic antenna, the field power in the unit of *dBμV / m* to antenna termination power in the unit of *dBm* conversion factor is 108.75–5=103.75 dB. For a fixed field strength, the power delivered by an isotropic antenna is proportional to the square power of the wavelength. Therefore, the same field strength will produce 2.5 dB and 6 dB more power delivered by an isotropic antenna at frequencies of 7.5 MHz and 6 MHz, respectively. In the other direction, the same field strength will produce 6 dB and 14 dB less power at frequencies of 20 MHz and 50 MHz, respectively.

By comparing radio field strength with induced power at a cable termination, we can find the conversion factor. By comparing the conversion factor of a particular cable with that of an equal power conversion, we can find the cable *Radio Frequency Interference* (RFI) loss, which is equivalent to the negative antenna gain.

Table 15.2 summarizes power losses for different cables at different frequencies along with the average and worst cable power losses. Results in Table 15.2 are calculated based on induced power measurements made by Broadband Technologies for a known strength of radio field.[15]

Table 15.2   Cable RFI Power Loss (dB)

Frequency (MHz)	BKMA 100 Pair	ARTM 25 Pair	Steel Flat Drop	Twisted Drop	Twisted Customer
1.9	74	55.92	36.48	45.46	39.57
3.9	55.92	73.98	50.10	47.96	53.15
7.2	52.04	52.04	40.91	60.00	52.04
10.125	54.90	59.17	41.01	52.04	60.00
14.2	47.96	48.97	35.01	49.00	49.12
18.13	59.17	67.96	40.91	54.96	55.43
21.3	61.13	57.08	48.09	61.03	60.00
24.96	74.27	75.85	48.56	53.55	63.10
29.0	59.08	55.98	47.90	56.90	55.56
Average	59.83	60.77	43.22	53.43	5421
Worst	47.96	48.97	35.01	45.46	39.57

Through the ionospheric reflection, the SW radio interference field strength can be calculated by combining the ray-path distance loss and ionospheric absorption loss for a one-hop propagation. For a ray-path distance loss of between 80–120 dB and an ionospheric absorption loss between 20–40 dB, the combined loss is between 100–160 dB. For a SW radio transmit power of 300 kw, or 84.77 dBm, the incident power at a twisted pair could vary between –75.23 and –15.23 dBm/m² or 43.54 and 103.54 $dB\mu V / m$.

Assuming a radio station transmit power of 500 kW, a bandwidth of 10 kHz, and a cable power loss of 40 dB, we can calculate the RFI induced noise density. For d=10 miles =16090 m at a frequency of 1.9 MHz, we have the following:

$$p \approx 5.82 \times 10^{-5} \times 1.609 \times 10^{4} (1.9)^{2} = 3.38$$

$$b \approx \tan^{-1}\left(5.56 \times 10^{-2} \times 1.9\right) = \tan^{-1}(0.1056) = 6.03^{o}$$

$$|A_{s}| = \frac{2 + 0.3 \times 3.38}{2 + 3.38 + 0.6 \times 3.38^{2}} - \sqrt{\frac{3.38}{2}} e^{-0.6 \times 3.38} \sin 6.03^{o} = 0.228$$

$$P_{inc} = \frac{500 \times 10^{3}}{\pi \times 16090^{2}} 0.228^{2} = 3.196 \times 10^{-5} Watts / m^{2} = -14.95 dBm / m^{2}$$

$$|E| = \sqrt{2 \times 377 \times 3.196 \times 10^{-5}} = 0.1552 Volt/m = 103.82 dB\mu V/m$$

The RFI power density is

$$P_{RFI} = 103.82 - 108.75 - 40 - 10\log_{10}10^4 = -84.93 dBm/Hz$$

Table 15.3 summarizes the RFI power density levels for other frequencies and distances.

Table 15.3   RFI Power Density (dBm/Hz)

Frequency (MHz)	0.01 Mile 500 W	0.1 Mile 500 W	1 Mile 500 kW	10 Miles 500 kW
1.9	−42.14	−62.31	−53.63	−84.93
3.9	−42.28	−63.04	−59.09	−98.96
7.2	−42.75	−65.44	−69.60	−111.02
10.125	−43.36	−68.83	−75.24	−117.32
14.2	−44.47	−74.78	−81.82	−123.41
18.13	−45.79	−79.63	−86.66	−127.74
21.3	−47.02	−81.69	−89.76	−130.57
24.96	−48.62	−82.92	−92.74	−133.36
29.0	−50.60	−84.28	96.62	−135.98

AM MW and SW radio stations as well as some high-power amateur radio stations can generate radio frequency interference to a VDSL receiver. On the other hand, the VDSL signal radiated from telephone subscriber loops can also affect some sensitive radio receptions, such as that of an amateur radio receiver. With the worst and average cable power loss factors, we can also estimate VDSL signal–generated field strength. We have

$$|E| = 20\log_{10}\frac{\sqrt{10^{\frac{P}{10}} \times 0.001 \times B_W R_t 10^{-\frac{K_{cable}}{10}}}}{10^{-6}\sqrt{4\pi r}}$$

The values are as follows:

$|E|$ is the field strength in the unit of $dB\mu V/m$.

P is the VDSL transmit power density in the unit of dBm/Hz.

B_W is the bandwidth of interest in the unit of Hz.

R_t is the twisted-pair termination resistance.

r is the distance from the twisted-pair cable in the unit of m.

K_{cable} is the cable power loss in the unit of dB.

For $P = -70dBm / Hz$, $B_W = 2.2kHz$, $R_t = 100\Omega$, we have

$$|E| = P - 30 + 10\log_{10} B_W R_t - K_{cable} + 120 - 10\log_{10}(4\pi) - 20\log_{10} r$$
$$= -70 - 30 + 53.42 - K_{cable} + 120 - 10.99 - 20\log_{10} r$$
$$= 62.43 - K_{cable} - 20\log_{10} r$$

For $K_{cable} = 35dB$ and $r = 10m$, we have

$$|E| = 62.43 - 35 - 20\log_{10} 10 = 7.43dB\mu V / m$$

Table 15.4 shows estimated worst and average VDSL signal–caused field strength for different type of twisted-pair cables along with the worst-case measurements.[16]

Table 15.4 Field Strength Caused by a VDSL Signal (dBµV/m)

	BKMA 100 Pair at 10 m	ARTM 25 Pair at 6 m	Steel Flat Drop at 6 m	Twisted Drop at 6 m
Measured	1	−1	10	1
Worst Case	−5.53	−2.1	11.86	1.41
Average	−17.4	−13.9	3.65	−13.23

Measured values are also from the *Broadband Technologies T1E1.4 Contribution*. Estimations for worst VDSL-caused field strengths are very close to that of measured worst cases except for the BKMA 100 twisted pair. That big difference might be considered as a special case where the field strength is enhanced by an unknown cause. In comparison to twisted-pair cables, flat cables can induce a much stronger radio field.

15.2 General System Architecture

Before any specific VDSL transceiver parameters can be determined, some system issues need to be resolved. The understanding of the transmission potential under the VDSL channel and noise condition is a very important aspect of defining the system architecture. The VDSL transmission throughput is mainly limited by the combination of loop plant background and self-NEXT noises.

A high transmit power can lead to a high transmission throughput. On the other hand, the transmission power level is limited not only by the capability of the hardware implementation, but also by the amount of egress from the twisted-pair loop. Using expressions developed in Chapter 4, "Transceiver Front-End Noise Models," VDSL loop plant SNRs and channel capacities are calculated in this section.

The received signal power density is determined by the transmit power spectrum and the twisted-pair loop channel characteristics. We have

$$S(f) = Q(f)|H(f)|^2$$

$Q(f)$ is the transmit power spectral density, and $H(f)$ is the channel transfer function. The higher the received signal power, the higher the transmission throughput. The effectiveness of the received signal power, however, is relative to the noise power also present at the input of a receiver. For VDSL, we are interested in effects of FEXT, loop plant background, and RFI noise.

We consider the loop plant background noise as white noise because its spectrum is almost flat. The strength of a white noise of density W can be described by its total power σ^2 within a particular bandwidth of B. We have the received-signal-to-white-noise ratio as

$$\frac{S(f)}{W} = \frac{Q(f)|H(f)|^2}{W}$$

Figure 15.6 shows signal-to-noise ratios under the white noise condition for 24-gauge twisted-pair loop channel models, assuming a transmit power density of -70 dBm/Hz and a white noise power density of -140 dBm/Hz.

Under the self-FEXT condition for which the same transmit power spectrum also affects both received signal and noise power, we have the received-signal-to-noise ratio as follows:

$$\frac{S(f)}{N_F(f)} = \frac{Q(f)|H(f)|^2}{Q(f)FEXT(f)} = \frac{1}{klf^2}$$

The values are as follows:

$$k = 8 \times 10^{-20}.$$

l is in units of ft.

f is in units of Hz.

The channel model becomes irrelevant.

Figure 15.6 Signal-to-White-Noise Ratio for 24-Gauge Twisted-Pair Loops

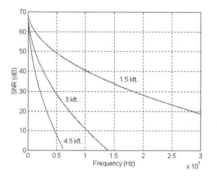

In practice, especially at a low-frequency region and a high-frequency region for which the FEXT noise power density is very small, the effect of white background noise also needs to be considered. By including the background noise power density, the received-signal-to-noise ratio becomes

$$\frac{S(f)}{N_F(f) + W} = \frac{Q(f)|H(f)|^2}{Q(f)FEXT(f) + W} = \frac{1}{klf^2 + \dfrac{W}{Q(f)|H(f)|^2}}$$

Figure 15.7 shows signal-to-noise ratios under the self-FEXT plus white noise condition for 24-gauge twisted-pair loop channel models with a transmit power density of –70 dBm/Hz and a background white noise level of –140 dBm/Hz.

For the receiver front-end white noise limited condition, the channel capacity for VDSL can be described as

$$C = \int_{f_1}^{f_2} \log_2\left(1 + \frac{S(f)}{W(f)}\right) df$$

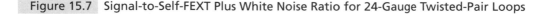

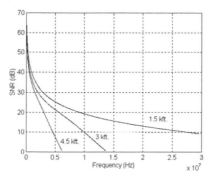

The values are as follows:

$f_1 = 1.5 MHz$ is the lower-corner frequency of the VDSL signal spectrum above that of ADSL.

f_2 is the higher-corner frequency.

For the self-FEXT plus receiver front-end white noise limited condition, the channel capacity can be described as

$$C = \int_{f_1}^{f_2} \log_2 \left(1 + \frac{S(f)}{N_F(f) + W} \right) df$$

Figure 15.8 shows channel capacities under the self-FEXT plus white noise condition for 24-gauge twisted-pair loop channel models also assuming a transmit power density of –70 dBm/Hz and a white noise power density of –140 dBm/Hz.

Figure 15.9 shows channel capacities also under the self-FEXT plus white noise condition for a 2 kft, 24-gauge twisted-pair loop with different lengths of bridged taps also assuming a transmit power density of –70 dBm/Hz and a white noise power density of –140 dBm/Hz.

According to channel capacity results, transmission throughputs for 1.5 kft, 3 kft, and 4.5 kft, 24-gauge twisted-pair loops are limited to 160 Mbps, 68 Mbps, and 25 Mbps, respectively, for a transmission bandwidth of less than 30 MHz. The frequency band below 1.5 MHz is also reserved for ADSL with concerns about spectral compatibility. We also observe that the inclusion of bridged taps will reduce the channel capacity. With advanced modulation and coding techniques, the transmission throughput of a DSL system can be made within 2 to 6 dB to less than the channel capacity.

Figure 15.8 Self-FEXT Plus White Noise Channel Capacity for the 24-Gauge Twisted-Pair Loop

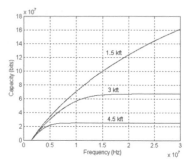

Figure 15.9 Self-FEXT Plus White Noise Channel Capacity for a 2 kft, 24-Gauge Twisted-Pair Loop

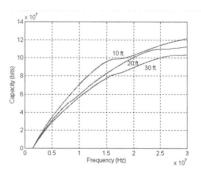

We might also reserve a 6 dB performance margin for VDSL to account for some non-characterized loop and system impairments. Figure 15.10 shows channel capacities under the same self-FEXT plus white noise condition for 24-gauge twisted-pair loop channel models except with a 6 dB performance margin. The effect of the 6 dB performance margin is emulated by reducing signal-to-noise ratio by a factor of 4 at all frequencies.

According to channel capacity results with 6 dB performance margin, transmission throughput for 1.5 kft, 3 kft, and 4.5 kft, 24-gauge twisted-pair loops is limited to 108 Mbps, 44 Mbps, and 18 Mbps, respectively, also for a transmission bandwidth of less than 30 MHz. The total of realized transmission throughput in both upstream and downstream directions might be less than what we have observed due to the allocation of a guardband between upstream and downstream channels if frequency division multiplex is involved.

Figure 15.10 Self-NEXT Channel Capacity with 6 dB Noise Margin

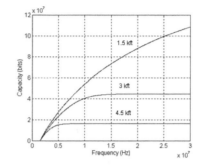

Symmetrical transmission throughput of 13 Mbps and 26 Mbps as well as asymmetrical transmission throughput of 52 Mbps/6.4 Mbps, 26 Mbps/3.2 Mbps, and 13 Mbp/1.6 Mbps have been considered for VDSL depending on loop and noise environment. Transmit power density of –60 dBm/Hz in non-HAM bands and –80 dBm/Hz in HAM bands has been considered. Figure 15.11 shows such a transmit power spectrum mask defined by the ETSI VDSL document.[9] An alternative –70 dBm/Hz transmit power density was also considered.

Figure 15.11 VDSL Transmit Power Density with Notches

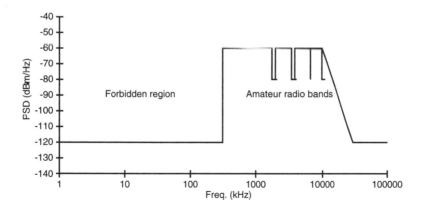

To take advantage of a better transmission environment at low frequencies, a staircase VDSL transmit power density mask has also been proposed, as shown in Figure 15.12.[17] This proposed PSD mask has not been agreed to at any standard meetings.

Figure 15.12 A Staircase VDSL Transmit Power Density Mask

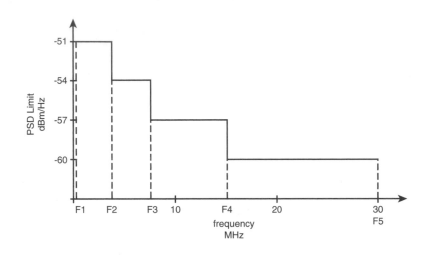

Table 15.5 defines the staircase VDSL PSD mask in more detail.

Table 15.5 The Definition of a Staircase VDSL PSD MASK

Frequency Band (MHz)	Power Density (dBm/Hz)
0.2–3.5	−51
3.5–7.0	−54
7.0–14	−57
14–30	−60
30–	−120

Table 15.6 specifies PSD at HAM bands for the same staircase VDSL mask.

Table 15.6 The Definition for HAM Bands

Frequency Band (MHz)	Power Density (dBm/Hz)
1.8–2.0	−71
3.5–4.0	−74
7.0–7.3	−77
10.1–10.15	−77
14–14.35	−80
18.068–18.168	−80
21.0–21.45	−80
28.0–29.7	−80

15.3 VDSL System Line Code Proposals

There are generally two proposals, CAP/QAM and DMT, for the VDSL line code. The CAP/QAM proposal is associated with the Frequency Division Multiplex for the upstream and downstream channels. The DMT proposal is associated with the Time Division Multiplex, although the division between upstream and downstream is independent from the choice of line code. In addition, there is also a multiple QAM VDSL proposal to avoid international amateur radio bands.[18]

There are proposals to improve the performance of a DMT VDSL system using *window filters*.[19,20] It was also considered possible to interlace downstream and upstream DMT subcarriers together for a FDM approach, but without any band splitting filter.[21] It was shown that downstream and upstream frames can be aligned by extending the size of the cyclic prefix.

15.3.1 CAP/QAM Proposal

The CAP/QAM VDSL proposal is still under development. Currently, the transmission throughput, the constellation size, and the center frequency have been defined for different serving distance in both upstream and downstream directions.

Figure 15.13 shows the general architecture of a VDSL-based broadband transmission system.[22]

Figure 15.13 VDSL Generic Reference Model

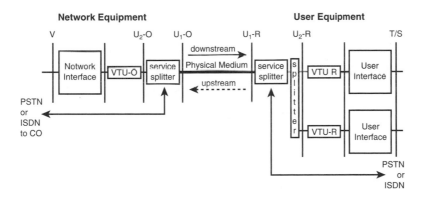

Service splitters, for either a POTS or an ISDN channel, terminate a VDSL subscriber loop at both ends. The VDSL at the network end, within an *Optical Network Unit* (ONU), is called *VDSL Terminal Unit-ONU* (VTU-O). The VDSL at the subscriber end within a residential premises is called *VDSL Terminal Unit-Remote* (VTU-R). Multiple deployment of VTU-Rs was considered feasible with the use of a VDSL splitter. This is also sometimes called a *point-to-multipoint configuration*.

Figure 15.14 shows a VDSL protocol reference model, which further depicts the existence of a frame structure, separate upstream and downstream error control mechanisms, and some management and operational control functions.

Figure 15.14 VDSL Protocol Reference Model

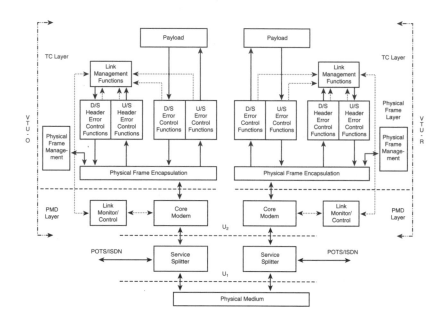

Figure 15.15 shows the general structure of a CAP VDSL transmitter. The CAP VDSL transmitter consists of a bit-to-symbol encoder, a pair of passband, in-phase and quadrature, transmit shaping filters, and an additional passband spectrum shaping filter.

Figure 15.16 shows the general structure of a QAM VDSL transmitter. The QAM VDSL transmitter also consists of a bit-to-symbol encoder, a pair of baseband transmit shaping filters followed by a pair of modulators implemented with the in-phase and quadrature multiplication of the carrier, and an additional passband spectrum shaping filter.

The impulse response of the baseband shaping filter for the QAM transmitter can be described as

$$g(t) = \frac{\sin\left(\pi\frac{4t}{5T}\right) + \left(\frac{4t}{5T}\right)\cos\left(\pi\frac{6t}{5T}\right)}{\left(\pi\frac{t}{T}\right)\left[1 - \left(\frac{4t}{5T}\right)^2\right]}$$

T is the baud period.

Figure 15.15   CAP VDSL Transmitter

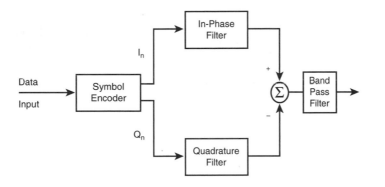

Figure 15.16   QAM VDSL Transmitter

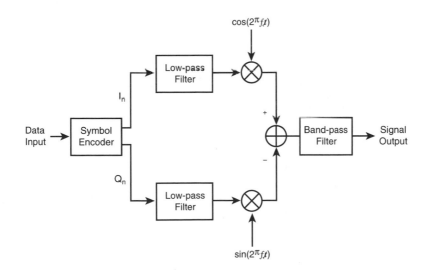

The QAM transmit signal can be described as

$$S_{QAM}(t) = \left[\sum_n I_n g(t - nT) \right] \cos(2\pi f_c t) - \left[\sum_n Q_n g(t - nT) \right] \sin(2\pi f_c t)$$

The impulse response of the in-phase CAP transmit filter can be described as

$$f(t) = g(t)\cos(2\pi f_c t)$$

The value f_c is the center frequency.

The impulse response of the quadrature CAP transmit filter can be described as

$$f'(t) = g(t)\sin(2\pi f_c t)$$

The CAP transmit signal can be described as

$$S_{CAP}(t) = \sum [I_n f(t - nT) - Q_n f'(t - nT)]$$

A 16-point constellation carrying four bits per symbol is used for both QAM and CAP line codes in the downstream direction, as illustrated in Figure 15.17.

Figure 15.17 CAP/QAM Downstream 16-Point Constellation

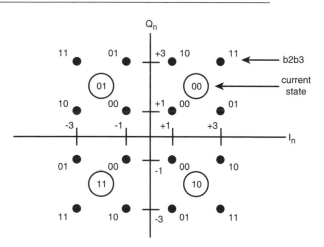

Even though the same constellation is adapted, VDSL CAP and QAM transceivers are generally not compatible, which means that a VDSL QAM receiver cannot be used to recover signals from a VDSL CAP transmitter and vice versa.

Table 15.7 summarizes the CAP/QAM VDSL downstream transmission throughput values, baud rates, and transmit spectrum characteristic frequencies.

Table 15.7 Downstream Transmission Parameters

Loop Length kft (km)	Downstream Rate (Mbps)	Symbol Rate (MHz)	Lowest Freq. (MHz)	Center Freq. (MHz)	Highest Freq. (MHz)
Long, 4.5 (1.5)	6.48	1.62	2	2.972	3.944
Long, 4.5 (1.5)	12.96	3.24	2	3.944	5.888
Medium, 3 (1)	25.92	6.48	2	5.888	9.772
Short, 1 (0.3)	51.84	12.96	2	9.776	17.552

The downstream baud rates of a VDSL transceiver can range from 1.62 MHz to 12.96 MHz. Transmit spectrum bandwidths defined by differences between highest and lowest frequencies are 120 percent of corresponding baud rates. Different transmit filter coefficients should be maintained for different loop conditions. The transmit spectrum of the VDSL downstream channel is allocated at above 2 MHz.

A 256-point constellation carrying eight bits per symbol is used for both QAM and CAP line codes in the upstream direction (see Figure 15.18). Again, VDSL CAP and QAM upstream transceivers are not compatible.

Table 15.8 summarizes CAP/QAM VDSL upstream transmission throughput values, baud rates, and transmit spectrum characteristic frequencies. The upstream baud rates of a VDSL transceiver can range from 202.5 kHz to 810 kHz. The transmit spectrum of the VDSL upstream channel is centered at 1.314 MHz.

Figure 15.18   CAP/QAM Upstream 256-Point Constellation

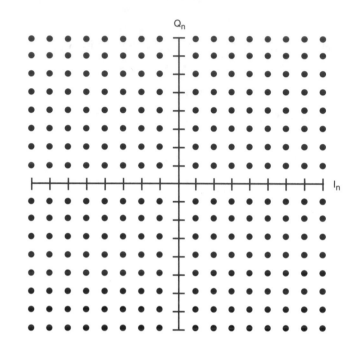

Table 15.8   Upstream Transmission Throughput

Loop Length kft (km)	Downstream Rate (Mbps)	Baud Rate (MHz)	Lowest Freq. (MHz)	Center Freq. (MHz)	Highest Freq. (MHz)
Long, 4.5 (1.5)	1.62	0.2025	1.1925	1.314	1.4355
Medium, 3 (1)	3.24	0.405	1.071	1.314	1.557
Short, 1 (0.3)	6.48	0.81	0.828	1.314	1.8

Symmetric transmission throughput values of 12.96 Mbps and 25.92 Mbps are considered possible for medium- and short-length VDSL loops, respectively. Detailed constellation and spectrum parameters, however, have not yet been decided.

15.3.2 DMT Proposal

The DMT VDSL proposal is also under further development. Currently, the IFFT/FFT size, the transmission throughput, the transmit power spectrum, and the super frame structure have been defined for different serving distances in both upstream and downstream directions.

Figure 15.19 illustrates the reference model of a DMT VDSL[23] transceiver, VTU-O. In addition to the core mode, physical layer of the DMT VDSL, Forward Error Correction (FEC)–based error control mechanisms are also depicted. Dual latency systems are defined for both downstream and upstream channels.

Figure 15.19 Reference Model

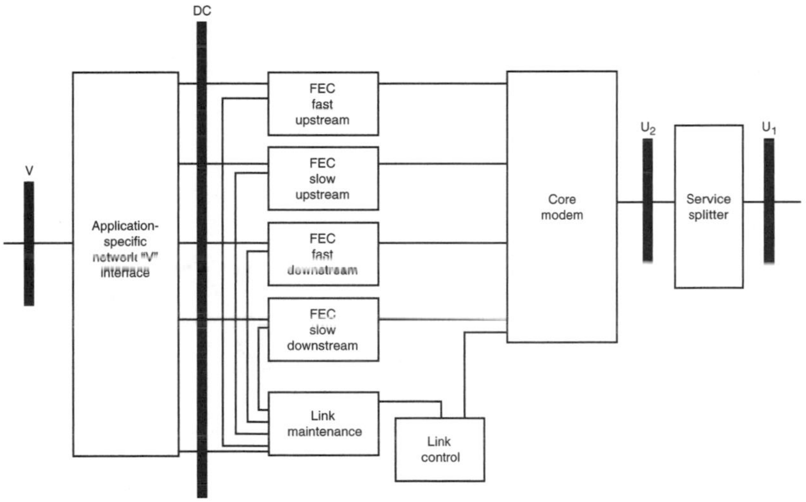

The reference model of a VTU-R is similar to that depicted in Figure 15.19, except that the name of α interface is replaced by the name β interface, and the V interface connecting to the backbone network is replaced by the S/T interface connecting to the premises wiring.

Table 15.9 summarizes the transmission parameters of the DMT VDSL. Three possible sampling rates (5, 10, and 20 times that of ADSL) are considered while IFFT/FFT size is maintained to be the same. Up to 11 bits can be allocated for each DMT subcarrier depending on the line-signal-to-noise ratio. A bit loading algorithm defining the constellation and corresponding bit mapping similar to that used for ADSL is also proposed.

Table 15.9 DMT VDSL Transmission Parameters

Sampling Rate	11.04 MHz	22.08 MHz	44.16 MHz
Baud Rate	20 kHz	40 kHz	80 kHz
Bandwidth	5.02 MHz	11.04 MHz	22.08 MHz
Cyclic Prefix Size	40 Samples	40 Samples	40 Samples
IFFT/FFT Size	256	256	256
Number of Tones	256	256	256
Tone Bandwidth	21.5625 kHz	43.125 kHz	87.25 kHz

Utilizing Time Division Multiplex (TDM), the transmit power spectrum mask shown in Figure 15.20 is defined for both upstream and downstream directions. The transmit power density level is –60 dBm/Hz with an allowed variation of +/–3 dB to realize the full potential of each subcarrier without the use of a fractional bit loading algorithm.

Figure 15.20 DMT VDSL Transmit Power Spectrum

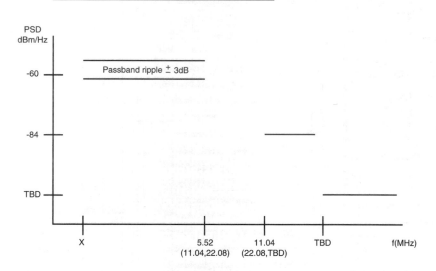

Figure 15.21 shows the timing relationship of downstream transmission, upstream transmission, propagation delay, and guard time.

A guard time period between the reception of the incoming packet and the transmission of the next outgoing packet is necessary to account for different round trip delays among all VDSL loops because the synchronization between all VDSL transceivers is required to avoid the effect of NEXT. There are two guard time periods, as shown in Figure 15.21. The total guard time $(T_{g1}+T_{g2})$ is a multiple of DMT symbols.

Figure 15.21 The DMT VDSL Time Division Multiplex System

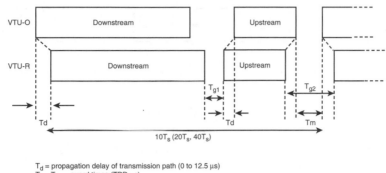

T_d = propagation delay of transmission path (0 to 12.5 µs)
T_{g1}, T_{g2} = guard times (TBD µs)
T_m = guard time (0 to TBD µs)

The transmission throughput ratio between downstream and upstream is regulated through the allocation of a different number of DMT data symbols for different directions. The transmission throughput is in multiples of 64 Kbps and is fully user programmable.

Asymmetric DMT VDSL Super Frames

Figure 15.22 shows an asymmetric super frame with a downstream-to-upstream transmission throughput ratio of 8:1. 16 DMT symbols are allocated for the downstream channel (DMT), while only two DMT symbols are allocated for the upstream channel (UMT). One silent symbol is used following the group of downstream symbols and the group of upstream symbols.

Figure 15.22 An Asymmetric VDSL Super Frame

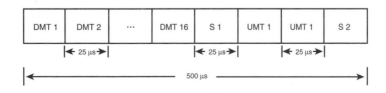

Symmetric VDSL Super Frames

Figure 15.23 shows a symmetric super frame. Nine DMT symbols are allocated for the downstream channel, and nine DMT symbols are allocated also for the upstream channel. One silent symbol is used also following the group of downstream symbols and the group of upstream symbols.

Figure 15.23 A Symmetric VDSL Super Frame

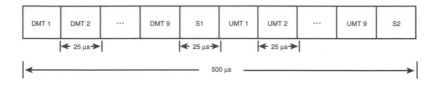

The mixing of asymmetric and symmetric transmission throughput services in the same VDSL is believed to be feasible. Under the all-VDSL transceiver synchronized condition, the implementation of mixed services will induce some extra NEXT noise for VDSL receivers located at the ONU side.

Minimizing RFI Noise

The effect of RFI can be minimized with some noise cancellation techniques.[24] A combination of analog and digital RFI cancellation as well as subcarrier nullifying techniques has been proposed for the DMT VDSL.[25]

Figure 15.24 shows the general arrangement of an analog RFI canceller. The weight can be trained using adaptive signal processing algorithms during the silent periods. The weight can also be simplified to a frequency-independent scaling factor.

Figure 15.24 Analog Radio Interference Cancellation

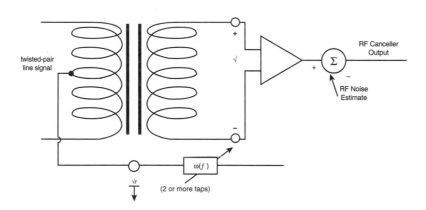

15.4 Twisted-Pair Primary Constants for VDSL

Twisted-pair cable primary parameters presented by two Bellcore contributions[2, 3] are summarized in Tables 15.10 through 15.18 for a quick reference. The frequency range is up to 30 or 40 MHz. More frequency points are available from these contributions.

Table 15.10   0.4 mm (24-Gauge) Twisted Pair

Frequency (kHz)	R (ohm/km)	L (μH/km)	G (nMho/km)	C (μF/km)
5	180.98	724.63	74.72	130.66
10	181.14	721.82	72.89	236.51
15	181.40	719.42	71.88	334.65
20	181.76	717.27	71.19	428.10
30	182.79	713.46	70.26	605.74
50	185.96	707.05	69.15	938.00
70	190.44	701.66	68.46	1251.12
100	199.02	694.78	67.75	1697.87
150	216.34	685.43	66.97	2402.43
200	235.21	677.78	66.45	3073.31
300	272.90	665.70	65.74	4348.62
500	340.88	648.79	64.89	6733.92
700	399.36	637.08	64.35	8981.78
1000	474.74	624.65	63.81	12189.01
1500	579.72	611.03	63.22	17247.00
2000	668.71	601.99	62.81	22063.22
3000	818.39	590.45	62.27	31218.65
5000	1056.13	578.22	61.62	48342.67
7000	1249.50	571.59	61.21	64480.06
10000	1493.35	565.74	60.79	87504.68
15000	1828.92	560.39	60.34	123815.92
20000	2111.83	557.33	60.03	158391.52
30000	2586.43	553.87	59.61	224118.21

Table 15.11 0.5 mm (26-Gauge) Twisted Pair

Frequency (kHz)	R (ohm/km)	L (μH/km)	G (nMho/km)	C (μF/km)
5	174.62	616.69	50	29.88
10	174.81	615.96	50	77.77
15	175.12	615.17	50	136.10
20	175.55	614.35	50	202.42
30	176.76	612.66	50	354.21
50	180.49	609.16	50	716.83
70	185.67	605.63	50	1140.44
100	195.45	600.42	50	1865.68
150	214.64	592.18	50	3264.69
200	235.03	584.64	50	4855.77
300	274.83	571.60	50	8496.96
500	345.18	552.20	50	17195.51
700	405.11	538.85	50	27357.20
1000	482.06	525.44	50	44754.46
1500	588.99	512.26	50	78314.52
2000	679.53	504.61	50	116481.71
3000	831.75	496.23	50	203827.92
5000	1073.45	489.11	50	412491.45
7000	1270.01	486.02	50	656253.52
10000	1517.88	483.72	50	1073584.8
15000	1858.97	481.99	50	1878634.5
20000	2146.54	481.15	50	2794201.6
30000	2628.95	480.34	50	4889491.3

Table 15.12 DW10 Reinforced 0.5 mm Twisted Pair

Frequency (kHz)	R (ohm/km)	L (μH/km)	G (nMho/km)	C (μF/km)
5	286.22	673.73	49	16.70
10	286.33	672.27	49	27.13
15	286.53	670.88	49	36.04
20	286.80	669.55	49	44.07
30	287.58	667.01	49	58.54

Frequency (kHz)	R (ohm/km)	L (µH/km)	G (nMho/km)	C (µF/km)
50	290.04	662.29	49	83.70
70	293.60	657.93	49	105.93
100	300.77	651.94	49	135.98
150	316.47	643.08	49	180.60
200	335.14	635.31	49	220.90
300	376.06	622.20	49	293.40
500	457.03	602.52	49	419.51
700	530.29	588.28	49	530.93
1000	626.85	572.87	49	681.50
1500	763.06	556.00	49	905.17
2000	879.19	545.00	49	1107.11
3000	1075.10	531.41	49	1470.46
5000	1386.83	517.85	49	2102.56
7000	1640.56	511.01	49	2660.95
10000	1960.61	505.33	49	3415.61
15000	2401.10	500.51	49	4536.62
20000	2772.49	497.93	49	5548.68
30000	3395.54	495.20	49	7369.76

Table 15.13   DW8 1.14 mm Flat Telephone Cable

Frequency (kHz)	R (ohm/km)	L (µH/km)	G (nMho/km)	C (µF/km)
5	41.26	998.74	35.04	95.36
10	41.59	997.17	34.13	175.50
15	42.11	995.49	33.62	250.75
20	42.81	993.76	33.28	322.98
30	44.63	990.30	32.81	461.47
50	49.32	983.63	32.26	723.38
70	54.52	977.56	31.91	972.66
100	62.28	969.67	31.55	1331.30
150	74.18	959.34	31.16	1902.11
200	84.75	951.67	30.89	2450.09
300	102.99	941.30	30.53	3500.60

continues

Table 15.13 Continued

Frequency (kHz)	R (ohm/km)	L (µH/km)	G (nMho/km)	C (µF/km)
500	132.41	930.35	30.10	5487.44
700	156.49	924.83	29.83	7378.40
1000	186.92	920.41	29.55	10098.94
1500	228.86	916.87	29.25	14429.00
2000	264.23	915.12	29.04	18585.84
3000	323.59	913.40	28.76	26554.77
5000	417.74	912.10	28.43	41626.46
7000	494.27	911.58	28.22	55970.88
10000	590.76	911.21	28.00	76608.31
15000	723.53	910.94	27.77	109455.14
20000	835.46	910.81	27.61	140988.04
30000	1023.22	910.70	27.39	201438.54

Table 15.14 22-Gauge PIC Cable by Bellcore

Frequency (kHz)	R (ohm/km)	L (µH/km)	G (nMho/km)	C (µF/km)
0.3	197.30	0.537	96	50.27
0.5	236.91	0.528	161	50.94
0.7	289.54	0.518	226	51.41
1	357.25	0.506	323	51.61
1.5	422.08	0.494	485	51.80
2	494.48	0.488	653	51.89
3	604.82	0.481	977	51.92
5	773.35	0.474	1610	51.85
7	914.91	0.471	2265	51.75
10	1097.92	0.469	3262	51.63
15	1332.03	0.467	4809	51.50
20	1555.59	0.466	6441	51.38
30	1918.18	0.465	9624	51.27
40	2278.32	0.464	12866	51.19

Table 15.15 | 24-Gauge PIC Cable by Bellcore

Frequency (kHz)	R (ohm/km)	L (μH/km)	G (nMho/km)	C (μF/km)
0.3	269.87	0.581	98	51.30
0.5	335.32	0.559	162	51.20
0.7	395.73	0.544	226	51.47
1	465.11	0.528	324	51.70
1.5	557.87	0.514	486	51.84
2	640.57	0.506	653	51.91
3	776.39	0.497	977	51.90
5	990.41	0.489	1607	51.76
7	1173.18	0.485	2260	51.62
10	1407.60	0.482	3252	51.46
15	1712.96	0.480	4790	51.30
20	1998.94	0.479	6411	51.15
30	2484.74	0.477	9573	50.99
40	2935.00	0.477	12792	50.90

Table 15.16 | 26-Gauge PIC Cable by Bellcore

Frequency (kHz)	R (ohm/km)	L (μH/km)	G (nMho/km)	C (μF/km)
0.3	353.22	0.579	94	49.55
0.5	408.00	0.573	159	50.71
0.7	492.54	0.567	224	50.96
1	613.31	0.554	318	50.70
1.5	728.78	0.540	476	50.55
2	848.40	0.530	636	50.54
3	1019.26	0.518	953	50.64
5	1288.27	0.505	1580	50.87
7	1520.23	0.497	2235	51.04
10	1809.56	0.489	3238	51.25
15	2176.92	0.482	4808	51.50
20	2516.51	0.477	6474	51.64
30	3093.75	0.471	9737	51.87
40	3606.84	0.68	13077	52.03

Table 15.17   Two-Pair Twisted Drop Cable by Bellcore

Frequency (MHz)	R (ohm/kft)	L (mH/kft)	C (nF/kft)
0.772	112.64	0.1436	14.16
0.978	128.30	0.1400	13.89
1.481	163.02	0.1377	13.79
1.991	194.34	0.1384	13.94
3.013	250.16	0.1374	13.94
5.135	349.72	0.1364	13.93
6.905	426.53	0.1359	13.92
9.850	539.99	0.1353	13.90
14.91	720.14	0.1345	13.86
20.05	890.36	0.1338	13.82
30.34	1191.67	0.1328	13.74
40	1488.43	0.1321	13.68

Table 15.18   Flat-Pair Drop Cable by Bellcore

Frequency (MHz)	R (ohm/kft)	L (mH/kft)	C (nF/kft)
0.772	170.5	0.129	10.5
0.999	190.1	0.134	10.34
1.497	253.6	0.144	10.37
1.993	324.2	0.151	10.43
2.987	462	0.159	10.51
4.987	702.9	0.167	10.55
6.98	900.9	0.172	10.56
10.05	1153	0.175	10.56
15.06	1478	0.179	10.55
20.05	1738	0.181	10.54
30.06	2141	0.183	10.53
40	2455	0.184	10.5

End Notes

1. P. S. Chow, J. C. Tu, and J. M. Cioffi, "Performance Evaluation of a Multichannel Transceiver System for ADSL and VHDSL," *IEEE JSAC,* vol. 9, no. 6 (August 1991): 909–919.

2. "Specification Part 8: Lower Layer Protocols and Physical Interfaces," *DAVIC 1.0* (January 1996).

3. J. Cioffi, "VDSL System Requirements: Draft Technical Report," T1E1.4/96-153 (June 1996).

4. "Transmission and Multiplexing: Very-High-Bit-Rate Digital Transmission on Metallic Local Lines (VDSL)," *ETSI Draft Technical Report DTR/TM-03068* (December 7, 1995).

5. J. W. Cook, "Parametric Modeling of Twisted-Pair Cables for VDSL," *BT Labs T1E1 Contribution,* T1E1.4/96-015 (January 1996).

6. K. T. Foster, "Primary Line Constant Tabulations for US 24 & 26 AWG Twisted-Pair Cables," *BT Labs T1E1 Contribution,* T1E1.4/96-097 (January 1997).

7. C. F. Valenti, "Primary and Secondary Parameters for 26-, 24-, and 22-AWG PIC Cables," *Bellcore T1E1 Contribution,* T1E1.4/97-296 (September 1997).

8. C. F. Valenti, "Primary and Secondary Parameters for Service Drop Cables," *Bellcore T1E1 Contribution,* T1E1.4/97-297 (September 1997).

9. J. Cioffi, "VDSL System Requirements," *Draft Technical Report-Revision 9,* T1E1.4/97-131 (May 1997).

10. G. H. Im and J. J. Werner, "Effect of Bridged Taps at VDSL Frequencies," *Lucent Technologies T1E1 Contribution,* T1E1.4/97-324 (September 1997).

11. C. F. Valenti, "Cable Crosstalk Parameters and Models," *Bellcore T1E1 Contribution,* T1E1.4/97-302 (September 1997).

12. I. K. Czajkowski, "Demographic Analysis of AM Broadcast RFI for a North American Scenario," *Nortel T1E1 Contribution,* T1E1.4/97-083.

13. R. E. Collin, *Antennas and Radiowave Propagation* (McGraw-Hill, 1985).

14. P. N. Saveskie, *Radio Propagation Handbook* (Blue Ridge Summit, PA: TAB Books, Inc., 1980).

15. G. Robb, "EMC Measurement Results on Various Aerial Telephony Plant," *Broadband Technologies T1E1 Contribution,* T1E1.4/96-318 (November 1996).

16. "Balance Measurements on BT Drop Wire 10," *ETSI TM3 TD52* (Helsinki, 1995).

17. "Spectral Mask for VDSL with Power Boost," *A Joint T1E1 Contribution,* T1E1.4/97-304 (September 1997).

18. J. Lindholm, J. Nieminen, and A. Tommiska, "MQAM Line Code Proposal for VDSL," *NOKIA T1E1 Contribution,* T1E1.4/97-190 (May 1997).

19. P. Spruyt, P. Reusens, and S. Braet, "Performance of Improved DMT Transceiver for VDSL," *Alcatel T1E1 Contribution,* T1E1.4/96-104 (April 1996).

20. L. D. Humphrey, "Description of 'Whistler' DMT Receiver Algorithm," *Nortel T1E1 Contribution,* T1E1.4/96-195 (July 1996).

21. M. Isaksson, D. Bengtsson, P. Deutgen, M. Sandell, F. Sjoberg, P. Odling, and H. Ohman, "Zipper: A Duplex Scheme for VDSL Based on DMT," *Telia Research AB T1E1 Contribution,* T1E1.4/97-016 (February 1997).

22. R. McConnell, Editor, "VDSL Draft Specification (Version 1.0)," T1E1.4/97-168 (May 1997).

23. K. S. Jacobsen, "DMT Group VDSL PMD Draft Standard Proposal," T1E1.4/96-329R2 (May 1997).

24. W. Y. Chen, "VDSL and Radio Interference Cancellation," *Texas Instrument T1E1 Contribution,* T1E1.4/96-022 (January 1996).

25. J. Cioffi, M. Mallory, and J. Bingham, "Analog RF Cancellation with SDMT," *Amati T1E1 Contribution,* T1E1.4/96-084 (April 1996).

Glossary

Numbers/Symbols

2B1Q line code A baseband line code with two bits per quaternary, four levels, symbols.

3B2T line code A baseband line code with three bits for every two ternary, three levels, symbols.

4B3T line code A baseband line code with four bits for every three ternary, three levels, symbols.

A

ABCD parameters A two-by-two matrix describing input voltage and current-to-output voltage and the current relationship of a two-port network.

ADC (Analog to Digital Converter) An analog integrated circuit that samples, quantizes, and holds analog signals for digital signal processing.

AFE (analog front end) The part that connects digital signal processing circuits to an analog signal. AFE mainly consists of an ADC and a DAC.

AGC (Automatic Gain Control) A part of the AFE that adjusts the received signal level to that suitable for the input of the ADC.

AMI (Alternate Mark Inversion) line code A simple baseband line code that alternates the parity of data symbols for adjacent 1s. For example, a sequence of 1011000 is encoded as +A 0 −A +A 0 0 0 for the AMI line code for which A is the magnitude of the line code.

Amplifier nonlinearity The nonlinear amplifier input-to-output relationship.

ASIC (Application Specific Integrated Circuit) An integrated circuit (IC) that is designed for a specific application in contrast to some general purpose ICs that are available from an IC catalog.

ASSP (Algorithm Specific Signal Processor) An integrated circuit (IC) that is designed for a specific algorithm for a category of general applications. An example is an adaptive filter IC.

Asymptotic coding gain A coding gain that can only be obtained when the SNR value approaches infinity.

Attenuation The signal loss caused by a transmission channel at a particular frequency.

AWG (American Wire Gauge) A measuring system designed to distinguish twisted-pair telephone cables with different diameters of conductors.

B

B8ZS (bipolar with 8-zero substitution) line code A baseband line code in which ones and zeros are encoded with opposite parities and every consecutive of eight zeros is replaced with a special non-all-zero sequence.

Background noise A random noise in front of, and external to, a receiver.

Balance condition The condition in which a hybrid circuit is most effective at separating transmitted and received signals.

Bandwidth The frequency band size of a signal.

Baseband signals Data symbols that are sent to the channel without modulation.

Baud rate equalizers Adaptive channel equalizers operating at the symbol of baud rate.

BCH (Bose, Chaudhuri, and Hocquenghem) code A class of cyclic codes that is easy to define and implement.

BER (bit error rate) A performance measurement, usually in terms of the number of errors per second, of a transmission system.

Bessel filter A filter whose frequency response is described by Bessel functions.

Biphase line code A baseband line code with different phases for zeros and ones. *See also* Manchester line code.

Bit stuffing Inserting an extra number of bits to adjust the frame size.

Brickwall filter An ideal filter frequency response with 0 loss passband, infinite loss stopband, and no transition region in between.

Bridged taps Unused twisted-pair cables attached to a telephone subscriber loop.

Byte A group of eight bits.

C

CAP (Carrierless AM/PM) system A variation of the passband QAM line code.

Capacitance The capacity of electrical energy storage in positive and negative charges.

Channel capacity The maximum transmission throughput of a channel with a correctable number of transmission errors.

Channel intersymbol interference Interference between adjacent data symbols caused by channel frequency and phase distortion.

Clipping noise Noise caused by the clipping of signal peaks by DAC or ADC.

CMOS (Complementary Metal Oxide Semiconductor) A semiconductor technology whose element circuit is based on the complementary combination of p and n types of semiconductor material.

CO (Central Office) A telephone company office for terminating telephone subscriber loops and for housing telephone switching equipment.

Code book A mapping between input information sequences and output code words.

Companding A method to compress a large amplitude signal to increase the dynamic range of a voice encoder through non-uniform quantization.

Conductance The capacity of electrical energy storage in the strength electromagnetic fields.

Convolution code A coding mechanism whose output codewords depend on input information sequences as well as the state of the encoder.

Crosstalk noise Noise caused by a signal carried over adjacent telephone subscriber loops.

CSA (Carrier Serving Area) A design guideline for the constraining of the length of telephone subscriber loops to accommodate digital telephone transmission equipment.

Cyclic code An error correction code. The cyclic shift of a codeword from a particular cyclic code is also a codeword of the same cyclic code.

D

DA (Distribution Area) The area served by a remote terminal.

DAC (Digital to Analog Converter) An analog integrated circuit that takes in a group of binary digits and generates an analog signal of corresponding magnitude.

dBrnc The Log format power ratio with respect to 1 nano-watt including a C-message filter.

DC resistance The resistance at direct current or zero frequency.

DFE (Decision Feedback Equalizer) A channel equalizer consisting of a feedforward filter (FFF) whose input is the received signal and a feedback filter whose input is the sequence of estimated data symbols.

DFT (Discrete Fourier Transform) The discrete version of the Fourier transform. It is usually implemented with the FFT algorithm using digital hardware.

Differential channel capacity The channel capacity within a unit frequency. The differential channel capacity is derivative of the conventional channel capacity. The differential channel capacity can be used to examine the frequency characteristic aspect part of a channel.

Differential hybrid circuit A hybrid circuit that connects to ADC and DAC with differential input and output, respectively.

Discrete time domain Signal values that are defined at sampling instances of periodic intervals.

Distribution cable A part of the telephone subscriber loop that connects feeder cables to drop wires.

Disturbers Signal sources of crosstalk noises.

DLC (Digital Loop Carrier) system A high-throughput digital transmission system developed to connect a Central Office to a remote terminal. A DLC system can be implemented using existing twisted-pair telephone subscriber loops or optical fiber cables.

DMT (Discrete MultiTone) systems A multi-carrier line code whose modulation and demodulation are implemented using Inverse Fast Fourier Transform (IFFT) and Fast Fourier Transform (FFT), respectively. The twisted-pair channel inter-symbol interference of a DMT system is mitigated by dividing the transmission spectrum into many sub-channels.

double-Barker code A synchronization word whose contents are the double bit assignment of a Barker code. The double-Barker code is defined for the HDSL frame structure.

Drop wire A telephone cable (twisted or flat) that connects a distribution cable to a subscriber premises.

DS1 (Digital Signal 1) circuit The first level of the North American digital hierarchy with a nominal rate of 1.544 Mbps. A specific implementation of DS1 is further referred to as DSX-1.

DSL (Digital Subscriber Lines) The original name for the physical layer of the Basic Rate Access ISDN channel. DSL uses a 2B1Q baseband line code with a transmission throughput of 160 kbps. Most recently, the term DSL is used as a generic name for any Digital Subscribe Loop system (ADSL, HDSL, and so forth).

DSP (Digital Signal Processor) A programmable semiconductor circuit capable of implementing multiple signal processing algorithms with software

DTMF (dual tone multifrequency) A method used for telephone touch dialing.

E

EC (echo cancellation) Separation of the transmit signal from the received signal through the use of an adaptive filter.

Echo canceller The digital signal processing circuit implementing the echo cancellation algorithm.

Echo path impulse response The time-domain impulse response of the echo path (from transmit to receive).

Echo path transfer function The frequency domain description of the echo path.

Echo return loss The average signal loss of the echo path.

Eigenvalues The characteristic vector of a matrix. The eigenvalues are obtained by solving a set of linear equations derived from the matrix.

EOC (Embedded Operations Channel) A virtual communication channel embedded in the physical layer for inter-transceiver and network maintenance purposes.

Euclidean distance The geometric distance in a multidimensional signal space.

exclusive-or operation The binary operation that returns a 1 only when one of its two operands is 1.

F

FBF (FeedBack Filter) The feedback filter of a DFE. An FBF cancels the tail portion of the channel impulse response using recovered data symbols. An FBF can be implemented only at the baud rate.

FDD (Frequency Division Duplex) systems Transmission channels in opposite directions are separated by frequency division.

FDI (Feeder Distribution Interface) A twisted-pair telephone loop plant interface point between feeder and distribution cables.

FDM (Frequency Division Multiplex) transmissions Transmission channels separated by frequency division.

Feeder cables Twisted-pair telephone cables coming out of COs.

FEXT (Far End Crosstalk) noise The crosstalk noise from the other end of the twisted-pair telephone loop.

FFF (FeedForward Filter) The feedforward filter of a DFE. An FFF compensates for the channel distortion with linear equalization. An FFF can be implemented at a multiple of the baud rate.

FFT (Fast Fourier Transform) An efficient digital implementation of the Fourier transform, which converts a time-domain signal to its frequency-domain equivalence.

FIR (Finite Impulse Response) filter A digital filter with a finite number of delay and multiplication elements. The output of an FIR filter is the convolution of the input and filter coefficients.

Fourier transform A linear transform based on the sinusoid expansion of a signal.

Fractionally spaced equalizer A channel equalizer operating on multiples of the signaling rate.

G

GAFF (General Adaptive FIR Filter) chip A semi-programmable semiconductor circuit for the implementation of DSL transceivers.

Galois field A closed algebra field for describing encoding and decoding operations.

Gaussian distribution A bell-shaped statistical distribution function. Also called the *normal distribution*.

Guard period A period used in a DMT system to elevate the effect of channel distortion.

H–I

Hamming distance The minimum number of bits that are different between every pair of codewords.

IDFT (Inverse Discrete Fourier Transform) The discrete version of the inverse Fourier transform. It is usually implemented with the IFFT algorithm using digital hardware.

IFFT (Inverse Fast Fourier Transform) An efficient digital implementation of the Inverse Fourier transform that converts a frequency-domain signal to its time-domain equivalence.

Impedance The relationship between the applied voltage and the induced current of an electrical device.

Impulse noise Short-duration, high-magnitude noise whose occurrence does not follow the normal distribution.

Impulse response The time-domain response at the output of a network corresponding to an impulse applied at the input of a network.

INA (Intelligent Network Architecture) A general telephone networking concept that coordinates trunk, network, service, and management capabilities.

Inductance The measurement of the amount of energy stored in the magnetic field format.

IPC (ISDN to POTS Converter) A device that converts an ISDN interface to a POTS interface.

ISDN (Integrated Service Digital Network) A digital network with integrated services, switch, and maintenance functions.

ISI (Inter Symbol Interference) Interference between adjacent data symbols caused by channel distortion.

L

LC ladder An analog filter structure where inductance and capacitance are connected in an alternate cascading fashion.

LEC (Linear Echo Canceller) An echo canceller dealing only with a linear echo path.

Linear channel equalizer A channel equalizer with only received signals as its input.

LMS (Least Mean Square) algorithm Algorithm commonly used for the adaptive filters for its simplicity and robustness.

Load coils Inductance coils used in telephone loops to improve the transmission performance of the voice band channel.

Look-up table A map of the input-output logic relationship stored in memory or described by a table instead of a logic expression.

Loopback A direct connection between the transmit path and the receive path. Loopback can be used for testing purposes. Loopback is also used to describe the direct connection of the transmit clock to the clock recovered from the received signal.

LSB (Least Significant Bit) The bit that determines the presence of the zero power of two terms in a binary polynomial representation.

LT (line termination) The Central Office–side DSL transceiver defined for ISDN Basic Rate Access channel.

M

Magnitude The amplitude of a signal.

Manchester line code A line code that maps a data bit 1 into a pulse containing both a positive and a negative level and a data bit 0 into the same pulse with inverted polarity.

MDB (Modified Duobinary) line code A baseband line code in which each data symbol is followed by its negative replica after a two-symbol delay.

MMSE (Minimum Mean Square Error) An optimization objective to minimize the average power of error.

MSB (Most Significant Bit) The bit that determines the presence of the highest power of two terms in a binary polynomial representation.

N

NEC (Nonlinear Echo Canceller) An echo canceller capable of dealing with an echo path with a certain degree of nonlinearity.

NEXT (Near End Crosstalk) noise Crosstalk noise coming from near-end transmitters.

NID (Network Interface Device) A telephone company supplied module for interconnection between the telephone subscriber loop and in-house wiring at the loop entry point.

NML (Near Maximum Likelihood) algorithm A receiver algorithm whose performance is close to that of a maximum likelihood algorithm, but with a simplified implementation.

Noise Random signal with no detectable information.

Noise floor The background noise level across a frequency band.

Nonlinearity The input/output value deviations for Digital to Analog Conversions (DAC) and Analog to Digital Conversions (ADC).

NT (network termination) The subscriber-side DSL transceiver defined for an ISDN Basic Rate Access channel.

Nyquist shaping filter A digital FIR filter that introduces no intersymbol interferences at particular periodic sampling points.

O–P

OAM (Operation, Administration, Maintenance, and Provisioning) channels An embedded utility channel for carrying out auxiliary functions.

PAR (peak to average voltage ratio) The measure for the dynamic range of a line signal.

Parity check code An encoding method for which the coding redundancy is the parity check bits of message bits.

Passband signal A line code that is modulated with a carrier of cosine and/or sine waves.

PBX (Private Branch Exchanges) A telephone switch for private business applications.

PCM (Pulse Code Modulation) A binary code word representation of a baseband multi-level signal.

PDM (Pulse Duration Modulation) A pulse width representation of a baseband multi-level signal. In other words, the magnitude of a signal is translated into the width of a fixed-height pulse.

Peak-to-peak voltage The voltage level measured from the negative peak to the positive peak.

Phase The starting angle of a sinusoidal signal.

Phase delay The starting time shift of a sinusoidal signal.

Phase invariant Trellis codes Trellis codes that preserve the angular information of data symbols.

PLL (Phase Locked Loop) A feedback loop with a very tight bandwidth that can be used to track the clock signal.

Post-cursor (channel impulse response) The portion after the peak of an impulse response.

POTS (Plain Old Telephone Service) The traditional general-purpose telephone set.

Pre-cursor (channel impulse response) The portion before the peak of an impulse response.

Propagation constant The attenuation and phase shift of a cable with ideal terminations.

PSD (power spectrum density) The power density of a signal at different frequencies.

PSTN (Public Switched Telephone Network) The general telephone switched network connecting COs.

Q

QAM (Quadrature Amplitude Modulation) line code A passband line code generated through modulating in-phase and quadrature data symbols with cosine and sine phases of a carrier frequency, respectively.

QPSK (Quadrature Phase Shift Keying) signals A passband signal generated through modulating complex data symbols with four different angles of a carrier frequency.

Quantization noise The noise generated when converting an analog signal to a digital signal by rounding to the nearest signal level.

Quaternary symbol A four-level symbol.

R

Rate conversion filters A digital filter that has different input and output data rates.

RC balance network A network of resistors and capacitors for the purpose of balancing a hybrid circuit.

Receiver front-end noise A combination of background and electronics noise at the input of a transceiver.

Reed-Solomon code A class of non-binary BCH codes with features for easy code definition and implementation.

Resolution The accuracy, in terms of number of bits, of a digital circuit.

Ring trip The disconnection of ringing voltage from the loop when the called party picks up the phone.

RJ45 plugs A compact telephone style plug designed for connecting up to four twisted pairs.

Roll off A point at which the energy of a spectrum or the magnitude of the transfer function is reduced by a certain amount, usually 3 dB.

S

Sigma-delta modulator An analog-to-digital conversion technique that trades high processing speed for high resolution.

Single-ended hybrid circuit A hybrid circuit that connects to a single-ended line driver.

SNR (signal-to-noise ratio) A measure of the quality of the received signal.

Superframe format A data/synchronization structure build upon data/synchronization frames of a lower hierarchy.

SW (Synchronization Word) A particular bit/symbol pattern designed for the synchronization of data frames.

Syndrome vector A decoder-derived vector whose pattern is uniquely related to a particular error sequence.

T

T1 line A specially equipped telephone line capable of a transmission throughput of T1 rate.

TCM (Time Compression Multiplex) transmissions Transmission in opposite directions are achieved through time division multiplex. The transmission throughput over the channel is faster than the data rate.

TR (Timing Recovery) An algorithm to derive the clock from the received signal.

Transfer function The frequency response of a linear system or a linear channel.

Transmit power density The transmit power level at a particular frequency.

Transmit symbol pulse shape Defined for a baseband line code as a time-domain mask to ensure inter-operability between different equipment vendors.

Trellis code modulation A combination of a specially selected convolution code and a bit-to-symbol mapping algorithm for achieving significant coding gain with no bandwidth expansion.

U–V

Unger NEXT model A simplified piece-wise linear NEXT model derived on extensive computer simulation results.

Variable frame structure A flexible frame structure whose length can be altered to accommodate asymmetry transmission throughputs in opposite directions.

VCCO (Voltage Controlled Crystal Oscillator) A high-accuracy crystal oscillator whose frequency can be slightly adjusted through applying different amounts of voltage.

Viterbi algorithm A received data symbol recovery procedure whose decision making is based on a sequence of received data symbols.

VLSI (Very Large Scale Integrated) circuit A high-density semiconductor circuit that can include multiple signal processing capabilities in a single chip.

W–Z

White noise A noise whose power spectrum is flat.

Wiener Filter A filter whose frequency response is based on the signal-to-noise ratio of the received signal for the optimal detection of data symbols.

Zero forcing channel equalizer A linear channel equalizer whose filter coefficients are designed to produce zero inter-symbol interference at every sampling point.

Index